Editorial Committee

Per Bech

Rating Scales for Psychopathology, Health Status and Quality of Life

A Compendium on Documentation
in Accordance with the DSM-III-R
and WHO Systems

Springer-Verlag
Berlin Heidelberg New York
London Paris Tokyo
Hong Kong Barcelona
Budapest

Per Bech, M. D., Ph. D.
Professor of Psychiatry
Frederiksborg General Hospital
Department of Psychiatry
48, Dyrehavevej
DK-3400 Hillerød, Denmark

ISBN 3-540-55903-5 Springer-Verlag Berlin Heidelberg New York
ISBN 0-387-55903-5 Springer-Verlag New York Berlin Heidelberg

Library of Congress Cataloging-in-Publication Data. Bech, Per. Rating scales for psychopathology, health status, and quality of life: a compendium on documentation in accordance with the DSM-III-R and WHO systems/P. Bech p. ... cm. Includes bibliographical references and index. ISBN 3-540-55903-5 (Berlin: alk. paper. – ISBN 0-387-55903-5 New York: alk. paper) 1. Psychiatric rating scales. 2. Health status indicators. 3. Quality of life – Evaluation. I. Title. [DNLM: 1. Health Status. 2. Mental Disorders – classification. 3. Psychiatric Status Rating Scales – classification. 4. Psychopathology – classification. 5. Quality of life. WM 15 B391r] RC473.P78B43 1993 616.89'075 – dc20

Typesetting: Data conversion by M. Masson-Scheurer, Kirkel
25/3130-5 4 3 2   – Printed on acid-free paper

The thing of deepest
or, at any rate, of comparatively
deepest significance in life
does seem to be its character of progress

                    James (1899)

There will be time,
there will be time to prepare a face
to meet the faces
... and time for all the works
and days of hands that lift and
drop a question on your plate;
...and time yet for a hundred indecisions,
and for a hundred visions
and revisions.

And indeed there will be time to wonder,
Do I dare? ...
Time to turn back and descend the stair,
with a bald spot in the middle of my hair ...
Do I dare
disturb the universe?

In a minute there is time
for decisions and revisions which
a minute will reverse ...

For I have known them all ...
have known the evenings, mornings, afternoons,
I have measured out my life ...

                    Eliot (1917)

A chain of summa genera,
genera, species, sub-species, and varieties
is not a chain of axioms, theorems, and riders.
But what is more,
it cannot, in general,
be deductively established
or established by reductio ad absurdum.
The work of a Linnaeus
cannot be done a priori.

                    Ryle (1965)

Preface

This book has grown out of a previous publication, the Mini-compendium (Bech et al. 1986), which was developed as a guide both for clinical research and for the documentation of routine activities in assessing psychiatric disability, whether in a general hospital, by a district psychiatrist or a nurse, by a liaison-consultant psychiatrist, by a clinical psychologist, by a health worker, or in general practice. One of its outstanding merits was that its scales were authoritative: During its preparation Max Hamilton corrected and finally accepted the English versions of his scales and Ole Rafaelsen corrected the English versions of the remaining scales. While preparing this publication we were constantly reminded of how difficult it is to accept that Max and Ole are no longer with us.

One indication of the success of the Mini-compendium is the fact that it was translated into a number of languages, including Spanish (Ballus and Tressera, 1988), Italian (Fava and Grandi, 1988), French (Pichot et al. 1989), Dutch (D'haenen and Verhoeven, 1989), and German (Maier et al. 1991). Another indication was its correspondence to the DSM-III (APA, 1980) criteria for anxiety, depression, mania and schizophrenia. This volume refers to DSM-III-R (APA, 1987) and ICD-10 (WHO, 1992).

This compendium has, furthermore, followed the DSM-III-R principle in describing health and disease by a multi-dimensional approach, including psychosocial stressors, social functioning and coping styles. In addition, health-related quality of life scales as well as scales measuring side-effects of treatment have been included. Within each dimension rating scales have been selected because of their high validity and reliability. The content validity of the scales has reference to DSM-III-R and ICD-10. However, the construct validity of the included scales has been tested by reference to modern psychometric models. Thus, each rating scale has been selected by its ability to measure the underlying construct sufficiently. For measuring dimensions of health and disease Likert rating scales have been found sufficient (i.e. brief scales including around 10 items each of which is defined by categories from 0 (not present) to 4 (present to an extreme degree)). By use of such scales health status profiles can be scored. The global integration of this profile from the patient's point of view gives the quality of life assessment.

It is only three decades since Max Hamilton introduced the rating scale method into clinical research. The first chapter of this compendium summarizes the psychometric literature on the scientific use of rating scales in health and disease (from Hamilton's use of classical psychometric methods to the modern use of latent structure or trait methods). This compendium is intended not only for clinicians interested in the scientific background for DSM-III-R or ICD-10, but also for those wishing to know more about the psychometric or clinimetric properties of the different dimension of health and disease. Therefore, it is intended for all health workers who have a primary interest in rating scales measuring clinical disability, health status profile, and health-related quality of life.

The compendium has been completed in collaboration with an editorial committee consisting of European colleagues who made the very difficult task of translating the Mini-compendium to their respective languages. The compendium has been through many revisions which secretary Pernille Slej, Hillerød, has faithfully and effectively performed. Thomas Thiekötter, Springer-Verlag, has from the very beginning endeavoured that this compendium should cover all relevant aspects of health and disease as measured by rating scales. Dr. Wilson and his team in Springer-Verlag have carefully edited the compendium. In the final stage Johan Sonne Mortensen, University of Odense, has organized the lay-out of the scales in collaboration with Pernille Slej, and made the proof corrections. The subject index (including lists of authors, scales and their abbreviations) has been developed by Gabriele Bech-Andersen, Psychiatric Institute, Hillerød.

Copenhagen   Per Bech

References

American Psychiatric Association. Diagnostic and Statistical Manual of Mental Disorders. Third edition (DSM-III). Washington DC, American Psychiatric Association, 1980.

American Psychiatric Association: Diagnostic and Statistical Manual of Mental Disorders. Third edition, revised version (DSM-III-R). Washington DC, American Psychiatric Association, 1987.

Ballus C, Tressera J. Breve compendio de las escalas de evaluacio para los estados de ansiedad, depression, mania y esquizofrenia con los sindroms correspondientes en el DSM-III. Barceloa, Espanxs, 1988.

Bech P, Kastrup M, Rafaelsen OJ. Mini-compendium of rating scales. Acta Psychiat Scand 1986; 73 (suppl. 326): 7–37.

D'haenen HAH, Verhoeven WMA. Mini-compendium van beoordelingsschalen in de psychiatrie. Brussels, VUB Press, 1989.

Eliot TS. Prufrock and other observations. London, Hogarth Press, 1917.

Fava GA, Grandi S. Minicompendio delle scale de valutazione di stati di ansia, depressione, mania, schizofrenia con le corrispondenti sindromi del DSM-III. Milano, CE.D.RIM, 1988.

James W. Talks to Teachers. New York: Holt 1899.

Maier W, Gastpar M, Bech-Andersen G. Minikompendium für psykiatrische Ratingskalen. Berlin, Springer 1991.

Pichot P, Chambon O, Poncet F, Kiss L. Echelles d'anxiety, de manie, de dépression, de schizophrenie correspondance avec le DSM-III. Paris, Masson, 1989 (second edition 1991).

Ryle G. The academy and dialectic. In: Bambrough R (ed). New essays on Plato and Aristotle. London, Routledge & Kegan Paul, 1965.

World Health Organization: International Classification of Disease, tenth revision. The ICD-10 Classification of Mental and Behavioural Disorders. Clinical descriptions and diagnostic guidelines. Geneva, World Health Organization, 1992.

Contents

2 **Rating Scales for Psychopathological States**   45

3 **Rating Scales for Mental Disorders**   107

1 Introduction:
Rating Scales Versus DSM-III-R and ICD-10

The *Mini-compendium* (Bech et al. 1986a) was innovative in two ways: firstly, in its attempt to guide the psychopathologist in making quantitative ratings of psychiatric syndromes such as anxiety, depression, mania and schizophrenia; and secondly in its attempt to integrate the quantitative rating scale approach with the procedural algorithms in DSM-III, because the core items of the corresponding DSM-III syndromes are rather similar to the rating scale items (content validity). These clinimetric approaches have also been adopted in this, the revised version of the compendium, which has, however, been enlarged to include all the DSM-III axes of health and disease. Furthermore, the revised DSM-III (DSM-III-R; APA 1987) categories and the draft versions of ICD-10 (WHO 1990a,b) have also been considered. The result is thus of such scope that it in fact represents a compendium or handbook rather than a mini-compendium.

The *Index Medicus* heading 'Psychiatric state rating scales' was adopted in 1969. Rating scales measure psychopathological states by assigning numbers to clinical symptoms (reported or observed) or psychosocial events according to formal rules, while data expressed in categories refer to empirical symptoms or events which psychopathologists have found to be valid (content validity). Counting, as opposed to measuring, may be used when the classification, for example, of plants into species or genus has been established, and a sample of plants can then be expressed in relative frequencies of species and genus. In counting, numbers of categories are used to maintain identity. Code numbers in diagnostic classification systems (e.g. DSM-III) are also used for this purpose. In measurement, however, numbers also have the property of sequential order, one number being greater than another. It should therefore be possible to order the data to which they refer along a continuum. A rating scale contains items that cover such orderable data. Rating scales also make use of the fact that numbers have the further property of additivity, which means that the summing of the numbers assigned to a group of items can express a total score. This property is the basis of the rating scales included in this compendium. Rating scale values are thus measurements that can be analysed in the form of metric data.

In his introductory remarks to Clinimetrics, Feinstein (1987) says that patients use clinimetric forms of measurement when they say they have severe pain, a slight headache, a large gain in weight, or a great improvement in appetite. According to Feinstein clinimetrics can be defined as the domain concerned with indexes, rating scales, and other expressions that are used to describe or measure symptoms, physical signs, and other clinical phenomena in clinical medicine. In this compendium the validity of rating scales are often referred to as construct validity which includes clinimetric as well as domain validity.

1.1 Concordance Between Rating Scales and DSM-III-R or ICD-10

In contrast to DSM-III-R, which provides only one set of diagnostic criteria for both clinical and research purposes, ICD-10 offers separate clinical and research criteria. The rating scale principle in this compendium makes use of the same set of criteria for use in both contexts. However, scientific evidence remains the basic principle.

1.1.1 Phenomenology

In his classic textbook on psychometric methods, Guilford (1954) declared that "of the psychological measurement methods that depend upon human judgment, rating scale procedures exceed them all for popularity and use". The most commonly technique of measurement used by social and behavioural scientists to determine the direction and strength of people's beliefs and preferences is, according to Lodge (1981), one or another form of category scaling in which a respondent rates an item or expresses a judgment by selecting one of a fixed number of options, i.e. a rating scale. DSM-III introduced the rating scale approach into psychiatric nomenclature by emphasizing the phenomenological method. The descriptive psychiatric diagnoses in axes 1 and 2 were neutral with regard to aetiology. DSM-III is to a large extent aetiologically atheoretical. Hence, organic aetiology is to be found only in the criteria of organic mental disorders, and psychological aetiology is built into the criteria only for adjustment disorders, post-traumatic stress disorders and conversion disorders. Thus, anxiety, depression, mania and schizophrenia are disorders defined without reference to aetiology. The criteria for these states are, according to DSM-III, the shared phenomenology of the clinical symptoms and signs. By shared phenomenology, DSM-III refers to groups of symptoms (symptom clusters, or symptoms defining a cluster) that are associated with one another, and that covary over time. However, the theory of symptom clustering is not mentioned in DSM-III or DSM-III-R.

Hegel (1807) proposed the language of phenomenology as the basic language for describing precise perceptions; in this sense the language of clinical symptoms and signs belongs at the basic level at which one also describes trees, birds, rivers and flowers. This phenomenological language is thus at the same level for psychic and for physical perceptions, according to Hegel, and in this respect Hegel was opposed to Descarte's language of dualism. As discussed by Kersten (1989), descriptive phenomenology was used by Husserl (1913) in the sense of Hegel, (for further discussion see Berrios 1989). In the clinical context, the work of Jaspers (1923) on phenomenology is most relevant. He used the term phenomenology, like Hegel, as an empirical method of enquiry based solely on patients' communication, the language of symptoms and complaints. The collection of itemized information (phenomenology) during the communication between the psychiatrist and the patient is a common feature of rating scales and of DSM-III-R and ICD-10. Phenomenology is therefore the inductive observation of clinical data during an interview.

1.1.2 Psychopathology

In a comprehensive review of British psychopathology, Berrios (1990) has shown that two opposite approaches have been taken. That of 'pathological psychology' defines psychopathology as a branch of psychology dealing with experiential and behavioural phenomena that result from the disturbed expression of 'normal' mental functions. (For example, negative symptoms of schizophrenia are manifestations of decreased normal mental functions such as an-hedonia, conceptual disorganization, or concentration difficulties). The 'psychological pathology' approach, on the other hand, defines psychopathology as an independent science dealing with mental phenomena appearing de novo in the evolution of mental illness, and hence unrelated to 'normal' mental functions. (For example, positive symptoms of schizophrenia are manifestations of abnormal mental functions such as hallucinations or delusions).

DSM-III involves both approaches. Axis 1 is principally one psychological pathology. Hence, shared phenomenology has higher priority in DSM-III than presumed psychological genesis (resulting from the disturbed expression of 'normal' mental functions). However, axis 2 (personality disorders), axis 4 (psychosocial stressors) and axis 5 (social functioning) in DSM-III can be seen as an attempt to take a 'pathological psychology' approach, for instance, with reference to the stress model.

There is a clear correspondence between the rating scale procedure and DSM-III or DSM-III-R in considering psychopathology as a multidimensional continuum. It is necessary to break psychopathology down into axes or groups of related phenomena in order to be able to grasp it and particularly to discuss it properly.

It is interesting to compare modern psychopathology with introductory remarks in the classic textbook on general psychopathology by Jaspers (1923). As the following excerpts from his textbook demonstrate, the psychopathology approach in DSM-III-R axis 1 (clinical psychiatric syndromes) is very close to Jaspers' view:

Psychopathology is concerned with the ill person as a whole, in so far as he suffers from a psychic illness or one that is psychically determined.... Theoretically psychology is as necessary for the psychopathologist as physiology for the pathologist, but in fact we find many instances to the contrary. This is due to the fact that psychopathologists are concerned with much material of which the normal counterpart has not yet been studied by psychologists and they often have to provide their own psychology.... We can grasp and investigate only what has become an object to us. Psychic life as such is not an object. It becomes an object to us through that which makes it perceptible in the world, the accompanying somatic phenomena, meaningful gestures, behaviour and actions. It is further manifested through communication in the form of speech. It says what it means and thinks and it produces works. These demonstrable phenomena present us with the effects of the psyche. We either perceive it in these phenomena directly or at least deduce its existence from them; the psyche itself does not become an object.... Psychopathology is limited in that there can be no final analysis of human beings as such, since the more we reduce them to what is typical and normative the more we realise there is something hidden in every human individual which defines recognition. We have to be content with partial knowledge of an infinity which we cannot exhaust. As a person, not as a psychopathologist, one may well see more; and, if others see more which is exceptional and unique, we should refrain from letting this interfere with our psychopathology. Ethical, aesthetic and metaphysical values are established independently from psychopathological assessment and analysis....

Chapters 2 and 3 of this compendium include the psychopathological rating scales corresponding to axis 1 of DSM-III-R. These chapters are relevant for psychopathologists, both clinicians and researchers, with various orientations, (biological, cognitive, behavioural, psychodynamic, etc.). In other words, the psychopathological chapters of this compendium may be useful for psychiatrists, other physicians, psychologists, nurses, social workers and other mental health professionals. However, realizing that there is 'something hidden in every human individual which defines recognition' is relevant for the concept of quality of life (Chapter 9).

1.1.3 Health-Status Profiles

When the World Health Organization (WHO) was established in 1948, two major lines of action were undertaken. One was to compose an international classification of diseases. WHO adopted the International List of Causes of Death from 1893 and published the *International Statistical Classification of Diseases, Injuries and Causes of Death*, sixth edition (ICD-6; WHO 1948a). It is the draft version of the tenth edition (ICD-10) which this compendium refers to for psychopathological states. The second line of action sought to establish a definition of health. The resulting statement put forth the following practical formulation: "state of complete physical, mental and social well-being and not merely the absence of disease" (WHO 1948b).

A health status profile has been developed since 1948 by WHO (*International Classification of Impairments, Disabilities and Handicaps*, ICIDH; WHO 1980). The ICIDH refers to the sequence underlying an illness-related dimension: disease, impairment, disability and handicap. Thus, disease is seen as an intrinsic situation; impairment is any loss or abnormality of structure caused by disease; disability is any restriction or lack (resulting from an impairment) of ability to perform an activity in the manner or within the range considered normal for a human being; and handicap is a subjective disadvantage resulting from disability that limits or prevents the fulfilment of a role that is normal (depending on age, sex, and social and cultural factors) for a given individual. Although initial results with the ICIDH have been rather disappointing (Wood 1990), this approach has been adopted in this compendium. The concept of handicaps was the weakest part of ICIDH, according to Wood. In this compendium handicaps are considered as health-related quality of life problems.

It has been found to be of great value to distinguish between clinical disability (axis 1 syndromes) and social functioning (axis 5 problems). In other words, the ICIDH has been used to focus on consequences of chronic disorders, or, more precisely, to look at pathopsychological states with reference to the stress model, which is another way to use the DSM-III axes.

1.1.4 Health-Related Quality of Life: A Measurement Problem

Although Guilford (1936) maintained that "there seems to be little doubt that the first rating scale employed in a psychological problem was that of Galton (1883), used in the evaluation of the vividness of images", Bentham in his monograph on descriptive psychology (published posthumously in 1834) had already given instructions for measuring well-being. (As a procedure for scaling systematic impression in research dates back at least 150 B.C. when Hipparchus used a six-point scale to judge the brightness of stars, Lodge (1981)). Bentham emphasized that the individual member of the community is usually the best judge of what his or her own well-being consists in and how it can best be pursued.

Essentially, health-related quality of life is the patient's subjective (global) assessment of his or her own health profile: this is often referred to as 'subjective well-being'. Self-characterization is thus a major area of quality of life assessments, and it is the field in which self-rating scales have their major relevance. In this context Kelly's 'first principle' should be mentioned (Kelly 1955; Bannister and Fransella 1986). This is the simple statement that "if you don't know what is wrong with a patient, ask him, he *may* tell you." Therefore, quality-of-life assessment scales are mainly self-rating scales.

It is very interesting that psychologists have disagreed on methods of measuring direct personal statements. For example, idiographic research (each patient is psychopathologically unique) and nomothetic research (patients can be psychopathologically compared) have been distinguished since Windelband (1894, 1921) introduced these concepts. Self-rating scales imply a nomothetic dimension on which different patients can be compared. The problem in this has been illustrated by Eysenck, who throughout his life has constructed many nomothetic scales, including a lie scale, to measure personality dimensions. In his recent autobiography Eysenck (1990) observes that: "in writing one's autobiography, one inevitably has to take the idiographic path of trying to see regularities in one's own life, look for behaviour patterns that repeat themselves, and try to discover variables that are important for oneself, even though they might not be of general interests." Brock (1988) has formulated the impact of quality of life on clinical trials in saying: "Quality of life in the medical context is viewed as an effort to influence the practice of clinical medicine with a particular emphasis on a more humane, empathetic, pragmatic approach that heightened the focus on the patients' autonomy with regard to what they want to do with their lives and bodies...".

WHO has initiated quality of life studies that go beyond the concept of handicaps, although with some reference to the 'subjective disadvantage of being ill'. Sartorius (1987) has summarized the WHO approach to quality of life in its generic form: (a) quality of life can be expressed in terms of the distance between a patient's position before and that during treatment with reference to his or her intended goal; (b) the patient should (or should be helped to) define his or her goals in terms that are clear enough to allow an estimation of how close or distant he or she is from them; (c) the relationship between illness and quality of life is not necessarily linear (for example, depending on the stage of illness); (d) the measurement of quality of life is subject to no other difficulties than those inherent in all measurements of emotions.

The problems inherent in all measurements of emotions need to be reviewed here briefly. It is generally accepted that Thurstone (1928) was among the first to measure attitudes or subjective feelings by means of questionnaires. As a psychologist, he had great experience with psychophysics and was inspired by Fechner's law on subjective discrimination of physical stimuli. Thurstone defined attitudes as the sum total of a person's inclinations and feelings about any special topic. (Bentham in 1834 had measured subjective well-being as "the difference in value between the sum of the pleasures of all sorts and the sum of pains of all sorts which a man experienced in a given period of time.") Thurstone's attitude scales used paired comparisons, which were related to Fechner's subjective discrimination technique in psychophysics. Likert's (1932) scaling method used item response categories (e.g. strongly agree, agree), and this soon became more popular than the Thurstone method. Likert required that items of an attitude scale have an additive relationship when the summed total score of the scale is the measurement of the attitude under investigation.

In this compendium rating scales of the Likert type are used not only for the measurement of health-related quality-of-life distances, as suggested by Sartorius (1987), but also for the measurement of severity of health status and for the measurement of diagnoses. This is a quantitative approach to psychopathology. The main objective of this compendium concerning scaling methods is a further development of Likert scaling. Likert (1932) used the correlation between each item and the total score of all items in a rating scale as evidence for the additive relationship between items measuring a dimension (e.g. subjective well-being, severity of schizophrenia or diagnosis of melancholia). In this compendium, latent structure analysis (Rasch 1960) is used to assess the additive relationship between items (construct validity). This approach is closer to Popper's (1976) requirements of scientific evidence than to correlational analysis.

1.2 Divergence Between Rating Scales and DSM-III-R

The question of concordance between rating scales and DSM-III-R is mainly in regard to content validity for the psychopathologist or others interested in health profiles and health-related quality-of-life problems. The scientific evidence for the system of DSM-III or DSM-III-R is fragile. Thus, it is emphasized that the major methodological innovation of DSM-IV will be "its efforts to move beyond expert consensus by placing greater emphasis on the careful, objective accumulation of empirical evidence" (Frances et al. 1990). In a historical perspective, however, it should be mentioned that DSM-I (APA 1952) was considered by Stengel (1959) to be the most useful of the various national classification systems in psychiatry. On the other hand, DSM-I was found insufficient for the needs of rational psychopharmacological therapies when the major tranquillizers were introduced in the late 1950s.

Reviewing studies on factor analysis using comprehensive rating scales, Frank (1975) concluded that DSM-II (APA 1968) contained the following target syndromes (a) a general psychotic syndrome, which could be organic (e.g. dementia) or non-organic; (b) specific psychotic syndromes such as schizophrenia and depression; and (c) neurotic syndromes such as depression, anxiety, phobia and obsessive-compulsive states. However, DSM-II contains 182 different diagnoses. Table 1.1 compares the various DSM editions and the system developed by de Sauvages (1747), who constructed his system by arranging the individual symptoms into classes, orders and genera with reference to the biological system of Linnaeus. However, the system of Linnaeus was an empirically based classification. The development shown in Table 1.1 has been described by Frances et al. (1990) as follows: "Some separately labelled co-occuring disorders may just as plausibly be considered part of a single complex syndrome that has been split apart of a single complex syndrome."

Table 1.1. Number of different diagnosis in DSM editions and by de Sauvages (1747). (From Frances et al. 1990)

	Number of diagnoses
DSM-I	106
DSM-II	182
DSM-III	265
DSM-III-R	292
Bossier de Sauvages	2400

In his chapter on general psychopathology Bleuler, (1924) stated:

It must be borne in mind that although superficially two phenomena may look alike, they may nevertheless have entirely different meanings, depending on their psychic environments and on their genesis. Moreover, and this is even more true here than in physical pathology, every symptom is really only a special part of a general process. What we, for example, described in the spheres of association, is but a general psychic disturbance, from which we pick out one part, namely that which concerns the associations.

1.2.1 Target Syndromes: The Phenomenological Spectrum of Core Symptoms Versus the Discriminating Points of Diagnosis

The DSM-III criteria of the many (too many) axis 1 syndromes (psychiatric syndromes) are based on clinical symptoms. This is perhaps the most revolutionary aspect of DSM-III-R (or DSM-III). In contrast, rating scales, as a conservative method, are defined by their functions. Thus, scales measuring severity of clinical syndromes are symptom scales or global scales. However, scales measuring diagnosis include a variety of non-symptoms such as personality features, psychosocial stressors, duration of symptoms, diurnal fluctuation in symptoms, etc. Hence, the Melancholia Scale (Bech 1981) is an example of a pure severity scale measuring the phenomenological spectrum of depression, while the Diagnostic Melancholia Scale (Bech et al. 1988) illustrates a diagnostic scale having no core symptoms.

Frances et al. (1990) have pointed out that DSM-III-R uses two separate approaches at the same time, namely including core symptoms based on shared phenomenology and symptoms with discriminating (diagnostic) power. These authors emphasize that "Unfortunately, items at the core of the definition are sometimes poor at discriminating the disorder, and items that are more discriminating may not be close to the core." In this context, the classical paper by Prusoff and Klerman (1974) on differentiating depressed from anxious neurotic patients should be recalled. In this study, Prusoff and Klerman used a symptom checklist to show that anxiety was part of the depressive spectrum, thus employing a quantitative approach (total item scores). However, using a discriminant function analysis on the same set of items, a few symptoms (without any logical connection) seemed to discriminate, emphasizing the fact that discriminant function analysis is statistically too powerful to show differences.

There is no close correspondence between severity scales and diagnostic disorders analogous to the lack of structural association between fever ('thermometer measurement') and causal agents (e.g. toxins or microorganisms). Severity scales refer mainly to the core or target syndromes and usually tap several disorders.

Most of the scales included in this compendium in Chaps. 2 and 3 are severity scales, i.e. symptom scales. The correspondence to DSM-III, DSM-III-R or ICD-10 is at the level of core (target) syndromes. The phenomenological spectrum of these target syndromes reduces the number of axis 1 syndromes. Frances et al. (1990) argue that the attempt to use a prototypal approach in DSM-III-R through polythetic criteria and multiple disorders to be diagnosed is a way to counterbalance the evident lack of spectrum thinking.

1.2.2 Procedural Algorithms Versus Rating Scale Spectrum

The use of criteria (in the form of procedural algorithms) in DSM-III was intended for improvement of inter-observer reliability of the diagnosis of mental disorders. Neither DSM-II nor ICD-9 included specific criteria or rules of convention; these are both examples of the so-called textbook approach, in which inter-observer reliability is not a natural part of the system. These textbook systems have shown low inter-observer reliability (Bech 1981).

There are various models of classification for combining items into a set of criteria (Snaith 1962). The monothetic model contains several criteria, and each needs to be present in order to make the diagnosis. The polythetic model is that adopted by DSM-III, the procedural algorithm, in which ten items, for instance, are listed but only four required in order to make the diagnosis. Cantor et al. (1980) and Widiger and Frances (1985), among others, have considered the DSM-III model as an example of the prototypical model which accepts that diagnostic groups are heterogeneous in membership, have overlapping boundaries, and are characterized by items correlated with group membership.

The distinction between monothetic and polythetic models illustrates the different philosophical theories of definition: The monothetic model is used by Widiger and Frances (1985) as an example of the classical, Aristotelian approach of definition with individually necessary and jointly sufficient items. The textbook approach is similar to the monothetic model in requiring obligatory criteria. The procedural algorithms of DSM-III or DSM-III-R are to some extent indeterminate by not requiring obligatory criteria (as one criterion can substitute another) and might in this respect be closer to Wittgenstein's epistemological model for concepts of mind. The textbook approach considers items as part of a psychiatric terminology by which a lexicographic definition is possible, in the Aristotelian sense. However, Wittgenstein (1953) showed that concepts of mind are not lexicographic concepts; in his view, the items should be considered as indicators of a dimension which is not observable. It is the behaviour of the items that yields the concept.

Probability is therefore the key. There are, as discussed by Popper (1990), different theories of probability, for example, the subjectivistic and the objectivistic theories. In the subjectivistic theory of probability there is no structure among items. The DSM-III or DSM-III-R approach assumes a subjectivistic theory, i.e. it is unimportant which four of the ten items classify a patient on the dimension being examined. The objectivistic theory requires a structure among items, with some items being more important but in terms of an indeterminate or probabilistic theory.

The key here is quantification. Although the procedural algorithms of DSM-III or DSM-III-R resist quantification, it can be tested whether they fit statistical

models of latent classes. However, as a field becomes better understood, the need
for quantification or measurement increases (Kuhn 1961). Rating scales are based
on quantitative, psychometric theories of validity. Rating scales assign numbers to
clinical data (reported or observed) according to specified rules to yield a metric
indicator of the dimension being investigated. The theory behind rating scales is
the model of set theories, which, as observed by Quine (1963), derives from
Skolem's axiomatized set theory (Skolem 1922). This was the first definition of
the term model. When applied to the spectrum of an illness, Skolem's model assumes neither that one among the symptoms which is pathognomonic, nor that all
thinkable symptoms of the illness must be considered. Quine's set theory is a further development of Skolem's model and stresses the role of quantification in describing the essential behaviour of the items.

The basic point here is that no item of a rating scale is alone sufficient, but that
a limited number of items are together sufficient if representative of the universe
of items being investigated, and if clustered. In psychometric terms, the representative set of items should be tested for their content validity (representativeness)
and the clustering of items for their construct validity (the sufficient statistic of
measurement).

The size of a rating scale (the number of items it contains) should in the
framework for set theories be few. The principle of limitation of size in set theories emphasizes that sets are parts of classes and that the number of items in a set
is consequently few (Lewis 1991). The rating scales included in this compendium
are brief (small, short) scales containing around 10 items (see also Sect. 1.5.1,
number of items in a rating scale).

Using numbers, in accordance with Quine (1963), to express the clustering of
symptoms in a set (i.e. a clinical syndrome), the psychometric literature has
adopted two different methods: correlation coefficients (e.g. factor analysis) and
latent structure analysis (e.g. Rasch analysis; Rasch 1960). Table 1.2 compares the
(classical) psychometric method of correlational analysis and the (modern) psychometric method of latent structure analysis. Both methods use terms such as
homogeneity, construct validity and criterion-related validity.

The concept of validity (*Geltung*), as discussed by Jaspers, (1947), has implications for determining the appropriateness of a test. The analysis of content validity is a practical or pragmatic approach, which in psychopathology refers to
clinical knowledge. As shown in Table 1.2, content validity plays a major role in
the modern psychometric literature while Likert scales contain only a very limited
number of items (around 10) measuring only one dimension. In the classical psychometric literature, on the other hand, content validity played a minor role because a large number of items were included (the most proper scale has most
items), and the construct analysis determined how many dimensions or factors
were needed.

The term homogeneity has different meanings in the classical and the modern
psychometric literature, although it is rooted basically in coherence theories of
truth. In classical test theories (Guilford 1936, 1954; Nunnally 1967) homogeneity
refers to the degree of positive correlation between items. Among the most fre-

Table 1.2. Classical correlational analysis and modern latent structure analysis in psychometric models

Type of Validity	Classical psychometric methods	Modern psychometric methods
Content validity (practical clinical knowledge)	Minor importance because of greater role of construct validity	Major importance because construct validity is part of content validity
Construct validity (coherence of items)	Coherence of items is based on correlation coeffeicients expressing the homogeneity, e.g. item total coefficients, Cronbach's alpha, factor analysis	Coherence of items in terms of their hierarchical tapping of information along one dimension (homogeneity), e.g. Loevinger, Rasch; the homogeneity should be maintained across populations (transferability), e.g. Rasch
Criterion validity ☐ Concurrent	Correspondence with other tests, standardization of homogeneity, e.g. by sex	Correspondence with other tests, especially global clinical assessment
☐ Predictive validity	Correspondence with other criteria over time, e.g. outcome of treatment (dynamic standardization)	Correspondence with other criteria over time, e.g. outcome of treatment (dynamic standardization)

Item score

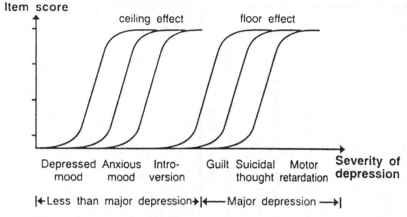

|←Less than major depression→|←——Major depression ——→|

Fig. 1.1. Latent structure analysis

quently used statistical tests for measuring homogeneity in this sense is the Cronbach alpha coefficient (Cronbach 1951). In this context it should be emphasized that the square root of alpha in most textbooks has been labeled the "index of reliability", but it is as already stated by Tryon (1957) an index of domain or construct validity. However, if items have a high alpha value they may measure only a very limited aspect of the dimension being examined, thereby showing low content validity. Another consequence of a high alpha value is that only one item may be needed while the other items are redundant. In modern psychometric theories the homogeneity of items refers to items belonging to the same dimension but with differing degrees of inclusiveness. Dividing the dimension into units of information, each item should be independent of each other in the tapping of information. Using the dimension of depressive states (severity of depression) as an example, the homogeneity of items is shown in Fig. 1.1. The most inclusive items, such as depressed mood, anxious mood and introversion, provide information of the lesser degree of depression. In the psychometric literature such items are said to have a ceiling effect. The items of guilt, suicidal thoughts and motor retardation are exclusive items, showing a floor effect (Fig. 1.1).

It should be emphasized that there are coefficients which express homogeneity in its modern sense (e.g. Loevinger 1948, 1957; Mokken 1971). In this meaning of homogeneity it constitutes a major aspect of construct validity. Although the American Psychological Association (1974) considers construct validity to be an essential requirement of a rating scale, it is difficult to use their recommendations practically. The term construct validity was introduced by Cronbach and Meehl (1955) to measure hypothesized dimensions (constructs) in situations in which external validity criteria were lacking (criterion validity). While homogeneity in the classical psychometric literature refers to construct validity, homogeneity in modern psychiatry is only one aspect of construct validity. In the modern approach, construct validity is the measuring process of content validity, i.e. the coherence among components (items) of the content of the scale. In other words, construct validity is the scaling aspect and it is determined by an analysis of the measurement operations of the items (components). Such an item analysis could be named the "survival of the fittest". As noted in Table 1.2, a proper analysis of construct validity involves testing for transferability (Bech 1981), which refers to the degree to which homogeneity is represented in different subpopulations, for example, males versus females and young versus elderly and across different diagnoses. The most appropriate method for testing transferability is latent structure analysis (Rasch 1960; Lord and Novick 1968; Lazarsfeld and Henry 1968; Rust and Golombok 1989). This is the only method in which homogeneity and transferability are integral parts of the construct validity analysis. The Loevinger analysis, on the other hand, provides only some information on homogeneity.

It is a general principle of this compendium to show the components (and their relationships to items) for describing content validity. Likert items (i.e. each item measured on a scale from 0–4) and Likert rating scales (i.e. short scales with approximately ten items; Ghiselli et al. 1981) have been used for analyses of construct validity concerning both psychopathological dimensions and the health-status dimension or health-related quality-of-life dimensions. If a scale fulfils the Rasch analysis, the total score is an adequate indicator of the dimension being evaluated (Fig. 1.1).

The correspondence between the sufficient statistic of a scale (its total score as an expression of construct validity) and an external criterion is termed criterion validity. If the external criterion is another hypothetical dimension (a construct), criterion validity refers to the same conceptual level. In this situation one could argue that the analysis is within the range of construct validity in its classical sense (Cronbach and Meehl 1955). In this compendium, however, the construct validity of a rating scale is defined in its narrow sense as the unidimensional scaling principle of content validity. Hence, criterion validity is defined in its wider range. Criterion validity can be subdivided into concurrent validity (i.e. the correspondence between scale score and criterion is at the same point in time) and predictive validity (i.e. the correspondence is delayed, the criterion being measured after a follow-up period). Furthermore, concurrent validity can be subdivided into convergent validity (expressing an acceptable correspondence between scale score and criterion if the criterion is defined within the same content universe as the scale) and discriminant validity (the ability of the scale to discriminate between different conditions, for example, the criterion being defined as the difference between active treatment and placebo). The latter aspect of concurrent validity is also referred to as sensitivity to measure change. Only for scales fulfilling the Rasch model does a change in scores between two assessments represent a real change (the total scores refer to only one dimension).

One of the consequences of working with proper Likert scales is that parametric tests of statistical inference can be used. Otherwise, non-parametric tests should be used (Siegel 1956; Siegel and Castellan 1988).

1.2.3 Administration: Types of Information

The DSM-III-R and ICD-10 systems are administered by psychiatrists or psychologists on the basis of an interview with the patient and, if needed, other information obtained from ward personnel, relatives of the patient, written documents, case records, etc. The use of self-rating assessments of symptoms for reaching a diagnosis may be misleading as the thresholds of clinicians may differ from those of the patients. Scales based on interview assessments are called observer-rating scales. In some observer-rating scales it is a general principle that all obtainable information (including other information than that from the interview situation) be considered (e.g. the Hamilton Depression Scale). Other observer scales specify which items are based on the interview situation and which on other information (e.g. the Positive and Negative Syndrome Scale). For scales in which information is often based on other sources than the interviews it is artificial to speak of inter-observer reliability. Inter-rater (or inter-judge) reliability is then a more appropriate term, and for such scales case vignettes rather than interviews are needed for inter-rater reliability studies in a joint rater situation (Hjortsø et al. 1989).

The rating scale method involves other forms of scales. If the information is the patient's self-report, one speaks of self-rating scales or self-administered questionnaires. If the information source is a patient's relative, the term relative-rating scale is often used, and if the information is based on ward observations, the term nurse-rating scale is used. It is generally considered that patients and nurses are more likely either to miss important signs of psychopathology or to attribute too much importance to minor signs of mental illness because they lack appropriate training in psychopathology (Raskin 1986). However, with the appropriate training nurses can be excellent raters, and patients' self-assessments are vital when measuring quality of life components. Self-rating scales are therefore essential in the discussion in Chapter 9 on health-related quality-of-life scales. Table 1.3 presents an overview of the various types of scales in relation to their respective types of information.

In this compendium observer rating scales are used for comparing scales with DSM-III-R and ICD-10 at the level of axis 1 disorders, i.e. the scales discussed in Chaps. 2 and 3. However, for some syndromes (e.g. mania and aggression) nurse-

Table 1.3. Administration of rating scales in relation to types of information

Type of information	Scales
Self-report	Self-rating scales
Report from relatives	Relative rating scales
Ward observations	Nurse rating scales
Interview with the patient	Observer rating scales
All kinds of information including documents, case record, interviews	Case vignette scales

rating scales are included. Chapter 4 deals with self-rating scales relevant for axis 1 disorders, and Chapter 5 covers axis 2 disorders in which both observer rating scales and self-rating scales are included.

It should be emphasized that a comprehensive textbook on clinical interviews using DSM-III-R has just been released (Othmer and Othmer 1989). It is outside the scope of this compendium to deal with this approach, but the book is highly recommended.

1.3 Comparison Between ICD-9, DSM-III and Rating Scales: Degrees of Quantification

Theoretically, the use of criteria for mental states concerning content validity (at which level of validity, DSM-III-R and rating scales agree) was introduced by Wittgenstein (1953). In paragraph 580 he states that "An inner process stands in need of outward criteria." The notion of consistency between inner and outer processes was further developed by Strawson (1959). Outward criteria are based on the observation of behaviour including patient's self-reports.

The use of criteria in DSM-III was intended for the improvement of inter-observer reliability of the diagnosis of mental disorders, in comparison to the previous classification systems such as those of DSM-II or ICD-8 (WHO 1974) in which no specific criteria or rules of convention were listed (the so-called text-book approach). In contrast to DSM-III the criteria drawn from rating scales refer to measurement, as shown in the preceding section.

Table 1.4 presents the description of depressive states by ICD-9 (WHO 1978), DSM-III and the Melancholia Scale. The ICD-9 description includes a number of items without further specifications. The DSM-III description is a list of items, of which item A and at least four items of group B should be present for the definition of major depression. A patient who does not fulfil the DSM-III criteria may have a less than major depression, for which, however, there are no specific DSM-III categories (such as atypical depression, dysthymia, and generalized anxiety). This is indeed a serious disadvantage as most of the patients treated for depression by family doctors do not fulfil the criteria of major depression or dysthymia. The rank order of items on the Melancholia Scale is in accordance with results obtained by Maier and Philipp (1985). This is analogous to the example shown in Fig. 1.1.

In this compendium the various target syndromes have been described as in Table 1.4, however, with ICD-10 and DSM-III-R replacing ICD-9 and DSM-III, respectively.

Table 1.4. Comparison of ICD-9, DSM-III and rating scales for the classification of depression

ICD-9 Classical textbook classification	DSM-III Prototypic classification		Rating scale Adequacy of indicator	
Severe disturbance of mood (usually compounded of depression and anxiety) which is accompanied by one or more of the following symptoms: delusions, perplexity, disturbed attitude to self, disorders of perception and behaviour; these are all in keeping with patient's prevailing mood. There is a strong tendency to suicide. For practical reasons, mild disorders of mood may also be included here if the symptoms match closely the description given.	A: Dysphoric mood	(0-1)	Work and interests	(0-4)
	B: Appetite/weight	(0-1)	Lowered mood	(0-4)
	Insomnia/hypersomnia	(0-1)	Sleep disturbances	(0-4)
	Psychomotor agitation/ retardation	(0-1)	Anxiety	(0-4)
			Emotional retardation	(0-4)
	Loss of interests	(0-1)	Intellectual retardation	(0-4)
	Loss of energy	(0-1)	Tiredness and pains	(0-4)
	Guilt feelings	(0-1)	Guilt feelings	(0-4)
	Concentration disturbances	(0-1)	Decreased verbal activity	(0-4)
	Suicidal thoughts and impulses	(0-1)	Suicidal thoughts and impulses	(0-4)
			Decreased motor activity	(0-4)
			Total score	(0-44)
			No depression =	0-5
			Mild depression =	6-9
			Probable major depression =	10-14
			Major depression =	15 or more

1.4 The Taxonomic Arrangement of Rating Scales: The Multi-Axial Approach

The multi-axial system introduced by DSM-III was a methodological innovation for official classification systems, as were the concepts of disability and handicaps introduced by the ICIDH (WHO 1980). However, scientific studies are still lacking for a comparison between the rating scale approach and the DSM-III-R/WHO systems. In this context it should be emphasized that the multi-axial approach was first advocated by the two Swedish psychiatrists Sjöbring (1919) and Essen-Möller (1949), but their suggestions were never adopted by the official Swedish classification system.

Table 1.5 shows seven different axes which are considered in this compendium. The litterature on rating scales has indicated the association between the conceptual basis of an axis and its scaling problem. The rating scale approach includes both observer ratings and self-ratings, whereas DSM-III-R and ICD-10 are only based on observer assessment of the various axes. In Chaps. 2 and 3 the clinical scales corresponding to DSM-III-R and ICD-10 diagnoses are mostly observer scales. However, Chapter 4 is devoted to self-rating scales for depression, anxiety and neurasthenia.

Concerning axis 1 (psychiatric disorders) the target syndromes and diagnostic syndromes are mixed in DSM-III-R. Psychometrically, item scaling of 0–4 is most appropriate for target syndromes (severity scales), while a 0–2 scaling is most appropriate for diagnostic indices. In general, observer scales are most appropriate for psychiatric disorders, although self-rating might be useful in minor disorders (e.g. anxiety and neurasthenia). In this compendium the dimensional approach to psychiatric axis 1 disorders is used, which in Chapter 3 is shown in relation to the Newcastle scales and the Diagnostic Melancholia Scale.

The scientific evidence for the many personality disorders included in DSM-III-R axis 2 is very fragile. In this compendium personality scales measuring vulnerability to stress are considered to cover the pathological psychology approach of psychopathology. Self-ratings are of particular interest here. However, for the borderline or the psychopathic personality observer ratings are considered most appropriate. The axis 2 disorders are analysed best using a dimensional approach.

Axis 3 in DSM-III-R is not an axis comparable to axis 1. Both axis 1 and axis 3 are meant to measure clinical disability in – psychiatric and somatic disorders, respectively. However, it is usually the ICD codes for somatic disorders that have been used (e.g. Bech et al. 1987). In this compendium axis 3 refers to the impact of somatic illness on the chronically ill. The concept of impairment is used for disturbances at the level of organs. In general, impairments can be classified by the ICD system (e.g. ICD-9). Disability refers to restriction in the patient's ability to perform functions in a manner considered normal for normal persons. In this compendium the principles of using disorder-specific scales for somatic disability has been compared to the ailment-oriented scales (Chapter 6). Ailment-oriented scales contain components that are relevant in clinical care of the patient whereas

Table 1.5. Conceptual basis and scaling of the different axes

	Conceptual basis	Scaling
Axis 1: Psychiatric disorders	Target syndromes for which treatments needed Diagnostic indices	Item scaling: 0-4 - Observer ratings (self) Item scaling: 0-2 - Observer ratings
Axis 2: Personality	Basic propensities to react with clinical syndromes. Vulnerability to stress	Item scaling: 0-1 - Self/observer ratings
Axis 3: Somatic disorders	Impact of somatic illness on the chronically ill	Item scaling: 0-1 - Self-ratings
Axis 4: Psychosocial stressors	Separating acute events from enduring circumstances. Separating independent (alpha) from dependent (beta) press	Item scaling: 0-1 - Self/observer ratings
Axis 5: Social functioning	Separating function in ward, at home, at work	Item scaling: 0-4 - Observer ratings
Axis 6: Quality of life scale	Separating physical, social and psychic well-being	Item scaling: 0-4 - Self-ratings
Axis 7: Sode effects of treatment	Unintended effects of treatment	Item scaling: 0-4 - Observer ratings

disorder-specific scales contain components that are relevant in the diagnosis making process.

Of the five axes in DSM-III-R, it is the dimension of axis 4 (severity of psychosocial stressors) that most resembles a rating scale. In DSM-III-R acute events are distinguished from persisting circumstances. Murray (1938) differentiated between alpha press (the event in itself) and beta press (the subjective effect of the event). Alpha press should be measured by observer ratings and beta press by self-ratings (see Chapter 7).

Axis 5 (social functioning) was a pure axis in DSM-III, but in DSM-III-R it consists of a mixture between symptoms and social functioning. The WHO (1980) concept of handicap refers to the social disadvantage due to disability. Strictly speaking, axis 5 should cover the patient's ability to fulfil a normal social role. It is therefore an observer rating scale. Social status scales are mentioned in Chapter 8.

Quality of life refers to the patient's own perception globally of the psychic, physical and social disadvantage of being ill and has therefore no reference to a specific DSM-III-R axis, rather quality of life is an integration of the five DSM-III-R axes. As discussed elsewhere (Bech 1991), the DSM-III-R definition of alcohol abuse illustrates the difference between disability and quality of life. According to DSM-III-R (code 305), alcohol abuse is the continued use of alcohol despite knowledge of having a persistent social, occupational, psychological or physical problem that is caused or exacerbated by the use of alcohol. In other words, the persistent social and occupational problem is measured in axis 5 (social functioning); the persistent psychological problem is measured in axis 1 (psychiatric disorders); and the persistent physical problem is measured in axis 3 as an ICD-9 code number and/or as a disability problem. It might well be (Bech 1991) that alcohol grants the patient a relief from discomfort effect which increases his or her quality of life. Hence, Peyser (1982) claims that "mood changes associated with relief of discomfort often appear with the first drinking episode and remain something that the alcoholic will later remember and report on his recovery." Recovery here refers to a return to health (axes 1 and 3). Discomfort scales are self-rating scales, as quality of life is a self-rating dimension.

Axis 7 in this compendium refers to symptoms of side effects of treatment. So far, only the side effects to biological treatments have been scientifically investigated. Observer ratings are often recommended in this context, but self-rating scales should also be taken into account. Rating scales for adverse drug reactions are mentioned in Chapter 10.

1.5 The Psychometric Characteristics and Criteria for the Selected Rating Scales

Many rating scales have been published – too many to be included in a single compendium. For each of the many axes covered by this compendium the modern psychometric criteria of homogeneity, construct validity, criterion validity and inter-observer reliability have been considered. The classical psychometric criteria have therefore not been dealt with thoroughly; the classical psychometrician Nunnally (1967) offered the following warning in this regard: "Without powerful methods of analysis, such as factor analysis and analysis of variance, it would be all but impossible to assess the results of research."

In making this selection of rating scales it becomes clear that modern psychometric verification is remarkably weak for many scales. However, this is also the case even in reference to classical psychometric studies on psychopathological rating scales (e.g. von Riezen and Siegel 1988; Wetzler 1989), on measurements of health (e.g. McDowell and Newell 1987), and on quality of life scales (Spilker 1990). From a scientific point of view the work on instruments of psychiatric research (Thompson 1989) is important for stressing the content validity of scales and the relative weights of clinical components included in the individual scales.

1.5.1 Content Validity

It is the rather high correspondence between DSM-III-R, ICD-10 and the most frequently used rating scales that constitutes the basis of this compendium. One of the major differences between the classical and the modern psychometric approach is the greater importance of content validity required by the modern approach. Rating scales, as noted by Hamilton (1976), "are not really suitable for exploring a new field of knowledge. Their construction requires much practical experience and an appropriate body of theory; in a sense they are an end-product."

A Likert scale contains rather few items (around 10) and is often referred to as a brief (short, small) scale. Dimensions in health and disease can be sufficiently measured by Likert scales which have been evidenced by Rasch analysis (Bech 1981). This size of a scale (around 10 items) has also been supported from other frames of reference than set theories and Rasch models, e.g. information theory models (Miller 1956), decission-making models (Widiger et al. 1984), and judgment analysis (Hammond et al. 1980). Most of the syndromes in DSM-III-R and ICD-10 are likewise domained by around 10 items (Table 1.6). In contrast, the

Table 1.6. Content validity item characteristic of diagnosis and severity scales

Content validity item characteristic	Diagnostic scales, incl. DSM-III-R and ICD-10	Severity scales
Number of items	10	10
Calibration of items	Nominal, checklist	Ordinal, Likert
Time framing of items	2 weeks or more (retroduction)	3 days (inspection)

classical approach to measurement requires the largest size of items for a rating scale; the most proper scale according to this principle is the scale containing most items.

Calibration of Items: Likert Versus Checklist. The type of response categories for of the individual items depends on the purpose of the scale (nominal: not present or present; ordinal: not present, very mild or doubtful, mild to moderate, moderate to marked, marked to extreme). For severity scales, ordinal item definition is most appropriate. From a modern psychometric point of view, ordinal categories from 0–4 are most appropriate, as these values are still considered as categorical data in statistical analysis. From a clinical point of view, one can consider steps between 0 and 6 or 0 and 8. Hamilton (1967) found it clinically superfluous to have more than three steps (0–2) for items such as insomnia. In this compendium, therefore, items with more than five categories are excluded. For diagnostic scales the three-step (0–2) item definition is most appropriate. In this compendium only very few diagnostic scales are included because still rather few scales have been constructed. The Newcastle scales originally had 0–1 definitions, but the Diagnostic Melancholia Scale has item definitions from 0 to 2, as have the Newcastle scales included in this compendium.

Scales with ordinally defined items are often referred to as Likert scales after Likert (1932), one of the pioneers of rating scales (see above). Lissitz and Green (1975) have emphasized that Likert scales have five categories. Scales with nominally items defined are often referred to as checklist scales.

Studies of symptoms (items), as opposed to studies of diagnostic categories, regard psychopathological symptoms as probably best conceived of as continuous with non-pathological phenomena, a point made by Strauss (1969). Experience with the scales included in this compendium (Chapter 2), however, has shown that the definition of the score '0' should signify 'not present' instead of, for example, 'normal motor activity'. In the case of a depressed patient showing signs of slight motor retardation but no sign of motor agitation, it is not reasonable to score '0' in the item of agitation if the definition here is 'normal motor activity'. Consequently, the scales in this compendium use 'not present' apart from items for which it is evident that a specific definition is necessary.

The calibration of items is a major topic of this compendium. For severity items no more than five steps (0–4) have been considered (handling more than five steps or levels consistently may be beyond the cognitive capacity of many raters; Miller 1956). The Brief Psychiatric Rating Scale, which originally included 0-6 steps for each item was modified to 0–4 items (Bech et al. 1986). The Positive and Negative Syndrome Scale (Chapter 3) has also been modified from a 0–6 to a 0–4 calibration. When applying psychometric methods such as factor analysis or latent structure analysis, 0–4 categories are more acceptable than 0–6 categories.

Time Frame of Items. Different classification schedules may vary in the time frame required for the various diagnoses. Thus, as discussed by Angst et al. (1990), the various classification systems for the diagnosis of depression cover different time frames ranging from 2 weeks for the DSM-III-R to 4 weeks for the Feighner criteria (Feighner et al. 1972). The Newcastle scales focus on the current episode of depression. In contrast, scales measuring the severity of clinical states are usually less variable in their time frames and cover 3–7 days. In this compendium a time frame of 3 days is recommended; however, one of 7 days may be more appropriate for certain research projects in which case this should be specified.

Severity scales measure symptoms which, following Ryle (1949), are occurrences or reported states ("protocol sentences" in the terminology of Carnap (1934)). Diagnosis refers to the mode of reasoning about underlying hypothesis formation. It proceeds from the observations of a fact, as collected by means of a severity scale, to a hypothesis for explaining that fact. Severity scales involve inspection and induction, diagnostic scales retroduction.

The content validity of severity scales refers to items that are sensitive to change over time, whereas in the case of diagnostic scales the reference to time is less important.

The time frame is a major problem in DSM-III-R. On the one hand, it is not clearly stated, for example, when defining major depression versus endogenous depression; on the other the strict criterion of 2 weeks' duration for the target syndrome of major depression is less valid from a therapeutic point of view. This problem has recently been discussed by Wing et al. (1990), who have suggested the following nomenclature for time frames:

Primary period (the most recent period)
– Present state, e.g. the last 3 days (Melancholia Scale)
– Present episode, from date of onset of episode (e.g. Diagnostic Melancholia Scale)
– Lifetime ever, from date of onset of first episode (symptom) to present state (e.g. Newcastle Depression Diagnostic Scale)
Secondary period (a period earlier than the primary period)
– Representative period, if more characteristic than the primary period, or if representing a different type of symptom profile
– Lifetime before, from date of onset of first episode (symptom) to the beginning of the primary period

1.5.2 Criterion and Construct Validity

The traditional definition of criterion validity is the association of a scale with a 'gold standard', the 'cash value' of a scale (Bech, 1981). Criterion validity is divided into concurrent validity and predictive validity both of which are relevant for the standardization of a scale. The construct validity refers to how well a scale measures the proposed underlying factors or dimensions (hypothetical or latent constructs) of health and disease. Methodologically but not ontologically construct validity differs from criterion validity. Thus, Guion (1977) has stated that:

"...All validity is as its base some form of construct validity... It is the basic meaning of validity..."

The paradigm shift in modern psychometric theories towards construct validity lay in the introduction of statistical thinking for the integration of items, inclusion of clinically relevant components (content validity) and the adequacy of indicators (criterion validity).

Latent trait analysis (Rasch 1960) is referred to in this compendium as latent structure analysis to ensure that it can be used without misunderstanding for evaluating construct validity concerning both psychopathological states and traits. From a historical point of view latent trait models came from the tradition of mental test theory and latent class models were mostly applied to sociological research data. Lazarsfeld and Henry (1968) were among the first to treat both approaches within a common framework, the latent structure analysis. A further development in this direction has recently been made by Langeheine and Rost (1988). The Rasch model is the model referred to in this compendium as this model from a rating scale point of view is most appropriate and relevant. The model is based on what Popper (1990) has called "the propensity interpretation of probability". The hierarchical structure of the items in Fig. 1.1 shows that depression (as with the inner structure of the loaded die in Popper's example) has the effect of producing unequal probabilities of item affirmation. Hence, some items 'come first', are most inclusive and show a ceiling effect.

There are three levels of description. At the lowest level are the items. At the second level is the distribution of items in relation to the components of the dimension (syndrome) being empirically analysed. At the third level is the Rasch analysis of homogeneity and transferability by which the construct validity is tested in terms of the adequacy of the indicator.

Feinstein (1987) has used the term transparency for the ability to 'see through' a total score to determine what it contains. If the total score is an adequate indicator, the information contained in the individual items is transformed into the total score. In other words, there is no information left in the individual items; the total score has optimal transparency. Feinstein (1987) maintains that transparency is generally obtained by scales containing a limited number of items, for example around ten. Construct validity, then, is the demonstration that a rating scale is unidimensional although including several components.

In the classical psychometric literature standardization of a scale has two elements: first obtaining information on the total scores of the general population by taking appropriate samples, and second establishing a set of principles for transforming raw data into a scale with a normal distribution. Modern psychometric methods eliminate the need for normal score distribution abandonned because the construct validity obtained by Rasch analysis allows parametric testing. Although the scales for the Rasch model are sufficient in terms of transferability across populations, it is often of clinical significance to establish some criterion-related validity of the total scores. Concerning the need for score references, two methods are often used in the classical psychometric literature; of these, the norm-referencing procedure is the more frequent; the population used to specify the scale score may consist of different diagnostic groups and/or matched non-patient populations. The other form of standardization is the criterion-referencing procedure, which is essentially a method of predictive validity, and which is the method relevant for this compendium. An example of this is provided by the study of Paykel (1990), who found that depressed patients with a score of 13 or higher on the Hamilton Depression Scale had a significantly better outcome on active drug therapy than those on placebo.

Rasch analysis is the only statistical model in which homogeneity and transferability can be tested as aspects of construct validity to determine whether the total score represents an adequate indicator. Rasch analysis is most relevant for severity scales, where measurement is the essential aspect, for example, in measuring outcome of treatment.

While transparency or adequacy of total scores is a criterion of construct validity in severity rating scales, this concept is not meaningful in categorical classification systems where the goal is to preserve rather than to reduce information. On the other hand, the procedural algorithm of DSM-III-R seems based on a platonic idealism, where each diagnosis is adequately described by the lexicographic symptom of the diagnosis being examined. In this connection it should be mentioned that latent class analysis (Andersen 1990) is an approach by which symptoms are considered only as indicators of illness (as in the Rasch model). However, the adequacy but local independence of total scores is not a requirement of latent class analysis, which is therefore a weaker test than Rasch analysis. An example of latent class analysis is the study by Young et al. (1983) on establishing diagnostic criteria for mania.

Another model that may be found appropriate for testing the validity of diagnostic criteria is that the examing degree of membership, which is a mathematical version of Wittgenstein's theory of definition.

The rating scale approach follows Wittgenstein's non-lexicographic approach to mental concepts (Wittgenstein 1953), in which items are indicators of the underlying dimension which in principle is unobservable.

Figure 1.2 presents a modification of Brunswik's lens model (Brunswik 1952); this shows that the rating scale method is one for skilled perception and indicates the probabilistic nature of perception (Brunswik 1934). Brunswik was a member of the Vienna Circle of philosophers of mind, along with Schlick (1932), Carnap (1934), Ayer (1936), Quine (1963) and Wittgenstein (1953). These philosophers emphasized the importance of inter-observer reliability and the fact that while construct validation can never be complete, it may in a way be cumulative over the numerous studies available (an example of verification in science).

The six symptom points in Fig. 1.2 are the items having the most content validity of the dimension being studied. The rater who selects the six item scale has a greater trust in these items than in others. However, because patients may differ in their ability to signal their symptoms, the validity of the items is never absolutely certain, and the area of uncertainty is probabilistic in nature. The most appropriate analysis of the area of uncertainty of severity scales is that of Rasch, in which the informational utility of the items is analysed by the hierarchy of cues, as

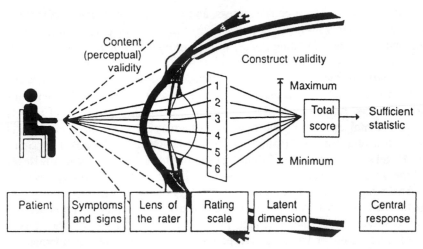

Fig. 1.2. The Brunswik (1934, 1952) lens model of perception modified for rating scales (skilled perception)

described by Brunswik (1934, 1952). The Rasch model, however, analyses the group of items as a whole group; therefore, if the group of items does not fulfil the Rasch model, no information on the individual items is given. Another problem is that Rasch analysis requires a relatively large number of patients. The features of Rasch analysis has been described by Allerup and Sorber (1977) and recently by Andersen (1990).

Statistical methods that may be considered 'pre-Rasch' models are those of Guttman and Loevinger (further developed by Mokken 1971). Of these, the Guttman method (Guttman 1944) is non-probabilistic, leaving no room for errors. Mokken (1971) notes that "When we try to apply this Guttman model of a perfect scale to empirical data, its deterministic features will lead to imperfections. Perfect scales and perfect items rarely exist in practice. One has to face the fact that the ideal, as usual, can only be approximated." Probabilistic models based on Guttman's principle of a perfect scale (i.e. homogeneity) were developed by Loevinger (1948, 1957), using a coefficient of homogeneity (in Guttman's sense, i.e. hierarchical structure); this coefficient expresses the degree of inter-item hierarchy. A Loevinger coefficient value under 0.30 indicates no hierarchical structure; one between 0.30 and 0.39, a slight tendency towards hierarchical structure; one between 0.40 and 0.49, a moderate tendency; and one of 0.50 or higher, a marked tendency. Mokken (1971) also developed a coefficient of homogeneity for the individual items of a scale. It should, however, be emphasized that the adequacy of scale total scores can only be shown by the Rasch model, which is therefore the most appropriate test for construct validity of severity scales.

Development of a rating scale with true construct validity takes years. It is interesting in this context to compare the rating scale model in Figure 1.2 with the experience of a novelist: "Experience is never limited, and it is never complete; it is an immense sensibility, a kind of huge spider-web of the finest silken threads suspended in the chamber of consciousness, and catching every air-borne particle in its tissue" (James 1884). As Jaspers (1923) emphasized, psychopathology is limited, and therefore also rating scales, which are bound to their construct validity.

In the course of the development from platonic idealism to Kant's subjective idealism a priori concepts or categories came to be seen as the basis for the combination of items. According to Kant (1781),it is the pathologist himself who is the transcendental ego. Thus, the atomistic diversity of items or symptoms is formed into a unity or combination by the individual rater. As noted by Stern (1990), Hegel's (1817) critique of Kant focused on this subjective idealism. Hegel argued that no transcendental subject is in need of this item combination because the internal structures are inherent in nature. Hegel's approach is often referred to as absolute idealism, but Stern (1990) points out that his is a realist's approach according to which objects are structured by concepts. Hegel thus not only depersonalized Kant's transcendental ego but perhaps also inspired the development of modern statistical models by which the inherent structures of concepts can be studied (for example, by latent structure analysis). This development was foreseen by James (1911) when he concluded, "With concepts we go in quest of the absent, meet the remote, actively turn this way or that, bend our experience, and make it tell us whether it is bound. We change its order, run it backwards, bring far bits together and separate near bits, ... string its items on as many ideal diagrams as our mind can frame." In this compendium the assessment of similarity between patients has been made using only one dimension per assessment, the index approach. Assessing similarity between profiles (by diagrams) is, of course, much more complex and little has been done in this field since the classical paper by Cronbach and Gleser (1953).

The best example of the combined use of factor analysis and latent structure analysis (Loevinger, Mokken, Rasch) to evaluate the construct validity of rating scales is the development of aggression scales by ERAG (1992).

1.5.3 Inter-observer Reliability

Disagreement between observers or raters (Andreasen and Spitzer 1979; Bech 1981) may arise as the result of (a) information variance, occurring when observers gather their information from different sources; (b) observation variance, occurring when clinicians look at the same set of information but observe it differently; (c) terminological variance, occurring when clinicians observe the same phenomena but come to different conclusions because they employ different terminologies; and (d) the ignorance of clinical phenomena. The use of Likert rating scales eliminates some of these, but studies have shown that the level of inter-observer reliability is rarely optimal. In general, there have been very few studies even with the most frequently used scales, such as the Hamilton scales and the Brief Psychiatric Rating Scale.

In the psychometric literature many different methods have been used for the statistical evaluation of inter-observer reliability. Table 1.7 presents the classical approach (Fleiss 1986; Bech 1988). Fleiss has used parametric tests such as the intra-class coefficient (ICC, Bartko and Carpenter 1976) and analysis of variance (ANOVA). Using data published by Fleiss, Bech (1988) has shown that non-parametric tests (Kendall's concordance test and the Friedman test; Siegel 1956) give comparable results. In principle, however, the non-parametric methods should be used for scales without construct validity in terms of Rasch analysis. As noted by Levy (1973), latent structure analysis tests whether a rating scale is an interval scale.

The ICC or Kendall's concordance test measures the inter-observer reliability for a group of psychopathologists examining a heterogeneous group of patients. It is customary to make joint ratings, with one rater performing the interview with the patients while the other raters are passive participators. Strictly speaking, each interview should be restricted to only one rater (Williams 1990), but this is rather difficult in daily practice; the use of video-taped interviews has become more popular (e.g. Bech et al. 1986b). The inter-observer coefficient, however, provides no information on whether one rater differs systematically from the others. Table 1.7 compares ANOVA and the Friedman test as methods for measuring rater bias in this sense.

In general, rating scales for latent structure analysis have a higher inter-rater reliability because strongly hierarchical structure tends to overestimate rater agreement (Hammond et al. 1980). According to classical test theories, however, a low number of items in a scale (around ten) reduces inter-observer reliability.

Judgement analysis is a most interesting method for investigating the reason for disagreement between raters (Joyce and Hammond 1984; Bech et al. 1986b). In this method reliability is considered as a dependent variable. Basically, judgement analysis is a method in the development phase of a rating scale or to be used in feedback training when introducing new raters to a study (Wigton et al. 1986). Part of the problem of inter-observer disagreement is the so-called halo effect, described as early as 1936 by Guilford as a major problem. This refers to the reflection of the patient's global impression in items that are not currently present. Judgement analysis deals with this problem by the use of global ratings.

Table 1.8 demonstrates the interaction between the observer and the scale. Murray (1959) refers to the nomothetic approach as the alpha situation and the idiographic situation as the beta situation; in the former the interview is conducted by an experienced psychiatrist and in the latter by a lay person. In the beta situation structured interviews such as the Diagnostic Interview Schedule can compensate for lay interviewers; this has been shown to have a sufficient number of specific alpha elements to be scored directly by lay interviewers without requiring considerable judgement (Robbins 1988). Without a structured interview schedule the DSM-III-R cannot be used by a lay interviewer. DSM-III-R cautions that "The proper use of these criteria requires specialized clinical training that provides both a body of knowledge and clinical skills." In this compendium the alpha approach

Table 1.7. Statistical requirements for inter-observer reliability studies

Level of scale measurement	Group of raters	Sufficient number of patients	Reliability coefficient	Rater bias
Interval scales: total score as adequate indicator (parametric scales)	Fixed or varying	10	Intra-class coefficient	ANOVA
Ordinal scales: total score as inadequate indicator (non-parametric scales)	Fixed	15	Kendall concordance test	Friedman test

Table 1.8. Inter-rater reliability. (Modified from Murray 1959)

	Alpha situation (Nomothetic approach)	Beta situation (Idiographic approach)
Observer	Experienced psychiatrist	Unexperienced psychiatrist
	Balanced view of pharmaco-, psychotherapy	Biased attitude towards treatment
	Experience with clinical trials	No experience with clinical trials
	Competence and good performance in goal-directed interviews	Vagueness and ambivalence in conducting interviews (conversations)
Scale	Few and relevant items	Many items
	Likert scale definition	Vague item definitions
	Adequacy of total scores	Inadequacy of total scores
	Transparency regarding treatment interventions	No transparency regarding treatment

has been used in selecting scales. Specialized clinical training as recommended for users of DSM-III-R is also recommended here.

Other errors related to the rater-scale situation have been discussed in the psychometric literature, include those of the central tendency, contrast error and therapeutic contrast effect. The central tendency, often seen in inexperienced raters, involves avoidance of extreme response categories (to be sure that he does not differ too much from other raters). It is for this reason that the Hamilton scale includes a middle category (1, very mild; 2, mild to moderate; 3, moderate to marked; 4, marked to extreme). Contrast error refers to the tendency often found in personality rating scales to underrate a trait which is also present in the rater himself. With depression scales, for example, this means the tendency of a de-pressed rater to score the depressed patient as less depressed than would a non-de-pressed rater. The therapeutic contrast effect is a very important factor recently described by Hamilton (1974). This refers to the bias of ratings before treatment versus those after treatment. If a rater is uncertain as to how to score a response, he tends to give a higher score before treatment (to ensure that the patient fulfils inclusion criteria) and a lower score after treatment (to ensure that the patient shows a response to treatment). According to Hamilton, this contrast effect can explain the difference in total score of about 5 units (the therapeutic contrast ef-fect) often seen in the patients receiving placebo treatment.

It should be emphasized that video interviews are particularly useful for train-ing raters in rating scale administrations (Bech et al. 1986c). The production of videotaped interviews with simulated patients is an indirect but highly effective way of teaching raters (Bech et al. 1986b). The skills that an effective interviewer should learn include according to Heilveil (1984) such issues as: 1) Preparing the patient: Try to relax the patient. 2) Asking questions: Focus on the "here and now" situation versus historical data. 3) Listening skills: Maintaining good emotional eye contact. Concentrate on the patient's response, and not the next question. 4) Sum-marize at the end of the interview. 5) Express gratitude to the patients for their participation.

There exist now several high quality video interviews with real patients cov-ering the Hamilton Anxiety Scale, Hamilton Depression Scale with Melancholia Scale, Mania Scale and Brief Psychiatric Rating Scale. New scales like the Posi-tive and Negative Symptom Schizophrenia Scale (PANSS) have been introduced by video interviews. An example of a training procedure based on videotapes cov-ering the Hamilton Depression Scale is the work by Hooijer et al. (1991).

1.6 General Considerations on Quantifying Psychopathological States

The general problem of quantifying such psychopathological states as anxiety, de-pression, mania and schizophrenia has been studied extensively over the past three decades. Several scale types have been developed or examined. The Likert-type rating scales, analogue graphic scales, continuous or visual analogue scales (VAS), and discretized analogue scales (Discan).

1.6.1 Likert-type Rating Scales or Categorical Scales

Categorical scales were introduced by Likert (1932) and are therefore usually referred to as Likert scales. Likert himself suggested five categories for each item: no, mild, moderate, severe and extreme (scored 0, 1, 2, 3 and 4). It is a set of such five-category items for obtaining summed ratings that is referred to as a Likert scale (Ghiselli et al. 1981). In essence, these scores still represent categorical data; however they can be treated as though they were metric data, as shown in Rasch analyses (Rasch 1960).

Studies on the Hamilton Depression Scale (HDS) revealed that some of its items did not fulfil the Rasch criteria (Bech et al. 1981), and the HDS was therefore modified. The Melancholia Scale (MES) is 11-item Likert scale in which each item has five categories (Bech 1981). It has been confirmed that the MES fulfils the Rasch criteria (Maier and Philipp 1985). The Hamilton Anxiety Scale (HAS; Hamilton 1959) is another Likert scale with five categories for each item and with the total score taken the rating indicator. Explicit criteria for each item have been developed (Bech et al. 1984a). Studies on scales for mania have verified the 11-item Mania Scale (MAS; Bech et al. 1979) with items defined in terms of five categories. Among scales for schizophrenia states, the Brief Psychiatric Rating Scale (BPRS; Overall and Gorham 1962) is the most frequently used. This is an 18 item Likert scale in which each item originally had seven categories; this has since been reduced, and in preliminary studies five categories like the Melancholia or Mania scales have been used. Preliminary results (Andersen et al. 1989) indicate that the modified BPRS is reliable and valid.

Another rating scale designed by Montgomery and Åsberg (1979) has items with 7 item categories from 0 (not present) to 6 (extremely present). However, anchoring definitions are only stated for 0, 2, 4 and 6. The intermediate steps 1, 3, 5 are open spaces. It has been found (Allerup 1986) that the score distribution shows lower frequency for the categories of 1, 3, 5 compared to 0, 2, 4, 6. This bias has also been found by Huskisson (1974) when defining some aspects of a visual analogue scale. Explicit Likert items are therefore preferable.

In using Likert scales such as the HDS or HAS in studies on antidepressant or anti-anxiety drugs, statistics based on mean scores (mean changes or mean percentage changes) are often presented. However, such a mean score is not experienced by any individual patient, and the median also still does not describe how effective a treatment has been in a group of patients. Among patients suffering from depression, for example, Hamilton (1982) has shown that the response to treatment is often an all-or-none phenomenon. In a drug trial (Bech et al. 1984b) we therefore indicated the percentage of complete responders, partial responders, and non-responders from week to week; for each of the rating scales selected, the cut-off scores for not present, possible, and definite were shown. In the following, the term no depression or no anxiety is used when the rating scale score is within normal limits. In the assessment of clinical states of depression or anxiety the rater should, however, always attempt to let the patient express changes from his or her habitual way of functioning.

1.6.2 Analogue or Graphic Scales

Guilford (1954) has presented a detailed description of analogue, or graphic scales. The format of these scales permits numerous variations as there are many ways in which one can display a straight line and combine this with the various cues to aid the rater. The line can be continuous (VAS) or segmented (Discan).

1.6.2.1 Continuous or Visual Analogue Scales

A visual analogue scale (VAS) consists of a continuous line indicating the dimension under study. The line can be placed either vertically (thermometer-type) or horizontally (yardstick-like), but generally preferred is a horizontal line of 10 cm with the descriptive cues at the ends.

The use of single item visual analogue scales was introduced by Freyd (1923) in the field of educational research and by Aitken (1969) or Zeally and Aitken (1969) in psychiatric research. The latter authors conclude that a visual analogue scale, "provides the patient with a language by which to communicate his feelings frequently; its scores are amenable to parametric statistics, allowing precise examination of the significance og any differences."

Visual analogue scales have been most frequently used in the measurement of pain which in essence is a purely subjective sensory. In this field VAS has been advocated by Huskisson (1974) but criticized by others. Thus by Grimshaw (1976) who stressed that, "at some stage one is faced with the problem of aggregating across patients and this implies that one patient's 3.5 cm is equivalent to another's. This seems rather more unlikely than implying that two ratings of 'moderate pain' are equivalent to each other. It is not at all certain that relying on semantic differences is any less meaningful than applying an arbitrary numerical scale."

In a comprehensive review of the clinical application of single VAS McCormack et al. (1988) have concluded that, "There is no disagreement in the literature as to whether VAS provide ordinal scores which can be ranked and analysed using non-parametric, rank based methods." The disagreement has been on the assumption that VAS can produce interval or ratio level data. In a recent study on patients with chronic pain disorders it was found that VAS pain data fit the Rasch model when categorized into no (0–2 cm), minor (3–7 cm) and major (8–10 cm) degrees of pain (Bech et al. 1992).

In the first validity studies on rating scales for depression and mania a global clinical assessment scale for severity of illness (GCSI) with an 11-point scoring system was used (Bech et al. 1975): 0 or 1, no depression; 2–4, mild depression;

5–7, moderate depression; 8–10, severe depression. A score of 4 or higher indicates the need for treatment (Bech 1981). The features of the GCSI are as follows:

1. Instructions: Considering your total clinical experience with depressive disorders, how depressed is the patient today?
2. Applicability: For all patients already diagnosed as suffering from depressive illness
3. Administration time: Once at pretreatment and at appropriate occasions during treatment
4. Administration personnel: Psychiatrists, psychologists, nurses or other skilled observers

The VAS is an attempt to combine some semantic cues (guidewords) with a numerical scale. It is interesting, as Huskisson (1974) has shown, that when guidewords such as mild, moderate and severe are included in a graphic (thermometer-like) scale, the guideword levels were used by the majority of individuals. In spite of these considerations it has been decided to use the VAS.

1.6.2.2 Discretized Analogue Scales

The use of Discan scales is based on a system of repeated comparisons. These scales have been described by Singh and Bilsbury (1989), who consider the Likert scale and the VAS as special types of Discan scales. The GCSI described above is, in a sense, a Discan scale. However, using repeated comparisons, the actual Discan scale offers a high degree of sensitivity. With Discan scales, patients can distinguish 14 grades of a psychological dysfunction. However, in aggregating the scores across patients, one patient's score is considered equivalent to another's. The main indications for Discan scales, administered by the patient, are in assessing a target symptom such as pain in single-case research designs. Wen administered by an observer, Discan scale such as the GCSI can be considered as an alternative to the VAS.

1.6.2.3 Global Severity Versus Global Improvement Scales

The GCSI can be regarded as a compromise between a vertical VAS of 10 cm and a Discan scale. On the other hand, the Clinical Global Impression Scale for Severity of Illness (CGI-SI; Guy 1976) refers to the administrator's global impression of the patient and emphasizes that he rely upon his total clinical experience with the syndrome under assessment (e.g. depression). This scale is scored as follows: 0, not assessed; 1, not at all ill; 2, doubtfully (borderline) mentally ill; 3, mildly ill; 4, moderately ill; 5, markedly ill; 6, severely ill; 7, among the most extremely ill patients. The features of the scale are as follows:

1. Instructions: Considering your total clinical experience with this particular population, how mentally ill is the patient at this time?
2. Applicability: For all research populations

3. Administration time: Once at pretreatment and at least one post-treatment assessment
4. Administration personnel: Psychiatrists, psychologists, nurses

In comparing the GCSI and the CGI-SI, the definition of the respective research populations of patients may be unclear. This is because the former presents a specific example and states explicitly that the assessment should be made only for patients already diagnosed as having a depressive illness. It is recommended to use global severity scales only for the target population.

The concept of improvement refers to the clinical distance between the patient's current condition and that prior to treatment. The evaluation of this distance is often described by a single index describing the pattern of a series of single-state ratings, for example, before, during and after treatment. Feinstein (1987) uses the term polyadic component index when more than two ratings are performed, dyadic component index when only pre- and post- treatment ratings are compared, and monadic component index when only a post-treatment evaluation is used. The Clinical Global Improvement Scale (CGIS; Guy 1976) is an example of a monadic index, although it refers essentially to a comparative category, with change being heavily weighted in terms of improvement.

The five-point scoring system for the CGIS is: 0, unchanged or worse; 1, minimally or doubtfully improved (less than 25); 2, mildly improved (more than 25% but less than 50%; 3, moderately to markedly improved (more than 50% but less than 75%); 4, greatly to excellently improved (more than 75%. Its further features are:
–   Instruction: Compared to patient's condition before treatment, how much has he or she changed today?
–   Rate total improvement as to whether or not, in your own judgment, it is due entirely to the treatment under examination.

Strictly speaking, the CGIS is a change scale, not an improvement scale. As pointed out by Feinstein (1987), it represents a form of measurement that is unique in clinical medicine. From a logical point of view the CGIS can be completed only following (or during) treatment; however, in its first version (Guy and Bonato 1970) its use was suggested also prior to starting treatment, as a predictor (with the instruction "Answer the question according to your prediction of the patient's response to treatment").

Symptom rating scales are used as polyadic component indices, with the differences between pretreatment ratings and the various ratings during treatment indicating the degree of improvement. For scales fulfilling the Rasch model the change in scores between two ratings is a real change.

The global ratings depend, of course, on the skill of the rater and his or her capacity of empathy. The clinical, phenomenological knowledge has the global assessment before the itemized perceptions as already emphasized by James (1902) in his pragmatic, hermeneutical approach. Rümke (1941/1990) has focussed on the doctor's internal attitude induced by the patient as a sensitive global tool: "Patients suffering from schizophrenia, mania, hysteria, psychopathy or dementia are approached by us in radically different ways. How many of us are a bit manic when confronted with a manic patient, somewhat psychopathic with a psychopath or neurotic if our patient is neurotic." This condition-specific response on the part of the interviewer should be separated from the concept of 'countertransferance' introduced by Freud (1910) as the therapist's transferance to his or her patient using material from the therapists own past. Thus 'countertransferance' reflects the therapist's own personal story and only very little of the patient's condition. In contrast, the condition-specific response is, as discussed by Rümke (1941/1990), the interviewer's emotional reponse to the patient's verbal and non-verbal signals during the rating scale interview. It is one of the principles of the rating scale approach to consult this global feeling, to control for it and not to exclude it. As stressed by Tähka (1978) this emotional, condition-specific response is not identical to empathic understanding even though they are inter-related. The selection of the most appropriate scale is based on global ratings.

1.7 The User's Perspective for This Compendium

This compendium is intended for psychopathologists or other clinicians interested in the DSM-III-R or ICD-10 system and wishing to know more about the psychometric properties of the different axes. It is also intended for psychopathologists who have a primary interest in rating scales, but who have been confused, on the one hand, by the contrast between classical and modern psychometric methods, and, on the other, by the apparent correspondence in content validity between rating scales and DSM-III-R or ICD-10 syndromes. Finally, the compendium seeks to integrate the concepts of clinical disability, health status profile and health-related quality of life; this integration was initiated by the World Health Organization a decade ago, but it still remains at a developmental stage.

The practical functions of this compendium include the following:
- To cover clinically meaningful target syndromes to satisfy the cognitive needs of the psychopathologist or clinician in the treatment and care of patients
- To indicate the construct validity of these syndromes
- To stimulate further research for standardization of criteria
- To enable cross-referencing between studies and facilitate meta-analysis, thereby satisfying the cognitive needs of the person planning of treatment and care of patients in the community

It can be argued that the modern psychometric methods described in this compendium for validity and reliability are still in their developing stage. However, the relative merits of the scales included have been discussed with their different strengths. It should be emphasized, furthermore, that if no scale has been found appropriate for a study which the reader intends to carry out, methods other than rating scales should be considered. In this respect the reader should consult the article by Shapiro (1975) concerning a method for constructing an individualized questionnaire for each patient. In this idiographic approach one should consider the repertory grid technique (Bech 1990), judgement analysis (Hammond et al. 1980) or verbal content analysis (Gottschalck and Gleser 1969). However, the homogeneity and transferability of these methods across patients are very problematic.

The choice between self-rating and observer-rating scales is discussed above (see Table 1.4). In general, only one rating scale per dimension is selected in this compendium – the psychometrically most appropriate. In comparing the outcome of two different treatments the scale with the better construct validity poses the null hypothesis a greate challenge (i.e. the position that there is no difference between the treatments). This function of measurement is in accordance with Popper's dialectic of conjecture and refutation (Popper 1976). A recent study has supported this principle (Bech et al. 1991). The cash value of a rating scale (Bech, 1981) indicates whether it pragmatically is better than already existing scales. This incremental form of validity was recommended by Mischel (1972) and has been considered throughout this compendium.

The exclusive reliance on a single rating scale means a restriction in validity. In other words, if the construct validity of a scale has not been sufficiently investigated, it is recommended to include additional scales (and where it has been felt relevant, more than one scale is included). The use of more than one scale per dimension permits, of course, evaluation not only of the extent to which the scales are in agreement (i.e. convergent validity) but also of the extent to which they do not seem to measure the same construct (divergent validity). When using more than one rating scale as outcome measure in a drug trial the problem statistically to handle, the multiple endpoint evaluation, can be rather complex. However, O'Brien (1984) has shown a non-parametric method, Tandon (1990) has shown a parametric solution, and the Bonferroni adjustment of the P-value of the individual scales (multiplying every P-value by the number of endpoints) has been discussed by Pocock et al. (1987). In this context it is important to emphasize that latent structure analysis (or factor analysis) are statistical methods for combining items of a rating scale into a sufficient statistic (total score), whereas the Bonferroni method, for example, is an attempt to make global statistics of multiple scales at endpoint (posttreatmently) in clinical trials. The term index is often used, but logically an index can refer both to a total scale score (item combination) and to global statistics (the overall statistical power of multiple scales at endpoint).

Another guiding principle of this compendium is the selection of scales offering international utility for purposes of secondary research, for instance, in carrying out meta-analyses (drawing conclusions across studies). Many of the selected scales, such as the Hamilton scales or the Brief Psychiatric Rating Scale, are included in the subject indices of psychiatric journals.

If the reader intends to use a structured clinical interview, he may consult other reviews (e.g. Hedlund and Vieweg 1981). However, in Chapter 2 an example of a structured interview for the Hamilton/Melancholia Scale has been shown. The self-rating scales or questionnaires included in this compendium may be considered structured methods in the sense that the questions to be answered by the patients are fixed. In other words, a structured interview is an orally administered questionnaire. The clinical interview recommended in this compendium is the traditional interview, often referred to as goal-directed (or semi-structured). According to Hamilton (1967) the rating scale interview has the following limitations:

The sufficient information obtained during the interview will obviously depend on the skill of the rater and the condition of the patient. The patient should not be pressed and should be allowed sufficient time to say what he wants to say, but he should not be allowed to wander too far from the point. The number of direct questions should be kept to a minimum and such questions should be asked in different ways, in particular, both in positive and negative form, e.g. "How badly do you sleep?" or "How well do you sleep". Questions should be asked in language which the patient understands, and ordinary words should never be used in a technical sense. Patients should be helped and encouraged to admit to symptoms of which they are ashamed.

The description of rating scales selected in this compendium follows two approaches. The classificatory principle in Chapter 2 is the so-called bottom-up approach which means that symptoms of anxiety are recorded first and at a higher level then depression, etc. Chapter 3, however, adopts the DSM-III-R approach, the so-called top-down approach whereby dementia is recorded first and then schizophrenia, etc. at the next level down.

Finally, it should be emphasized that the scales in this compendium have been selected on the basis of psychometric criteria. Thus, scales with items calibrated from 0–6 have been modified to 0–4 because there is no reason from a modern psychometric point of view to use more categories than can be obtained meaningfully. The quantitative aspect of the scale is its construct validity, where adequacy of total scores is considered. The Rasch model has been preferred to other models of latent structure analysis because the adequacy of total score here is the scientifically most verified. This model combines theories of measurement with those of clinical phenomenology. In Putman's terms (1980) latent structure models, such as that of Rasch "are not lost noun waifs looking for someone to name them; they are constructions within our theory itself, and they have names from birth." If a scale covering a clinically relevant area has not been analysed by Rasch criteria, Loevinger's coefficient of homogeneity is considered.

The principal theme of this compendium is the relationship between the DSM-III-R or ICD-10 approach and the rating scale approach. It is not an ad hoc collection of scales such as that of von Riesen and Siegel (1989) but is closer to the scientific approach of Thompson (1989) and Benkert et al. (1990). However, in some cases the principle of international utility is considered; some scales are included for this reason despite inadequate psychometric properties. In the description of each scale the criteria of administration, time framing, item selection, item calibration, validity (content, construct, discriminant and predictive) and inter-observer reliability have been stated.

References

Allerup P. Statistical analysis of rating scales. Copenhagen: Danish Institute of Educational Research, 1986.

Allerup P, Sorber G. The Rasch Model for Questionnaires. Report No. 16. Copenhagen, Danish Inst Educ Res, 1977.

Aitken RCB. A growing edge of measurement of feelings. Pro Royal Soc Med 1969; 62: 989–996.

American Psychiatric Association. Diagnostic and Statistical Manual. Mental Disorders (DSM-I). Washington DC, Am Psychiat Ass, 1952.

American Psychiatric Association: Diagnostic and Statistical Manual of Mental Disorders (DSM-II). Washington DC, Am Psychiat Ass, 1968.

American Psychiatric Association: Diagnostic and Statistical Manual of Mental Disorders. Third edition (DSM-III). Washington DC, Am Psychiat Ass, 1980.

American Psychiatric Association. Diagnostic and Statistical Manual of Mental Disorders (DSM-III-R). Washington DC, Am Psychiat Ass, 1987.

American Psychological Association. Standards for Educational and Psychological Tests. Washington DC, Am Psychol Ass, 1974.

Andersen EB. The Statistical Analysis of Categorical Data. Berlin, Springer, 1990.

Andersen J, Larsen JK, Schultz V, Nielsen BM, Kørner A, Behnke K, Munk-Andersen E, Butler B, Allerup P, Bech P. The Brief Psychiatric Rating Scale. Dimensions of schizophrenia – reliability and construct validity. Psychopathol 1989; 22: 168–176.

Ayer AJ. Language, Truth and Logic. London, Gollancz, 1936.

Bannister D, Fransella F. Inquiring Man: the Psychology of Personal Constructs. London, Croom Helm, Third Edition, 1986.

Bartko JJ, Carpenter WT. On the methods and theory of reliability. J Nerv Ment Dis 1976; 163: 307–317.

Bech P. Rating scales for affective disorders: their validity and consistency. Acta Psychiat Scand 1981; 64 (suppl 295): 1–101.

Bech P. Rating scales in psychopharmacology: statistical aspects. Acta Psychiat Belg 1988; 88: 291–302.

Bech P. Measurement of psychological distress and well-being. Psychother Psychosom 1990; 54: 77–89.

Bech P. Alkoholisme og affektive lidelser: Patologisk psykologi eller psykologisk patologi. Månedsskr Prakt Lægegern, 1991 (in press).

Bech P, Gram LF, Dein E, Jacobson O, Vitger J, Bolwig TG. Quantitative rating of depression states. Acta Psychiat Scand 1975; 51: 161–170.

Bech P, Bolwig TG, Kramp P, Rafaelsen OJ. The Bech-Rafaelsen Mania Scale and the Hamilton Depression Scale. Acta Psychiat Scand 1979; 59: 420–430.

Bech P, Allerup P, Gram LF et al. The Hamilton Depression Scale. Evaluation of objectivity using logistic models. Acta Psychiat Scand 1981; 63: 290–299.

Bech P, Grosby H. Husum B, Rafaelsen L. Generalized anxiety or depression measured by the Hamilton Anxiety Scale and the Melancholia Scale in patients before and after cardiac surgery. Psychopathol 1984a; 17: 253–263.

Bech P, Allerup P, Reisby N, Gram LF. Assessment of symptom change from improvement curves on the Hamilton Depression Scale in trials with antidepressants. Psychopharm 1984b; 84: 276–281.

Bech P, Gastpar M, Mendlewics J. The role of training courses in multicenter trials: WHO experiences. In: Chagas C, Josiassen RC, Bridger WH et al. (eds). Amsterdam, Elsevier 1986a, pp 1513–1515.

Bech P, Kastrup M, Rafaelsen OJ. Mini-compendium of rating scales. Acta Psychiatr Scand 1986b; 73 (suppl 326): 7–37.

Bech P, Haaber A, Joyce CRB. Experiments on clinical observation and judgment in the assessment of depression. Psychol Med 1986c; 16: 873–883.

Bech P, Hjortsø S, Lund K, Vilmar T, Kastrup M. An integration of the DSM-III and ICD-8 by global severity assessments for measuring multidimensional outcomes in general hospital psychiatry. Acta Psychiat Scand 1987; 75: 297–306.

Bech P, Allerup P, Gram LF and DUAG. The Diagnostic Melancholia Scale (DMS). Dimensions of endogenous and reactive depression with relationship to the Newcastle Scales. J Aff Dis 1988; 14: 161–170.

Bech P, Allerup P, Loldrup D. The dynamic Rasch model in the analysis of improvement curves based on single item visual analogue scales in patients with chronic pain disorders. Int J Educ Res 1992 (in press).

Bech P, Allerup P, Maier W, Albus M, Lavori P, Ayuso JL. The Hamilton scales and the Hopkins symptom checklist (SCL-90): a cross-national validity study in patients with panic disorders. Br J Psychiat 1992; 160: 206–211.

Benkert O, Maier W, Rickels K (eds). Methodology of the Evaluation of Psychotropic Drugs. Berlin, Springer, 1990.

Bentham J. Denontology. London, Bowring, 1834 (reprinted by Clarendon Press, Oxford, 1983).

Berrios GE. What is phenomenology? A review. J Roc Soc Med 1989; 82: 425–428.

Berrios GE. British psychopathology: a conceptual history. Paper presented at 5th European Psychiatric Association Congress October 1990, Strasbourg.

Bleuler E. Textbook of Psychiatry. New York, MacMillan, 1924.

Brock DW. Paternism and autonomy. Ethics 1988; 98: 550–568.

Brunswik E. Wahrnehmung und Gegenstandswelt: Grundlinien einer Psychologie vom Gegenstand. Leipzig, Deuticke, 1934.

Brunswik E. The Conceptual Framework of Psychology. Chicago, Univ Chicago Press, 1952.

Cantor N, Smith EE, Franch RS, Mezzich J. Psychiatric diagnosis as prototype categorization. J Ab Psychol 1980; 89: 181–193.

Carnap R. On the character of philosophical problems. Phil Science 1934; 1: 5–19.

Cronbach LJ. Coefficient alpha and the internal structure of tests. Psychometrika 1951; 16: 297–334.

Cronbach LJ, Gleser GC. Assessing similarity between profiles. Psychol Bull 1953; 50: 546–473.

Cronbach LJ, Meehl PE. Construct validity in psychological tests. Psychol Bull 1955; 52: 281–302.

Essen-Möller E, Wohlfart S. Suggestions for the amendment of the official Swedish classification of mental disorders. Acta Psychiat Scand 1947; 47 (suppl): 551–555.

European Rating Aggression Group (ERAG). Social Dysfunction and Aggression Scale (SDAS-21) in generalized aggression and in aggressive attacks. A validity and reliability study. Int J Methods in Psychiat Res 1992, 2:15–29.

Eysenck HJ. Rebel with a Cause: an Autobiography. London, W. H. Allen, 1990.

Feighner J, Robins E, Guze S. Diagnostic criteria for use in psychiatric research. Arch Gen Psychiat 1972; 26: 57.

Feinstein AR. Clinimetrics. New Haven, Yale Univ Press, 1987.

Fleiss JL. The Design and Analysis of Clinical Experiments. New York, J. Wiley, 1986.

Frances A, Pincus HA, Widiger TA, Davis WW, First MB. DSM-IV: work in progress. Am J Psychiat 1990; 147: 1439–1448.

Frank G. Psychiatric Diagnosis: Review of Research. Oxford, Pergamon Press, 1975.

Freud S. The Future Prospects of Psychoanalytic Therapy (First published in Zentralblatt, 1910). New York, Basic Books 1959, vol 2, pp. 285–297.

Freyd M. The graphic rating scale. J Educat Psychol 1923; 14: 83–102.

Galton F. Inquiries into Human Faculty and its Development. London, MacMillan, 1883, p. 93.

Ghiselli EE, Campbell JP, Zedeck S. Measurement Theory for the Behavioural Sciences. San Francisco, W. H. Freeman and Company, 1981.

Gottschalck LA, Gleser GC. The Measurement of Psychological States through the Content Analysis of Verbal Behaviour. Berkeley, Univ California Press, 1969.

Grimshaw JJ. Statistical analysis of trial results. In: Good CS (ed). The Principles and Practice of Clinical Trials. Edinburgh, Churchill Livingstone 1976, pp. 129–137.

Guilford JP. Psychometric Methods. First edition. New York, McGraw-Hill, 1936.

Guilford JP. Psychometric Methods. Second edition. New York, McGraw-Hill, 1954.

Guion RM. Content validity: Three years of talk – what's the action. Public Personnel Management 1977; 6: 407–414.

Guttman L. The basis for scalogram analysis. In: Stouffer SA, Guttman L, Suchman EA, Lazarsfeld PF, Starr SS, Clausen JA (eds). Measurement and Prediction. Princeton, Princeton Univ Press 1950, pp. 60–90.

Guy W. Early Clinical Drug Evaluation (ECDEU) Assessment Manual. Rockville, Nat Inst Ment Health, 1976.

Guy W, Bonato RR. Manual for the Early Clinical Drug Evaluation (ECDEU) Assessment Battery. Bethesda, Nat Inst Ment Health, 1970.

Hamilton M. Diagnosis and rating of anxiety. Br J Psychiat 1969 (special publ): 76–79.

Hamilton M. Development of a rating scale for primary depressive illness. Brit J Soc Clin Psychol 1967; 6: 278–296.

Hamilton M. General problems of psychiatric rating scales. In: Pichot P (ed). Psychological Measurements in Psychopharmacology. Basel, Karger, 1974 pp. 125–138.

Hamilton M. The role of rating scales in psychiatry. Psychol Med 1976; 6: 347–349.

Hamilton M. The effect of treatment of the melancholias (depressions). Br J Psychiat 1982; 140: 223–230.

Hammond KR, McClelland GH, Mumpower J. Human Judgment and Decision Making. New York, Prager, 1980.

Hedlund JL, Vieweg BW. Structured psychiatric interview: a comparative review. J Operat Psychiat 1981; 12: 39–67.

Hegel GWF. Die Phänomologie des Geistes (Phenomenology of Spirit, First German edition, 1807). Translated by Wallace W, Miller AV. Oxford, Oxford Univ Press, 1971.

Hegel GWF. Philosophy of Nature. First edition 1817 (translated by M. J. Petry). London, George Allen, 1970.

Heilveil I. Video in mental health practice. London: Tavistock Publications 1984.

Hjortsø S, Butler B, Clemmesen L, Jepsen PW, Kastrup M, Vilmar T, Bech P. The use of case vignettes in studies of interrater reliability of psychiatric target syndromes and diagnoses. A comparison of ICD-8, ICD-10 and DSM-III. Acta Psychiat Scand 1989; 80: 632–638.

Hooijer C, Zitman FG, Griez E et al. The Hamilton Depression Rating Scale (HDRS): Changes in scores as a function of training and version used. J Aff Dis 1991; 22: 21–29.

Huskisson EC. Measurement of pain. Lancet 1974; 11: 1127–1131.

Husserl E. Logische Untersuchungen, Zweiter Band. Halle, Max Niemayer, 1913.

International Statistical Institute. The International Classification of Diseases (ICD-1). Health Organization of the League of Nations, Paris, 1893.

James H. The Art of Fiction. London, Longmans, 1884.

James W. The Varieties of Religious Experience. London, Longmans, 1902.

James W. Some Problems of Philosophy. London, Longmans, 1911.

Jaspers K. Allgemein Psycho-Pathologie. Berlin, Springer, 1923.

Jaspers K. Von der Wahrheit. Munich, R. Piper, 1947.

Joyce CRB, Hammond KR. Judgment analysis in clinical trials: how to save the baby from the bathwater. Controlled Clinical Trials 1984; 5: 307–308.

Kant I. Critique of Pure Reason. First edition 1781. (translated by N. Kemp Smith). London, MacMillan, 1933).

Kelly GA. The Psychology of Personal Constructs. New York, Norton, 1955.

Kersten F. Phenomenological Method: Theory and Practice. Boston, Kluwer Academic Publishers, 1989.

Kuhn TS. The function of measurement in modern physical science. In: Woolf H (ed). Quantification: a History of the Meaning of Measurement in the Natural and Social Sciences. Indianapolis, Bobbs-Merrild, 1961 pp. 31–63.

Langeheine R, Rost J (eds). Latent Trait and Latent Class Models. New York: Plenum Press, 1988.

Lazarsfeld PF, Henry NW. Latent Structure Analysis. Boston, Houghton Mifflin, 1968.

Levy P. On the relation between test theory and psychology. In: Kline P (ed). New Approaches in Psychological Measurement. London, J. Wiley, 1973 pp. 1–42.

Lewis D. Parts of Classes. Oxford, Basil Blackwell, 1991.

Likert RA. Technique for the measurement of attitudes. Arch. Psychol. 1932; 140: 1–55.

Lissitz RW, Green SB. Effects of the number of scale points of reliability: a Monte Carlo approach. J Appl Psychol 1975; 60: 10–13.

Lodge M. Magnitude Scaling. Quantitative Measurement of Opinions. Beverly Hills, Sage Publications, 1981.

Loevinger J. The technique of homogenous tests compared with some aspects of scale analysis and factor analysis. Psychol Bull 1948; 45: 507–529.

Loevinger J. Objective tests as measurements of psychological theory. Psychol Reports 1957; 3: 635–694.

Lord FM, Novick MR. Statistical Theories of Mental Test Scores. Reading, Massachusetts, Addison-Wesley Publishing Comp, 1968.

Luborsky L. Clinicians' judgment of mental health. Arch Gen Psychiat 1962; 7: 407–417.

Lyerly SB, Abbott PS. Handbook of Psychiatric Rating Scales (1950–1964). Bethesda, Nat Inst Ment Health, 1964.

Maier W, Philipp M. Comparative analysis of observer depression scales. Acta Psychiat Scand 1985; 72: 239–245.

McCormack HM, de Horne DJ, Sheather S. Clinical applications of visual analogue scales. A critical review. Psychol Med 1988; 18: 1007–1019.

McDowell I, Newell C. Measuring Health: a Guide to Rating Scales and Questionnaires. New York, Oxford Univ Press, 1987.

Miller GA. The magical number seven, plus or minus two. Psychol Rev 1956; 63: 81–97.

Mischel W. Direct versus indirect personality assessment: evidence and implications. J Consult Clin Psychol 1972; 38: 319–324.

Mokken RJ. A Theory and Procedure of Scale Analysis with Applications in Political Research. Berlin, Mouton, 1971.

Montgomery SA, Åsberg M. A new depression scale designed to be sensitive to change. Brit J Psychiat 1979; 134: 382–389.

Murray HA. Explorations in Personality. New York, Oxford, 1938.

Murray HA. Preparations for the scaffold of a comprehensive system. In: Koch S (ed). Psychology: a Study of Science. New York, McGraw Hill, 1959, pp. 7–54.

Nunally JC. Psychometric Theory. New York, McGraw-Hill, 1967.

O'Brien PC. Procedures for comparing samples with multiple endpoints. Biometrics 1984; 40: 1079–1087.

Othmer E, Othmer SC. The Clinical Interview Using DSM-III-R. Washington DC: American Psychiatric Press 1989.

Overall JE, Gorham DR. The Brief Psychiatric Rating Scale. Psychol Rep 1962; 10: 799–812.

Paykel ES. Use of the Hamilton Depression Scale in general practice. In: Bech P, Coppen A (eds). The Hamilton Scales. Berlin, Springer, 1990 pp. 40–47.

Peyser H. Stress and alcohol. In: Goldberger L, Breznitz S (eds). Handbook of Stress: Theoretical and Clinical Aspects. New York, The Free Press, 1982 pp. 585–598.

Pocock SJ, Geller NJ, Tsiatis AA. The analysis of multiple endpoints in clinical trials. Biometrics 1987; 43: 487–498.

Popper K. The Unended Quest. London, Fontane, 1976.

Popper K. A world of Propensities. Bristol, Thoemmes, 1990.

Prusoff B, Klerman GL. Differentiating depressed from anxious neurotic outpatients. Use of discriminant function analysis for separating of neurotic affective states. Arch Gen Psychiat 1974; 30: 302–308.

Putman H. Models and reality. J Symbolic Logic 1980; 45: 464–482.

Quine WV. Set Theory and its Logic. Cambridge, Mass, Harvard Univ Press, 1963.

Rasch G. Probabilistic Models for Some Intelligence and Attainment Tests. Danish Inst Educ Res, Copenhagen 1960 (reprinted by Univ Chicago Press, Chicago 1980).

Raskin A. Sensitivity to treatment effects of evaluation instruments completed by psychiatrists, psychologists, nurses, and patients. In: Sartorius N, Ban TA (eds). Assessment of Depression. Berlin, Springer, 1986; pp. 367–376.

Robins LN. Diagnostic grammar and assessment. Translating criteria into questions. In: Robins LN, Barret JE (eds). The Validity of Psychiatric Diagnosis. New York, Raven Press, 1989 pp. 263–278.

Rust J, Golombok S. Modern Psychometrics. The Science of Psychological Assessment. London, Routledge, 1989.

Ryle G. The Concept of Mind. London, Hutchinson, 1949.

Rümke HC. The nuclear symptom of schizophrenia and praecoxfeeling (First published 1941). History Psychiat 1990; 1: 334–341.

Sartorius N. Cross-cultural comparisons of data about quality of life: sample of issues. In: Aaronson NK, Beckmann J (eds). The Quality of Life of Cancer Patients. New York, Raven Press, 1987 pp. 19–24.

Sauvages de Boissier. Nosologia methodica. Univ Montpellier, 1747.

Schlich M. The future of philosophy. College Pacific Publ Phil 1932; 1: 45–62.

Shapiro MB. The requirements and implications of a systematic science of psychopathology. Bull Br Psychol Soc 1975; 28: 149–155.

Siegel S. Non-parametric Statistics. New York, McGraw Hill, 1956.

Siegel S, Castellan NJ. Non-parametric Statistics for the Behavioural Sciences. New York, McGraw-Hill, 1988.

Singh AC, Bilsbury CD. Measurement of subjective variables: the Discan Method. Acta Psychiat Scand 1989; 79 (suppl 347): 1–38.

Sjöbring H. Mental constitution and mental illness. Svenska Läkare Sällskap 1919; 45: 462–493 (Translated by E. Essen-Möller. In: Hirsch SR, Shepherd M (eds). Theories and Variations in European Psychiatry. Bristol, John Wright & Sons, 1974, pp. 265–294).

Skolem T. Einige Bemerkungen zur axiomatischen Begründung der Mengenlehre. Proceedings, 5th Scandinavian Congress in Mathematics, Helsinki, 1922. (English version: Some remarks on anxiomatized set theory. In: Van Heijenoort J (ed). From Frege to Gödel, Cambridge, Mass: Harvard University Press, 1967, pp 290–301.

Snaith PHS. Microbiological Classification. Cambridge, Cambridge Univ Press, 1962.

Spilker R (ed). Quality of Life Assessments in Clinical Trials. New York, Raven Press, 1990.

Stengel E. Classification of mental disorders. Bull Wld Hth Org 1959; 21: 601–663.

Stern R. Hegel, Kant and the Structure of the Object. London, Routledge, 1990.

Strauss JS. Hallucinations and delusions as points on continua function: rating scale evidence. Arch Gen Psychiat 1969; 21: 581–586.

Strawson PF. Individuals: an Essay in Descriptive Metaphysics. London, Methuen, 1959.

Tandon PK. Applications of global statistics in analysing quality of life data. Statistics in Medicine 1990; 9: 819–827.

Thompson C. The Instruments of Psychiatric Research. Chichester, J. Wiley, 1989.

Thurstone LL. Attitudes can be measured. Am J Sociol 1928; 33: 529–554.

Tryon RC. Reliability and behaviour domain validity. Psychol Bull 1957; 54: 229–249.

Tähka VA. On the narcissistic aspects of self-destructive behaviour and their influence on its predictability: In: Achte K, Lönnqvist J (eds). Psychopathology of Direct and Indirect Self-Destruction. Helsinki, Psychiatria Fennica 1978, pp. 59–62.

Van Riezen H, Siegel M. Comparative Evaluation of Rating Scales for Clinical Psychopharmacology. Amsterdam, Elsevier, 1988.

Wetzler S. Measuring Mental Illness. Washington DC, Am Psychiat Press, 1989.

Widiger TA, Hurt SW, Frances A, Clarkin JF, Gilmore M. Diagnostic efficiency and DSM-III. Arch Gen Psychiat 1984; 41: 1005–1012.

Widiger TA, Frances A. The DSM-III personality disorders: perspectives from psychology. Arch Gen. Psychiat. 1985; 42: 615–623.

Wigton RS, Patil KD, Hoellerich VL. The effect of feedback in learning clinical diagnosis. J Med Educ 1986; 61: 816–822.

Williams JBW. Structured interview guides for the Hamilton rating scales. In: Bech P, Coppen A (eds). The Hamilton Scales. Berlin, Springer, 1990 pp. 48–63.

Windelband W. Geschichte und Naturwissenschaft. Strassburg, Heitz, 1894.

Windelband W. An Introduction to Philosophy. London, Fisher Unwin, 1921.

Wing JK, Babor T, Brugha T, Burke J, Cooper JE, Giel R, Jablenski A, Regier D, Sartorius N. SCAN: schedules for clinical assessment in neuropsychiatry. Arch Gen Psychiat 1990; 47: 589–593.

Wittgenstein L. Philosophical Investigations. Oxford, Blackwell, 1953.

Wood PHN. The international classification of impairments, disabilities, and handicaps of the World Health Organization. In: Leidl R, Potthoff P, Schwefel D (eds). European Approaches to Patient Classification Systems. Berlin, Springer, 1990, pp. 83–101.

World Health Organization. Manual of the International Statistical Classification of Diseases, Injuries, and Causes of Death (ICD-6). Bull Wld Hth Org, Suppl 1, 1948a.

World Health Organization. Construction in Basic Documents. Geneva: World Health Organization, 1948b.

World Health Organization. Glossary of Mental Disorders and Guide to their Classification for Use in Conjunction with the International Classification of Diseases. Eighth Revision. Geneva, World Health Organization, 1974.

World Health Organization. Mental Disorders: Glossary and Guide to their Classification in Accordance with the Ninth Revision of the International Classification of Diseases. Geneva, World Health Organization, 1978.

World Health Organization. International Classification of Impairments, Disabilities, and Handicaps (ICIDH/WHO). Geneva, World Health Organization, 1980.

World Health Organization: International Classification of Disease, Tenth Revision (ICD-10). Draft of chapter V. Mental and behavioural disorders. Clinical description and diagnostic guidelines. Geneva, World Health Organization, 1990a.

World Health Organization: International Classification of Disease, Tenth Revision (ICD-10). Draft of chapter V. Mental and bahavioral disorders. Diagnostic criteria for research. Geneva, World Health Organization, 1990b.

Young MA, Abrams R, Taylor MA, Meltzer HY. Etablishing diagnostic criteria for mania. J Nerv Ment Dis 1983; 171: 676–682.

Zeally AK, Aitken RCB. Measurement of mood. Proc Roy Soc Med 1969; 62: 993–996.

2 Rating Scales for Psychopathological States

The scales discussed in Chap. 2 – the Hamilton Anxiety Scale (HAS), Hamilton Depression Scale (HDS), Melancholia Scale (MES), Mania Scale (MAS), and Brief Psychiatric Rating Scale (BPRS) – have been selected because research has shown them relevant for assessing changes in the patient's condition during the treatment, by psychiatrists all over the world. These are not diagnostic scales. Their main function in measuring the severity of psychopathology is to indicate when treatment is required, and when treatment can be discontinued. The oldest scales (HAS, HDS and BPRS) were originally published without sufficient Likert item criteria. Therefore many different versions of these scales exist. The most frequently used versions, at least outside Scandinavia, are the so-called HAM-A (Hamilton Anxiety Scale), HAM-D (Hamilton Depression Scale) and the BPRS with seven anchored items, which have been published in the American (Guy 1976) and the German systems (CIPS 1981). The manuals in these systems are, however, unacceptable as they do not fulfil the Likert criteria.

The MAS and the MES fulfil the Likert criteria, and both are included in the WHO system of rating scales (Israel et al. 1984). This compendium seeks to modify the HAS, HDS, and BPRS to fulfil the Likert criteria. Some guidelines are presented below for using these five scales, including not only manuals for item definitions but also item combinations for case identifications. In contrast to the original HDS manual, all our item definitions are applicable to both men and women. (For the sake of convenience, however, the patient is often referred to as "he".) Moreover, the DSM-III and DSM-III-R (APA 1987) for the corresponding syndromes are indicated.

In assessing 'total' psychopathology the interview required to complete all five scales may be obtained in the dealt with below order. Start by completing the form in "Appendix 2.1", which identifies the patient and the rater; finish this form with an assessment of the validity of the interview; in between, use the scoring sheets relevant for the particular study ("Appendices 2.2–2.7"). Using the scales in the order presented provides an assessment of the current symptoms from anxiety to schizophrenia, i.e. the bottom-up approach. The time framing is usually the past 3 days, including the morning of assessment. The severity of syndromes is then indicated by the total scale score and, if needed, a global assessment by a VAS or a global scale (GCSI or CGI-SI; see Sect. 1.6). This procedure involves repeated assessments during the treatment period. The differences between total scores indicate the change in the clinical picture during treatment. There are several ways to define outcome of treatment (Bech et al. 1992). Weekly mean scores are often taken, but the area under the curve should also be considered. The percentage of reduction in pretreatment score is most frequently used, typically the index of a 50% or higher reduction. This index corresponds closely to global improvement scores of moderate to excellent (Bech 1989). However, as already mentioned, an index of recovery is a very practical indicator, recovery being defined as return to health. Standardization of rating scale scores into no, minor, less than major, and major states provides the degrees of recovery ('no' meaning full recovery, 'minor' or 'less than major' referring to degrees of partial recovery, and 'major' indicating no recovery). Use of the CGIS is recommended as an important supplement to the substantive rating scales.

The combined assessment of the four syndromes of anxiety, depression, mania and schizophrenia can be made with the help of the Clinical Syndrome Circle (CSC; "Appendix 2.8"; see also Fig. 2.1). These scales are listed in such a way, that contiguous syndromes share a number of characteristics. The set of symptoms measured by a given scale here is most similar to those on either side of it. The CSC facilitates a diagnostic judgment by the interviewer on the basis of all information obtained from the various rating procedures. This assessment often covers a longer retrospective period than do the symptom scales and therefore represents a longitudinal evaluation. The CSC diagnosis is the final assessment.

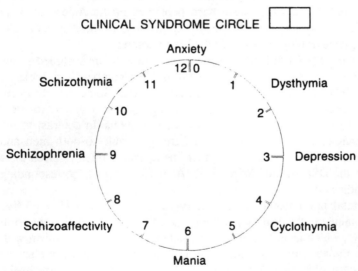

Fig. 2.1

Anxiety can be scored as either '0' or '12', depression as '3', mania as '6', and schizophrenia as '9'. These syndromes have intermediate states. When anxiety is considered as part of depression, it can be scored as: '0' no certain anxiety; '1', anxiety without depression; '2', mixed anxiety-depression or dysthymic state; '3', depression; '4', depression with some hypomanic features; '5', mania; '7', mania with some schizophrenic symptoms; '8', schizophrenia with some manic features; '9', schizophrenia; '10',schizophrenia with borderline features; '11', more border-line than schizophrenia; '12', no certain anxiety-borderline features.

The Clinical Syndrome Circle was introduced in the mini-compendium (Bech et al. 1986) and a self-rating version of these syndromes has often been found needed. In section 2.5 self-rating scales for the Clinical Syndrome Circle have been included.

Finally, in section 2.5 a structured interview for the Hamilton/Melancholia Scale (HDS/MES) has been included as an example of this approch because at-tempts have been made to develop also structured interview for the Hamilton Scale (e.g. Williams 1990).

2.1 Hamilton Anxiety Scale

As discussed elsewhere (Bech et al. 1984a), it is not possible to use the original HAS in patients with panic attacks because there are no instructions for distin-guishing between attacks of anxiety and generalized or persistent anxiety. There-fore, the following procedure is recommended.

Panic attacks are assessed by a subset of the Hamilton Anxiety Scale (HAS-P; "Appendix 2.2"). A spondateous panic attack is defined as a sudden anxiety attack developing in about 10 min, occurring with little or no provoking stress, and in-cluding three or more symptoms of anxiety ("Appendix 2.2" A–L). The number of panic attacks in the preceding 3 weeks is recorded. (At weekly ratings, for exam-ple, during a trial, the number of attacks in the past week is recorded). The HAS-P is completed by assessing the 'average' attack. Thereafter, it is recorded whether the DSM-III/DSM-III-R criteria (see "Appendix 2.2") are fulfilled. Finally, the VAS is used to indicate how severe the typical panic attack is.

If there have been panic attacks in the past 3 days, the interviewer must ask about anxiety symptoms between attacks. In such cases, or if there have been no attacks, the interviewer makes use of the HAS for assessing generalized anxiety (HAS-G; "Appendix 2.3"). According to the HAS-G criteria, total scales scores are interpreted as follows: 0–5, no anxiety; 6–14, minor anxiety; 15 or more, ma-jor anxiety.

The interviewer should assess the presence and intensity of the various features in terms of the patient's condition at the time of the interview. Only few of the 14 items are clinical signs to be observed directly during the interview; the majority are symptoms (patient complaints), and the assessment of these must be based on the condition in the past days (minimum period, 3 days). The interview should not last longer than 30 min. The interview technique does not differ basically from the traditional clinical approach. The patient should not feel under pressure, and as far as possible the patient should be encouraged to describe his situation in his own words. Spontaneous intermissions should be accepted as they constitute an important part of the observation of the patient. Considering a diurnal variation in the symptoms, the interview should always take place at a fixed time, for example, between 8:00 a.m. and 9.30 a.m.

The scale is semi-quantitative; it was constructed solely to assess the severity of the clinical condition and not to serve as a diagnostic tool. When the scale is used repeatedly with the same patient, for example, at weekly intervals, the individual assessment must be independent of the others, and the interviewer should never have these at his disposal. As far as possible one should avoid asking about changes since the last interview; rather, the patient should be asked to describe the condition during the week that has just passed. It is a general rule for all items that a scale level encompasses the lower levels, for instance, level '3' always includes levels '2' and '1'. Some items (e.g. somatic anxiety manifestation) are more pronounced in panic attacks while others are less pronounced or even absent (e.g. sleep). If the condition to which an item refers is not present, the item is scored '0'.

1 Anxious Mood
This item covers the emotional condition of uncertainty about the future, ranging from worry, insecurity, irritability and apprehension to overpowering dread.
0. The patient is neither more nor less insecure or irritable than usual.
1. It is doubtful whether the patient is more insecure or irritable than usual.
2. The patient expresses more clearly to be in a state of anxiety, apprehension or irritability, which he may find difficult to control. It is thus without influence on the patient's daily life, because the worrying still is about minor matters.
3. The anxiety or insecurity is at times more difficult to control because the worrying is about major injuries or harms which might occur in the future. E.g.: The anxiety may be experienced as panic, i.e. overpowering dread. Has occasionally interfered with the patient's daily life.
4. The feeling of dread is present so often that it markedly interferes with the patient's daily life.

2 Tension
This item includes inability to relax, nervousness, bodily tensions, trembling and restless fatigue.
0. The patient is neither more nor less tense than usual.
1. The patient seems somewhat more nervous and tense than usual.
2. The patient expresses clearly unable to relax and full of inner unrest which he finds difficult to control, but it is still without influence on the patient's daily life.
3. The inner unrest and nervousness is so intense or so frequent that it occasionally interferes with the patient's daily work.
4. Tensions and unrest interfere with the patient's life and work at all times.

3 Fears
This item refers to type of anxiety which arises when the patient finds himself in specific situations. The patient experiences relief from the expectation of anxiety

by avoiding the situation. Among the situations to be considered is fear of being in places from which escape may be difficult (or embarrassing) or in which help may not be available in the event of a panic attack. These agoraphobic situations include fear of being alone at home or being outside the home alone. In these situations it can be fear of being in a crowd, in public places, in a tunnel, on a bridge, in a bus, train or car, in an elevator, or when travelling. It is important to note whether there has been more phobic anxiety (agoraphobia) during the present episode than usual.

0. Not present.
1. Doubtful whether present.
2. The patient experiences phobic anxiety but is able to fight it.
3. It is difficult for the patient to fight or overcome his phobic anxiety, which thus to some extent interferes with his daily life and work.
4. The phobic anxiety clearly interferes with the patient's daily life and work.

4 Insomnia

This item covers only the patient's subjective experience of sleep length (hours of sleep per 24-h period) and sleep depth (superficial and interrupted sleep versus deep and steady sleep). The rating is based on the 3 preceding nights. (Note: administration of hypnotics or sedatives is disregarded.)

0. Usual sleep length and sleep depth.
1. Sleep length is doubtfully or slightly reduced (e.g. due to difficulties falling asleep), but there is no change in sleep depth.
2. Sleep depth is also reduced, sleep being more superficial. Sleep as a whole is somewhat disturbed.
3. Sleep duration as well as sleep depth is markedly changed. The broken sleep periods total only a few hours per 24-h period.
4. It is difficult to ascertain sleep duration as sleep depth is so shallow that the patient speaks of short periods of slumber or dozing, but no real sleep.

5 Difficulties in Concentration and Memory

This item covers difficulties in concentration, making decisions about everyday matters, and memory.

0. The patient has neither more nor less difficulty in concentration and/or memory than usual.
1. It is doubtful whether the patient has difficulty in concentration and/or memory.
2. Even with a major effort it is difficult for the patient to concentrate on his daily routine work.
3. There are pronounced difficulties with concentration, memory, or decision making, for example, in reading a newspaper article or watching a television programme to the end. (Score '3' as long as the loss in concentration or memory does not clearly influence the interview.
4. The patient during the interview shows difficulty in concentration or memory, or decisions are reached only with considerable delay.

6 Depressed Mood

This item covers both the verbal and the non-verbal communication of sadness, depression, despondency, helplessness and hopelessness.

0. Not present.
1. It is doubtful whether the patient is more despondent or sad than usual; for example, the patient appears vaguely to be more depressed than usual.
2. When the patient more clearly is concerned with unpleasant experiences, although he still lacks helplessness or hopelessness.
3. The patient shows clear non-verbal signs of depression and/or hopelessness.
4. The patient's remarks on despondency and helplessness or the non-verbal signs dominate the interview, and the patient cannot be distracted.

7 General Somatic Symptoms: Muscular Symptoms

This item includes weakness, stiffness, soreness or real pain, which is more or less diffusely localized in the muscles, for example, jaw ache or neck ache.

0. The patient is neither more nor less sore or stiff in his muscles than usual.
1. The patient seems somewhat more sore or stiff in his muscles than usual.
2. The symptoms have the character of pain.
3. The muscle pain interferes to some extent with the patient's daily life and work.
4. The muscle pain is present most of the time and clearly interferes with the patient's daily life and work.

8 General Somatic Symptoms: Sensory

This item includes increased fatigability and weakness or real functional disturbances of the senses. This includes: tinnitus, blurring of vision, hot and cold flushes and prickling sensations.

0. Not present.
1. It is doubtful whether the patient's indications of pressing or prickling sensations (e.g. in ears, eyes or skin) are more pronounced than usual.
2. The sensations of pressure reach the character of buzzing in the ears, visual disturbances in the eyes, and prickling or itching sensations in the skin (paraesthesias).
3. The generalized sensory symptoms interfere to some extent with the patient's daily life and work.
4. The generalized sensory symptoms are present most of the time and clearly interfere with the patient's daily life and work.

9 Cardiovascular Symptoms

This item includes tachycardia, palpitations, oppression, chest pain, throbbing in the blood vessels, and feelings of faintness.

0. Not present.
1. Doubtful whether present.
2. Cardiovascular symptoms are present, but the patient can still control the symptoms.

3. The patient has occasional difficulty controlling the cardiovascular symptoms, which thus to some extent interfere with his daily life and work.
4. The cardiovascular symptoms are present most of the time and interfere clearly with the patient's daily life and work.

10 Respiratory Symptoms
This item includes feelings of constriction or contraction in throat or chest, dyspnoea or choking sensations and sighing respiration.
0. Not present.
1. Doubtful whether present.
2. Respiratory symptoms are present, but the patient can still control the symptoms.
3. The patient has occasional difficulty controlling the respiratory symptoms, which thus to some extent interfere with his daily life and work.
4. The respiratory symptoms are present most of the time and interfere clearly with the patient's daily life and work.

11 Gastro-intestinal Symptoms
The item includes difficulties in swallowing, 'sinking' sensation the stomach, dyspepsia (heartburn or burning sensations in the stomach, abdominal pains related to meals, fullness, nausea and vomiting), abdominal rumbling and diarrhoea.
0. Not present.
1. Doubtful whether present (or doubtful whether different from the patient's ordinary gastro-intestinal sensations).
2. One or more of the above-mentioned gastro-intestinal symptoms are present, but the patient can still control the symptoms.
3. The patient has occasional difficulty controlling the gastro-intestinal symptoms, which thus to some extent interfere with his daily life and work, for example, tendency to lose control over the bowels.
4. The gastro-intestinal symptoms are present most of the time and interfere clearly with the patient's daily life and work, for example losing control over the bowels.

12 Genito-urinary Symptoms
This item includes non-organic or psychic symptoms such as frequent or more pressing passing of urine, menstrual irregularities, anorgasmia, dyspareunia, premature ejaculation, loss of erection.
0. Not present.
1. Doubtful whether present (or doubtful whether different from the ordinary genito-urinary sensations).
2. One or more of the above-mentioned genito-urinary symptoms are present, but they do not interfere with the patient's daily life and work.
3. The patient occasionally has one or more of the above mentioned genito-urinary symptoms to such a degree that they interfere to some extent with his daily life and work, for example tendency to lose control over micturation.

4. The genito-urinary symptoms are present most of the time and interfere clearly with the patient's daily life and work, for example, losing control over micturation.

13 Other Autonomic Symptoms

This item includes dryness of mouth, blushing or pallor, sweating and dizziness.
0. Not present.
1. Doubtful whether present.
2. One or more of the above-mentioned autonomic symptoms are present, but they do not interfere with the patient's daily life and work.
3. The patient occasionally has one or more of the above-mentioned autonomic symptoms to such a degree that they interfere to some extent with his daily life and work.
4. The autonomic symptoms are present most of the time and clearly interfere with the patient's daily life and work.

14 Behaviour During Interview

During the interview the patient appears tense, nervous, agitated, restless, fidgeting, tremulous, pale, hyperventilating or sweating. On the basis of such observations a global estimate is made.
0. The patient does not appear anxious.
1. It is doubtful whether the patient is anxious.
2. The patient is moderately anxious.
3. The patient is markedly anxious.
4. The patient is overwhelmed by anxiety, for example, with shaking and trembling all over.

2.2 Hamilton Depression Scale with Melancholia Scale

During the interview for completing the HAS-G, a number of depressive symptoms are also assessed. The HDS/MES ("Appendix 2.4") covers the depressive spectrum. The first 17 items constitute the original HDS, and 18–23 are from the MES.

According to the HDS criteria for depression, total scale scores are interpreted as follows: 0–7, no depression; 8–12, minor depression; 13–15, less than major depression; 16 or more, major depression. Interpretation of total scores on the six item HDS subscale, indicated as HDS (a–f) in "Appendix 2.4", is: 0–3, no depression; 4–8, minor depression; 9 or more, major depression. The MES criteria for depression are: 0–5, no depression; 6–9, mild depression; 10–14, less than major depression; 15 or more, major depression.

This enlarged HDS consists of the 17 original Hamilton items and the 11 Bech-Rafaelsen items, for a total of 23 items (some are identical in the two depression scales). The interviewer should assess the presence and intensity of these items in terms of the patient's condition at the time of the interview. Some items, however, are less suitable for a 'here and now' evaluation, for example, sleep disturbances, and with these it is necessary to judge the conditions retrospectively over recent days0 (we recommend a minimum period of 3 days for this). When in doubt, the interviewer should obtain information from the ward personnel or from relatives. The rating should take place at a fixed time, for example, between 8:00 a.m. and 9:30 a.m., to avoid the influence of diurnal variation.

Although in our opinion the selected items cover the set of depressive symptoms, there may, of course, be situations in which one or more features seem to be lacking. We have, for example, no items for obsessional or compulsive symptoms because these have diagnostic rather than quantitative properties. However, if obsessional thoughts seem to refer to the severity of the depressive state under assessment, it should be considered whether the patient's obsessions are part of his insecurity or apprehension; in this case the obsessional thoughts should be taken into account when assessing item 10 (psychic anxiety). If obsessional thoughts are part of the patient's self-depreciation (often expressing his delusional guilt feelings), they should be rated in item 2 (self-depreciation and guilt feelings). If obsessional thoughts are part of depressive thoughts, they are rated in item 1 (depressed mood) or item 3 (suicidal impulses). Obsessions or compulsions may also refer to the patient's depressive inability in making decisions, and in this case they should be scored in item 21 (intellectual retardation or impairment).

The scale is basically quantitative; it was constructed for the sole purpose of rating the actual clinical picture, and it is not to be considered a diagnostic tool. When the scale is used in repeated (weekly) ratings, each assessment must be independent of the others. The rater should therefore avoid taking a look at or recalling former interviews and should not ask about changes that have taken place since the last interview; instead he should elicit the patient's condition over the preceding 3 days for all items. Each scale step encompasses the lower steps, for example scale step '3' includes scale steps '2' and '1'. Normal function is always rated as '0'. In general, five categories are provided for each item. If the symptom is not present, score '0'; if the symptom is present to a very mild degree, for instance, it is doubtful whether it differs from the patient's normal state, score '1'; if the symptom is clearly present, but only to a moderate degree (i.e. has no influence on the patient's daily life), score '2'; when the symptom is present in a marked degree (i.e. occasionally influencing the patient's daily life), score '3'; when the symptom is present in an extreme degree (i.e. more constantly interferes with the patient's life), socre '4'. In reference to insomnia items (items 4, 5, 6, 18) administration of drugs (e.g. sedatives) is disregarded.

1 Depressed Mood
This item covers both the verbal and the non-verbal communication of sadness, depression, despondency, helplessness and hopelessness.
0. Not present.

1. It is doubtful whether the patient is more despondent or sad than usual; for example, the patient appears vaguely to be more depressed than usual.
2. The patient more clearly is concerned by unpleasant experiences, although he still lacks helplessness or hopelessness.
3. The patient shows clear non-verbal signs of depression and/or is at times overpowered by helplessness or hopelessness.
4. The patient's remarks on despondency and helplessness or the non-verbal signs dominate the interview, and the patient cannot be distracted.

2 Self-Depreciation and Guilt Feelings
This item covers the lowered self-esteem with guilt feelings.
0. No self-depreciation or guilt feelings.
1. It is doubtful whether guilt feelings are present because the patient is concerned only with the fact that during the current illness he has been a burden to family or colleagues due to reduced work capacity.
2. Self-depreciation or guilt feelings are more clearly present because the patient is concerned with incidents in the past prior to the current episode. For instance, the patient reproaches himself for minor omissions or failures, for not having done his duty or for having harmed others.
3. The patient suffers from more severe guilt feelings. He may express the feeling that the current suffering is some sort of punishment. (Score '3' as long as the patient intellectually can see that his view is unfounded.)
4. The guilt feelings are firmly maintained and resist any counter argument, so that they become paranoid ideas.

3 Suicidal Impulses
0. No suidical impulses.
1. The patient feels that life is not worthwhile, but he expresses no wish to die.
2. The patient wishes to die but has no plans of taking his own life.
3. It is probable that the patient contemplates committing suicide.
4. In the days prior to the interview the patient has tried to commit suicide cr in the ward is under special observation due to suicidal risk.

4 Initial Insomnia
0. Not present.
1. At least 1 of the last 3 nights the patient lay in bed for more than 30 min before falling asleep.
2. Each of the 3 nights the patient lay in bed for more than 30 min before falling asleep.

5 Middle Insomnia
The patient wakes up one or more times between midnight and 5 a.m. (if for voiding purpose followed by immediate sleep, score '0').
0. Not present.

1. Once or twice during the last 3 nights.
2. At least once every night.

6 Delayed Insomnia (Premature Awakening)
The patient wakes up before planned by himself or his surroundings.
0. Not present.
1. Less than 1 h too early (and may fall asleep again).
2. Constantly, or more than 1 h too early.

7 Work and Interests
This item includes both work carried out and motivation. Note, however, that the assessment of tiredness and fatigue in their physical manifestations is included in item 13 (general somatic symptoms) and in item 23 (tiredness and pain).

A At First Rating
0. Not unusual.
1. The patient expresses motivation and/or trouble in carrying out his usual work load without reduction.
2. The patient shows more pronounced reduction in motivation and/or trouble in carrying out the usual work. Here the patient has reduced work capacity, cannot keep normal speed, copes with less on the job or in the home; the patient may stay home some days or may try to leave early.
3. Difficulties in simple routine activities. If hospitalized score 3.
4. The patient is fully hospitalized and generally unoccupied, without participation in ward activities (unable to do anything without help). If at home: unable to do anything without help.

B At Weekly Ratings
0. Not unusual. (a) The patient has resumed work at his normal activity level. (b) The patient would have no trouble resuming normal work.
1. (a) The patient is working but at reduced activity level, due either to lack of motivation or to difficulties in the accomplishment of his normal work. (b) The patient is not working, and it is still doubtful whether he could resume his normal work without difficulties.
2. (a) The patient is working but at a clearly reduced level, due either to episodes of non-attendance or to reduced working hours. (b) The patient is still hospitalized or sick-listed, participates more than 3–4 h per day in ward (or home) activities, but is capable of resuming normal work only at a reduced level. If hospitalized, the patient is able to change from full stay to day-patient status.
3. Difficulties in starting simple routine activities which are carried out with great efforts.
4. The patient is still fully hospitalized and generally unable to participate in ward activities (unable to do anything without help). If at home: unable to do anything without help.

8 Retardation: General

0. Not present.
1. Conversational speed doubtfully or slightly reduced and facial expression doubtfully or slightly stiffened (retarded).
2. Conversational speed clearly reduced, with intermissions; reduced gestures and slow pace.
3. The interview is clearly prolonged due to long latencies and brief answers; all movements are very slow.
4. The interview cannot be completed; retardation approaches (and includes) stupor.

9 Agitation

0. Not present.
1. Doubtful or slight agitation, for example, tendency to changing position in chair or at times scratching his head.
2. Fidgeting; wringing hands, changing position in chair again and again; restless in ward, with some pacing.
3. Patient cannot stay in chair during interview (and/or much pacing in ward).
4. Interview must be conducted 'on the run'. Almost continuous pacing; pulling off clothes, tearing his hair.

10 Anxiety: Psychic

This item includes tenseness, irritability, worry, insecurity, fear and apprehension approaching overpowering dread. It may often be difficult to distinguish between the patient's experience of anxiety ('psychic' or 'central' anxiety phenomena) and the physiological ('peripheral') anxiety manifestations which can be observed, such as hand tremor and sweating. Most important is the patient's report of worry, insecurity, uncertainty, experiences of dread, i.e. psychic ('central') anxiety.

0. The patient is neither more nor less insecure or irritable than usual.
1. It is doubtful whether the patient is more insecure or irritable than usual.
2. The patient is more clearly in a state of anxiety, apprehension or irritability, which he may find difficult to control. It is thus without influence on the patient's daily life because the worrying still is about minor matters.
3. The anxiety or insecurity is at times more difficult to control because the worrying is about major injuries or harms which might occur in the future; thus the anxiety may be experienced as panic, i.e. overpowering dread. This occassionally interferes with the patient's daily life.
4. The feeling of dread is present so often that it markedly interfere with the patient's daily life.

11 Anxiety: Somatic

This item includes all physiological concomitants of anxiety.All feeling states should be rated under item 10 and not here.

0. The patient is neither more nor less prone than usual to experience somatic concomitants of psychic anxious states.

1. The patient occasionally experiences slight manifestations such as abdominal symptoms, sweating or trembling; however, the description is vague and doubtful.
2. The patient from time to time experiences abdominal symptoms, sweating, trembling, etc. Symptoms and signs are clearly described but are not marked or incapacitating, i.e. still without influence on the patient's daily life.
3. Physiological concomitants of anxious psychic states are marked and sometimes very worrying. They interfere occasionally with the patient's daily life.
4. Physiological concomitants of anxious psychic states are numerous, persistent and often incapacitating; they interfere markedly with the patient's daily life.

12 Somatic Symptoms: Gastro-intestinal

Symptoms may stem from the entire gastro-intestinal tract. Dry mouth, loss of appetite, and constipation are more common than abdominal cramps and pains. They must be distinguished from gastro-intestinal anxiety symptoms ('butterflies in the stomach' or loose bowel movements) and from nihilistic ideas (no bowel movements for weeks or months taken as indicating that the intestines have withered away) which should be rated under 15 (hypochondriasis).

0. No gastro-intestinal complaints (or symptoms unchanged from before onset of depression).
1. The patient eats without encouragement by staff; food intake is about normal, but without relish (all dishes taste alike and cigarettes are without flavour). Occasional constipation.
2. Food intake is reduced; the patient must be urged to eat. As a rule, he is clearly constipated. Laxatives are often tried but are of little help.

13 Somatic Symptoms: General

Central are feelings of fatigue and exhaustion, loss of energy, but also diffuse muscular aches and pains in neck, back or limbs, such as muscular headache.

0. The patient is neither more nor less tired or troubled by bodily discomfort than usual.
1. Doubtful or very vague feelings of muscular fatigue or other somatic discomfort.
2. The patient is clearly or constantly tired and exhausted, and/or troubled by bodily discomforts (e.g. muscular headache).

14 Sexual Interest

The subject of sexual interest is often difficult to approach, especially with elderly patients. In men, try to ask questions concerning sexual preoccupation and drive, in women, ask about responsiveness (both to engage in sexual activity and to obtain satisfaction in intercourse).

0. Not unusual.
1. Doubtful or mild reduction in sexual interest and enjoyment.
2. Clear loss of sexual appetite. Often functional impotence in men and lack of arousal or plain disgust in women.

15 Hypochondriasis
Preoccupation with bodily symptoms or functions (in the absence of somatic disease).
0. The patient pays no more interest than usual to the slight bodily sensations of everyday life.
1. Slightly or doubtfully more occupied than usual with bodily symptoms and functions.
2. The patient is quite worried about his physical health. He expresses thoughts of organic disease, with a tendency to somatize the clinical presentation.
3. The patient is convinced of suffering from a physical illness which can explain all his symptoms (brain tumour, abdominal cancer, etc.), but he can briefly be reassured that this is not the case.
4. The preoccupation with bodily dysfunction clearly reaches paranoid dimensions. The hypochondriac delusions often have a nihilistic quality or guilt associations: to be rotting inside; insects eating the tissues; bowels blocked and withering away; other patients are being infected by the patient's bad odour or his syphilis. Counter-argumentation is without effect.

16 Loss of Insight
This item is only meaningful if the observer is convinced that the patient during the interview is still in a depressive state.
0. The patient agrees that he has depressive symptoms or a nervous illness.
1. The patient agrees that he is depressed but feels this to be secondary to conditions unrelated to the illness such as malnutrition, climate, or overwork.
2. The patient denies being ill at all. Delusional patients are by definition without insight. Enquiries should therefore be directed to the patient's attitude to his symptoms of guilt (item 2) or hypochondriasis (item 15), but other delusional symptoms should also be considered.

17 Weight Loss
Try to obtain objective information; if such is not available, be conservative in estimation. (Evaluation at first interview refers to the whole period of current illness.)

A At First Rating
0. No weight loss.
1. Weight loss of 1–2.5 kg.
2. Weight loss of 3 kg or more.

B At Weekly Interviews
0. No weight loss.
1. Weight loss of 0.5 kg per week.
2. Weight loss of 1 kg or more per week.

18 Insomnia: General
This item covers only the patient's subjective experience of the duration of sleep (hours of sleep per 24-h period) and sleep depth (superficial and interrupted sleep versus deep and steady sleep). The rating is based on three preceding nights, irrespective of administration of hypnotics or sedatives.

0. Usual sleep duration and sleep depth.
1. Sleep duration is doubtfully or slightly reduced (for example, to difficulty in falling asleep, but no change in sleep depth).
2. Sleep depth is also reduced, sleep being more superficial. Sleep as a whole is somewhat disturbed. The total duration of sleep per 24-h period is still more than 50% of the habitual duration.
3. Sleep duration as well as sleep depth is markedly changed. The broken sleep periods total only a few hours per 24-h period.
4. It is difficult to ascertain sleep duration, as sleep depth is so shallow that the patient speaks of short periods of slumber or dosing, but no real sleep.

19 Retardation: Motor
0. Not present.
1. Doubtfully decreased motor activity, for example, facial expression slightly or doubtfully retarded.
2. More clearly motor retardation (e.g. reduced gestures; slow pace).
3. All movements very slow.
4. Motor retardation approaching or including stupor.

20 Retardation: Verbal
This item includes changes in flow of speech and the capacity to verbalize thoughts and emotions.

0. Not present.
1. Doubtfully reduced verbal expression or inertia in conversation.
2. More pronounced inertia in conversation, for example a trend to longer intermissions.
3. The interview is clearly prolonged due to long pauses and brief responses.
4. The interview can be completed only with marked difficulty.

21 Retardation: Intellectual
This item covers difficulties in concentration, making decisions about everyday matters, and memory, i.e. intellectual impairment.

0. The patient has neither more nor less difficulty in concentration and/or memory than usual.
1. It is doubtful whether the patient has difficulty in concentration and/or memory.
2. Even with a major effort it is difficult for the patient to concentrate on his work, but this is still without influence on the patient's daily life.
3. More pronounced difficulty with concentration, memory, or decision making.

For example, the patient has difficulty reading a newspaper article or watching a television programme to the end. (Score '3' as long as loss of concentration or poor memory does not clearly influence the interview).
4. The patient during the interview shows difficulty in concentration and/or memory, or decisions are reached only with considerable delay.

22 Retardation: Emotional

This item covers the reduced interest and emotional contact with other human beings. The reduced wish or ability to communicate one's own feelings and opinions and to share joy and sorrow is normally experienced by the patient as alien and painful.
0. The patient is neither more nor less emotionally interested in contact with other persons.
1. It is doubtful whether the patient is more emotionally introverted than usual.
2. The patient has clearly less wish or ability than usual to be together with other people.
3. The patient isolates himself to a certain degree. He has no need or ability to establish closer contact with friends or family.
4. The patient feels emotionally indifferent even to near friends and family.

23 Tiredness and Pains

This item includes weakness, faintness, tiredness, fullness and soreness as well as real pains more or less diffusely located in muscles or inner organs. Muscular fatigue is normally located in the extremities. The patient may give this as the reason for difficulty in his work, as he has a feeling of tiredness or heaviness in arms and legs. Muscle pains are often located in the back, neck or shoulders, perceived as tensions or headache. The feeling of fullness and heaviness increasing to actual sensations of pain is often broadly located as 'chest discomfort' (different from heart pains), abdominal pains, head pains (muscular headache). It is often difficult to discern between 'psychic' and 'physical' pains. Special notice should be taken of vague 'psychic' pains.
0. The patient is neither more nor less tired or troubled by bodily discomfort than usual.
1. Doubtful or very vague feelings or muscular fatigue or other somatic discomfort.
2. Feelings of muscular fatigue or somatic discomfort are more pronounced. Painful sensations sometimes occur, such as muscular headache, but these are still without influence on the patient's daily life.
3. Muscular fatigue or diffuse pain is clearly present, which interferes occasionally with the patient's daily life.
4. Muscular fatigue and diffuse pains constantly cause the patient severe distress, so that it markedly interferes with his daily life.

2.3 Mania Scale

If there are manic symptoms, the MAS ("Appendix 2.5") should be considered. Total scale scores are interpreted: 0–5, no mania; 6–9, hypomania (mild); 10–14, probable mania; 15 or more, definite mania.

The MAS consists of 11 items. The interviewer should assess the presence and grade of the individual items in terms of the patient's condition at the time of the interview. Some items are, however, less suitable for a 'here and now' evaluation, for example, sleep disturbances. It is necessary here to judge the condition during the 3 days prior to the interview. When in doubt, information from ward personnel or relatives should be solicited. The duration of the interview should be no less than 15 min and no more than 30 min. The interview technique does not differ in principle from clinical tradition. Compared to the interview with a depressed patient (where pressure should not be exerted on the patient), the problem in assessing the manic patient is the balance between, on the one hand, allowing him sufficient time to say what he wants to say, and, on the other, preventing him from wandering too far from the point. The rating should always take place at a fixed time, for example, between 8:00 a.m. and 9:30 a.m., to avoid the influence of diurnal variation.

The scale is basically quantitative; it was constructed for the sole purpose of rating the current clinical picture, and it is not to be considered as a diagnostic tool. When the scale is used in repeated (weekly) ratings, each assessment must be independent of the others. The rater should therefore avoid seeing or recalling former interviews and should not ask about changes since the last interview; rather, he should refer to the patient's condition during the preceding 3 days. For all items each scale step encompasses the lower steps, for example, scale step '3' includes scale steps '2' and '1'. Normal function is always rated as '0'.

1 Activity: Motor
0. Not unusual.
1. Slightly or doubtfully increased motor activity (e.g. lively facial expression).
2. Moderately increased motor activity (e.g. lively gestures).
3. Clearly excessive motor activity, on the move most of the time, rises once or several times during interview.
4. Constantly active, restlessly energetic. Even if urged, the patient cannot sit still.

2 Activity: Verbal
0. Not unusual.
1. Somewhat talkative.
2. Very talkative, no spontaneous intervals in the conversation.
3. Difficult to interrupt.
4. Impossible to interrupt, completely dominates the conversation.

3 Flight of Thoughts
0. Not present.
1. Somewhat lively descriptions, explanations and elaborations without losing the connection with the topic of the conversation. The thoughts are thus still cohesive.
2. Again it is occasionally difficult for the patient to stick to the topic, he is distracted by random associations (often rhymes, clangs, puns, pieces of verse or music).
3. The line of thought is regularly disrupted by diversionary associations.
4. It is difficult or impossible to follow the patient's line of thought, as he constantly jumps from one topic to another.

4 Voice/Noise Level
0. Not unusual.
1. Speaks somewhat loudly without being noisy.
2. Voice discernible at a distance, and somewhat noisy.
3. Vociferous, voice discernible at a long distance, is noisy, singing.
4. Shouting, screaming; or using other sources of noise due to hoarseness.

5 Hostility/Destructiveness
0. No signs of impatience or hostility.
1. Somewhat impatient or irritable, but control is maintained.
2. Markedly impatient or irritable. Provocation badly tolerated.
3. Provocative, makes threats, but can be calmed down.
4. Overt physical violence; physically destructive.

6 Mood Level (Feeling of Well-Being)
0. Not unusual.
1. Slightly or doubtfully elevated mood, optimistic, but still adapted to situation.
2. Moderately elevated mood, joking, laughing.
3. Markedly elevated mood, exuberant both in manner and speech.
4. Extremely elevated mood, quite irrelevant to situation.

7 Self-Esteem
0. Not unusual.
1. Slightly or doubtfully increased self-esteem, for example occasionally overestimates his own habitual capacities.
2. Moderately increased self-esteem, for example, overestimates more constantly his own habitual capacities or hints at unusual abilities.
3. Markedly unrealistic ideas, for example, that he has extraordinary abilities, powers or knowledge (scientific, religious, etc.), but can briefly be corrected.
4. Grandiose ideas which cannot be corrected.

8 Contact (Intrusiveness)
0. Not unusual.
1. Slightly or doubtfully meddling, for example, interrupting or slightly intrusive.
2. Moderately meddling and arguing or intrusive.
3. Dominating, arranging, directing, but still in context with the setting.
4. Extremely dominating and manipulating, not in context with the setting.

9 Sleep (Average of Past 3 Nights)
0. Habitual duration of sleep.
1. Duration of sleep reduced by 25%.
2. Duration of sleep reduced by 50%.
3. Duration of sleep reduced by 75%.
4. No sleep.

10 Sexual Interest
0. Habitual sexual interest and activity.
1. Slight or doubtful increase in sexual interest and activity, for example, slightly flirtatious.
2. Moderate increase in sexual interest and activity, for example, clearly flirtatious.
3. Marked increase in sexual interest and activity; excessively flirtatious; dress provocative.
4. Completely and inadequately occupied by sexuality.

11 Decreased Work Ability

A At First Rating
0. Not present.
1. Slightly or doubtfully increased drive, but work quality is slightly down as motivation is changing, and the patient somewhat distractable.
2. Increased drive, but motivation clearly fluctuating. The patient has difficulties in judging own work quality and the quality is indeed lowered. Frequent quarrels at work.
3. Work capacity clearly reduced; the patient occasionally loses control. He must stop work and be written off sick. If hospitalized, he can participate for some hours per day in ward activities.
4. The patient is (or ought to be) hospitalized and is unable to participate in ward activities.

B At Weekly Ratings
0. (a) The patient has resumed work at his normal activity level. (b) The patient would have no trouble resuming normal work.
1. (a) The patient is working, but the effort is somewhat reduced due to changable motivation. (b) It is doubtful whether the patient can resume normal work on a full scale due to distractability and changable motivation.

2. (a) The patient is working, but at a clearly reduced level, for example, due to episodes of non-attendance. (b) The patient is still hospitalized or written off sick. He is able to resume work only if special precautions are taken: close supervision and/or reduced working hours.
3. The patient is still hospitalized or written off sick and is unable to resume work. In hospital he participates for some hours per day in ward activities.
4. The patient is still fully hospitalized and generally unable to participate in ward activities.

2.4 Brief Psychiatric Rating Scale

Although the BPRS ("Appendix 2.6") also includes depression symptoms (items 1, 2, 5, 6, 9 and 13), the scale is constructed essentially for schizophrenic states; the total scale score should therefore be considered as a schizo-affective scale. Interpretation of total scale scores is: 0–9, not a schizo-affective case; 10–20, possible schizo-affective case; 21 or more, definite schizo-affective case. For schizophrenic states, the ten schizophrenic items on the BPRS should be summed. "Appendix 2.7" lists the ten BPRS items for schizophrenia, or, more appropriately, for 'psychotic disintegration', as a scale in its own right. (Andersen et al. 1989).

The BPRS consists of 18 items. The interviewer should assess the presence and degree of the individual items in terms of patient's condition at the time of the interview. The following six items, however, should be evaluated on the basis of the condition during the past 3 days: items 2 (psychic anxiety), 10 (hostility), 11 (suspiciousness), 12 (hallucinatory behaviour), 15 (unusual thought content) and 16 (blunted or inappropriate affect). When in doubt, the interviewer should solicit information from ward personnel or relatives. It is recommended to use the first minutes of the interview to establish a rapport with the patient before direct questions are introduced. The interview should last no more than 30 min. The interview technique does not differ in principle from clinical tradition. Pressure should not be exerted on the patient, who as far as possible should be allowed to explain his situation in his own words. The interviewer should remain unaffected by spontaneous intermissions, as these represent an integral part of the observation. The rating should always take place at a fixed time, for instance between 8:00 a.m. and 9:30 a.m., to avoid the influence of diurnal variation.

The scale is basically quantitative; it was constructed for the sole purpose of rating the current clinical picture, and it is not to be considered as a diagnostic tool. When the scale is used in repeated (weekly) ratings, each assessment must be independent of the others. The rater should therefore avoid looking at or recalling former interviews and should not ask about changes that might have taken place since the last interview; rather, he should refer to the patient's condition during the preceding 3 days. For all items each scale step encompasses the lower steps, for example, scale step '3' includes scale steps '2' and '1'. Normal function is always rated as '0'.

1 Somatic Concern
This item includes hypochondriasis. Scale steps '1' and '2' refer to non-delusional hypochondriasis and scale steps '3' and '4' to delusional hypochondriasis.

0. Not present.
1. Mild or doubtful degree of overconcern for physical health.
2. The patient expresses thoughts of organic disease (e.g. cancer or heart disease) but without delusional interpretations.
3. The complaints are bizarre (e.g. rotting inside), but the patient can briefly be reassured that this is not the case.
4. The patient is convinced that, for instance, the organs are rotted or missing, or that worms are eating the brain. He cannot even for a briefly be reassured that this is not the case.

2 Anxiety: Psychic
This item includes tenseness, irritability, worry, insecurity, fear and apprehension approaching overpowering dread. It is often difficult to distinguish between the patient's experience of anxiety ('psychic' or 'central' anxiety phenomena) and the physiological ('peripheral') anxiety manifestations which can be observed, such as hand tremor and sweating. Most important is the patient's report of worry, insecurity, uncertainty, experiences of dread, i.e. of psychic ('central') anxiety.

0. The patient is neither more nor less insecure or irritable than usual.
1. It is doubtful whether the patient is more insecure or irritable than usual.
2. The patient seems more clearly in a state of anxiety, apprehension or irritability, which he may find difficult to control. It is thus without influence on the patient's daily life, because the worrying is still about minor matters.
3. The anxiety or insecurity is at times more difficult to control because the worrying is about major injuries or harms which might occur in the future. For example, the anxiety may be experienced as panic, i.e. overpowering dread. This occasionally interferes with the patient's daily life.
4. The feeling of dread is present so often that it markedly interferes with the patient's daily life.

3 Emotional Withdrawal
This item includes the introspective experience of emotional contact with the patient during the interview. Emotional withdrawal is represented by the feeling on the part of the rater that an invisible barrier exists between the patient and the observer.

0. Not present.
1. Some (or doubtful) emotional distance.
2. Emotional reactions reduced, for example, doubtful eyecontact.
3. Emotional reactions more limited, for example, occasionally inadequate eyecontact or other indicators of a barrier of contact.
4. The emotional contact is strongly reduced or nearly absent, for example, the patient avoids eyecontact or shows other indicators of a barrier of contact.

4 Conceptual Disorganization (Incoherence)

Presenting disturbances of the thought process, from some vagueness in verbal expression to completely disorganized verbal productions.

0. Not present.
1. The thinking is characterized by some minor vagueness, but the language is conceptually not unusual.
2. Moderate disturbance in thinking. There is some difficulty in directing thoughts towards goals, resulting in emptiness in the communicative information transmitted. There may be a tendency to unusual conceptbehaviour, but most characteristical is that language resembles an engine idling in communication.
3. Marked difficulty in organizing thoughts, as evidenced by frequent irrelevancies, loosening of associations, possibly with a tendency to thought blockings or neologisms.
4. Conceptual disorganization extremely severe, resulting in gross irrelevancies and total failure of communication, (e.g. 'word salad').

5 Self-Depreciation and Guilt Feelings

This item covers the lowered self-esteem with guilt feelings.

0. Not present.
1. It is doubtful whether guilt feelings are present, as the patient is concerned only with the fact that during the current illness he has been a burden to family or colleagues due to reduced work capacity.
2. Self-depreciation or guilt feelings are more clearly present, as the patient is concerned with incidents in the past prior to the current episode. For example, the patient reproaches himself for minor omissions or failures, for not having done his duty or for having harmed others.
3. The patient suffers from more severe guilt feelings. He may express the feeling that the current suffering is some sort of punishment. Score '3' as long as the patient intellectually can see that his view is unfounded.)
4. The guilt feelings are firmly maintained and resist any counter argument, so that they become paranoid ideas.

6 Anxiety: Somatic

This item includes physiological concomitants of anxiety which are present during the interview. All anxious states should be rated under item 2 and not here.

0. The patient is neither more nor less prone than usual to experiencing somatic concomitants of anxious states.
1. The patient occasionally experiences slight manifestations such as abdominal symptoms, sweating or trembling; however, pathology is questionable.
2. The patient occasionally experiences abdominal symptoms, sweating, trembling, etc. Symptoms and signs are clearly described but are not marked or incapacitating.
3. Physiological concomitants of anxious states are marked and sometimes very worrying.

4. Physiological concomitants of anxious states are numerous, persistent and often incapacitating.

7 Specific Movement Disturbances

These represent various degrees of bizarre motor behaviour, ranging from some eccentricity in posture to severe catatonic agitation.

0. Not present.
1. Mild or doubtfully present during interview.
2. Moderate; clearly present during parts of the interview.
3. Severe; continuous motor abnormalities. Can be interrupted.
4. Extremely severe; persistent, uncontrolled motor abnormalities.

8 Exaggerated Self-Esteem

This item includes various degrees of exaggerated self-opinion, ranging from remarkable self-complacency or smugness to grotesque delusions of grandeur.

0. Not present.
1. Slightly or doubtfully increased self-esteem, for example, occasionally overestimates his own habitual capacities.
2. Moderately increased self-esteem, for example, overestimates more constantly his own habitual capacities or hints at unusual abilities.
3. Markedly unrealistic ideas, for example, that he has extraordinary abilities, powers or knowledge (scientific, religious, etc), but can briefly be corrected.
4. Grandiose ideas which cannot be corrected.

9 Depressive Mood

This item covers both the verbal and the non-verbal communication of sadness, depression, despondency, helplessness and hopelessness.

0. Not present.
1. The patient vaguely indicates that he is more despondent and depressed than usual.
2. The patient more clearly is concerned with unpleasant experiences, although he still lacks helplessness or hopelessness.
3. The patient shows clear non-verbal signs of depression and/or is at times overpowered by helplessness or hopelessness.
4. The patient's remarks on despondency and helplessness or the non-verbal signs dominate the interview, in which the patient cannot be distracted.

10 Hostility

This item represens the patient's verbal report of hostile feelings or actions towards other persons outside the interview and is a retrospective judgment of the previous 3 days. Distinguish from item 14 (uncooperativeness), which includes the formal contact during the interview.

0. Not present.
1. The patient has been somewhat impatient or irritable, but control has been maintained.

2. The patient has been moderately impatient or irritable, but provocation has been tolerated.
3. The patient has been verbally hostile, has made threats, and may nearly be physically destructive, but can still be calmed down.
4. The patient extremely hostile, with overt physical violence; physically destructive.

11 Suspiciousness
This item represents suspiciousness, distrustfulness or misinterpretations, ranging from a remarkable lack of confidence in others to florid delusions of persecution.
0. Not present.
1. Vague ideas of reference. The patient tends to suspect others of talking about him or laughing at him, feels that 'something is going on'. However, thoughts, interactions and behaviour are only minimally affected.
2. Distrustfulness is clearly evident, but there is no evidence of persecutory delusions because the beliefs are still an 'as-if' experience, thus still without influence on behaviour or interpersonal relations.
3. Persecutory delusions are present (reassurance is difficult), but they still have limited impact on interpersonal relations or behaviour.
4. Florid, systematized delusions of persecution (correction impossible) which, significantly interfere with interpersonal relations and behaviour.

12 Hallucinations
This item represents sensory perceptions without correspondence to external stimulus. The hallucinatory experiences must have occurred within the past 3 days, and with the exception of hypnagogic hallucinations, not during states of clouding of consciousness (delirium).
0. Not present.
1. Mild or doubtful degree. Hypnagogic hallucinatory experiences or isolated elementary hallucinatory experiences (e.g. hearing sounds).
2. Occasional but fully developed hallucinations (e.g. hearing voices), not affecting behaviour, i.e. limited to a few brief moments.
3. Hallucinations (e.g. hearing voices) that influence behaviour, i.e. are present most part of the day.
4. Constantly absorbed in hallucinatory experiences throughout the day.

13 Motor Retardation
Reduction in motor activity as reflected in showing or lessening of movements. Manifestations during the course of interview.
0. Not present.
1. Very slight or questionable diminution in rate of movements.
2. Mild to moderate slowness in movements.
3. Moderate to marked retardation in movements.
4. Movements are extremely slow. Motor retardation approaches (and includes) stupor.

14 Uncooperativeness

This item represens the patient's attitude and responses to the interviewer and the interview situation, in contrast to item 10 (hostility) which covers the uncooperativeness with other persons during the previous 3 days.

0. Not present.
1. Overly formal and reserved in the interview situation. Patient answers somewhat briefly.
2. Moderate resistance. Patient answers evasively or objects to some questions. Moderately hostile attitude to the interviewer.
3. Pronounced resistance. Patient answers irrelevantly or refuses to answer. Markedly hostile attitude to the interviewer.
4. Interview impossible. Patient refuses to stay in the interview situation.

15 Unusual Thought Content

This item concerns the content of the patient's verbalization and not with the organization of the language, which is rated in item 4 (conceptual disorganization). The item refers to the qualities of unusual thought content, ranging from overvalued ideas to various levels of delusional ideas. Notice that 'grandiose delusions' is rated in item 8 (exaggerated self-estccm), 'delusions of guilt' in item 5 (guilt feeling) and 'delusions of persecution' in item 11 (suspiciousness). The delusions of particular interest here are those of control, influence or depersonalization, morbid jealousy, sexual delusions, expansive or religious delusions. Rate only the degree of unusualness in thought content expressed, the significance it constitutes in the patient's mind or its influence on behaviour.

0. Not present.
1. Mild or doubtful degree (e.g. overvalued ideas).
2. Moderate degree (e.g. some delusional quality, but still an 'as-if' experience).
3. Delusions determine most of thought content and occasionally influence behaviour.
4. Overwhelming delusions determine thought content and behaviour.

16 Blunted or Inappropriate Affect

This item represents lowered ability or motivation to feel or express emotions such as grief, happiness and anger. The emotions, verbally and non-verbally expressed, are inappropriate to the situation or thought content. Essentially, emotions do not correspond to ideas. Thus, the patient might laugh or weep without recognizable cause (parathymia). This element includes: (a) any ability of emotional display not evidently related to the situation as the interviewer sees it, or to the manifest content of thought as the interviewer understands the patient's words, or (b) any more or less steady, unvarying emotional state which seems to be other than that called for by the setting of the interview, the nature of the background as known by the interviewer, and the manifest content of the patient's speech. Distinguish from item 3 (emotional withdrawal) which refers to the introspective experience of emotional contact with the patient during interview. The concept of blunted affect may be difficult or impossible to distinguish from anhedonia if it refers to the capacity to conceal emotions, for example, the patient may be in a state of excessive anxiety without any clinical manifestations (his countenance is serene and he talks composedly about neutral topics).

0. Not present.
1. Diminished emotional responsiveness of questionable pathology. Outside the interview: less ability to express affective tone in contact with others.
2. Tendency to conceal emotional reaction or to unvary emotional modulations. Outside interview: less ability to establish closer contact with or indifference of affection for collegues, fellow patients, or ward personnel.
3. Clearly blunted affect with a general flatness in emotional tone, possibly with a tendency to affective discharge, for example, inappropriate or uncontrolled laughter or weeping. Outside interview: less ability to establish closer contact with or indifference of affection for friends or family.
4. Clearly blunted affect and clearly affective discharges, such as excitement, rage or inappropriate, uncontrolled laughter or weeping. Outside interview: clearly lack of any feeling of having human contact or extreme indifference of affection for other persons.

17 Psychomotor Agitation
This item represents elevation in psychomotor activity level.
0. Not present.
1. Slightly or doubtfully increased motor activity, for example, lively facial expression or somewhat talkative.
2. Moderately increased motor activity, for example, lively gestures or very talkative or speech loud and fast.
3. Clearly excessive motor activity, on the move most of the time; rises once or several times during interview; flight of ideas; difficult to understand.
4. Constantly active, restlessly energetic; speech disintegrated; meaningful communication impossible.

18 Disorientation and Confusion
This item represents various degrees of clouding of consciousness with reduction in or lack of orientation in time, place or personal data.
0. The patient is completely orientated in time, place and personal data.
1. The patient has occasional difficulties but can spontaneously correct statements about orientation in time, place or personal data.
2. The patient has impairments which are not spontaneously corrected. For example, he does not know the name of the day or the date although he still names the month and year correctly; he has spatial difficulties although he is still orientated in the ward (or own home); or he has difficulty remembering names although he still knows his own name.
3. The patient is markedly disorientated. For example, he does not know the month or year although he does know which season it is, or has difficulty

finding his way to toilet and bed without help, and/or remembers his name only with some help.
4. The patient is completely disorientated in time, or place, or personal data.

2.5 Other Versions of Rating Scales

2.5.1 Hamilton Depression Scale

The original Hamilton scale manual (Hamilton 1960, 1967) is rarely used, and the American version (Guy 1976) is now the most frequently used (Zitman et al. 1990). Hamilton himself, however, never accepted the American version, preferring instead the one included in this compendium. Hamilton's two original versions are presented here to illustrate the principle behind this scale. Hamilton (1977) used the following cut-off points: 0–11, minor or no depression; 12–18, less than major depression; 19–24, major depression; 25 or more, severe depression.

1 Depressed Mood (1960)
Gloomy attitude, pessimism about the future. Feeling of sadness, tendency to weep. The most useful indicator is tendency to weep, but it must always be considered against the cultural background, and patients may also 'go beyond weeping'.
0. Not present.
1. Sadness.
2. Occasional weeping.
3. Frequent weeping.
4. Extreme symptoms.

1 Depression (1967)
Depressed mood is not easy to assess. One looks for a gloomy attitude, pessimism about future, feelings of hopelessness and a tendency to weep. As a guide, occasional weeping could count as '2', frequent weeping as '3', and severe symptoms alloted '4' points. When patients are severely depressed they may 'go beyond weeping'. It is important to remember that patients interpret the word 'depression' in all sorts of strange ways. A useful common phrase is 'lowering of spirits'. It is generally believed that women weep more readily than men, but there is little evidence that this is true in the case of depressive illness. There is no reason to believe, at the moment, that an assessment of the frequency of weeping could be misleading when rating the intensity of depression in women.

2 Guilt (1960)
0. Not present.
1. Self-reproach.
2. Ideas of guilt.
3. Delusions of guilt.
4. Hallucinations of guilt.

2 Guilt (1967)
This is fairly easy to assess but judgement is needed, for the rating is concerned with pathological guilt. From the patient's point of view, some action of his which precipitated a crisis may appear as a 'rational' basis for self-blame, which persists even after recovery from his illness. For example, he may have accepted a promotion, but the increased responsibility precipitated his breakdown. When he 'blames' himself for this, he is ascribing a cause and not necessarily expressing pathological guilt. As a guide to rating, feelings of self-reproach count '1', ideas of guilt '2', belief that the illness might be a punishment '3', and delusions of guilt, with or without hallucinations, '4' points.

3 Suicide (1960)
0. Not present.
1. Feels life is not worth living.
2. Wishes he were dead.
3. Suicidal ideas.
4. Attempts at suicide. An attempt at suicide scores '4', but such an attempt may sometimes occur suddenly against a background of very little suicidal tendency; in such cases it should be scored as 3. There will be great difficulty sometimes in differentiating between a real attempt at suicide and a demonstrative attempt; the rater must use his judgement.

3 Suicide (1967)
The scoring ranges from feeling that life is not worth living '1', wishing he were dead '2', suicidal ideas and half-hearted attempts '3', serious attempts '4'. Judgement must be used when the patient is considered to be concealing this symptom, or conversely when he is using suicidal threats as a weapon, to intimidate others, obtain help and so on.

4 Initial Insomnia (1960)
0. Not present.
1. Mild difficulty in falling asleep.
2. Clear difficulty in falling asleep.

5 Middle Insomnia (1960)
0. Not present.
1. Patient restless and disturbed during the night.
2. Waking during the night.

6 Delayed Insomnia (1960)

0. Not present.
1. Mild waking in early hours of the morning and unable to fall asleep again.
2. Clear waking in early hours of the morning and unable to fall asleep again.

4–6 Initial, Middle, Delayed Insomnia (1967)

Mild, trivial and infrequent symptoms are given '1' obvious and severe symptoms are rated '2' both severity and frequency should be taken into account. Middle insomnia (disturbed sleep during the night) is the most difficult to assess, possibly because it is an artefact of the symptom of rating. When insomnia is severe, it generally affects all phases. Delayed insomnia (early morning wakening) tends not to be relieved by hypnotic drugs and is not often present without other forms of insomnia.

7 Work and Interests (1960)

Difficulties at work and loss of interest in hobbies and social activities are both included.

0. Not present.
1. Feeling of incapacity.
2. Listlessness, indecision and vacillation . Loss of interest in hobbies.
3. Decreased social activities, productivity decreased.
4. Unable to work. Stopped working because of present illness.

7 Work and Interests (1967)

It could be argued that the patient's loss of interest in his work and activities should be rated separately from his decreased performance, but it has been found too difficult to do so in practice. Care should be taken not to include fatiguability and lack of energy here; the rating is concerned with loss of efficiency and the extra effort required to do anything. When the patient has to be admitted to hospital because his symptoms render him unable to carry on, this should be rated 4 points, but not if he has been admitted for investigation or observation. When the patient improves he will eventually return to work, but when he does so may depend on the nature of his work; judgement must be used here.

Most women are housewives and therefore their work can be varied, both in quantity and intensity, to suit themselves. Women do not often complain of work being an effort, but they say they have to take things easy, or neglect some of their work. Other members of the family may have to increase the help they give. It is rare for a housewife to stop looking after her home completely. If she has an additional job outside the home, she may have to change it to parttime, or reduce her hours of work or even give it up completely. Women engage in hobbies less frequently than men. Loss of interest, therefore, may not be as obvious. Patients may complain of inability to feel affection for their families. This could be rated here, but it could also be rated under other symptoms, depending upon its meaning and setting. Care should be taken not to rate it in two places. It is a very valuable and important symptom if patients mention it spontaneously, but could be very misleading as a reply to a question.

8 Retardation (1960)
Slowness of thought, speech, and activity including apathy and stupor.
0. Not present.
1. Slight retardation at interview.
2. Obvious retardation at interview.
3. Interview difficult. Patient needs much care and patience to rate, but it can be done.
4. Complete stupor. Not suitable for rating.

8 Retardation (1967)
Severe forms of this symptom are rare, and the mild forms are difficult to perceive. A slight flattering of affect and fixity of expression rate as '1', a monotonous voice, a delay in answering questions, a tendency to sit motionless count as '2'. When retardation makes the interview extremely prolonged and almost impossible, it is rated '3', and '4' is given when an interview is impossible (and symptoms cannot be rated). Although some patients may say that their thinking is slowed or their emotional responsiveness has been diminished, questions about these manifestations usually produce misleading answers.

9 Agitation (1960)
This is defined as restlessness associated with anxiety. Unfortunately, a five-point scale was found impracticable, and therefore this variable is rated on a three-point scale. The mildest degrees of agitation cause considerable difficulty.
0. Not present.
1. Slight agitation.
2. Obvious agitation.

9 Agitation (1967)
Severe agitation is extremely rare.
0. Not present.
1. Fidgetiness at interview.
2. Obvious restlessness with picking at hands and clothes.
3. The patient has to get up during the interview.
4. The interview has to be conducted 'on the run', with the patient pacing up and down, picking at his face and hair and tearing at his clothes. Although agitation and retardation may appear to be opposed forms of behaviour, in mild form they can co-exist.

10 Anxiety: Psychic (1960)
0. Not present.
1. Slight tension and irritability.
2. Obvious tension, worrying about minor matters.

3. Apprehensive attitude.
4. Fears.

10 Anxiety: Psychic Symptoms (1967)
Many symptoms are included here, such as tension and difficulty in relaxing, irritability, worrying over trivial matters, apprehension and feelings of panic, fears, difficulty in concentration and forgetfulness, 'feeling jumpy'. The rating should be based on pathological changes that have occurred during the illness, and an effort should be made to discount the features of a previous anxiety disposition.

11 Anxiety: Somatic (1960)
Gastro-intestinal, wind, indigestion, cardiovascular, palpitations, headaches, respiratory, genito-urinary, etc.

11 Anxiety: Somatic Symptoms (1967)
These consists of the well-recognized effects of autonomic over-activity in the respiratory cardiovascular, gastro-intestinal and urinary systems. Patients may also complain of attacks of giddiness, blurring of vision and tinnitus.

12 Somatic Symptoms: Gastrointestinal (1960)
These occur in connection with both anxiety and depression. Considerable clinical experience is required to evaluate them satisfactorily. The definitions given have been found very useful in practice.
0. Not present.
1. Slight loss of appetite, heavy feelings in abdomen, constipation.
2. Obvious loss of appetite, heavy feelings in abdomen, constipation.

12 Gastro-intestinal Symptoms (1967)
The characteristic symptom in depression is loss of appetite and this occurs very frequently. Constipation also occurs but is relatively uncommon. On rare occasions patients will complain of 'heavy feelings' in the abdomen. Symptoms of indigestion, wind and pain, etc. are rated under 'anxiety'.

13 Somatic Symptoms: General (1960)
In depression these are characteristically vague and ill defined, and it is extremely difficult to get a satisfactory description of them from the patient.
0. Not present.
1. Slight heaviness in limbs, back or head. Diffuse backache. Loss of energy and fatiguability.
2. Obvious heaviness in limbs, back or head. Loss of energy and fatiguability.

13 General Somatic Symptoms (1967)
These fall into two groups: The first is fatiguability, which may reach the point where the patients feel tired all the time. In addition, patients complain of 'loss of energy' which appears to be related to difficulty in starting up an activity. The

other type of symptom consists of diffuse muscular achings, ill-defined and often difficult to locate, but frequently in the back and sometimes in the limbs; these may also feel 'heavy'. It is not uncommon for women to complain of backache and to ascribe it to a plevic disorder. This symptom requires careful questioning.

14 Genital Symptoms (1960)

0. Not present.
1. Slight loss of libido, menstrual disturbances.
2. Obvious loss of libido, menstrual disturbances.

14 Loss of Libido (1967)

This is a common and characteristic symptom of depression, but it is difficult to assess in older men and especially those, e.g. unmarried, whose sexual activity is usually at a low level. The assessment is based on a pathological change, i.e. a deterioration obviously related to the patient's illness. Inadequate or no information should be rated as zero. In women whose sexual experience is satisfactory, this symptom will appear as increasing frigidity, progressing to active dislike of sexual intercourse. Women who are partially or completely frigid find that their customary toleration of sex also changes to active dislike. It is difficult to rate this symptom in women who have no sexual experience or, indeed, in widows since loss of libido in women tends to appear not so much as a loss of drive but as a loss of responsiveness.

Disturbed menstruation and amenorrhoea have been described in women suffering from severe depression, but they are very rare. Dispite the difficulties in rating, it has been found that the mean score for women is negligibly less than men.

15 Hypochondriasis (1960)

This is easy to rate when it is obviously present, but difficulties arise with mild hypochondriacal preoccupation. Phobias of specific disease can cause difficulties. A phobia of veneral disease or of cancer will sometimes be rated under 'guilt' by the nature of doubt, and judgement requires care. Fortunately, phobias are not common, but the whole subject of hypochondriasis could well repay clinical investigation.

0. Not present.
1. Self-absorption.
2. Preoccupation with health.
3. Querulous attitude.
4. Hypochondriacal delusions.

15 Hypochondriasis (1967)

The severe states of this symptom, concerning delusions and hallucinations of rotting and blockages, etc., which are extremely uncommon in men, are rated as '4'. Strong convictions of the presence of some organic disease which accounts for the patient's condition are rated '3'. Much preoccupation with physical symptoms and with thoughts of organic disease are rated '2'. Excessive preoccupation with bodily functions is the essence of a hypochondriacal attitude, and trivial or doubtful symptoms count as '1' point.

16 Loss of Insight (1960)

This must always be considered in relation to the patient's thinking and background of knowledge. It is important to distinguish between a patient who has no insight and one who is reluctant to admit that he is 'mental'.
0. Not present.
1. Partial or doubtful loss.
2. Loss of insight.

16 Loss of Insight (1967)

This is not necessarily present when the patient denies that he is suffering from mental disorder. It may be that he is denying that he is insane and may willingly recognize that he has a 'nervous' illness. In case of doubt, enquiries should be directed to the patient's attitude to his symptoms of guilt and hypochondriasis.

17 Loss of Weight (1960)

Ideally this would be measured in pounds or kilogrammes, but few patients know their normal weight and keep a check on it. It was therefore necessary to use a three-point scale.

17 Loss of Weight (1967)

The simplest way to rate this would be to record the amount of loss, but many patients do not know their normal weight. For this reason, an obvious or severe loss is rated as '2', and a slight or doubtful loss as '1' point.

2.5.2 Brief Psychiatric Rating Scale

The original BPRS included 16 items, and the following 18-item version had Likert definitions of 0–6 without anchoring description ('not present', 'very mild', 'mild', 'moderate', 'moderately severe', 'severe', 'extremely severe'). For this reason the original BPRS is not included in the Mini-compendium. However, to illustrate the principle of the BPRS, the final version (Overall and Hollister 1986) is presented below.
1. Somatic Concern: preoccupation with physical health, fear of physical illness, hypochondriasis.
2. Anxiety: Worry, fear, overconcern for present or future.
3. Emotional Withdrawal: Lack of spontaneous interaction, isolation, deficiency in relating to others.
4. Conceptual Disorganization: Thought processes, confused, disconnected, disorganized, disrupted.

5. Guilt feelings: Self-blame, shame, remorse for past behaviour.
6. Tension: Physical and motor manifestations or nervousness, overactivation, tension.
7. Mannerisms and Posturing: Peculiar, bizarre, unnatural motor behaviour (not including tics).
8. Grandiosity: Exaggerated self-opinion, arrogance, conviction of unusual power or abilities.
9. Depressive Mood: Sorrow, sadness, despondency, pessimism.
10. Hostility: Animosity, contempt, belligerence, disdain for others.
11. Suspiciousness: Mistrust, belief others having malicious or discriminatory intent.
12. Hallucinatory Behaviour: Perceptions without normal external stimulus correspondence.
13. Motor Retardation: Slowed, weakened movements or speech, reduced body tone.
14. Uncooperativeness: Resistance, guardedness, rejection of authority.
15. Unusual Thought Content: Unusual, odd, strange, bizarre thought content.
16. Blunted Affect: Reduced emotional tone, reduction in normal intensity of feelings, flatness.
17. Excitement: Heightened emotional tone, agitation.
18. Disorientation: Confusion

2.5.3 Melancholia Scale for General Practice

Because most depressed patients now are treated by their family doctor the need for a modified version of the Melancholia Scale for General Practice has emerged (Bech et al. 1989). In the first draft version it was decided to use a check-list scale, i.e. each item was defined as 'present' versus 'not present'. Later, a self-rating version of the MES was developed because many doctors preferred to have the patient's own assessment. In a pilot study (Bent-Hansen et al. 1991) it was found that depressed patients prefer a 'global' rating of the individual items to an anchoring definition. It has hereafter been concluded that in general practice the MES version should be designed to be administered both by the treating doctors and by the patients themselves. Each item is, therefore, described by the questions relevant for the symptom being assessed. The severity from '0' (not present) and to '4' (present in marked to extreme degree) is defined 'globally'. When used in accordance with DSM-III-R the degrees of '0' and '1' means not clearly present (= 0) and degrees '2', '3', '4' means clearly present (= 1). Using this dichotomized translation a score of '5' equals a score of 10 on the original MES.

The items of the MES have the same content validity as the short 10-item Present State Examination (PSE-10) which has been shown to be a very efficient predictor of psychiatric morbidity, e.g. in liaison psychiatry or in general practice (Cooper & Mackenzie 1981). The cut-off score of MES for General Practice using "no" = 0 and "yes" = 1 is 4 analogue to the PSE-10. The scoring sheet for the MES for General Practice (MES-GP) is shown in Appendix 2.9, where the DSM-III-R is included as well.

2.5.4 Clinical Syndrome Circle: Self-Rating Scales

The Clinical Syndrome Circle (Fig. 2.1) includes anxiety (generalized and panic), depression or melancholia, mania, schizophrenia or psychotic disintegration, and borderline. Self-rating scales of these states have been developed because the patients' own assessment of their psychopathology often is important to take into account, especially in long-term trials.

2.5.4.1 The Panic Attack Scale (PAS)

This questionnaire has been designed to identify panic attacks. Have you during the past four weeks been suffering from panic attacks? Yes, no. If yes, please complete the following symptoms: Each symptom or item is scored in intensity: 0 = not at all; 1 = a little bit or doubtfully; 2 = mildly to moderately; 3 = moderately to markedly; 4 = markedly to extremely.
  1. Shortness of breath; trouble getting your breath.
  2. Dizziness or faintness.
  3. Palpitations; heart pounding or racing.
  4. Trembling or shaking.
  5. Sweating.
  6. Nausea or abdominal distress.
  7. Hot or cold spells.
  8. Numbness or tingling in parts of your body.
  9. Pains in heart or chest.
  10. Fear of dying.
  11. Fear of going crazy or of doing something uncontrolled.

Please indicate: During the last four weeks how many panic attacks have you experienced? How many have been mild to moderate? How many have been moderately to markedly? How many have been markedly to extremely?

2.5.4.2 Generalized Anxiety Scale (GEAS)

This questionnaire has been designed to identify how you have been feeling or behaving during the past three days including to-day.
  In total eleven symptoms have been found to cover relevant aspects of generalized anxiety. For each symptom please indicate the box which describes your state most appropriately taking the past three days into account.

Each symptom or item is scoreed in intensity: 0 = not present; 1 = doubtful or very mild depression; 2 = mild to moderate depression; 3 = moderate to marked depression; 4 = marked to extreme depression.

1 Performance and/or Interest in Your Daily Activities
This symptoms or problem covers such questions as: "Have you tended to lose interest in your ordinary day-to-day activities"? "Have you reduced or even stopped doing activities you used to do?"

2 Sleep Disturbances
This symptom or problem covers the three proceding nights, irrespective of administration of hypnotics or sedatives. It is your subjective experience of the duration and quality of sleep which you should try to indicate. "Have you been sleeping poorly?"

3 Restlessness
This symptom covers such questions as "Have you been more restless?" "Needed to be moving?" "Difficult to keep still?"

4 Inner Restlessness
This symptom covers such questions as "Have you had unpleasant feelings of inner unrest?" "Nervousness or shakiness inside?" "Inability to relax?" "Feeling tense in your muscles?"

5 Worrying or Preoccupations
This symptom is your preoccupations with painful thoughts and covers such questions as "Have you been worrying too much about things?" "Been worrying about your health, family, work or economical situation?"

6 Phobias
This symptom is situational anxiety and covers such questions as "Have you been feeling afraid in open spaces or on the streets?" "Feeling afraid to go out of your home alone?" "Feeling afraid to travel alone?" "Have to avoid certain things?" "Feeling uneasy in crowds?"

7 Palpitations
This symptom covers such questions as "Have you been bothered with heart pounding or racing?" "Have your pulse been beating faster than usual?"

8 Abdominal Discomfort
This complex of symptoms cover such questions as "Have you experienced sinking feeling in stomach?" "Sick in stomack?" "Nausea or upset stomach?" "Loose bowel movements?"

9 Other Symptoms from the Autonomic Nervous System

This symptom complex covers such questions as "Have you been sweating more than usual?" "Trouble getting your breath?" "Faintness or dizziness?" "Hot or cold spells?" "Frequent urination?" "Trembling?"

10 Irritability

This symptom complex covers such questions as "Have your feelings been easily hurt?" "Feeling easily annoyed or irritated?" "Feeling critical of others?" "Have severe temper outbursts?" "Feeling tense or keyed up?"

11 Anxious Mood

This symptom covers such questions as "Have you been feeling suddenly scared for no reason?" "Been feelng somewhat insecure and apprehensive?" "Fearful for no reason?"

2.5.4.3 Melancholia Scale (MES)

This questionnaire has been designed to identify how you have been feeling or behaving during the past three days including today.

In total eleven symptoms have been described which have been found to cover relevant aspects of melancholia or depression. For each symptom please indicate which describes your state most appropriately taking the past three days into account.

Each symptom or item is scored in intensity: 0 = not present; 1 = doubtful or very mild degree; 2 = mild to moderate degree; 3 = moderate to marked degree; 4 = marked to extreme degree.

1 Performance and/or Interest in Your Daily Work

This symptom or problem covers such questions "Have you tended to lose interest in your ordinary day-to-day activities?" "Have you reduced or even stopped doing activities you used to do?"

2 Lowered Mood

This symptom covers such questions as "Have you been feeling down or depressed?" "Lowering of spirits?" "Crying?" "Have you been feeling hopeless about the future?"

3 Sleep Disturbances

This symptom and problem covers the three preceding nights, irrespective of administration of hypnotics or sedatives. It is your own subjecyive experience of the duration and quality of sleep which you should try to indicate. "Have you been sleeping poorly?"

4 Anxiety or Inner Unrest

This symptom covers such questions as "Do you feel more nervous or anxious than usual?" "Have you had unpleasant feelings of inner unrest?" "Have you been worrying too much about things?" "Suddenly scared for no reason?" "Can you put your worries out of your mind when you want to get on with something?"

5 Emotional Indifference (Introversion)

This symptom covers such questions as "Have you been feeling lonely?" "Have you reduced or stopped contacts with your surroundings (friends, family)?"

6 Concentration Disturbances

This symptom or problem covers such questions as "Have you had difficulty in concentration?" "Do you find it difficult to make dicisions?" "Trouble remembering things?" "Have you been able to think clearly?"

7 Tiredness and/or Pains

This symptom covers such questions as "Do you feel pain (e.g. headaches, neck or back pains)?" "Do you have a heavy feeling in arms or legs?" "Do you feel easily tired?" "Get tired for no reason?"

8 Low Self-Esteem or Guilt Feelings

This symptom or problem covers such questions as "Have you been critical of yourself for weakness or mistakes?" "Have you been very concerned of previous events in a self-critical way?" "Been feeling inferior to others?" "Blaming yourself for things?" "Have you been been very self-conscious?"

9 Reduced Verbal Activity

This symptom covers such questions as "Have you been more quiet in conversations?" "Don't want to use telephone?" "Have you experienced inner resistance to speak?" "Have others told you that you are very quiet?"

10 Suicidal Thoughts or Impulses

This problem concerns thoughts saying that what you want from life has been fulfilled. It covers such questions as "Have you felt that life for you has become pointless?" "Do you want to get away from it all?" "Thoughts of ending your life?"

11 Reduced Motor Activity

This symptom covers such questions as "Have your body been more slow?" "Have you felt that your appearance has been older?" "Do you have to stop doing things because your movements are too slow?" "Do you experience an inner resistance when moving?"

2.5.4.4 The Mania Scale (MAS)

This questionnaire has been designed to identify how you have been feeling or behaving during the past three days including today.

In total eleven symptoms have been described which have been found to capture relevant aspects of mania. For each symptom please indicate which describes your state most appropriately taking the past three days into account.

Each symptom or item is scored in intensity: 0 = not present; 1 = doubtful or very mild degree; 2 = mild to moderate degree; 3 = moderate to marked degree; 4 = marked to extreme degree.

1 Performance and/or Interest in Your Daily Work
This symptom or problem covers such questions as "Have you had quarrels at work because you have too many activities going at the same time?" Have you been spending too much money?" "Have your housing been insufficient?" "Have you stopped working?"

2 Talkativeness
This symptom covers such questions as "Have you been more active in conversations?" "Have you used the telephone more than usual?" "Have you had difficulties in stopping to speak?" "Have others told you that you have been more lively in conversations?"

3 Mood (Well-Being)
This problem covers such questions as "Have you been feeling more cheerful than usual?" "High spirits?" "On the top of the world?" "That things are working out very well?"

4 Social Contact
This problem covers such questions as "Have you been more outgoing than usual?" "Been putting your oar in?" "Been dominating or arranging in groups (in the family, in leisure activities)?" "Invited friends to dinner etc.?"

5 Restlessness
This symptom covers such questions as "Have you difficulties sitting down?" "Like to be in move?" "Have you more than average energy?" "Bursting with energy, have to walk a lot?"

6 Plans and Perspectives
This symptom or problem covers such questions as "Have you many plans for the future?" "Many ideas about your professional activities (e.g. work, studies)?" "Have you started new activities (sport, music or other artistic or cultural activities)?" "Have others told you that you jump too quickly from one subject to another?"

7 Sleep

This symptom or problem covers the three preceding nights, irrespective of administration of hypnotics or sedatives. It is your subjective experience of the duration and quality of sleep which you should try to indicate.

8 Self-Esteem

This symptom covers such questions as "Do you feel you are a person with special talents or abilities?" "That life for you has unique points?" "That you are selected to perform special acts?" "That you have extraordinary abilities, powers or knowledge (political, scientific, religious)?"

9 Irritability and Aggression

This problem covers such questions as "Do you easily lose your temper?" "Do you have difficulties in controlling your urge to harm others?" "Do you often find yourself disagreeing with people?" "Have you been physically violent to other persons?"

10 Sexual Interest

This problem concerns such questions as "Have you been more interested in sex than usual?" "Easily falling in love?" "Been more flirtatious?" "Do you have difficulties in controlling your urge to dress in a provocative way?"

11 Noise Level

This problem covers such questions as "Have your been speaking or behaving more loudly that usual?" "Been playing radio or television in a much higher volume that usual?" "Been shouting or singing in a manner that is quite apart from your habitual level?"

2.5.4.5 The Psychotic Disintegration Scale (PDS)

This questionnaire has been designed to identify how you have been feeling or behaving during the past three days including today.

In total ten problems or symptoms have been described. For each symptom please indicate which describes your state most appropriately taking the past three days into account. Each symptom or item is scored in intensity: 0 = not present; 1 = doubtful or very mild degree; 2 = mild to moderate degree; 3 = moderate to marked degree; 4 = marked to extreme degree.

1 Emotional Withdrawal with Therapist

This problem covers such questions as "Do you feel to have problems in emotional contact with your therapist?"

2 Disruption in Your Thinking
This symptom covers such questions as "Do you have difficulties to explain things to others?" "Do you feel that your trains of thought suddenly can stop, as when a telephone is cut off?" "Do you feel that 'alien' thoughts are intrusing your mind?"

3 Specific Movement Disturbances
This problem covers such questions as "Do you feel that your motor behaviour is bizarre?" "That you can sleep in bed without touching the pull with your head?" "That you for quite a long time can stay in the same position?"

4 Expansiveness
This problem covers such questions as "Have you the feeling that you have extraordinary talents or abilities?" "In religious matters?" "In science?" "In art or music?" "In other fields?"

5 Hostility
This problem covers such questions as "Are you more easily hostile or provoked by other people?" "Have you been threatening others?" "Have you been physically hostile?"

6 Suspiciousness
This problem covers such questions as "Have you had reason to suspect any hostility from other people?" "Has other people been threatening you?" "Have you sometimes felt that others wished to harm you?" "Been feeling that people talked about you in television?"

7 Hallucinations
This problem covers such questions as "Have you sometimes heard voices that others do not seem to hear?" Or seen things others do not seem to see?

8 Unusual Thought Content
This problem covers such questions as "Have you sometimes felt that other people influenced or controlled you in an odd way?" "As if you were hypnotised?" "Have you felt that your feelings were changed so that you yourself had been changed in some peculiar way?"

9 Blunted or Inappropriate Affect
This problem covers such questions as "Have you noticed that your feelings were inappropriate to the occasion?" "That you had laughed, although you actually inside was frightening?" "That you in contact with others felt so frightening that you did not show your emotions?"

10 Cooperativeness with Your Therapist
This problem concerns such questions as "Have you been feeling that your therapist has provoked you?" "That you feel uneasy when he or she ask you ques-

tions?" "Have you been uncomfortable with this questionnaire?" "Have you felt that it provoked you, because at time furious when completing it?"

2.5.4.6 The Borderline Anhedonia Scale (BAS)

This questionnaire has been designed to identify how you have been feeling or behaving during the past three days including today.

In total seven problems or symptoms have been described. For each symptom please indicate which describes your state most appropriately taking the past three days into account. Each item is defined in intensity: 0 = not present; 1 = doubtful or very mild degree; 2 = mild to moderate degree; 3 = moderate to marked degree; 4 = marked to extreme degree.

1 Excessive Social Anxiety
This problem covers such questions as "In social situations, e.g. at school, at work, by public transportation (bus, train, etc.), do you experience anxiety or insecurity?"

2 Affective Instability Thinking
This problem covers such questions as "Are you very ' moody'?" "Can you within minutes or hours change from baseline to dysphoria?" "From baseline to euphoria?" "From dysphoria to euphoria or vice versA?"

3 Inappropriate Anger or Lack of Control of Anger
This problem covers such questions as "Have you experienced inappropriate anger?" "Have you had difficulties to control your temper?" "Have you experienced 'temper outbursts'?"

4 Self-Mutilating Behaviour
This problem covers such questions as "Have you had tendencies to hurt yourself?" "By banging the head against the wall?" "Scrating your skin?" "Plucking out your hair?" "Burning yourself with a cigarette?"

5 Feelings of Emptiness or Boredom
This problem covers such questions as "Have you felt that life was empty?" "Have had the feeling that you in a way do not exist?" "Found life without meaning?"

6 Lack of Empathy
This problem covers such questions as "Have you had difficulties to understand other people's feelings?" "Have you had difficulties to understand your friends or family when they have problems?"

7 Expansiveness

This problem covers such questions as "Have you the feeling that you have special talents or abilities?" "Within art or music?" "In religious matters?" "In other fields?"

2.5.5 Structured Interview of the Hamilton/Melancholia Scale (HDS/MES)

The version included in this compendium is based on a draft version designed by Williams analoque to her HDS version (Williams 1990).

Although the order of items suggested in the following is not mandatory it has been suggested because experience has shown that the items follow each other in a logical way. However, the questions and the rank order depend of course on the condition of the patient. In brackets is shown the items number in accordance with the HDS/MES version.

The initial contact with the patient when starting the interview should be the following: "I would like to ask you some questions about the past three days including today."

Lowered Mood (item 1)

"What's your mood been like the past three days?" "Have you been feeling down or depressed?" "Lowering spirits?" "Crying?"

0. Absent.
1. Very mildly.
2. Clearly concerned with unpleasant things but without hopelessness.
3. Moderately to markedly depressed. Some hopelessness.
4. Severe degree of lowered mood. Pronounced hopelessness.

Activities and Interests (item 7)

"How have you been spending your time?" "Have you felt interested in doing things or do you feel you have to push yourself to do them?" "Have you been less interested in your ordinary day-to-day activities?" "Have you reduced or even stopped doing activities you used to do?" At weekly ratings the work activities should be assessed as at the first rating, howeever, for inpatients the status should be examined, so at a score of 2 is possible.

0. No difficulty.
1. Mild insufficiencies in the day-to-day activities.
2. Clear but still moderate insufficiencies. Reduced work activity.
3. Moderate to marked insufficiencies. Decrease in actual time spent in activities if hospitalized but is still able to participate for some hours in ward activities.
4. Stopped working because of present illness. In hospital no activities except ward chores.

Sleep Disturbances
This symptom is scored irrespective of hypnotics or sedatives. "How have you been sleeping over the past three nights?" "have you had trouble falling asleep at the beginning of the night. (Right after you go to bed, how long has it taking you to fall asleep)?" "How many nights have you had trouble falling asleep?"

Insomnia Initial (item 4)
0. No difficulty falling asleep.
1. One or two of the last three nights difficulty falling asleep.
2. Constantly difficulties.

"During the past three nights, have you been waking up in the middle of the night? If yes: Do you get out of bed? What do you do? When you get back in bed, are you able to fall right back asleep?"

Insomnia Middle (item 5)
0. No difficulty.
1. Once or twice during the past three days have complaints of disturbed sleep.
2. Constantly disturbed sleep during the night.

"What time have you been waking up in the morning for the past three nights? If early: Is that with an alarm clock, or do you just wake up spontaneously?"

Insomnia Delayed (item 6)
0. No difficulty.
1. Less than one hour (and may fall asleep again).
2. Constantly - or more than one hour too early.

Insomnia General (item 18)
"During the past three days how many hours have you been sleeping during night?" "How has the quality of your sleep been?" Indicate the mean duration of sleep over the past three days.
0. Usual sleep duration.
1. Duration of sleep slightly reduced.
2. Duration of sleep been moderately reduced and/or quality of sleep disturbed.
3. Duration of sleep less than 50% of the usual sleep.
4. Duration of sleep extremely reduced, e.g. as if not been sleeping at all.

Somatic Symptoms General
"How has your energy been during the past three days?" "Have you been tired all the time?" "Have you had any backaches, headaches, or muscleaches?" "Have you felt any heaviness in your limbs, back or head?"

A (item 13)
0. Absent.
1. Very slight feelings of tiredness and/or pains.
2. Clearly present.

B (item 23)
0. Absent.
1. Very slight feelings of tiredness or pains.
2. Mild to moderate feelings of tiredness or pains.
3. Moderate to marked feelings of tiredness or pains.
4. Extreme feelings of tiredness or pains.

Anxiety, Psychic (item 10)
"Have you been feeling especially nervous or anxious?" "Have you had unpleasant feelings of inner unrest?" "Have you been worrying too much about things?" "Suddenly scared for no reason?" "Panic?"
0. Absent.
1. Very slight.
2. Mild to moderate anxiety, but still without influence on the patient's daily life.
3. Moderate to marked insecurity influencing daily life. At the edge of panic.
4. Extreme, had within the past three days experienced panic anxiety.

Anxiety, Somatic (item 11)
"In the past three days, have you had any physical symptoms of anxiety? Palpitations, heart beating, abdominal discomfort, sick in stomach, upset stomach, loose bowel movement, trouble getting your breath, faintness or dizziness, hot or cold spells, frequent urination, trembling?" "How much have these things been bothering you?" "How bad have they gotten?" "How much of the time, or how often, have you had them?"
0. Absent.
1. Very mild, only occasionally.
2. Moderate degree but still without influencing the patient's daily life.
3. Marked degree, interfering occasionally with patient's daily life.
4. Extreme degree, interfering greatly with patient's daily life.

Gastro-Intestinal Symptoms (item 12)
"How has your appetite been the past three days (What about compared to your usual appetite)?" "Have you had to force yourself to eat?" "Have other people had to urge you to eat?"
0. None.
1. Mild reduction in appetite.
2. Clear loss of appetite.

Loss of Weight (item 17)
"Have you lost any weight since this (depression) began?" If yes: "How much?" If not sure: "Do you think your clothes are any looser on you?" At follow up: "Have you gained any of the weight back? Or are you still reducing your weight?"

A When rating by history
0. No weight loss.

1. 1 to 2.5 kg weight loss.
2. Weight loss of 3 kg or more.

B On follow-up
0. No weight loss.
2. 0.5 kg per week.
2. 1 kg or more per week.

Sexual Interest (item 14)
"How has your interest in sex been the past three days?" (I am not asking about performance, but about your interest in sex -how much do you think about it). "Has there been any change in your interest in sex (from when you were not depressed)?" "Is it something you have thought much about?" If so: "Is that usual for you?"
0. Absent.
1. Mild reduction in sexual interest.
2. Clear loss of sexual interest:

Hypochondriasis (item 15)
"During the past three days, how much have your thoughts been focussed on your physical health or how your body is working (compared to your normal thinking)?" "Do you complain much about how you feel physically?" "Have you found yourself asking for help by doctors?" If yes: "Like what, for example?" "How often has that happened?"
0. Absent.
1. Slightly occupied with bodily symptoms and functions.
2. Mild to moderate tendency to 'somatize' but still at the 'neurotic' level.
3. The patient is clearly convinced to be physically ill, but can for a brief while be reassured that this is not the case.
4. The preoccupation with bodily dysfunction is within the paranoid dimension.

Feelings of Guilt (item 2)
"Have you been especially critical of yourself the past three days, feeling you have done things wrong, or let others down?" If yes: "What have your thoughts been?" "Have you been feeling guilty about anything that you have done or not done in the past?" "Have you thought that you have brought (this depression) on yourself in some way?" "Do you feel you are being punished by being sick?"
0. Absent.
1. Concerned with the fact of being a burden to the family or colleagues due to reduced interest or capacity.
2. Concerned with incidents in the past prior to the current depression.
3. Feels that present depression is a punishment, but can still intellectually see that this view is unfounded.
4. Guilt feelings have become paranoid ideas.

Insight (item 16)
Rating is based on observation during interview. The objective is to find out whether the patient (if in the depressive state) acknowledge to being depressed, or (if in the neutral phase) acknowledge to not being currently depressed.
0. Accept to be in the current state as rated by the interviewer.
1. Acknowledges illness but attributes cause to bad food, climate, overwork, etc.
2. Denies being ill at all or to have recovered, respectively.

Emotional Indifferences (item 22)
"Have you during the past three days reduced or even stopped emotional contacts with your surroundings (friends, family)?" "Have you been feeling lonely?" "More introverted?" "Have you been feeling indifferent even to those closest to you?"
0. Absent.
1. Slight.
2. Mild to moderate in relation to colleagues or other people but still glad to be with friends, or family.
3. Moderate to marked, i.e. less need or ability to feel warmth to friends, or family.
4. The patient feels isolated or emotionally indifferent even to near friends or family.

Concentration Disturbances (item 21)
"Have you during the past three days had difficulty in concentration?" "Have you had difficulty in making decisions?" "Trouble remembering things?"
0. Absent.
1. Slight difficulties.
2. Even with a major effort difficult to concentrate occasionally.
3. Difficulties in concentration even in things that usually need no effort (reading a newspaper, watching television program).
4. When it is clear that patient also during interview is showing difficulties in concentration.

Suicide (item 3)
"Have you during the past three days had any thoughts that life is not worth living, or that you had been better off dead?" "Have you felt that it would be best if you did not wake up next morning?" "Have you had any plans actively to hurt yourself?"
0. Absent.
1. Feels that life is not worth while, but has no wish to die.
2. Wish to die, but has no plans of taking own life.
3. Has probably plans actively to hurt himself.
4. Has definitely plans to kill himself.

Agitation (item 9)

Rating is based on observation during interview. The objective is to observe motoric manifestations of anxiety.
0. Absent.
1. Slight agitation, e.g. tendency to playing with hands, hair, etc.
2. Mild to moderate fridgetiness, changing position in chair again and again.
3. Patient cannot stay in chair throughout interview.
4. Part of interview has to be conducted "as on the run".

Reduced Verbal Formulation Activity (item 20)

Rating is based on observations during interview. The objective is to observe reduction in flow of speech and capacity to verbalize or formulate thoughts or feelings.
0. Absent.
1. Slight.
2. Mild to moderate inertia in conversation.
3. Moderate to marked.
4. When interview is difficult to maintain or conduct.

Reduced Motor Activity (item 19)

Rating is based on observations during interview. The objective is to observe decreased motor activity of the body, in movements, etc.
0. Absent.
1. Slight.
2. Mild to moderate, e.g. reduced gestures.
3. Moderate to marked, all movements slow.
4. Severe, approaching stupor.

Retardation General (item 8)

Rating is based on observations during interview. The objective of this item is to integrate total behaviour at interview (including slowness of thoughts and speech).
0. Absent.
1. Slight.
2. Obvious retardation at interview, but interview can be obtained without difficulty.
3. Interview occasionally difficult.
4. Interview extremely difficult.

References

American Psychiatric Association. Diagnostic and Statistical Manual of Mental Disorders. 3rd ed. Washington DC, Am Psychiat Ass, 1980.
American Psychiatric Association. Diagnostic and Statistical Manual of Mental Disorders. Third Revised Version (DSM-III-R. Washington DC, Am Psychiat Ass, 1987.

Andersen J, Larsen JK, Schultz V, Nielsen BM, K.rner A, Behnke K, Munk-Andersen E, Butler B, Allerup P, Bech P. The brief psychiatric rating scale. Dimension of schizophrenia, reliability and construct validity. Psychopathol 1989; 22: 168–176.

Bech P. Rating scales for affective disorders. Their validity and consistency. Acta Psychiat Scand 1981: Suppl 295; 64: 1–101.

Bech P. Clinical effects of selective serotonin reuptake inhibitors. In: Dahl SG, Gram LF. (eds). Clinical Pharmacology in Psychiatry. Berlin, Springer, 1989 pp. 83–93.

Bech P. The Cronholm-Ottosson Depression Scale. The first depression scale designed to changes during treatment. Acta Psychiat Scand 1991; 84: 439–445.

Bech P, Gram LF, Dein E, Jacobsen O, Vitger J, Bolwig TG. Quantitative rating of depressive states. Acta Psychiat Scand 1975; 51: 161–170.

Bech P, Rafaelsen OJ, Kramp P, Bolwig TG. The mania rating scale: scale construction and inter-observer agreement. Neuropharm 1978; 17: 430–431.

Bech P, Bolwig TG, Kramp P, Rafaelsen OJ. The Bech-Rafaelsen Mania Scale and the Hamilton Depression Scale. Acta Psychiat Scand 1979; 59: 420–430.

Bech P, Rafaelsen OJ. The use of rating scales exemplified by a comparison of the Hamilton and the Bech-Rafaelsen melancholia scale. Acta Psychiat Scand 1980; 62 (suppl 285): 128–131

Bech P, Allerup P, Gram LF et al. The Hamilton Depression Scale. Evaluation of objectivity using logistic models. Acta Psychiat Scand 1981; 63: 290–299.

Bech P, Gjerris A, Andersen J et al. The Melancholia scale and the Newcastle scales. Item-combinations and inter-observer reliability. Br J Psychiat 1983; 143: 48–63.

Bech P, Grosby H, Husum B, Rafaelsen L. Generalized anxiety or depression measured by the Hamilton Anxiety Scale and the Melancholia Scale in patients before and after cardiac surgery. Psychopathol 1984a; 17: 253–263.

Bech P, Allerup P, Reisby N, Gram LF. Assessment of symptom change from improvement curves on the Hamilton Depression Scale in trials with antidepressants. Psychopharm 1984b: 84: 276–281.

Bech P, Gastpar M, Morozov PV. Clinical assessment scales for biological psychiatry to be used in WHO studies. Progr Neuro-Psychopharmacol & Biol Psychiat 1984c; 8: 190–196.

Bech P, Haaber A, Joyce CRB. DUAG: Observation and judgment in psychiatry: profiled videotapes and judgment analysis in the assessment of depression. Psychol Med 1986; 16: 873–883.

Bech P, Kastrup M, Rafaelsen OJ. Mini-compendium. Acta Psychiat Scand 1986; 73 (suppl 326): 1–37.

Bech P, Larsen JK, Andersen J. The BPRS: psychometric developments. Psychopharm Bull 1988; 24: 118–121.

Bech P, Jørgensen B, Nørrelund N, Loldrup D, Langemark M, Hansen HJ, Olesen J. Pains as presentation symptoms of depression in liaison psychiatry as evidenced by outcome of clomipramine treatment. Nord Psychiat Tidsskr 1989; 43 (suppl. 20): 89–94.

Bech P, Allerup P, Maier W, Albus M, Lavori P, Ayuso JL. The Hamilton scales and the Hopkins symptom checklist (SCL-90): a cross-national validity study in patients with panic disorders. Br J Psychiat 1992; 160:206–211.

Bent-Hansen J, Lauritzen L, Kørner A. A self-rating version of the Hamilton/Melancholia (HDS/MES) scale. 1991 (in preparation).

Bischoff R, Bobon D, Görtelmeyer R, Horn R, Müller AA, Stoll KD, Woggon B. Rating Scales for Psychiatry: European Edition. Weinheim, Beltz Test, 1990.

Collegium Internationale Psychiatriae Scalarum (CIPS): Internationale Skalen für Psychiatrie. Weinheim: Beltz Test, 1981.

Cooper JE, Mackenzie S. The rapid prediction of low scores on a standardized psychiatric interview (Present State Examination) In: Wing JK, Bebbington P, Robins LN (eds.). What is a case? London: Grant McIntyre, 1981, pp. 143–151.

Feinstein AR. Clinimetrics. New Haven, Yale Univ Press, 1987.

Ghiselli EE, Campbell JP, Zedeck S. Measurement Theory for the Behavioural Sciences. San Francisco, W.H. Freeman and Comp, 1981 pp. 413.

Gjerris A, Bech P, Bøjholm S et al. The Hamilton Anxiety Scale. J Aff Dis 1983; 5: 163–170.

Guilford JP. Psychometric methods. New York, Mc Graw Hill, 1954.

Guy W, Bonato RR. Manual for ECDEU Assessment Battery. Maryland, Nat Inst Ment Health, 1970.

Guy W. Early Clinical Drug Evaluation (ECDEU) Assessment Manual for Psychopharmacology. Publication No 76–338. Rockville, Nat Inst Ment Health, 1976.

Hamilton M. The assessment of anxiety states by rating. Br J Med Psychol 1959; 32: 50–55.

Hamilton M. A rating scale for depression. J Neurol Neurosurg Psychiat 1960; 23: 56–62.

Hamilton M. Development of a rating scale for primary depressive illness. Br J Soc Clin Psychol 1967; 6: 278–296.

Hamilton M. Diagnosis and rating of anxiety. Br J Psychiat 1969 (special publ): 76–79.

Hamilton, M. Die Beurteilung einer Behandlungsart und die Messung von Symptomen: In: Hippius H (ed). Symposium über Ergebnisse der experimentellen und klinische Prüfung der Nomifensin. Stuttgart, F.K. Schattauer Verlag 1977, pp. 11–17.

Hamilton M. The effect of treatment of the melancholias (depressions). Br J Psychiat 1982; 140: 223–230.

Hardy MC, Lecrubier Y, Widlöcher D. Efficacy of clonidine in 24 patients with acute mania. Am J Psychiat 1986; 143: 1450–1453.

Huskisson E C. Measurement of pain. Lancet 1974; 11: 1127–1131.

Israël L, Kozarevic D, Sartorius N. Source Book of Geriatric Assessment. Basel, Karger, 1984.

Likert R. A technique for the measurement of attitudes. Arch Psychol 1932; 140: 1–55.

Luborsky L. Clinicians' judgments of mental health. Arch Gen Psychiat 1962; 7: 407–417.

Maier W, Philipp M. Comparative analysis of observer depression scales. Acta Psychiat Scand 1985: 72: 239–245.

Maier W, Buller R, Philipp M, Heuser I. The Hamilton Anxiety Scale: Reliability, validity and sensitivity to change in anxiety and depression disorders. J Aff Dis 1988a; 14: 61–68.

Maier W, Philipp M, Heuser I, Schlegel S, Buller R, Wentzel H. Improving depression severity assessment. Reliability, internal validity and sensitivity to change of three observer depression scales. J Psychiatr Res 1988b; 22: 3–12.

Marcos T, Salamero M. Factor study of the Hamilton Rating Scale for Depression and the Bech Melancholia Scale. Acta Psychiat Scand 1990; 82: 178–181.

Overall JE, Gorham DR. The Brief Psychiatric Rating Scale. Psychol Rep 1962; 10: 799–812.

Overall JE, Hollister LE. Assessment of depression using the Brief Psychiatric Rating Scale. In: Sartorius N, Ban TA (eds). Assessment of Depression. Berlin, Springer, 1986, pp. 159–178.

Paykel ES. Use of the Hamilton Depression Scale in general practice. In: Bech P, Coppen A. (eds). The Hamilton Scales. Berlin, Springer, 1990 pp. 40–47.

Rasch G. Probabilistic Models for Some Intelligence and Attainment Tests. Copenhagen: Danish Inst Educ Res, 1960. (Reprinted: Chicago, Univ Chicago Press, 1980).

Singh AC, Bilsbury CD. Measurement of subjective variables: the Discan method. Acta Psychiat Scand 1989; 79 (suppl 347): 1–38.

Wiliams JBW. Structured interview guides for the Hamilton Rating Scales. In: Bech P, Coppen A (eds). The Hamilton Scales. Berlin: Springer 1990, pp. 48–63.

World Health Organization. Mental Disorders: Glossary and Guide to their Classification in Accordance with the Ninth Revision of the International Classification of Diseases. Geneva, World Health Organization, 1978.

Zeally AK, Aitken RCB. Measurement of mood. Proc Roy Soc Med 1969; 62: 993–996.

Zitman FG, Mennew MFG, Griez E, Hooijer C. The different versions of the Hamilton Depression Rating Scale. In: Bech P, Coppen A (eds). The Hamilton Scales. Berlin, Springer, 1990, pp. 28–34.

Appendix 2.1   *General Case Information*

Code no.
□□□□

Patient
□□□□□□□□□□□□□□□□□□□□□□□

Date of birth   Identity no.
□□□□□□   □□□□

Surname: ————————————————————————————

First name:————————————————————————————

Rater:————————————————————

Date of rating   Rater no.
□□□□□□   □□

Research no.
□□□□

Rater's final assessment of the validity of the interview:

Compared to other subjects how well did this subject cooperate during the interview? (Use A or B - select the one which best characterizes the patient.)

A   0:   Did not appear to be attention demanding.

    1:   Slight tendency to enjoy being observed, slight stimulation of symptoms.

    2:   Obviously stimulating, engaged insistently in description of symptoms, 'yes'-sayer.

B   0:   Did not appear to be attention demanding

    1:   Slight tendency to dissimulate, to 'leave the judgement to the doctor'.

    2:   Obviously dissimulating, neglecting symptoms, 'no'-sayer.

Validity of interview: A   □   (0-2)

                                       B   □   (0-2)

Appendix 2.2   *Scoring Sheet for Anxiety Attacks (DSM-III: Panic Attacks) Defined by the Hamilton Anxiety Scale*

A DSM-III panic attack is defined by a discrete period of apprehension or fear and at least four of the 12 symptoms (A to L):

(1)	A	Dyspnoea	(9)	G	Paraesthesias
(3)	B	Palpitations	(10)	H	Hot and cold flushes
(11)	C	Chest pain or discomfort	(5)	I	Sweating
(6)	D	Choking or smothering sensations	(2)	J	Faintness
(2)	E	Dizziness, vertigo or unsteady feelings	(4)	K	Trembling and shaking
(8)	F	Feelings of unreality	(12)	L	Fear of dying
		(depersonalization/derealization)	(13)		Going crazy or doing
(7)		Nausea or abdominal discomfort			something uncontrolled

The Hamilton Anxiety Scale (HAS-P) can be used to assess the severity of the 'average' attack, i.e. the typical attack for the period tested (3 weeks at first rating, and the last week at weekly ratings). The HAS-P major anxiety attack is defined by a score of 2 or more on item 1, and a score of 2 or more on three of the items 2, 8, 9, 10 and 13 (DSM-III) or of the items 2, 8, 9, 10, 11 and 13

DSM-III	No.	Item	Score	DSM-III-R
	1	Anxious mood		
K	2	Tension		(4)
	3	*Fear		
	4	Insomnia		
	5	Difficulties in concentration and memory		
	6	Depressed mood		
	7	General somatic symptoms: muscular		
G, H	8	General somatic symptoms: sensory		(9)(10)
B, J	9	Cardiovascular symptoms		(3)(2)
A, C, D	10	Respiratory symptoms		(1)(11)(6)
	11	Gastro-intestinal symptoms		(7)
	12	Genito-urinary symptoms		
E, I	13	Other automatic symptoms		(2)(5)
	14	Bevaiour during interview		
		Total score		

Number of anxiety attacks   ☐☐
Are DSM-III criteria fulfilled?   ☐   (Yes = 1, No = 0)
Are DSM-III-R criteria fulfilled?   ☐   (Yes = 1, No = 0)

Visual Analogue Scale (panic attacks)

No   Extreme

A DSM-III-R panic attack is defined by a discrete period of apprehension of fear and at least four of the 13 symptoms (1-13).

*Specify if agoraphobic situations have occurred: alone (at home) ☐
                                                     outside home   ☐

Appendix 2.3   *Scoring Sheet for Generalized Anxiety (DSM-III)*
Defined by the Hamilton Anxiety Scale

Generalized anxiety consists of four categories (A to D) of which three should be present for fulfilling DSM-III. The four categories are:

A   Motor tension   C   Apprehensiveness
B   Autonomic hyperactivity   D   Vigilance

The HAS can be used for assessing the four categories. As indicated, category A includes items 2, 7 and 14. Category B includes items 8, 9, 10, 11, 12 and 13. Category C includes items 1 and 3. Category D includes items 4 and 5.

When using HAS-G for assessing DSM-III generalized anxiety the following should be considered. Category A, C and D are fulfilled when one of the corresponding items is present of which one must have a score of 2 or more..

DSM-III	No.	Item	Score	DSM-III-R
C	1	Anxious mood		(14)(15)(18)
A	2	Tension		(1)(2)
C	3	*Fear		
D	4	Insomnia		(17)
D	5	Difficulties in concentration and memory		(16)
	6	Depressed mood		
A	7	General somatic symptoms: muscular		(4)
B	8	General somatic symptoms: sensory		(11)
B	9	Cardiovascular symptoms		(6)
B	10	Respiratory symptoms		(5)
B	11	Gastro-intestinal symptoms		(10)(13)
B	12	Genito-urinary symptoms		(12)
B	13	Other automatic symptoms		(7)(8)(9)
A	14	Bevaiour during interview		(3)
		Total score		

Are DSM-III criteria fulfilled?   ☐   (Yes = 1, No = 0)
Are DSM-III-R criteria fulfilled?   ☐   (Yes = 1, No = 0)

Visual Analogue Scale (generalized anxiety)

No   Extreme

Generalized anxiety after DSM-III-R is defined by a discrete period of apprehension at least six of the following symptoms (1-18):

A   Motor tension: (1) trembling, (2) muscle tension, (3) restlessness, (4) fatigability.

B   Autonomic hyperactivity: (5) dyspnoea, (6) palpitations, (7) sweating, (8) dry mouth, (9) dizziness, (10) nausea, abdominal discomfort, (11) flushes or chills, (12) frequent urination, (13) trouble swallowing.

C   Vigilance: (14) feeling keyed up or on edge, (15) exaggereated startle response, (16) difficulty in concentration, (17) trouble falling or staying asleep, (18) irritability.

Appendix 2.4 *Scoring Sheet for Major Depression (DSM-III) Defined by the Hamilton Depression Scale and the Melancholia Scale*

The DSM-III criteria for major depression are:

(1) A Dysphoric mood
(3) B(1) Poor appetite or significant weight loss
(4) B(2) Insomnia
(5) B(3) Psychomotor agitation or retardation
(2) B(4) Loss of interest or pleasure

(6) B(5) Loss of energy; fatigue
(7) B(6) Self-reproach or guilt
(8) B(7) Diminished ability to think or concentrate
(9) B(8) Suicidal impulses

Major depression (DSM-III) assessed by HDS/MES is defined by a score of 1 or more on A and on at least four B items.
Major depression (DSM-III-R) assessed by HDS/MES is defined by a score of 1 or more on at least five (1) to (9) items.

DSM-III	No.	Item		HDS	MES	DSM-III-R
A	1	Depressed mood	(0-4)	a ☐	☐	(1)
B(6)	2	Self-depreciation, guilt feelings	(0-4)	b ☐	☐	(7)
B(8)	3	Suicidal impulses	(0-4)	☐	☐	(9)
B(2)	4	Insomnia: initial	(0-2)	☐		(4)
B(2)	5	Insomnia: middle	(0-2)	☐		(4)
B(2)	6	Insomnia: late	(0-2)	☐		(4)
B(4)	7	Work and interest	(0-4)	c ☐	☐	(2)
B(3)	8	Retardation: general	(0-4)	d ☐		(5)
B(3)	9	Agitation	(0-4)	☐		(5)
	10	Anxiety: psychic	(0-4)	e ☐	☐	
	11	Anxiety: somatic	(0-4)	☐		
B(1)	12	Somatic symptoms: gastro-intestinal	(0-2)	☐		(1)
B(5)	13	Somatic symptoms: general	(0-2)	f ☐		(6)
	14	Sexual interest	(0-2)	☐		
	15	Hypochondriasis	(0-4)	☐		
	16	Loss of insight	(0-2)	☐		
B(1)	17	Weight loss	(0-2)	☐		(3)
B(2)	18	Insomnia: general	(0-4)		☐	(4)
	19	Retardation: motor	(0-4)		☐	
	20	Retardation: verbal	(0-4)		☐	
	21	Retardation: intellectual	(0-4)		☐	(8)
	22	Retardation: emotional	(0-4)		☐	
B(5)	23	Tiredness and pains	(0-4)			(6)

Are DSM-III criteria fulfilled? ☐ (Yes = 1, No = 0) HDS(a-f) MES HDS(1-17)
Are DSM-III-R criteria fulfilled? ☐ (Yes = 1, No = 0) ☐☐ ☐☐ ☐☐

Visual Analogue Scale (depression)

No   Extreme

Appendix 2.5   *Scoring Sheet for Mania (DSM-III) Defined by the Mania Scale*

The DSM-III criteria for mania involve the sympoms A + B:

A1	A(1)	Elevated mood
A2	A(2)	Irritability
(6)	B(1)	Increased motor activity
(3)	B(2)	Increased verbal activity
(4)	B(3)	Flight of ideas
(1)	B(4)	Exaggerated self-esteem
(2)	B(5)	Decreased need for sleep
(5)	B(6)	Distractability
(7)	B(7)	Excessive involvement in social activities

If A(1) is scored higher than A(2) three B items are needed for fulfilling the DSM-III criteria for mania.
If A(2) is scored higher than A(1) four B items are needed.

DSM-III	No.	Item		Score	DSM-III-R
B(1)	1	Activity: motor	(0-4)		(6)
B(2)	2	Activity: verbal	(0-4)		(3)
B(3, 6)	3	Flight of thoughts	(0-4)		(4)
	4	Voice/noise level	(0-4)		
A(2)	5	Hostility/destructiveness	(0-4)		A2
A(1)	6	Mood level	(0-4)		A1
B(4)	7	Self-esteem	(0-4)		(1)
B(1)	8	Contact	(0-4)		(6)
B(5)	9	Sleep	(0-4)		(2)
B(7)	10	Sexual interest	(0-4)		(7)
	11	Decreased work ability	(0-4)		(7)
		Total score			

Are DSM-III criteria fulfilled?   ☐   (Yes = 1, No = 0)
Are DSM-III-R criteria fulfilled?   ☐   (Yes = 1, No = 0)

Visual Analogue Scale (mania)

No   Extreme

The DSM-III-R criteria for mania involve A1 and A2 as well as symptoms (1) to (7). If A2 is higher than A1 a manic episode needs at least four items from (1) to (7). If A1 is higher than A2 only three (1) to (7) items are needed.

Appendix 2.6   *Scoring Sheet for Schizophrenia (DSM-III) Defined by the Brief Psychiatric Rating Scale*

S = Schizophrenic symptoms (psychotic disintegration).
The DSM-III criteria for schizophrenia involve the following symptoms:

(2)	I	Bizarre delusions (item 15)	
(1a) (1a)	II	Somatic (item 1) or grandiose (item 8) delusions	
(1a) (1a)	III	Delusions with persecutory ideas (item 11)	
(2)	IV	Auditory hallucinations (item 12)	
(1c)	V	Incoherence (item 4) associated with at least one of the following	
(1e)		(a)	Flat affect (item 3)
(1b)		(b)	Delusions (items 1, 8, 11, 15) or hallucinations (item 12)
(1d)		(c)	Catatonic behaviour (item 7)

When using BPRS for DSM-III schizophrenia a score of 3 or more on one of the five DSM-III symptoms is needed.

DSM-III	No.	Item			Score	DSM-III-R
II/V (b)	1	Somatic concern	(0-4)			(1a)
	2	Anxiety: psychic	(0-4)			
V (a)	3	Emotional withdrawal	(0-4)	S		(1e)
V	4	Conceptual disorganization	(0-4)	S		(1c)
	5	Self-depreciation, guilt feelings	(0-4)			
	6	Anxiety: somatic	(0-4)			
V (c)	7	Specific movement disturbances	(0-4)	S		(1d)
II/V (b)	8	Exaggerated self-esteem	(0-4)	S		(1a)
	9	Depressed mood	(0-4)			
	10	Hostility	(0-4)	S		
III/V (b)	11	Suspiciousness	(0-4)	S		(1a)
IV/V (b)	12	Hallucinations	(0-4)	S		(3)(1b)
	13	Motor retardation	(0-4)			
	14	Uncooperativeness	(0-4)	S		
I/V (b)	15	Unusual thought content	(0-4)	S		(2)
	16	Blunted or inappropriate affect	(0-4)	S		
	17	Psychomotor agitation	(0-4)			
	18	Disorientation and confusion	(0-4)			
		Total score				

Are DSM-III criteria fulfilled?   ☐   (Yes = 1, No = 0)
Are DSM-III-R criteria fulfilled?   ☐   (Yes = 1, No = 0)

Visual Analogue Scale (schizophrenia)

No   Extreme

The DSM-III-R criteria for schizophrenia involve at least one of the (1) to (3) symptoms. When using BPRS for DSM-III-R schizophrenia a score of 3 or more on one of the following items: 3 or 4, 2 and 12.

Appendix 2.7   *Scoring Sheet for the Brief Psychiatric Rating Scale: Psychotic Disintegration Scale*

No.	Item	Score
1	Emotional withdrawal	
2	Conceptual disorganization	
3	Specific movement disturbances	
4	Exaggerated self-esteem	
5	Hostility	
6	Suspiciousness	
7	Hallucinations	
8	Uncooperativeness	
9	Unusual thought content	
10	Blunted or inappropriate affect	
	Total score	

Visual Analogue Scale (psychotic disintegration)

No   Extreme

Appendix 2.8 *Clinical Syndrome Circle*

Scales	Total score	Scale criteria (0 = no 1 = minor 2 = major)	VAS (0-100)	DSM-III-R (0 = not fulfilled 1 = fulfilled)	
HAS-P	☐☐	☐	☐☐☐	☐	Panic anxiety
HAS-G	☐☐	☐	☐☐☐	☐	Generalized anxiety
HDS	☐☐	☐	☐☐☐	☐	Depression (broad)
HDS (a-f)	☐☐	☐	☐☐☐	☐	Depression (core)
MES	☐☐	☐	☐☐☐	☐	Depression (melancholia)
MAS	☐☐	☐	☐☐☐	☐	Mania
BPRS	☐☐	☐	☐☐☐	☐	Schizo-affective
BPRS-S	☐☐	☐	☐☐☐	☐	Schizophrenia

Appendix 2.9 *Scoring Sheet for the MES for General Practice*

No.	Item	MES	DSM-III-R
1	Work and interests	☐	☐
2	Lowered mood	☐	☐
3	Sleep disturbances	☐	☐
4	Anxiety: psychic	☐	
5	Emotional retardation (introversion)	☐	
6	Intellectual retardation	☐	☐
7	Tiredness and pains	☐	☐
8	Self-depreciation and guilt feelings	☐	☐
9	Decreased verbal activity	☐	☐
10	Suicidal thoughts	☐	☐
11	Decreased motor activity	☐	☐
	Total score	☐☐	☐☐

Appendix 2.10   *Scoring Sheet for the GEAS*

No.	Item	GEAS	DSM-III-R
1	Performance	☐	☐ D
2	Sleep	☐	☐ D
3	Restlessness (outer)	☐	☐ A
4	Restlessness (inner)	☐	☐ A
5	Worrying	☐	☐ C
6	Phobias	☐	
7	Palpitations	☐	☐ B
8	Abdominal discomfort	☐	☐ B
9	Other autonomic discomfort	☐	☐ B
10	Irritability	☐	☐ D
11	Anxious mood	☐	☐ C
	Total score	☐☐	☐☐

0, not present; 1, present

A, motor tension

B, autonomic hyperactivity

C, apprehensiveness

D, vigilance

DSM-III-R criteria: at least six in total score

GEAS criteria: at least five in total score

3 Rating Scales for Mental Disorders

This chapter deals with the scales and syndromes of axis 1 disabilities. As conceptualized in DSM-III-R, a mental disorder is a clinically significant behavioural or psychological syndrome or pattern that is associated with current distress (a painful symptom) or disability (disturbance in one or more important areas of functioning) or with a significantly increased risk of suffering death, pain, disability or an important loss of freedom. In addition, this syndrome or pattern must not be merely an expectable response to a particular event. Whatever its original cause, it must currently be considered a manifestation of a behavioural, psychological or biological dysfunction in the patient. As discussed by Spitzer and Williams (1988), clinically significant means some pathological disturbance and behavioural or psychological syndrome or pattern that refers to the core symptoms. These symptoms are associated with either distress or disability.

Symptoms of psychiatric syndromes may therefore refer, on the one hand, to organic (disease specific) impairments, and, on the other hand, to social functioning (performance) or subjective handicaps or discomforts (the essential quality-of-life elements). Figure 3.1 depicts the relationship of the clinical syndromes of dementia, schizophrenia, depression and anxiety with axis 0 (the organic impairment), axis 1 (behavioural or psychological disability), axis 5 (social functioning), and axis 6 (quality of life). In principle, only dementia can be considered as an organic disorder, while schizophrenia, depression and anxiety are seen as such only if these states are considered as primary disorders (i.e. not merely an expectable response to a particular event – axis 4 in DSM-III-R). The severity syndromes thus refer not only to behavioural and psychological symptoms but also in varying degrees to social functioning and general well-being.

The classificatory principle adopted in Chap. 2 was the bottom-up approach, whereby the four syndromes of anxiety, depression, mania and schizophrenia are symptomatically scored without reference to aetiology. Chapter 3 follows the DSM-III-R approach because all psychiatric disease entities have been included; this is the top-down approach which uses the disease specificity order shown in Fig. 3.1. In other words, the first syndrome to be considered is dementia, followed by withdrawal syndrome, etc. Each syndrome is considered with references to DSM-III-R and ICD-10 and to the various rating scales for measuring the syndrome. A summary of the psychometric properties of the selected scale is presented, using the format shown in Table 3.1.

Table 3.1. Psychometric description format

Type	The purpose of the scale
Content validity	Specification of the clinical components into which the items can be grouped
Administration	Observer (interviewer) scale or self-rating scale
Time frame	Period of retrospection
Item selection	First- or second-generation scale
Item calibration	Likert or checklist items
Number of items	Total scale and possibly subscales
Construct validity	The statistical model used to evaluate the item structure in regard to total score
Sensitivity to change/diagnostic validity	Whether the scale is a severity scale or a diagnostic test
Inter-observer reliability	References to most relevant studies

Disease specificity

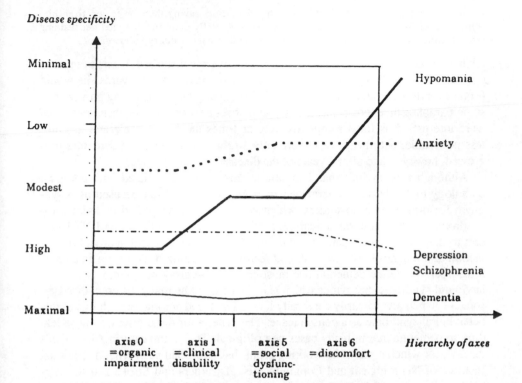

Fig. 3.1. The correlation between axes and disease specificity

Reference

Spitzer RL, Williams JBW. Basic principles in the development of DSM-III. In: Mezzich JE, von Cranach M (eds). International Classification in Psychiatry. Cambridge, Cambridge Univ Press, 1988, pp. 81–86.

3.1 Dementia (Chronic Organic Mental Syndrome)

Alzheimer's original paper (1907) described one patient's illness and the pathology of her brain. The description was as follows:

A woman, 51 years old, showed jealousy toward her husband as the first noticeable sign of the disease. Soon a rapidly increasing loss of memory could be noticed. She could not find her way around in her own apartment. She carried objects back and forth and hid them. At times she would think that someone wanted to kill her and she would begin screaming loudly. In the institution her entire behaviour bore the stamp of utter perplexity. She was totally disorientated to time and place. Occasionally she stated that she could not understand and did not know her way around. At times she greeted the doctor like a visitor and excused herself for not having finished her work, at times she screamed loudly that he wanted to cut her, or she repulsed him with indignation, saying that she feared from him something against her chastity. Periodically she was totally delirious, dragged her bedding around, called her husband and daughter and seemed to have auditory hallucinations.

Alzheimer also reported that her memory was severely disturbed. If one pointed to objects, she named most of them correctly, but immediately afterwards she would forget everything again. When talking, she frequently used perplexing phrases and some paraphrastic expressions. During her subsequent course the phenomena that were interpreted as focal symptoms were at times more noticeable and at times less noticeable, but always they were only slight. The generalized dementia progressed, however, and after 4 years of the disease, the patient died.

Although it is obvious that dementia in this case is associated with a known pathology of the brain, the term dementia as such should not be used as a synonym for organic brain disorders, which is a broader concept and includes focal syndromes such as aphasia and amnesia. It should be emphasized that ICD-10 refers to dementia as an organic mental disorder. This aetiological approach to dementia as a diagnosis, however, should result in the listing of dementia as an axis 3 disorder. To define dementia one must consider an array of symptoms in a behavioural syndrome, behaviour which is in fact caused by many different diseases, some of which are primarily cerebrally located and lead among other things to this behavioural syndrome as a consequence. The criteria for these diseases, those leading to dementia, are in many cases neurological. This is the case in Alzheimer's disease, for which a scientific working group has published such criteria (National Institute of Neurological and Communicative Disorders and Stroke and the Alzheimer's Disease and Related Disorders Association; McKhann et al. 1984). These criteria include dementia, defined by cognitive deficits but no disorientation: "A diagnosis of dementia cannot be made when consciousness is impaired by delirium, drowsiness, stupor or coma." This, however, poses some problems for dementia as a concept, since disorientation is an important symptom in the assessment of severity of dementia states. In fact, Alzheimer (1907, 1911), stated that the demented patient periodically was totally delirious, which would lead to the conclusion that she could periodically be diagnosed as suffering from dementia, while at other times the diagnosis could not be made. Dementia is a behavioural syndrome and as such an axis 1 syndrome.

DSM-III-R distinquishes between organic mental syndromes and organic mental disorders. Organic mental syndrome refers to a pattern of behavioural and psychological signs or symptoms, without reference specifically to aetiology. Organic mental disorder designates a particular organic mental syndrome in which the aetiology is known or presumed (e.g. multi-infarct dementia). The rating scale approach covers the organic mental syndrome, i.e. dementia. The scales reviewed are therefore dementia scales measuring severity of signs and symptoms without reference to aetiology. The same approach is used by the Diagnostic Interview Schedule (DIS), which simply includes the Mini-Mental State Examination to detect dementia, thereby reducing 44 DSM-III categories to one, the spectrum of dementia (Robbins 1988).

The dementia scales bear witness to the fact that the concept of dementia is viewed differently, and that so far there has been no efficacious psychopharmacological treatment of dementia which has made it possible to test the scales as outcome measures. One of the first dementia scales developed along the lines of the Hamilton scales to make it simple to administer was the Mental Status Checklist (MSCL; Lifshitz 1960). This scale included components of cognitive functions such as orientation, calculation, abstraction, writing performance, registration, and general information level. The scale correlated significantly (0.82) with the Wechsler Adult Intelligence Subtest Scale (WAIS), including components of arithmetric, digit span, picture completion, block design and information. The use of more comprehensive tests in this group of elderly patients (55–75 years of age) with a variety of dementia symptoms led to such symptoms as irritability, inattentiveness and frequently manifest hostility.

The MSCL should still be considered as a rating scale for measuring the severity of cognitive dysfunction (Hollingsworth 1980; Petrie 1983). However, another scale – the Mini Mental State (MMSE) – has since been developed (Folstein et al. 1975) which includes components of orientation, calculation, registration, memory and praxis. This scale has been considered acceptable for screening procedures; it is easy to administer, takes a short time to complete and meets criteria for inter-rater reliability, but focuses exclusively on the cognitive components of dementia. The MMSE is used more frequently than the MSCL, but its focus is even more exclusively on the cognitive components of dementia than the MSCL.

This is understandable as the core symptoms of dementia must be considered those of cognitive decline, however, it is an established fact that psychotic behaviour and depressive symptoms play an important part in patients suffering from dementia (Reifler et al. 1982, 1986; Reisberg 1983; Reisberg et al. 1987). In his original description, discussed above, Alzheimer lists several of the signs and symptoms which are present in patients suffering from dementia: cognitive decline, delusions, hallucinations, disorientation, arousal, perplexity, and loss of ability to manage alone. In modern rating scales these items constitute the set to be considered for content validity. The Brief Cognitive Rating Scale (BCRS) includes orientation, calculation, memory (recent and past) and general functioning (Reisberg 1983); hence the aspect of self-care has been added in this scale to the basic cognitive items. The Sandoz Clinical Assessment – Geriatric (SCAG; Shader et al. 1974) for assessing the efficacy of psychopharmacological treatment and the Gottfries-Bråne-Steen scale (GBS; Gottfries et al. 1982) add components of motor functioning, arousal, and affective symptoms. However, neither the MSCL, MMSE, nor the SCAG have shown sufficient content and construct validity. The Alzheimer's Disease Assessment Scale (ADAS) is not a diagnostic scale but a severity scale (Rosen et al. 1984; Mohs and Cohen 1988). In other words, the ADAS is only applicable to patients already diagnosed as suffering from Alzheimer's disease.

At present there is no established scale for dementia. On the basis of content validity (Table 3.2) and the criteria of item definition for observer scales, Lauritzen and Bech (1990) have developed the Brief Dementia Scale (BDS; Appendix

3.1a; Table 3.2) which is a compromise between the BCRS (lacking many non-cognitive dementia items) and more comprehensive scales (such as the GBS lacking psychotic behaviour and strict, i.e. 0–4, item definitions). Table 3.3a compares ICD-10, DSM-III-R and BDS.

The impact of DSM-III-R on the development of dementia rating scales has been increasing. Among the new scales is the CAMDEX (The Cambridge Dementia Scale, Roth et al. 1986) which is a very comprehensive scale and therefore not to be included in this compendium in its full range. In Appendix 3.1b the items of the CAMDEX corresponding to the DSM-III-R criteria for dementia is shown. In Sect. 3.8 the Gottfries-Bråne-Steen Scale (GBS), the Cognitive Subscale of the ADAS, and the MMSE have been included. In Table 3.3b the items of ADAS, MMSE, BDS and CAMDEX have been shown grouped in accordance with DSM-III-R.

Table 3.4 shows the components of dementia scales (content validity) and the relative emphasis in terms of item distribution of the different scales. The item contribution of both ICD-10 and DSM-III-R is weighted on the cognitive components of dementia. DSM-III-R furthermore includes a list of items concerned with organic brain disorders (e.g. apraxia and agnosia). Finally, it should be emphasized that comprehensive rating scales like the AMDP (Association for Methodology and Documentation in Psychiatry) includes items of psychopathology bearing on the components of dementia (e.g. Pietzcker et al. 1983).

The BDS defines dementia as a clinical syndrome without reference to aetiology. The scale is not a diagnostic scale but one for measuring the severity of dementia, as was the first scale in this field, the MSCL. The BDS has sufficient content validity (Table 3.3). Its construct validity has not yet been evaluated by latent structure analysis, but neither has that of any other dementia scale in this respect, and studies with the BDS are in progress.

The scoring sheet for the BDS is illustrated in "Appendix 3.1a". Instructions for scoring its 21 items are presented below.

1 Registration
Ask the patient to repeat the following three words: Apple, Table, Penny. Take one second to say each word, then ask the patient to repeat them. If the patient does not remember all three words after trying once, you repeat all the words. Two trials allowed.
0. No error.
1. Doubtful or very slight subjective trouble repeating the words.
2. Minor objective signs of difficulty or hesitation or confuses succession of words.
3. Clear deficit, misses one or even two words or has to have words repeated to be able to repeat them.
4. Cannot tell words even after going through the procedure twice.

Table 3.2. Psychometric description: BDS

Type	Symptom scale
Content validity	The measurement of severity of dementia syndromes including the following components:
	- cognitive symptoms (registration, concentration, memory, attention, conceptual disorganisation, language)
	- orientation
	- arousal (perplexity, hostility)
	- social (self-care, introversion)
	- motor (agitation)
	- mood (depression, anxiety, emotional incontinence)
	- psychotic symptoms (suspiciousness, hallucinations, unusual thought content)
	- vegetative symptoms
	- judgement
	- other specific symptoms (e.g. aphasia)
Administration	Interviewer scale to be used by skilled observers (goal-directed interview)
Time frame	Previous 3 days
Item selection	Items have been selected mainly from the BCRS, BPRS and MES
Item calibration	Likert scale definition, 0-4
Number of items	The full scale consists of 21 items which cover the components as shown in Table 3.3a. However, a subscale covering the essential components of dementia is recommended. This dementia index contains items 1-13
Construct validity	The BDS consists of a general dimension (items 1-16) and a second-order dimensions (psychotic, items 17-21). Preliminary results have shown (Lauritzen and Bech 1990) that the affective dimension is relevant in mild degrees of dementia while the psychotic items are most relevant in moderate to marked degrees of dementia. So far Rasch models for analysing the construct validity of the BDS in terms of sufficiency of total scores of the full scale or subscales have not been investigated

Table 3.3a. Dementia items in ICD-10, DSM-III-R and BDS

ICD-10	DSM-III-R	BDS
Orientation	A (1) Short-term memory	1 Registration
Calculation	(2) Long-term memory	2 Calculation
Memory		3 Recall of words
Thinking	B (1) Impairment in abstract thinking	4 Recent memory
Comprehension	(2) Impaired judgement	5 Past memory
Language	(3) - Aphasia	6 Orientation
Learning capacity	- Apraxia	7 Self-care
Judgement	- Agnosia	8 Speech
	- Constructional difficulty	9 Depressed mood
		10 Emotional retardation
	(4) Personality change	11 Anxiety
		12 Motor agitation
		13 Hostility
		14 Perplexity
		15 Distractability
		16 Affective incontinence
		17 Conceptual disorganisation
		18 Suspiciousness
		19 Hallucination
		20 Unusual thought content
		21 Judgement

Table 3.3b. Dementia scales with their items corresponding to DSM-III-R components of dementia

	ADAS (cognitive)	BDS	CAMDEX	MMSE
A (1) Impairment in short term memory	1, 7, 11	1, 2, 3, 4	156, 157, 158, 161, 178	3, 5
(2) Long-term memory impairments	-	5	148, 149	-
B (at least one of the following)				
(1) Impairment in abstract thinking	5, 9	17	142-143, 179-182	-
(2) Impaired judgement		21	211	-
(3) Other disturbances of higher cortical function	2, 3, 4, 8, 10	8	130, 134, 137, 176	4, 6, 7, 8, 9, 10, 11
(4) Personality change		13	238, 244	-
C The disturbances in A and B significantly interfere with work or usual social activities	-	7	251, 258, 262, 263, 264	-

Table 3.4. Item distributions of rating scales: components of dementia

Components	MMS	SCAG	BDS	BCRS	GBS	ADAS
Cognitive symptoms	82%	22%	24%	60%	31%	47%
Orientation	18%	5%	5%	20%	12%	5%
Arousal	0%	11%	19%	0%	4%	10%
Social	0%	27%	10%	20%	30%	0%
Motor	0%	0%	5%	0%	4%	5%
Mood	0%	17%	18%	0%	12%	10%
Psychotic symptoms	0%	0%	19%	0%	0%	10%
Vegetative symptoms	0%	17%	0%	0%	4%	5%
Other specific symptoms	0%	0%	10%	0%	4%	10%

2 Concentration

Ask the patient to begin with 100 and count backwards by 7. Stop after five substractions.

0. No problems doing substractions.
1. Doubtful or very slight decrement in subjective concentration ability.
2. Mild to moderate concentration deficit taking the patient's social background into account.
3. Marked concentration deficit for a person of that background. Gets one or two answers correct.
4. Very severe concentration deficits. Must give up without even giving one answer correctly or forgets the task.

   If the patient cannot or will not perform this task or says that he has always been totally incapable of doing substractions, then ask the patient to spell the word 'world' backwards. The score is the number of letters in correct order.

3 Recall of Words

Ask the patient if he can recall the three words you previously asked for in item 1.

0. No error.
1. Doubtful or very slight subjective trouble repeating the words.
2. Minor objective signs of difficulty hesitates for a while or confuses succession of words.
3. Clear deficit, misses one or even two words.
4. Does not remember words.

4 Recent Memory

0. Not unusual.
1. Doubtful or very slight subjective impairment. E.g. forgetting names more than formerly.
2. Minor objective signs of poor memory for recent events, i.e. deficit in recall of specific events evident upon detailed questionning.
3. Cannot recall major events of previous weekend or week; scanty knowledge (not detailed) of current events, for TV-shows etc.
4. Severe memory deficit of recent events, e.g. unaware of weather, may not know current national head of government or head of state.

5 Past Memory

0. Not unusual.
1. Doubtful or very slight subjective impairment, e.g. can recall two or more primary school teachers.
2. Minor gaps in past memory upon detailed questioning, e.g. able to recall at least one childhood teacher and/or one childhood friend.
3. Clear deficit, confuses chronology in reciting personal history.
4. Severe deficit, major past events not recalled, e.g. former occupation.

6 Orientation

0. The patient is completely orientated in time, place and personal data.
1. The patient occasionally has some slight difficulty but can spontaneously give correct statement about time, place and personal data.
2. The patient has impairments such that he does not spontaneously give correct statement, e.g. he does not know the day or the date although he still knows the month and year, or has spatial difficulties although he is still orientated in the ward (or own home), or has difficulty remembering names although he still knows his own name.
3. The patient is markedly disorientated, e.g. does not know the month or year although he still knows the season, or has difficulty finding his way to the toilet and bed without help, or remembers his name only with some help.
4. The patient is completely disorientated in time and place or the identity of self or others.

7 Functioning and Self-care

0. Not unusual.
1. Doubtful or very slight subjective difficulty.
2. Minor difficulty in job functioning whether it is in job functioning or functioning at home.
3. The patient is unable to undertake normal work or functioning normally in activities of daily living if hospitalized, he can still participate to some extent in ward activities.
4. The patient requires assistance in self-care, hospitalization, or other constant assistance is needed. If hospitalized, he is unable to participate in ward activities.

8 Speech

Show a pencil and a watch and ask the patient: what are these called? Use the whole interview as well to assess this item.

0. Normal capacity.
1. Doubtful or very slight subjective deficits in recalling names of persons and objects.
2. Minor overt word finding difficulties which may result in intermittant interruptions of speech or mild stuttery.
3. Overt paucity of spontaneous speech or obvious word finding difficulties. However, sentence production abilities remain intact.
4. Inability to speak in sentences.

9 Depressed Mood

0. Not unusual.
1. It is doubtful whether the patient is more despondent or sad than usual, e.g. the patient appears vaguely more depressed than usual.

2. The patient is more clearly concerned with unpleasant experiences, although he still lacks helplessness or hopelessness and/or looks sad to a mild/moderate degree.
3. The patient looks clearly depressed to a moderate/marked degree and/or communicate hopelessness.
4. The patient's remarks of despondency and helplessness or non-verbal signs dominate the interview in which the patient cannot be distracted.

10 Emotional Retardation

0. Not present.
1. It is doubtful whether the patient is more emotionally introverted and without interest than usual.
2. The patient clearly has less wish and interest than usual to be together with new or distant acquaintances.
3. The patient isolates himself to a certain degree from other persons. He meets away from home (work mates, fellow patients, ward personnel).
4. The patient isolates himself also in relation to family members. He feels emotionally indifferent and uninterested even in near friends or family.

11 Anxiety: Psychic

0. The patient is or looks neither more nor less insecure or irritable than usual.
1. It is doubtful whether the patient is or looks more insecure or irritable than usual.
2. The patient looks more clearly to be in a state of anxiety, apprehension or irritability, which he may find difficult to control. It is thus without influence on his daily life because the worrying still is about minor matters.
3. The anxiety or insecurity is at times more difficult to control because the worrying is about major injuries or harms which might occure in the future; the anxiety may be experienced as panic, i.e. overpowering dread. It occasionally interferes with his daily life. Non-verbal signs of moderate to marked anxiety should be looked for in the verbally incompetent patient.
4. The feeling of dread is present so often that it markedly interferes with the patient's daily life and/or severe non-verbal signs of anxiety.

12 Motor Agitation

0. Not present.
1. Slightly or doubtfully increased motor activity, e.g. tendency to changing position in chair.
2. Restless in ward with some pacing. During the interview the patient can still maintain a position, although changing repeatedly.
3. Patient cannot stay in chair during interview.
4. Interview must be conducted on the run.

13 Hostility/Destructiveness
0. Not present.
1. Somewhat impatient but control is maintained.
2. Provocation badly tolerated.
3. Provocative, threatening, but can be calmed down.
4. Overt physical violence. Physically destructive.

14 Perplexity
0. Not present.
1. Doubtful or very mild degree of perplexity. Occasional difficulty in under-standing what should be simple questions.
2. Mild to moderate degree of perplexity. Simple questions must be repeated to be understood. Answers occasionally unrelated to the question.
3. Moderate to marked degree of perplexity. Answers more frequently unrelated to the question.
4. Extreme degree of perplexity. Speech and behaviour clearly inappropriate, as if in a dream.

15 Distractability
0. Not present.
1. Doubtful or very mild degree of distractability.
2. Mild to moderate degree of distractability. Attention occasionally distracted by irrelevant stimuli (such as background noises).
3. Easily distracted.
4. Continually distracted by incidental events and objects which makes inter-viewing difficult or impossible.

16 Affective Incontinence
0. Not present.
1. Doubtful or very mild degree of affective incontinence. Tendency to rapid mood changes.
2. Weeps or laughs in an uninhibited manner on moderate emotional stimula-tions.
3. Markedly uncontrolled affect on mild emotional stimulations.
4. Severely uncontrolled affect without context to the setting.

17 Conceptual Disorganization
0. Not present.
1. Doubtful or very mild degree of conceptual disorganization. Pedantic and slightly circumlocutory speech.
2. Some idiosyncratic but comprehensible use of words or phrases, especially under stress.
3. Illogical associations between words and phrases even when not under stress.
4. Obviously disjointed and illogical speech. Fragmentation of phrases or words which seriously interferes with communication.

18 Suspiciousness
Representing suspiciousness, distrustfulness or misinterpretations ranging from a remarkable lack of confidence in others to florid delusions of persecution.
0. Not present.
1. Vague ideas of reference. Tends to suspect other people of talking about him or laughing at him or steeling from him. Feels that 'something is going on'. Responds to reassurance, but it is doubtful whether there are ideas of reference or related delusions.
2. Ideas of reference with vague, unsystematized delusions of persecution. Someone might have intentions! It is intimated in TV and newspapers. Still an 'as-if' experience.
3. Delusions with some systematization. Reassurance difficult.
4. Florid systematized paranoid delusions of persecution. Correction impossible.

19 Hallucinations
This represents sensory perceptions without external stimulus correspondence. The hallucinatory experiences must have occurred within the past 3 days and, with the exception of hypnagogic hallucinations, not during states of clouding of consciousness (delirium).
0. Not present.
1. Mild or doubtful degree. Hypnagogic hallucinatory experiences or isolated elementary hallucinatory experiences (hearing sounds, seeing lights).
2. Occasional but fully developed hallucinations (hearing voices, seeing shapes), not affecting behaviour.
3. Occasional hallucinations that influence behaviour.
4. More or less constantly absorbed in hallucinatory experiences.

20 Unusual Thought Content
This item is concerned with the content of the patient's verbalization and not with the organization of his language, which is rated in item 17 (conceptual disorganization). The item refers to the qualities of unusual thought content ranging from overvalued ideas to various levels of delusional ideas. The delusions of particular interest here are those of control, influence or depersonalization, morbid jealousy, sexual delusions, expansive or religious delusions. Rate only degree of unusualness in thought content expressed, its significance in the patient's mind or its influence on his behaviour.
0. Not present.
1. Mild or doubtful degree (e.g. overvalued ideas).
2. Moderate degree (e.g. some delusional quality but still an "as if" experience).
3. Delusions determine most of thought content and occasionally influence behaviour.
4. Overwhelming delusions determine thought content and behaviour.

21 Judgement

0. No impairment of judgement.
1. The patient realizes that for some time (months) he has suffered from an intellectual impairment. He experiences problems with his normal activities because of this intellectual decline.
2. The patient may occasionally realize that for some time (months) he has been suffering from an intellectual impairment. His planning and broad view of things are affected by this impairment. His intellectual level allows him to manage on his own.
3. The patient has only little knowledge or seldom notices his own intellectual reduction. Planning and broad view bear witness to this lack of realization. The patient needs help managing on his own.
4. The patient has no knowledge of his intellectual impairment. His attitude to his own abilities is totally unrealistic, and he does not acknowledge any need for help but is in need of constant surveillance.

References

Alzheimer A. Über eine eigenartige Erkrankung der Hirnrinde. Allgemeine Zeitschrift für Psychiatrie und psychisch gerichtlich Medizin 1907; 64: 146–148.

Alzheimer A. On Certain Peculiar Diseases of Old Age (Über eigenartige Krankheitsfälle des späteren Alters, original 1911). English version 1991. History of Psychiatry 1991; 2: 74–98.

Folstein MF, Folstein SE, McHugh PR. Mini-Mental State. A practical method for grading the cognitive state of patients for the clinician. J Psychiat Res 1975; 12: 189–198.

Gottfries CG, Bråne G, Gullberg B, Steen G. A new rating scale for dementia syndromes. Arch Gerontol Geriat 1982; 1: 331–330.

Hollingsworth SW. Response of geriatric patients from the satellite nursing homes of Maricopa County to Hydergine therapy. A double blind study. Cur Ther Res 1980; 27: 401–410.

Lauritzen L, Bech P. Paper presented at WPA regional symposium, Oslo, August 1990.

Lifshitz K. Problems in the quantitative evaluation of patients with psychoses of the senium. J Psychol 1960; 49: 295–303.

McKhann G, Drachman D, Folstein M, Katzman R, Price D, Stadlan EM. Clinical diagnosis of Alzheimer's disease. Neurol 1984; 34: 939–944.

Mohs RC, Cohen L. Alzheimer's Disease Assessment Scale (ADAS). Psychopharmacol Bull 1988; 24: 627–628.

Petrie WM. Psychiatric rating scales for inpatient research. In: Crook T, Ferris S, Bartus R (eds). Assessment in Geriatric Psychopharmacology. New Canaan, Connecticut, Mark Powley, 1983, pp. 59–68.

Pietzcker A, Gebhardt R, Strauss A, Stöckel M, Langer C, Freudenthal K. The syndrome scales in the AMDP system. In: Bobon D, Bauman U, Angst U, Helmchen H, Hippius H (eds). AMDP-System in Pharmacopsychiatry. Basel, Karger, 1983, pp. 88–99.

Reifler BV, Larsen E, Hanley R. Co-existence of cognitive impairment and depression in geriatric outpatients. Am J Psych 1982; 139: 623–629.

Reifler BV, Larsen E, Teri L et al. Dementia of the Alzheimer's type and depression. J Am Geriat Soc 1986; 34: 855–859.

Reisberg B. The Brief Cognitive Rating Scale and Global Deterioriation Scale. In: Cook T, Ferris S, Bartus R (eds). Assessment in geriatric psychopharmacology. New Canaan, Connecticut, Mark Powley, 1983, pp. 59–68.

Reisberg B, Bolenstein J, Salob SP et al. Behavioural symptoms in Alzheimer's disease: phenomenology and treatment. J Clin Psychiat 1987; 48(5): 9–15.

Robins LN. An overview of the Diagnostic Interview Schedule and the Composite International Diagnostic Interview. In Mezzich JE, van Cranach M (eds). International Classification in Psychiatry. Cambridge, Cambridge Univ Press, 1988, pp. 205–220.

Rosen WG, Mohs RC, Davis KL. A new rating scale for Alzheimer's disease. Am J Psychiat 1984; 141: 1356–1364.

Roth M, Tym E, Mountjoy CQ, Huppert SA, Hendrie H, Verma S, Goddard R. CAMDEX: A standardized instrument for the diagnosis of mental disorder in the elderly with special reference to the early detection of dementia. Br J Psychiat 1986; 149: 698–709.

Shader RI, Harmatz JS, Salzman C. A new scale for assessment in geriatric population: Sandoz Clinical Assessment – Geriatric (SCAG). J Am Geriat Soc 1974; 22: 107–113.

3.2 Delirium (Acute Organic Mental Syndrome)

Among the organic mental syndromes, delirium refers to the acute (reversible) state while dementia refers, as described in Sect. 3.1, to the chronic (irreversible) state. According to ICD-10 delirium can be subdivided into "alcohol or drugs induced" and "other than induced by alcohol and drugs". The following components are listed in ICD-10 for the definition of delirium: (A) impairment of consciousness and attention; (B) hallucination, delusion, impairment of immediate recall and disorientation; (C) psychomotor disturbances (autonomic hyperactivities); (D) disturbances of sleep-wake cycle, e.g. insomnia, nocturnal worsening, nightmares; (E) rapid onset (hours); (F) total duration up to six months (typically few days to four weeks); and (G) objective evidence for organic impairment.

In this compendium only the alcohol or drug induced delirium will be dealt with because most research with rating scales have been carried out in this field. Of the ICD-10 components the organic impairment here is alcohol depencence (or related drug dependence). As shown in Table 3.5 withdrawal symptoms are included in the DSM-III-R definition of alcohol dependence.

Table 3.5. Alcohol dependence (according to DSM-III-R:309.90)

Amount of use	Continued alcohol use despite knowledge of having a persistent or recurrent social, psychological or physical problem that is caused or exacerbated by the alcohol use
Tolerance	Need for increased ($\geq 50\%$) alcohol dosage in order to achieve desired effect
Withdrawal	Withdrawal symptoms when expected to fulfil major role obligations Characteristic withdrawal symptoms Alcohol often taken to relieve or avoid withdrawal symptoms

Table 3.6 shows the different mental syndromes associated with psychoactive substances in accordance with DSM-III-R. In the literature on rating scales the withdrawal syndrome has received most attention. Delusional and mood syndromes are described in other chapters of this volume. The spectrum of withdrawal symptoms includes states of delirium. As indicated in Table 3.6, alcohol, sedatives and hypnotics (e.g. barbiturates and benzodiazepines) are the most serious substances in the withdrawal stage. In early research, Schneider (1913, 1916) showed that barbiturates but not opoids can induce withdrawal states with delirium.

The Withdrawal Syndrome Scale (WSA; Table 3.7) was the first scale in which construct validity was analysed by the Rasch model. It has been demonstrated that the rank ordering of items (Table 3.8) fulfil the Rasch model (Bech et al. 1989), although increased temperature seems more inclusive in women than in men. In general, increased pulse, tremor and motor restlessness are seen in minor withdrawal states, while increased temperature and sweating are seen in the moderate degrees. Disorientation and hallucinations are most exclusive, indicating delirium states. This structure of the withdrawal spectrum is similar in alcohol dependence and in benzodiazepine or related substance dependence.

ICD-10 differentiates between withdrawal states with and those without delirium. In the section on diagnostic criteria, ICD-10 points out that the withdrawal syndrome should be coded only if it is of sufficient severity. It should not be coded merely upon evidence of 'rebound' effects after substance use. Simple 'hangover' after heavy consumption of alcohol, for instance, should not be coded as a withdrawal syndrome. It should be emphasized that DSM-III-R uses different criteria. Thus tremor is a necessary (monothetic) condition for withdrawal states after alcohol, but not for sedative withdrawal. No such subtyping is used in ICD-10. Table 3.9 compares scales developed to measure the withdrawal syndrome after alcohol, sedatives or hypnotics. These include, in addition to the WSA, the Thomas and Freedman (1964) scale and the Martin et al. (1979) scale. The items of these scales can be grouped into (a) nonspecific items (e.g. headache, dizziness and nausea), dysphoric or neurasthenia items (e.g. lack of energy, irritability, concentration difficulty and depressed mood), complicational symptoms (e.g. convulsions), and (b) specific core items. The specific items can be grouped into the following components: (a) autonomic hyperactivity, (b) motor symptoms (restlessness), (c) orientation, and (d) psychotic symptoms (e.g. hallucinations).

A version of the WSA for use with alcohol and sedative substances has been constructed for nursing staff (Kristensen et al. 1986). The problem of anti-abstinence treatment by substitution therapy has been reviewed elsewhere (Bech et al. 1990). In the influential study by Thomas and Freedman (1964) a fixed dosage of substitution therapy was recommended; otherwise "clinical judgement is the sole basis for dosage", which, according to Thomas and Freedman, is a too non-pharmacological approach. However, Kristensen et al. (1986), using the WSA as the dependent variable, showed the scale to be a reliable and valid indicator for efficacy in treating the withdrawal syndrome after alcohol or sedatives (e.g. barbiturates and benzodiazepines) with phenobarbital.

Table 3.6. Organic mental syndromes associated with psychoactive substances according to DSM-III-R

	Withdrawal without delirium	Withdrawal with delirium	Intoxication	Intoxication		
				Delusional syndrome	Mood syndrome	Delirium
Alcohol	+	+	+	-	-	-
Amphetamine	+	-	+	+	-	+
Caffeine	-	-	+	-	-	-
Cannabis	-	-	+	+	-	-
Cocaine	+	-	+	+	-	+
Hallucinogens	-	-	+	+	+	-
Nicotine	+	-	(+)	-	-	-
Opioid	+	-	+	-	+	-
Phencyclidine	-	-	+	+	+	+
Sedative, hypnotic (barbiturates/benzodiazepines)	+	+	+	-	-	-

Table 3.7. Psychometric description: WSA

Type	Symptom scale
Content validity	The measurement of severity of withdrawal states after alcohol or related substance use, including the following components: - autonomic hyperactivity (pulse, tremor, sweating, increased temperature) - motor (restlessness) - orientation - psychotic symptoms (delirious)
Administration	Observer scale to be used by the nursing team
Time frame	Inspection every 2 h during the withdrawal stage
Item selection	The scale is a modified version of the scale constructed by Kramp et al. (1979)
Item calibration	Likert scale definition, 0-4
Number of items	The full scale consists of seven items
Item distribution	The items cover the four components in the following proportions: - autonomic hyperactivity: 58% - motor: 14% - orientation: 14% - psychotic: 14%
Construct validity	By use of Rasch models it has been shown (Bech et al. 1989) that the total score of the WSA is a sufficient statistic. The Rasch analysis uses as external criteria such variables as sex, age, and alcohol versus psychoactive drugs (e.g. benzodiazepines)
Inter-observer reliability	The intra-class coefficient was found acceptable (Kristensen et al. 1986)

Table 3.8. Withdrawal syndrome items in ICD-10, DSM-III-R and WSA

ICD-10	DSM-III-R	WSA
Withdrawal state	*Uncomplicated alcohol withdrawal*	
A group of symptoms of variable clustering and degree of severity occurring on absolute or relative withdrawal of a substance. Physical symptoms vary according to the substance being used. Psychological disturbances are also common features of withdrawal.	Tremor and at least one of the following items: (1) Nausea or vomity (2) Malaise or weakness (3) Autonomic hyperactivity (4) Anxiety (5) Depressed mood or irritability (6) Transient hallucinations or illusions (7) Headache (8) Insomnia DSM-III-R Alcohol withdrawal delirium: the uncomplicated syndrome plus hallucination and disorientation. DSM-III-R uncomplicated withdrawal: item 2 plus one of the items 1, 3, 4, 5. DSM-III-R withdrawal delirium: the uncomplicated syndrome plus hallucination and disorientation.	1 Increased pulse (0-4) 2 Tremor (0-4) 3 Motor restlessness (0-4) 4 Temperature (0-4) 5 Sweating (0-4) 6 Disorientation (0-4) 7 Hallucination (0-4)

Table 3.9. Item distributions of rating scales: components of withdrawal syndrome

Component	WSA	Thomas-Freedman scale	Martin et al. scale
Autonomic hyperactivity (palpitations, tremor, restlessness, hyperpyrexia, sweating)	71%	38%	50%
Delirious (psychotic) symptoms	29%	15%	20%
Convulsions	0%	8%	10%
Depressive and/or anxious mood	0%	8%	10%
Other symptoms (e.g. headache, nausea, insomnia, loss of appetite)	0%	31%	10%
Number of items	7	13	10

It should be emphasized that in patients with several episodes of withdrawal syndromes after alcohol or related substances, the kindling process may change the hierarchy of symptoms in the scale. Kindling is the invoking of major motor seizures as a result of repeated electrophysiological stimulation in the brain (Goddard et al. 1969; Racine 1978). Thus, the seizures manifested in the withdrawal state often do not correspond to the hierarchical list in the WSA. So far, no empirical analysis of the influence of kindling on the items of the WSA has been carried out.

It should also be emphasized that the withdrawal syndrome after alcohol or related sedative substances covers the clinical picture of 'acute psycho-organic syndromes' which can be caused by intoxication of these psychoactive substances as well as by other impairments not only in the brain but also in the kidneys or endocrine system or by fever, severe anaemia, or physical or mental exhaustion etc.

The scoring sheet for the WSA is illustrated in "Appendix 3.2". Instructions for scoring its seven items are presented below.

1 Increased Pulse
0. Below 90 (bpm).
1. 90–100.
2. 101–110.
3. 111–120.
4. Above 120.

2 Tremor
0. No tremor.
1. Tremor at movements (e.g. hand tremor when drinking).
2. Light tremor of the upper extremities.
3. Heavy tremor of the extremities.
4. Heavy tremor of the whole body.

3 Motor Restlessness
0. Calm, natural movements.
1. Slight motor unrest.
2. Constant movements and/or constant motor tension.
3. Constant movements, walking around.
4. Maximal unrest, must be fixed (belt).

4 Temperature
0. Below 37.3 °C
1. 37.3–37.6 °C
2. 37.7–38.0 °C
3. 38.1–38.4 °C
4. Above 38.4 °C

5 Sweating
0. No sweating.
1. Skin warm and damp.
2. Localized, pearling sweat (facies, thorax, etc.).
3. Whole body damp and localized visible sweating.
4. Maximal sweating (clothes, linen wet).

6 Disorganization
0. Fully orientated.
1. Fully orientated in personal data, unstable orientation in time and place.
2. Orientated in personal data, not aware of time or place.
3. Unstable orientation in personal data, not aware of time or place.
4. Totally disorientated, cannot be contacted relevantly.

7 Hallucinations
0. No hallucinations.
1. Periodic, unstructured experiences of illusionary character.
2. Periodic, structured hallucinations.
3. More constant hallucinations.
4. Constant hallucinations.

References

Bech P, Rasmussen S, Dahl A, Lauritsen B, Lund K. The Withdrawal Syndrome Scale for alcohol and related psychoactive drugs. Nord Psykiat Tidsskr 1989; 43: 291–294.

Bech P, Rasmussen S, Dahl A, Lauritsen B, Lund K. Withdrawal States after Alcohol and Minor Tranquilizers: Shared Phenomenology as Index of Standardized Substitution Therapy. Proceeding World Psychiatric Association Athens. Amsterdam, Elsevier 1990. In: Stefanis CN, Rabavila AD, Soldatos CR (eds) Psychiatry: A World Perspective. Proceedings of the WPA Congress, Athens. Amsterdam, Excerpta Medica 1990, pp. 1211–1218.

Goddard GV, McIntyre DC, Leech CK. A permanent change in brain function resulting from daily stimulation. Experim Neurol 1969; 25: 295–330.

Kramp P, Hemmingsen R, Rafaelsen OJ. Delirium tremens: Some clinical features. Acta Psychiat Scand 1979; 60: 405–422.

Kristensen CB, Rasmussen S, Dahl A, Lauritsen B, Lund K, Stubgaard M, Bech P. The Withdrawal Syndrome Scale for alcohol and related psychoactive drugs. Total scores as guidelines for treatment with phenobarbital. Nord Psychiat Tidsskr 1986; 40: 139–146.

Martin PR, Kapur BM, Witeside EA, Sellars EM. Intravenous phenobarbital therapy in barbiturate and other hypnosedative withdrawal reactions: A kinetic approach. Clin Pharmacol Ther 1979; 26: 256–264.

Racine RJ. Kindling: The first decade. Neurosurg 1978; 3: 234–252.

Schneider K. Zur Frage der chronischen Morphinpsychose und des Zusammenhangs von Sinnestäuschungen und Wahnideen. Z Gesamt Neurolog Psychiatrie 1913; 19: 25–41.

Schneider K. Ein Veronaldelirium. Allgem Z Psychiatrie 1916; 72: 87–99.

Thomas DW, Freedman DX. Treatment of the alcohol withdrawal syndrome. J Am Med Ass 1964; 188: 244–246.

3.3 Schizophrenia

As pointed out by Berner and Kieffer (1986), all attempts to define schizophrenia ultimately refer either to Kraepelin (1913), Bleuler (1911), or Schneider (1939), who agreed on an organic or endogenous underlying pathological impairment. Indeed, schizophrenia is the 'functional' disorder in axis 1 closest to the organic mental disorders, a view also was accepted by Jaspers (1923) and reflected in his hierarchical principle. This principle is followed by DSM-III-R and ICD-10 and therefore also in this compendium.

However, Kraepelin, Bleuler or Schneider differed to some extent concerning the phenomenological, symptomatic, cross-sectional description of schizophrenic states. Thus, Kraepelin's model of description is the classical text-book definition by showing the typical cases. Bleuler's model is a valid diagnostic description. Hence he separated basic symptoms (e.g. association disturbances, affect disturbances, ambivalence, autism) from accessory symptoms (e.g. hallucinations and delusions). Bleuler considered the basic symptoms as necessary and sufficient criteria for schizophrenia. Finally, Schneider's model included his first-rank symptoms of schizophrenia which were neither necessary nor sufficient but had a certain diagnostic probability of schizophrenia. Of these models the Schneiderian has the highest inter-observer reliability (his first-rank symptoms has been selected because of their reliability, not because of their validity).

In DSM-III, DSM-III-R and ICD-10 the Schneiderian first-rank symptoms have been included because these systems prefer reliability to validity. The predictive validity of schizophrenia in relation to response to neuroleptics was considered by Crow (1980) when he introduced the concept of negative and positive symptoms into schizophrenia. Crow (1980) separated two types of schizophrenia: Type 1 patients had a good response to neuroleptics and were characterized by positive symptoms and no dementia, whereas type 2 patients had poor response to neuroleptics and were characterized by negative symptoms and dementia.

The separation of negative and positive symptoms in neurology goes back to Reynolds (1858) who stated: "...Negative symptoms derive from a loss of vital properties of nervous arrangements (in CNS), while positive symptoms derive from an excess of such properties..." According to Reynolds (1858) there is no relation between negative and positive symptoms (at least in epilepsy) but this was already questioned by Jackson (1889).

Concerning schizophrenia the basic symptoms can be considered as negative symptoms and the accessory symptoms consequently as positive symptoms (Bleuler 1924). Within the context of theories of psychopathology (see Chapter 1) the negative and positive symptoms seem easy to understand. Thus, negative symptoms are delayed development or even no development of certain normal mental functions, of which the anhedonia is most fundamental.

Pathological psychology deals with disturbed expression of normal mental functions, and hedonia is one of the most fundamental attributes of man as a social creature (the instinctual drive of life satisfaction in interpersonal relations). Anhedonia is the first negative of vital brain properties and is described in clinical terms in Chapter 4 (personality disturbances). The negative symptoms can be subdivided into emotional withdrawal, disturbances of verbal communication (conceptual disorganization, loosening of associations) and of non-verbal communication (autism). In the more severe cases the negative symptoms are the deterioration into dementia.

The psychological pathology deals with symptoms appearing "de novo" as manifestation of a disease process. The positive symptoms are unique disease symptoms of psychotic illness (hallucinations and delusions). In relation to validity the positive symptoms respond to neuroleptics (dopamine hyperactivity in the brain) while negative symptoms might respond to serotonin (Bech 1992).

In the following, rating scales for negative and positive symptoms will be discussed although the various scales so far have not referred to the psychopathological theories (pathological psychology vs. psychological pathology). However, the relationship of scales to DSM-III, DSM-III-R and ICD-10 will first be dealt with although none of these systems have adopted the negative-positive approach to schizophrenia. Also the global 'praecox feeling' as described by Rümke (1941/1989) has been excluded from DSM-III, DSM-III-R and ICD-10 because the lack of inter-observer reliability. The praecox feeling is, according to Rümke, not only obtained by a direct observation of the patient, but by examining the examiner's own inner world during the interview. It is a global feeling. This aspect of rating has been discussed in Chapter 1.

Table 3.10 lists the eight items in DSM-III, DSM-III-R and ICD-10. Only in ICD-10 are 'negative' symptoms considered; however, these are not accepted as monothetic criteria. Monothetic criteria are based on pathognomonic symptoms; thought disturbances, delusion of control and hallucinatory voices are considered by DSM-III, DSM-III-R and ICD-10 as pathognomonic symptoms. The increased use in DSM-III-R of polythetic criteria is also seen in the case of schizophrenia where 'other persistent delusions' is a non-pathognomonic symptom (Table 3.10). The criteria of thought disturbances, delusion of control and hallucinatory voices do not have the predictive validity concerning prognosis of schizophrenia as should be expected from diagnostic criteria. Table 3.11 shows the ICD-10 and DSM-III-R criteria for schizophrenia with reference to Schneider's principal symptoms.

The most frequently used rating scale for measuring outcome of antipsychotic drugs treatment in schizophrenia is the Brief Psychiatric Rating Scale (BPRS; see Chapter 2). In principle, the items of the BPRS are positive symptoms of schizophrenia. This scale was the first scale to be sensitive to antipsychotic drugs (Overall and Gorham 1962). The BPRS is a subscale derived from the Multi-dimensional scale for rating psychiatric patients (Lorr 1953). The Lorr scale was found valid in other studies comparing antipsychotics (major tranquilizers) with sedatives (minor tranquilizers, e.g. phenobarbital) in schizophrenia (Turner et al. 1958). In other words, the BPRS was shown to have discriminant validity concerning treatment differences. The first elaborate glossary for the BPRS was developed by Turner (1963). A psychiatric glossary is, as described by Strömgren

Table 3.10. The psychotic disintegration scale of BPRS in relation to ICD-10, DSM-III and DSM-III-R criteria of schizophrenia

Items of psychotic disorganization		Monothetic approach	Polythetic approach
BPRS (number)	ICD-10		
Blunted affect (16)	'Negative' symptoms		ICD-10/DSM-III/DSM-III-R
Emotional withdrawal (3)	'Negative' symptoms		ICD-10/DSM-III/DSM-III-R
Conceptual disorganization (4)	Incoherence		ICD-10/DSM-III/DSM-III-R
	Thought echo, insertion	ICD-10/DSM-III/DSM-III-R	
Unusual thought content (15)	Delusion of control	ICD-10/DSM-III/DSM-III-R	
	Other persistent delusions	ICD-10/DSM-III	DSM-III
Hallucinations (12)	Voices	ICD-10/DSM-III/DSM-III-R	
	Other persistent hallucinations		ICD-10/DSM-III/DSM-III-R
Suspiciousness (11)	Other delusions	ICD-10/DSM-III	DSM-III-R
Specific movement disturbances (7)	Catatonic behaviour		ICD-10/DSM-III/DSM-III-R
Exaggerated self-esteem (8)	Other delusions	ICD-10/DSM-III	DSM-III-R
Hostility (10)			
Uncooperativeness (14)			

Table 3.11. Schizophrenia items in ICD-10, DSM-III-R and among Schneider's first-rank symptoms

ICD-10	DSM-III-R	Schneider symptoms
Although no strictly pathognomic symptoms can be identified, a number of psychopathological phenomena have particular significance. These include:	A Two of the following:	Delusional perception
	(1) Delusions	Voice arguing
(1) Thought echo, thought insertion, thought broadcasting, delusional perception.	(2) Prominent hallucinations	Voices commenting
	(3) Incoherence of association	Audible thoughts
	(4) Catatonic behaviour	Thought broadcasting
(2) Delusions of control.	(5) Flat or grossly inappropriate affect	Thought insertion
(3) Hallucinatory voices.	B Bizarre delusions (e.g. thought broadcasting, being controlled	Thought withdrawal
(4) Fleeting non-affective or half-formed delusions or overvalued ideas.	C Prominent hallucinations of voice	Somatic passivity
(5) Blunted or incoherent emotional response; apathy, paucity of speech.	Presence of either at least two A symptoms or B or C	Disturbance of affect and feelings
(6) Breaks or interpolations in the train of thought.		Disturbance of volition

(1988), a list of selected items with explanatory notes on how to combine them into categories or dimensions. The combinations of items in Table 3.10 can be used either to evaluate the outcome of treatment (total score of BPRS) or as diagnostic criteria (the monothetic versus the polythetic approach in ICD-10, DSM-III or DSM-III-R).

In a study by Andersen et al. (1989) using the glossary of BPRS items relevant for schizophrenia (Overall 1979) the ten items in Table 3.10 fulfilled the Rasch criteria of construct validity (i.e. the total score being an adequate indicator). The rank order of the ten BPRS items (with the original item numbers in parentheses) is the hierarchical structure. The first three items – blunted affect, emotional withdrawal and conceptual disorganization – are components of Bleuler's concept of 'basic' symptoms of schizophrenia. The other seven items in the BPRS are positive symptoms of schizophrenia. In other words, the Rasch analysis accepts this combination of negative and positive symptoms as constituting one dimension.

Crow (1980) used a dimensional approach to negative versus positive symptoms of schizophrenia, whereas Andreasen and Olsen (1982) referred to negative and positive categories or subtypes of schizophrenia. Andreasen (1981, 1982) constructed the Scale for the Assessment of Negative Symptoms (SANS) and the Scale for the Assessment of Positive Symptoms (SAPS). The apathetic factor of AMDP can be considered as a negative syndrome of AMDP (Pieztker et al. 1983). Another scale for measuring positive and negative symptoms of schizophrenia is the Bonn Scale for the Assessment of Basic Symptoms of Schizophrenia (Gross et al. 1987).

A most interesting approach from the point of view of rating scales is the Positive and Negative Syndrome Scale (PANSS; Table 3.12; Kay et al. 1988) which modifies the BPRS to include more negative symptoms. This scale consists of 30 items (Table 3.13), 7 of which cover the negative syndrome of schizophrenia (N1–N7), another 7 the positive syndrome (P1–P7), and the remaining 16 a general psychopathological subscale (G1–G16). Of the 30 items in the PANSS, 18 are from the BPRS, and 12 are new items. In contrast to the original BPRS (Overall and Gorham 1962), the PANSS provides strict item definition; however, it follows the original version in having a 0–6 calibration for each item. Furthermore, the basis for rating does not strictly follow the original BPRS version, such as in the balance between reported and observed items.

The PANSS approach to the BPRS focuses on the measurement of schizophrenia, while the Mini-compendium uses the BPRS as a general scale for psychotic disintegration. The PANSS considers the negative and positive syndromes as important dimensions in schizophrenia, but the general subscale emphasizes that other facets of schizophrenia are important. The level of inter-observer reliability of the PANSS has been found acceptable (Kay et al. 1987). In a recent factor analysis (which is important because of the 30 items) the negative and positive syndromes were the two first factors to emerge, the negative factor explaining 23.6% of variance and the positive factor 12.5% (Kay and Sevy 1990). From a psychometric point of view the PANSS contains many items with overlapping definition, for example those of delusions, tension versus psychic anxiety, tension

Table 3.12. Psychometric description: PANSS and the BPRS subscale for schizophrenia

Type	Symptom scale (severity).
Content validity	Negative and positive dimensions of schizophrenia. Item distribution according to the components (see Tables 3.14, 3.15).
Administration	Interviewer scale to be used by skilled observers (goal-directed interview).
Time frame	For each item it is indicated whether the assessment is observation at interview alone, or whether the basis for rating also includes reports from others, e.g. family (only item G16 in PANSS is solely based on reports).
Item selection	The BPRS is included in PANSS. The innovation is the negative syndrome.
Item calibration	Likert scale definition, 0-4.
Number of items	The negative syndrome scale contains items N1-N7, the positive syndrome scale contains items P1-P7, and the BPRS-10 (negative and positive syndromes) contains items N1, N3, P2, P3, P5, P6, P7, G5, G8, G9.
Content validity	The PANSS subscales of negative and positive syndromes have been factor analysed (Kay et al. 1991). The first factor was the negative scale and the second factor the positive syndrome. Rasch analysis has not yet been performed. The BPRS-10 fulfils the Rasch model, total score is a sufficient statistic for a dimension of predominantly positive symptoms (70%; Andersen et al. 1989).
Inter-observer reliability	The PANSS has adequate reliability (Kay et al. 1987), as does the BPRS-10 (Andersen et al. 1989).

Table 3.13. PANSS: negative, positive, and general psychopathological subscales (BPRS wording and number in parenthesis)

N1	Blunted affect (blunted affect, 16)
N2	Emotional withdrawal
N3	Poor rapport (emotional withdrawal, 3)
N4	Passive social withdrawal
N5	Difficulty in abstract thinking
N6	Lack of spontaneity and flow of conversation
N7	Stereotyped thinking
P1	Delusions (unusual thought content, 15)
P2	Conceptual disorganisation (conceptual disorganization, 4)
P3	Hallucinatory behaviour (hallucinations, 12)
P4	Excitement (increased psychomotor activity, 17)
P5	Grandiosity (exaggerated self-esteem, 8)
P6	Suspiciousness (suspiciousness, 11)
P7	Hostility (hostility, 10)
G1	Somatic concern (somatic concern, 1)
G2	Anxiety (anxiety: psychic, 2)
G3	Guilt feelings (guilt feelings, 5)
G4	Tension (anxiety: somatic, 6)
G5	Mannerism and posturing (specific motor disturbances, 7)
G6	Depression (lowered mood, 9)
G7	Motor retardation (decreased psychomotor activity, 13)
G8	Uncooperativeness (uncooperativeness, 14)
G9	Unusual thought content (unusual thought content, 15)
G10	Disorientation (disorientation and confusion, 18)
G11	Poor attention
G12	Lack of judgement and insight
G13	Disturbance of volition
G14	Poor impulse control
G15	Preoccupation
G16	Active social avoidance

versus agitation, and depressed mood versus motor retardation. In this compendium, a modified PANSS version is used, with item calibration of 0–4 instead of 0–6 and with mutually exclusive items. The guidelines for the 0–4 item calibration are: '0', not present; '1', questionable pathology; '2', mild to moderate (not influencing behaviour); '3', moderate to marked (occasionally influencing behaviour); and '4', marked to extreme (constantly influencing behaviour).

Among other rating scales considered as alternatives to the BPRS are the Manchester scale (Krawiecka et al. 1977) and the Comprehensive Psychiatric Rating Scale subscale (CPRS; Montgomery et al. 1978). Table 3.14 compares the negative subscale of PANSS, the Manchester scale and the Montgomery scale in terms of the four components of schizophrenia from the Kraepelin and Bleuler criteria. It appears that all three scales include in common only autism and cognitive impairments (dementia praecox). The PANSS is superior to the other scales. Construct validity in terms of Rasch analysis is still lacking. In this connection it should be mentioned that Levine et al. (1983) have used Rasch analysis in a preliminary study with the Schedule for Affective Disorders and Schizophrenia (SADS). As with Andersen et al. (1989) in the case of the BPRS, it was found that the items of conceptual disorganization comprise a negative symptom and not, as claimed by the PANSS, a positive symptom of schizophrenia. This is also in accordance with DSM-III-R, where hebephrenic schizophrenia (the model for negative symptoms) is called disorganized schizophrenia.

Table 3.15 compares the item distribution of the PANSS positive syndrome, BPRS (10 items of psychotic disintegration), Manchester scale and Montgomery scale in relation to positive components of schizophrenia: (a) psychotic symptoms, (b) cognitive beliefs (e.g. self-esteem), as distinguished from cognitive impairments (dementia-like), (c) motor symptoms, and (d) aggression. These components have special reference to the effects of neuroleptics (major tranquilizers). When the items of conceptual disorganization are considered as a negative symptom of schizophrenia (Table 3.15), the PANSS positive subscale is seen to include 14% negative symptoms and the BPRS-10 30%. The distribution of the PANSS and BPRS items regarding the four components is more homogeneous than that of the Manchester or the Montgomery scale. This compendium therefore includes these PANSS and BPRS subscales. According to Frances et al. (1990), negative symptoms of schizophrenia will be given prominence as defining features of schizophrenia in DSM-IV.

The predictive nature of a diagnosis in psychiatry is most obvious for organic mental disorders such as dementia and substance use disorders. These diagnostic terms focus on the aetiology and pathogenetic elements of the disorders in a way comparable to the role of diagnosis in the rest of medicine. Among the 'non-organic' or 'functional' disorders (Fig. 3.1), schizophrenia is the most 'organic'. The model for negative symptoms is Kraepelin's dementia praecox, with the emphasis on cognitive deficits. From a psychometric point of view the two dimensions of negative and positive syndromes can be used to form a 2 x 2 table (Table 3.16). However, no study has examined the mathematical relationship between these two axes. Patients with schizophrenia score rather high on both axes, as seen in the study of Andersen et al. (1989); such findings have resulted in construction of the BPRS psychotic disintegration scale (see Chap. 2). Non-schizophrenic patients score high on the positive axis and low on the negative (often referred to as delusional states).

As discussed by Gray et al. (1991), neuroleptics seem to act on the positive dimension alone. This dimension therefore has a predictive validity from a neuropsychopharmacological point of view.

Recurrent delusional states, often with a mixture of positive symptoms of schizophrenia and affective (mood) symptoms of mania and/or depression are often

Table 3.14. Item distributions of rating scales: Kraepelins's and Bleuler's components of negative syndrome of schizophrenia

Component	PANSS	Manchester scale	CPRS subscale
Autism (conceptual disorganization, blunted affect)	57%	13%	17%
Ambivalence	0%	0%	0%
Anhedonia (lack of drive and intrusiveness, praecox-feeling)	0%	0%	0%
Cognitive impairment or deficits (dementia feeling)	43%	13%	8%
Number of items	7	8	12

Table 3.15. Item distributions of rating scales: Schneider's components of positive syndrome of schizophrenia

Component	PANSS positive subscale	BPRS-10	Manchester scale	CPRS subscale
Psychotic symptoms (hallucinations)	43%	20%	13%	58%
Cognitive beliefs (self-esteem)	14%	20%	13%	0%
Motor symptoms (mannerism, agitation, retardation)	14%	10%	25%	0%
Aggression	14%	20%	0%	0%
Negative symptoms	14%	30%	25%	25%
Number of items	7	10	8	12

Table 3.16. A categorical approach to the dimensions of negative and positive syndromes of schizophrenia

Negative syndrome

Schizophrenia (disintegrational) states	Schizophrenia (disintegrational paranoid) states
Borderline states	Delusional (paranoid) states

Positive syndrome

referred to as schizo-affective disorders. Kleist (1928) was the first to use the term cycloid psychosis for these states of delusional affective psychoses, and Leonhard (1957) provided their first clinical discriptions. Perris (1974) found regarding treatment that these patients had the best outcome to lithium and other therapies for affective states. In DSM-III-R and ICD-10 schizo-affective disorder is a subtype of schizophrenia. As regards rating scales, the BPRS with all its 18 items covers the range of schizo-affective symptoms (see Chapter 2).

The scoring sheet for the PANSS is illustrated in "Appendix 3.3". Instructions for scoring its 7 items for the negative syndrome (N1–N7), 7 for the positive syndrome (P1–P7) and 16 for general psychopathology (G1–G16) are presented below.

N1 Blunted Affect
Diminished emotional responsiveness as characterized by a reduction in facial expression, modulation of feelings, and communicative gestures. Basis for rating: observation of physical manifestations of affective tone and emotional responsiveness during the course of the interview.
0. Not present.
1. Diminished emotional responsiveness, of questionable pathology.
2. Tendency to conceal emotional reactions or to unvary emotional modulations or to have expressionsless face.
3. Clearly blunted affect with a general flatness in emotional tone, possibly with tendency to affective discharge, e.g. uncontrolled laughter or weeping.
4. Clearly blunted affect as well as clear affective discharges, such as excitement, rage or inappropriate, uncontrolled laughter or weeping.

N2 Emotional Withdrawal
Lack of interest in, involvement with, and affective commitment to life's events. Basis for rating: reports of functioning from primary care workers or family and observation of interpersonal behaviour during the course of interview.

0. Not present.
1. Very mild or questionable pathology.
2. Patient is mildly distanced emotionally from his surroundings and its challenges but with encouragement becomes involved.
3. Patient is clearly (a moderate to marked degree) detached emotionally from persons and events in his surroundings, resisting all efforts to involve him. He appears distant, docile and purposeless but can be involved in communication at least briefly and tends to personal needs, sometimes with assistance.
4. Marked to extreme deficiency of interest and emotional commitment results in limited conversation with others and frequent neglect of personal functions, for which the patient requires supervision.

N3 Poor Rapport

This item is assessed by interpersonal behaviour during the course of interview. It represents lack of interpersonal empathy, openness in conversation, and sense of closeness, interest or involvement with the interviewer.
0. Not present.
1. Very mild degree of poor emotional communication, questionable pathology.
2. Conversation is characterized by a stilted, strained, or artificial tone. Interview tends to remain on an impersonal, intellectual plane.
3. Moderate to marked degree of poor emotional communication, for example, patient tends to avoid eye or face contact. This clearly impedes the productivity of the interview.
4. Marked to extreme distance in emotional communication. Eye and face contact are frequently avoided.

N4 Passive Social Withdrawal

Diminished interest and initiative in social interactions due to passivity, apathy, listlessness or rejection. This leads to reduced interpersonal involvements and neglect of activities of daily life. Basis for rating: reports on social behaviour from primary care workers or family.
0. Not present.
1. Very mild or questionable reduction in interest in social activities.
2. Passively goes along with most social activities, in a disinterested or mechanical way.
3. Passively participates in only a minority of activities and shows virtually no interest or initiative. Generally spends little time with others.
4. Tends to be apathetic and isolated, participating very rarely in social activities and occasionally neglecting personal needs. Has very few or no spontaneous social contacts.

N5 Difficulty in Abstract Thinking

This item is assessed by response to questions on similarities and proverb interpretation, and use of concrete versus abstract mode during the course of the interview. It represents impairment in the use of the abstract-symbolic mode of thinking, as evidenced by difficulty in classification, forming generalizations, and proceeding beyond concrete or egocentric thinking in problem-solving tasks.

0. Not present.
1. Very mild or questionable degree of difficulty in abstract thinking.
2. Tends often to utilize a concrete mode. Has difficulty with many proverbs and some categories. Tends to be distracted by functional aspects and salient features.
3. Deals primarily in a concrete mode, exhibiting difficulty with most proverbs and many categories.
4. Unable to grasp the abstract meaning of any proverbs or figurative expressions and can formulate classifications for only the most simple of similarities. Thinking is either vacuous or locked into functional aspects, salient features and idiosyncratic interpretations.

N6 Lack of Spontaneity and Flow of Conversation

This item is assessed by cognitive-verbal processes observed during the course of interview. It represents a reduction in the normal flow of communication associated with apathy, rejection, defensiveness, or cognitive deficit. This is manifested by diminished fluidity and productivity of the verbal-interactional process.

0. Not present.
1. Conversation shows little initiative, but to a very mild degree, questionable pathology.
2. Conversation lacks free flow and appears uneven or halting.
3. Moderate to marked degree of lack of spontaneity, replying to the interviewer's questions with only one or two brief sentences.
4. Marked to extreme lack of spontaneity of conversation. Patient's responses are limited to a few words. Interview very unproductive and very restricted, or cannot be completed.

N7 Stereotyped Thinking

This item is assessed by cognitive-verbal processes observed during the interview. It represents decreased fluidity, spontaneity and flexibility of thinking, as evidenced in rigid, repetitious or barren thought content.

0. Not present.
1. Some tendency to rigidity shown in attitudes or beliefs, however, questionable pathology.
2. Conversation revolves around a recurrent theme, resulting in difficulty in shifting to a new topic.
3. Thinking is rigid and repetitious to the point that, despite the interviewer's efforts, conversation is limited to only two or three dominating topics.
4. Uncontrolled repetition of demands, statements, ideas, or questions which severely impairs conversation.

P1 Delusions: General

This item is assessed by inspection of thought content expressed in the interview and its influence on social relations and behaviour. It represents beliefs which are unfounded, unrealistic, and idiosyncratic. It is scored independently of the subtypes rated in items P2, P5, P6, G1, G3 or G9.

0. Not present.
1. Very mild or doubtful degree (e.g. overvalued ideas) at the upper extreme of normal limits; questionable pathology.
2. Presence of poorly formed unstable delusions ('as if' experience) that only rarely interfere with social relations.
3. Presence of more well-formed delusions that are tenaciously held and occasionally interfere with thinking, social relations or behaviour.
4. Presence of a stable set of delusions tenaciously held and clearly interfering with thinking, social relations and behaviour.

P2 Conceptual Disorganization

This item is assessed by cognitive-verbal processes observed during the course of the interview. It represents disorganized process of thinking characterized by vagueness in verbal expression (disruption of goal-directed sequences) including completely disorganized verbal production (e.g. thought blocking).

0. Not present.
1. Doubtful or very mild degree of vagueness, but language is grammatical, without pathology.
2. Mild to moderate disturbance in cognitive-verbal processes. There is some difficulty in directing thoughts towards goals, resulting in emptiness in the communicative information transmitted.
3. Clear difficulty in organizing thoughts, as evidenced by frequent irrelevancies, loosening of associations; possibly with a tendency to thought blockings or neologisms.
4. Marked to extreme degree of conceptual disorganization, resulting in gross irrelevancies and total failure of communication (e.g. 'word salad').

P3 Hallucinatory Behaviour

Verbal report or behaviour indicating perceptions which are not generated by external stimuli. Basis for rating: verbal report and physical manifestations during the course of the interview as well as reports of behaviour by primary workers or family.

0. Not present.
1. Very mild or doubtful degree. Vague abnormal perception which, however, is isolated and of questionable pathology, not affecting behaviour.
2. One or two clearly formed but very infrequent hallucinations, but still not affecting behaviour.
3. Hallucinations are frequent, may involve more than one sensory modality, and tend to distort thinking and/or disrupt behaviour.

4. Hallucinations are present almost continuously, causing major disruption of thinking and behaviour, including obedience to command halluciantions.

P4 Excitement (Agitation)

Hyperactivity as reflected in accelerated motor behaviour, hypervigilance. Basis of rating: behaviour manifestations during course of interview as well as reports of behaviour by primary care workers or family.
0. Not present.
1. Very slightly or doubtfully increased motor activity, e.g. lively facial expression or somewhat talkative, but of questionable pathology.
2. Mildly to moderately increased motor activity, e.g. lively gestures or rather talkative.
3. Moderate to marked hyperactivity or frequent outbursts of restlessness, making it difficult for the patient to sit still for longer than several minutes, hence rises one or several times during interview.
4. Marked to extreme agitation dominates the interview. Can to some extent carry out personal functions such as eating and sleeping.

P5 Grandiosity (Exaggerated Self-Esteem)

This item is assessed by thought content expressed during the interview and its influence on behaviour. It represents exaggerated self-opinion and unrealistic beliefs of superiority, including delusions of extraordinary abilities, wealth, knowledge, fame, power, and moral righteousness.
0. Not present.
1. Tendency to expansiveness or boastfulness, but without grandiose pathology.
2. Feels to a moderate degree unrealistically superior to others. Some poorly formed delusions about special status or abilities seems present, but without affecting attitude or behaviour.
3. Clear delusions concerning remarkable abilities, status, or power are expressed and influence attitudes but not behaviour.
4. Clear delusions of remarkable superiority involving more than one issue (wealth, knowledge, fame, etc.) are expressed, notably influencing social relations and behaviour.

P6 Suspiciousness

This item is assessed by thought content expressed in the interview and its influence on behaviour. It represents unrealistic or exaggerated ideas of persecution as reflected in guardedness, a distrustful attitude, suspicious hypervigilance, or frank delusions that others mean one harm.
0. Not present.
1. Presents a guarded or even openly distrustful attitude. Feels that 'something is going on', but thoughts, interactions and behaviour are minimally affected.
2. Distrustfulness is clearly evident, but there is no evidence of persecutory delusions because the beliefs are still an 'as if' experience, thus still without influence on behaviour.

3. Clear persecutory delusions but these have limited impact on interpersonal relations or behaviour.
4. Clear persecutory delusions which significantly interfere with interpersonal relations and behaviour.

P7 Hostility

Verbal and non-verbal expressions of anger and resentment including sarcasm, passive-aggressive behaviour, verbal abuse, and threats. Basis for rating: interpersonal behaviour observed during the interview and reports by primary care workers or family.

0. Not present.
1. Somewhat impatient or irritable but control is maintained, e.g. indirect communication of anger such as in sarcasm or disrespect.
2. Overtly impatient or irritable but provocations are tolerated.
3. Clearly hostile, makes verbal threats, and may nearly be physically destructive but can still be calmed down.
4. Clear hostility with overt physical violence. Physically destructive.

G1 Somatic Concern

This item is assessed by thought content expressed in interview. It represents physical complaints and beliefs about bodily illness or malfunctions (hypochondriasis).

0. Not present.
1. Very mildly concerned with physical health; questionable pathology.
2. Complaints about poor health or bodily malfunction, but there is no delusional convinctions.
3. Clear delusions of hypochondriasis but with limited impact on behaviour. Thus the patient can briefly be reassured that his beliefs are unjustified.
4. Clear delusions of hypochondriasis; cannot even briefly be reassured that his beliefs are unjustified, thereby having a significant influence on behaviour.

G2 Anxiety: Psychic

This item is assessed by a verbal report during the course of the interview and corresponding physical manifestations. It represents subjective (psychic) experience of nervousness, worry, apprehension.

0. Not present.
1. Very mild or doubtful degree of worry; questionable pathology.
2. The patient is more clearly in a state of nervousness, worry and apprehension. The patient is, however, able to control himself. It is without influence on behaviour.
3. The apprehension and insecurity are moderately to markedly present. The patient may experience feelings of panic. It occasionally interferes with behaviour or social relations.

4. Marked to extreme anxiety which reaches panic proportions or manifests itself in actual panic attacks.

G3 Guilt Feelings
This item is assessed by a verbal report of guilt feelings during the course of the interview and the influence on attitudes and thoughts. It represents a sense of reproach or self-blame for real or imagined misdeeds in the past.
0. Not present.
1. Doubtful whether guilt feelings are present, as the patient is concerned only with the fact that during the current illness he has been a burden to family or colleagues due to reduced work capacity; questionable pathology.
2. Guilt feelings are more clearly present as the patient is concerned with incidents in the past prior to the current episode. For example, the patient reproaches himself for small omissions or failures, for not having done his duty or for having harmed others.
3. Moderate to marked guilt feelings. Patient may report that he feels the current suffering to be some sort of punishment. Hence, the guilt feelings may have a delusional basis. (Score '3' as long as the patient can see that his view is unfounded.)
4. The guilt feelings are firmly maintained and resist any counter-argument, so that they become strong delusional ideas.

G4 Tension (Somatic Anxiety)
This item is assessed by a verbal report of somatic anxiety expressed in severity of autonomic hyperactivity. It represents overt physical (somatic) manifestations of anxiety, e.g. palpitations, tremor, sweating, inner restlessness, abnormal sensations.
0. Not present.
1. The patient occasionally experiences slight manifestations of tension such as palpitations or trembling. Questionable pathology.
2. The patient occasionally experiences mild to moderate tension symptoms, or sighs are clearly present, but this does not incapacitate behaviour.
3. Moderate to marked degree of tension which may influence behaviour or social relations.
4. Marked to severe degree of tension to the point that interpersonal interactions are disrupted. The symptoms are persistent and very incapacitating.

G5 Mannerisms and Posturing (Specific Movement Disturbances)
Unnatural movements or posture as characterized by an awkward, stilted, disorganized, or bizarre appearance. Basis for rating: observation of physical manifestations during the course of the interview as well as reports from primary care workers or family.
0. Not present.
1. Very mild, questionable pathology.

2. Mild to moderate degree. Movements are notably awkward or disjointed, but only for very brief periods.
3. Clearly bizarre rituals or contorted posture sustained for extended periods.
4. Clearly bizarre repetition of rituals, mannerisms or stereotyped movements sustained most of the time.

G6 Depression (Depressed Mood)

This item is assessed by a verbal report of depressed mood during the course of the interview and its observed influence on attitude and behaviour. It represents feelings of sadness, discouragement, helplessness and pessimism.
0. Not present.
1. The patient vaguely indicates that he is more despondent and depressed than usual, however, of questionable pathology.
2. The patient more clearly is concerned with unpleasant experience, although he still lacks helplessness or hopelessness.
3. The patient shows clear non-verbal signs of depression or is at times overpowered by helplessness or hopelessness.
4. The patient's remarks on despondency and pessimism or the non-verbal signs dominate the interview.

G7 Motor Retardation

Reduction in motor activity as reflected in showing or lessening of movements and speech, diminished responsiveness to stimuli and reduced body tone. Basis for rating: manifestations during the course of the interview as well as reports by primary care workers or family.
0. Not present.
1. Very slight or questionable diminution in rate of movement.
2. Mild to moderate slowness in movements (e.g. reduced gestures, slow pace).
3. Clear motor retardation of moderate to marked degree, nearly all movements are affected. Limits functioning in social and occupational situations.
4. Movements are extremely slow, resulting in a minimum of activity, approaching or including stupor.

G8 Uncooperativeness

Active refusal to comply with the will of significant others, including the interviewer, hospital staff or family, which may be associated with negativism and rejection of authority. Basis of rating: inter-personal behaviour observed during the course of the interview as well as reports by primary care workers or family.
0. Not present.
1. Reserved or impatient in interview situation or reports of very mild attitudes of uncooperativeness. Questionable pathology.
2. Mild to moderate resistance. Answers evasively or objects to some sensitive questions; or reports of occasionally outright refusal to comply with normal social demands, such as making his own bed, attending scheduled programmes, etc.

3. Moderate to marked uncooperativeness as reflected in obvious defensiveness or irritability with the interviewer and possible unwillingness to address many questions; or reports on the patient having 'a serious attitude problem'.
4. Patient is extremely uncooperative, negativistic. The patient may refuse to stay in the interview situation, or he refuses to comply with most social demands.

G9 Unusual Thought Content

This item is assessed by the thought content expressed during the course of the interview. It represents strange, fantastic or bizarre ideas. This concerns the content of the patient's verbalization and not the organization of his language, which is rated in item P2 (conceptual disorganization). Notice that 'grandiose delusions' is rated in item P5, 'delusions of persecution' in P6, 'delusions of hypochondriasis' in G1, and 'delusions of guilt' in G3, and that another general item of delusions is considered in P1. The delusions of particular interest in G9 are those of control, influence or depersonalization, morbid jealousy, sexual delusions, expansive (religious) delusions. Rate only degree of unusualness in thought content expressed, the significance it has in the patient's mind or its influence on his social relations or behaviour.

0. Not present.
1. Very mild or doubtful degree (e.g. overvalued ideas) at the upper extreme or normal limits, questionable pathology.
2. Presence of poorly formed unstable delusions ('as if' experience) that only rarely interfere with social relations.
3. Presence of more well-formed delusions that are tenaciously held and occasionally interfere with social relations or behaviour.
4. Presence of a stable set of delusions, tenaciously held and clearly interfering with social relations and behaviour.

G10 Disorientation

This item is assessed by response to interview questions on orientation. It represents lack of awareness of one's relationship to the surroundings, including persons, place and time.

0. The patient is completely orientated in time, place and personal data.
1. The patient occasionally has some difficulty, but can spontaneously give correct statements about orientation in time, place and personal data.
2. The patient has impairments such that he does not spontaneously give correct statements. For example, he does not know the name of the day or the date although he still knows the month and year correctly, or has spatial difficulties although he still knows his own name.
3. The patient is markedly disoriented. For example, he does not know the month or year although he still knows which season it is, or has difficulty finding his way to the toilet and bed without help, or remembers his name only with some help.
4. The patient is completely disoriented in time, place, or personal data.

G11 Poor Attention
This item is assessed by manifestations during the course of the interview. It represents a failure in focused alertness manifested by poor concentration, distractability from internal and external stimuli, and difficulties in harnessing, sustaining or shifting focus to new stimuli.
0. Not present.
1. Some very mild tendency to vulnerability to distraction or faltering attention towards the end of interview. Questionable pathology.
2. Conversation is affected by the tendency to be easily distracted, difficulty in sustaining concentration long on a given topic.
3. Conversation is clearly hampered by poor concentration, distractability, and difficulty in shifting focus appropriately.
4. Patient's attention can be harnessed for only brief moments or with great effort, due to marked distraction by internal or external stimuli.

G12 Lack of Judgement and Insight
This item is assessed by thought content expressed during the interview. It represents impaired awareness or understanding of one's own psychiatric condition and life situation. This is evidenced by failure to recognize past or present psychiatric illness or symptoms, denial of need for psychiatric hospitalization or treatment, decisions characterized by poor anticipation of consequences, and unrealistic short-term and long-range planning.
0. Not present.
1. Recognizes having a psychiatric disorder but underestimates its seriousness to some extent. Questionable pathology.
2. Shows only vague or shallow recognition of illness. Patient may rationalize the need for treatment in terms of its relieving lesser symptoms, such as anxiety and sleep difficulty.
3. Shows clear lack of insight. (Delusional patients should score at least '3'.) The need for psychiatric treatment is unrecognized.
4. Denies ever having psychiatric disorders; emphatic denial of past and present psychiatric illness.

G13 Disturbance of Volition
This item is assessed by thought content and behaviour manifested in the course of interview. It represents disturbance in the wilful initiation, sustaining and control of one's thoughts, behaviour, movements and speech.
0. Not present.
1. Some indecisiveness in conversation and thinking. Questionable pathology.
2. Shows difficulty in reaching decisions. Conversation may be marred by alternation in thinking.
3. Disturbance of volition interferes in thinking as well as in behaviour. Patient shows pronounced indecision that impedes the initiation and continuation of social and motor activities.

4. Disturbance of volition interferes in the execution of simple, automatic motor functions, such as dressing and grooming, and markedly affects speech.

G14 Poor Impulse Control
Disordered regulation and control of action on inner urges, resulting in sudden unmodulated, arbitrary, or misdirected discharge of tension and emotions without concern about consequences. The assessment is based on behaviour during the course of the interview and reports by primary care workers and family.
0. Not present.
1. Patient tends to be easily angered and frustrated when facing stress, but questionable pathology.
2. Patient becomes angered and verbally abusive with minimal provocation. May be occasionally threatening or destructive.
3. Patient exhibits repeated impulsive episodes involving abuse, destruction of property or physical threats.
4. Patient frequently is impulsively aggressive, threatening, demanding and destructive, without any apparent consideration of consequences.

G15 Preoccupation
This item is assessed by interpersonal behaviour observed during the course of the interview. It represents absorption with internally generated thoughts and feelings and with autistic experiences to the detriment of reality orientation and adaptive behaviour.
0. Not present.
1. There is a very mildly diminished concern exhibited towards others; questionable pathology.
2. Patient occasionally appears self-absorbed, as if day-dreaming, which, however, interferes with communication only to a minor extent.
3. Patient often appears to be engaged in autistic experiences, as evidenced by behaviours that significantly intrude on social and communicational functions.
4. Marked to extreme preoccupation with autistic experiences, which seriously delimits concentration, ability to converse, and orientation to the surroundings.

G16 Active Social Avoidance
Diminished social involvement associated with unwarranted fear, hostility or distrust. Basis for rating: reports of social functioning by primary care workers or family.
0. Not present.
1. Patient tends to feel ill at ease in the presence of others or prefers to spend time alone. Very mild degree, questionable pathology.
2. Patient begrudgingly attends all or most social activities.
3. Patient fearfully or angrily keeps away from many social interactions despite other's efforts to involve him.
4. Patient participates in very few social activities because of fear or distrust.

References

Andersen J, Larsen JK, Schultz V, Nielsen BM, Kørner A, Behnke K, Munk-Andersen E, Butler B, Allerup P, Bech P. The Brief Psychaitric Rating Scale. Dimension of schizophrenia. Psychopathol 1989; 22: 168–176.

Andreasen NC. Negative symptoms in schizophrenia. Arch Gen Psychiat 1982; 39: 788–794.

Andreasen NC, Olsen SA. Negative versus positive schizophrenia: Definition and validation. Arch Gen Psychiat 1982; 39: 789–794.

Bech P. Den kliniske betydning af negative og positive symptomer ved skizofreni. Nord Psyk Tidsskr, 1992; 46 (Suppl 26):23–27.

Berner P, Kieffer W. International perspectives on schizophrenia and related psychotic disorders. In: Mezzich JE, von Cranach M (eds). International Classification in Psychiatry. Cambridge, Cambridge University Press, 1988, pp. 89–98.

Bleuler E. Dementia praecox oder Gruppe der Schizophrenia. In: Aschaffenburg, T (ed). Handbuch der Psychiatrie. Leipzig, Deuticke, 1911.

Bleuler E. Textbook of Psychiatry. New York, Mac Millan, 1924.

Frances A, Pincus HA, Widiger TA, Davis WW, First MB. DSM-IV: work in progress. Am J Psychiat 1990; 147: 1439–1448.

Gray JA, Feldon J, Rawlins JNP, Hemsley DR, Smith AD. The neuropsychology of schizophrenia. Behavioural and Brain Sciences 1991; 14: 1–84.

Gross G, Huber G, Klusterkötter J, Linz M. BSABS, Bonner Skala für die Beurteilung von Basissymptomen. Berlin, Springer, 1987.

Jackson JH. On postepileptic states: A contribution to the comparative study of insanities. J Ment Sci, 1889; 34: 490–500.

Jaspers K. Allgemeine Pathology (First edition, 1923). Berlin, Springer. English edition. Manchester Univ Press, 1963.

Kay SR, Opler LA, Fiszbein A. Positive and Negative Syndrome Scale (PANSS). Rating Manual. New York, San Rafael, Social and Behavioural Science Documents, 1987.

Kay SR, Opler LA, Lindenmayer JP. Reliability and validity of the positive and negative syndrome scale for schizophrenics. Psychiat Res 1988; 23: 99–110.

Kay SR, Sevy S. Pyramidical model of schizophrenia. Schizophrenia Bull 1990; 16: (in press).

Kleist K. Über zykloide, paranoide und epileptoide Psychosen und über die Frage der Degenerationspsychosen. Schw Arch Neurol Psychiat 1928; 23: 1–35.

Kraepelin E. Psychiatrie, Bd 3. Leipzig, Barth, 1913. Crow TJ. Molecular pathology of schizophrenia: more than one disease process? Brit Med J 1980; 280: 66–68.

Krawiecka M, Goldberg D, Vaugham M. A standardized psychiatric assessment scale for rating chronic psychotic patients. Acta Psychiat Scand 1977; 55: 299–308.

Leonhard K. The cycloid psychosis usually misdiagnosed as schizophrenias. Psychiat Neurol Med Psychol 1957; 9: 359–365.

Levine RJ, Fogg L, Meltzer HY. Assessment of negative and positive symptoms in schizophrenia. Schizophrenia Bull 1983; 9: 368–376.

Lorr M. Multidimensional scale for rating psychiatric patients. Veterans Admin Tech Bull 1953; 43: 10–507.

Montgomery SA, Taylor P, Montgomery D. Development of a schizophrenia scale sensitive to change. Neuropharma 1978; 17: 1061–1063.

Overall JE. Criteria for the selection of subjects for research in biological psychiatry. In: van Praag H, Lader M, Rafaelsen OJ, Sachar S (eds). Handbook of Biological Psychiatry. New York, Dekker, 1979, pp. 359–391.

Overall JE, Gorham DR. The Brief Psychiatric Rating Scale. Psychol Rep 1962; 10: 799–812.

Perris C. Study of cycloid psychosis. Acta Psychiat Scand 1974 (suppl 253).

Pietzker A, Beghardt R, Strauss A, Stöckel M, Langer C, Freudenthal K. The syndrome scales in the AMDP system. In: Bobon D, Bauman U, Angst U, Helmschen H, Hippius H (eds). AMDP-System in Pharmacopsychiatry. Basel, Karger, 1983, pp. 88–99.

Reynolds JR. On the pathology of convulsions, with special reference to those of children. Liverpool Med Chir J, 1858; 2: 1–14.

Rümke HC. Het kernsymptoom der schizophrenie en het praecoxgevoel (The nuclear symptom of schizophrenia and the precoxfeeling). Original publication in Dutch (1941). English translation: History of Psyciatry 1990; 1: 334–341.

Schneider K. Klinische Psychopathologie (First edition, 1939). English edition. New York, Grune and Stratton, 1959.

Strömgren E. The lexicon and issues in the relation of psychiatric concepts and terms. In: Mezzich JE, von Cranach M (eds). International Classification in Psychiatry. Cambridge, Cambridge University Press, 1988, pp. 175–179.

Turner WJ. Glossaries for Use with the Overall and Gorham Brief Psychiatric Rating Scale and a Modified Melamud-Sands Rating Scale. New York, Central Islip State Hospital, 1963.

Turner WJ, Carl A, Merlis S, Wilcoxon F. Chemotherapeutic trials in psychosis. Acta Neurol Psychiat 1958; 79: 507–602.

3.4 Mood (Affective) Disorders

The term 'affective disorders' was used in DSM-III, but the entry was changed in DSM-III-R to 'mood disorders' because mood refers to a state of longer duration (weeks) than affective state (days). In ICD-10 the term 'mood' is also preferred, but 'affective' is placed in parentheses; this usage is also adopted here to consider brief major depression as part of mood disorders. Attempts to define mood disorders refer ultimately to either Kraepelin (1913,1921), Wimmer (1916), or Freud (1917). Both DSM-III-R and ICD-10 have followed Freud in excluding anxiety states from mood disorders.

3.4.1 Manic States

Among the mood states mania is considered as the most 'organic' (Fig. 3.1). However, Freud considered mania as a contra-phobic reaction, and Wimmer described some cases of reactive (e.g. non-endogenous) mania. Among mood disorders the clinical features of mania form a more distinct entity than those of endogenous depression (Häfner et al. 1967). The clinical states of mania were subdivided by Kraepelin (1913, 1921) into hypomania (minor), mania (major) and delusional (psychotic), i.e. a quantitatively defined spectrum. This approach has also been adopted by DSM-III-R and ICD-10.

The first mania rating scale was a rather comprehensive scale designed for administration by the nursing staff; this was the Mania State Rating Scale (Beigel et al. 1971). From this the Mania Scale (MAS; Table 3.17) was constructed as a brief rating scale to be administered as the BPRS or the Hamilton Depression Scale

Table 3.17. Psychometric description: MAS

Type	Severity scale, symptoms.
Content validity	The scale items are equally distributed across the Kraepelin components of mania (Table 3.19).
Administration	Observer-rating scale to be used by skilled observers.
Time frame	The previous 3 days including the days of interview.
Item selection	Derived from the nursing scale (Beigel et al. 1971).
Item calibration	Likert scale definition, 0-4.
Number of items	Eleven.
Content validity	Latent class analysis has supported the hierarchy, and latent structure analysis for the total score being a sufficient statistic of severity in terms of Loevinger coefficient is 0.58 (Cronbach α = 0.93).
Sensitivity to change	Superior to the BPRS (Small et al. 1988).
Item-observer reliability	Acceptable in terms of inter-class coefficient (0.98).

Table 3.18. Manic state items in ICD-10, DSM-III-R and MAS

ICD-10	DSM-III-R	MAS	
Mania	A: Elevated, expansive or irritable mood	1 Increased mood level	(0-4)
1 Increased energy and activity	B: At least three of the following:	2 Talkativeness	(0-4)
2 Increased feelings of well-being	(1) Inflated self-esteem or grandiosity	3 Increased social contact	(0-4)
3 Increased sociability	(2) Decreased need for sleep	4 Increased motor activity	(0-4)
4 Increased talkativeness	(3) Talkative	5 Decreased need for sleep	(0-4)
5 Increased sexual energy	(4) Flight of ideas	6 Decreased work activity	(0-4)
6 Decreased need for sleep	(5) Distractability	7 Hostility	(0-4)
7 Increased distractability	(6) Psychomotor hyperactivity	8 Increased sexual activity	(0-4)
8 Inflated self-esteem (grandiosity)	(7) Excessive involvement in pleasurable activity	9 Increased self-esteem	(0-4)
9 Flight of ideas		10 Flight of thoughts	(0-4)
10 Delusions and hallucinations		11 Increased noise level	(0-4)
			0-44
Hypomania: Mild severity of the first seven items. Research criteria: at least three of the first seven items.			
Mania without psychotic symptoms: Moderate to severe degree of the first nine items. Research criteria: at least three of the nine items.			
Mania with psychotic symptoms: Research criteria: at least three of the first nine items plus item 10.			

(Bech et al. 1978; see Chap. 2)). Another modification is the enlarged version published by Blackburn et al. (1977).

Table 3.18 compares the MAS to the ICD-10 and DSM-III-R. The rank ordering of MAS items is in accordance with Bech (1989), with the first six items being seen in hypomanic states and the next five principally in marked states of mania. This rank ordering is in accordance with the results of a latent class analysis performed by Young et al. (1983). It should be emphasized, however, that the latter study was intended for the diagnosis of mania, for which latent class analysis is appropriate. A Rasch analysis to evaluate the value total scores of the MAS is still lacking, but a preliminary result on 84 patients with mania showed a Loevinger coefficient of homogeneity of 0.58 (Bech 1992).

A mania scale analogous to the MAS is that of Young et al. (1978). A comparison of the MAS and the Young scale is presented in Table 3.19 in terms of the Kraepelin (1913, 1921) components. The two scales are rather similar apart from the social disability symptoms, which were not considered in the Young scale.

The sensitivity of the MAS in measuring changes in manic states during treatment has been shown by Small et al. (1988). They found the MAS more sensitive than the BPRS in measuring changes in manic states. The inter-observer reliability has been found excellent (Bech et al. 1979), in terms of intra-class coeffecient a level of 0.98 has been found (Bech 1992).

The interactions between manic and melancholic states were described excellently by Deny and Camus (1907) and by Kraepelin (1913, 1921). They observed that these states of mood are not necessarily mutually exclusive; thus, mixed states such as agitated melancholia or akinetic mania can be seen. The combined use of the Melancholia Scale (MES) and the MAS has been recommended (Bech 1981; Bischoff et al. 1990), especially in long term relapse-prevention therapies. (See also Section 3.4.2.1 The Depressive Syndrome.)

It should be emphasized that the Mania Scale has mainly been used in clinical studies to evaluate the antimanic effect of different treatment modalities. Thus, ECT and lithium (Small et al. 1988), haloperidol (Gjerris et al. 1981), clonidine

Table 3.19. Item distributions of rating scales: Kraepelin's components of mania

Component	MAS	Young et al. Mania Rating Scale
Mood (primary: elated; secondary: irritable)	18%	36%
Motor (agitation, talkativeness, noise)	27%	18%
Cognitive beliefs (self-esteem, flight of thoughts)	18%	27%
Social functioning (work, intrusiveness)	18%	0%
Vegetative symptoms (sleep, sexual interests)	18%	18%
Number of items	11	11

(Hardy et al. 1986), and zuclopenthixol (Amdisen et al. 1987). These studies have confirmed that the Mania Scale is sensitive to measure changes during treatment. The scoring sheet for the MAS is illustrated in "Appendix 3.4".

References

Amdisen A, Nielsen MS, Dencker SJ. Zuclopenthixol acetate in Viscoler – a new drug formulation in patients with acute psychoses including mania. Acta Psychiat Scand 1987; 75: 99–107.

Bech P. Rating scales for affective disorders: their validity and consistency. Acta Psychiat Scand 1981; 64 (suppl. 295): 1–101.

Bech P. Methods of evaluation of psychoactive drugs. Recenti Progressi in Medicina 1989; 80: 706–711.

Bech P. The Mania Scale. Reliability and Validity. 1992 (in preparation).

Bech P, Rafaelsen OJ, Kramp P, Bolwig TG. The mania rating scale: scale construct and inter-observer agreement. Neuropharmacol 1978; 17: 430–431.

Bech P, Bolwig TG, Kramp P, Rafaelsen OJ. The Bech-Rafaelsen Mania Scale and the Hamilton Depression Scale. Acta Psychiat Scand 1979; 59: 420–430.

Beigel A, Murphy DL, Bunney WE. The manic-state rating scale. Arch Gen Psychiat 1971; 25: 256–262.

Bischoff R, Bobon D, Görtelmeyer R, Horn R, Müller AA, Stoll KD, Woggon B. Rating scales for psychiatry: European edition. Weinheim, Germany, Beltz Test, 1990.

Blackburn IM, Loudon JB, Ashworth CM. A new scale for measuring mania. Psychol Med 1977; 7: 453–458.

Deny G, Camus P. Les folies intermittentes: la psychose maniaque-depressive. Paris, J-B Bailliere, 1907.

Freud S. Mourning and Melancholia. (First published 1917). Collected papers (Vol 4). New York, Basic Books, 1959, pp. 152–170.

Gjerris A, Bech P, Broen-Christensen V. Haloperidol plasma levels in relation to antimanic effect. In: Usdin E, Dahl SG, Gram LF, Lingjærde O (eds). Clinical Pharmacology in Psychiatry. London, McMillan 1981, pp. 227–232.

Häfner H, Cesarin AC, Cesarino-Krantz M. Konstanz und Variabilität klinisch psychiatrischer Diagnosen über sechs Jahrzehnte. Soc Psychiat 1967; 2: 14–25.

Hardy MC, Lecrubies Y, Widlöcher D. Efficacy of clonidine in 24 patients with acute mania. Am J Psychiat 1986; 143: 1450–1455.

Kraepelin E. Psychiatrie. Vol. 3, Eight edition. Leipzig, Barth, 1913.

Kraepelin E. Manic-depressive insanity and paranoia. Edinburgh, Livingstone, 1921.

Lusznat RM, Murphy DP, Nunn CMH. Carbamazepine vs. lithium in the treatment and prophylaxis of mania. Brit J Psychiat 1988; 153: 198–204.

Small JG, Klapper MH, Kellanus JJ, Miller MJ, Milstein V, Sharpley PN, Small IP. Electroconvulsive treatment compared with lithium in the management of mania states. Arch Gen Psychiat 1988; 45: 727–732.

Wimmer A. Psykogene sindssygdomsformer. In: Sct. Hans Mental Hospital 1816–1916, Jubilee Publication. Copenhagen, Gad, 1916, pp. 85–216.

Young MA, Abrams R, Taylor MA, Meltzer HY. Stablishing diagnostic criteria for mania. J Nerv Ment Dis 1983; 171: 676–682.

Young RC, Biggs JT, Ziegler VE, Meyer DA. A rating scale for mania: reliability, validity and sensitivity. Brit J Psychiat 1978; 133: 429–435.

3.4.2 Depression (Melancholic States)

Among the various mood states (depression, anxiety, and aggression) depression is considered the most 'organic' (Fig. 3.1). However, Freud (1917) considered depression (melancholia) as a psychogenic (neurotic) manifestation, and Wimmer (1916), influenced by Kierkegaard, considered subtypes of depression as existential human reactions to psychosocial stressors.

The depressive syndrome (melancholia) is the most complex in psychopathology. It illustrates the diagnosing process as this was formulated by Wing (1977): "to put forward a diagnosis is, first of all, to recognize a condition, and then to put forward a theory about it." It is very interesting (Bech 1989) that Kraepelin (1913,1921), Wimmer (1916) and Freud (1917) were rather in agreement in recognizing melancholia (Table 3.20). At the descriptive level (shared phenomenology) the only disagreement was that Freud considered anxiety mood as pathognomonic for anxiety states. At the theoretical level, however, Kraepelin assumed an organic factor of melancholia (endogenous depression), while a psychogenic factor was considered by Wimmer and Freud.

DSM-III-R continues the tendency initiated in DSM-III to make a dichotomy between a mild degree of depression and a moderate to marked (major) degree of depression. The theory behind the mild forms implicates a psychological genesis and suggests psychotherapy, while major depression is considered an 'organic' disorder for which drug therapy is the appropriate treatment. Both DSM-III-R and ICD-10 classify major depression as an endogenous depression. In contrast, the rating scale approach has considered the diagnostic part of depressive states as a spectrum itself, with endogenous and reactive depressions at either end of an aetiological dimension.

Table 3.20. Clinical recognition of melancholia

Symptoms and signs	Melancholia simplex (Kraepelin 1913/1921)	Depression simplex (Wimmer 1916)	Melancholia (Freud 1917)
Depressed mood	+	+	+
Lack of interest	+	+	+
Anxious mood	+	+	-
Introversion	+	+	+
Tiredness and pains	+	+	+
Guilt feelings	+	+	+
Motor retardation	+	+	+

+ , included; -, excluded.

References

Bech P. Modern classification of affective disorders. In: Lopez-Ibor JJ (ed). Depresiones y otros trastornos. Madrid: Universidad Complutense 1989, pp. 53–68.

Freud, S. Mourning and Melancholia (First published 1917). Collected papers (vol 4). New York, Basic Books, 1959, pp. 152–170.

Kraepelin E. Psychiatrie. Vol 3, Eight edition. Leipzig, Barth, 1913.

Kraepelin E. Manic-Depressive Insanity and Paranoia. Edinburgh, Livingstone, 1921.

Wimmer A. Psykogene sindssygdomsformer. In: Sct. Hans Mental Hospital 1816–1916, Jubilee Publication. Copenhagen, Gad, 1916 pp. 85–216.

Wing JK. The limits of standardization. In: Rakoff WM, Stancer HC, Kedward HD (eds). Psychiatic diagnosis. New York, Breunner-Mazel 1977.

3.4.2.1 The Depressive Syndrome

The Melancholia Scale (MES; Table 3.21; Bech and Rafaelsen 1980), as integrated in the Hamilton Depression Scale (HDS/MES), is discussed in Chapter 2. As in the case of manic states, the severity of the depressive syndrome can be graded according to minor, major and psychotic degrees. This approach has been adopted by DSM-III-R and ICD-10. Table 3.22 compares ICD-10, DSM-III-R and the MES. It should be emphasized that in this compendium 'melancholia' refers to depressive illness which is in accordance with Hamilton (1989) but not with DSM-III-R.

Table 3.23 presents the distribution of items in the depressive syndrome (melancholia) on the most frequently used scales for measuring the severity of melancholia. The components are in accordance with the content validity analysis of Thompson (1989). Motor symptoms include both general and verbal retardation, and vegative symptoms include tiredness, pain and sleep disturbances. Cognitive disability includes negative beliefs (guilt, suicidal thoughts) and concentration difficulties (intellectual retardation), and social disability includes decreased work ability, interests and introversion. As shown by Thompson (1989), the MES has an equal distribution of items on the various components of clinical depression. However, the HDS, the Zung (1974) scale, and the Montgomery-Åsberg (1979) scale have a rather high percentage of vegetative or somatic symptoms. Silverstone (1990) has shown that the Montgomery-Åsberg scale in its present form is not valid for measuring depression in medically ill patients. As seen in Table 3.23, the Montgomery-Åsberg scale and the Zung scale are rather similar. The construct validity of the HDS and the Montgomery-Åsberg scale has been found inadequate by Rasch analysis (Maier and Philipp 1985; Allerup 1986; Maier et al. 1988), but that the construct validity of the MES has been found adequate (Maier and Philipp 1985; Maier et al. 1988; Chambon et al. 1990). It has been found that the set of items covered by the combined HDS/MES includes those of the Montgomery-Åsberg Scale (Kørner et al. 1990). However, the insufficiency of the latter scale (MADRS) both concerning content validity and inter-rater reliability has recently been demonstrated (Lang et al. 1991), whereas the validity of the retardation symptom in MES has been confirmed (Schlegel et al. 1991).

Table 3.21. Psychometric descriptions: MES

Type	Symptom scale measuring severity of depression.
Content validity	Covers the essential components of the depressive syndrome (see Table 3.23).
Administration	Interview to be performed by skilled observers (goal-directed interview).
Time frame	Covers the previous 3 days.
Item selection	Second-generation scale derived from the Hamilton Depression Scale (Bech et al. 1981).
Item calibration	Likert scale definition. 0-4.
Content validity	Adequate by Rasch analysis (Maier et al. 1988; Chambon et al. 1990).
Sensitivity to change and discriminant validity	Superior to the Hamilton Depression Scale and the Montgomery-Asberg Scale (Maier et al. 1988; Maier 1990; Schlegel et al. 1989; Mendlewicz et al. 1990).
Inter-observer reliability	Adequate (Kørner et al. 1990; Bech et al. 1986).
Standardization	Total score: 0-5 = No depression 6-9 = Mild depression 10-14 = Less than major depression >14 = Major depression

Table 3.22. Depressive (melancholic) state items in ICD-10, DSM-III-R and MES

ICD-10	DSM-III-R	MES	
Depression	At least five of the following:	1 Work and interests	(0-4)
1 Lowered mood	(1) Depressed mood	2 Lowered mood	(0-4)
2 Loss of interests	(2) Markedly diminished interest	3 Sleep disturbances	(0-4)
3 Decreased energy	(3) Significant weight loss or weight gain	4 Anxiety	(0-4)
4 Decreased self-esteem		5 Emotional retardation	(0-4)
5 Guilt feelings	(4) Insomnia or hypersomnia	6 Intellectual retardation	(0-4)
6 Suicidal thoughts	(5) Psychomotor agitation or retardation	7 Tiredness and pains	(0-4)
7 Impaired concentration		8 Guilt feelings	(0-4)
8 Motor retardation or agitation	(6) Fatigue or loss of energy	9 Decreased verbal acitivity	(0-4)
9 Disturbed sleep	(7) Feelings of worthlessness or excessive guilt	10 Suicidal thoughts	(0-4)
10 Decreased or increased appetite	(8) Diminished ability to concentrate	11 Decreased motor activity	(0-4)
	(9) Recurrent thoughts of death		0-44
Mild depression: Research criteria: at least two of the first three items, and at least two of the following seven items.		No depression: 0-5 Mild depression: 6-9 Less than major depression: 10-14 Major depression (severe): 15-24 Major depression (extreme): 25 or more	
Moderate depression: Research criteria: as mild depression plus at least three of the ten items should be present to a marked degree, or a total of at least seven of the ten items should be mildly or moderately present.			
Severe depression: Research criteria: the first three items should be present, at least three of the following ten items, at least two of the symptoms should be severe, and others should be marked.			

Table 3.23. Item distributions of rating scales: components of depressive syndrome (melancholia)

Component	HDS	MES	Montgomery-Åsberg Depression Scale	Zung Depression Scale
Mood symptoms	8%	18%	30%	15%
Anxiety symptoms	16%	9%	10%	10%
Motor symptoms	12%	18%	0%	5%
Cognitive disability	28%	27%	30%	35%
Social disability	8%	9%	0%	0%
Vegetative symptoms	28%	18%	30%	35%
Number of items	17	11	10	20

The concept of depression in elderly patients has often been discussed, as most psychometric studies on depression have been carried out in patients aged between 18 and 70 years (Gerson et al. 1988). Marcos and Salamero (1990) using the HDS/MES in persons aged between 60 and 95 demonstrated with factor analysis that the first factor includes most of the MES items. They also draw attention, however, to the indices of anxiety and sleep. For comparing different antidepressant drugs it is customary to use Kielholz's classification system of anxiolytic and sedative subtypes of drugs (Kielholz 1986). Here, the HDS/MES is most useful; the items included here are listed in Table 3.24.

The standardization of the MES using total scores has been evaluated by Bech et al. (1983) and Loldrup et al. (1991). An MES score of 15 or higher is equivalent to major depression in DSM-III and score of 10–14 to 'less than major depression'. This refers to pretreatment scores for antidepressant treatment. In depressed patients scoring below 10 on the MES no difference was found between clomipramine treatment and placebo, while in those scoring 10 or higher clomipramine was superior to placebo (Loldrup et al. 1991). A MES score of 10 is equivalent to a HDS score of 13. Paykel (1990) found amitriptyline superior to placebo in depressed patients treated in general practice who had a HDS score of 13 or higher; below this score no difference was seen. These studies are examples of criterion-related standardization of scale scores (see Chap. 1). Hence, for scales with adequate construct validity (i.e. unidimensional scales where the total score is an adequate indicator of the construct) it is possible to make simple predictions of the relationship between the total score and an external variable (e.g. response to treatment). A score of 10 to 14 on MES or 13 to 17 on HDS equals probable major depression (Paykel 1990) or less than major depression (Loldrup et al. 1991).

Table 3.24. HDS/MES items on severity of melancholia

Depression index	*Sleep index*
1 Depressed mood[ab]	14 Insomnia: initial[a]
2 Work and interests[ab]	15 Insomnia: middle[a]
3 Emotional retardation[b]	16 Insomnia: late[a]
4 Intellectual retardation[b]	17 Insomnia: general[b]
5 Tiredness and pains[b]	
6 Guilt feelings[ab]	*Non-specific index*
7 Decreased verbal activity[b]	18 Gastro-intestinal[a]
8 Suicidal thoughts[ab]	19 Sexual interests[a]
9 Decreased motor activity[b]	20 Hypochondriasis[a]
10 Retardation: general[a]	21 Loss of insight[a]
	22 Loss of weight[a]
Anxiety index	23 Somatic symptoms: general[a]
11 Anxious mood[ab]	
12 Anxiety: somatic[a]	
13 Agitation[a]	

a, HDS item; b, MES item

DSM-III-R identifies a new type of depression classified by symptoms: seasonal depression. This type of depression can be considered as a melancholia arousal syndrome involving symptoms from mania and melancholia without reference to the respective dimensions. The MES has been adapted in a version to cover the DSM-III-R criteria for seasonal depression; this is the Melancholia Scale with Arousal Symptoms (MES-A). Its components include changes in appetite, weight, sleep, verbal and motor activities. The content validity of this scale has been indirectly confirmed by Rosenthal (1991). Thus, if these components are associated with lowered mood, decreased work and interests, anxiety, introversion, reduced concentration, tiredness or pain, and possibly with suicidal thoughts, a seasonal (winter) depression is present. Empirical studies on the construct validity of this scale are still lacking. It should, however, be emphasized that combined assessment of manic and depressive states often are recommended for the measurement of mixed or transion states, rapid – cycling states or other variations in mood, apart from seasonal depression. Here Goodwin and Jameson (1990) recommended the MES and MAS.

The scoring sheet for the MES-A is illustrated in "Appendix 3.5". That for the 11-item MES (i.e. without arousal symptoms) comprises "Appendix 3.6"; the 11 items here correspond to those numbered as follows in the MES-A: 2, 1, 8, 10–15, 19, 17. Instructions for scoring the 19 items of the MES-A are presented below.

1 Lowered Mood
This item covers both the verbal and the non-verbal communication of sadness, depression, despondency, helplessness and hopelessness.
0. Neutral mood.
1. It is doubtful whether the patient is more despondent than usual; for example, the patient seems vaguely more depressed than usual.
2. The patient is more clearly concerned with unpleasant experiences, although he still lacks helplessness and hopelessness.
3. The patient shows clear non-verbal signs of depression or is at times overpowered by helplessness or hopelessness.
4. The patient's remarks or non-verbal signs of despondency and helplessness dominate the interview, and the patient cannot be distracted.

2 Work and Interests
This item includes both work carried out and motivation. Note, however, that the physical manifestations of tiredness and fatigue are assessed in item 13 (tiredness and pain). Work covers the ordinary day-to-day activities.

A At First Rating
0. Normal work and activity.
1. The patient expresses inadequacy due to lack of motivation, or trouble in carrying out the usual work load, which he, however, manages to do without reduction.
2. More pronounced insufficiency due to lack of motivation, or trouble in carrying out the usual work activities. The patient has reduced work capacity, can-

not keep normal speed, copes with less on the job or at home; he may stay home some days or may try to leave early.
3. Difficulties in simple routine activities. If hospitalized score 3.
4. The patient is fully hospitalized and generally unoccupied, without participation in the ward activities (unable to do anything without help). If at home: unable to do anything without help.

B At Weekly Ratings
0. Normal work activity. a) The patient has resumed work at his normal activity level. b) The patient would have no trouble resuming normal work.
1. a) The patient is working but at reduced activity level, due either to lack of motivation or to difficulties in accomplishing his normal work. b) The patient is not working, and it is still doubtful whether he can resume his normal work without difficulties.
2. The patient is working but at a clearly reduced activity level, due either to episodes of non-attendance or to reduced working hours. b) The patient is still hospitalized or sick-listed, participates more than 3–4 h per day in ward (or home) activities, but is capable of resuming normal work only at a reduced level. If hospitalized the patient is able to change from full hospitalization to day-patient status.
3. Difficulties in starting simple routine activities which are carried out with great efforts.
4. The patient is still fully hospitalized and generally unable to participate in ward activities (unable to do anything without help). If at home: unable to do anything without help.

3 Appetite: Decreased
0. No decrease in appetite.
1. Eating somewhat less than usual.
2. Eating much less than usual.

4 Appetite: Increased
0. No increase in appetite.
1. Eating somewhat more than usual.
2. Eating much more than usual.

5 Weight: Decreased
Try to obtain objective information; if such is not available, be conservative in estimation. (Evaluation 'A' covers the whole current period of illness.)

A At First Rating
0. No weight loss.
1. 1–2.5 kg weight loss.
2. Weight loss of 3 kg or more.

B At Weekly Ratings
0. No weight loss.
1. Weight loss of 0.5 kg per week.
2. Weight loss of 1 kg or more per week.

6 Weight: Increased
(Evaluation 'A' covers the whole current period of illness.)

A At First Rating
0. No weight gain.
1. 1–2.5 kg weight gain.
2. Weight gain of 3 kg or more.

B At Weekly Ratings
0   No weight gain.
1. Weight gain of 0.5 kg per week.
2. Weight gain of 1 kg or more per week.

7 Carbohydrate Craving
0. No change in food preferences.
1. Eating more carbohydrates.
2. Eating much more carbohydrates than before.

8 Sleep: Insomnia
This item covers only the patient's subjective experience of the duration of sleep (hours of sleep per 24-h period) and sleep depth (superficial and interrupted sleep versus deep and constant sleep). The rating is based on the 3 preceding nights, irrespective of the administration of hypnotics or sedatives.
0. Usual sleep duration and sleep depth.
1. Sleep duration is doubtfully or slightly reduced (e.g. due to difficulties in falling asleep, but no change in sleep depth).
2. Sleep depth is now also reduced, sleep being more superficial. Sleep as a whole is somewhat disturbed. The total duration of sleep per 24-h period is still more than 50% of the habitual duration.
3. Sleep duration as well as sleep depth is markedly changed. The broken sleep periods total only a few hours per 24-h period.
4. It is difficult to ascertain sleep duration as sleep depth is so shallow that the patient speaks of short periods of slumber or dozing, but no real sleep.

9 Sleep: Hypersomnia
Compare sleep length to euthymic and *not* to hypomanic sleep lengths; if this cannot be established, use 8 h.
0   No increase in sleep length.
1. At least 1 h increase of sleep length.
2. At least 2 h increase of sleep length.

3. At least 3 h increase of sleep length.
4. At least 4 h increase of sleep length.

10 Anxiety

This item includes tenseness, irritability, worry, insecurity, fear and apprehension approaching overpowering dread. It may often be difficult to distinguish between the patient's experience of anxiety ('psychic' or 'central' anxiety phenomena) and the physiological ('peripheral') anxiety manifestations which can be observed, e.g. hand tremor and sweating. Most important is the patient's report of worry, insecurity, uncertainty, experiences of dread, i.e. the psychic ('central') anxiety.

0. The patient is neither more nor less insecure or irritable than usual.
1. It is doubtful whether the patient is more insecure or irritable than usual.
2. The patient seems more clearly in a state of anxiety, apprehension, or irritability which he might find difficult to control. However, this has no influence on his daily life because the worrying is still about minor matters.
3. The anxiety or insecurity is at times more difficult to control because the worrying is about major injuries or harms which might occur in the future, for example, the anxiety may be experienced as panic, i.e. overpowering dread. It occasionally interferes with the patient's daily life.
4. The feeling of dread is present so often that it markedly interferes with the patient's daily life.

11 Introversion

This item covers the reduced interest and emotional contact with other human beings. The reduced wish or ability to communicate one's own feelings and opinions and to share joy and sorrow is usually experienced as alien and painful by the patient.

0. The patient is emotionally neither more nor less interested in contact with other persons.
1. It is doubtful whether the patient is emotionally more introverted than usual.
2. The patient clearly has less wish or ability than usual to be together with new or distant acquaintances, interacting less with other people in social situations.
3. The patient isolates himself to a certain degree, interacting less with friends or family.
4. Marked withdrawal even from friends or family.

12 Concentration Difficulties

This item covers difficulties in concentrating, making decisions about everyday matters, and with memory, i.e. intellectual impairment.

0. The patient has neither more nor less difficulty in concentrating and/or remembering than usual.
1. It is doubtful whether the patient has difficulties in concentrating and/or remembering.
2. Even with a major effort it is difficult for the patient to concentrate on his work, but it is still without influence on the patient's daily life.

3. More pronounced difficulties with concentration, memory, or decision making. For example, he has difficulty reading a newspaper article or watching a television programme to the end. (Score '3' as long as the loss of concentration or poor memory does not clearly influence the interview.)
4. During the interview the patient shows difficulty concentrating or remembering, or reaches decisions only with considerable delay.

13 Tiredness and Pains

This item includes weakness, faintness, tiredness, fullness and soreness verging on real pain more or less diffusely located in muscles or inner organs. Muscular fatigue is normally located in the extremities. The patient may give this as the reason for difficulties at work, as he has a feeling of tiredness or heaviness in arms and legs. Muscle pains are often located in the back, neck or shoulders and perceived as tension or headache. The feeling of fullness or heaviness increasing to real sensation of pain is often broadly located as 'chest discomfort' (different from heart pain), abdominal pain, head pain (muscular headache). It is often difficult to discern between 'psychic' and 'physical' pain. Special notice should be taken of vague 'psychic' pain.

0. The patient is neither more nor less tired or troubled by bodily discomfort than usual.
1. Doubtful or very vague feelings of muscular fatigue or other somatic discomfort.
2. Feelings of muscular fatigue or somatic discomfort are more pronounced. Painful sensations sometimes occur, e.g. muscular headache, but they are still without influence on the patient's daily life.
3. Muscular fatigue or diffuse pain is clearly present, which occasionally interferes with the patient's daily life.
4. Muscular fatigue and diffuse pain constantly cause the patient severe distress, markedly interfering with his daily life.

14 Guilt Feelings

This item covers lowered self-esteem with guilt feelings.

0. No self-depreciation or guilt feelings.
1. Doubtful whether guilt feelings are present because the patient is concerned only with the fact that during the current illness he has been a burden to family or colleagues due to reduced work capacity.
2. Self-depreciation or guilt feelings are more clearly present because the patient is concerned with incidents in the past prior to the current episode. For example, the patient reproaches himself for small omissions or failures, for not having done his duty, or for having harmed others.
3. The patient suffers from more severe guilt feelings. He may report feeling that the current suffering is some sort of punishment. (Score '3' as long as the patient intellectually can see that this view is unfounded.)
4. The guilt feelings are firmly maintained and resist any counter-argument, so that they have become paranoid ideas.

15 Verbal Activity: Decreased
This item includes changes in flow of speech and the capacity to verbalize thoughts and emotions.
0. Normal verbal activity.
1. Doubtfully reduced verbal expression or languor in conversation.
2. More pronounced languor in conversation, e.g. a trend to longer intermissions.
3. The interview is clearly prolonged due to long pauses and brief responses.
4. The interview can be completed only with marked difficulty.

16 Verbal Activity: Increased
0. Normal verbal activity.
1. Somewhat talkative.
2. Very talkative, no spontaneous intervals in the conversation.
3. Difficult to interrupt.
4. Impossible to interrupt, completely dominates the conversation.

17 Motor Activity: Decreased
0. Normal motor activity, adequate facial expression.
1. Doubtfully decreased motor activity (e.g. facial expression slightly or doubtfully retarded.
2. Clearer motor retardation (e.g. reduced gestures, slow pace).
3. All movements very slow.
4. Motor retardation approaching or including stupor.

18 Motor Activity: Increased
0. Normal motor activity, adequate facial expression.
1. Slightly or doubtfully increased motor activity, e.g. lively facial expression.
2. Moderately increased motor activity, e.g. lively gestures.
3. Clearly excessive motor activity, in motion most of the time; rises once or several times during the interview.
4. Constantly active, restlessly energetic. Even if urged, the patient cannot sit still.

19 Suicidal Thoughts
0. No suicidal thoughts.
1. The patient feels that life is not worthwhile, but he expresses no wish to die.
2. The patient wishes to die but has no plans of taking his own life.
3. It is probable that the patient has contemplated committing suicide.
4. If the patient is in the ward, he is under special observation due to suicide risk.

References

Allerup P. Rasch model analysis of a rating scale. Copenhagen, Danish Inst Educ Res, 1986.

Bech P. Psychometric developments of the Hamilton Scales. In: Bech P, Coppen A (eds). The Hamilton Scales. Berlin, Springer 1990 pp. 72–79.

Bech P. Symptoms and assessment of depression. In: Paykel ES (ed). Handbook of affective disorders. Edinburgh, Churchill Livingstone, 1992, pp. 3–13.

Bech P, Rafaelsen OJ. The use of rating scales exemplified by a comparison of the Hamilton and the Bech-Rafaelsen Melancholia Scale. Acta Psychiat Scand 1980; 62 (suppl 285): 128–131.

Bech P, Allerup P, Gram LF, Reisby N, Rosenberg R, Jacobsen O, Nagy A. The Hamilton Depression Scale. Evaluation of objectivity using logistic models. Acta Psychiat Scand 1981; 63: 290–299.

Bech P, Gastpar M, Mendlewicz J. The role of training courses in multicenter trials: WHO experiences. In: Chagas C, Josiassen R, Bech P, Gjerris A, Andersen J. The Melancholia Scale and the Newcastle Scales. Br J Psychiat 1983; 143: 58–63.

Bridger W, Weis K, Stoff D, Simpson G (eds). Biological Psychiatry. Amsterdam, Elsevier, 1986; 7: 1510–1512.

Chambon O, Cialdella P, Kiss L, Poncet F. Study on the unidimensionality of the Bech Rafaelsen Melancholia Scale using Rasch analysis in a French sample of major depressive disorders. Pharmacopsychiat 1990; 23: 243–245.

Freud S. Mourning and melancholia. (First published 1917). Collected Papers Vol 4. New York, Basic Books, 1959, pp. 152–170.

Gerson SC, Plotkin DA, Jarvik LF. Antidepressant drug studies, 1964 to 1986: empirical evidence for aging patients. J Clin Psychopharmacol 1988; 8: 311–322.

Goodwin FK, Jamison KR. Manic-Depressive Illness. New York, Oxford University Press 1990.

Hamilton M. A rating scale for depression. J Neurol Neurosurg Psychiat 1960; 23: 56–62.

Hamilton M. Development of a rating scale for primary depressive illness. Br J Soc Clin Psychol 1967; 6: 278–296.

Hamilton M. Frequency of symptoms in melancholia (depressive illness). Br J Psychiat 1989; 154: 201–206.

Kielholz P. Latest findings in the treatment of depression. In: Hippius H, Klerman GL, Matussech N (eds). New results in depression results. Berlin, Springer, 1986, pp. 99–111.

Kørner A, Nielsen BM, Eschen F, Møller-Madsen S, Stender A, Christensen EM, Aggernæs H, Kastrup M, Larsen JK. Quantifying depressive symptomatology: interrater reliability and inter-item correlation. J Aff Dis 1990; 20: 143–149.

Lang F, Pellet J, Postic Y. Widlöcher's Depression Retardation Scale and Montgomery Åsberg's Depression Rating Scale. An inter-rater study. Eur Psychiat 1991; 6: 47–52.

Loldrup D, Hansen HJ, Langemark M, Olesen J, Kastrup M, Elsborg L, Bech P. Depression as predictive factor in idiopathic pain disorder: psychometric and therapeutical perspectives. Eur Psychiat 1991; 6:119–125.

Maier W, Philipp M. Comparative analysis of observer depression scales. Acta Psychiat Scand 1985; 72: 239–245.

Maier W, Philipp M, Heuser I, Schlegel S, Buller R, Wentzel H. Improving depression severity assessment. Reliability, internal validity and sensitivity to change of three observer depression scales. J Psychiat Res 1988; 22: 3–12.

Maier W. The Hamilton Depression Scale and its alternatives: a comparison of their reliability and validity. In: Bech P, Coppen A (eds). The Hamilton Scales. Berlin, Springer, 1990, pp. 64–71.

Marcos T, Salamero M. Factor study of the Hamilton Rating Scale for Depression and Bech's Melancholia Scale (MES). Acta Psychiat Scand 1990; 82: 178–181.

Mendlewicz J, Kerhofs M. Sleep EEG in depressive illness. a WHO collaborative study. In: Stefanis CN, Soldatos CR, Rabavi–las AD (eds). Psychiatry: A World Perspective. Amsterdam, Elsevier, 1990; 2: 350–357.

Montgomery S, Åsberg M. A new depression scale designed to be sensitive to change. Br J Psychiat 1979; 134: 382–389.

Rosenthal N. Winter blues. Seasonal Affective Disorder. Glasgow, Fontana/Collins, 1991.

Paykel ES. Use of the Hamilton Depression Scale in general practice. In Bech P, Coppen A (eds). The Hamilton Scales. Heidelberg, Springer, 1990 pp. 40–47.

Schlegel S, Maier W, Philipp M, Aldenhoff JB, Heuser I, Kretzschmar K, Benkert O. Computed tomography in depression: Association between ventricular size and psychopathology. Psychiat Res 1989; 29: 221–230.

Schlegel S, Nieber D, Hermann C, Bakanski E. Latencies of the P 300 component of auditory event-related potential in depression are related to the Bech-Rafaelsen Melancholia Scale but not to the Hamilton Rating Scale for Depression. Acta Psychiat Scand 1991; 83: 484–440.

Silverstone PH. Changes in depression scores following life-threatening illness. J Psychosom Res 1990; 34: 659–663.

Thompson C. The instruments of psychiatric research. Chichester, J. Wiley, 1989.

Zung WWK. The measurement of affects: depression and anxiety. In: Pichot P (ed). Psychological measurements in psychopathology. Basel, Karger, 1974, pp. 170–188.

3.4.2.2 The Diagnosis of Depression

The problem with DSM-III in differentiating cases of major depression as endogenous (biological) or non-endogenous (stress-related) was due to the nearly identical descriptions of major depression (core symptoms) and endogenous depression (discriminating items).

The classical work on endogenous depression was Kraepelin's study (1921), and that on reactive/neurotic depression were the studies of Wimmer (1916) and Freud (1917). In this context it should be emphasized that Wimmer (1916) differentiated between severity (including psychotic degrees) and diagnosis (e.g. psychogenic). The many attempts at operational diagnosis along the continuum of endogenous–reactive/neurotic depression have been reviewed by Ban (1989); a total of 198 different subtypes have been suggested. The term 'endogenous' depression has, for instance, been used to describe 'psychotic', 'primary', 'bipolar', 'vital', 'pure', 'endogenomorphic', and 'typical' depression; 'reactive' depression to describe 'secondary', 'participatory', and 'atypical' depression; and 'neurotic' depression to describe 'chronic', 'hypochondriacal', and 'atypical' depression.

The first rating scale to integrate features other than symptoms into a total score for the spectrum of endogenous–neurotic depression was the Newcastle Depression Diagnostic Scale of Carney et al. (1965). This scale equates endogenous and psychotic depression. The HDS, on the other hand, considers psychotic items as indicators of severity, not of diagnosis: "a schizophrenic patient who has delusions is not necessarily worse than one who has none, but a depressive patient who has is much worse" (Hamilton 1960). Whereas the 1965 version of the Newcastle Depression Diagnostic Scale (1965) differentiates between endogenous and neurotic depression, the 1971 version (Gurney 1971; Bech et al. 1980) distinguishes endogenous from reactive depression. The construct validity of these two Newcastle scales has been examined by factor analysis and discriminant function analysis, and these methods have been used to assign the various items positive or

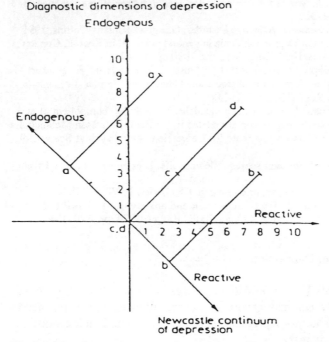

Fig. 3.2. The diagnostic diagram for depression. (Bech et al. 1988)

negative diagnostic weights. This allows the information obtained in the scales to be reduced to a single diagnostic dimension, with endogenous depression at one pole and neurotic or reactive depression at the other (Fig. 3.2).

The predictive value of the Newcastle scales concerning response to treatment has been investigated. The 1965 version was found to predict the response to electroconvulsive therapy and the 1971 version to describe the therapeutic range of plasma levels of antidepressants (Bech 1981). The Newcastle scales original lacked detailed item definitions; this compendium includes those provided by Bech et al. (1983). Scores on the Newcastle scales have been used as a validation criterion by Carney et al. (1965) and Gurney (1971). This presumes a boundary between endogenous and reactive depression manifesting itself in a 'point of rarity' around the middle of the score range. In fact, a bimodal distribution in the 1965 Newcastle scale scores was found by Carney et al., with the point of rarity of scores around +6; a score of +6 or higher indicates endogenous depression and one below +6 neurotic depression. For the 1971 Newcastle scale the point of rarity was a score of –20; a score of –20 or lower indicates endogenous depression and one above –20 reactive depression. There has, however, been an extensive debate in the literature about the 'true' meaning of Newcastle scales scores. Kendall (1970), for instance, was not able to replicate the Newcastle results. This debate has recently been summarized by Carney (1986).

Table 3.25. Psychometric description: DMS

Type	Diagnostic scale, differentiating depression into endogenous and reactive type.
Content validity	Covers the essential components of endogenous and reactive depression related to the current episode (see Table 3.27).
Administration	Interview to be performed by a skilled observer (goal-directed interview).
Time frame	The current episode.
Item selection	The Newcastle scale.
Item calibration	Likert scale definition, 0-2.
Construct validity	Adequate by Rasch analysis (Bech et al. 1988).
Inter-observer reliability	Adequate (Bech et al. 1988; Kørner et al. 1990).

Standardization	Pure endogenous depression:
	  Endogenous score: 5 or more
	  Reactive score: less than 5
	Pure reactive depression:
	  Endogenous score: less than 5
	  Reactive score: 5 or more
	Mixed endogenous/reactive depression:
	  Endogenous score: 5 or more
	  Reactive score: 5 or more
	Uncertain diagnosis:
	  Endogenous score: less than 5
	  Reactive score: less than 5

The most impressive argument against using the score on a single spectrum measuring two different dimensions was put forth by Eysenck (1970), who suggested studying the construct validity of the individual dimensions (endogenous and reactive depression) as indicated in Fig. 3.2. This suggestion was followed by Bech et al. (1988) in constructing the Diagnostic Melancholia Scale (DMS; Table 3.25) on the basis of the two Newcastle scales. The five items of the DMS measuring endogenous depression are three biological symptoms (quality of depression, early awakening, weight loss) and the biological course of symptoms (diurnal variation and day-to-day persistence). The five items of the DMS measuring reactive/neurotic depression are three reactive items (psychosocial stressors, reactivity of symptoms and somatic, i.e. stress, anxiety) and two neurotic items (personality deviation and duration of symptoms). It has been shown (Bech et al. 1988) that both sets of items fulfil the Rasch model; however, no simple mathematical relationship was found between the total score on endogenous items and the total score on reactive/neurotic items. It was found (Bech et al. 1988) that 32% of patients with major depression had high scores on both dimensions, indicating that patients of Eysenck's type d (Fig. 3.2) do exist. This is also in accord with studies from general practice (Watts 1966). In addition it has been found that patients with high endogenous scores but low reactive scores (pure endogenous depression) show the clearest response to antidepressant treatment (Bech et al. 1988).

Table 3.26 compares the DSM-III-R concept of endogenous depression (melancholia) and the DMS. Compared to the DSM-III concept of endogenous depres-

Table 3.26. Melancholia items in DSM-III-R and DMS

DSM-III-R	DMS	
Endogenous melancholia:	*Endogenous dimension:*	
At least five of the following items:	E1 Quality of depression	(0-2)
(1) Loss of interests	E2 Early awakening	(0-2)
(2) Lack of reactivity	E3 Weight loss	(0-2)
(3) Depression regularly worse morning	E4 Diurnal variation, morning worse	(0-2)
(4) Early morning awakening	E5 Persistence of clinical picture	(0-2)
(5) Psychomotor retardation or agitation		0-10
(6) Significant anorexia or weight loss	*Reactive dimension:*	
(7) No significant personality disturbances	R1 Psychological stressors	(0-2)
(8) One or more previous episodes of major depression	R2 Reactivity	(0-2)
	R3 Somatic anxiety	(0-2)
(9) Previous good response to antidepressants, ECT or lithium	R4 Duration of episode	(0-2)
	R5 Character neurosis	(0-2)
		0-10

Table 3.27. Item distributions of rating scales: components of depression diagnosis

Component	Newcastle scale (1965)	Newcastle scale (1971)	DMS
Psychosocial stressors	10%	10%	10%
Personality	10%	0%	10%
Onset, duration, persistence of current episode	0%	30%	10%
Previous episodes	10%	0%	0%
Diurnal variation of symptoms	0%	10%	10%
Reactivity of symptoms	0%	10%	10%
Biological symptoms (quality, early awakening, weight loss)	20%	10%	30%
Psychological symptoms (anxiety, phobias, aggression)	20%	10%	10%
Severity symptoms (psychotic, motor, guilt)	30%	20%	0%
Number of items	10	10	2x5

sion the DSM-III-R criteria include fewer severity items (Zimmermann et al. 1989) although there is still an overlap (e.g. psychomotor retardation/agitation and loss of interest). Table 3.27 compares the DSM with both versions of the New-castle Scale in terms of the relative distribution of items on the various com-po-nents. The inter-observer reliability of the Newcastle scales and of the DMS has been shown to be adequate (Bech 1981; Bech et al. 1988; Kørner et al. 1990).

The Newcastle scales as well as the DMS differentiate depressive states of less than 2 years of duration. However, both DSM-III-R and ICD-10 include a diag-nostic subcategory, persistent mood disorder (cyclothymia and dysthymia). The severity of these states are hypomania (cyclothymia) or less than major depression (dysthymia). It should be emphasized that cyclothymia includes both mild depres-sion and hypomania. The severity of these states is, of course, measured by the MAS and the MES, respectively. Dysthymia is equivalent to neurotic depression. It is very interesting that reactive states (stress-related disorders) are considered as anxiety states in DSM-III-R and ICD-10. In this context ICD-10 has a more com-prehensive approach than DSM-III-R. The relationship between depression and anxiety is described further in the following section.

As discussed in Chapter 1, there is no close relationship between severity scales (e.g. MES) and diagnostic scales (e.g. DMS), just as there is no structural relationship between fever and its causative agents. Aetiologically, depression can be considered either as a biological disorder (endogenous or primary depression) or as a post-traumatic stress disorder (reactive or secondary depression). The DMS takes both diagnoses into account and includes no items on the severity of depression. The MES, on the other hand, includes the target symptoms of depres-sion and therefore covers both diagnostic types of depression.

1965 Newcastle Depression Diagnostic Scale

The scoring sheet for the 1965 version of the Newcastle scale is illustrated in "Appendix 3.7". Instructions for scoring its ten items are presented below.

1 Deviant Personality
The patient's personality is considered deviant if there is information on earlier nervous breakdowns, severe neurotic symptoms or important problems in social adjustment.
0. Adequate personality
1. In doubt.
2. Deviant personality clearly present.

2 Psychological Stresses
Psychological stresses include any situation or event considered by the inter-viewer to be stressful to the patient. The situation or event must have appeared within the past 6 months and may or may not still be present and maintaining the episode of illness. The stressful situation may, for example, be worries concerning one's health, worries concerning the health of near relatives or friends, a death,

international conflicts, worries over job or financial situation. The same event may, of course, be a very different experience for the different persons involved, and the patient's subjective experiences and feelings must be taken into consideration, but the interviewer's evaluation is decisive.

0. Psychological stresses have not been present.
1. In doubt.
2. Psychological stresses have been or are present.

3 Quality of Depression

The decisive factor is whether the patient describes his present depressive state as qualitatively different from 'ordinary' sadness as experienced in adverse situations, e.g. death within the family or circle of friends.

0. The present depressive condition by and large is experienced similarly to ordinary situational sadness.
1. The interviewer or patient questions the qualitative difference.
2. Evident/positive.

4 Weight Loss

0. No weight loss related to present episode.
1. Less pronounced weight loss.
2. The patient indicates a weight loss of 3 kg or more related to the present episode or 0.5 kg or more per week during the past 3 weeks.

5 Previous Depressive Episodes

A previous depressive episode is understood as a depression of at least 2 weeks' duration which stands out clearly in the patient's past history. The lowering of mood must have remained constant during the episode. The patient should have asked for or have been referred to treatment or assistance during the episode or demonstrated impairment in family relations or other social functions.

0. The patient has had no clearly defined depressive episodes.
1. In doubt concerning the typology of earlier episodes.
2. One estimates that the former depressive episode was of endogenous type.

6 Motor Activity

This includes both motor retardation and motor agitation. The item includes more than the mere subjective feeling of being slow or restless. The interviewer may tend to concentrate on the patient's appearance during the interview, but if the interviewer obtains sufficient information on the patient's condition during the present episode, this information must be included in the final evaluation.

0. Neither retardation nor agitation has been or is present.
1. In doubt.
2. The patient clearly has marked changes in motor activity.

7 Anxiety

The patient's behaviour during the interview is decisive at this item.

0. The patient does not appear to be anxious.
1. In doubt.
2. The patient during the interview is clearly anxious (tense, sweating, nervous, etc.).

8 Nihilistic Delusions

This denotes the experience of need, destruction and misery. It includes (a) somatic nihilism: the assumption that the body no longer exists (e.g. the stomach and/or intestines have withered away); (b) economic/financial nihilism: the assumption that he or the whole family will end in misery and disaster.

0. The experience is not present.
1. The patient's views may be modified.
2. The assumption is vigorously maintained even after it has been tried to correct the assumption.

9 Accusations of Others

The patient is easily angered and blames others for things going wrong, for instance, that others are responsible for the patient's present problems.

0. The experience is not present.
1. In doubt.
2. This is clearly expressed.

10 Feelings of Guilt

The patient is tormented by feelings of guilt, for example, the patient expresses the view that the present suffering is a form of punishment due to or caused by former misdeeds.

0. The experience is not present.
1. It is doubtful whether the patient harbours feelings of guilt.
2. The patient stresses the events prior to the present episode as misdeeds.

1971 Newcastle Depressive Diagnostic Scale

The scoring sheet for the 1971 version of the Newcastle scale is illustrated in "Appendix 3.8". Instructions for scoring its ten items are presented below.

1 Sudden Onset

Sudden onset of the present episode means a development within days or at most a week. By development of symptoms is understood primarily the change from neutral modd but it also encompasses a clear exacerbation from previous doubtful or very mild symptoms. Not to be included is a deterioration in the course of a depressive episode, well described by the patient, ffor example, when the patient indicates the abrupt start of the present episode (within a week), but with further acceleration of the depression, sudden onset should still be scored.

0. More protracted development.
1. Symptoms developing within 1-2 weeks.
2. Sudden onset.

2 Duration of Present Episode

Duration of the present episode is noted between the time when the patient first experienced a clear change from normal life and mood and the time of investigation. If the disease is phasic, the present episode must be preceded by a clear (non-disease) interval of at least 3 months.

0. The episode has lasted more than 2 years.
1. The episode has lasted between 1 and 2 years.
2. The episode has lasted between 3 months and 1 year.
3. The episode has lasted less than 3 months.

3 Psychological Stressors

By psychological stresses are understood any situation or event which the interviewer considers stressful to the patient. The situation or event must have appeared within the past 6 months and may or may not still be present and maintaining the episode of illness. The stressful situation may, for example, be worries concerning one's health, worries concerning the health of near relatives or friends, a death, interpersonal conflicts, worries over job or financial situation. The same event may, of course, be a very different experience for the different persons involved, and the patient's subjective experiences and feelings must be taken into consideration, but the interviewer's evaluation is decisive.

0. Psychological stresses have not been present.
1. In doubt.
2. Psychological stresses have been or are present.

4 Phobias

A phobia is a state of anxiety elicited when the patient finds himself in specific situations or circumstances. Evasion of such situations, on the other hand, protects the patient against acute anxiety and thus provides a relative amelioration. Simple phobias such as fear of high places or of spiders or mice are quite common. Such everyday phobias should not be scored except when accompanied by pronounced neurotic phobias, e.g. of open spaces, of crossing busy streets, of travelling by bus or train, or of air travel. At the assessment it is unimportant whether the present episode has been characterized by an excess of neurotic phobia or not.

0. The patient has had no neurotic phobia.
1. In doubt.
2. It is evident that the patient also outside the depressive episodes has had neurotic phobia.

5 Persistence of Depression

The clinical picture has in general been constant during the present episode, and thus there has been no change between 'good' and 'bad' days or weeks.

0. There have been clear fluctuations.
1. It is doubtful whether persistence has characterized the present episode.
2. The present state (apart from possible diurnal variation) has been quite con-
    stant.

6 Reactivity of Symptoms

Reactivity means that the depression waxes and wanes in relation to circumstances; for example, the patient feels less depressed when something pleasant or
positive appears or takes place. The patient thus retains the capacity to react positively when something positive takes place or for a while to feel less depressed in
good company.
0. There is no reactivity, and the depression is thus autonomous.
1. Reactivity is only very transient.
2. The interviewer is convinced that reactivity is present.

7 Diurnal Variation

Diurnal variation means that the patient during the present episode usually feels
most depressed in the morning, and that the depression diminishes in intensity
during the day. The criterion for diurnal variation is not fulfilled if the patient only
reports a brief amelioration just before going to bed.
0. There is ni diurnal rhythmicity.
1. It is doubtful whether a truly autonomous diurnal variation is present.
2. The interviewer is convinced that the patient during the present episode has
    shown diurnal rhythmicity in the severity of his symptoms. (Take habitual
    diurnal variation and possible reactivity into account.)

8 Early Awakening

This refers to the patient waking up at least 1 h earlier than usual. It should be
taken into consideration whether earlier awakening has been a persistent feature
during the present episode. (Disregard whether the patient has been receiving
sedative/hypnotic medication.)
0. Early awakening has not been present.
1. In doubt, or the patient has had this symptom only during the past few days.
2. The interviewer is convinced that the patient during the present episode as a
    persistent feature has woken up at least 1 h too early.

9 Motor Inhibition

Motor inhibition covers more than the subjective feeling of being slower in
movements than usually. The interviewer must judge solely from the interview
situation.
0. With no motor inhibition.
1. In doubt.
2. There is information available that the patient has had persistent motor inhibi-
    tion; during the interview is clearly (motorically) inhibited.

10 Delusions
This comprises ideas related to self-esteem, guilt feelings, ideas of hypocondriac and nihilistic nature, and even paranoid ideas.
0. There are no delusional ideas.
1. The patient is less entrenched in his ideas.
2. Such ideas (of either type) are maintained vigorously even after it has been tried to correct them.

Diagnostic Melancholia Scale

The scoring sheet for the DMS is illustrated in "Appendix 3.9". Instructions for scoring its ten items are presented below.

1 Quality of Depression
This item includes the patient's experience of the current depressive episode as qualitatively distinct from normal despondency when under adversity or distress, e.g. the death of a loved one. The patient should, therefore, be asked for qualitative feelings different from the range of his ordinary affective responses to adversity. It is a difficult item to assess, especially, of course, if the patient denies ever having had severe adversities. It is of importance to ensure whether prior to the current depressive episode, i.e. in the habitual state, the patient has edxperienced the same kind of symptoms as now, or whether the current symptoms are more of a 'foreign body', a distinct quality of depression.
0. The current depressive episode has been described as 'ordinary' sadness as experienced in adverse situations such as death in the family or circle of friends.
1. The interviewer or the patient is in doubt whether this experience is present.
2. The patient cannot identify himself with the current depressive syndrome, which therefore is conceived as qualitatively distinct from feelings of grief.

2 Early Awakening
Early awakening refers to the patient waking up at least 1 h earlier than usual. The assessment of this item should include the general ('average') sleep pattern during the current depressive episode, and not only the previous days. (Disregard whether the patient has been using sedative/hypnotic medication.)
0. Early awakening has not been present.
1. In doubt, or the patient has had this symptom only during the past few days.
2. The interviewer is convinced that during the present episode as a persistent feature the patient has woken up at least 1 h too early.

3 Weight Loss
0. No weight loss related to the current episode.
1. A less pronounced weight loss.
2. The patient indicates a weight loss of 3 kg or more related to the current depressive episode, or 0.5 kg or more per week during the past 3 weeks.

4 Diurnal Variation

Diurnal variation means that during the current depressive episode the patient has generally ('on average') been most depressed in the morning hours, and that the severity diminishes during the day. The criterion for diurnal variation is not fulfilled if the patient indicates only a brief amelioration just before going to bed.

0. There is no diurnal rhythmicity.
1. When it is doubtful whether a truly autonomous diurnal variation is present.
2. The interviewer is convinced that during the current episode the patient has diurnal rhythmicity in the severity of his symptoms. (Take habitual diurnal variation and possible reactivity into account.)

5 Persistence of Clinical Picture

This item refers to the clinical picture, the depressive syndrome, being in general constant during the current episode, apart from minor day-to-day variations and/or diurnal variation.

0. There have been clear fluctuations.
1. It is doubtful whether persistence has characterized the current episode.
2. There has been no significant change (fluctuations between 'good' and 'bad' days or weeks).

6 Psychological Stressors

Psychological stressors are any situation or event which is considered by the interviewer to have been a significant contributor to the development of the current depressive episode. The stressors must have appeared within the 6 months prior to this episode and may or may not still be present and maintaining the depressive syndrome. The stressors may be worries concerning one's health, worries concerning the health of near relatives or friends, a death of a loved one, interpersonal conflicts in the family or at work, or financial problems. The same stressor may, of course, be a very different experience for different patients, and the patient's subjective experiences and feelings must be taken into consideration. However, the interviewer's evaluation is decisive.

0. Psychological stressors have not been present.
1. The interviewer is in doubt.
2. Psychological stressors have been or are still present.

7 Reactivity of Symptoms

Reactivity means that the severity of the depressive symptoms waxes and wanes in relation to circumstances; for example, the patient feels less depressed when something pleasant or positive appears or takes place. The patient thus retains the capacity to react positively when something positive takes place or to feel less depressed for a while in good company.

0. There is lack of reactivity to usually pleasurable stimuli, that is, the patient does not feel much better, even temporarily, when something good happens.
1. Reactivity is only transient.
2. The interviewer is convinced that reactivity is present.

8 Somatic Anxiety

Somatic anxiety should be assessed independently of psychic anxiety. Somatic anxiety includes all physiological concomitants of anxiety: motor tension and autonomic hyperactivity (especially palpitations, nausea or vomiting, sweating, and dizziness). It is often difficult to distinguish between somatic anxiety and psychomotor agitation, but in this connection it is immaterial whether agitation is perhaps included in the score. It is also immaterial to distinguish between attacks of somatic anxiety and generalized anxiety. It is, however, decisive to assess whether during the current depressive episode the patient has experienced somatic anxiety, and the past week should be stressed most.

0. The patient has not experienced somatic anxiety.
1. In doubt.
2. During the past week and/or the interview the patient has been clearly anxious (experienced motor tension, palpitations, nausea, sweating, etc.).

9 Duration of Current Episode

Duration of the current episode is noted between the time when the patient first experienced a clear change from normal life or mood and the time of investigation. If the illness is phasic, the current episode must have been preceded by a clear illness-free interval of at least 3 months.

0. The episode has lasted less than 6 months.
1. The episode has lasted between 6 and 12 months.
2. The episode has lasted 1 year or more.

10 Character Neurosis

Character neurotic features may have emerged before the current episode from the patient's choice of spouse or life partner (a peaceful or considerate partner rather than a dominating or self-assertive partner) because character neurotics avoid persons who provoke them. During the current episode the neurotic features may have manifested themselves in the way in which the patient presents his complaints, namely by striving for an emotional secondary gain. At the interview this striving can be observed by the patient's cooperation on an attention-demanding dimension.

0. The patient has no sign of character neurosis.
1. It is uncertain whether the patient has a character neurosis.
2. The patient has shown clear signs of character neurosis.

References

Ban TA. Composite diagnostic evaluation of depressive disorders. Nashvill, CODE Distributers IUNCP, 1989.

Bech P, Gram LF, Reisby N, Rafaelsen OJ. The WHO Depression Scale: Relationship to the Newcastle scales. Acta Psychiat Scand 1980; 62: 140–153.

Bech P. Rating scales for affective disorders: their validity and consistency. Acta Psychiat Scand 1981; 64 (suppl 295): 1–101.

Bech P, Gjerris A, Andersen J. The Melancholia Scale and the Newcastle Scales. Brit J Psychiat 1983; 143: 58–63.

Bech P, Allerup P, Gram LF, Kragh-S.rensen P, Rafaelsen OJ, Reisby N, Vestergaard P and DUAG: The Diagnostic Melancholia Scale (DMS). Dimensions of endogenous and reactive depression with relationship to the Newcastle Scales. J Aff Dis 1988; 14: 161–170.

Carney MWP. The Newcastle Scale. In: Sartorius N, Ban TA (eds). Assessment of depression. Berlin, Springer, 1986, pp. 201–212.

Carney MWP, Roth M, Garside RR. The diagnosis of depressive syndromes and prediction of ECT response. Br J Psychiat 1965; 111: 659–674.

Eysenck HJ. The classification of depressive illness. Br J Psychiat 1970; 117: 241–250.

Freud S. Mourning and melancholia (First published 1917). Collected papers (Vol 4). New York, Basic Books, 1959, pp. 152–170.

Gurney C. Diagnostic Scales for Affective Disorders. Mexico, World Conference of Psychiatry, 1971, p. 330.

Hamilton M. A rating scale for depression. J Neurol Neurosurg Psychiat 1960; 23: 56–62.

Kendell RE. The classification of depressive illness. Brit J Psychiat 1970; 117: 241–250.

Kraepelin E. Manic-depressive insanity and paranoia. Edinburgh, Livingstone, 1921.

Kømer A, Nielsen BM, Eschen F, Møller-Madsen S, Stender A, Christensen EM, Aggernæs H, Kastrup M, Larsen JK. Quantifying depressive symptomatology: interrater reliability and inter-item correlation. J Aff Dis 1990; 20: 143–149.

Watts CAH. Depressive disorders in the community. Bristol, J. Wright, 1966.

Wimmer A. Psykogene sindssygdomsformer. In: Sct. Hans Mental Hospital 1816–1916, Jubilee Publication. Copenhagen, Gad, 1916, pp. 85–216.

Zimmerman M, Black DW, Coryell W. Diagnostic criteria for melancholia: the comparative validity of DSM-III and DSM-III-R. Arch Gen Psychiat 1989; 46: 361–368.

3.5 Anxiety Disorders

Among the psychiatric disability syndromes anxiety is the most 'functional'. The first significant description of anxiety as a human reaction which may or may not have morbid degrees was given by Kierkegaard (1844). Westphal (1871) is commonly seen as the first to have described agoraphobia. The description of neurasthenia by Beard (1869, 1880) was a major contribution to psychopathology, providing around 50 symptoms (1880). He observed that the components of depression, morbid fear and vegetative symptoms (sleep, pain and tiredness) were the most sensitive to change over time ('shared phenomenology'). Importantly, Beard (1880) pointed out that "the test and measure of improvement is not so much the relief of any one symptom, taken by itself alone, as by the average of all symptoms." As discussed elsewhere (Bech 1991), the historical development with reference to Beard's neurasthenia included contributions by Freud (1885) on anxiety neurosis (panic attacks and generalized anxiety), Janet (1903) on obsessional states, Lange (1886) on non-psychotic (minor) recurrent depression, and Bonhoeffer (1912) on endogenous depression. Of the vegetative symptoms in Beard's concept of neurasthenia 'tiredness' remains as the major symptom of the ICD-10's diagnosis of neurasthenia, which is listed together with anxiety disorders under the heading of neurotic states. 'Pain' is by DSM-III-R considered as an axis 3 disorder and is consequently placed there in this compendium. Finally, 'sleep' is included as an axis 1 disorder in DSM-III-R and is in ICD-10 placed next to neurotic disorders as a non-organic syndrome of behaviour. Therefore, rating scale for sleep is included as the last paragraph in Section 3.5. DSM-III-R follows Freud in distinguishing anxiety from depression. Thus, the symptoms of anxious mood are not included in the set of depressive symptoms (this is also the case in ICD-10). However, the first attempt to apply the rating scale method in clinical psychiatry revealed a high positive correlation (0.73) between depressed mood and anxious mood in patients with depressive illness (Moore 1930).

The Hamilton Anxiety Scale (HAS; Hamilton 1959, 1969) is the most frequently used scale for measuring anxiety. Factor analysis has differentiated a somatic factor (autonomic hyperactivity; "Appendix 3.10a") and a psychic factor ("Appendix 3.11"), both in patients with anxiety neurosis (Hamilton 1959, 1969) and in those with panic disorders (Bech et al. 1992). In Chapter 2 the HAS is discussed with DSM-III-R criteria for panic anxiety for generalized anxiety. The HAS psychic anxiety factor can be considered as a scale specifically for measuring the spectrum of dysthymia and generalized anxiety. Table 3.28 compares ICD-10, DSM-III-R and the HAS psychic anxiety factor concerning the concept of dysthymia (minor depression). On the two HAS anxiety factors, the psychic factor fulfils the Rasch criteria, while the somatic factor does not (Maier et al. 1988b). The Zung anxiety scale (Zung 1974) is rather similar to the HAS, apart from the items of phobia and depressed mood. The Clinical Anxiety Scale (Snaith et al. 1982) is a psychic anxiety 'factor' derived from the Hamilton Anxiety Scale.

Table 3.29 compares the item distribution of these scales regarding the components of anxiety as captured by the two most frequently used anxiety rating scales. The component of anxious mood includes apprehension; phobia includes agoraphobia; motor tension includes trembling and outer restlessness; psychic tension includes inability to relax, inner restlessness; autonomic hyperactivity includes palpitation and abdominal discomfort; and arousal includes being keyed up, irritability, insomnia.

Many studies have been performed to differentiate depression and anxiety. The overlap of anxiety elements in the HDS and the depression elements in the HAS indicates the similarity between the concepts. It is very interesting that the classical study in this field, the one by Prusoff and Klerman (1974) differentiating depression from anxiety using total scores of depression, anxiety, obsessive-compulsive and inter-personal sensitivity scales, showed that the difference between depression and anxiety is due to intensity. Hence, depressed patients had higher scores both on depression and on anxiety scales. On the other hand, using a discriminant function analysis on the same data, Prusoff and Klerman (1974) demonstrated small or minimal differences between depressed and anxious patients. This result supports the argument that discriminant function analysis is too powerful in detecting differences between item scores.

The rating scale dichotomy of endogenous versus reactive (stress-related) depression is considered by DSM-III-R and ICD-10 a dichotomy between depression and anxiety. ICD-10 locates stress-related disorders under anxiety states.

Table 3.28. Dysthymia items in ICD-10, DSM-III-R and HAS (psychic factor)

ICD-10	DSM-III-R	HAS	
1 Reduction in energy	1 Depressed mood	1 Anxious mood	(0-4)
2 Insomnia	2 Poor appetite or overeating	2 Tension	(0-4)
3 Feelings of inadequacy	3 Insomnia or hypersomnia	3 Fears	(0-4)
4 Difficulty concentrating	4 Low energy or fatigue	4 Insomnia	(0-4)
5 Often in tears	5 Low self-esteem	5 Poor concentration	(0-4)
6 Loss of interests	6 Poor concentration	6 Depressed mood	(0-4)
7 Feelings of hopelessness	7 Feelings of hopelessness	7 Muscular symptoms	(0-4)
8 Inability to cope with the routine responsibility	Criteria: item 1 plus at least two of the following six items.		0-28
9 Pessimistic about future			
Research criteria: at least three of the nine items.			

Table 3.29. Item distributions of rating scales: components of anxiety syndrome

Component	HAS	HAS (psychic factor)	Zung Anxiety Scale	Clinical Anxiety Scale
Anxious mood	7%	14%	15%	33%
Phobia	7%	14%	0%	0%
Motor tension	14%	14%	15%	7%
Psychic tension	7%	14%	10%	33%
Autonomic hyperactivity	43%	0%	45%	0%
Arousal	14%	29%	15%	0%
Depressed mood	7%	14%	0%	0%
Number of items	14	7	20	6

Table 3.30. Classification of stress-related disorders with reference to ICD-10 with the F-codes and the MES

Axis 1 syndromes

Psychosocial stressors (axis 4)	Generalized anxiety, minor depression (MES 6-9)	Less than major depression (MES 10-14)	Major depression (MES >14)
Extreme	Post-traumatic stress disorder (mild) (F 43.10)	Post-traumatic stress disorder (moderate) (F 43.11)	Post-traumatic stress disorder (severe) (F 43.12)
Moderate	Acute stress reaction (mild) (F 43.00)	Acute stress reaction (moderate) (F 43.01)	Acute stress reaction (severe) (F 43.02)
Mild	Brief anxiety reaction (F 41.1)	Brief depressive reaction (F 43.20)	Prolonged depressive reaction (F 43.21)

There is no evidence supporting the exclusion of secondary depression or reactive depression from depressive disorders. The spectrum of symptoms in stress-related states extends from anxiety to depression (Carney et al. 1965; Gurney 1971; Horowitz et al. 1980a, b).

In ICD-10 (and less consistently in DSM-III-R) the nature or severity of the psychosocial stressor is the classificatory principle for subdividing the different stress-related disorders. This compendium follows the ICD-10 approach. Table 3.30 classifies the clinical symptoms in terms of the severity of the psychosocial stressor and MES score. For a more detailed discussion of the measurement of psychosocial stressors by rating scales, see Chapter 7.

3.5.1 Panic Attacks

Freud (1895) was the first to differentiate generalized anxiety (anxious mood, insomnia, apprehension) from anxiety attacks, which include panic with accompanying somatic symptoms such as increased respiration and heart activity and vasomotor innervation. Freud (1895) noted that:

"It is interesting and important diagnostically, that the degree to which these elements are combined in anxiety attacks varies extraordinarily, and that almost every accompanying symptom can alone constitute the attack just as well as the anxiety itself. There are consequently rudimentary anxiety attacks and equivalents of an anxiety attack."

The components of panic attacks are autonomic hyperactivity. James (1884) and Lange (1885) were the first to maintain that the symptoms of autonomic hyperactivity preceded the experience of panic (excessive dread). Beck et al. (1988) have likewise seen a mood of anxiety as representing catastrophic misinterpretations of bodily sensations.

From a psychopharmacological point of view, Klein's (1964) demonstration that imipramine but not placebo or chlorpromazine is highly effective in blocking panic attacks led to renewed interest in distinguishing anxiety attacks as a separate entity. These findings inspired DSM-III and later DSM-III-R and ICD-10 to incorporate criteria for panic disorders. Table 3.31 compares the DSM-III-R and ICD-10 criteria for panic attacks with the HAS somatic factor.

Latent structure analysis has so far failed to reveal a structure within the somatic anxiety factor of the HAS that can serve as an adequate indicator (Maier et al. 1988b; Bech et al. 1992, see Appendix 3.10). The number of panic attacks and their global severity might be considered as appropriate indicators (see Chap. 2).

The description of panic attacks in DSM-III inspired Sheehan (1983) to develop a panic anxiety scale (discussed in Chap. 4). This compendium presents the SCL-19/DSM-III-R panic scale below as an example of a scale based primarily on DSM-III-R using the set of symptoms from the Hopkins symptom checklist (SCL-90; Guy 1976; Lipman 1986). The SCL-90 was shown by Pichot (1986) to be an appropriate, comprehensive anxiety scale. Because anxiety is a stress-related human experience there are a great variety of symptoms in this spectrum.

Table 3.31. Panic attack items in ICD-10, DSM-III-R and HAS (somatic factor)

ICD-10	DSM-III-R	HAS
Recurrent attacks of severe anxiety (panic) which are not restricted to any particular situation and therefore are unpredictable	Discrete periods of intense fear or discomfort that were (1) unexpected and (2) not triggered by situation in which the person was the focus of others' attention.	1 Sensory symptoms
		2 Cardiovascular symptoms
		3 Respiratory symptoms
		4 Gastro-intestinal symptoms
The dominant items are:	At least four of the following items:	5 Genito-urinary symptoms
		6 Other autonomic symptoms
(1) Sudden onset of palpitations	(1) Shortness of breath	7 Behaviour at interview
(2) Chest pain	(2) Dizziness	
(3) Choking sensations	(3) Palpitations	
(4) Feeling of unreality	(4) Trembling	
	(5) Sweating	
	(6) Choking	
	(7) Nausea or abdominal distress	
	(8) Depersonalization	
	(9) Paraesthesias	
	(19) Flushes	
	(11) Chest pain	
	(12) Fear of dying	
	(13) Fear of going crazy	

The questions of the SCL-90 are presented below, with DSM-III-R categories inserted in parentheses. DSM-III-R criteria for panic disorders are: A plus B plus at least four C items. Scoring is: 0, not at all; 1, a little bit; 2, moderately; 3, markedly; 4, extremely. The scoring sheet is shown in Appendix 3.10b.

Below is a list of problems and complaints that people sometimes have. Circle the number to the right that best describes how much that problem bothered or disabled you during the past week including today. Mark only one number for each problem and do not skip any items.

1. Suddenly scared for no reason (A).
2. Spells of terror or panic (A).
3. Trouble getting your breath (C1).
4. Faintness or dizziness (C2).
5. Heart pounding or racing (C3).
6. Trembling (C4).
7. Bouts of excessive sweating (C5).
8. Choking sensation or lump in throat (C6).
9. Nausea or upset stomach (C7).
10. Feeling that familiar things are strange or unreal (C8).
11. Numbness or tingling in parts of your body (C9).
12. Hot or cold spells (C10).
13. Pains in heart or chest (C11).
14. Thoughts of death or dying (C12).
15. The idea that something is wrong with your mind (C13).
16. Sudden unexpected panic spells (A).
17. Sudden unexpected spells at the edge of panic (A).
18. Anxiety episodes that are built up in anticipation (B).
19. Surges of panic that occur when in a public situation (B)

3.5.2 Generalized Anxiety

The HAS was designed to measure generalized anxiety in patients with anxiety neurosis (Table 3.32; see also "Appendix 3.10c"). It is the state of anxiety syndrome, not the diagnosis of anxiety neurosis, that this scale is intended to measure (Hamilton 1959). As discussed by Ryle (1949), the symptoms of somatic anxiety are rather brief occurences. The psychic (mood) components of generalized anxiety are of longer duration than panic anxiety. Spielberger et al. (1970) constructed a state and trait scale; however, the trait anxiety part of this scale is not a diagnostic scale.

The HAS has been used mainly to measure the effect of minor tranquilizers (barbiturates, meprobamate and benzodiazepines) in patients with anxiety disorders. These drugs have been found superior to placebo in such components as motor tension and arousal (irritability; Berger 1970).

Table 3.32. Psychometric description: HAS

Type	Severity scale for measuring panic attacks and generalized anxiety.
Content validity	The components of the full scale are shown in Table 3.29. The psychic factor of the scale measures dysthymia, and the somatic factor panic symptoms. Chapter 2 describes how the full scale can be used both to attacks anxiety and generalized anxiety.
Administration	Interview to be performed by a skilled observer (goal-directed).
Time frame	Covers previous 3 days.
Item selection	Symptoms of anxiety neurosis.
Item calibration	Likert scale definition, 0-4.
Construct validity	The psychic factor of the scale, but not the somatic factor has adequate Rasch structure.
Sensitivity to change	Has discriminated validity in studies versus placebo.
Inter-observer reliability	Adequate (Gjerris et al. 1983; Bech et al. 1984).
Standardization	The full Hamilton scale: 0-5 = No anxiety 6-14 = Minor state >14 = Major states

Table 3.33. Generalized anxiety items in ICD-10, DSM-III-R and HAS

ICD-10	DSM-III-R	HAS
The essential feature is anxiety which is generalized and persistent but not restricted to any situations. Following symptoms accompany the feeling of anxiety: nervousness, trembling, muscular tension, sweating, lightheadedness, palpitation, dizziness, and epigastric discomfort.	(1) Anxiety	Item 3 Fear
	(2) Trembling	Item 2 Tension
	(3) Muscle tension	Item 7 Muscular symptoms
	(4) Restlessness	Item 14 Agitated behaviour
	(5) Fatigability	Item 2 Tension
	(6) Shortness of breath	Item 10 Respiratory symptoms
	(7) Palpitations	Item 9 Cardiovascular symptoms
	(8) Sweating	Item 13 Other autonomic symptoms
	(9) Dry mouth	Item 13 Other autonomic symptoms
	(10) Dizziness	Item 13 Other autonomic symptoms
	(11) Nausea	Item 11 Gastro-intestinal symptoms
	(12) Flushes	Item 8 Sensory symptoms
	(13) Frequent urination	Item 12 Genito-urinary symptoms
	(14) Trouble swallowing	Item 11 Gastro-intestinal symptoms
	(15) Feeling keyed up	Item 2 Tension
	(16) Exaggerated startle response	Item 14 Agitated behaviour
	(17) Difficulty concentrating	Item 5 Difficulties in concentrating
	(18) Insomnia	Item 4 Insomnia
	(19) Irritability	Item 1 Anxious mood
	Criteria: item 1 plus at least six of the following 18 items.	

The concept of generalized anxiety in DSM-III included components of motor tension, autonomic hyperactivity, and arousal. Table 3.33 compares DSM-III-R, ICD-10 and the HAS.

References

Beard GM. Neurasthenia or nervous exhaustion. Boston Med Surg J 1869; 3: 217–221.

Beard GM. A Practical Treatise on Nervous Exhaustion (Neurasthenia). New York, Trent E.B., 1880.

Bech P. Use of rating scales for neurasthenia, anxiety and depression in general practice. In: Kielholz P, Gastpar M (eds). Psychological Disorders in General Practice. New Aspects. Bern, Hans Huber, 1991, pp. 56–70.

Bech P, Grosby H, Husum B, Rafaelsen L. Generalized Anxiety or Depression measured by the Hamilton Anxiety Scale and the Melancholia Scale in patients before and after cardiac surgery. Psychopathol 1984; 16: 253–263.

Bech P, Allerup P, Maier W, Albus M, Lavori P, Ayuso JL. The Hamilton scales and the Hopkins symptom checklist (SCL-90): a cross-national validity study in patients with panic disorders. Br J Psychiat 1992; 160:206–211.

Beck AT, Brown G, Epstein N, Steer RA. An inventory for measuring clinical anxiety: psychometric properties. J Consult Clin Psychol 1988; 56: 893–897.

Berger FM. Anxiety and the discovery of the tranquilizers. In: Ayd FJ, Blackwell B (eds). Discoveries in biological psychiatry. Philadelphia, Lippincott, 1970 pp. 115–129.

Bonhoeffer K. Zur Differentialdiagnose der Neurasthenia und endogenen Depression. Berliner klinische Wochenschrift 1912; 49: 1–4.

Carney MWP, Roth M, Garside RR. The diagnosis of depressive syndromes and prediction of ECT response. Br J Psychiat 1965; 111: 659–674.

Freud S. The Justification for Detaching from Neurasthenia a Particular Syndrome: The Anxiety Neurosis (First published in Neurologisches Zentralblatt 1895). Collected papers (Vol 4) New York, Basic Books, 1959, pp. 76–106.

Gjerris A, Bech P, Bøjholm S. The Hamilton Anxiety Scale. J Aff Dis 1983; 5: 163–170.

Gurney C. Diagnostic scales for affective disorders. Mexico, World Conference of Psychiatry 1971, p. 330.

Guy W. Early Clinical Drug Evaluation (ECDEU) Assessment Manual for Psychopharmacology. Publication No. 76–338. Rockville, Nat Inst Ment Health, 1976.

Hamilton M. The assessment of anxiety states by rating. Br J Med Psychol 1959; 32: 50–55.

Hamilton M. Diagnosis and rating of anxiety. Br J Psychiat 1969 (special publication): 76–79.

Horowitz M, Wilner N, Kaltreider N, Alvarez W. Signs and symptoms of posttraumatic stress disorder. Arch Gen Psychiat 1980a; 37: 85–92.

Horowitz M, Wilner N, Marnar C, Krupnick J. Pathological grief and the activation of altern self-images. Am J Psychiat 1980b; 137: 1157–1162.

James W. What is an emotion? Mind 1884; 9: 188–205.

Janet P. Les obsessions et la psychiasthenie. Paris, Alcan, 1903.

Kierkegaard S. Concept of Anxiety (First edition). Copenhagen, C. A. Reitzel 1844). English version: Princeton, Princeton Univ Press, 1980.

Klein DF. Delineation of two drug-responsive anxiety syndromes. Psychopharmacol 1964; 5: 897–408.

Lange C. Om sindsbevægelser. Et psyko-fysiologisk studie. Copenhagen, J. Lund 1885 (German version: Über Gemütsbewegungen. Eine psycho-physiologische Studie). Leipzig, Theodor Thomas, 1887.

Lange C. Periodiske depressionstilstande. Copenhagen, Jacob Lunds Forlag, 1886 (German version: Periodische Depressionszustände, Leipzig, Leopold Voss, 1896).

Lipman RS. Depression scales derived from the Hopkins Symptom Checklist. In: Sartorius N, Ban TA (eds). Assessment of depression. Berlin, Springer, 1986, pp. 232–248.

Loldrup D, Langemark M, Hansen HJ, Olesen J, Bech P. Clomipramine and mianserin in chronic idiopathic pain syndrome. A placebo controlled study. Psychopharmacol 1989; 99: 1–7.

Maier W, Buller R, Philipp M, Heuser I. The Hamilton Anxiety Scale: Reliability, validity and sensitivity to change in anxiety and depressive disorders. J Aff Dis 1988; 14: 61–68.

Moore TV. The empirical determination of certain syndromes underlying praecox and manic-depressive psychoses. Am J Psychiat 1930; 86: 719–738.

Pichot P. Evaluation methods of the therapeutic effects of anxiety disorders treatment. In: Pepplinkhuizen L, Verhoeven WMA (eds). Biological psychiatry in Europe today. Leiderdorf, Netherlands, Vigeversig De Medicins, 1986, pp. 69–73.

Prusoff B, Klerman GL. Differentiating depressed from anxious neurotic outpatients. Use of discriminant function analysis for separating of neurotic affective states. Arch Gen Psychiat 1974; 30: 302–308.

Ryle G. The Concept of Mind. London, Hutchinson, 1949.

Sheehan DV. The Anxiety Disease. New York, C. Schribner's Sons 1983.

Snaith RP, Baugh S, Clayden AD, Hussain A, Sipple M. The Clinical Anxiety Scale: a modification of the Hamilton Anxiety Scale. Br J Psychiat 1982; 141: 518–523.

Spielberger CD, Gorsuch RL, Lushene RE. State-Trait Anxiety Inventory. Palo Alto, Consulting Psychologists Press, 1970.

Westphal C. Die Agoraphobie: eine neurapathische Erscheinung. Archiv für Psychiatrie und Nervenkrankheiten 1871; 3: 138–161.

Zung WWK. The measurement of affects: Depression and anxiety. In: Pichot P (ed). Psychological measurements in psychopathology. Basel, Karger, 1974, pp. 170–188.

3.5.3 Phobias

Phobia refers to anxiety or fear of an object or a situation. In their comprehensive dictionary of psychological terms, English and English (1958) point out that phobia may but does not necessarily connote morbid fear. In over 180 listed terms, they failed to find a single case in which the compound formed with '-phobia' is clearer, more convenient, or more univocal than the characterization in normal language, for example, open-space phobia versus agoraphobia. It is generally accepted that Westphal (1871) was the first to describe agoraphobia, although Lange (1864) had earlier noticed that Eskimos in Greenland sometimes experience states of open space phobia when they were alone in their kayaks. Westphal described agoraphobia as a morbid and recurrent fear of open public places (open-space phobia). He emphasized that the patients were aware of the irrationality of their own uncontrollable reaction of anxiety to open spaces. The pathological element of phobia is its irrationality. However, Westphal felt that agoraphobia had a neurological aetiology, that it was neuropathic in nature.

The most frequently used scale specifically developed to assess phobia is the Gelder-Marks Phobia Questionnaire or its modification ("Appendix 3.11"; Gelder and Marks 1966; Marks 1978; Sheehan 1983). The items of this scale can be assessed either by the patient (the questionnaire form) or by the treating physician

Table 3.34. Phobia items in ICD-10, DSM-III-R, Hopkins SCL-9 and the Fear Scale

ICD-10	DSM-III-R	Hopkins SCL-9	Fear Scale
Agoraphobia	*Agoraphobia*	*Agoraphobia*	*Agoraphobia*
(1) Crowds	Social phobias	[13] (1) Afraid of open spaces	[5] Afraid of open spaces
(2) Public places	Simple phobias	[70] (2) Uneasy in crowds	[6] Walking in busy streets
(3) Travelling alone		[47] (3) Fear of travelling	[8] Going in crowded shops
(4) Travelling away from home		[25] (4) Afraid to leave home	[5] Travelling alone
			[12] Going alone far from home
Social phobias		*Social phobias*	
(1) Eating or speaking in public		[61] (5) Uneasy when people are watching	*Social phobias*
			[7] Being watched or stared at
(2) Encountering known individuals in public		[82] (6) Afraid of fainting in public	[14] Speaking or eating to audience
(3) Entering or enduring small group situations		[73] (7) Feeling uncomfortable eating in public	[9] Talking to people in authority
			[3] Eating/drinking with other people
		Simple phobias	
		[50] (8) Avoiding certain things	
		(9) Nervous being left alone	

Table 3.35. Item distributions of rating scales: components of phobia syndrome

Component	Marks-Sheehan Scale	Hopkins SCL-9
Agoraphobia	42%	44%
Social phobia	25%	33%
Simple phobia	33%	22%
Number of items	12	9

(the interview form). The psychometric properties of this scale, with the range of response values exceeding 0–4, are inadequate. The phobia subscale of the Hopkins Symptom Checklist (SCL-90) includes item values ranging from 0 to 4, as does the Fear Scale. (Marks and Mathews 1979). Table 3.34 compares the ICD-10, the DSM-III-R, the Hopkins SCL, and the Fear Scale.

It should be recalled that Westphal (1871) extracted the agoraphobia elements from Beard's (1869) concept of neurasthenia; in his later publication (Beard 1880) the term topophobia was used. The three components of phobia (agoraphobia, social phobia, and simple phobia) are reasonably covered by SCL-9 (Table 3.35). However, latent structure analysis of this scale is still lacking.

The questions of the Fear Scale are presented below. Agoraphobia items are 5, 6, 8, 12, 15; social phobia items are 3, 7, 9, 11, 14; blood-injury items are 2, 4, 10, 13, 16; anxiety-depression items are 18–22; total phobia items are 2–16. Scoring on items 2–17 is; 0, would not avoid it; 1, slightly avoid it; 2, definitely avoid it; 3, markedly avoid it; 4, always avoid it. Scoring on items 18–23 is: 0, hardly at all; 1, slightly troublesome; 2, definitely troublesome; 3, markedly troublesome; 4, very severely troublesome. Scoring on item 24 is: 0, no phobia; 1, somewhat disturbing/disabling; 2, definitely disturbing/disabling; 3, markedly disturbing/disabling; 4, very severely disturbing/disabling.

Choose a number between 0 and 4 to show how much you would avoid each of the situations listed below because of fear or other unpleasant feelings.

1. Main phobia you want treated (specify in your own words)
2. Injections or minor surgery
3. Eating or drinking with other people
4. Hospitals
5. Travelling alone by bus or coach
6. Walking alone in busy streets
7. Being watched or stared at
8. Going into crowded shops
9. Talking to people in authority
10. Sight of blood
11. Being criticized
12. Going alone far from home

13. Thought of injury or illness
14. Speaking or acting to an audience
15. Large open spaces
16. Going to the dentist
17. Other situations (specify in your own words

Now choose a number between 0 and 4 to show how much you are troubled by each problem listed.

18. Feeling miserable or depressed
19. Feeling irritable or angry
20. Feeling tense or panicky
21. Upsetting thoughts coming into your mind
22. Feeling you or your surroundings are strange
23. Other feelings (specify)
24. My present state of phobic symptoms (global rating)

References

Beard GM. Neurasthenia or nervous exhaustion. Boston Med Surg J 1869; 3: 217–221.
Beard GM. A Practical Treatise One Nervous Exhaustion (Neurasthenia). New York, Trent E. B., 1880.
English HB, English AC. A Comprehensive Dictionary of Psychological and Psychoanalytical Terms. London, Longman, 1958.
Gelder MG, Marks IM. Severe agoraphobia: A controlled trial of behaviour therapy. Br J Psychiat 1966; 112: 309–319.
Lange C. Bemærkninger om Grønlands sygdomsforhold. Bibliotek for læger 1864; 5: 15–64.
Marks IM. Living with fear. New York, Mc Graw-Hill, 1978.
Marks IM, Mathews AM. Brief standard self-rating for phobic patients. Behav Rec Therap 1979; 17: 263–267.
Sheehan DV. The anxiety disease. New York, C. Schribner's Sons, 1983.
Westphal C. Die Agoraphobie: eine neuropathische Erscheinung. Archiv für Psychiatrie und Nervenkrankheiten 1871; 3: 138–161.

3.5.4 Obsessive-Compulsive States

Obsessive-compulsive states were recognized by Westphal (1871), but it is generally accepted that Janet (1903) made the first major contribution in this area. Janet first differentiated obsessive from hysterical states; the narrowing of the field of consciousness in terms of suggestibility and dissociation was the characteristic feature of hysterical states which Janet never observed in obsessional states. Depressive states are therefore, according to Janet, rarely seen in the hysterical personality, while a positive correlation between obsessive-compulsive states and depression is often observed (Bech 1981). The correlation between depression and obsessive-compulsive states has been verified in controlled clinical trials with antidepressants. Psychopathologically obsessions are connected with guilt feelings (inward aggression) and hysterical symptoms with outward aggression as shown by Kiloh and Garside (1977) when making a multivariate study of Aubrey Lewis's data on melancholia.

It seems that it is the serotonergic effects of antidepressants that stabilize the cognitive dyscontrol in obsessive-compulsive states (Coppen and Doogan 1988). From a psychopharmacological point of view, obsessive and compulsive states are recognized as forming a single psychopathological syndrome. This syndrome is manifested as a type of irrational behaviour in which anxiety and depression is associated with unwanted ideas (obsessions) and with persistent impulses to repeat certain acts over and over again (compulsions). In psychopharmacological research, the Obsessive-Compulsive Subscale (OCS) of the Comprehensive Psychopathological Rating Scale (Thoren et al. 1980) has been most frequently used and seems to cover the obsessive-compulsive syndrome in outcome trials with antidepressants. A modified (0 to 4 item version) of the OCS is included in this compendium.

From a pathological psychology point of view, two major theories have been advocated. Thus, Reed (1985) consideres that clinical compulsions are a pathological extension of a basic obsessive personality trait. In contrast, Rachman and de Silva (1978) have advocated that clinical obsessions are an extreme variant of non-clinical intrusive cognitions, i.e. a result of normal psychological processes. Non-clinical intrusive cognitions refer to mental events which are perceived as interrupting a person's stream of consciousness by capturing the focus of attention (see Section 3.7). From a rating scale point of view it therefore seems useful to differentiate between obsesssions and compulsion.

Questionnaires have been most frequently used for obsessive-sompulsive states. Previously, the Leyton Obsessional Inventory (Cooper 1970), with both trait and state items (Allen and Tune 1975) has been widely used. However, it seems now clear (Salkovskis 1990) that data do not support a relationship between obsessional traits and the obsessive-compulsive syndrome. The Maudsley Obsessive-Compulsive Inventory (Hodgson and Rachman 1977) measures mainly compulsions, and a modification largely following Sanavio and Vidotte (1985) is provided below. Another self-rating scale is the factor of obsessive-compulsive states from the Hopkins SCL which is rather similar to the OCS. This SCL-10 (Guy 1976) is also included below.

Table 3.36 compares ICD-10, DSM-III-R and the OCS. Table 3.37 compares the OCS, Maudsley, and Hopkins scales.

Recently, a global-like scale for obsessions have been developed at the Warneford Hospital in Oxford (Salkovskis 1990) where the patient is asked to write down the most troublesome obsession and then measure it on a global discomfort scale from 0 (no discomfort) to 8 (extreme discomfort). Thereafter, the patient is asked to indicate how much this obsesssion interfere with his life from 0 (not at all) to 8 (extremely). Finally, the patient is asked to estimate (a) for how long each day his is having the thought "in the front of your mind" (in hours and minutes); (b) for how long each day the obsession is "in the back of your mind" (in hours

Table 3.36. Obsessive-compulsive items in ICD-10, DSM-III-R and OCS

ICD-10	DSM-III-R	OCS
Obsessions and compulsions share the following features: (1) They are acknowledged as originating in the mind of the patient. (2) They are repetitive and unpleasant and senseless. (3) The subject tries to resist them. (4) Carrying out obsessive thoughts or compulsive acts is not in itself pleasurable.	*Obsessions* (1) Recurrent and persistent ideas, thoughts, impulses, or images. (2) The person attempts to ignore or suppress such thoughts. (3) The person recognizes that the obsessions are the product of his or her own mind. *Compulsions* (1) Repetitive, purposeful, and intentional behaviours that are performed in response to an obsession. (2) The behaviour is designed to neutralize or prevent discomfort. (3) The person recognizes that his or her behaviour is excessive or unreasonable.	1 Obsessive thoughts 2 Compulsive behaviour 3 Indecision 4 Concentration difficulties 5 Depressed mood 6 Psychic anxiety 7 Work activity

Table 3.37. Item distribution of rating scales: component of obsession and compulsion

Components	OCS	Maudsley	Hopkins SCL-10	Yale-Brown
Obsession (cognitions)	14%	42%	20%	53%
Compulsions (behaviour)	14%	58%	30%	47%
Concentration or decission making	28%	0%	50%	0%
Other	44%	0%	0%	0%
Number of items	7	12	10	15

and minutes); and (c) how many times per day he has the obsession (in hours and minutes).

The most comprehensive scale is probably the Yale-Brown Obsessive Compulsive Scale (Y-BOCS) which is developed by Goodman et al. (1989). This scale has been designed to rate the severity and type of symptoms in patients with obsessive-compulsive disorder. The scale contains two parts. In part A the items depend on the patient's report, and in part B the items are based on the clinical judgement of the interview.

Obsessive-Compulsive Scale

The scoring sheet for the OCS is illustrated in "Appendix 3.12a". Instructions for scoring its seven items are presented below.

1 Obsessive Thoughts
This item covers recurrent thoughts that are experienced as irrational or senseless but cannot be suppressed by the patient. The quality of being experienced as senseless is important. Hence, preoccupations, such as hypochondriasis, about potentially unpleasant things should be distinguished from obsessions because they lack the quality of being experienced as senseless on the part of the patient.
0. Not present.
1. Doubtful or very mild tendency to obsessions.
2. Occasional repetitive thoughts which, however, are not distressing.
3. More pronounced obsessions which therefore are socially disturbing.
4. Incapacitating obsessions which occupy the patient's mind entirely.

2 Compulsive Behaviour
This item covers repetitive and intentional behaviours which are performed in response to an obsession, according to certain rules, or in a stereotyped fashion. However, the patient recognizes that the behaviour is unreasonable. The most common compulsions involve handwashing, counting, checking and touching.
0. Not present.
1. Doubtful or very mild tendency to compulsive behaviour, e.g. checking.
2. Mild compulsive behaviour, e.g. checking, which, however, is not distressing.
3. More pronounced compulsions which, therefore, are socially disturbing.
4. Incapacitating compulsions which are very time consuming.

3 Indecision
This item covers difficulty in choosing between simple alternatives.
0. Not present.
1. Doubtful or very mild tendency to vacillation.
2. Occasional indecisiveness which, when present, restricts or prevents action but is still without influence on the patient's daily life.

3. Indecisiveness or vacillation is more markedly present and restricts or prevents action, makes it difficult to answer simple questions or to make simple choices, hence interfering with the patient's daily life.
4. Marked to extreme indecisiveness even in situations in which conscious deliberation is not normally required, such as whether to sit or stand, enter or stay outside.

4 Concentration Difficulties

This item covers difficulties in concentrating, making decisions about everyday matters, and memory.
0. The patient has neither more nor less difficulty in concentrating and remembering than usual.
1. It is doubtful whether the patient has difficulty in concentrating and remembering.
2. Even with a major effort it is difficult for the patient to concentrate on his daily routine work.
3. More pronounced difficulties with concentration, memory, or decision making. For example, he has difficulty reading a newspaper article or watching a television programme to the end. (Score '3' as long as the loss of concentration or poor memory does not clearly influence the interview.)
4. The patient shows difficulty during the interview in concentrating and remembering, or decisions are reached only with considerable delay.

5 Depressed Mood

This item covers both the verbal and the non-verbal communication of sadness, depression, despondency, helplessness and hopelessness.
0. Not present.
1. It is doubtful whether the patient is more despondent or sad than usual; for example, he seems vaguely more depressed than usual.
2. The patient is more clearly concerned with unpleasant experiences, although he still lacks helplessness and hopelessness.
3. The patient shows clear non-verbal signs of depression or hopelessness.
4. The patient's remarks on despondency and helplessness or the non-verbal signs dominate the interview in which the patient cannot be distracted.

6 Psychic Anxiety

This item includes tenseness, irritability, worry, insecurity, fear and apprehension approaching overpowering dread. It may often be difficult to distinguish between the patient's experience of anxiety ('psychic' or 'central' anxiety phenomena) and the physiological ('peripheral') anxiety manifestations which can be observed, e.g., hand tremor and sweating. Most important is the patient's report of worry, insecurity, uncertainty, experiences of dread, i.e. psychic ('central') anxiety.
0. The patient is neither more nor less insecure or irritable than usual.
1. It is doubtful whether the patient is more insecure or irritable than usual.

2. The patient seems clearly in a state of anxiety, apprehension or irritability, which he may find difficult to control. It is thus without influence on the patient's daily life because the worrying is still about minor matters.
3. The anxiety or insecurity is at times more difficult to control because the worrying is about major injuries or harms which might occur in the future; for examples, the anxiety may be experienced as panic, i.e. overpowering dread. It occasionally interferes with the patient's daily life.
4. The feeling of dread is present so often that it markedly interferes with the patient's daily life.

7 Work and Normal Day-to-Day Activities
This item includes both work carried out and motivation.

A At First Rating
0. Normal work activity.
1. The patient expresses inadequacy due to lack of motivation and/or trouble in carrying out the usual work load, which the patient, however, manages to do without reduction.
2. More pronounced inadequacy due to lack of motivation and/or trouble in carrying out the usual work. Here the patient has reduced work capacity, cannot keep normal speed, copes with less on the job or in the home; the patient may stay home some days or may try to leave early.
3. Difficulties in simple routine activities. If hospitalized score 3.
4. The patient is fully hospitalized and generally unoccupied, without participation in the ward activities (unable to do anything without help). If at home: unable to do anything without help.

B At Weekly Ratings
0. Normal work activity. (a) The patient has resumed work at his normal activity level. (b) The patient would have no trouble resuming normal work.
1. (a) The patient is working but at reduced activity level, due either to lack of motivation or to difficulties in accomplishing his normal work. (b) The patient is not working, and it is still doubtful whether he can resume his normal work without difficulties.
2. (a) The patient is working but at a clearly reduced level, due either to episodes of non-attendance or to reduced working hours. (b) The patient is still hospitalized or sick-listed, participates more than 3–4 h per day in ward (or home) activities, but is capable of resuming normal work only at a reduced level. If hospitalized, the patient is able to change from in-patient to day-patient status.
3. Difficulties in starting simple routine activities which are carried out with great efforts.
4. The patient is still fully hospitalized and generally unable to participate in ward activities (unable to do anything without help). If at home: unable to do anything without help.

Obsessive-Compulsive Inventory (Sanovio and Vidotto)

The questions of the modified Maudsley scale are presented below. Checking items are 2, 5, 9; cleaning items are 1, 6, 10; slowness items are 3, 7, 11; doubting items are 4, 8, 12. Scoring is: 0, not at all; 1, a little bit; 2, moderately; 3, markedly; 4, extremely.

Below is a list of problems and complaints that people sometimes have. Circle the number to the right that best describes how much that problem bothered or disabled you during the last week including today.

1. Excessively concerned about cleanliness.
2. Frequently have to check or double check things (gas, electricity, water taps).
3. Often late because I can't get through everything on time.
4. Often doubts about what to do.
5. Checking letters over and over before mailing them.
6. Use more than the average amount of soap.
7. It takes me longer than others to dress in the morning.
8. Even when I do something very carefully, I often feel that it is not quite right.
9. I have to go back and check doors and windows to make sure that they are really shut.
10. Unduly concerned about germs and disease.
11. Hanging and folding my clothes at night takes up a lot of time.
12. I find myself paying too much attention to detail.

Obsessive-Compulsive Inventory (Hopkins)

The question of the Hopkins SCL-10 are presented below. Scoring is: =, not at all; 1, a little bit; 2, moderately; 3, markedly; 4, extremely.

Below is a list of problems and complaints that people sometimes have. Circle the number to the right that best describes how much that problem bothered or disabled you during the last week including today.

1. Unwanted thoughts, words, or ideas that won't leave your mind.
2. Trouble remembering things.
3. Worried about sloppiness and carelessness.
4. Feeling blocked in getting things done.
5. Having to do things very slowly to ensure correctness.
6. Having to check and double-check what you do.
7. Difficulty making decisions.
8. Your mind going blank.
9. Trouble concentrating.
10. Having to repeat the same actions such as touching, counting, washing.

Yale-Brown Obsessive Compulsive Scale (Y-BOCS)

The scoring sheet for the Y-BOCS is illustrated in "Appendix 3.12b". Instructions for scoring are presented below.

Part (A). Please check all that apply both currently (last week) and past.

A1. Aggressive Obsessions
- fear might harm self
- fear might harm others
- fear might harm others
- violent or horrific images
- fear of blurting out obscenities or insults
- fear of doing something else embarrassing
- fear will act on unwanted impulses (e.g. to stab friend)
- fear will steal things
- fear will harm others because not careful enough (e.g.hit/run MVA)
- fear will be responsible for something else terrible happening (e.g.fire, burglary)
- other (specify)

A2. Contamination Obsessions
- concerns or disgust with bodily waste or secretions (e.g. urine, feces, saliva)
- concern with dirt or germs
- excessive concern with environmetal contaminants (e.g. asbestos, radiation, toxic waste)
- excessive concern with household items (e.g. cleansers, solvents)
- excessive concern with animals (e.g. insects)
- bothered by sticky substances or residues
- concerned will get ill because of contaminant
- concerned will get others ill by spreading contaminant (Aggressive)
- no concern with consequences of contamination other than how it might feel
- other

A3. Sexual Obsessions
- forbidden or perverse sexual thoughts, images, or impulses
- content involves children or incest
- content involves homosexuality
- sexual behavior toward others (Aggressive)
- other

A4. Hoarding/Saving Obsessions (distinguish from hobbies and concern with objects of monetary or sentimental value)

A5. Religious Obsessions (Scrupulosity)
- concerned with sacrilege and blasphemy
- excess concern with right/wrong, morality
- other

A6. Obsession with Need for Symmetry or Exactness
- accompanied by magical thinking (e.g., concerned that mother will have accident unless things are in the right place)
- not accompanied by magical thinking

A7. Miscellaneous Obsessions
- need to know or remember
- fear of saying certain things
- fear of not saying just the right thing
- fear of losing things
- intrusive (non-violent) images
- intrusive nonsense sounds, words, or music
- bothered by certain sounds/noises
- lucky/unlucky numbers
- colors with special significance
- superstitious fears
- other

A8. Somatic Obsessions
- concern with illness or disease
- excessive concern with body part or aspect of appearance (e.g. dysmorphophobia)
- other

A9. Cleaning/Washing Compulsions
- excessive or ritualized handwashing
- excessive or ritualized showering, bathing, toothbrushing, grooming, or toilet routine.
- involves cleaning of household items or other inanimate objects
- other measures to prevent or remove contact with contaminants
- other

A10. Checking Compulsions
- checking locks, stove, appliances, etc. – checking that did not/will not harm others
- checking that did not/will not harm self
- checking that nothing terrible did/will happen
- checking that did not make mistake
- checking tied to somatic obsessions
- other

A11. Repeating Rituals
- re-reading or re-writing
- need to repeat routine activities (e.g. in/out door, up/down from chair)
- other

A12. Counting Compulsions

A13. Ordering/Arranging Compulsions

A14. Hoarding/Collecting Compulsions
- (distinguish from hobbies and concern with objects of monetary or sentimental value (e.g., carefully reads junkmail, piles up old newspapers, sorts through garbage, collects useless objects))

A15. Miscellaneous Compulsions
- mental rituals (other than checking/counting)
- excessive listmaking
- need to tell, ask, or confess
- need to touch, tap, or rub
- rituals involving blinking or staring
- measures (not checking) to prevent: harm to self; harm to others; terrible consequences
- ritualized eating behaviors
- superstitious behaviors
- trichotillomania
- other self-damaging or self-mutilating behaviors
- other

Please indicate your target symptoms in order of priority, (a) through (c).
AI. Obsessions
AII. Compulsions
AIII. Avoidance

Part B. Interview past.
By making specific reference to the patient's target obsessions (AI(a) to (c)) the interviewer says: "I am now going to ask several questions about your obsessive thoughts."

B1. How much of your time is occupied by obsessive thoughts?
0 = None
1 = Mild, less than 1 hr/day or occasional intrusion.
2 = Moderate, 1 to 3 hrs/day or frequent intrusion.
3 = Severe, greater than 3 and up to 8 hrs/day or very frequent instrusion.
4 = Extreme, greater than 8 hrs/day or near constant intrusion.

B2. How much do your obsessive thoughts interfere with your social or work functioning?
0 = None
1 = Mild, slight interference with social or occupational activities, but overall performance not impaired.
2 = Moderate, definite interference with social or occupational performance, but still manageable.
3 = Severe, causes substantial impairment in social or occupational performance.
4 = Extreme, incapacitating.

B3. How much distress do your obsessive thoughts cause you?
0   = None
1   = Mild, not too disturbing
2   = Moderate, disturbing, but still manageable
3   = Severe, very disturbing
4   = Extreme, near constant and disabling distress

B4. How much of an effort do you make to resist the obsessive thoughts?
0   = Makes an effort to always resist, or symtomps so minimal doesn't need to actively resist.
1   = Tries to resist most of the time.
2   = Makes some effort to resist.
3   = Yields to all obsessions without attempting to control them, but does so with some reluctance.
4   = Completely and willingly yields to all obsessions.

B5. How much control do you have over your obsessive thoughts?
0   = Complete control.
1   = Much control, usually able to stop or divert obsessions with some effort and concentration.
2   = Moderate control, sometimes able to stop or divert obsessions.
3   = Little control, rarely successful in stopping or dismissing obsessions, can only divert attention with difficulty.
4   = No control, experienced as completely involuntary, rarely able to even momentarily alter obsessive thinking.

B6. How much time do you spend performing compulsive behaviors?
0   = None
1   = Mild (spends less than 1hr/day performing compulsions), or occasional performance of compulsive behaviors.
2   = Moderate (spends from 1 to 3 hrs/day performing compulsions), or frequent performance of compulsive behaviors.
3   = Severe (spends more than 3 and up to 8 hrs/day performing compulsions), or very frequent performance of compulsive behaviors.
4   = Extreme (spends more than 8 hrs/day performing compulsions), or near constant performance of compulsive behaviors (too numerous to count).

B7. How much do your compulsive behaviors interfere with your social or work functioning?
0   = None
1   = Mild, slight interference with social or occupational activities, but overall perfomance not impaired.
2   = Moderate, definite interference with social or occupational performance, but still manageable.
3   = Severe, causes substantial impairment in social or occupational performance.
4   = Extreme, incapacitating.

B8. How would you feel if prevented from performing your compulsion(s)?

0 = None

1 = Mild, only slighty anxious if compulsions prevented, or only slight anxiety during performance of compulsions.

2 = Moderate, reports that anxiety would mount but remain manageable if compulsions prevented, or that anxiety increases but remains manageable during performance of compulsions.

3 = Severe, prominent and very disturbing increase in anxiety if compulsions interrupted, or prominent very disturbing increase in anxiety during performance of compulsions.

4 = Extreme, incapacitating anxiety from any intervention aimed at modifying activity, or incapacitating anxiety develops during performance of compulsions.

B9. How much of an effort do you make to resist the compulsions?

0 = Makes an effort to always resist, or symtomps so minimal doesn't need to actively resist.

1 = Tries to resist most of the time.

2 = Makes some effort to resist.

3 = Yields to almost all compulsions without attempting to control them, but does so with some reluctance.

4 = Completely and willingly yields to all compulsions.

B10. How strong is the drive to perform the compulsive behavior?

0 = Complete control.

1 = Much control, experiences pressure to perform the behavior but usually able to exercise voluntary control over it.

2 = Moderate control, strong pressure to perform behavior, can control it only with difficulty.

3 = Little control, very strong drive to perform behavior, must be carried to completion, can only delay with difficulty.

4 = No control, drive to perform behavior experienced as completely involuntary and overpowering, rarely able to even momentarily delay activity.

References

Allen JJ, Tune GS. The Lynfield obsessional/compulsive questionnaire. Scott Med J 1975; 201: 21–26.

Bech P. Rating scales for affective disorders. Their validity and consistency. Acta Psychiat Scand 1981; 64 (suppl. 285): 1–101.

Cooper J. The Leyton Obsessional Inventory. Psychol Med 1970; 1: 48–64.

Coppen AJ, Doogan DP. Serotomin and its place in the pathogensis of depression. J Clin Psychiat 1988; 49 (Suppl 8): 4–11.

Goodman WK, Rasmussen SA, Price LH, Mazure C, Heninger G, Charmey DS. The Yale-Brown Obsessive Compulsive Scale (Y-BOCS). Clinical Neuroscience Research Unit, Connecticut Mental Health Center, New Haven, 1989.

Guy W. Early Clinical Drug Evaluation (ECDEU) Assessment Manual for Psychopharmacology. Publication No. 76–338. Nat Inst Ment Health; Rockville 1976.

Hodgon RJ, Rachman S. Obsessional-compulsive complaints. Beh Res Ther 1977; 15: 389–395.

Janet P. Les obsessions et la psychiasthenie. Paris, Alcan, 1903.

Kiloh LG, Garside RF. Depression: A multivariate study of Sir Aubrey Lewis's data on melancholia. Aust N Zealand J Psychiat 1977; 11: 149–156.

Rachman SJ, de Silva P. Abnormal and normal obsessions. Beh Res Ther 1978; 16: 233–238.

Reed GF. Obsessional experience and compulsive behaviour: a cognitive-structural approach. London, Academic Press, 1985.

Salkovskis PM. Obsessions, compulsions and intrusive cognitions. In: Peck DF, Shapiro CM (eds). Measuring Human Problems. Chichester, John Wiley, 1990, pp. 90–118.

Sanovio E, Vidotto G. The components of the Maudsley obsessional compulsive questionnaire. Beh Res Ther 1985; 23: 659–662.

Thoren P, Åsberg M, Cronholm B, Jörnestedt L, Träskman L. Clomipramine treatment of obsessive-compulsive disorder. Arch Gen Psychiat 1980; 37: 1281–1285.

Westphal C. Die Agoraphobie: eine neuropathische Erscheinung. Arch f Psychiatrie u Nervenkrankheiten. 1871; 3: 138–161.

3.5.5 Neurasthenia (Chronic Fatigue/Pain Syndromes)

The set of components in Beard's (1869, 1880) classical description of the psychopathology of neurasthenia is, in accordance with ICD-10 and DSM-III-R, subdivided here into panic disorders, generalized anxiety, phobias and obsessive-compulsive states. The residual components of neurasthenia are the chronic fatigue syndrome or the chronic pain syndrome. The overlap between these syndromes and depression is as marked as with the other neurasthenia syndromes derived from Beard's concept of neurasthenia (e.g. Wessely 1989; Bech 1991). The overlap between neurasthenia and depression is also impressive in Freudenberger's (1974) 'burn-out' syndrome. However, the modern (residual) concept of neurasthenia also seems to be associated with neurological concepts (e.g. post-viral fatigue syndrome or myalgic encephalomyelitis).

DSM-III-R includes chronic pain disorders but not chronic fatigue disorders; however, ICD-10 includes both. As an axis 1 disorder, the major component of somatoform pain disorder is, according to DSM-III-R, pain that has no organic pathology or known pathophysiological mechanism to account for the symptoms. The ICD-10 concept of neurasthenia includes fatigability and weakness. The classical rating scale in psychosomatic medicine is the Cornell Medical Index (Brodman et al. 1949). The 16 components of this index are presented in Table 3.38. Neurasthenia in Beard's sense is covered by the components of fatigability, habits, feelings of inadequacy, depressed mood, anxious mood, sensitivity feelings, anger (irritability), and tension. Both the Hopkins scale (Parloff et al. 1954; Guy 1976) and the General Health Questionnaire (Goldberg 1972) include items from the Cornell Medical Index. Table 3.39 compares ICD-10 and the asthenia scales of Pichot and Brun (1984) and Bech and Hey (1979), as well as the Fatigability Index from the Cornell Medical Index (Brodman et al. 1949), which seems

Table 3.38. The Cornell Medical Index

1	Eyes and ears	9	Fatigability
2	Respiratory system	10	Habits
3	Cardiovascular system	11	Inadequacy feelings
4	Digestive tract	12	Depressed moods
5	Musculoskeletal system	13	Anxiety moods
6	Skin	14	Sensitivity feelings
7	Nervous system	15	Anger moods
8	Genito-urinary system	16	Tension feelings

to correspond more with the ICD-10 concept of neurasthenia than do the other asthenia scales.

Table 3.40 compares the item distribution of the scales measuring pain (Zung 1983), fatigue (Wessely 1989) and asthenia (Pichot and Brun 1984; Bech and Hey 1979), as well as the checklist results from the comprehensive work on neurasthenia by Birket-Smith (1960). Birket-Smith described 75 patients with primary fatigability who were examined because of significantly reduced work activity. From Table 3.39 it appears that the Wessely and Pichot-Brun scales specifically measure the component of fatigue and weakness, while the other scales, including the Birket-Smith items, consider a broader spectrum, as is the case with the Thoren scale for obsessive-compulsive states (see Sect. 3.5.4). It should be mentioned that the Bech-Hey scale was developed from an extended Beck Depression Inventory (Bech 1988) in a follow-up study on obese patients after surgery operation. In a recent study on menopausal syndrome the scale was shown to fulfil the Rasch model (Munk-Jensen et al. 1991). The validity of the Pichot-Brun asthenia scale has been confirmed by factor analysis by Guelfi et al. (1989). The neurasthenia scales shown in Table 3.39 are self-rating scales. The Pichot-Brun asthenia scale is constructed as the Hopkins scale and is therefore in principle also an observer scale. The same is the case with the Zung pain scale.

Asthenia Scale (Pichot-Brun)

The questions of the Pichot-Brun Asthenia Scale are presented below. Scoring is: 0, not at all; 1, a little bit; 2, moderately; 3, markedly; 4, extremely.

Below is a list of problems and complaints that people sometimes have. Circle the number to the right that best describes how much that problem bothered or disabled you during the last week including today.

1. Feeling low in energy.
2. Feeling everything is an effort.
3. Feeling weak in parts of your body.
4. Heavy feelings in your arms or legs.
5. Feeling tired for no reason.

Table 3.39. Neurasthenia items in ICD-10, Pichot-Brun Asthenia Scale, Bech-Hey Asthenia Scale, and the Fatigability Index

ICD-10	Pichot-Brun Asthenia Scale	Bech-Hey Asthenia Scale	Fatigability Index
The following items are required: (1) Persistent and distressing complaints of increased fatigability after mental effort. (2) Persistent complaints of bodily weakness (e.g. muscle aches or pains) and inability to relax.	1 Feeling low in energy. 2 Feeling everything is an effort 3 Feeling weak in parts of the body 4 Heavy feeling in arms and legs 5 Tired for no reason 6 Having to rest 7 Trouble concentration 8 Feeling weary	1 Headache 2 Tiredness 3 Work inhibition 4 Sleep 5 Hypochondriasis 6 Dry mouth 7 Dizziness 8 Irritability 9 No sexual interest 10 Self-disappointment 11 Palpitation 12 Increased thirst	1 Spells of complete exhaustion 2 Working tiredness 3 Tired in the morning 4 Everything is an effort 5 Too tired to eat 6 Suffering from severe nervous exhaustion

Table 3.40. Item distributions of rating scales: components of neurasthenia

Component	Zung Pain Scale	Wesesly Fatigue Questionnaire	Pichot-Brun Asthenia Scale	Bech-Hey Asthenia Scale	Birket-Smith study
Pain: general	5%	0%	0%	8%	8%
Fatigue (weakness)	15%	65%	88%	8%	8%
Indecision, concentration, memory	15%	29%	12%	0%	8%
Depression	20%	6%	0%	8%	8%
Anxious mood	5%	0%	0%	0%	8%
Work inhibition	15%	0%	0%	8%	8%
Vegetative symptoms (sleep, sexual)	15%	0%	0%	25%	45%
Autonomic hyperactivity (dizziness, thirst)	0%	0%	0%	33%	0%
Arousal (irritability)	10%	0%	0%	8%	8%
Number of items	20	17	8	12	13

6. I feel like lying down and taking a rest.
7. Trouble concentrating.
8. Feeling weary, stiff, heavy.

Asthenia Rating Scale (Bech and Hey)

The questions of the Bech-Hey Asthenia Rating Scale are presented below.
1. a I don't get more tired than usual.
   b get tired more easily than I used to.
   c I get tired from doing anything.
2. a I can work about as well as before.
   b It takes extra effort to get started at doing something.
   c I have to push myself very hard to do anything.
3. a I am no more irritable now than I ever am.
   b I get annoyed or irritated more easily than I used to.
   c I feel irritated all the time.
4. a I can sleep as well as usual.
   b I wake up more tired in the morning than I used to.
   c I couldn't get more than 5 hours sleep.
5. a I am no more concerned about my health than usual.
   b I am concerned about aches and pains or upset stomach
   c I am so concerned with how I feel or what I feel that it is hard to think of
      much else.
6. a I have not noticed any recent change in my interest in sex.
   b I am less interested in sex than I used to be.
   c I am much less interested in sex now.
7. a I have no headache.
   b I feel a slight trace of headache.
   c From time to time I suffer from severe headaches.
8. a I do not feel dizzy.
   b I tend to get dizzy if I get up quickly.
   c I tend to loose my balance even if I get up slowly.
9. a My mouth does not feel dry.
   b My mouth feels somewhat dry.
   c My mouth feels very dry.
10 a I don't feel disappointed in myself.
   b I am disappointed in myself.
   c I am disgusted with myself.
11. a I consume the same quantity of liquid per day as I used to.
    b It is doubtful whether my consumption has increased.
    c My consumption of liquid has clearly increased.
12. a I feel no tension or oppression of my heart.
    b I feel a slight tension and oppression of my heart.
    c I feel a stronger heartbeating than normally.

Pain and Distress Scale (Zung)

The questions of the Zung Pain and Distress Scale are presented below. Scoring is as follows: 1, none or a little of the time; 2, some of the time; 3, a good part of the time; 4, most of the time.
1. I feel miserable, low and down.
2. I feel nervous, tense, and keyed up.
3. I get tired for no reason.
4. I can work for as long as I usually do.
5. I am as efficient in my work as usual.
6. I have trouble falling asleep.
7. I have trouble sleeping through the night.
8. I wake up earlier than I want to.
9. I feel rested when I get out of bed.
10. I am restless and can't keep still.
11. I find it hard to do the things I usually do.
12. I find it hard to think and remember things.
13. My mind is foggy and I can't concentrate.
14. I am as alert as I could be.
15. I still enjoy the things I used to.
16. I enjoy listening to the radio or watching TV.
17. I enjoy visiting friends and relatives.
18. I have aches and pains that bother me.
19. I am more irritable than usual.
20. Everything I do is an effort.

Fatigue Questionnaire (Wessely)

The questions of the Wessely Fatigue Questionnaire are presented below.

The following questions are all about fatigue, lack of energy and tiredness. We would like to know how much you have had these feelings, over the past few weeks. Please answer ALL the questions simply by underlining the answer which you think most nearly applies to you. Remember that we want to know about present and recent feelings of tiredness, not those that you had in the past. If you have been feeling tired for a long time, we want you to compare your present feelings with how you felt when you last felt normal. It is important that you try to answer ALL the questions.

Thank you very much for your co-operation.
1. How long have you been feeling tired? (Please enter length of time in weeks):
2. Do you feel tired every day?
   a Every day
   b Most days
   c Some days
3. Do you feel tired all the time?
   a Yes, never varies

    b Yes, but varies

    c No, sometimes goes completely

4. Do you get tired easily?

    a Less than usual

    b No more than usual

    c More than usual

    d Much more than usual

5. Do you need to rest more?

    a Less than usual

    b No more than usual

    c More than usual

    d Much more than usual

6. Do you feel sleepy or drowsy?

    a Less than usual

    b No more than usual

    c More than usual

    d Much more than usual

7. Do you have less strength in your muscles?

    a Not at all

    b No more than usual

    c More than usual

    d Much more than usual

8. Do you feel weak?

    a Less than usual

    b No more than usual

    c More than usual

    d Much more than usual

9. Do you lack energy?

    a Not at all

    b No more than usual

    c More than usual

    d Much more than usual

10. Do you start things easily, but get weak as you go on?

    a Less than usual

    b No more than usual

    c More than usual

    d Much more than usual

11. Do you have problems starting things?

    a Less than usual

    b No more than usual

    c More than usual

    d Much more than usual

12. Have you lost interest in the things that you used to do?

    a Not at all

    b No more than usual

   c More than usual
   d Much more than usual
13. Do you have difficulty in concentrating?
   a Less than usual
   b No more than usual
   c More than usual
   d Much more than usual
14. Do you have problems thinking clearly?
   a Less than usual
   b No more than usual
   c More than usual
   d Much more than usual
15. Do you make slips of the tongue while speaking?
   a Less than usual
   b No more than usual
   c More than usual
   d Much more than usual
16. Do you find it more difficult to find the right word?
   a Less than usual
   b No more than usual
   c More than usual
   d Much more than usual
17. How is your memory?
   a Better than usual
   b No more than usual
   c Worse than usual
   d Much worse than usual
18. What brings on your fatigue? (More than one answer may be needed!)
   a It may occur at rest
   b Moderate exercise, or normal housework (walking at normal pace)
   c Severe excercise (running for a bus; heavy lifting; 2 flights of stairs)
   d Moderate mental effort (reading a book; watching TV, sustaining a conversation)
   e Severe mental effort (studying; filling in long forms; complicated arithmetic)
(please circle ALL of the above that apply)

References

Beard GM. Neurasthenia or nervous exhaustion. Boston Med Surg J 1869; 3: 217–221.
Beard GM. A Practical Treatise on Nervous Exhaustion (Neurasthenia). New York, Trent, 1880.
Bech P. Rating scales for mood disorders: applicability, consistency and construct validity. Acta Psychiat Scand 1988 (suppl 345): 45–55.

Bech P. Use of rating scales for neurasthenia, anxiety and depression in general practice. In: Kielholz P, Gastpar M (eds). Psychological Disorders in General Practice. New Aspects. Bern, Hans Huber, 1991, pp. 56–70.

Bech P, Hey H. Depression or asthenia related to metabolic disturbances in obese patients after intestinal bypass surgery. Acta Psychiat Scand 1979; 59: 462–470.

Birket-Smith E. Det asteniske syndrom. Aarhus, Universitetsforlaget, 1960.

Brodman K, Erdmann AJ, Lorge I, Wolff HG. The Cornell Medical Index. An adjunct to medical interview. JAMA 1949; 140: 530–534.

Freudenberger HJ. Staff burnout. J Soc Issues 1974; 30: 159–165.

Goldberg D. The detection of psychiatric illness by questionnaires. Oxford, Oxford Univ Press, 1972.

Guelfi JD, von Frenckell R, Caille Ph. The Norris VAS and the ADA inventory. A factorial analysis in outpatients. Paper presented at World Psychiatric Association Congress, Athens, October 1989.

Guy W. Early Clinical Drug Evaluation (ECDEU) Assessment Manual for Psychopharmacology. Publication No. 76–338. Rockville, Natl Inst Ment Health, 1976.

Munk-Jensen N, Bech P, Obel E, Pors-Nielsen S. Effect of sequental or continous oestrogen/progestogen therapy on psychological discomfort in the climacteric women, 1991 (in preparation).

Parloff MB, Kelman HC, Frank JD. Comfort, effectiveness, and self-awareness as criteria of improvement in psychotherapy. Am J Psychiat 1954; 111: 343–351.

Pichot P, Brun JP. Questionnaire bref d'autoevaluation des dimensions depressive, asthenique et anxieuse. Am Medico-Psychol 1984; 142: 862–865.

Wessely S. The Epidemiology of Fatigue: Evidence of a Large UK Community Survey. M. Sc. Thesis. London, University of London, 1989.

Zung WWK. A self-rating pain and distress scale. Psychosom 1983; 24: 887–894.

3.5.6 Insomnia

Sleep disturbance is a common symptom of many mental and somatic disorders. Insomnia is included in rating scales for depression and anxiety.

Primary sleep disorders (sleep disturbances considered to be independent of any other mental or somatic condition) are included in both ICD-10 and in DSM-III-R (as axis 1 disorders). According to DSM-III-R these sleep disorders are subdivided into dyssomnia (a predominant disturbance in amount, quality or timing of sleep) and parasomnias (where the predominant disturbance is an abnormal event occuring during sleep).

Within primary dyssomnia ICD-10 and DSM-III-R have three subtypes: insomnia, hypersomnia and sleep-wake disturbances. In this section only insomnia is dealt with.

Both ICD-10 and DSM-III-R have as the main criteria of insomnia difficulty in initiating or maintaining sleep or a poor quality of sleep. The definition of poor quality of sleep is a non-restorative sleep, i.e. sleep which is apparently adequate in amount, but leaves the person feeling unrested (as manifested in daytime fatigue or in irritability, tension or other emotional disturbances).

The DSM-III-R or ICD-10 criteria of primary insomnia do not include data from laboratory procedures such as sleep recordings. The rating scale approach follows DSM-III-R/ICD-10 in this respect. Because the quality of sleep has a major impact on insomnia self-rating scales seem more valid than observer scales in the assessment of insomnia. Thus, Kupfer et al. (1970) found murses' observations of sleep invalid.

Among self-rating scales for measuring insomnia the St. Mary's Hospital Sleep Questionnaire (SMH; Ellis et al. 1981) and the Leeds Sleep Evaluation Questionnaire (SEQ; Hindmarch 1975; Parrott and Hindmarch 1978) have been selected. Both scales cover a specific night's sleep rather than retrospective sleep habits, which is essential in all symptom rating scales, especially concerning insomnia (Carskadon et al. 1976).

In a recent study by Patel et al. (1991) it has been demonstrated that SMH is an appropriate scale to describe insomnia quantitatively as well as qualitatively and that SEQ is a scale designed to be sensitive for detecting changes in insomnia during treatment.

The study by Patel et al. (1991) is of great interest also in assessment of sleep in secondary insomnia. It is recommended to use specific insomnia questionnaires like SMH and SEQ instead of subscales from other rating scales for measuring health status (e.g. the Nottingham Health Profile (Hunt et al. 1981) which includes many items for sleep performance but without subjective estimates).

The SMH Sleep Questionnaire

This questionnaire refers to your sleep over the past 24 hours.
At what time did you:
1 Settle down for the night? Hrs, Mins.
2 Fall asleep last night? Hrs, Mins.
3 Finally wake this morning? Hrs, Mins.
4 Get up this morning? Hrs, Mins.
5 Was your sleep – 1, very slight; 2, light; 3, fairly light; 4, light average; 5, deep average; 6, fairly deep; 7, deep; 8, very deep?
6 How many times did you wake up? 0, not at all; 1, once; 2, twice; 3, three times; 4, four times; 5, five times; 6, six times; 7, more than six times.
How much sleep did you have
7 Last night? Hrs, Mins.
8 During the day (yesterday)? Hrs, Mins.
9 How well did you sleep last night? 1, very badly; 2, badly; 3, fairly badly; 4, fairly well; 5, well; 6, very well.
10 How clear-headed did you feel after getting up this morning? 1, still very drowsy indeed; 2, still moderately drowsy; 3, still slightly drowsy; 4, fairly clear-headed; 5, alert; 6, very alert.
11 How satisfied were you with last noght's sleep? 1, very satisfied; 2, moderately unsatisfied; 3, slightly unsatisfied; 4, fairly satisfied; 5, completely satisfied.
12 Were you troubled by waking early and being inable to get off to sleep again? 1, no; 2, yes.

13 How much difficulty did you have in getting off to sleep last night? 1, none or very little; 2, some; 3, a lot; 4, extreme difficulty.

14 How long did it take you to fall alseep last night? Hrs, Mins.

The Sleep Evaluation Questionnaire

How would you compare getting to sleep using the medication with getting to sleep normally, i.e. without medication?

1 Harder than usual – easier than usual.

2 Slower than ususal – quicker than usual.

3 Felt less drowsy than usual – felt more drowsy than usual.

How would you compare quality of sleep using the medication with non-medication (your usual) sleep?

4 More restless than usual – more restful than usual.

5 More periods of wakefulness than usual – fewer periods of wakefulness than usual.

How did your awakening after medication compare with your usual pattern of awakening?

6 More difficult than usual – easier than usual.

7 Took longer than usual – took shorter than usual.

How did you feel on wakening?

8 Tired – alert.

How do you feel now?

9 Tired – alert.

How was your sense of balance and coordination upon getting up?

10 More clumsy than usual – less clumsy than usual.

Note: A 10 cm line separates the two halves of each question. The questionnaire instructions are: Each question is answered by placing a vertical mark on the answer line. If no change was experienced then place your mark in the middle of the line. If a change was experienced then the position of your mark will indicate the nature and extent of the change, i.e. large changes near the ends of the line, small changes near the middle.

References

Carskadon MA, Dement WC, Mitler MM, Guilleminault C, Zarcone VP, Spiegel R. Self-reports vs. sleep laboratory findings in 122 drug-free subjects with complaints of insomnia. Am J Psychiat 1976; 133: 1382–8.

Ellis BW, Johns MW, Lancaster R, Raptopoulos P, Angelopoulos N, Priest RG. The St. Mary's Hospital Sleep Questionnaire: A study of reliability. Sleep 1981; 4: 93–7.

Hindmarch I. A 1,4-benzodiazepine, temazepam, its effect on some psychological parametres of sleep and behaviour. Arzneim Forsch 1975; 25: 1836–9.

Hunt SM, McEwen J, McKenna SP. The Nottingham Health Profile: Subjective health status and medical consultations. Social Science & Medicine 1981; 15: 221–9.

Kupfer DJ, Wyatt RJ, Snyder F. Comparison between electroencephalographic and systemic nursing observations of sleep in psychiatric patients. J Nerv Men Dis 1970; 151: 361–8.

Parrott AC, Hindmarch I. Factor analysis of a sleep questionnaire. Psychol Med 1978; 8: 325–9.

Patel AG, Gurer R, Kurian T, Lambert MT, Steinert J, Priest RG. A comparison of the hypnotic effects of temazepam capsules and temazepam elixir. Int Clin Psychopharm 1991; 6: 1–9.

3.6 Aggression

Anger, hostility and aggression have been considered as personality traits that can explain psychosomatic disorders such as cardiovascular disorders (Alexander 1939). In psychopathology, anger and aggression have also been considered important in the aetiology of neuroses, depression and schizophrenia, as well as being seen as induced by psychopharmacological treatment (Rosenbaum 1991). However, these views have not been confirmed in recent studies using empirical methods. We discuss here the descriptive aspects of the clinical spectrum of anger, hostility and aggression.

The classical scale for measuring the different aspects of hostility is the Buss-Durkee (1957) scale. This, however, is a self-rating scale, and self-rating scales in the measurement of aggression may well measure something other than aggression, for instance, due to the patient's response set. Chapter 4 deals with the advantages and disadvantages of self-rating scales; this section considers only observer scales. In this context we should note that Platman et al. (1969) demonstrated a very low correlation between self-ratings and staff ratings in manic patients.

3.6.1 Aggressive States in Mental Handicap and Conduct Disorder

Mental retardation has been most successfully assessed by the Binet (1903) scale, which in principle is a standardized interview rather than a psychological test (Terman and Merrild 1957). The measurement of intelligence as an aspect of mental retardation is outside the scope of this compendium. However, aggressive behaviour is considered a dimension across mental handicap and conduct disorders.

Both ICD-10 and DSM-III-R regard aggression as an essential component of conduct disorders. Aggression is also measured by the Handicaps, Behaviour and Skills Schedule (HBS; Table 3.41) developed by Wing (1980). This scale has recently been analysed by Lund (1989) using the Rasch model in a study on mentally handicapped patients and shown to fulfil the Rasch model. Table 3.42 compares the ICD-10, DSM-III-R and HBS criteria of aggression. The rank order of HBS items here is from Lund (1989), the items of temper tantrums, destructive-

Table 3.41. Psychometric description: HBS

Type	Severity scale, symptoms.
Content validity	Outward aggression.
Administration	Observer rating scale to be used by skilled observers.
Time frame	The previous 3 days.
Item selection	First-generation scale based on litterature reviews and clinical experiences.
Item calibration	Likert definitions, 0-2.
Number of items	Twelve.
Construct validity	Rasch analysis has supported that the total score is a sufficient statistic (Lund 1989). The hierarchical structure is shown in Table 3.42.
Inter-observer reliability	Acceptable (Malt et al. 1990).

Table 3.42. Conduct disorders in ICD-10, DSM-III-R and HBS

ICD-10	DSM-III-R	HBS
Conduct disorders are characterized by a repetitive and persistent pattern of asocial, aggressive or defiant conduct. Examples of the behaviour on which the diagnosis is based includes excessive levels of fighting or bullying; cruelty to other people or animals; severe destructiveness to property; fire-setting; stealing; repeated lying; truancy from school and running away from home; frequent and severe temper tantrums and disobedience. Any one of these items, if marked, is sufficient for a diagnosis.	(1) Has stolen (2) Has run away from home (3) Often lies (4) Has deliberately engaged in fire-setting (5) Is often truant from school (6) Has broken into someone else's house, building or car (7) Has deliberately destroyed others' property (8) Has been physically cruel to animals (9) Has forced someone into sexual activity (10) Has used a weapon in more than one fight (11) Often initiates physical fights (12) Has stolen, with confrontation of victim (13) Has been physically cruel to people	1 Temper tantrums 2 Noisiness 3 Destructiveness 4 Hyperactivity 5 Lack of cooperation 6 Behaviour in public places 7 Aggressive behaviour 8 Wandering 9 Difficult or objectionable personal habits 10 Other behavioural problems 11 Scatters or throws objects 12 Crying and moaning

ness and hyperactivity are the most inclusive, whereas those of scattering or throwing objects and crying or mourning are the most exclusive.

The scoring sheet for the HBS subscale for conduct behaviour is illustrated in 'Appendix 3.13'. Below is a list of its 12 items, with clarifications as to the respective traits being evaluated. Scoring on each item is as follows. 0, no problem; 1, minor problem; 2, marked problem.

1 Temper Tantrums. Does the patient frequently have temper tantrums?
2 Noisiness: Does the patient frequently scream or shout or make other loud noises (not crying or moaning)?
3 Destructiveness: Does the patient tear books, wallpaper, spil furniture, own clothing, etc. unless constantly supervised?
4 Hyperactivity: Does the patient not sit still (even when interested in food, television, etc.)?
5 Lack of Cooperation: Does the patient strongly resist attempts to make him join in, learn new things, or change his behaviour – by screams, temper tantrums, scratches, bites or kicks if these attempts are made – or else passively resists?
6 Behaviour in Public Places: Is the patient too difficult to take out because of marked problems in public places (grabs things in shops, speaks loudly and tactlessly, screams, takes off clothes, etc.)?
7 Aggressive Behaviour: Is the patient frequently aggressive towards others (including spitting at them)?
8 Wandering: Does the patient run away or wander off unless constantly supervised?
9 Objectional Personal Habits: Does the patient spit, smear, make himself vomit, hoard rubbish, eat rubbish, continously eat and drink, show inappropriate swearing, inappropriate sexual behaviour without social awareness, etc.?
10 Other Behavioural Problems: Does the patient have any other behaviour problems with limited or no social awareness?
11 Scatters or Throws Objects: Does the patient create chaos aimlessly?
12 Crying and Moaning: Does the patient cry or moan a great deal, appearing miserable most of the time, with no known cause?

References

Alexander F. Psychological aspects of medicine. Psychosom Med 1939; 1: 7–18.
Binet A. L'etude experimentale de l'intelligence. Paris: Schleicher 1903.
Buss AH, Durkee A. An inventory for assessing different kinds of hostility. J Consult Psychol 1957; 21: 343–9.
Lund J. Measuring behaviour disorder in mental handicap. Br J Psychiat 1989; 155: 379–83.
Malt UF, Bech P, Dencker SJ, Elgen K, Ahlfors UG, Lingjærde O. Skalaer for diagnostik og sygdomsgradering ved psykiatriske tilstande. Nor Psyk Tidsskr 1990; 20: 99–238.
Platman SR, Plutchik R, Fieve RR, Lawlor WG. Emotion profiles associated with mania and depression. Arch Gen Psychiat 1969; 20: 210–4.

Rosenbaum M. Violence in psychiatric wards: Role of the lax milieu. General Hospital
    Psychiatry 1991; 13: 115–21.
Terman CM, Merrild MA. Measuring intelligence. New York: Houghton Mifflin, 1957.
Wing L. The MRC Handicaps, Behaviour & Skills (HBS) schedule. Acta Psychiatr Scand
    1980; 62 (suppl 285) 241–247.

3.6.2 Aggressive States: Generalized

In his review of rating scales corresponding to DSM-II Frank (1975) referred to
psychotic reaction with aggressive behaviour of general nature, i.e. independent of
diagnostic categories like schizophrenia or mood disorders. Among the various
rating scales the works by Wittenborn (1951) and Wittenborn and Holzberg
(1951) were of interest, as the first factor to emerge in their factor analyses carried
out in mental hospitals was one characterized by unawareness of the feelings of
others, oppositional behaviour, deceptive behaviour and assaultive behaviour.

Aggressiveness as manifested by psychiatric in-patients is most appropriately
assessed by ward staff members. It is, of course, preferable to record behaviours
during the observation period, and the nursing staff is frequently in contact with
the patient. In contrast, ratings with a scale covering the previous 3 days rely
heavily on information by the patients and in the field of aggression other forms
of information are often needed. Nurses' observations are the most natural, regis-
tering behaviour as it occurs. Among the first nurses' observation rating scales was
the 100-item Behavioural Rating Scale for Mental Patients (Shatin and Freed
1955). The inter-observer reliability of this scale is high (0.79), as is the Richard-
son-Kuder statistic (analogous to Cronbach's alpha; 0.97). The most frequently
used nurses' scale is the Nurses' Observation Scale for Inpatient Evaluation
(NOSIE; Honigfeld and Klett 1965; Honigfels et al. 1966); which is derived, inter
alia, from the Behavioural Rating Scale for Mental Patients. A characteristic of
NOSIE is that the items are graded in terms of the frequency of occurrence (0,
never; 1, occasionally; 2, sometimes; 3, often; 4, always). The original NOSIE
consisted of 80 items from which a 30 item version, NOSIE-30 (Honigfeld 1974;
see below) has been extracted. The NOSIE-30 is used in trials measuring changes
in generalized aggression in psychiatric inpatients. Honigfeld (1974) has presented an excellent review of the discriminant validity of the NOSIE-30 in measurement differences between antipsychotic drugs and placebo. The scale has an
adequate validity in this respect. In factor analysis of NOSIE-30 (Guy 1976) seven
factors emerged (social competence, social interests, personal neatness, irritability, manifest psychosis, retardation and depression). Table 3.43 compares the item
distribution of the Behavioural Rating Scale for Mental Patients and NOSIE-30
(including the factor structure) in relation to the relevant components.

The total score on the NOSIE-30 reflects not only aggressive behaviour but
also symptoms of illness. Table 3.44 shows the factor of irritability of NOSIE-30
in relation to the aggressive factor of the nursing scale for mania, the Manic State
Rating Scale (Beigel et al. 1971; Murphy et al. 1974) and the AMDP factor of
hostility (Ban and Guy 1982; Pietzcker et al. 1983). The latter is a scale adminis-

Table 3.43. Item distributions of rating scales: components of aggression

Component	Behavioral Rating Scale	NOSIE	NOSIE factor structure
Self-care (personal neatness)	18%	13%	13%
Communication (social competence)	28%	26%	17%
Reaction to environment (social interest)	14%	26%	17%
Orientation	8%	0%	0%
Psychotic behaviour	18%	13%	13%
Cooperativeness	14%	20%	20%
Disability (clinical symptoms)	0%	0%	20%
Number of items	100	30	30

Table 3.44. Irritability components of NOSIE-30, severity components of Manic State Rating Scale (MSRS) and hostility components of AMDP

NOSIE-30 irritability	MSRS severity	AMDP hostility
(2) Is impatient	(2) Is talkative	(94) Aggressiveness
(6) Gets angry or annoyed	(3) Moves from one place to another	(67) Dysphoria
(10) Becomes easily upset	(5) Shows poor judgement	(99) Uncooperativeness
(11) Refuses to do ordinary things	(9) Is distractable	(68) Irritability
(12) Is irritable and grouchy	(11) Is irritable	(27) Suspiciousness
(29) Quick to fly off the handle	(15) Is active	(97) Lack of feeling of illness
	(16) Is argumentative	(98) Lack of insight
	(13) Is angry	
	(20) Has diminished impulses	
	(24) Demands contact with others	
	(26) Jumps from one subject to another	

tered by psychiatrists. In general, aggression seems in all these scales to be connected with psychotic behaviour.

In DSM-III-R elements of aggressiveness are included in the Global Assessment of Functioning (GAF), an axis 5 dimension. According to DSM-III-R, axis 5 permits the clinician to indicate his or her overall judgement of a patient's psychological, social and occupational functioning on GAF. The scores on GAF "generally reflect the current need for treatment or care." (DSM-III-R). The GAF includes, however, a mixture of clinical symptoms and social functioning. The original version is shown in Table 3.45 and a modified version in Table 3.46. In the latter clinical symptoms and social functioning have been separated, as there is no scientific evidence for a 100% correlation between clinical disability and social functioning. From Table 3.46 it appears that symptom scores of 31–40 refer to psychotic behaviour (impairment in reality testing), 21–30 to markedly psychotic behaviour (delusions or hallucination), and 1–20 to aggressive behaviour (against self or others). If the GAF is a Likert scale, the transitivity of scores implies that psychotic behaviour precedes aggressive behaviour.

The questions for the NOSIE-30 are presented below (see also Appendix 3.14). Scoring is as follows: 0, never; 1, sometimes; 2, often; 3, usually; 4, always. Negative factors are irritability (items 2, 6, 10, 11, 12, 29), manifest psychoses (items 7, 20, 26, 28), retardation (items 5, 22, 27), and depression (items 3, 18, 23). Positive factors are social competence (items 13, 14, 21, 24, 25; all inverted scores), personal neatness (items 1, 8, 16, 30; inverted scores only in 1, 16), and social interest (items 4, 9, 15, 17, 19). The aggression subscale consists of items 2, 6, 11, 12, 29.

1. Is sloppy.
2. Is impatient.
3. Cries.
4. Shows interest in activities around him/her.
5. Sits, unless directed into activity.
6. Gets angry or annoyed easily.
7. Hears things that are not there.
8. Keeps his/her clothes neat.
9. Tries to be friendly with others.
10. Becomes easily upset if something does not suit him/her.
11. Refuses to do the ordinary things expected of him/her.
12. Is irritable and grouchy.
13. Has trouble remembering.
14. Refuses to speak.
15. Laughs or smiles at funny comments or events.
16. Is messy in his/her eating habits.
17. Starts up a conversation.
18. Says he/she feels blue or depressed.
19. Talks about his/her interests.
20. Sees things that are not there.
21. Has to be reminded what to do.

Table 3.45. GAF: original version

Performance code	Comments
90-81	None or minimal symptoms; good functioning in all areas.
80-71	If symptoms are present, they are transient and expectable reactions to psychosocial stressors; no more than slight impairment in occupational social functioning.
70-61	Some mild symptoms, or some difficulty in occupational or social functioning, but generally functioning pretty well.
60-51	Moderate symptoms or moderate difficulty in occupational or social functioning.
50-41	Serious symptoms, or any serious impairment in occupational or social functioning.
40-31	Some impairment in reality testing or communication, or major impairment in several social areas.
30-21	Behaviour is considerably influenced by delusions or hallucinations; or serious impairment in communication or judgement; or inability to function in almost all areas.
20-11	Some danger of hurting self or others; or occasionally fails to maintain minimal personal hygiene; or gross impairment in communication.
10-1	Persistent danger of severely hurting self or others; or persistent inability to maintain minimal personal hygiene; or serious suicidal act.

Table 3.46. GAF: modified version

Performance score	Symptoms	Social
90-61	Possibly some mild symptoms.	Generally functioning pretty well.
60-51	Moderate degree of symptoms.	Moderate difficulty in social functioning.
50-41	Marked symptoms.	Serious impairment in social functioning.
40-31	Some impairment in reality testing.	Major impairment in communication; major impairment in several social areas.
30-21	Behaviour is considerably influenced by delusions or hallucinations.	Serious impairment in communication or judgement; inability to function in almost all areas.
20-11	Some danger of hurting self or others.	Gross impairment in communication or judgement; occasionally fails to maintain personal hygiene.
10-1	Persistent danger of severely hurting self or others.	Almost no ability in communication or judgement; persistent inability to maintain minimal personal hygiene.

22. Sleeps, unless directed into activity.
23. Says that he/she is no good.
24. Has to be told to follow hospital routine.
25. Has difficulty completing even simple tasks on his/her own.
26. Talks, mutters or mumbles to himself/herself.
27. Is slow moving and sluggish.
28. Giggles or smiles to himself/herself without any apparent reason.
29. Quick to fly off the handle.
30. Keeps himself/herself clean.

3.6.3 Aggression States: Attacks or Peak Episodes

According to dictionaries (e.g. Reber 1985), the term attack has two meanings: (a) Sudden onset of a symptom (syndrome), such as epileptic fits or panic attacks; (b) aggressive action covering both verbal and physical varieties. In this compendium the term aggression is used to cover a syndrome which may be generalized, and which may have peak episodes (attacks) with a sudden, often dramatic, onset (aggressive actions).

Table 3.47 compares anxiety, depression and aggression in relation to generalized levels and behaviour of attacks. The correlation between the generalized level and attacks may not be linear. As mentioned above, Freud (1895) observed that the degree to which symptoms of generalized anxiety are combined in anxiety attacks varies extraordinarily, and that almost any symptom alone can constitute an attack. The same may well be the case in states of aggression.

The first scale developed to measure aggressive actions (attacks) was the Overt Aggression Scale (OAS) constructed by Yudofsky et al. (1986). This scale measures the aggressive overt (outward) attack on the basis of nursing staff observations of three items: verbal aggression, physical aggression against objects, and physical aggression against others; the scale has one further item for inward aggression. No psychometric evaluation of construct validity in the OAS has been published. A preliminary study found the differential weights assigned by Yudofsky et al. in summing the items to a total score to be of no advantage compared to equal weights. The Staff Observation Aggression Scale (SOAS) developed by

Table 3.47. Anxiety, depression and aggression: generalized levels and attack behaviour

Syndromes	Generalized	Attacks
Anxiety	Psychic anxiety	Panic (somatic anxiety)
Depression (inward aggression)	Melancholia	Suicidal impulses
Aggression (outward aggression)	Mania	Peak assaults

Palmstierna and Wistedt (1987) focuses on the factors that may provoke aggressive behaviour. The modified OAS/SOAS for recording aggressive incidents is presented below. In the combined OAS/SOAS the following items cover the psychopathology of aggression in the OAS: item 10 corresponds to item 1 on the original OAS (verbal aggression), item 11 to 2 (physical aggression against object), item 12 to 3 (physical aggression against self), 13 to 4 (physical aggression against others), and 19 to 5 (intervention). According to the original OAS instruction (Yudofsky et al. 1986) all five items were summed to give the rating for the patient. It is recommended, however, to separate psychopathology (items 1–4) from intervention (item 5); furthermore, it is recommended to separate item 3 from items 1, 2 and 4, as the three latter measure outward aggression while item 3 measures inward aggression.

Overt Aggresion Scale/Staff Observation Aggression Scale

The questions of the modified OAS/SOAS are presented below with the exception of those posed as open questions, these are scored as 'yes' ('1') or 'no' ('0'). (The omitted subject '1' is used for personal/registration data.) The OAS includes items 10–13 and 19. These are weighted as follows: item $10 - a1 = 1$, $a2 = 2$, $a3 = 3$, $a4 = 4$; item $11 - b1 = 2$, $b2 = 3$, $b3 = 4$, $b4 = 5$; items $12 - c1 = 3$, $c2 = 4$, $c3 = 5$, $c4 = 6$; item $13 - d1 = 3$, $d2 = 4$, $d3 = 5$, $d4 = 6$. It is recommended to score item 19 separately and to subtotal scores on items 10, 11, 13 for outward aggression.

2.1   Time when aggression started
2.2   Duration of aggressive incident (minutes)
3   Was the aggressive incident expected?
If yes it was because of:
3.1   Threats by the patient
3.2   Previous aggressive/violent incidents
3.3   Other
4.   Was the aggressive incident provoked?
If yes, who, what provoked the patient:
4.1   Other patient(s)
4.2   Relatives
4.3   Staff member
4.4   Other person
5   If provoked by staff, was it:
5.1   Help with ADL
5.2   Staff demanding patient to take medication
5.3   Staff demanding patient to be more active
5.4   Staff demanding patient to show responsibility
5.5   Restrictions
5.6   Other
6   Is the patient:
6.1   Psychotic
6.2   Intoxicated

6.3   Having withdrawal symptoms
6.4   Demented
6.5   Other
7   If psychotic:
7.1   Schizophrenia
7.2   Depression
7.3   Mania
7.4   Delirium tremens
7.5   Other
8   If intoxicated:
8.1   Alcohol
8.2   Minor tranquillizers
8.3   Heroine/morphine
8.4   Amphetamine
8.5   Hashish (marihuana)/cocaine
8.6   Other
9   If withdrawal symptoms:
9.1   Alcohol
9.2   Medicine/drugs
10A   Verbal aggression
10A.1   Makes loud noises, shouts angrily
10A.2   Yells mild personal insults, e.g. "You're stupid!"
10A.3   Curses viciously, uses foul language in anger, uses moderate threats to others or self
10A.4   Makes clear threats of violence towards others or self ("I'm going to kill you") or requests help to control self
11B   Physical- aggression against objects
11B.1   Slams door, scatters clothing, makes a mess
11B.2   Throws objects down, kicks furniture without breaking it, marks the wall
11B.3   Breaks objects, smashes windows
11B.4   Sets fires, throws objects dangerously
12C   Physical aggression against self
12C.1   Picks or scratches skin, hits self, pulls hair (with no or minor injury only)
12C.2   Bangs head, hits fist into objects, throws self onto floor or into objects (hurts self without serious injury)
12C.3   Small cuts or bruises, minor burns
12C.4   Mutilates self, makes deep cuts, bites that bleed, internal injury, fracture, loss of consciousness, loss of teeth
12C.5   Suicide/attempt
Specify
13D   Physical aggression towards other people
13D.1   Makes threatening gesture, swings at people, grabs at clothes 13D.2 Strikes, kicks, pushes, pulls hair (without injury to them)
13D.3   Attacks others causing mild-moderate physical injury (bruises, sprain, welts)

13D.4   Attacks others causing severe physical injury (broken bones, deep lacerations, internal injury)
14   Sexually provocative (kissing, touching)
If yes, in which way?
15   Aim of aggression
15.1   Nothing/nobody
15.2   Objects
15.3   Staff member
15.4   Other patient(s)
15.5   Other person(s)
Sex of victim:
16   Consequences for victim(s)
16.1   None
Objects:
16.2   Damaged, replaced
16.3   Damaged, not replaced
17   Persons
17.1   Felt threatened
17.2   Pain < 10 min
17.3   Pain > 10 min
17.4   Visible injury
17.5   Need for treatment
17.6   Need for treatment by physician
18   Staff
18.1   If staff member, what position/job
18.2   Reported vocational injury
19E   Intervention
19E.1   None
19E.2   Talking to patient
19E.3   Closer observation
19E.4   Holding patient
19E.5   Immediate oral medication
19E.6   Immediate injected medication
19E.7   Isolation without seclusion
19E.8   Seclusion
19E.9   Use of restraints
19E.10 Injury requires immediate treatment of patient
19E.11 Injury requires immediate treatment of other person
If E.5, what drug/dose
If E.6, what drug/dose
20   Where did the aggressive incident take place?

3.6.4 The Social Dysfunction and Aggression Scale (SDAS)

The Social Dysfunction and Aggression Scale (SDAS) was originally developed as an observer scale measuring generalized aggression (Wistedt et al. 1990). The first version contained 11 items (SDAS-11) of which nine items (SDAS-9) measured outward aggression and two items (SDAS-2) measured inward aggression. In the first study (Wistedt et al. 1990) it was found that SDAS-9 had adequate construct validity and inter-observer reliability, and no correlation was found between SDAS-9 and SDAS-2.

The second study with SDAS (ERAG 1992) examined a larger sample of items especially for inward aggression, in total 21 items were included (SDAS-21). This version of the scale considered the possibility to use the items twice, namely to measure both generalized aggression and attacks of aggression, analogue to the use of the Hamilton Anxiety Scale (Chapter 2) in both generalized anxiety and panic anxiety. By use of Rasch analysis it was shown (ERAG 1992) that the SDAS-9 (outward aggression) was homogenous both for generalized aggression and for attacks (peaks) of aggression. The inter-observer reliability of the scale was also found adequate. The SDAS-9 scoring sheet is shown in 'Appendix 3.15'.

Factor analysis of the SDAS-21 (ERAG 1992) not only supported the SDAS-9 (outward aggression factor) but identified also a second factor including the SDAS-2 items of inward aggression (suicidal impulses and self-mutilating behaviour). However, the Rasch analysis accepted six of these items in the following rank order: psychic anxiety, somatic anxiety, social withdrawal, depressed mood, self-dislike, and suicidal impulses. These items are the core symptoms of melancholia (cf. Chapter 2, the Hamilton/Melancholia Scale). The item of self-mutilation was, thus, not accepted by the Rasch analysis (ERAG 1992) implying that this item should be regarded not as an indicator of aggression but, for instance, as an indicator of borderline anhedonia (cf. Chapter 5, see also Gundersen and Phillips 1991 and Simeon et al. 1992).

Table 3.48 shows the psychometric description of SDAS-9.

Table 3.49 shows the components of outward aggression comparing the SDAS-9, the hostility factor of the AMDP system (Pietzcker et al. 1983), and the nurse-rating scale (Yudofsky et al. 1986).

Table 3.50 shows the components of inward aggression comparing the seven SDAS items (SDAS-7) inward scale, SDAS-2 inward scale and the Yudofsky scale. This part of aggression is still not psychometrically valid, therefore only SDAS-9 is included in this compendium.

The NOSIE-30, as a nurse scale measuring aspects of aggression or social dysfunction in the ward (see Sect. 3.6.2), is complementary to SDAS as the items of the NOSIE-30 are defined in terms of frequency and those of the SDAS in terms of severity.

In Chapter 4 the Spielberger et al. (1982) self-assessment scales for anger or aggression are described.

Table 3.48. Psychometric description: SDAS-9

Type	Severity scale.
Content validity	The scale includes the components shown in Table 3.49. The scale should be used as the Hamilton Anxiety Scale to measure both generalized aggression and peak of aggression (attacks).
Administration	Rating scale to be used by skilled raters on the basis of observation and other information. Thus, the generalized aggression to be administered by psychiatrists, and the attacks by nurses.
Time frame	For the generalized scale the level during the previous 3 days. For the peak aspect the number of attacks and their duration are indicated, and the typical feature for the attacks are then rated.
Item selection	First generation scale based on literature.
Item calibration	Likert definitions, 0-4.
Number of items	Nine.
Construct validity	Acceptable in terms of Rasch analysis (ERAG 1992) both for generalized and peak assessments
Concurrent validity	Acceptable congruence with global assessments (Spearman coefficient of 0.84).
Inter-observer reliability	Acceptable intra-class coefficient.

Table 3.49. Item distributions of rating scales: components of outward aggression

Component	OAS-3	SDAS-9	AMDP
Irritable mood (irritability, anger, dysphoria)	0%	22%	29%
Social dysfunction (uncooperative, provocative, e.g. sexually)	0%	22%	19%
Verbal: unspecified	33%	11%	*
Verbal: specified	0%	11%	*
Physical: objects	33%	11%	*
Physical: persons	33%	22%	*
Number of items	3	9	7

*in total 14%

Social Dysfunction and Aggression Scale

The scoring sheet for the SDAS-9 is illustrated in "Appendix 3.15". Instructions for scoring its 9 items are presented below, using the SDAS-21 original item number system in brackets.

1(1) Irritability
This item covers the reduced ability to cope with situations regarded as provocative by the patient, impatience, and the reduced ability to control responses;
0. Not present.
1. Slight or possible impatience and/or slight difficulty controlling responses.
2. Mildly impatient and irritated; some difficulty controlling reactions.

Table 3.50. Item distributions of rating scales: components of inward aggression

Component	OAS-3	SDAS-2	SDAS-7
Aggressive emotions (self-dislike, suicidal thoughts)	0%	50%	29%
Social dysfunction (withdrawal, attention seeking)	0%	0%	29%
Verbal (hypochondriasis)	0%	0%	14%
Physical (self-mutilation, addictive behaviour)	100%	50%	29%
Number of items	1	2	7

3. Moderately impatient, easily provoked, poor control over reactions, but this has still limited impact on personal relations.
4. Severe impatience and irritability, no control over reactions, feels constantly provoked which interferes significantly with interpersonal relations.

2(2) Negativism/Uncooperative Behaviour

Covers the reduced ability to cooperate or to conform to a group, e.g. refuses to comply with ward regulations or management plan.
0. Not present.
1. Slight or possible non-verbal/verbal opposition when discipline is required.
2. Mild negativism. Does not want to cooperate, but can control him-/herself when told to conform.
3. Moderate negativism; clearly fighting all authority, though still moderate; sometimes undisciplined.
4. Severe negativism; ostentatious in opposing the rules of social intercourse, fully uncooperative.

3(3) Dysphoric Mood

Covers a type of dysphoric mood where the patient is moody, testy, and fed up.
0. Not present.
1. Slight, or possibly present.
2. Mild; the patient has displayed a slight mood of dissatisfaction.
3. Moderate; the patient has given the impression of being moderately gloomy and testy but still with limited impact on interpersonal relations.
4. Severe; the patient has given the impression of being extremely sullen and crabby, displaying clear signs of intense discontent and dissatisfaction which significantly interfere with interpersonal relations.

4(6) Socially Disturbing/Provocative Behaviour

The patient behaves in a provocative manner towards others. Includes also sexually provocative behaviour.
0. Not present.
1. Slight, or possibly present.
2. The patient has acted provocatively, to a mild degree.
3. The patient has acted provocatively, to a moderate degree.
4. The patient has seriously acted provocatively.

5(7) Non-directed Verbal/Vocal Aggressiveness

This item covers verbal aggressiveness or noises assumed to represent agression which (instead of being directed towards defined persons) is/are directed towards people or things in general, e.g. the staff, the ward, or society in general.

0. Not present.
1. Very slight or possible verbal aggressiveness, though only implicitly present.
2. Mild aggressiveness which is explicitly present, but only intermittently.
3. Moderate level of verbal aggressiveness, sometimes vociferous, e.g. claiming "everything to be wrong" or shouting angrily.
4. Severe and somtimes screaming aggressiveness of general nature, this may include cursing or swearing.

6(8) Directed Verbal/Vocal Aggressiveness
Covers verbal aggressiveness directed towards particular people.
0. Not present.
1. Very slight or possible aggressiveness towards defined individuals.
2. Mild aggressiveness manifested by an explicit way of talking, though the aggressive contents are only present in short outbursts.
3. Moderate aggressiveness, e.g. insulting people personally, more constant, sometimes vociferous.
4. Severe and sometimes screaming aggressiveness, e.g. making serious insults or wishing people harm.

7(9) Physical Violence Towards Things
0. Not present.
1. Slight, or possibly present (threatening gestures).
2. Mild, occasional episode of throwing or hitting things.
3. Repeated episodes of throwing trivial things, hitting objects or slamming doors.
4. Severe, has been destroying significantly large or important objects, i.e. T.V., windows and furniture.

8(10) Physical Violence Towards Staff
0. Not present.
1. Slight, or possibly present (threatening gestures).
2. Mild; the patient has tried to hit out at/kick a member of staff, though without touching the person.
3. Moderate; the patient has kicked/punched a member of staff. No severe injuries.
4. Severe; the patient has dangerously assaulted a member of staff and/or has tried to strangle a member of staff who was injured.

9(11) Physical Violence Towards Others Than Staff (Non-staff)
E.g. visitors or other patients.
0. Not present.
1. Slight, or possibly present (threatening gestures).
2. Mild; the patient tried to hit out at/kick non-staff, though without touching the person.

3. Moderate; the patient has kicked/punched non-staff. No severe injuries.
4. Severe; the patient has dangerously assaulted non-staff, and/or has tried to strangle non-staff who was injured.

References

Ban TA, Guy W (eds.) The Manual for the Assessment and Documentation of Psychopathology (AMDP-system). Berlin: Springer, 1982.

Beigel A, Murphy DL, Bunney WE. The manic state rating scale. Arch Gen Psychiat 1971; 75: 256–262.

European Rating Aggression Group (ERAG). Social Dysfunction and Aggression Scale (SDAS-21) in generalized aggression and in aggressive attacks: A validity and reliability study. Int J Methods Psychiat Res 1992; 2: 15–29.

Frank G. Psychiatric Diagnosis: A Review of Research. Oxford: Pergamon Press, 1975.

Freud S. The justification for detaching from neurasthenia a particular syndrome: The anxiety neurosis (First published in Neurologisches zentralblatt, 1885). Collected Papers (vol. 4) New York: Basic Books, 1959 pp. 76–106.

Gundersen JG, Phillips KA. A current view of the interface between borderline personality disorder and depression. Am J Psychiat 1991; 148: 967–975.

Guy W. Early clinical drug evaluation (ECDEU) assessment manual for psychopharmacology. Publication No. 76–338. Rockville: National Institute of Mental Health, 1976.

Honigfeld G. NOSIE-30: History and current status of its use in pharmacopsychiatric research. In Pichot P (ed.) Psychological Measurements in Psychopharmacology. Basel: Karger, 1974, pp. 238–63.

Honigfeld G, Klett CJ. The Nurses' Observation Scale for Inpatient Evaluation. A new ward behaviour rating scale. J Clin Psychol 1965; 21: 65–71.

Honigfeld G, Gillis RD, Klett CJ. NOSIE-30. A treatment sensitive ward behaviour scale. Psychol Rep 1966; 19: 180–2.

Murphy DL, Beigel A, Weingartner H, Bunney WE. The quantification of manic behaviour. In Pichot P (ed.) Psychological Measurements in Psychopharmacology. Basel: Karger, 1974, pp. 203–20.

Palmstierna T, Wistedt B. Staff observation aggression scale (SOAS). Acta Psychiatr Scand 1987; 76: 657–63.

Pietzcker A, Gebhardt R, Strauss A, Stöckel M, Langer C, Freudenthal K. The syndrome scales in the AMDP system. In Bobon D, Baumann U, Angst J, Helmchen H, Hippius H (eds.) The AMDP System in Pharmacopsychiatry. Basel: Karger, 1983, pp. 88–99.

Reber A. Dictionary of Psychology. New York: Viking, 1985.

Shatin L, Freed EX. A behavioural rating scale for mental patients. J Ment Sci 1955; 101: 644–53.

Simeon D, Standley B, Frances A, Mann JJ, Winchel R, Standley M. Self-mutilation in personality disorders: psychological and biological correlates. Am J Psychiat 1992; 149: 221–226.

Spielberger CD, Jacobs G, Russel S, Crane RS. Assessment of anger: The state-trait scale. In Butcher JN (ed.) Personality Assessments. New York: Erolbaun Hillsdale, 1982.

Wistedt B, Rasmussen A, Pedersen L, Malm U, Träskman-Bendz L, Berggren M, Wakelin J, Bech P. The development of an observer scale for measuring social dysfunction and aggression (SDAS). Pharmacopsychiatry 1990; 23: 249–52.

Wittenborn JR. Symptoms patterns in a group of mental hospital patients. J Consult Psychol 1951; 15: 290–302.

Wittenborn JR, Holzberg JD. The generality of psychiatric syndromes. J Consult Psychol 1951; 15: 372–80.

Yudofsky SC, Silver JM, Jackson W, Endicott G, Williams D. The overt aggression scale for the objective rating of verbal and physical aggression. Am J Psychiat 1986; 143: 35–9.

3.7 Conclusion

Chapter 3 contains the DSM-III-R axis 1 syndromes and related ICD-10 syndromes. Most of these are target syndromes, i.e. the core components to which the treatment is related. Table 3.51 provides an overview of the various syndromes with reference to their respective components. Only for depression are diagnostic aspects included (endogenous versus reactive melancholia); this is an example of a dimensional approach for diagnostic purposes. The above syndromes follow DSM-III-R and ICD-10 to a large extent. However, the separation of negative and positive syndromes of schizophrenia is a recent rating scale approach. The syndromes of neurasthenia and aggression are dealt with only little in DSM-III-R and ICD-10.

One of the drawbacks in following DSM-III-R is the artificial separation of anxiety from depression. Many symptoms within the borderline of clinical psychiatry (e.g. obsessions, panic, irritability) should be evaluated for their clinical significance in the broad field of emotional dimensions. This has been illustrated by the anxiety-depression diagram shown in Figure 3.3 (Bech 1992).

Symptoms such as panic, pain, irritability or obsessions are often presentation symptoms by patients with psychosomatic disorders. It is the doctor's task to evaluate such symptoms in the anxiety-depression frames of reference. From a psy-

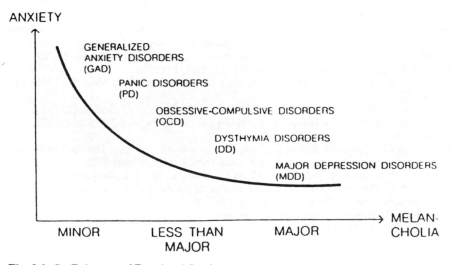

Fig. 3.3. Co-Existence of Emotional Syndromes

Table 3.51. Components of axis 1 syndromes

Dementia Chap 3, Table 3	Withdrawal syndrome Chap 3, Table 9	Schizophrenia Neg. syndrome Chap 3, Table 13	Schizophrenia Pos. syndrome Chap 3, Table 14	Mania Chap 3, Table 16	Depressive Syndrome (Melancholia) Chap 3, Table 21
Cognitive deficits Orientation Arousal Social Motor Mood Psychotic symptoms Vegetative Other specific	Autonomic hyperactivity Orientation Motor Psychotic (delirious)	Autism Ambivalence Anhedonia Cognitive deficits	Psychotic symptoms Cognitive beliefs Motor Aggression	Mood Motor Cognitive beliefs Social Vegetative	Mood Anxiety Motor Cognitive Social Vegetative

Table 3.51 (cont.)

Depression Diagnosis Chap 3, Table 24	Anxiety Panic Generalized Chap 3, Table 26b	Phobia Syndrome Chap 3, Table 32	Neurasthenia Syndrome Chap 3, Table 34	Aggression Outward Syndrome (Attack-Gen) Chap 3, Table 44	Intrusive Cognition Disorders
Psychosocial stressors	Anxious mood	Agoraphobia	Pain	Irritable mood	Obsessions
Personality	Phobia	Social phobia	Fatique	Social dysfunction	Compulsions
Previous episodes	Motor tension	Simple phobia	Memory	Verbal aggression (unspecified)	Panic
Diurnal Variation	Psychic tension		Depressive mood	Verbal aggression (specified)	Pain
Reactivity of sympt.	Autonomic hyperactivity		Anxious mood	Physical aggression (objects)	Irritability
Biological sympt.	Arousal		Social	Physical aggression (persons)	Preoccupation
Psycholog. sympt.	Depressed mood		Vegetative sympt.	Physical aggression (persons)	Hypochondriasis
Severity of sympt.			Autonomic hyperactivity		Worry
			Arousal		Discomfort

chometric point of view Figure 3.3 stimulates to careful measurements. The individual symptoms such as panic, pain and obsessions are specific, global-like indicators which most validly can be measured by visual analogue scales (Bech 1992). Furthermore, there is no linear relationship between these presentation indicators in contrast to the dimension of anxiety and depression (the Hamilton and Melancholia Scales). Thus, the use of anxiolytics can often provoke depression in obsessive states by removing anxiety symptoms. The desynchrony of the individual states in Figure 3.3 calls for including both anxiety and depression scales in states of panic, pain and obsessions.

Obsessions, compulsions, panic, or preoccupations have been brought together under the concept of intrusive cognitions by Salkovskis (1990) who defines these cognitions as mental events that are perceived as interrupting a person's stream of consciousness by capturing the focus of attention. These intrusive cognitions can take the form of 'verbal' thoughts, images, or impulses, or some combination of the three. The automatic thoughts claimed by Beck (1967) to be the aetiological basis for clinical depression should also be considered as intrusive cognitions. As discussed by Bech (1991a) the items of the Beck Depression Inventory (Beck et al. 1961) are a mixture of clinical symptoms of melancholia and intrusive thoughts. Salkovskis (1990) claims that the mechanisms governing the occurrence and persistence of clinical intrusive thoughts may be an integral part of normal problem-solving activity.

Figure 3.1 showed that anxiety disorders are the most non-organic syndromes in Chapter 3. Figure 3.3 illustrates how intrusive cognition disorders can be grouped in a diagram. Their covariation is not linear. Following Beck (1967) and Salkovskis (1990) the pathology of anxiety and depression is extreme variants of normal problem-solving processes by intrusive cognitions. It is important to measure the states included in Figure 3.3 by appropriate rating scales including global scales (Bech 1992). Self-rating scales are of special interest in this field and they will be more carefully described in Chapter 4.

3.8 Other Scales

The principle for selecting the rating scales in Chapter 3 emphasizes those with proper psychometric characteristics, among which are Likert definitions, i.e. with values of 0–4. Among scales excluded by this criterion are the dementia scale of Gottfries et al. (GBS; Gottfries et al. 1982) and the depression rating scale of Montgomery and Åsberg (1979). These scales have been included below. The Sheehan Clinician-Rated Anxiety Scale has been included. This scale was designed specifically for severity of panic attacks. It has so far not been sufficiently investigated regarding its construct validity. Preliminary results (Albus et al. 1990; Maier et al. 1990) have shown that the clinician version of this scale has higher validity than the self-rating version. The original PANSS and the Depressive Retardation Rating Scale have been included. Finally, the Cognitive Subscale of Alzheimer's Disease (ADAS) and the Mini Mental State (MMSE) have been included because they both are frequently used to measure severity of dimension.

3.8.1 Gottfries-Bråne-Steen Scale

This scale (GBS) contains 26 items (Gottfries et al. 1982). The items are grouped into the following subscales: motor function (6 items), intellectual functions (11 items) emotional functions (3 items), and general symptoms (6 items). Of these subscales 'intellectual functions' and 'emotional functions' are the most specific for measuring the dimension of dementia. These two subscales and their scoring instructions are presented below.

Intellectual Dysfunction Subscale

1. Impaired Orientation In Space (0, patient knows which geographical place, which hospital/department/ward he is in, i.e. patient is completely orientated in space; 1; 2, has some defects in spatial orientation but is orientated in his own department or in his own home; 3; 4, is disorientated, i.e. has defects of orientation in his own department or in his home; 5; 6, is completely disorientated in space).

2. Impaired Orientation in Time (0, patient knows day of week, date and year; 1; 2, knows what year and what month it is (but not the name of the day and the date); 3; 4, knows which season it is; 5; 6, is completely disorientated in time; 9, is not testable).

3. Impaired Personal Orientation (0, patient has accurate knowledge of his name, occupation, age and date of birth; 1; 2, knows his name but may lack knowledge of other personal details; 3; 4, remembers his name only with some help; 5; 6, is completely disorientated as to personal details).

4. Impaired Recent Memory (0, patient has no disturbance of recent memory, i.e. he/she knows what has happened during the last 24 hours; 1; 2, has some impairment of recent memory but this is evident only in more detailed conversation or testing; 3; 4, has such impairment of recent memory that this is evident in superficial conversation; 5; 6, recent memory has completely gone; patient cannot remember anything from one moment to the next).

5. Impaired Distant Memory (0, no disturbance of distant memory – in detailed conversation the patient remembers the names of persons important to him/her and important political or other events during the years of childhood and youth; 1; 2, cannot answer questions such as the above. He/she finds it difficult to remember important persons and important political events from earlier periods in life; 3; 4, has much impaired distant memory, which is evident in superficial conversations, e.g. does not remember names, numbers, places of residence, etc., of members of the family; 5; 6, distant memory has completely gone).

6. Impaired Wakefulness (0, patient is fully awake; 1; 2, from time to time the patient appears slightly drowsy; 3; 4, Shows signs of drowsiness but only slight encouragement is required to keep him awake; 5; 6, is somnolent, i.e. drowsy. It is possible to wake patient but he/she soon lapses again into drowsiness).

7. Impaired Concentration (0, there are no difficulties in concentration, i.e. patient has not difficulty in collecting his thoughts in the interview situation, in following a T.V. programme or in reading a written text; 1; 2, from time to time appears to lose concentration, i.e. wanders from the subject of discussion now and then and has some difficulty in reading or in following a T.V. programme; 3; 4, has obvious disturbance of concen-

tration, which makes it difficult to keep to the thread of the conversation or to find coherence in T.V. programmes, newspaper articles and the like; 5; 6, has such severe deficiencies in concentration power that no meaningful conversation can be conducted with him/her).

8. Inability to Increase Tempo (0, patient can hurry when this is required of him/her; 1; 2, when hustled, performance becomes obviously worse but patient manages to do what is required; 3; 4, when hustled, performance is so severely impaired that not even simple tasks can be carried out and the patient may become irritable, restless and/or confused; 5; 6 reactions are so blunted that he/she does not react at all when the attempt is made to hurry him/her).

9. Absentmindedness (0, patient is normally collected; 1; 2, from time to time may appear absentminded; 3; 4, is moderately but constantly absentminded; 5; 6, is continuously so absentminded that he/she is incapable of purposeful and meaningful occupation).

10. Long-Windedness (0, patient expressed himself/herself normally; 1; 2, may occasionally be wordy and overfull of detail in descriptions. He/she has, however, no difficulty at all in keeping to the subject; 3; 4, is constantly loquacious, with unending detail, has difficulty in 'coming to the point' and makes many digressions from the subject; 5; 6, is incapable of expressing what he/she wants to say and completely loses himself/herself in wordy detail; 9, is not testable).

11. Distractibility (0, patient's attention can be normally held at stimulation; 1; 2, attention is now and then captured by irrelevant stimuli; 3; 4, attention is striking and constantly captured; 5; 6, attention is so seriously captured, that meaningful activity is not possible).

Emotional Dysfunction Subscale

1. Emotional Blunting (0, no disturbance of emotional function; the patient is able to react appropriately in different situations, i.e. he/she is able to feel sorrow, joy, hate, fear, anger etc.; 1; 2, there is no occasional disturbance of function. May show signs of emotional functions but the 'fine' nuances previously characteristic of the patient have been lost; 3; 4, may show signs of joy, sorrow, etc., but does so in a crude and superficial manner; 5; 6, emotional functions have become completely extinguished, i.e. he/she is incapable of showing signs of sorrow, joy, hate, fear, anger, etc.).

2. Emotional Lability (0, patient can control his/her emotional reactions normally; 1; 2, with strong emotional stimulation, weeps or laughs in an ininhibited or exaggerated manner; 3; 4, even with moderate emotional stimulation the patient reacts in an uninhibited manner; 5; 6, ability to control emotional reactions is completely abolished; 9, is not testable).

3. Reduced Motivation (0, patient is in his/her situation normally motivated for activity and occupation; 1; 2, needs considerable encouragement to begin any task and usually shows only passive interest; 3; 4, is clearly lacking in motivation and needs constant exhortation to begin and complete any task; 5; 6, is not motivated at all and never spontaneously begins any task. Even with very strong stimulation the patient cannot be induced to take part).

3.8.2 The Positive and Negative Syndrome Scale

In Section 3.3 is shown a shortened version of this scale (each item defined from 0 to 4 and with no overlap between item definitions). The original scale (with items defined from 0 to 6) is shown in the following:

Positive Scale (P)

P1 Delusions. Beliefs which are unfounded, unrealistic, and idiosyncratic. *Basis for rating*: thought content expressed in the interview and its influence on social relations and behavior.
1   Absent – Definition does not apply.
2   Minimal – Questionable pathology; may be at the upper extreme of normal limits.
3   Mild – Presence of one or two delusions which are vague, uncrystallized, and not tenaciously held. Delusions do not interfere with thinking, social relations, or behavior.
4   Moderate – Presence of either a kaleidoscopic array of poorly formed, unstable delusions or of a few well-informed delusions that occasionally interfere with thinking, social relations, or behavior.
5   Moderate severe – Presence of numerous well-informed delusions that are tenaciously held and occasionally interfere with thinking, social relations, or behavior.
6   Severe – Presence of a stable set of delusions which are crystallized, possibly systematized, tenaciously held, and clearly interfere with thinking, social relations, and behavior.
7   Extreme – Presence of a stable set of delusions which are either highly systematized or very numerous, and which dominate major facets of the patient's life. This frequently results in inappropriate and irresponsible action, which may even jeopardize the safety of the patient or others.

P2 Conceptual Disorganization. Disorganized process of thinking characterized by disruption of goal-directed sequencing, e.g. circumstantiality, tangentiality, loose associations, non sequiturs, gross illogicality, or thought block. *Basis for rating*: cognitive-verbal processes observed during the course of interview.
1   Absent – Definition does not apply.
2   Minimal – Questionable pathology; may be at the upper extreme of normal limits.
3   Mild – Thinking is circumstantial, tangential, or paralogical. There is some difficulty in directing thoughts toward a goal, and some loosening of associations may be evidenced under pressure.
4   Moderate – Able to focus thoughts when communications are brief and structured, but becomes loose or irrelevant when dealing with more complex communications or when under minimal pressure.
5   Moderate severe – Generally has difficulty in organizing thoughts, as evidenced by frequent irrelevancies, disconnectedness, or loosening of associations even when not under pressure.
6   Severe – Thinking is seriously derailed and internally inconsistent, resulting in gross irrelevancies and disruption of thought processes, which occur almost constantly.

7   Extreme – Thoughts are disrupted to the point where the patient is incoherent. There is marked loosening of associations, which results in total failure of communication, e.g. 'word salad' or mutism.

P3 Hallucinatory Behaviour. Verbal report or behaviour indicating perceptions which are not generated by external stimuli. These may occur in the auditory, visual, olfactory, or somatic realms. *Basis for rating*: verbal report and physical manifestations during the course of interview as well as reports of behaviour by primary care workers or family.

1   Absent -Definition does not apply.
2   Minimal – Questionable pathology; may be at the upper extreme of normal limits.
3   Mild – One or two clearly formed but infrequent hallucinations, or else a number of vague abnormal perceptions which do not result in distortions of thinking or behavior.
4   Moderate – Hallucinations occur frequently but not continuously, and the patient's thinking and behavior are affected only to a minor extent.
5   Moderate severe – Hallucinations are frequent, may involve more than one sensory modality, and tend to distort thinking and/or disrupt behaviour. Patient may have delusional interpretation of these experiences and respond to them emotionally and, on occasion, verbally as well.
6   Severe – Hallucinations are present almost continuously, causing major disruption of thinking and behaviour. Patient treats these as real perceptions, and functioning is impeded by frequent emotional and verbal responses to them.
7   Extreme – Patient is almost totally preoccupied with hallucinations, which virtually dominate thinking and behavior. Hallucinations are provided a rigid delusional interpretation and provoke verbal and behavioral responses, including obedience to command halluciantions.

P4 Excitement. Hyperactivity as reflected in accelerated motor behaviour, heightened responsivity to stimuli, hypervigilance, or excessive mood lability. *Basis of rating*: behavioral manifestations during course of interview as well as reports of behavior by primary care workers or family.

1   Absent – Definition does not apply
2   Minimal – Questionable pathology; may be at the upper extreme of normal limits.
3   Mild – Tends to be slightly agitated, hypervigilant, or mildly overaroused throughout the interview, but without distinct episodes of excitement or marked mood lability. Speech may be slightly pressured.
4   Moderate – Agitation or overarousal is clearly evident throughout the interview, affecting speech and general mobility, or episodic outbursts occur sporadically.
5   Moderate severe – Significant hyperactivity or frequent outbursts of motor activity are observed, making it difficult for the patient to sit still for longer than several minutes at any given time.

6   Severe – Marked excitement dominates the interview, delimits attention, and to some extent affects personal functions such as eating and sleeping.

7   Extreme – Marked excitement seriously interferes in eating and sleeping and makes interpersonal interactions virtually impossible. Acceleration of speech and motor activity may result in incoherence and exhaustion.

P5 Grandiosity. Exaggerated self-opinion and unrealistic convictions of superiority, including delusions of extraordinary abilities, wealth, knowledge, fame, power, and moral righteousness. *Basis for rating*: thought content expressed in the interview and its influence on behavior.

1   Absent – Definition does not apply.

2   Minimal – Questionable pathology; may be at the upper extreme of normal limits.

3   Mild – Some expansiveness or boastfullness is evident, but without clearcut grandiose delusions.

4   Moderate – Feels distinctly and unrealistically superior to others. Some poorly formed delusions about special status or abilities seems present, but are not acted upon.

5   Moderate severe – Clear-cut delusions concerning remarkable abilities, status, or power are expressed and influence attitude but not behavior.

6   Severe – Clear-cut delusions of remarkable superiority involving more than one parameter (wealth, knowledge, fame, etc.) are expressed, notably influence interactions, and may be acted upon.

7   Extreme – Thinking, interactions, and behavior are dominated by multiple delusions of amazing ability, wealth, knowledge, fame, power, and/or moral stature, which may take on a bizarre quality.

P6 Suspiciousness/Persecution. Unrealistic or exaggerated ideas of persecution as reflected in guardedness, a distrustful attitude, suspicious hypervigilance, or frank delusions that others mean one harm. *Basis for rating*: thought content expressed in the interview and its influence on behaviour.

1   Absent – Definition does not apply.

2   Minimal – Questionable pathology; may be at the upper extreme of normal limits.

3   Presents a guarded or even openly distrustful attitude, but thoughts, interactions and behavior are minimally affected.

4   Distrustfulness is clearly evident and intrudes on the interview and/or behavior, but there is no evidence of persecutory delusions. Alternatively, there may be indication of loosely formed persecutory delusions, but these do not seem to affect the patient's attitude or interpersonal relations.

5   Moderate severe – Patient shows marked distrustful, leading to major disruption of interpersonal relations, or else there are clear-cut persecutory delusions that have limited impact on interpersonal relations or behaviour.

6   Clear-cut pervasive delusions of persecution which may be systematized and significantly interfere in interpersonal relations.

7   Extreme – A network of systematized persecutory delusions dominates the patient's thinking, social relations, and behavior.

P7 Hostility. Verbal and nonverbal expressions of anger and resentment, including sarcasm, passive-aggressive behavior, verbal abuse, and assaultiveness. *Basis for rating*: interpersonal behavior observed during the interview and reports by primary care workers or family.
1   Absent – Definition does not apply.
2   Minimal – Questionable pathology; may be at the upper extreme of normal limits.
3   Mild – Indirect or restrained communication of anger, such as sarcasm, disrespect, hostile expressions, and occasional irritability.
4   Moderate – Presents an overtly hostile attitude, showing frequent irritability and direct expression of anger or resentment.
5   Moderate severe – Patient is highly irritable and occasionally verbally abusive or threatening.
6   Severe – Uncooperativeness and verbal abuse or threats notably influence the interview and seriously impact upon social relations. Patient may be violent and destructive but is not physically assaultive toward others.
7   Extreme – Marked anger results in extreme uncooperativeness, precluding other interactions, or in episode(s) of physical assault toward others.

Negative Scale (N)

N1 Blunted Affect. Diminished emotional responsiveness as characterized by a reduction in facial expression, modulation of feelings, and communicative gestures. *Basis for rating*: observation of physical manifestations of affective tone and emotional responsiveness during the course of interview.
1   Absent – Definition does not apply.
2   Minimal – Questionable pathology; may be at the upper extreme of normal limits.
3   Mild – Changes in facial expression and communicative gestures seem to be stilted, forced, artificial, or lacking in modulation.
4   Moderate – Reduced range of facial expression and few expressive gestures result in a dull appearance.
5   Moderate severe – Affect is generally 'flat', with only occasional changes in facial expression and a paucity of communicative gestures.
6   Severe – Marked flatness and deficiency of emotions exhibited most of the time. There may be unmodulated extreme affective discharges, such as excitement, rage, or inappropriate uncontrolled laughter.
7   Extreme – Changes in facial expression and evidence of communicative gestures are virtually absent. Patient seems constantly to show a barren or 'wooden' expression.

N2 Emotional Withdrawal. Lack of interest in, involvement with, and affective commitment to life's events. *Basis for rating*: reports of functioning from primary care workers or family and observation of interpersonal behavior during the course of interview.

1 Absent – Definition does not apply.

2 Minimal – Questionable pathology; may be at the upper extreme of normal limits.

3 Mild – Usually lacks initiative and occasionally may show deficient interest in surrounding events.

4 Moderate – Patient is generallty distanced emotionally from his milieu and its challenges but, with encouragement, can be engaged.

5 Moderate severe – Patient is clearly detached emotionally from persons and events in the milieu, resisting all efforts at engagement. Patient appears distant, docile, and purposeless but can be involved in communication at least briefly and tends to personal needs, sometimes with assistance.

6 Severe – Marked deficiency of interest and emotional commitment results in limited conversation with others and frequent neglect of personal functions, for which the patient requires supervision.

7 Extreme – Patient is almost totally withdrawn, uncommunicative, and neglectful of personal needs as a result of profound lack of interest and emotional commitment

N3 Poor Rapport. Lack of interpersonal empathy, openness in conversation, and sense of closeness, interest or involvement with the interviewer. This is eviddenced by interpersonal distancing and reduced verbal and nonverbal communication. *Basis for rating*: interpersonal behaviour during the course of interview.

1 Absent – Definition does not apply.

2 Minimal – Questionable pathology; may be at the upper extreme of normal limits.

3 Mild – Conversation is characterized by a stilted, strained, or artificial tone. It may lack emotional depth or tend to remain on an impersonal, intellectual plane.

4 Moderate – Patient typically is aloof, with interpersonal distance quite evident. Patient may answer questions mechanically, act bored, or express disinterest.

5 Moderate severe – Disinvolvement is obvious and clearly impedes the productivity of the interview. Patient may tend to avoid eye or face contact.

6 Severe – Patient is highly indifferent, with marked interpersonal distance. Answers are perfunctory, and there is little nonverbal evidence of involvement. Eye and face contact are frequently avoided.

7 Extreme – Patient is totally uninvolved with the interviewer. Patient appears to be completely indifferent and consistently avoids verbal and nonverbal interactions during the interview.

N4 Passive/Apathetic Social Withdrawal. Diminished interest and initiative in social interactions due to passivity, apathy, anergy or avolition. This leads to reduced interpersonal involvements and neglect of activities of daily life. *Basis for rating:* reports on social behavior from primary care workers or family.

1   Absent – Definition does not apply.
2   Minimal – Questionable pathology; may be at the upper extreme of normal limits.
3   Mild – Shows occasional interest in social activities but poor initiative. Usually engages with others only when approached first by them.
4   Passively goes along with most social activities but in a disinterested or mechanical way. Tends to recede into the background.
5   Moderate severe – Passively participates in only a minority of activities and shows virtually no interest or initiative. Generally spends little time with others.
6   Severe – Tends to be apathetic and isolated, participating very rarely in social activities and occasionally neglecting personal needs. Has very few spontaneous social contacts.
7   Extreme – Profoundly apathetic, socially isolated, and personally neglectful.

N5 Difficulty in Abstract Thinking. Impairment in the use of the abstract-symbolic mode of thinking, as evidenced by difficulty in classification, forming generalizations, and proceeding beyond concrete or egocentric thinking in problem-solving tasks. *Basis for rating:* response to questions on similarities and proverb interpretation, and use of concrete vs. abstract mode during the course of the interview.

1   Absent – Definition does not apply.
2   Minimal – Questionable pathology; may be at the upper extreme of normal limits.
3   Mild – Tends to give literal or personalized interpretations to the more difficult proverbs and may have some problems with concepts that are fairly abstract or remotely related.
4   Moderate – Often utilizes a concrete mode. Has difficulty with many proverbs and some categories. Tends to be distracted by functional aspects and salient features.
5   Moderate severe – Deals primarily in a concrete mode, exhibiting difficulty with most proverbs and many categories.
6   Severe – Unable to grasp the abstract meaning of any proverbs or figurative expressions and can formulate classifications for only the most simple of similarities. Thinking is either vacuous or locked into functional aspects, salient features and idiosyncratic interpretations.
7   Extreme – Can use only concrete modes of thinking. Shows no comprehension of proverbs, common metaphors or similes, and simple categories. Even salient and functional attributes do not serve as a basis for classification. This rating may apply to those who cannot interact even minimally with the examiner due to marked cognitive impairment.

N6 Lack of Spontaneity and Flow of Conversation. Reduction in the normal flow of communication associated with apathy, avolition, defensiveness, or cognitive deficit. This is manifested by diminished fluidity and productivity of the verbal-interactional process. *Basis for rating*: cognitive-verbal processes observed during the course of interview.

1 Absent – Definition does not apply.
2 Minimal – Questionable pathology; may be at the upper extreme of normal limits.
3 Conversation shows little initiative. Patient's answers tend to be brief and unembellished, requiring direct and leading questions by the interviewer.
4 Moderate – Conversation lacks free flow and appears uneven or halting. Leading questions are frequently needed to elicit adequate responses and proceed with conversation.
5 Moderate severe – Patient shows a marked lack of spontaneity and openness, replying to the interviewer's questions with only one or two brief sentences.
6 Severe – Patient's responses are limited to a few words or short phrases intended to avoid or curtail communication. (E.g.,"I don't know," "I'm not at liberty to say.") Conversation is seriously impaired as a result, and the interview is highly unproductive.
7 Extreme – Verbal output is restricted to, at most, an occasional utterance, making conversation not possible.

N7 Stereotyped Thinking. Decreased fluidity, spontaneity, and flexibility of thinking, as evidenced in rigid, repetitious or barren thought content. *Basis for rating*: cognitive-verbal processes observed during the interview.

1 Absent – Definition does not apply.
2 Minimal – Questionable pathology; may be at the upper extreme of normal limits.
3 Mild – Some rigidity shown in attitudes or beliefs. Patient may refuse to consider alternative positions or have difficulty in shifting from one idea to another.
4 Moderate – Conversation revolves around a recurrent theme, resulting in difficulty in shifting to a new topic.
5 Moderate – Thinking is rigid and repetitious to the point that, despite the interviewer's efforts, conversation is limited to only two or three dominating topics.
6 Severe – Uncontrolled repetition of demands, statements, ideas, or questions which severely impairs conversation.
7 Extreme – Thinking, behavior, and conversation are dominated by constant repetition of fixed ideas or limited phrases, leading to gross rigidity, inappropriateness, and restrictiveness of patient's communication.

General Psychopathology Scale (G)

G1 Somatic Concern. Physical complaints and beliefs about bodily illness or malfunctions. This may range from a vague sense of ill being to clear-cut delusions of catastrophic physical disease. *Basis for rating*: thought content expressed in the interview.

1   Absent – Definition does not apply.
2   Minimal – Questionable pathology; may be at the upper extreme of normal limits.
3   Mild – Distinctly concerned about health or somatic issues, as evidenced by occasional questions and desire for reassurance.
4   Moderate – Complaints about poor health or bodily malfunction, but there is no delusional conviction, and overconcern cam be allayed by reassurance.
5   Moderate severe – Patient expresses numerous or frequent complaints about physical illness or bodily malfunction, or else patient reveals one or two clear-cut delusions involving these themes but is not preoccupied by them.
6   Severe – Patient is preoccupied by one or a few clear-cut delusions about physical disease or organic malfunction, but affect is not fully immersed in these themes, and thoughts can be diverted by the interviewer with some effort.
7   Extreme – Numerous and frequently reported somatic delusions, or only a few somatic delusions of a catastrophic nature, which totally dominate the patient's affect and thinking.

G2 Anxiety. Subjective experience of nervousness, worry, apprehension, or restlessness, ranging from excessive concern about the present or future to feelings of panic. *Basis for rating*: verbal report during the course of interview and corresponding physical manifestations.

1   Absent – Definition does not apply.
2   Minimal – Questionable pathology; may be at the upper extreme of normal limits.
3   Mild – Expresses some worry, overconcern, or subjective restlessness, but no somatic and behavioral consequences are reported or evidenced.
4   Moderate – Patient reports distinct symptoms of nervousness, which are reflected in mild physical manifestations such as fine hand tremor and excessive perspiration.
5   Moderate severe – Patient reports serious problems of anxiety which have significant physical and behavioral consequences, such as marked tension, poor concentration, palpitations, or impaired sleep.
6   Severe – Subjective state of almost constant fear associated with phobias, marked restlessness, or numerous somatic manifestations.
7   Extreme – Patient's life is seriously disrupted by anxiety, which is present almost constantly and, at times, reaches panic proportion or is manifested in actual panic attacks.

G3 Guilt Feelings. Sense of remorse or self blame for real or imagined misdeeds in the past. *Basis for rating*: verbal report of guilt feelings during the course of interview and the influence on attitudes and thoughts.

1 Absent – Definitiondoes not apply.

2 Minimal – Questionable pathology; may be at the upper extreme of normal limits.

3 Mild – Questioning elicits a vague sense of guilt or self-blame for a minor incident, but the patient clearly is not overly concerned.

4 Moderate – Patient expresses distinct concern over his responsibility for a real incident in his life but is not preoccupied with it, and attitude and behavior are essentially unaffected.

5 Moderate severe – Patient expresses a strong sense of guilt associated with self-deprecation or the belief that he deserves punishment. The guilt feelings may have a delusional basis, may be volunteered spontaneously, may be a source of preoccupation and/or depressed mood, and cannot be allayed readily by the interviewer.

6 Severe Strong ideas of guilt take on a delusional quality and lead to an attitude of hopelessness or wothlessness. The patient believes he should receive harsh sanctions for the misdeeds and may even regard his current life situation as such punishment.

7 Extreme – Patient's life is dominated by unshakable delusions of guilt, for which he feels deserving of drastic punishment, such as life imprisonment, torture, or death. There may be associated suicidal thoughts or attribution of others' problems to one's own past misdeeds.

G4 Tension. Overt physical manifestations of fear, anxiety, and agitation, such as stiffness, tremor, profuse sweating, and restlessness. *Basis for rating*: verbal report attesting to anxiety and, thereupon, the severity of physical manifestations of tension observed during the interview.

1 Absent – Definition does not apply.

2 Minimal – Questionable pathology; may be at the upper extreme of normal limits.

3 Mild – Posture and movements indicate slight apprehensiveness, such as minor rigidity, occasional restlessness, shifting of position, or fine rapid hand tremor.

4 Moderate – A clearly nervous appearance emerges from various manifestations, such as fidgety behavior, obvious hand tremor, excessive perspiration, or nervous mannerisms.

5 Moderate severe – Pronounced tension is evidenced by numerous manifestations, such as nervous shaking, profuse sweating, and restlessness, but conduct in the interview is not significantly affected.

6 Severe – Pronounced tension to the point that interpersonal interactions are disrupted. The patient, for example, may be constantly fidgeting, unable to sit still for long, or show hyperventilation.

7   Extreme – Marked tension is manifested by signs of panic or gross motor acceleration, such as rapid restless pacing and inability to remain seated for longer than a minute, which makes sustained conversation not possible.

G5 Mannerisms and Posturing. Unnatural movements or posture as characterized by an awkward, stilted, disorganized, or bizarre appearance. *Basis for rating*: observation of physical manifestations during the course of interview as well as reports from primary care workers or family.
1   Absent – Definition does not apply.
2   Minimal – Questionable pathology; may be at the upper extreme of normal limits.
3   Mild – Slight awkwardness in movements or minor rigidity of posture.
4   Moderate – Movements are notably awkward or disjointed, or an unnatural posture is maintained for brief periods.
5   Moderate severe – Occasional bizarre rituals or contorted posture are observed, or an abnormal position is sustained for extended periods.
6   Severe – Frequent repetition of bizarre rituals, mannerisms or stereotyped movements, or a contorted posture is sustained for extended periods.
7   Extreme – Functioning is seriously impaired by virtually constant involvement in ritualistic, manneristic, or stereotyped movements or by an unnatural fixed posture which is sustained most of the time.

G6 Depression. Feelings of sadness, discouragement, helplessness, and pessimism. *Basis for rating*: verbal report of depressed mood during the course of the interview and its observed influence on attitude and behavior.
1   Absent – Definition does not apply.
2   Minimal – Questionable pathology; may be at the upper extreme of normal limits.
3   Mild – Expresses some sadness or discouragement only on questioning, but there is no evidence of depression in general attitude or demeanor.
4   Moderate – Distinct feelings of sadness or hopelessness, which may be spontaneously divulged, but depressed mood has no major impact on behavior or social functioning, and the patient usually can be cheered up.
5   Moderate severe – Distinctly depressed mood is associated with obvious sadness, pessimism, loss of social interest, psychomotor retardation, and some interference in appetite and sleep. The patient cannot be easily cheered up.
6   Severe – Markedly depressed mood is associated with sustained feelings of misery, occasional crying, hopelessness, and worthlessness. In addition, there is major interference in appetite and/or sleep as well as in normal motor and social funtions, with possible signs of self-neglect.
7   Extreme – Depressive feelings seriously interfere in most major functions. The manifestations include frequent crying, pronounced somatic symptoms, impaired concentration, psychomotor retardation, social disinterest, self-neglect, possible depressive or nihilistic delusions, and/or possible suicidal thoughts or action.

G7 Motor Retardation. Reduction in motor activity as reflected in slowing or lessening of movements and speech, diminished responsiveness to stimuli, and reduced body tone. *Basis for rating*: manifestations during the course of interview as well as reports by primary care workers or family.

1   Absent –Definition does not apply.
2   Minimal – Questionable pathology; may be at the upper extreme of normal limits.
3   Mild – Slight but noticeable diminution in rate of movement and speech. Patient may be somewhat underproductive in conversation and gestures.
4   Moderate – Patient is clearly slow in movements, and speech may be characterized by poor productivity, including long response latency, extended pauses, or slow pace.
5   Moderate severe – A marked reduction in motor activity renders communication highly unproductive or delimits functioning in social and occupational situations. Patient can usually be found sitting or lying down.
6   Severe – Movements are extremely slow, resulting in a minimum of activity and speech. Essentially the day is spent sitting idly or lying down.
7   Extreme – Patient is almost completely immobile and virtually unresponsive to external stimuli.

G8 Uncooperativeness. Active refusal to comply with the will of significant others, including the interviewer, hospital staff, or family, which may be associated with distrust, defensiveness, stubbornness, negativism, rejection of authority, hostility, or belligerence. *Basis of rating*: interpersonal behavior observed during the course of interview as well as reports by primary care workers or family.

1   Absent – Definition does not apply.
2   Minimal – Questionable pathology; may be at the upper extreme of normal limits.
3   Mild – Complies with an attitude of resentment, impatience, or sarcasm. May inoffensively object to sensitive probing during the interview.
4   Moderate – Occasional outright refusal to comply with normal social demands, such as making own bed, attending scheduled programs, etc. The patient may project a hostile, defensive, or negative attitude but usually can be worked with.
5   Moderate severe – Patient frequently is incompliant with the demands of his milieu and may be characterized by others as an 'outcast' or having 'a serious attitude problem'. Uncooperativeness is reflected in obvious defensiveness or irritability with the interviewer and possible unwillingness to address many questions.
6   Severe – Patient is highly uncooperative, negativistic, and possibly also belligerent. Refuses to comply with most social demands and may be unwilling to initiate or conclude the full interview.
7   Extreme – Active resistance seriously impacts on virtually all major areas of functioning. Patient may refuse to join in any social activities, tend to personal

hygiene, converse with family or staff, and participate even briefly in an interview.

G9 Unusual Thought Content. Thinking characterized by strange, fantastic or bizarre ideas, ranging from those which are remote or atypical to those which are distorted, illogical, and patently absurd. *Basis for rating*: thought content expressed during the course of the interview.

1 Absent – Definition does not apply.
2 Minimal – Questionable pathology; may be at the upper extreme of normal limits.
3 Mild – Thought content is somewhat peculiar or idiosyncratic, or familiar ideas are framed in an odd context.
4 Moderate – Ideas are frequently distorted and occasionally seem quite bizarre.
5 Moderate severe – Patient expresses many strange and fantastic thoughts (e.g., being the adopted son of a king, being an escapee from death row) or some which are patently absurd (e.g., having hundreds of children, receiving radio messages from outer space through a tooth filling).
6 Severe – Patient expresses many illogical or absurd ideas or some which have a distinctly bizarre quality (e.g., having three heads, being a visitor from another planet).
7 Extreme – Thinking is replete with absurd, bizarre, and grotesque ideas.

G10 Disorientation. Lack of awarenses of one's relationship to the milieu, including persons, place, and time, which may be due to confusion or withdrawal. *Basis for rating*: responses to interview questions on orientation.

1 Absent – Definition doesnot apply.
2 Minimal – Questionable pathology; may be at the upper extreme of normal limits.
3 Mild – General orientation is adequate but there is some difficulty with specifics. For example, patient knows his location but not the street address; knows hospital staff names but not their functions; knows the month but confuses the day of week with an adjacent day; or errs in the date by more than two days. There may be narrowing of interest evidenced by familiarity with the immediate but not extended milieu, such as ability to identify staff but not the Mayor, Governor, or President.
4 Moderate – Only partial success in recognizing persons, places, and time. For example, patient knows he is in a hospital but not its name; knows the name of his city but not the borough or district; knows the name of his primary therapist but not many other direct care workers; knows the year and season but is not sure of the month.
5 Moderate severe – Considerable failure in recognizing persons, place, and time. Patient has only a vague notion of where he is and seems unfamiliar with most people in his milieu. He may identify the year correctly or nearly so but not know the current month, day or week, or even the season.

6 Severe – Marked failure in recognizing persons, place, and time. For example, patient has no knowledge of his whereabouts; confuses the date by more than one year; can name only one or two individuals in his current life.

7 Extreme – Patient appears completely disoriented with regard to persons, place, and time. There is gross confusion or total ignorance about one's location, the current year, and even the most familiar people, such as parents, spouse, friends, and primary therapist.

G11 Poor Attention. Failure in focused alertness manifested by poor concentration, distractability from internal and external stimuli, and difficulty in harnessing, sustaining, or shifting focus to new stimuli. *Basis for rating*: manifestations during the course of the interview.

1 Absent – Definition does not apply.

2 Minimal – Questionable pathology; may be at the upper extreme of normal limits.

3 Mild – Limited concentration evidenced by occasional vulnerability to distraction or faltering attention toward the end of interview.

4 Moderate – Conversation is affected by the tendency to be easily distracted, difficulty in long sustaining concentration on a given topic, or problems in shifting attention to new topics.

5 Moderate severe – Conversation is seriously hampered by poor concentration, distractability, and difficulty in shifting focus appropriately.

6 Severe – Patient's attention can be harnessed for only brief moments or with great effort, due to marked distraction by internal or external stimuli.

7 Extreme – Attention is so disrupted that even brief conversation is not possible.

G12 Lack of Judgement and Insight. Impaired awareness or understanding of one's own psychiatric condition and life situation. This is evidenced by failure to recognize past or present psychiatric illness or symptoms, denial of need for psychiatric hospitalization or treatment, decisions characterized by poor anticipation of consequences, and unrealistic short-term and long-range planning. *Basis for rating*: thought content expressed during the interview.

1 Absent – Definition does not apply.

2 Minimal – Questionable pathology; may be at the upper extreme of normal limits.

3 Mild – Recognizes having a psychiatric disorder but underestimates its seriousness, the implications for treatment, or the importance of taking measures to avoid relapse. Future planning may be poorly conceived.

4 Moderate – Patient shows only vague or shallow recognition of illness. There may be fluctuations in acknowledgement of being ill or little awareness of major symptoms which are present, such as delusions, disorganized thinking, suspiciousness, and social withdrawal. The patient may rationalize the need for treatment in terms of its relieving lesser symptoms, such as anxiety and sleep difficulty.

5   Moderate severe – Acknowledges past but not present psychiatric disorder. If challenged, the patient may concede the presence of some unrelated or insignificant symptoms, which tend to be explained away by gross misinterpretation or delusional thinking. The need for psychiatric treatment is unrecognized.

6   Severe – Patient denies ever having had psychiatric disorder. He disavows the presence of any psychiatric symptoms in the past or present and, though compliant, denies the need for treatment and hospitalization.

7   Extreme – Emphatic denial of past and present psychiatric illness. Current hospitalization and treatment are given a delusional interpretation (e.g., as punishment for misdeeds, as persecution by tormentors, etc.), and the patient may thus refuse to cooperate with therapist, medication, or other aspects of treatment.

G13 Disturbance of Volition. Disturbance in the wilful initiation, sustenance, and control of one's thoughts, behavior, movements and speech. *Basis for rating*: thought content and behavior manifested in the course of interview.

1   Absent – Definition does not apply.

2   Minimal – Questionable pathology; may be at the upper extreme of normal limits.

3   Mild – There is evidence of some indecisiveness in conversation and thinking, which may impede verbal and cognitive processes to a minor extent.

4   Moderate – Patient is often ambivalent and shows difficulty in reaching decisions. Conversation may be marred by alternation in thinking, and in consequence verbal and cognitive functioning are clearly impaired.

5   Moderate severe – Disturbance of volition interferes in thinking as well as behavior. Patient shows pronounced indecision that impedes the initiation and continuation of social and motor activities, and which also may be evidenced in halting speech.

6   Severe – Disturbance of volition interferes in the execution of simple, automatic motor functions, such as dressing and grooming, and markedly affects speech.

7   Extreme – Almost complete failure of volition is manifested by gross inhibition of movement and speech, resulting in immobility and/or mutism.

G14 Poor Impulse Control. Disordered regulation and control of action on inner urges, resulting in sudden unmodulated, arbitrary, or misdirected discharge of tension and emotions without concern about consequences. *Basis for rating*: behavior during the course of the interview and reported by primary care workers and family.

1   Absent – Definition does not apply.

2   Minimal – Questionable pathology; may be at the upper extreme of normal limits.

3   Patient tends to be easily angered and frustrated when facing stress or denied gratification but rarely acts on impulse.

4   Moderate – Patient gets angered and verbally abusive with minimal provoca-
    tion. May be occasionally threatening or destructive, or have one or two
    episodes involving physical confrontation or a minor brawl.
5   Moderate severe – Patient exhibits repeated impulsive episodes involving ver-
    bal abuse, destruction of property, or physical threats. There may be one or
    two episodes involving serious assault, for which the patient requires isolation,
    physical restraint or p.r.n. sedation.
6   Severe – Patient frequently is impulsively aggressive, threatening, demanding,
    and destructive, without any apparent consideration of consequences. Shows
    assaultive behavior and may also be sexually offensive and possibly respond
    behaviorally to hallucinatory commands.
7   Extreme – Patient exhibits homicidal attacks, sexual assaults, repeated brutal-
    ity, or self-destructive behavior. Requires constant direct supervision or exter-
    nal constraints because of inability to control dangerous impulses.

G15 Preoccupation. Absorption with internally generated thoughts and feelings
and with autistic experiences to the detriment of reality orientation and adaptive
behavior. *Basis for rating*: interpersonal behaviour observed during the course of
the interview.
1   Absent – Definition does not apply.
2   Minimal – Questionable pathology; may be at the upper extreme of normal
    limits.
3   Mild – Excessive involvement with personal needs or problems, such that
    conversation veers back to egocentric themes and there is diminished concern
    exhibited toward others.
4   Moderate – Patient often appears self-absorbed, as if day-dreaming or
    involved with internal experiences, which interferes with communication to a
    minor extent.
5   Moderate severe – Patient often appears to be engaged in autistic experiences,
    as evidenced by behaviors that significantly intrude on social and communica-
    tional functions, such as the presence of a vacant stare, muttering or talking to
    oneself, or involvement with stereotyped motor patterns.
6   Severe – Marked preoccupation with autistic experiences, which seriously de-
    limits concentration, ability to converse, and orientation to the milieu. The pa-
    tient frequently may be observed smiling, laughing, muttering, talking, or
    shouting to himself.
7   Extreme – Gross absorption with autistic experience, which profoundly affects
    all major realms of behavior. The patient constantly may be responding ver-
    bally and behaviorally to hallucinations and show little awareness of other
    people or the external milieu.

G16 Active Social Avoidance. Diminished social involvement associated with
unwarranted fear, hostility or distrust. *Basis for rating*: reports of social functioning by primary care workers or family.

1   Absent – Definition does not apply.
2   Minimal – Questionable pathology; may be at the upper extreme of normal limits.
3   Mild – Patient seems ill at ease in the presence of others or prefers to spend time alone, although he participates in social functions when required.
4   Moderate – Patient begrudgingly attends all or most social activities but may need to be persuaded or may terminate prematurely on account of anxiety, suspiciousness, or hostility.
5   Moderate severe – Patient fearfully or angrily keeps away from many social interactions despite other's efforts to engage him. Tends to spend unstructured time alone.
6   Severe – Patient participates in very few social activities because of fear, hostility, or distrust. When approached, the patient shows a strong tendency to break off interactions, and generally he appears to isolate himself from others.
7   Extreme – Patient cannot be engaged in social activities because of pronounced fears, hostility, or persecutory delusions. To the extent possible, he avoids all interactions and remains isolated from others.

3.8.3 Montgomery-Åsberg Depression Scale

This scale is a subscale of the Comprehensive Psychopathological Rating Scale developed by Montgomery and Åsberg (1979). The scale consists of the following items:
1   Apparent sadness. Representing despondency, gloom and despair, (more than just ordinary transient low spirits) reflected in speech, facial expression, and posture. Rate by depth and inability to brighten up. (0, no sadness; 1; 2, looks dispirited but brightens up occasionally; 3; 4, appears sad and unhappy all the time; 5; 6, continuous experience of misery or extreme despondency).
2   Reported sadness. Representing subjectively experienced mood, regardless of whether it is reflected in appearance or not. Includes depressed mood, low spirits, despondency, and the feeling of being beyond help and without hope. Rate according to intensity, duration and extent to which the mood is influenced by events. Elated mood is scored zero on this item. (0, occasional sadness may occur in the circumstances; 1; 2, predominant feeling of sadness, but brighter moments occur; 3; 4, pervasive feelings of sadness or gloominess. The mood is hardly influenced by external circumstances; 5; 6, continuous experience of misery or extreme despondency).
3   Inner tension. Representing feelings of ill-defined discomfort, edginess, inner turmoil, mental tension mounting to panic, dread and anguish. Rate according to intensity, frequency, duration and the extent of reassurance called for. (0, placid. Only fleeting inner tension; 1; 2, occasional feelings of edginess and ill-defined discomfort; 3; 4, continuous feelings of inner tension, or intermittent panic which the patient can only master with some difficulty; 5; 6, unrelenting dread or anguish. Overwhelming panic).

4   Reduced sleep. Representing a subjective experience of reduced duration or
    depth of sleep compared to the subject's own normal pattern when well. (0,
    sleeps as usual; 1; 2, slight difficulty dropping off to sleep or slightly reduced,
    light or fitful sleep; 3; 4, sleep reduced or broken by at least 2 hours; 5; 6, less
    than two or three hours sleep).

5   Reduced appetite. Representing the feeling of a loss of appetite compared with
    when well. (0, normal; 1; 2, slightly reduced appetite; 3; 4, no appetite. Food is
    tasteless. Need to force oneself to eat; 5; 6, must be forced to eat. Food re-
    fusal).

6   Concentration difficulties. Representing difficulties in collecting one's
    thoughts mounting to incapacitating lack of concentration. Rate according to
    intensity, frequency, and degree of incapacity produced. (0, no difficulties in
    concentrating; 1; 2, occasional difficulties in collecting one's thoughts; 3; 4,
    difficulties in concentrating and sustaining thought which interfere with read-
    ing or conversation; 5; 6, incapacitating lack of concentration).

7   Lassitude. Representing a difficulty getting started or slowness initiating and
    performing everyday activities. (0, hardly any difficulties in getting started:
    No sluggishness; 1; 2, difficulties in starting activities; 3; 4, difficulties in
    starting activities; 3; 4, difficulties in starting simple routine activities, which
    are carried out only with effort; 5; 6, complete lassitude. Unable to start activ-
    ity without help.)

8   Inability to feel. Representing the subjective experience of reduced interest in
    the surroundings, or activities that normally give pleasure. The ability to react
    with adequate emotion to circumstances or people is reduced. (0, normal inter-
    est in the surroundings and in other people; 1; 2, reduced ability to enjoy usual
    interests. Reduced ability to feel anger; 3; 4, loss of interest in the surround-
    ings. Loss of feelings for friends and acquaintances; 5; 6, the experience of
    being emotionally paralyzed, inability to feel anger or grief, and a complete or
    even painful failure to feel for close relatives and friends).

9   Pessimistic thoughts. Representing thoughts of guilt, inferiority, self-reproach,
    sinfulness, remorse and ruin. (0, no pessimistic thoughts; 1; 2, fluctuating
    ideas of failure, self-reproach or self-depreciation; 3; 4, persistent self-accusa-
    tions, or definite but still rational ideas of guilt or sin. Increasingly pessimistic
    about the future; 5; 6, delusions of ruin, remorse and unredeemable sin.
    Absurd self-accusations).

10 Suicidal thoughts. Representing the feeling that life is not worth living, that a
    natural death would be welcome, suicidal thoughts, and preparations for sui-
    cide. Suicidal attempts should not in themselves influence the rating. (0, en-
    joys life or takes it as it comes; 1; 2, weary of life. Only fleeting suicidal
    thoughts; 3; 4, much better off dead. Suicidal thoughts are common, and sui-
    cide is considered as a possible solution, but without specific plans or inten-
    tion; 5; 6, explicit plans for suicide when there is an opportunity. Active prepa-
    rations for suicide).

3.8.4 Sheehan Clinician Rated Anxiety Scale

How severe has the patient's symptom been over the past week? 0, absent; 1, mild; 2, moderate; 3, severe; 4, very severe.

 1 Spells of dizziness/faintness, lightheadedness.
 2 Spells of rubbery legs.
 3 Spells of imbalance.
 4 Spells of dyspnea/hyperventilation.
 5 Spells of PVC's/tachycardia.
 6 Chest pain/pressure.
 7 Spells of choking sensation/lump in throat.
 8 Spells of parasthesias/numbness.
 9 Hot or cold spells.
10 Nausea.
11 Diarrhea.
12 Pains in head/neck/back.
13 Tires easily.
14 Spells of increased sensitivity to sound, light, touch (startle).
15 Sweating.
16 Derealization.
17 Depersonalisation.
18 Hypochondriasis.
19 Feeling of mental decompensation (self control/sanity).
20 Spells of fear of dying or impending disaster.
21 Spells of tremor/shaking.
22 Waves of depression with little or no provocation.
23 Emotional lability.
24 Dependent on others.
25 Compulsive rituals.
26 Obsessive thoughts.
27 Initial insomnia.
28 Middle insomnia.
29 Phobias.
30 Tension/nervousness/anxiety.
31 Signs of anxiety at interview (Tremor, facial pallor, dilated pupils, respiration or sighing, restlessness, fidgety, swallowing, burping, high pitch and speed of speech).
32 Spontaneous panic attacks – Major attacks (3+ symptoms).
33 Spontaneous anxiety or symptom attacks – Minor attacks (1–2 symptoms).
34 Anticipatory anxiety attacks.
35 Situational panic attacks.

3.8.5 Depressive Retardation Rating Scale

This scale has been developed by Widlöcher (1983) and has been included here because it is a very interesting scale when evaluating the activating components of antidepressant drugs. The Hamilton Depression Scale includes many of the relevant profiles of antidepressants, e.g. the mood brightening, the anxiolytic and the sedative. However, the Hamilton scale has only one item measuring retardation. Therefore, the combined Hamilton and Melancholia Scale (HDS/MES) is so far the most valid scale to measure profiles of antidepressants taking the Kielholz model into account (Bech 1991b). However, the Depressive Retardation Rating Scale should be considered in this field. The scale consists of the following 15 items:

1 Gait, stride (within a standard distance) (0, normal; 1, mild slowing (retardation of movement), but of an uncertain pathologic nature; 2, *one* of the following attributes is observed: (a) a lack of suppleness to the stride, or to the swing of the arms, (b) the patient drags his feet, (c) stride of normal amplitude, but slowed down, (d) slowed stride with small steps; 3, *more than one* of the signs in No. 2 are noted; 4, the patient must be supported in order to walk).

2 Slowness and paucity of movements (of limbs, trunk) (0, movements are appropriate, normal in amplitude, supple, and rhythmic – the trunk is nestled (wedged) comfortably in the chair, the shoulders relaxed. Attitude and movements are in harmony with the conversation; 1, there may be a mild degree of cramping to the movements, not readily noticeable; 2, a certain fixity (tightness of the body) is unmistakably present; 3, the patient moves his limbs only rarely, in a slowed down manner, with an awkwardness of gesture and below normal amplitude of movement *or* the proximal portions of the arms are fixed, and only the hands move. The trunk is immobile, either plastered against the back of the chair or with the shoulders drooping; 4, the patient refuses to get out of bed, or lies completely fixed in his chair. No truncal movements at all, and no mobility to the head-trunk axis).

3 Slowness and paucity of movements of the head and neck (mimetic) (0, the head moves freely, resting flexibly on the body with the gaze either exploring the room or fixed on the examiner or on other objects of interest – in an appropriate fashion. Movements of the mouth are of a normal amplitude; 1, there may be some reduction of mobility, not easily confirmed; 2, reduction of mobility is definite but mild. The gaze, while often fixed, is still capable of shifting; there is a monotonous quality, though still with some expressiveness, to the facial gestures; 3, the patient does not move his head. He does not explore the room and usually straes toward the floor, seldom looking at the examiner. He articulates poorly, barely moving his mouth; he never smiles; the expression is unchanging; 4, the face is completely immobile and painfully inexpressive).

4 Language and verbal flow (0, flow of speech appears normal; 1, barely perceptible slowing of speech; 2, a definite slowing of speech that nevertheless

does not interfere with conversation; 3, the subject speaks only upon the most forceful urging by the examiner; 4, stereotyped responses).

5   Modulation of the voice (intensity and modulation of speech) (0, appears normal; 1, barely perceptible weakening; 2, voice is weak and monotonous – listener must place his ear closer; 3, speech is barely audible – listener must request certain phrases to be repeated; 4, speech is inaudible).

6   Brevity of responses (0, the subject has no difficulty in making responses of appropriate length; 1, responses appear to be somewhat briefer than would be expected; 2, responses are brief but not to the point of compromising the course of the conversation (interfering with dialogue); 3, subject very laconic – responses are restricted to just one or two (to justa few) words; 4, only monosyllabic responses).

7   Variety of themes (topics) spontaneously approached (0, association of ides proceeds smoothly; there is a richness and variety to the themes (topics) broached by the subject; 1, conversational themes (topics) are relatively rich and varied but the patient may have some difficulty in making a quick transition from one idea to another; 2, there is a rarity and impoverishment to new themes (topics) spontaneously brought up by the patient; 3, no spontaneous offer of new themes (topics) along with a tendency to rumination on certain ideas; 4, no elaboration, Conversation is meagre, monotonous; exploration of topics isresisted).

8   Richness of associations to topics proposed by the examiner (viz,: occupation, family) 0, associations are made easily (and readily); 1, themes (topics) are relatively rich and varied, but the patient may have difficulty in moving from one idea to the next; 2, new topics rarely brought up and show little variety; 3, no new spontaneously offered topics; tendency toward rumination; 4, extremely meagre conversation).

9   Subjective experience of ruminations (0, the patient has the impression that he can think freely, without encumbrance now, just as before; 1, some uncertainty between 0 and 2; 2, the patient has the impression that his thoughts dwell on two or three themes that recur over and over, adversely affecting his current life and invading his internal world; 3, the patient has the feeling that his spontaneous thoughts tend always to collect around a single and painful preoccupation; 4, the patient experiences a total incapacity to free himself from his painful rumination(s).

10 Fatigability (0, fatigue is not mentioned spontaneously or after direct questioning; 1, fatigue is not mentioned spontaneously, but evidence for it does emerge in the course of the interview; 2, the patient is distressed by fatigability in his everyday life (eating, washing, dressing, climbing stairs); 3, fatigability is such that the patient must curb some of his activities; 4, near total reduction of activities owing to an overwhelming fatigue).

11 Interest in habitual activities (0, despite being in the hospital or in treatment the patient retains his usual interests; 1, the patient blames a certain measure of loss of interest to being in the hospital or some other pretext; 2, the cessation of certain activities (television, newspaper, knitting) is attributed to a general

lack of interest rather than (or as much as to) fatigue; 3, loss of interest is very extensive, affecting also the patient's future; 4, total loss of interest).

12 Patient's perception of the flow of time (0, the same as usual; 1, the present time passes slowly but this relates to inactivity, to being in the hospital, and so on; 2, the perceived passage of time seems slower, but this does not emerge except upon specific questioning; 3, the patient indicates spontaneously or quite readily a slowing in the (apparent) passage of time in response to a direct question; 4, passage of present time is suspended (painful perception of an infinite "present").

13 Memory (0, the subject states he has no memory difficulty; the examiner detects no evidence of memory deficit; 1, a difficulty in memory is alluded to be the patient, but this is not easily objectified; 2, memory deficit can be confirmed (for example, difficulty recalling what was served for breakfast), but is not very troublesome to the patient; 3, the memory difficulty disdescribed as a handicap (cannot find certain things; forget who visited him and when); 4, veritable amnesia).

14 Concentration (0, normal; 1, the patient believes his concentration is normal, but certain tasks requiring this capacity seem difficult to carry out; 2, the patient admits to problems with certain tasks because of trouble concentrating (reading, doing calculations, professional tasks); 3, a serious difficulty in concentration, interfering even with ordinary pursuits such as reading a newspaper, watching the television, and so on; 4, trouble concentrating affects even the interview).

15 General appreciation of retardation (0, none; 1, questionable; 2, definite; 3, moderate; 4, very serious).

3.8.6 The Cognitive Subscale
of Alzheimer's Disease Assessment Scale (ADAS)

1 Impairment in Short-term Memory
Ask the patient to read 10 words aloud giving the patient 2 seconds to look at each word. Then ask him to repeat as many words as he remembers. Three trials are performed.

Scoring: The mean score of the three attempts is used.

2 Naming of Objects and Fingers
The patient is asked to name twelve objects and all the fingers.

Scoring: $0 = 0–2$ items wrong; $1 = 3–5$ items wrong; $2 = 6–8$ items wrong; $3 = 9–11$ items wrong; $4 = 12–14$ items wrong; $5 = 15–17$ items wrong.

3 Following Commands
Receptive speech is assessed also on the patient's ability to carry out 1–5 step commands.

Scoring: 0 = all 5 correct; 1 = 1 wrong, 4 correct; 2 = 2 wrong, 3 correct; 3 = 3 wrong, 2 correct; 4 = 4 wrong, 1 correct; 5 = all wrong.

4 Constructional Praxis

The patient's ability of constructing four geometric figures is tested.

Scoring: 0 = all 4 correct; 1 = 1 figure wrong; 2 = 2 figures wrong; 3 = 3 figures wrong; 4 = 4 figures wrong; 5 = No drawings at all.

5 Ideational Praxis

The patient is instructed to pretend that he is going to mail a letter to himself. The instruction may be repeated if the patient forgets the task. The five components are: (a) folding the letter; (b) putting the letter in the envelope; (c) close the envelope; (d) write his own address and (e) show where the stamp goes.

Scoring: 0 = all components correct; 1 = fails to do one thing; 2 = fails to do 2 things; 3 = fails to do 3 things; 4 = fails to do 4 things; 5 = fails in doing it all.

6 Orientation

The components to be tested are: Name, month, date, year, day of the week, season, place and time of the day.

Scoring: The score is the number of answers which are not correct.

7 Word Recognition Task

The patient reads 12 words aloud. These words are mixed with 12 new words. The patient indicates whether the word is "new" or" old".

Scoring: 24 minus the number of correct answers.

8 Spontaneous Language Ability

This item is a global rating of the quality of speech, i.e. clarity, difficulty in making oneself understood. Quantity is not rated on this item.

Scoring: 0 = normal function; 1 = slight difficulty – one example of lack of clarity; 2 = minor difficulties – the patient is experiencing trouble less than 25% of the time; 3 = moderate degree of trouble – problems 25–50% of the time; 4 = moderate to serious degree of trouble – problems more than 50% of the time; 5 = serious trouble – one or two utterances, maybe fluent but empty talk, maybe mute.

9 Comprehension of Spoken Language

This item evaluates the patient's ability to understand speech. Do not include responses to commands.

Scoring: 0 = normal function; 1 = slight difficulties – one example of lack of understanding speech; 2 = minor difficulties – 3 to 5 examples of lack of understanding speech; 3 = moderate degree of difficulty – the patient has to be given several repetitions or paraphrases; 4 = moderate to serious troubles – only occasionally the patient answers correctly; 5 = serious troubles – the patient seriously answers questions in a irrelevant manner. This is notdue to paucity of speech.

10 Word Finding Difficulty in Spontaneous Speech

The patient has difficulty in finding the desired word in spontaneous speech. The problem maybe overcome by circumlocution, i.e. giving explanatory phrases or using nearly satisfactory synonyms. Do not include finger and object naming in this rating.

Scoring: 0 = normal function; 1 = minor problems – one or two examples, but not clinically significant; 2 = minor problems – paraphrasing or replasing words with synonyms; 3 = moderate degree of problems – now and again loss of words without trying to compensate; 4 = moderate to serious degree of problems: frequent loss of words without compensation; 5 = serious trouble – almost completely loss of words with contents, speech sounds empty, one or two utterences.

11 Recall of Test Instructions

The patient's ability to remember the requirements of the recognition task is evaluated. On each recognition trial, the patient is asked prior to presentation of the first two words: "Did you see this word before or is this word a new one?" For the third word, the patient is asked: "How about this one?" If the patient responds appropriately, i.e. "yes" or "no", the recall of the instruction is accurate. If the patient fails to respond this signifies that the instructions have been forgotten. Then instruction is repeated. The procedure used for the third wordis repeated for words 4–24. Each instance of recall failure is noted.

Scoring: 0 = no problems; 1 = slight degree of trouble – forgets once; 2 = minor degree of trouble – has to be reminded twice; 3 = moderate degree of trouble – three to four repetitions; 4 = moderate to serious degree of trouble – five to six repetitions; 5 = serious degree of trouble – seven or more repetitions.

3.8.7 Mini Mental State Examination (MMSE)

The interviewer should initially make the patient comfortable, to establish rapport, to praise successes, and to avoid pressing on items the patient finds difficult. The scale is divided into two parts. The first part requires vocal responses only and covers orientation, memory, and attention; the maximum score is 21. The second part tests ability to name, follow verbal and written commands, write a sentence spontaneously and copy a complex polygon similar to a Bender Gestalt Figure; the maximum score is 9. In total (parts 1 and 2) the maximum score is 30.

The scale consists of the following 19 individual items and their scoring:
 1 Ask for the year. Give one point for correctanswer.
 2 Ask for the season. Give one point for correct answer.
 3 Ask for the date. Give one point for correct answer.
 4 Ask for the day. Give one point for correct answer.
 5 Ask for the month. Give one point for correct answer.
 6 Ask for the state. Give one point for correct answer.
 7 Ask for the county. Give one point for correct answer.
 8 Ask for the town or city. Give one point for correct answer.

9 Ask for the hospital (or address). Give one point for correct answer.

10 Ask for the floor. Give one point for correct answer.

11 Name three objects, taking one second to say each. Then ask the patient all three after you have said them. Give one point for each correct answer. Repeat the answers until the patient learns all three (maximum score 3).

12 Ask the patient to begin with 100 and count backwards by 7. Stop after five subtractions. Give one point for each correct answer. Alternate: spell 'world' backwards. (Maximum score 5.)

13 Ask for names of three objects learned in item 11. Give one point for each correct answer.

14 Point to a pencil and a watch. Have the patient name them as you point. Give one point for each correct answer. (Maximum score 2.)

15 Have the patient repeat "No ifs, ands, or buts". Give one point for correct response. (Maximum score 1.)

16 Have the patient follow a three-stage command: "Take the paper in your right hand. Fold the paper in half. Put the paper on the floor." Give one point for each correct response. (Maximum score 3.)

17 Have the patient read and obey the following: "CLOSE YOUR EYES" (write it in capitals). Give one point for correct response. (Maximum score 1.)

18 Have the patient write a sentence of his own choice. (The sentence should contain a subject and an object and should make sense. Ignore spelling errors when scoring.) Give one point for correct response. (Maximum score 1.)

19 Have the patient copy the design printed below, adjust it to 1.5 cm per side. Give one point if the all sides and angles are preserved and if the intersected sides form a quadrangle.

References

Albus M, Maier W, Shera D, Bech P. Consistencies and discrepancies in self- and observer-rated anxiety scales: A comparison between the self and observer rated Marks-Sheehan scale. Eur Arch Psychiat Clin Neurosci 1990; 240: 96–102.

Bech P. Zones of interest in future research on depression. In: Kragh-Sørensen P, Gjerris A, Bolwig TG (eds.). Depression. Copenhagen: Munksgaard 1991a, pp. 188–196.

Bech P. Use of rating scales for neurasthenia, anxiety, and depression in general practice. In: Gastpar M, Kielholz P (eds). Problems of Psychiatry in General Practice. Bern: Hogrefe and Huber, 1991b, pp. 56–70.

Bech P. Selective serotonin reuptake inhibitors for the depressive spectrum disorders. Psykiatria 1992 (in press).

Beck AT. Depression: Clinical, Experimental, and Theoretical Aspects. Philadelphia: Univ Pennsylvania Press, 1967.

Beck AT, Ward CH, Mendelson M, Mock J, Erbaugh J. An inventory for measuring depression. Arch Gen Psychiat 1961; 4: 561–71.

Gottfries CG, Bråne G, Gullberg B, Steen G. A new rating scale for dementia syndromes. Arch Gerontol Geriatr 1982; 1: 311–330.

Maier W, Albus M, Buller R, Nutzinger D, Shera D, Bech P. Self- and observer assessment in anxiolytic drug trials: A comparison of their validity. Eur Arch Psychiat Clin Neurosci 1990; 240 :103–8.

Montgomery SA, Åsberg M. A new depression scale designed to be sensitive to change. Br J Psychiat 1979; 134: 382–9.

Salkovskis PM. Obsessions, compulsions and intrusive cognitions. In: Peck DF, Shapiro M (eds). Measuring Huam Problems. Chichester, John Wiley, 1990, pp. 90–118.

Sheehan DV. The Anxiety Disease. New York: Charles Schribner's Sons, 1983.

Widlöcher DJ. Psychomotor retardation: Clinical, theoretical, and psychometric aspects. Psychiatric Clinics of North America 1983; 6: 27–40.

Appendix 3.1a   *Scoring sheet for the BDS*

DSM-III-R	No.	Item	Score
	1	Registration	
	2	Calculation	
	3	Recall of words	
A1	4	Recent memory	
A2	5	Past memory	
	6	Orientation	
	7	Self-care	
B3	8	Speech	
	9	Depressed mood	
	10	Emotional retardation	
	11	Anxiety	
	12	Motor agitation	
	13	Hostility	
B2	14	Perplexity	
	15	Distractibility	
	16	Affective incontinence	
B1	17	Conceptual disorganization	
	18	Suspiciousness	
	19	Hallucinations	
	20	Unusual thought content	
	21	Judgement	
	Total score		

DSM-III-R criteria for dementia
A1 and A2 plus at least one B item
Are the DSM-III-R criteria fulfilled? - yes = 1; no = 0 ☐

Appendix 3.1b   *The Cambridge Dementia Scale: CAMDEX*
                         DSM-III-R criteria (in brackets CAMDEX items)

A (1) Impairment in Short-term Memory
Name the following three objects: Appla, Table, Penny [158]
What were the three objects I asked you to repeat a little while ago? (Apple, Table, Penny) [161]
Write this name and address: Mr John Brown, 42 West Street, Bedford. What was the name and address wrote on the envelope a short time ago? [178]
What is the name of the Prime Minister? [156]
What has been in the news in the past week or two? [157]

A (2) Impairment in Long-tern Memory
Can you tell me when the First World War began? [148]
Can you tell me when the Second World War began? [149]

B (1) Impairment in Abstract Thinking
In what way are an apple and a banana alike? [179]
In what way are a shirt and a dress alike? [180]
In what way are a table and a chair alike? [181]
In what are a plant and an animal alike? [182]
What is a bridge? [142]
What is an opinion? [143]

B (2) Impaired Judgment
The patient shows impaired judgment of situations and/or persons [211]

B (3) Other Disturbances of Higher Cortical Functions
Please nod your head? [130]
Is this place a hotel? [134]
Show a pencil: What is this called? [137]
Show a wristwatch: What is this called? [137]
Show some coins: How much money does this make? [176]

B (4) Personality Change (from informants)
Have you noticed changes in his personality? [238]
Has there been any noticeable exaggeration in his normal character? [239]
Has he become more (or less) changeable in mood? [240]
Has he become more (or less) irritable or angry? [241]
Does he show less concern for others? Or more? [242]
Does he get involved in difficult or embarrassing situations in public because of his behaviour? [243]
Has he become more stubborn or perhaps a little awkward? Or less? [244]

C The Disturbances in A and B Significantly Interferes with Work or Usual Social Activities
Does he have difficulty finding the way around the neighbourhood? [251]
Is there a loss of any special skill or hobby he could manage before? [258]
Does he have any difficulty performing common household chores, e.g. can he make a cup of tea? [263]
Does he have more difficulty managing small amounts of money [264]

Appendix 3.2   *Scoring sheet for the WSA*

DSM-III-R	No.	Item	Score
B2	1	Increased pulse	
A	2	Tremor	
	3	Motor restlessness	
B3	4	Temperature	
B1	5	Sweating	
C2	6	Disorientation	
C1	7	Hallucination	
	Total score		

DSM-III-R criteria:

Item A (tremor) plus at least one B item: uncomplicated state of withdrawal.

Item A (tremor) plus at least one B plus C, and C2: delirium state.

Are DSM-III-R criteria for uncomplicated state fulfilled? - yes = 1; no = 0 ☐

Are DSM-III-R criteria for delirium state fulfilled? - yes = 1; no = 0 ☐

Appendix 3.3   *Scoring sheet for the PANSS*

Negative Syndrome of Schizophrenia

DSM-III-R	No.	Item	Score
A	N1	Blunted affect	
	N2	Emotional withdrawal	
	N3	Poor rapport	
	N4	Passive social withdrawal	
	N5	Difficulty in abstract thinking	
	N6	Lack of spontaneity and flow of conversation	
	N7	Stereotyped thinking	
	Total score		

Positive Syndrome of Schizophrenia

DSM-III-R	No.	Item	Score
B	P1	Delusions: general	
A	P2	Conceptual disorganisation	
C	P3	Hallucinatory behaviour	
	P4	Excitement	
	P5	Grandiosity	
A	P6	Suspiciousness	
	P7	Hostility	
	Total score		

DSM-III-R criteria for schizophrenia: either at least two A symptoms or B or C
(indicated with a score of 3 or more)
Are DSM-III-R criteria fulfilled? - yes = 1; no = 0 ☐

Appendix 3.3   *cont.*

General psychopathology

No.	Item	Score
G1	Somatic concern	
G2	Anxiety: psychic	
G3	Guilt feeling	
G4	Tension	
G5	Mannerism and posturing	
G6	Depression	
G7	Motor retardation	
G8	Uncooperativeness	
G9	Unusual thought content	
G10	Disorientation	
G11	Poor attention	
G12	Lack of judgement and insight	
G13	Disturbance of volition	
G14	Poor impulse control	
G15	Preoccupation	
G16	Active social avoidance	
Total score		

Appendix 3.4   *Scoring sheet for the MAS*

DSM-III-R	No.	Item	Score
A (1)	1	Elevated mood	
B (3)	2	Talkativeness	
	3	Increased social contact	
B (6)	4	Increased motor activity	
B (2)	5	Sleep disturbances	
C	6	Work activity	
A (2)	7	Hostility	
B (7)	8	Increased sexual activity	
B (1)	9	Increased self-esteem	
B (4)	10	Flight of thoughts	
	11	Noise	
	Total score		

DSM-III-R criteria:
Hypomania: A (1) or A (2) and at least three B items.
Mania: A (1) or A (2), at least three B items, and C.
Are DSM-III-R criteria for hypomania fulfilled? - yes = 1; no = 0 ☐
Are DSM-III-R criteria for mania fulfilled? - yes = 1; no = 0 ☐

Appendix 3.5   *Scoring sheet for the MES-A*

DSM-III-R	No.	Item	Score
(1)	1	Lowered mood	
(2)	2	Work and interests	
(3)	3	Appetite: decreased	
(3)	4	Appetite: increased	
(3)	5	Weight: decreased	
(3)	6	Weight: increased	
(3)	7	Carbohydrate craving	
(4)	8	Sleep: insomnia	
(4)	9	Sleep: hypersomnia	
-	10	Anxiety	
-	11	Introversion	
(8)	12	Concentration difficulties	
(6)	13	Tiredness and pains	
(7)	14	Guilt feelings	
(5)	15	Verbal acitivity: decreased	
(5)	16	Verbal activity: increased	
(5)	17	Motor activity: decreased	
(5)	18	Motor activity: increased	
(9)	19	Suicidal thoughts	
		Total score	

DSM-III-R criteria: at least five of the indicated ( ) symptoms.
Are DSM-III-R criteria fulfilled? - yes = 1; no = 0 ☐

Appendix 3.6   *Scoring sheet for the MES*

DSM-III-R	No.	Item	Score
(2)	1	Work and interests	
(1)	2	Lowered mood	
(3)	3	Sleep disturbances	
	4	Anxiety	
	5	Introversion	
(7)	6	Concentration difficulties	
(5)	7	Tiredness and pains	
(6)	8	Guilt feelings	
(4)	9	Decreased verbal activity	
(8)	10	Suicidal thoughts	
(4)	11	Decreased motor activity	
		Total score	

DSM-III-R criteria for major depression: at least five of the indicated ( ) symptoms.
MES criteria for major depression: a total score of 15 or more.
MES criteria for less than major depression: a total score of 10 or more.
Are DSM-III-R criteria fulfilled? - yes = 1; no = 0 ☐

Appendix 3.7 *Scoring sheet for the 1965 Newcastle Depression Diagnostic Scale*

DSM-III	DSM-III-R	No.	Item	Score	Calculation value
		1	Deviant personality	2 1 0	0 +½ +1
		2	Psychological stresses	2 1 0	0 +1 +2
(1)		3	Quality of depression	2 1 0	+1 +½ 0
(3)	(2)	4	Weight loss	2 1 0	+2 +1 0
	(3)	5	Previous episodes	2 1 0	+1 +½ 0
(2)	(1)	6	Motor activity	2 1 0	+2 +1 0
		7	Anxiety	2 1 0	-1 -½ 0
		8	Nihilistic delusions	2 1 0	+2 +1 0
		9	Accusations of others	2 1 0	-1 -½ 0
(4)		10	Feelings of guilt	2 1 0	+1 +½ 0

DSM-III criteria: at least three of the () items.
DSM-III-R criteria: the three () items plus lack of interests and lack of reactivity.
Endogenous depression: +6 or more.
Doubtful depression: +5½
Reactive depression: +5 or less

Appendix 3.8   *Scoring sheet for the 1971*
Newcastle Depression Diagnostic Scale

DSM-III	DSM-III-R	No.	Item	Score	Calculation value
		1	Sudden onset	2 1 0	-6 -3 0
		2	Duration of episode	3 2 1 0	-6 -4 -2 0
		3	Psychological stressors	2 1 0	+12 +6 0
		4	Phobias	2 1 0	+8 +4 0
		5	Persistence of depression	2 1 0	-2 -1 0
(1)	(1)	6	Reactivity of symptoms	2 1 0	+14 +7 0
(2)	(2)	7	Diurnal variation	2 1 0	-16 -8 0
(3)	(3)	8	Early awakening	2 1 0	-10 -5 0
(4)	(4)	9	Motor inhibition	2 1 0	-9 -4½ 0
		10	Delusions	2 1 0	-7 -3½ 0

DSM-III criteria of endogenous depression: all four () systems.
DSM-III-R criteria of endogenous depression: all four () symptoms plus lack of interest.
Endogenous depression: -20 or less.
Reactive depression: -19 or more.

Appendix 3.9   *Scoring sheet for the DMS*

Endogenous axis

DSM-III	DSM-III-R	No.	Item	Score
(1)		1	Quality of depression	
(3)	(3)	2	Early awakening	
		3	Weight loss	
(2)	(2)	4	Diurnal variation	
		5	Persistence of clinical picture	
		Total score		

Reactivity axis

DSM-III	DSM-III-R	No.	Item	Score
		1	Psychological stressors	
	(1)	2	Reactivity of symptoms	
		3	Somatic anxiety	
		4	Duration of episode	
	(4)	5	Character neurosis	
		Total score		

DSM-III-R criteria of endogenous depression: all three () symptoms.
Are DSM-III criteria fulfilled? - yes = 1; no = 0 ☐
DSM-III-R criteria of endogenous depression: symptoms (2) and (3) present, but symptoms (1) and (4) not present, plus loss of interest or pleasure in all, or almost all activities.
Are DSM-III-R criteria fulfilled? - yes = 1; no = 0 ☐

Appendix 3.10a   *Scoring sheet for the HAS Panic Dimension*

DSM-III-R	No.	Item	Score
(9)(10)	1	Sensory symptoms (paraesthesias, hot and cold flushes)	
(3)	2	Cardiovascular symptoms	
(1)(6)(11)	3	Respiratory symptoms	
(7)	4	Gastro-intestinal symptoms	
	5	Genito-urinary symptoms	
(2)(5)	6	Other autonomic symptoms (dizziness, sweating)	
(4)	7	Behaviour at interview (trembling or shaking)	
	Total score		

DSM-III-R criteria for panic disorder: at least four of the () items developed during at least one attack.

Are the DSM-III-R criteria fulfilled? - yes = 1; no = 0 ☐

Number of panic attacks during the last week: ☐☐

Appendix 3.10b   *Hopkins SCL-19 Panic Anxiety Scale*

Instructions:
Below is a list of problems and complaints that people sometimes have. Circle the number
to the right that best describes how much that problem bothered or disabled you during the
past week including today. Mark only one number for each problem and do not skip any
items.

0, not at all; 1, a little bit; 2, moderately; 3, markedly; 4, extremely

DSM-III-R		Items	Score
A	1	Suddenly scared for no reason	0 1 2 3 4
A	2	Spells of terror or panic	0 1 2 3 4
C1	3	Trouble getting your breath	0 1 2 3 4
C2	4	Faintness or dizziness	0 1 2 3 4
C3	5	Heart pounding or racing	0 1 2 3 4
C4	6	Trembling	0 1 2 3 4
C5	7	Bouts of excessive sweating	0 1 2 3 4
C6	8	Choking sensation or lump in throat	0 1 2 3 4
C7	9	Nausea or upset stomach	0 1 2 3 4
C8	10	Feeling that familiar things are strange and unreal	0 1 2 3 4
C9	11	Numbness or tingling in parts of your body	0 1 2 3 4
C10	12	Hot or cold spells	0 1 2 3 4
C11	13	Pains in heart or chest	0 1 2 3 4
C12	14	Thoughts of death or dying	0 1 2 3 4
C13	15	The idea that something is wrong with your mind	0 1 2 3 4
A	16	Sudden unexpected spells	0 1 2 3 4
A	17	Sudden unexpected spells at the edge of panic	0 1 2 3 4
B	18	Anxiety episodes that are built up in anticipation	0 1 2 3 4
B	19	Surges of panic that occur when in a public situation	0 1 2 3 4
		Total score	

DSM-III-R criteria (full) for panic disorders. A + B + at least 4 C items.
Are the DSM-III-R criteria fulfilled? Yes = 1; No = 0.

Appendix 3.10c   *Scoring sheet for the HAS*

DSM-III-R	No.	Item	Score
A	1	Anxious mood	
D1	2	Tension	
D2	3	Fears	
D3	4	Insomnia	
D4	5	Concentration difficulties	
	6	Depressed mood	
B2,4	7	Muscular fatigue	
	8	Sensory symptoms	
C2	9	Cardiovascular	
C1,7,9	10	Respiratory	
C6	11	Gastro-intestinal	
C8	12	Genito-urinary	
C3,4,5	13	Other autonomic	
B1,3	14	Behaviour at interview	
	Total score		

DSM-III-R criteria for generalized anxiety: item A (anxiety) plus at least six of the B (motor tension), C (autonomic hyperactivity) or D (vigilance and scanning) items.

Are the DSM-III-R criteria fulfilled? - yes = 1; no = 0 ☐

Generalized Dimension

Appendix 3.11 *Marks-Sheehan Phobia Scale*

To fill out the phobia scale below, write a number between 0 and 10 in the *fear* column to show how much you fear a situation, and a number between 0 and 4 in the *avoid* column to show how much you avoid the situations named below.

Fear: 0 = not at all   Avoid: 0 = never
        1-3 = mildly   1 = sometimes
        4-6 = moderately   2 = often
        7-9 = markedly   3 = very often
        10 = extremely   4 = always

DSM-III-R	No.	Item	Fear	Avoid
	1	Main phobias you want treated:		
		Phobia 1 specify: _____		___
		Phobia 2 specify: _____		___
		Phobia 3 specify: _____		___
		Phobia 4 specify: _____		___
Agoraphobia	2	Going far from home alone		
Agoraphobia	3	Situations associated with sudden unexpected attacks of panic/anxiety that occur with little or no stress		
Agoraphobia	4	Traveling on buses, subways, trains, or in cars		
Agoraphobia	5	Crowded places (e.g., shopping, sports events, theatres)		
Agoraphobia	6	Large open spaces		
Simple phob.	7	Feeling trapped or caught in closed spaces		
Simple phob.	8	Being left alone		

Appendix 3.11   *cont.*

DSM-III-R	No.	Item	Fear	Avoid
Simple phob.	9	The thought of physical injury or illness		
Simple phob.	10	Hearing or reading about health topics or disease		
Social phob.	11	Eating, drinking, or writing in public		
Social phob.	12	Being watched or being the focus of attention		
Social phob.	13	Being with others because you are very self-conscious		
	14	Specify situations other than those listed above that frighten you ____ ____ ____		
	15	Specify farthest distance you can go alone ____		

Rate the present state of your phobias overall on the scale below. Circle the number you select

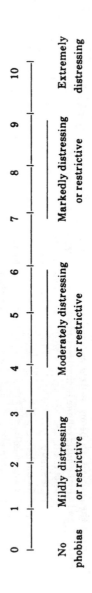

0	1	2	3	4	5	6	7	8	9	10

No phobias   Mildly distressing or restrictive   Moderately distressing or restrictive   Markedly distressing or restrictive   Extremely distressing

Appendix 3.12a   *Scoring sheet for the OCS*

DSM-III-R	No.	Item	Score
A	1	Obsessive thoughts	
B	2	Compulsive behaviour	
	3	Indecision	
	4	Concentration difficulties	
	5	Depressed mood	
	6	Psychic anxiety	
	7	Work and normal day-to-day activity	
		Total score	

DSM-III-R criteria for obsessive compulsive disorder: either A or B plus C.
Are the DSM-III-R criteria fulfilled? - yes = 1; no = 0 ☐

Appendix 3.12b *Scoring Sheet for Yale-Brown Obsession Compulsive Scale (Y-BOCS)*

No.	Items	Score	No.	Items	Score
B1	Time spent on obsession		B6	Time spent performing compulsions	
B2	Interference from obsessions		B7	Interference from compulsions	
B3	Distress of obsessions		B8	Distress from compulsive	
B4	Resistance against obsession		B9	Resistance against compulsions	
B5	Control over obsessions		B10	Control over compulsions	
Subtotal - obsessions			Subtotal - compulsions		
Total					

Appendix 3.13 Scoring sheet for the HBS subscale on conduct behaviour

DSM-III-R	No.	Item	Score
	1	Temper tantrums	
	2	Noisiness	
(3)	3	Destructiveness	
	4	Hyperactivity	
(4)	5	Lack of cooperation	
(6)	6	Behaviour in public places	
(2)	7	Aggressive behaviour	
(1)	8	Wandering	
	9	Objectional personal habits	
	10	Other behavioural problems	
(5)	11	Scattering or throwing of objects	
	12	Crying and moaning	
	Total score		

DSM-III-R criteria for conduct disorder: at least three of the ( ) items.
Are the DSM-III-R criteria fulfilled? - yes = 1; no = 0 ☐

Appendix 3.14   *NOSIE-30*

0, never; 1, sometimes; 2, often; 3, usually; 4, always

No.	Items	Subscales	Score
1	Is sloppy		
2	Is impatient	a	
3	Cries		
4	Shows interest in activities around him		
5	Sits, unless directed into activity		
6	Gets angry or annoyed easily	a	
7	Hears things that are not there		
8	Keeps his/her clothes neat		
9	Tries to be friendly with others		
10	Becomes easily upset if something does not suit him		
11	Refuses to do ordinary things expected of him	a	
12	Is irritable and grouchy	a	
13	Has trouble remembering		
14	Refuses to speak		
15	Laughs or smiles at funny comments or events		
16	Is messy in his eating habits		
17	Starts up a conservation with others		
18	Says he feels blue and depressed		
19	Talks about his interests		
20	Sees things that are not there		
21	Has to be reminded what to do		
22	Sleeps, unless directed into activity		
23	Says that he is no good		
24	Has to be told to follow hospital routine		
25	Has difficulty completing even simple tasks on his own		
26	Talks, mutters or mumbles to himself		
27	Is slow moving and sluggish		
28	Giggles or smiles to himself without any apparent reason		
29	Quick to fly off the handle	a	
30	Keeps himself clean		
Aggression subscale			
Total score			

Subscales

Negative factors:
Aggression (items 2, 6, 11, 12, 29) - a
Irritability (items 2, 6, 10, 11, 12, 29)
Manifest psychoses (items 7, 20, 26, 28)
Retardation (items 5, 22, 27)

Positive factors:
Social competence (inverted score on items 13, 14, 21, 24, 25)
Personal neatness (inverted score on items 1, 16; non-inverted score on items 8, 30)
Social interest (items 4, 9, 15, 17, 19)

Appendix 3.15 *Scoring sheet for the SDAS-9 (outward aggression)*

No.	Item	General 0-4	Peak episode 0-4
1	Irritability		
2	Negativism/Uncooperative behaviour		
3	Dysphoric mood		
6	Socially disturbing/provocative behaviour		
7	Non-directed verbal/vocal aggressiveness		
8	Directed verbal/vocal aggressiveness		
9	Physical violence towards things		
10	Physical violence towards staff		
11	Physical violence towards non-staff		

Number of attacks ☐☐
Severity of attacks (average) - 1 = minor, 2 = major ☐
Duration of attacks (average) - minutes ☐☐

4 Psychopathological Self-Rating Scales

Structured interviews are basically orally administered questionnaires. The Diagnostic Interview Schedule (Robins et al. 1981) is an orally administered questionnaire to be used by lay interviewers for making diagnoses according to DSM-III. The rating scales discussed in Chapters 2 and 3 of this compendium rely on clinical, goal-directed interviews which depend for their accuracy very strongly upon the skill and experience of the rater (psychiatrist, psychologist or other skilled observer). However, in Chapter 2 is shown an example of a structured interview for the Hamilton Melancholia Scale. DSM-III-R emphasizes that the user should be trained in psychopathology before making diagnostic assessments. In some cases, however, the psychiatrist or psychologist is less skilled than nurses in the observation and assessment of clinical syndromes. Thus, in assessing the psychiatric inpatient's competence in social or interpersonal relations and ability to perform basic activities of daily life, the nurse is the most appropriate rater, observing his behaviour in a natural way as it occurs. Rating scales such as the Hamilton Depression Scale have a high cross-national reliability because the clinical interview can be adapted with culturally specific idioms and questions, with the goal of improving the information obtained for the items of the scale.

Self-rating scales, i.e. questionnaires to be completed by the patients themselves, can be of value in measuring minor psychiatric syndromes, but their main importance is in the measurement of personality dimensions, psychosocial stressors, and health-related quality of life (which by definition is a self-reported dimension).

Table 4.1 lists the psychopathological syndromes (axis 1 syndromes) discussed in Chapters 2 and 3, indicating which are observer scales and which questionnaires. Table 4.2 lists the self-rating scales for each of the axis 1 disorders. Self-rating scales are of value particularly in the measurement of neurotic (minor) states (phobias, obsessive-compulsive states and neurasthenia). In this context, neurosis is considered as a state of illhealth which is differentiated from psychosis by the retention of insight. Hence, a neurotic patient regards the neurotic symptoms as abnormal, as representing illness in some form, regardless of whether he considers its cause as being physical or mental. A patient suffering from psychosis regards the environment as being really changed (derealization) or the self as being changed (depersonalization). This experience is not referred to by the psychotic patient as an illness. The use of self-rating scales in psychotic degrees of depression or mania and in schizophrenia is therefore very problematic. The term

Table 4.1. Observer and self-rating scales in psychopathological syndromes

Axis 1 disorder		Observer scale	Self-rating scale
Dementia		+	-
Withdrawal states		+	-
Schizophrenia		+	-
Mania		+	-
Depression		+	+
Anxiety	Panic attack	+	+
	Generalized	+	+
	Phobias	(+)	+
	Obsessive-compulsive	(+)	+
	Neurasthenia	(+)	+
Aggression	Conduct	+	-
	Generalized	+	-
	Attacks	+	-

Psychometric description: +, adequate; (+), not really adequate; -, inadequate

insanity is often used synonymously with psychosis, but this is a legal term referring to the condition of a patient certified by legal procedures as mentally incompetent in matters of judgement. Also in this case, self-rating scales have limited
validity.

In non-psychotic and sane patients the person himself is the best source for the
rating of his own inner feelings, beliefs or emotional states. Carroll et al. (1973)
have, however, argued that such feeling states are not particularly relevant for
purposes of defining a disease entity or for differential diagnosis. This chapter
considers the relevance of the most frequently used questionnaires for measuring
depression and anxiety not only in of measuring DSM-III-R and ICD-10 syndromes but also in measuring the outcome of treatment. The advantages and disadvantages of the various questionnaires are discussed.

4.1 Methodological Considerations

The set of items in self-administered questionnaires consists of reported symptoms. Assessing the severity of symptoms is largely analogous to assessing the
strength of attitudes, which were the object of the original Likert (1932) scales.
The problems involved in asking questions for attitude scales have been reviewed
by Sudman and Bradburn (1985), including the order of questions, open versus
closed questions, and bipolar versus unipolar questions.

Table 4.2. Self-rating for psychopathological syndromes

Axis 1 disorder	Observer scale	"Beck Depression Inventory"-like scales	"Hopkins Symptom Checklist"-like scales	"General Health Questionnaire"-like scales
Depression	HDS/MES; Zung	Carroll; HDS/MES; BDI	Zung	GHQ-30
Panic anxiety	HAS; Sheehan	-	Sheehan; SCL-19-P	-
Generalized anxiety	HAS; Zung	(BDI subscale) BAS	Zung; SCL-10-G	-
Phobias	(Marks scale) SCL-9	-	SCL-9-Ph	-
Obsessive-compulsive	(Thoren scale)	-	Maudsley; SCL-10-OC	-
Neurasthenia	-	Bech-Hey	Zung; Pichot-Brun	Wessely

4.1.1 Severity of Symptom Occurrence

Table 4.3 shows four different ways to measure severity of symptoms by self-administered scales. These four types have in common the use of closed questions, but they differ in terms of polarity and the symptom dimension. Very few studies have compared intensity versus the frequency of symptom occurrence. Kellner (1986) found intensity to be preferable. In psychopathological states such as depression periods of time have a higher ontological existence than events or points of time. (According to DSM-III-R major depression includes symptoms with a period of duration of at least two weeks.) In depression, therefore, intensity of symptoms has clinical meaning unlike frequency. However, as discussed in Chapter 9, quality of life scales measure emotions of hours' duration and here frequency has an ontological priority. Hence, the Hospital Anxiety Depression Scale measures emotions in medically ill patients (secondary depression), the CES-D measures emotions in non-patient populations, and Zung Depression Scale has also an applicability in minor emotional states. Those three scales have frequency as item definitions. In a recent review on the psychology of time van Benthem (1985) concludes that surprisingly little attention has been paid in the literature to the obvious temporal quantifiers: 'always', 'mostly', 'often', 'seldom', 'sometimes', 'never'.

Scales have been constructed with neither intensity nor frequency definition, but with a 'neutral' response formulation such as 'Definitely does not apply to me', 'Does *not* apply to me', 'Applies to me', and 'Definitely applies to me' (e.g. Watson 1988).

The standard (i.e. non-tailored) formulations of items are very close to adjective scales in that the patient responds to adjectives rather than to statements. The Clyde Mood Scale (Guy 1976) is among the first widely used adjective mood scales; this consists of 48 adjectives (e.g. tired, lonely, afraid, depressed) and resembles the SCL in format (intensity type). The Adjective Mood Scale (Befindlichkeitskala) developed by von Zerssen (1986) is an example of bipolar item formulation, as the adjectives are arranged in two columns with words of opposite meanings (e.g. happy versus unhappy, irritated versus calm), and the patient is asked to select the most appropriate alternative. The items included in the Adjective Mood Scale have been selected from the Beck Depression Inventory (BDI) and the Zung scale. The advantage of the Adjective Mood Scale is that it is a 'here and now' assessment and can be repeated at very short intervals of time (e.g. hours). One of the most frequently used adjective scales is the Profile of Mood States (POMS; McNair et al. 1971, Guy 1976). The Kellner Symptom Questionnaire (see Sect. 4.5.4) is also in principle an adjective scale.

Table 4.3. Self-administered rating scales – questions of severity of a symptom

Tailored item calibration (e.g. Beck et al. 1961)	Standard calibration by intensity (e.g. Hopkins SCL; Lipman 1986)	Standard calibration by frequency (e.g. Zung 1983)	Standard (bipolar) calibration using habitual as the middle alternative (e.g. Goldberg 1972)
Please read the group of statements and pick out the one which best describes the way you have been feeling the past week.	How much were you bothered by feeling lonely during the past week?	How often has this sentence applied to you within the past week: "I enjoy visiting friends and relatives?"	Have you recently been able to feel warmth and affection for those near to you?
0 I have not lost interest in other people.	0 Not at all.	0 None or little of the time.	0 Better than usual.
1 I am less interested in other people.	1 A little bit.	1 Some of the time.	1 About same as usual.
2 I have lost most of my interest in other people.	2 Moderately.	2 Good part of the time	2 Less well than usual.
3 I have lost all my interest in other people.	3 Quite a bit.	3 Most of the time.	4 Much less well than usual.
	4 Extremely.		

4.1.2 Response Set

Self-administered scales entail the same problems of content and construct validity as do observer scales. The specific psychometric problem in self-administrated scales is that of response set, a pattern of responses deriving from factors other than the content of the items. Three types of response set that should be taken into account in measuring depression and anxiety are (a) acquiescence, (b) social desirability and (c) impact of item order.

Acquiescence is the tendency to agree independently of the content of the question. This effect seems to be constant for a given individual, and Eysenck and Eysenck (1976) have used acquiescence as a dimension of neuroticism. This type of response set therefore seems to have no adverse effect on reliability. The Zung scales and the Goldberg (1972) scale limit the effect of acquiescence by wording one half of items positively and the other half negatively. This does not reduce acquiescence but simply cancels out its effect.

Social desirability is the tendency to respond to items in a socially desirable way. While some patients purposely score items so as to create for themselves a positive image, others attempt to present themselves as very ill (a 'sick set' response). Unfortunately, this sort of response set is difficult to control. The most direct procedure is to inform the patient of the significance and intended use of scale scores. Very few studies have examined the effect of social desirability (undesirability in depressive or anxiety questionnaires). Beck and Beamesderfer (1974) found little effect on the BDI while Langevin and Stancer (1979) demonstrated that the low self-esteem in depression and social undesirability (sick-set) are closely interrelated in the BDI.

The impact of item order on response sets has been investigated by very few researchers. The original order of items in the BDI, which begins with very serious items, has always presented some problems; however, proper instructions to the patient can overcome this problem. On the other hand, in the modified and enlarged version of the BDI (Bech 1988) the order of items has been changed beginning with 'neutral' somatic items such as appetite and headache. A systematic study has recently been published on the effect of order of items in the BDI (Dahlstrom et al. 1990), a random order of items to give a significantly higher depression score than either the original or the 'reversed-order' versions.

4.1.3 Self-Report Versus Others' Reports and Clinical Interview

Self-reports can be supplemented by reports from relatives (relative rating scales; Table 4.4). Such scales have been discussed in psychiatry (e.g. Fadden et al. 1987), but much more attention has been devoted to them in psychosomatic research. The most provocative study in this respect was that of Jachuck et al. (1982), who found a great divergence among physicians, patients and relatives in measuring subjective well-being during treatment with hypotensive drugs. In a study using the Jachuck scale as well as visual analogue scales patient versus rel-

Table 4.4. Type of information obtained in self-reports and clinical observation

Type of information	Scale
Self-report	Self-rating scales
Relative-report	Relative rating scales
Ward observation	Nurse rating scales
Interview assessment	Physician rating scales
All obtainable information (records, interview with an informant) case vignettes	Judgement scales

ative assessments correlated only at the level of 0.50 in terms of Spearman coefficients (Frimodt-Møller et al. 1991). The same low level of correlation between doctor and patient has been found for anxiety and depression scales in cancer research (Slevin et al. 1988).

4.2 Depression Scales

The psychometric properties of self-administered depression scales are detailed in Table 4.5. Table 4.6 presents the most frequently used scales in terms of the method for measuring severity of symptoms. The Carroll scale (Feinberg and Carroll 1986) is constructed as a self-administered Hamilton Depression Scale (HDS), and the Hamilton–Melancholia Inventory (Bech et al. 1975; see below) is a self-administered HDS/MES scale; the latter is still under development. The Self-Rating Depression Scale (SDS; Zung 1972; see below, was originally the Zung (1965) Depression Scale and the observer version was designed as an adjunct to the self-administered scale (the Depression Status Scale; Zung 1972). The 30-item version of the General Health Questionnaire (GHQ-30; Goldberg 1972) can be considered a self-administered version of the MES (Bech 1987). The BDI (Beck et al. 1961) was originally designed as an orally administered questionnaire but was found to be a workable self-administered scale. The Symptom Rating Test was originally designed to measure changes in the symptoms of neurotic patients (Kellner 1986).

The item distributions of these scales is shown in Table 4.7; the HDS and the Melancholia Scale (MES) are included for comparisons of the components selected by Thompson (1989). The BDI lacks anxiety and motor symptoms but has the highest percentage of cognitive symptoms, which is in accordance with the Beck's (1967) theory of cognitive elements of depression. The GHQ-30 places the

Table 4.5. Psychometric description of self-administered depression scale

Type	Symptom scale measuring severity of depression.
Content validity	Covers the essential components of depression less well than observer scales (see tables 4.7).
Administration	To be completed by the patients themselves.
Time frame	The past week.
Item selection	As the observer scales.
Item calibration	Likert scale definition with different aspects of symptom profile (see Table 4.3).
Construct validity	Most studies have focused on convergent validity to observer scales. So far latent structure analysis has been very limited (e.g. the Melancholia Inventory, Loldrup et al. 1991).
Severity to change	Defined as discriminant validity in drug-placebo; end-point analyses show that some studies have found self-administered scales superior to observer scales (e.g. Dick and Ferrero 1983).

Table 4.6. Self-administered depression scales

Tailored item calibrated scales	Intensity scales	Frequency scales	Bipolar scales
Beck Depression Inventory (21 items) Hamilton/Carroll Rating Scale (17 items) Hamilton/Melancholia Inventory (23 items)	The symptom Rating Test (30 items)	Zung Self-Rating Depression Scale (20 items)	General Health Questionnaire (30 items)

Table 4.7. Item distributions of rating scales: depressive symptoms in depressive syndrome (melancholia)

Component*	HDS	MES	BDI	Carroll	SDS	CHQ-30
Mood symptoms	8%	18%	10%	8%	15%	20%
Anxiety symptoms	16%	9%	0%	15%	5%	10%
Motor	12%	18%	0%	15%	5%	0%
Cognitive	28%	27%	52%	27%	35%	27%
Social	8%	9%	5%	0%	0%	36%
Vegetative	28%	18%	29%	35%	35%	7%
Irritability	0%	0%	5%	0%	5%	0%
Number of items	17	11	21	17	20	30

* from Thompson (1989)

most weight on social symptoms, which is in accordance with the emphasis of this scale on components of social inadequacy and quality of life (Bech 1987).

The construct validity of these self-administered questionnaires has been evaluated only to a limited extent. The BDI has been analysed by Bouman and Kok (1987) for latent structure validity, and the scale did not fulfil the Rasch model. This finding is in agreement with those of Loldrup et al. (1991) who found a low Loevinger coefficient for the full scale. However, these researchers found the Melancholia Inventory (Bech et al. 1975) and the GHQ-30 to have an acceptable Loevinger coefficient. The question of the concurrent validity of self-administered scales versus observer scales has been of special interest in depressive disorders. Excellent reviews have been published by Paykel and Norton (1986) and by Raskin (1986). The correlation between HDS and self-administered scales was highest for the Carroll scale, followed by the BDI. A high correlation was seen between the two Zung scales. Studies on the two versions of HDS/MES are now going on. The highest correlation between observer scales and self-administered scales thus seems to be obtained when the construct and the item formulations are similar. So far, little is known about patients' preferences among the question formulations shown in Table 4.3. However, in a recent study (Bendt-Hansen et al. 1992) it has been shown that patients prefer global formulations rather than the specified formulation (see Appendix to Chapter 2).

Table 4.8 presents Paykel and Norton's (1986) comparison between self-administered and observer scales in depression. Self-administered scales obviously have limitations in observable items and in circumstances. The lack of psychopathological specificity and the restricted range of severity mean that self-administered scales should be used before treatment only in minor levels of depression. Posttreatmently, self-rating scales for depression are less sensitive than the Hamilton scale to measure outcome of short term trials. The use of self-rating scales is most relevant in medium or long term trials (Bech 1988). It is of great interest that the CES-D (Center for Epidemiologic Studies) scale for depression differentiates between clinical and normal population but does not measure severity of depression (Radloff 1977, Hamilton and Shapiro 1990). The CES-D has been included to be used in epidemilogic studies.

In patients with milder forms of depression, comprehensive scales are often used which also cover anxiety states. A scale with balanced depression and anxiety symptoms is the Hospital Anxiety and Depression Scale (HAD; Zigmond and Snaith 1983). The most frequently used self-rating scales for depression are the BDI and SDS. Both Beck and Beamsderfer (1974) and Bech (1981) have constructed brief scales of approximately 12 items for the clinical manifestations of depression (melancholia). Both versions can be derived from the enlarged (42-item) BDI, which is included in this compendium (Bech 1988). In a study on secondary depression the various subscales of the enlarged BDI were investigated psychometrically, and the 12-item Melancholia Inventory was found to have the highest Loevinger coefficient (Loldrup et al. 1991). This scale, the HAD, the SDS (Self-Rating Depression Scale; Zung 1971) and the Kellner Symptom Questionnaire are included here as examples of brief self-rating depression scales.

Table 4.8. Self-administered and observer-rated in depression

	Self-administered scales	Observer-rated scales
Components		
Subjective feelings/emotions	Well	Less well
Verbal reports of symptoms	Well	Well
Observable behaviours	Minimal	Well
Psychopathological specificity	Less specific	Specific
Range of severity	Restricted to minor degrees	Full Range
Circumstances	Requires patient cooperation, motivation, ability to concentrate and read	Bed-side orientated (can be completed with minimal patient cooperation
Costs	Cheap in professional time	Requires professional and skilled rater
Potential biases	Response set	Rater bias

Melancholia Inventory

The questionnaire for the Melancholia Inventory is presented below. This is a questionnaire arranged in subgroups of 12 items. Please read the entire group of statements in each item. Then pick out the one statement in that item which best describes the way you have been feeling the last three days including today. Put your mark beside the statement you have chosen. If statements in an item seem to apply equally well, put a mark at each one. Be sure to read the statements in each item before making your choice.

1. a) I don't get more tired than usual. b) I get tired more easily than I use to. c) I get tired from doing anything.
2. a) I can work about as well as before. b) It takes extra effort to get started at doing something. c) I have to push myself very hard to do anything.
3. a) I am no more concerned about my health than usual. b) I am concerned about discomfort in my body, giving thoughts about illness. c) I am so concerned with how I feel in my body that it's hard to think of much else.
4. a) I am no more easily irritable than I ever am. b) I get irritated more easily than I used to. c) I feel irritated all the time.
5. a) I am not particularly pessimistic about future. b) I feel discouraged about the future. c) I feel I have nothing to look forward to.
6. a) I don't feel disappointed in myself. b) I am dissapointed in myself. c) I am disgusted with myself.
7. a) I do not feel sad. b) I feel sad and depressed. c) I feel constantly sad and feel unable to get out of it.
8. a) I make decisions about as well as ever. b) I try to put off making decisions. c) I have great difficulty in making decisions.
9. a) I don't feel I look any worse than I used to. b) I am worried that I am looking old and unattractive. c) I feel there are permanent changes in my appearance.
10. a) I don't feel particularly guilty. b) I feel bad or unworthy a good part of the time. c) I feel quite guilty.
11. a) I don't feel like a failure. b) I feel I have failed more than the average person. c) As I look back on my life, all I can see is a lot of failures.
12. a) I don't feel I am being punished. b) I have a feeling that something may happen to me. c) I feel I am being punished or will be punished.

Hospital Anxiety Depression Scale

Instruction: This questionnaire is designed to help your doctor to know how you feel. Read each item and reply which of the categories in each item comes closest to how you have been feeling the past week.

1. I feel tense or 'wound up'. 3, most of the time; 2, a lot of the time; 1, from time to time, occasionally; 0, not at all.
2. I still enjoy the things I used to enjoy. 0, definitely; 1, not quite so much; 2, only a little; 3, hardly at all.

3. I get a sort of frightened feeling as if something awful is about to happen. 3, very definitely and quite badly; 2, yes, but not too badly; 1, a little, but it doesn't very me; 0, not at all.

4. I can laugh and see the funny side of things. 0, as much as I always could; 1, not quite so much now; 2, definitely not so much now; 3, not at all.

5. Worrying thoughts go through my mind. 3, a great deal of the time; 2, a lot of the time; 1, from time to time but not too often; 0, only occasionally.

6. I feel cheerful. 3, not at all; 2, not often; 1, sometimes; 0, most of the time.

7. I can sit at ease and feel relaxed. 0, definitely; 1, usually; 2, not often; 3, not at all.

8. I feel as if I am slowed down. 3, nearly all the time; 2, very often; 1, sometimes; 0, not at all.

9. I get a sort of frightened feeling like 'butterflies' in the stomach. 0, not at all; 1, occasionally; 2, quite often; 3, very often.

10. I have lost interest in my appearance. 3, definitely; 2, I don't take so much care as I should; 1, I may not take quite so much care; 0, I take just as much care as ever.

11. I feel restless as if I have to be on the move. 3, very much indeed; 2, quite a lot; 1, not very often; 0, not at all.

12. I look forward with enjoyment to things. 0, as much as I ever did; 1, rather less than I used to; definitely less than I used to; 3, hardly at all.

13. I get sudden feelings of panic. 3, very often indeed; 2, quite often; 1, not very often; 0, not at all.

14. I can enjoy a good book or radio or TV programme. 0, often; 1, sometimes; 2, not often; 3, very seldom.

The anxiety subscale includes items 1, 3, 5, 7, 9, 11, 13 and the depression subscale includes items 2, 4, 6, 8, 10, 12, 14.

Self-Rating Depression Scale (Zung)

The questionnaire for the SDS is presented below. Response categories are: 1, none or a little of the time; 2, some of the time; 3, good part of the time; 4, most or all of the time.

1. I feel feel down-hearted and blue.

2. Morning is when I feel the best.

3. I have crying spells or feel like it.

4. I have trouble sleeping through the night.

5. I eat as much as I used to.

6. I enjoy looking at, talking to and being with attractive women (or men).

7. I notice that I am losing weight.

8. I have trouble with constipation.

9. My heart beats faster than usual.

10. I get tired for no reason.

11. My mind is as clear as it used to be.

12. I find it easy to do the things I used to.

13. I am restless and can't keep still.
14. I feel hopeful about the future.
15. I am more irritable than usual.
16. I find it easy to make decisions.
17. I feel that I am useful and needed.
18. My life is pretty full.
19. I feel that others would be better off if I were dead.
20. I still enjoy the things I used to do.

In an overview article on self-rating scales comparing the discriminating validity between antidepressant and placebo, McNair (1974) found that global improvement ratings were most sensitive. Then came Beck Depression Inventory, Zung Depression Scale, Hopkins Symptom Checklist, and Adjective Scales.

Finally, the CES-D has been included as a scale to identify clinical depression without having the ability to measure outcome of treatment. Response categories of CES-D are: 1, rarely, none of the time (less than 1 day); 2, some or little of the time (1–2 days); 3, occasionally or a moderate amount of time (3–4 days); 4, most or all of the time (5–7 days). The scale thus covers the past week.

1. I was bothered by things that don't usually bother me.
2. I did not feel like eating; my appetite was poor.
3. I felt that I could not shake off the blues, even with help from my family or friends.
4. I felt that I was just as good as other people.
5. I had trouble keeping my mind on what I was doing.
6. I felt depressed.
7. I felt that everything I did was an effort.
8. I felt hopeful about the future.
9. I thought my life had been a failure.
10. I felt fearful.
11. I sleep very restless.
12. I was happy.
13. I talked less than usual.
14. I felt lonely.
15. People were unfriendly.
16. I enjoyed life.
17. I had crying spells.
18. I felt sad.
19. I felt that people disliked me.
20. I could not get 'going'.

4.3 Anxiety Scales

Table 4.9 presents the psychometric properties of self-administered anxiety scales, and Table 4.10 classifies various such scales according to item construction. An example of tailored-item scales is the Beck Anxiety Inventory (Beck et al. 1988), constructed along the lines of the BDI. So far, no self-administered version of the Hamilton Anxiety Scale (HAS) has been developed, probably because the original version (e.g. Hamilton 1969) contained no tailored items (in contrast to the version presented in Chap. 2). It should be mentioned, however, that Lader and Marks (1971) have used the HAS with visual analogue scales of each item. Among intensity type scales, the Hopkins subscale of anxiety and the anxiety factor of the Pichot-Brun inventory (Guelfi et al. 1989) are preferable. Of special interest is the Patient-Rated Anxiety Scale (PRAS; Sheehan 1983; see below) because this scale, while emphasizing generalized anxiety, measures panic anxiety. In Chap. 3 a Hopkins SCL-19 is presented for measuring panic anxiety in accordance with DSM-III-R. Among frequency scales the Suchman scale has special interest because it fulfils Guttman's criteria for a perfect scale (Suchman 1950; Bech et al. 1986). This scale and the State-Trait Anxiety Scale (Spielberger et al. 1970) is constructed for cases of non-pathological anxiety. The Self-Rating Scale for Anxiety (SAS; Zung 1972; see below) has, like the Zung SDS, an observer version. The anxiety factor of the GHQ-30 (Goldberg 1978) illustrates the bipolar item formulation.

Table 4.11 presents the item distributions of several self-administered anxiety scales. Nearly half of the items refer to autonomic hyperactivity, i.e. to the somatic factor of anxiety, which may be either generalized or peak-related (panic attacks). The most somatic in this sense is the Post-traumatic Anxiety Scale (Suchman 1950), which fulfils the latent structure analysis of Guttman; the scale has been further discussed by Bech et al. (1986). Suchman (1950) concluded: "The symptoms come from a single universe and permit a rank ordering of respondents along a single continuum. There is an intrinsic interpendence among the different fear symptoms which permits them to be ordered from more to less severe. In this case the underlying continuum is probably physiological." The Suchman scale was used to measure anxiety in American soldiers during World War II. The instruction for the scale was: "Soldiers who have been under fire report different physical reactions to the danger of the battle. Some of these are given in the following list. How often have you had these reactions when you were under fire?"

It is of interest that latent structure analysis of the somatic factor of the HAS in patients with panic disorders has demonstrated lack of hierarchical structure (Maier et al. 1988; Bech et al. 1992). In contrast, both the Suchman scale and the Withdrawal Syndrome Scale (Kristensen et al. 1986) fulfil the latent structure model; Table 4.12 compares these two scales. The symptoms of the Suchman scale include gastro-intestinal items which have only a low weight in DSM-III or DSM-III-R concepts of panic anxiety (see Chaps. 2 and 3).

It should be emphasized that the Sheehan scale, the Hopkins scale, and the Zung scale have both self-administered and interview versions. The concurrent validity between self-administered and interview versions is adequate for the Hopkins and Zung scales, but that of the Sheehan scale has been found less adequate, the physician-administered version having highest discriminant validity (Albus et al. 1990; Maier et al. 1990).

Table 4.9. Psychometric description of self-administered anxiety scales

Type	Symptom scale measuring severity of anxiety.
Content validity	Covers the essential components of anxiety compared to observer scales (Table 4.11).
Administration	To be completed by the patients themselves.
Time frame	The past week.
Item selection	As the observer scale.
Item calibration	Likert scale definition with different aspects of the symptom profile (see Table 4.10).
Construct validity	Latent structure analysis has been carried out only for the Suchman scale. The concurrent validity between self-administered and observer-administered scales is adequate.
Sensitivity to change	In terms of discriminant validity some studies have found observer scales superior, and others have found self-administered scales superior.

Table 4.10. Self-administered anxiety scales

Tailored-item calibrated scales	Intensity scales	Frequency scales	Bipolar scales
Beck Anxiety Inventory (Beck et al. 1988)	Hopkins anxiety factor SCL-11 (Guy 1976) Patient-Related Anxiety Scale (Sheehan 1983) Anxiety factor (Pichot and Brun 1984)	Post-traumatic Stress Anxiety Scale (Suchman 1950) Self-Rating Anxiety Scale (Zung 1971) State-Trait Anxiety Inventory (Spielberger et al. 1970)	Anxiety factor of General Health Questionnaire (Goldberg 1978)

Table 4.11. Item distributions of rating scales: anxiety symptoms in anxiety syndromes

Component	Hamilton Anxiety Scale	Beck Anxiety Inventory	Post-traumatic Anxiety Scale	Hopkins SCL-11	SAS
Anxious mood	7%	24%	0%	18%	15%
Phobia	7%	0%	0%	0%	0%
Motor tension	14%	11%	33%	9%	15%
Psychic tension	7%	11%	0%	9%	10%
Autonomic hyperactivity	43%	48%	66%	55%	45%
Arousal	14%	0%	0%	9%	15%

Table 4.12. Components of Post-traumatic Anxiety Scale (Suchman 1950) and Withdrawal Syndrome Scale (Kristensen et al. 1986)

Post-traumatic Anxiety Scale	Withdrawal Syndrome Scale
Palpitations	Palpitations
Sinking feeling in stomach	Tremor
Dizziness	Agitation
Sick in stomach	Sweating
Vomiting	Increased temperature
Trembling	Disorientation
Urinating in pants	Hallucinations
Losing control of the bowels	
General feeling of stiffness	

Patient-Rated Anxiety Scale (Panic; Sheehan)

The questionnaire for the PRAS is presented below. Response categories are: 0, not at all; 1, a little bit; 2, moderately; 3, markedly; 4, extremely. Total scores are interpreted as follows: 0–5, no anxiety; 6–30, mild anxiety; 31–50, moderate anxiety; 51–80, marked anxiety; 81–134, severe anxiety.

Instructions: Below is a list of problems and complaints that people sometimes have. Circle the number to the right that best describes how much that problem bothered or distressed you during the past six months. Mark only one number for each problem and do not skip any items.

How much were you bothered by:
1. Lightheadedness, faintness or dizzy spells.
2. Sensation of rubbery or 'jelly' legs.
3. Feeling off balance or unsteady as if about to fall.
4. Difficulty in getting breath or overbreathing.
5. Skipping or racing of the heart.
6. Chest pain or pressure.
7. Smothering or choking sensation or lumb in throat.
8. Tingling or numbness in parts of the body.
9. Hot flushes or cold chills.
10. Nausea or stomach problems.
11. Episodes of diarrhoea.
12. Headaches or pains in neck or head.

13. Feeling tired, weak, and exhausted easily.
14. Spells of increased sensitivity to sound, light or touch.
15. Bouts of excessive sweating.
16. Feeling that surroundings are strange, unreal, foggy, or detached.
17. Feeling outside or detached from part or all of your body or a floating feeling.
18. Worrying about your health too much.
19. Feeling you are losing control or going insane.
20. Having a fear that you are dying or that something terrible is about to happen.
21. Shaking or trembling.
22. Unexpected waves of depression occurring with little or no provocation.
23. Emotions and moods going up and down a lot in response to changes around you.
24. Being dependent on others.
25. Having to repeat the same action in a ritual (e.g. checking, washing, counting repeatedly, when it's not really necessary).
26. Recurrent words or thoughts that persistently intrude on your mind and are hard to get rid of (e.g. unwanted aggressive, sexual, or poor impulse control thoughts).
27. Difficulty in falling asleep.
28. Waking up in the middle of the night or restless sleep.
29. Avoiding situations because they frighten you.
30. Tension and inability to relax.
31. Anxiety, nervousness, restlessness.
32. Sudden unexpected panic spells that occur with little or no provocation (e.g. anxiety attacks with three or more of the symptoms listed above occurring together).
33. Sudden unexpected spells like those listed above, without full panic that occur with little or no provocation (e.g. attacks associated with only one or two symptoms).
34. Anxiety episodes that build up as you anticipate doing something and that are more intense than most people experience in such situations.
35. Surges of panic that occur while you are in the phobic situation.

Patient-Rated Scale for Generalized Anxiety

This questionnaire is a modified SCL-19 scale using DSM-III-R as basis for item selection. The instruction is therefore analogous to the Hopkins scale (see Sect. 4.5.2) and the response categories are therefore: 0, not at all; 1, a little bit; 2, moderately; 3, quite a bit; 4, extremely.

How much were you during the last week bothered by:
1. Trembling?
2. Nervousness or shakiness inside?
3. Feeling so restless you couldn't sit still?
4. Feeling low in energy or slowed down?
5. Trouble getting your breath?

6. Heart pounding or racing?
7. Sweating?
8. Dry mouth?
9. Faintness or dizziness?
10. Nausea?
11. Hot or cold spells?
12. Frequent urination?
13. A lump in your throat?
14. Feeling tense or keyed up?
15. Feeling everything is an effort?
16. Trouble concentrating?
17. Trouble falling asleep?
18. Feeling easily annoyed or irritated?
19. Feeling fearful?

The DSM-III-R criteria for generalized anxiety: Item 19 should be present (a score of 2 or more) and at least 6 of the remaining items as well.

Self-Rated Anxiety Scale (Zung)

The questionnaire for the SAS is presented below. Response categories are: 1, none or a little of the time; 2, some of the time; 3, a good part of the time; 4, most or all of the time.

1. I feel more nervous and anxious than usual.
2. I feel afraid for no reason at all.
3. I get upset easily or feel panicky.
4. I feel like I'm falling apart and going to pieces.
5. I feel that everything is all right and nothing bad will happen.
6. My arms and legs shake and tremble.
7. I am bothered by headaches, neck and back pains.
8. I feel weak and get tired easily.
9. I feel calm and can sit still easily.
10. I can feel my heart beating fast.
11. I am bothered by dizzy spells.
12. I have fainting spells or feel like it.
13. I can breathe in and out easily.
14. I get feelings or numbness, and tingling in my fingers, toes.
15. I am bothered by stomach aches or indigestion.
16. I have to empty my bladder often.
17. My hands are usually dry and warm.
18. My face gets hot and blushes.
19. I fall asleep easily and get a good night's rest.
20. I have nightmares.

4.4 Aggression Scales

Section 3.6 discusses the assessment of aggressive states by observer-rating scales, including those by ward or nurses. The use of self-rating scales in the measurement of aggression, on the other hand, is problematic. Most self-administered scales for aggression to measure irritability rather than aggression. Thus, the Anger Scale from the Cornell Medical Index (CMI; Brodman et al. 1949), the Anger-Hostility Scale from the Hopkins Symptom Checklist (SCL-6; Guy 1976; see below) and the Irritability Scale (Snaith and Taylor 1985; see below). All seem to measure irritability, as defined by Snaith and Taylor (1985):

Irritability is a feeling state characterized by reduced control over temper which usually results in irascible verbal or behavioural outbursts, although the mood may be present without observed manifestation. It may be experienced as brief episodes, in particular circumstances, or it may be prolonged or generalized. The experience of irritability is always unpleasant for the individual and overt manifestation lacks the cathartic effect of justified outbursts of anger.

Spielberger et al. (1982) have constructed an anger scale for measuring both trait (e.g. "I am usually quick tempered" – never/sometimes/often/always) and state (e.g. "I feel angry right now" – not at all/somewhat/moderately so/very much so). Recently, Spielberger et al. (1986) developed a further self-rating scale for retrospectively measuring an episode of anger (e.g. "When I was angry, I lost my temper" – almost never/sometimes/often/almost always). Irritability defined by Snaith and Taylor (1985) has recently been included in Index Medicus under the medical subject heading of 'Irritable Mood' (1991). It is as an irritable mood that 'aggression' or 'anger' can be measured by self-rating scales. As a personality dimension anger or hostility can be considered as proneness to (a) experience anger, (b) behave in an antagonistic manner, and (c) view others in a negative light. This aspect is discussed in Chap. 5.

Anger-Hostility Scale

The questions of the Anger-Hostility Scale (SCL-6) are presented below.
1. Feeling easily annoyed or irritated?
2. Temper outburst that you could not control?
3. Having urges to beat, injure, or harm someone?
4. Having urges to break or smash things?
5. Getting into frequent arguments?
6. Shouting or throwing things.

Irritability Scale

The questions of the Irritability Scale are presented below. Items 1–4 refer to outwardly directed irritability and items 5–8 to inwardly directed irritability.

1. I lose my temper and snap at others.
2. I am impatient with other people.
3. I feel I might lose control and hit or hurt someone.
4. People upset me so that I feel like slamming doors or banging about.
5. I feel like harming myself.
6. The thought of hurting myself occurs to me.
7. Lately I have been getting annoyed with myself.
8. I get angry with myself and call myself names.

CMI Anger Scale

The questions from the CMI that make up the Anger Scale are presented below.
1. Do you have to be on your guard even with friends?
2. Do you always do things on sudden impulse?
3. Are you easily upset or irritated?
4. Do you go to pieces if you don't constantly control yourself?
5. Do little annoyances get on your nerves and make you angry?
6. Does it make you angry to have anyone tell you what to do?
7. Do people often annoy and irritate you?
8. Do you flare up in anger if you can't have what you want right away.
9. Do you often get into a violent rage?

4.5 Comprehensive Scales and Their Subscales

4.5.1 Cornell Medical Index

The first comprehensive scale covering symptoms measured by the patients themselves was the CMI, which is a health questionnaire containing a total of 195 items (Brodman et al. 1949). The areas covered by the CMI are listed in Table 3.38. Section 9 measures fatigability or neurasthenia and the items in this subscale are shown in Table 3.39. Section 15 measures anger or hostility and the items of this subscale are presented in the preceding section. The items of the CMI are of four kinds: those related to (a) bodily symptoms; (b) past illness; (c) family history; and (d) behaviour, mood and feeling. The items were selected to correspond to those usually asked in a detailed and comprehensive medical interview. The CMI covers, in DSM-III terms, axes 1, 2 and 3 conditions, but its validity in predicting illness was found to be most evident in the psychological aspects of diseases (Brodman et al. 1951).

Experience with the CMI shows that a psychological disturbance may be suspected with any of the following:
–   A syndrome of 'yes' answers in the sections of mood and feeling patterns (inadequacy, depression, anxiety, sensitivity, anger or tension).

- Thirty or more 'yes' responses on the entire CMI (195 items).
- Three or more 'yes' responses in the sections on fatigability and frequency of illness (16 items).
- Three or more 'yes' responses in the sections on mood and feeling patterns (51 items).
- Four or more questions not answered, answered both 'yes' and 'no', or with changes or remarks written in by the patient

The CMI provides a set of items from which many other scales have been derived; these include the GHQ (Goldberg 1972), the Hopkins Symptom Checklist (SCL-90; Guy 1976) and the Eysenck Personality Questionnaire (EPQ; Eysenck and Eysenck 1976). Of these scales the GHQ is the nearest to the CMI for predicting psychological disturbance (discomfort, quality of life). Although the SCL-90 can be used in this context, this scale is a comprehensive psychopathological self-rating scale for both prediction the measurement of outcome of treatment. The EPQ is a personality scale and is discussed in Chap. 5.

4.5.2 Hopkins Symptom Checklist

The Hopkins SCL was originally constructed by Parloff et al. (1954) for the measurement of discomfort or lack of psychological well-being as a criterion of improvement in psychotherapy. Hence, the scale serves basically as an outcome measure and not as a diagnostic tool, which was the intention with the CMI, from which it was to some extent derived. The Hopkins SCL originally included 41 items (Frank et al. 1957; see below) this grew to 58 items (Derogatis et al. 1971), and then to 90 items (Guy 1976). The final version (SCL-90; see below) is that of Lipman (1986). The item formulation was changed from that of the SCL-41 a calibration of 0–4. In one of the first factor analyses of this version a group of 35 items was isolated (Guy 1976). From this group a 17-item subscale was selected to measure psychological discomfort, which was the original intention of the scale (Cyr 1985; Bech 1987). This discomfort scale (SCL-17) is discussed further in Chap. 8 (health-related quality of life).

The official subscales of the SCL-90 are based on factor analysis (Guy 1976). In total, nine factors or subscales are recommended when using the scale to describe the diagnostic profile of a patient: somatization, obsessive-compulsive, interpersonal sensitivity, depression, anxiety, anger-hostility, phobic anxiety, paranoid ideation, and psychoticism. In a recent study on patients with panic disorders the factors of discomfort (e.g. interpersonal sensitivity), phobia and anxiety were the most consistent (Bech et al. 1992); in another study on patients with phobia, the factor of discomfort was the most consistent (Arrindell 1980). Table 4.13 compares the item distributions of the SCL-41 (Parloff et al. 1954), the SCL-90 (Lipman 1986) and the Checklist for the Evaluation of Somatic Symptoms (CHESS; Guelfi et al. 1983; see Sect. 4.5.5), in terms of the sections (components) of the CMI from which it was derived. The SCL-41 covers all the various sections of CMI apart from 'eyes and ears' and the non-symptomatic sections of 'frequency

Table 4.13. Item distribution of rating scales: CMI components

Component	SCL-41	SCL-90	CHESS-52
Eyes and ears	0%	0%	6%
Respiratory	2%	1%	4%
Cardiovascular	7%	3%	8%
Digestive tract	7%	3%	21%
Musculoskeletal	5%	2%	6%
Skin	5%	0%	0%
Nervous system	10%	7%	30%
Genito-urinary	2%	0%	2%
Fatigability	2%	7%	4%
Habits	5%	3%	9%
Inadequacy	10%	17%	5%
Depression	10%	14%	0%
Anxiety	5%	4%	0%
Sensitivity	5%	7%	0%
Anger	14%	8%	0%
Tension	10%	6%	6%
Psychoticism	0%	18%	0%

of illness' and 'miscellaneous diseases'. The set of items of the SCL-41 differs from that of the CMI in being better formulated and in being measured from 0 to 3 (instead of 'yes' versus 'no'. The SCL-90 differs from SCL-41 principally in having specific items for psychoticism. The component of inadequacy in the CMI contains phobic symptoms which are more heavily weighted in the SCL-90. A recent study comparing the SCL-90 and the Present State Examination showed a reasonable concordance (Peveler and Fairburn 1990).

Hopkins Symptom Checklist (41 Items)

The questionnaire for the 41-SCL is presented below. (The sequence of possible answers are as example question 1 in items 1, 3, 4, 6, 7, 9, 10, 12, 14, 15, 17, 18, 19, 20, 21, 22, 23, 25, 27, 28, 29, 30, 31, 32, 35, 36, 37, 38, 39, 41; and inverted in the remaining items – like in example question 2: 2, 5, 8, 11, 13, 16, 24, 26, 33, 34, 40.)Listed below are 41 symptoms or problems that people sometimes have.

Directly under each symptom or problem is a scale showing how distressed a person may feel as a result of having the particular symptom. Please read each of the 41 questions carefully and decide whether you had the complaint *during the past week including today.*

If you have not had the complaint at all *during the past week including today,* place an x in the parentheses above the statement "Have not had this complaint" on the scale. If you have had the complaint one or more times during the past week including today, then decide whether the complaint was slightly, moderately, or severely distressing and place an x in the parentheses above the statement which most nearly describes the amount of distress, worry or suffering you experienced. Since the same statement is not in the same place on each scale, please read each one carefully.

EXAMPLE: If you were severely distressed by a headache during the past seven days, then in completing the scale number 1 regarding headaches, you would place an x over the statement 'Severely distressed' as indicated below.

1. Headaches
   Have not had this complaint
   Slightly distressed
   Moderately distressed
   Severely distressed

If you have been slightly distressed by pains in the heart or chest, then in completing scale number 2 you would enter an x in the parentheses over 'Slightly distressed' as indicated below.

2. Pains in the heart or chest
   Severely distressed
   Moderately distressed
   Slightly distressed
   Have not had this complaint

Do not spend much time on any one question. Before you turn in your completed questionnaire, please check to see that you have answered every question.

During the past week, including today, how much were you distressed, troubled, annoyed, worried, pained, etc by each of the following complaints:

1. Headaches
2. Pains in the heart or chest
3. Heart pounding or racing
4. Trouble getting your breath
5. Constipation
6. Nausea or upset stomach
7. Loose bowel movements
8. Twitching of the face or body
9. Faintness or dizziness
10. Hot or cold spells
11. Itching or hives
12. Frequent urination

13. Pains in the lower part of your back
14. Difficulty in swallowing
15. Skin eruptions or rashes
16. Soreness or your muscles
17. Nervousness and shakiness under pressure
18. Difficulty in falling asleep or staying asleep
19. Sudden fright for no apparent reason
20. Bad dreams
21. Blaming yourself for things you did or failed to do
22. Feeling generally worried or fretful
23. Feeling blue
24. Being easily moved to tears
25. A need to do things very slowly in order to be sure you were doing them right
26. An uncontrollable need to repeat the same actions, e.g., touching, counting, handwashing, etc.
27. Unusual fears
28. Objectionable thoughts or impulses which keep pushing themselves into your mind
29. Your feelings being easily hurt
30. Feeling that people were watching or talking about you
31. Generally preferring to be alone
32. Feeling lonely
33. Feeling compelled to ask others what you should do
34. People being unsympathetic with your need for help
35. Feeling easily annoyed or irritated
36. Severe temper outbursts
37. Feeling critical of others
38. Frequently took alcohol or medicine to make you feel better
39. Difficulty in speaking when you were excited
40. Feeling you were functioning below your capacities, i.e., feeling blocked or stymied in getting things done
41. Having an impulse to commit a violent or destructive act, for example, desire to set a fire, stab, beat or kill someone, mutilate an animal, etc.

Please check to see that you have answered every question.

Notice that this original HSCL-41 measures intensity of symptom incidence and not frequency.

Hopkins Symptom Checklist (90-Items)

The questionnaire for the 90-SCL is presented below. Response categories are: 0, not at all; 1, a little bit; 2, moderately; 3, quite a bit; 4, extremely.

Below is a list of problems and complaints that people sometimes have. Please read each one carefully. After you have done so, please fill in one of the numbered spaces to the right that best describes how much that problem has bothered or distressed you during the past week including today. Mark only one numbered space for each problem and do not skip any items. Make your marks carefully using a no. 2 pencil. Do not use a ballpoint pen. If you change your mind, erase your first mark carefully. Please do not make any extra marks on the sheet. Please read the example below before beginning.How much were you bothered by:

1. Headaches
2. Nervousness or shakiness inside
3. Unwanted thoughts, words, or ideas that won't leave your mind
4. Faintness or dizziness
5. Loss of sexual interest or pleasure
6. Feeling critical of others
7. The idea that someone else can control your thoughts
8. Feeling others are to blame for most of your troubles
9. Trouble remembering things
10. Worried about sloppiness or carelessness
11. Feeling easily annoyed or irritated
12. Pains in heart or chest
13. Feeling afraid in open spaces or on the streets
14. Feeling low in energy or slowed down
15. Thoughts of ending your life
16. Hearing voices that other people do not hear
17. Trembling
18. Feeling that most people cannot be trusted
19. Poor appetite
20. Crying easily
21. Feeling shy or uneasy with the opposite sex
22. Feeling of being trapped or caught
23. Suddenly scared for no reason
24. Temper outbursts that you could not control
25. Feeling afraid to go out of your house alone
26. Blaming yourself for things
27. Pains in lower back
28. Feeling blocked in getting things done
29. Feeling lonely
30. Feeling blue
31. Worrying too much about things
32. Feeling no interest in things
33. Feeling fearful
34. Your feelings being easily hurt
35. Other people being aware of your private thoughts
36. Feelings others do not understand you or are unsympathetic
37. Feeling that people are unfriendly or dislike you
38. Having to do things very slowly to insure correctness
39. Heart pounding or racing
40. Nausea or upset stomach
41. Feeling inferior to others

42. Soreness of your muscles
43. Feeling that you are watched or talked about by others
44. Trouble falling asleep
45. Having to check and double-check what you do
46. Difficulty making decisions
47. Feeling afraid to travel on buses, subways, or trains
48. Trouble getting your breath
49. Hot or cold spells
50. Having to avoid certain things, places, or activities because they frighten your
51. Your mind going blank
52. Numbness or tingling in parts of your body
53. A lump in your throat
54. Feeling hopeless about the future
55. Trouble concentrating
56. Feeling weak in parts of your body
57. Feeling tense or keyed up
58. Heavy feelings in your arms or legs
59. Thoughts of death or dying
60. Overeating
61. Feeling uneasy when people are watching or talking about you
62. Having thoughts that are not your own
63. Having urges to beat, injure, or harm someone
64. Awakening in the early morning
65. Having to repeat the same actions such as touching, counting, washing
66. Sleep that is restless or disturbed
67. Having urges to break or smash things
68. Having ideas or beliefs that others do not share
69. Feeling very self-conscious with others
70. Feeling uneasy in crowds, such as shopping or at a movie
71. Feeling everything is an effort
72. Spells of terror or panic
73. Feeling uncomfortable about eating or drinking in public
74. Getting into frequent arguments
75. Feeling nervous when you are left alone
76. Others not giving you proper credit for your achievements
77. Feeling lonely even when you are with people
78. Feeling so restless you couldn't sit still
79. Feelings or worthlessness
80. Feeling that familiar things are strange or unreal
81. Shouting or throwing things
82. Feeling afraid you will faint in public
83. Feeling that people will take advantage of you if you let them
84. Having thoughts about sex that bother you a lot
85. The idea that you should be punished for your sins
86. Feeling pushed to get things done

87. The idea that something serious is wrong with your body
88. Never feeling close to another person
89. Feelings of guilt
90. The idea that something is wrong with your mind

Somatization: 1, 4, 12, 27, 40, 42, 48, 49, 52, 53, 56, 58 Obsessive-compulsive
states: 3, 9, 10, 28, 38, 45, 46, 51, 55, 65
Interpersonal sensitivity: 6, 21, 34, 36, 37, 41, 61, 69, 73
Depression: 5, 14, 15, 20, 22, 26, 29, 30, 31, 32, 54, 71, 79
Anxiety: 2, 17, 23, 33, 39, 57, 72, 78, 80, 86
Anger-hostility: 11, 24, 63, 67, 74, 81
Phobic anxiety: 13, 25, 47, 50, 70, 75, 82
Paranoid ideation: 8, 18, 43, 68, 76, 83
Psychoticism: 7, 16, 35, 62, 77, 84, 85, 87, 88, 90

Anxiety states (Bech et al. 1992): 2, 11, 17, 23, 31, 33, 39, 57, 72, 78
Phobia (Bech et al. 1992): 4, 13, 23, 25, 29, 33, 47, 50, 70, 71, 72, 75, 82
Discomfort (Bech 1990): 5, 6, 9, 11, 14, 15, 24, 26, 29, 30, 34, 38, 44, 46, 51, 54, 55
The Harvard subscale for anxiety (Mollica et al. 1992): 1, 2, 4, 17, 23, 33, 39, 57, 72, 78.
The Harvard subscale for depression (Mollica et al. 1992): 5, 14, 19, 20, 22, 26, 29, 30, 31, 32, 44, 54, 59, 71, 79.

4.5.3 Symptom Rating Scale for Depression and Anxiety

The Symptom Rating Scale for Depression and Anxiety is based on the BDI (Beck et al. 1961) and enlarged to include 42 items, i.e. double the number in the BDI. Apart from the original 21-item BDI, the scale contains several subscales (Bech 1988; Table 4.14). The asthenia subscale (Bech and Hey 1979) is described in Chap. 3 (see Table 3.39). The Melancholia Inventory is presented in Sect. 4.2. The Anxiety Inventory has been described by Lau (1989). The vegetative subscale was developed to measure side effects of antidepressants (Bech et al. 1976; see Chap. 10). A mania subscale has also been included, which is considered a relevant scale for measuring the effect of long-term treatment with lithium or other relapse-prevention drugs and as a correction subscale to measure response sets. Scoring of the various subscale items is as follows:

1. The 21-item Beck Depression Scale includes items 1, 8, 11, 13, 14, 17, 18, 19, 20, 21, 22, 23, 25, 26, 27, 28, 29, 31, 32, 34, 41. These are scored: a = 0, b = 1, c = 2, d = 3.
2. The 13-item Beck Depression Scale includes items 1, 8, 11, 13, 14, 19, 20, 22, 28, 29, 32, 34, 41. These are scored: a = 0, b = 1, c = 2, d = 3.

Table 4.14. Subscale items in the BDI

Item no.		Depression	Melancholia	Anxiety	Side effects	Asthenia
1	22	x •		•		
2	23	•			x	x
3	24			x •	x •	•
4	25	•		x •		•
5	26	•	•	x	x	x
6	27	•		•		•
7	28	•			x	•
8	29	x •	x •			•
9	30				x	x
10	31	•				
11	32	x •	x •			•
12	33			x •	•	
13	34	x •	x •			
14	35	x			•	
15	36			x	x •	
16	37					
17	38	x	x	x	•	x •
18	39	x		•	•	
19	40	x	x	•	•	
20	41	x •	x			
21	42	x	x	x •	•	x

3. The 12-item Melancholia Subscale includes items 8, 11, 13, 17, 19, 20, 21, 22, 26, 29, 32, 34. These are scored: a = 0, b = 1, c = 2, d = 3.

4. The 12-item Asthenia Subscale includes items 2, 5, 9, 17, 21, 24, 25, 27, 28, 29, 32, 38. These are scored: a = 0, b = 1, c = 2, d = 3.

5. The 14-item Anxiety Subscale includes items 3, 4, 5, 12, 15, 17, 21, 24, 25, 27, 33, 39, 40, 42. These are scored: a = 0, b = 1, c = 2, d = 3.

6. The 6-item Mania Subscale includes items which all are graded 6, 10, 16, 30, 37. These are scored a = 1, b = 0, c = 0, d = +1

This is a questionnaire. On the questionnaire are groups of statements. Please read the entire group of statemets in each category from no. 1 to no. 42. Then pick out the one statement in that group which best describes the way you feel today – that is, right now. Circle the letter beside the statement you have chosen. If several statements in the group seem to apply equally well, circle each one. Be sure to read all the statements in each group before making your choice.

1. a) My appetite is as it used to be. b) My appetite is not as good as it used to be. c) My appetite is much poorer now. d) I have lost my appetite completely.

2. a) I have no headache. b) I feel a slight trace of headache. c) From time to time I suffer from severe headaches. d) I suffer almost constantly from severe headaches.

3. a) I do not suffer from perspiration. b) My palms are wet. c) I often find myself bathed in perspiration. d) I have to change my clothes several times a day because of perspiration.

4. a) I feel calm and confident. b) I feel somewhat insecure and apprehensive. c) From time to time I feel very insecure, actually on the verge of panic. d) I am unable to control my feeling of insecurity; I sometimes even panic.

5. a) I do not feel dizzy. b) I tend to get dizzy if I get up quickly. c) I tend to lose my balance even if I get up slowly. d) I have a tendency to faint whenever I try to get up.

6. a) I feel unhappy. b) On the whole I feel alright. c) I feel cheerful most of the time. d) I feel on top of the world.

7. a) My appetite is normal. b) My appetite has increased slightly. c) I feel hungry almost constantly. d) I feel hungry all the time.

8. a) I do not feel sad. b) I feel sad and depressed. c) I feel constantly sad and depressed and feel unable to get out of it. d) I feel so blue and unhappy that I cannot bear it.

9. a) My mouth does not feel dry. b) My mouth feels somewhat dry. c) My mouth feels very dry. d) My mouth feels so unpleasantly dry that I find it difficult to speak.

10. a) I don't seem to have much energy. b) I have a fair amount of energy. c) I have more than average energy. d) I am bursting with energy.

11. a) I am not particularly pessimistic or discouraged about the future. b) I feel discouraged about the future. c) I feel I have nothing to look forward to. d) I feel that the future is hopeless, and that things cannot improve.

12. a) I find no difficulty in breathing. b) I find it difficult to breathe deeply. c) From time to time I suffer from a difficulty in breathing. d) Sometimer I have suffered from such difficulty in breathing that I thought I was going to die.

13. a) I do not feel like a failure. b) I feel I have failed more than the average person. c) As I look back on my life, lall I can see is a lot of failures. d) I feel I am a complete failure as a person.

14. a) I have not lost interest in other people. b) I am less interested in other people than I used to be. c) I have lost most of my interest in other people, and I have little feeling for them. d) I have lost all of my interest in other people and don't care about them at all.

15. a) My hands are steady. b) My hands are somewhat shaky, but I can overcome that it I am determined to. c) My hands go shaky whenever I want to use them for drinking, writing etc. d) My hands are shaking all the time.
16. a) I find that most people irritate or annoy me. b) I take people as I find them. c) I get on well with nearly everyone. d) It's very easy for me to get on with everyone.
17. a) I am no more concerned about my health than usual. b) I am concerned about aches and pains or upset stomach or constipation. c) I am so concerned with how I feel or what I feel that it's hard to think of much else. d) I am completely absorbed in what I feel.
18. a) I have not lost much weight, if any, during the last month. b) I have lost about one kilogramme during the last month. c) I have lost about two kilogramme during the last month. d) I have lost more than two kilogramme during the last month.
19. a) I enjoy things the way I used to. b) I don't enjoy things the way I used to. c) I hardly get satisfaction out of anything anymore. d) I have no experience of pleasure anymore.
20. a) I make decisions about as well as ever. b) I try to put off making decisions. c) I have great difficulty in making decisions. d) I cannot make any decisions at all anymore.
21. a) I am no more irritable now than I ever was. b) I get annoyed or irritated more easily than I used to. c) I feel irritated all the time. d) I don't get irritated at all about at the things that used to irritate me.
22. a) I don't feel particularly guilty. b) I feel bad or unworthy a good part of the time. c) I feel quite guiltyl. d) I feel constantly as though I am guilty and worthless.
23. a) I don't cry any more than usual. b) I cry more now than I used to. c) I cry all the time now; I cannot stop it. d) I used to be able to cry, but now I cannot cry at all, even though I want to.
24. a) I feel no tension or pressure in my heart. b) I feel a slight tension and pressure in my heart. c) I feel a stronger heart beat than normally. d) I feel a painful pressure in my heart which is also beating excessively.
25. a) I have not noticed any recent change in my interest in sex. b) I am less interested in sex than I used to be. c) I am much less interested in sex now. d) I have lost interest in sex completely.
26. a) I don't feel I am being punished. b) I have a feeling that something bad may happen to me. c) I feel I am being punished or will be punished. d) I feel I deserve to be punished.
27. a) I can sleep as well as usual. b) I wake up more tired in the morning than I used to. c) I wake up 1–2 hours earlier than usual and find it hard to sleep. d) I wake up early every day and cannot get more than 5 hours' sleep.
28. a) I don't feel disappointed in myself. b) I am disappointed in myself. c) I am disgusted with myself. d) I hate myself.

29. a) I can work about as well as before. b) It takes extra effort to get started at doing something. c) I have to push myself very hard to do anything. d) I can't do any work at all.
30. a) I feel dissatisfied with most things. b) I can't complain about my future. c) Everything is working out well. d) The future looks wonderful.
31. a) I don't feel I am any worse than anybody else. b) I am critical of myself for my weakness or mistakes. c) I blame myself for my faults. d) I blame myself for everything bad that happens.
32. a) I don't get more tired than usual. b) I get tired more easily than I used to. c) I get tired from doing anything. d) I get too tired to do anything.
33. a) I pass water as often as I used to. b) I pass water frequently, but in less quantity than before. c) I find urination somewhat difficult. d) I find urination extremely difficult.
34. a) I don't feel I look any worse than I used to. b) I am worried that I am looking old or unattractive. c) I feel that there are permanent changes in my appearance. d) I feel that I am ugly or repulsive looking.
35. a) My stomach functions normally. b) I suffer from constipation. c) My bowels move only if I take a laxative. d) In spite of treatment my bowels do not move.
36. a) My eyesight is as it used to be. b) I have to strain my eyes in order to read. c) I have become a slower reader than I was because of my eyesight. d) I have to pause frequently when reading because the text blurs.
37. a) I feel miserable most of the time. b) Once in a while I'm down, but most of the time I feel good. c) I feel pretty good most of the time. d) I have never felt better in my life.
38. a) I consume the same quantity of liquid per day as I used to. b) It is doubtful whether my consumption of liquid has increased. c) My consumption of liquid has clearly increased. d) I feel thirsty constantly, and my consumption of liquid has increased extremely.
39. a) I feel as relaxed as I normally do. b) I feel slightly more tense than usual. c) From time to time I feel very tense and find it very difficult to relax. d) I feel constantly tense and find it impossible to relax.
40. a) I do not feel nausea. b) I have a slight feeling of nausea, but I have not vomited. c) I have an unpleasant feeling of nausea, but I have not vomited. d) I have an unpleasant feeling of nausea and have actually vomited.
41. a) I don't have any thoughts of harming myself. b) I feel I would be better off dead. c) I have definite plans for committing suicide. d) I would kill myself if I had the chance.
42. a) My memory and powers of concentration are as good as they used to be. b) I have to make an effort in order to remember things I have heard, read or seen on television. c) I tend to forget what I have heard, read or seen in television. d) I find it so hard to concentrate that it is difficult for me to follow what is going on in general conversation or on television.

4.5.4 Kellner Symptom Questionnaire

The Kellner Symptom Questionnaire (Kellner 1987) attempts to improve self-rating scales in the measurement of mild degrees of depression. The item responses are reduced to 'yes' or 'no'. The number of items is increased from from 30 in the Kellner Symptom Rating Test (Kellner 1986) to 92, thereby rendering the Symptom Questionnaire a comprehensive rating scale. Studies by Fava et al. (1986) in depressed patients during a drug trial and by Grandi et al. (1990) in somatically ill patients have demonstrated adequate validity when tested against observer scales. These findings are in agreement with results by Loldrup et al. (1991) with the Symptom Rating Scale for Depression and Anxiety, where a reduction in item calibration from 0–3 into 0–2 did not decrease its validity.

The items of the Symptom Questionnaire are the following:
 1 nervous
 2 weary
 3 irritable
 4 cheerful
 5 tense, tensed up
 6 sad, blue
 7 happy
 8 frightened
 9 feeling calm
10 feeling healthy
11 losing temper easily
12 feeling of not enough air
13 feeling kind to people
14 feeling fit
15 heavy arms or legs
16 feeling confident
17 feeling warm to people
18 shaky
19 no pains anywhere
20 feeling aggressive or angry
21 arms and legs feel strong
22 appetite poor
23 feeling peaceful
24 feeling unworthy
25 annoyed
26 feelins of rage
27 cannot enjoy yourself
28 tight head or neck
29 relaxed
30 restless
31 feeling that people are friendly
32 feeling of hate

33 choking feeling
34 afraid
35 patient
36 scared
37 furious
38 feeling charitable, forgiving
39 feeling guilty
40 feeling well
41 feeling of pressure in head or body
42 worried
43 contented
44 weak arms or legs
45 feeling desperate, terrible
46 no aches anywhere
47 thinking of death or dying
48 hot tempered
49 terrified
50 feeling of courage
51 enjoying yourself
52 breathing difficult
53 parts of body feel numb or tingling
54 takes a long time to fall asleep
55 feeling hostile
56 infuriated
57 heart beating fast or pounding
58 depressed
59 jumpy
60 feeling a failure
61 not interested in things
62 highly strung
63 cannot relax
64 panicky
65 pressure on head
66 blaming yourself
67 thoughts ending your life
68 frightening thoughts
69 enraged
70 irritated by other people
71 looking forward toward the future
72 nauseated, sick to stomach
73 feeling that life is bad
74 upset bowels or stomach
75 feeling inferior to others
76 feeling useless
77 muscle pains

78 no unpleasant feelings in head or body
79 headaches
80 feel like attacking people
81 shaking with anger
82 mad
83 feeling of goodwill
84 feeling like crying
85 cramps
86 feeling that something bad will happen
87 wound up, uptight
88 get angry quickly
89 self-confident
90 resentful
91 feeling of hopelessness
92 head pains

The scoring of the various subscales are (Y = yes; N = no; or T = true; F = false):

Anxiety: 1Y, 5Y, 8Y, 9N, 16N, 18Y, 23N, 29N, 30Y, 34Y, 36Y, 42Y, 49Y, 50N, 54Y, 59Y, 62Y, 63T, 64Y, 68Y, 86Y, 87Y, 89N.

Depression: 2Y, 4N, 6Y, 7N, 24Y, 27T, 39Y, 40N, 43N, 45Y, 47Y, 51N, 58Y, 60Y, 61T, 66Y, 67Y, 71N, 73Y, 75Y, 76Y, 84Y, 91Y.

Somatic: 10N, 12T, 14N, 15Y, 19F, 21N, 22Y, 28Y, 33Y, 41Y, 44Y, 46F, 52Y, 53Y, 57Y, 65Y, 72Y, 74Y, 77Y, 78F, 79Y, 85Y, 92Y.

Anger-Hostility: 3Y, 11Y, 13N, 17N, 20Y, 25Y, 26Y, 31N, 32Y, 35N, 37Y, 38N, 48Y, 55Y, 56Y, 69Y, 70Y, 80Y, 81Y, 82Y, 83N, 88Y, 90Y.

Well-being: 9, 16, 23, 29, 50, 89, 4, 7, 40, 43, 51, 71, 10, 14, 19, 21, 46, 78, 13, 17, 31, 35, 38, 83.

4.5.5 Checklist for the Evaluation of Somatic Symptoms (CHESS)

The CHESS was developed in France beginning in 1978 (Guelfi et al. 1983). In its final version it contains 55 items (Guelfi et al. 1991). The scale is used both in a self-rating version and in an observer version. In this compendium the interview version has been included (Table 4.15) which most logically is discussed in Chap. 10.

Table 4.15. Checklist for the Evaluation of Somatic Signs and Symptoms (CHESS R-89)

a) Does the patient report any somatic disturbances during the interview, before being questioned about their presence?

☐ No - ☐ Yes - Which one(s)? (list ALL somatic complaints as reported by the patient)

b) Ask every single standardized question from pages 1 to 3. Add "IN ADDITION TO" (i.e. A DISTURBANCE ALREADY REPORTED UNDER a). Example: "You said you were constipated. In addition to being constipated, do you have other problems with your bowels?"

Rate the severity of the disturbances (1) using the following guidelines:
I, severity: 0, absent; 1, mild; 2, moderate; 3, marked; 4, very important.

Ratings are determined by present symptomatology, i.e. by features observed during the interview and symptoms reported by the patient. THE ASSESSMENT PERIOD usually covers 7 DAYS, in some trials it may cover 2 or 4 weeks. The time span considered is defined by using one of the following: DURING THE LAST WEEK or DURING THE LAST 2 (or 4) WEEKS or SINCE WE LAST SPOKE TOGETHER

Table 4.15 (cont.)

Questions		Items
How has your appetite been lately?	1	Decreased appetite
Have you lost weight?	2	Reported weight loss
	3	Reported weight gain
	4	Bulimia
Do you have problems with your bowels?	5	Nausea
Do you pass stools normally?	6	Vomiting
	7	Stomach pain
	8a	Gastric discomfort, bloating, other gastrointestinal symptoms
	8b	Constipation
	9	Diarrhea
Is your eyesight normal?	10	Blurred vision (accomodation)
Do you have a dry mouth?	11	Dry mouth
Do you sweat more than usual?	12	Sweating

Table 4.15 (cont.)

Questions	Items	
Do you feel dizzy at times?	13	Dizziness
	14	Faintness
	15	Tinnitus
Is your heart beating too hard or too fast? Do you have difficulties breathing?	16	Palpitations
	17	Cardiac pain
	18	Dyspnea
	19	Lump in the throat
	20	Difficulty swallowing
	21	ENT disturbances. Altered voice
Do you sleep well at night?	22	Difficulty falling asleep
	23	Waking in the middle of the night
	24	Early morning awakening
	25	Change in dreaming
	26	Hypersomnia
	27	Ineffective sleep
Do you feel sleepy during the day?	28	Drowsiness

Table 4.15 (cont.)

Questions	Items	
Have your legs been swelling?	29	Oedema of the lower limbs
Do you urinate normally?	30	Difficulty urinating: pollakiuria
Do you feel abnormally tired? In your muscles or all over?	31	General fatigue
Are you bothered by spasms, tingling?	32	Masticatory spasms
	33	Spasms (tetaniform)
	34	Paresthesias (arms, legs)
Do you have difficulties remembering things, concentrating?	35	Reported memory disturbances
	36	Inability to tolerate noise
	37	Difficulty concentrating
Are you bothered by any other pain?	38a	Physical agitation or tension
	38b	Headache
	39	Low back pain
	40	Abdominal pain
	41	Diffuse muscular pain
	42	Undefined physical pain

Table 4.15 (cont.)

Questions	Items
Neurological examination	43 Akathisia (restlessness)
	44 Oral dyskinesia
	45 Hypertonia (muscular)
	46 Amimia
	47 Hyperkinesia
	48 Hyperreflexia
	49 Observed tremor
	50 Micrography
	51 Dysarthria
	52 Observed memory impairment
	53 Other disturbance reported
	54 Other disturbance reported
	55 Other disturbance reported

c) Relationship (R) to medication.

Report (column Disturbances) items corresponding in your opinion to possible, probable or definite UNWANTED EFFECTS. Rate the relationship to medication using the following guidelines: 0, definitely none; 1, possible; 2, probable; 3, definite.

DISTURBANCE   R ☐ ☐ ☐ ☐

DISTURBANCE   R ☐ ☐ ☐ ☐

References

Albus M, Maier W, Shera D, Bech P. Consistences and discrepances in self-and observer-related anxiety scales: a comparison between the self and the observer rated Markes-Sheehan scale. Eur Arch Psychiat Clin Neurosci 1990; 240: 96–102.

Angst J. Meta-analysis of oxaprotyline. Paper presented at Strassbourg Forum, June 1992.

Arrindell WA. Dimensional structure and psychopathology correlates of the Fear Survey Schedule (FSS-III) in phobic population: a factorial definition of agoraphobia. Beh Res Ther 1980; 18: 229–242.

Bech P. Quality of life in psychosomatic research. Psychopath 1987; 20: 169–179.

Bech P. Rating scales for mood disorders: applicability, consistency and construct validity. Acta Psychiat Scand 1988; 78 (suppl 345): 45–55.

Bech P, Gram LF, Dein E, Jacobsen O, Vitger J, Bolwig, TG. Quantitative rating of depressive states. Acta Psychiat Scand 1975; 51: 161–170.

Bech P, Vendsborg PB, Rafaelsen OJ. Lithium maintenance treatment of manic-melancholic patients: Its role in the daily routine. Acta Psychiat Scand 1976; 53: 70–81.

Bech P, Hey H. Depression or asthenia related to metabolic disturbances in obese patients after intestinal bypass surgery. Acta Psychiat Scand 1979; 59: 462–470.

Bech P, Kastrup M, Loldrup D. Use of headache rating scales: a multiaxial approach. Cephalalgia 1986; 6: 69–80.

Bech P, Allerup P, Maier W, Albus M, Lavori P, Ayuso JL. The Hamilton Scales and the Hopkins Symptom Checklist (SCL-90): a cross-national validity study in patients with panic disorders. Br J Psychiat 1992; 160: 206–211.

Beck AT. Depression: Clinical, Experimental, and Theoretical Aspects. Univ Pennsylvania Press, Philadelphia, 1967.

Beck AT, Ward CH, Mendelson M, Mock J, Erbaugh J. An inventory for measuring depression. Arch Gen Psychiat 1961; 4: 561–571.

Beck AT, Beamesderfer A. Assessment of depression: the depression inventory. In: Pichot P (ed). Psychological Measurements in Psychopharmacology. Basel, Karger, 1974, pp. 151–169.

Beck AT, Brown G, Epstein N, Steer RA. An inventory for measuring clinical anxiety: psychometric properties. J Consult Clin Psychol 1988; 56: 893–897.

Bouman TK, Kok AR. Homogeneity of Beck's Depression Inventory (BDI): applying Rasch analysis in conceptual exploration. Acta Psychiat Scand 1987; 76: 568–573.

Brodman K, Erdmann AJ, Lorge I, Wolff HG. The Cornell Medical Index. An adjunct to medical interview. J Am Med Ass 1949a; 140: 530–534.

Brodman K, Erdman AJ, Lorge I, Wolff HG. The Cornell Medical Index – Health Questionnaire as a diagnostic instrument. J Am Med Ass 1951; 145: 152–157.

Carroll BJ, Fielding JM, Blashki TG. Depression rating scales: a critical review. Arch Gen Psychiat 1973; 28: 361–366.

Cook WW, Medley DM. Proposed hostility and pharisaic-virtue scales from the MMPI. J Appl Psychol 1954; 38: 414–418.

Cyr JJ, McKenna-Foley JM, Peacock E. Factor structure of the SCL-90: Is there one? J Pers Ass 1985; 49: 571–578.

Dahlstrom WG, Brooks JD, Petersen CD. The Beck Depression Inventory: item order and impact of response sets. J Pers Ass 1990; 55: 224–233.

Derogatis LR, Lipman RS, Covi L, Rickels K. Neurotic symptom dimensions as perceived by psychiatrists and patients of various social classes. Arch Gen Psychiat 1971; 24: 454–464.

Dick P, Ferrero E. A double-blind comparative study of the clinical efficacy of fluvoxamine and clomipramine. Br J Clin Pharmacol 1983; 15: 419–425.

Eysenck HJ, Eysenck SBG. Psychoticism as a Dimension of Personality. London, Hodder & Stroughton, 1976.

Fadden G, Bebbington P, Kuipers L. Caring and its burdens. A study of the spouses of depressed patients. Brit J Psychiat 1987; 151: 660–667.

Fava GA, Kellner R, Lisansky J, Park S, Perini GI, Zielezny M. Rating depression in normals and depressive: observer versus self-rating scales. J Aff Dis 1986; 11: 29–33.

Feinberg M, Carroll BJ. The Carroll Rating Scale for Depression. In: Sartorius N, Ban TA (eds). Assessment of depression. Berlin, Springer, 1986, pp. 188–200.

Frank JF, Gliedman LH, Imber SD, Nash EH, Stone AR. Why patients leave psychotherapy. Arch Neurol Psychiat 1957; 77: 283–299.

Frimodt-Møller J, Loldrup D, Kornerup HJ, Bech P. Quality of life, side effects and efficacy of lisinopril compared with metoprolol in patients with mild to moderate essential hypertension. J Human Hypertension 1991; 5: 215–221.

Goldberg D. The Detection of Psychiatric Illness by Questionnaire. Oxford, Oxford Univ Press, 1972.

Goldberg D. Manual of the General Health Questionnaire. Windsor, NFER, 1978.

Grandi S, Fava GA, Cunsolo A, Saviotti FM, Ranieri M, Trombini G, Gozzetti G. Rating depression and anxiety after mastectomy: observer versus self-rating scales. Int J Psychat Med 1990; 20: 163–171.

Guelfi JD, Pull CB, Guelfi C, Rushels, Dreyfus JF. La CHESS. Utilization dans la pathologie anxiense et depressive. Structure factorielle. Am Med Psychol 1983; 141: 257–278.

Guelfi JD, von Frenckell R, Caille Ph. The Norris VAS and the ADA inventory. A factorial analysis in outpatients. Paper presented at World Psychiatric Association Congress, Athens, October, 1989.

Guy W. Early Clinical Drug Evaluation Program (ECDEU) Assessment Manual. Rockville, Department of Health, Education and Welfare, 1976.

Hamilton M. Diagnosis and rating of anxiety. Br J Psychiat, 1969 (special publication): 76–79.

Hamilton M, Shapiro CM. Depression. In: Peck DF, Shapiro CM (eds). Measuring Human Problems. A Practical Guide. Chichester, John Wiley & Sons, 1990, pp. 25–65.

Jachuck SJ, Brierly H, Jachuck S, Willcox PM. The effect of hypotensive drugs on quality of life. J Roy Col Gen Pract 1982; 32: 103–105.

Kellner R. The Symptom Rating Test. In: Sartorius N, Ban TA (eds). Assessment of Depression. Berlin, Springer, 1986, pp. 213–220.

Kellner R. A Symptom Questionnaire. J Clin Psychiatry 1987; 48: 268–274.

Kristensen CB, Rasmussen S, Dahl A, Lauritsen G, Lund B, Stubgaard M, Bech P. The Withdrawal Syndrome Scale for alcohol and related psychoactive drugs. Total scores as guidelines for treatment with phenobarbital. Nord Psykiat Tidsskr 1986; 40: 139–146.

Lader M, Marks M. The rating of clinical anxiety. Acta Psychiat Scand 1974; 50: 112–137.

Langevin R, Stancer H. Evidence that depression rating scales primarily measure a social undesirability response set. Acta Psychiat Scand 1979; 59: 70–79.

Lau M. Livskvalitet? Hos lungekræftpatienter. Copenhagen, FADL, 1988.

Likert R. A technique for the measurement of attitudes. Arch Psychol 1932; 140: 1–55.

Lipman RS. Depression scales derived from the Hopkins Symptom Checklist. In: Sartorius N, Ban TA (eds). Assessment of Depression. Berlin, Springer, 1986, pp. 232–248.

Loldrup D, Langemark M, Hansen HJ, Kastrup M, Jeppesen K, Elsborg L, Bonnevie O, Olesen J, Bech P. The validity of the Melancholia Scale (MES) in predicting outcome of antidepressants in chronic idiopathic pain disorders. Eur Psychiat 1991; 6: 119–125.

Maier W, Buller R, Philipp M, Heuser I. The Hamilton Anxiety Scale: Reliability, validity and sensitivity to change in anxiety and depressive disorders. J Aff Dis 1988; 14: 61–68.

Maier W, Albus M, Buller R, Nutzinger D, Shera D, Bech P. Self-and observer assessment in anxiolytic drug trials: a comparison of their validity. Eur Arch Psychiatry Clin Neurosci 1990; 240: 103–108.

McNair DM. Self-evaluations of antidepressions. Psychopharma (Berl.) 1974; 37: 281–302.

McNair DM, Lorr M, Droppleman LF. Profile of Mood States. San Diego, Educ Indus Test Serv, 1971.

Mollica RF, Caspi-Yavin Y, Balini P, Troung T, For S, Lavelle J. The Harvard Trauma Questionnaire: Validating a cross-cultural instrument for measuring torture, trauma, and posttraumatic stress disorder in Indochinese refugees. J Nerv Ment Dis, 1992; 180: 111–116.

Parloff MB, Kelman HC, Frank JD. Comfort, effectiveness, and self-awareness as criteria of improvement in psychotherapy. Am J Psychiat 1954; 111: 343–351.

Paykel ES, Norton KRW. Self-report and clinical interview in the assessment of depression. In: Sartorius N, Ban TA (eds). Assessment of Depression. Berlin, Springer, 1986, pp. 356–366.

Peveler RC, Fairburn CG. Measurement of neurotic symptoms by self-report questionnaire: validity of the SCL-90R. Psychol Med 1990; 20: 873–879.

Pichot P, Brun JP. Questionnaire bref d'auto-evaluation des dimensions depressive, asthenique, et anxiose. Am Med Psychol 1984; 142: 862–865.

Radloff LS. The CES-D scale. a self-report depression scale for research in the general population. Appl Psychol Measurement, 1977; 1: 385–401.

Raskin A. Sensitivity to treatment effects of evaluation instruments completed by psychiatrists, psychologists, nurses, and patients. In: Sartorius N, Ban TA (eds). Assessment of Depression. Berlin, Springer, 1986, pp. 367–376.

Robins LN, Helzer JE, Croughan J, Ratcliff K. The NIMH Diagnostic Interview Schedule: Its history, characteristics, and validity. Arch Gen Psychiat 1981; 38: 381–389.

Sheehan DV. The Anxiety Disease. New York, Charles Schribner's Sons, 1983.

Siegel SM. The relationship of hostility to authoritarianism. J Abnorm Soc Psychol 1956; 52: 368–372.

Slevin ML, Plant H, Lynch D, Drinkwater J, Gregory WM. Who should measure quality of life, the doctor or the patient? Brit J Cancer 1988; 57: 109–112.

Snaith RP, Tayler CM. Irritability: Definition, assessment and associated factors. Br J Psychiat 1985; 147: 127–136.

Spielberger CD, Borsuch RL, Lushene RE. State-Trait Anxiety Inventory. Palo Alto, Consulting Psychologists Press, 1970.

Spielberger CD, Jacobs G, Russel S, Crane RS. Assessment of anger: The state-trait scale. In: Butcher JN (ed). Personality Assessments. New York, Erolbaun Hillsdale, 1982.

Spielberger CD, Johnson EH, Jacobs GA, Krasner SS, Oesterle SE, Worden TJ. The State-Trait Anger Inventory. Palo Alto, Consulting Psychologists Press, 1986.

Suchman EA. The utility of scalogram analysis. In: Stouffer SA, Guttman L, Suchman EA, Lazarsfeld PF, Star SA, Clausen JA (eds). Measurement and Prediction. Princeton, Princeton Univ Press, 1950, pp. 122–171.

Sudman S, Bradburn NM. Asking Questions. San Francisco, Jossey-Bass Publishers, 1985.

Thompson C. The instruments of psychiatric research. Chichester, John Wiley & Sons, 1989.

van Benthem J. Semantics of time. In: Michon JA, Jackson JL (eds). Time, Mind and Behavior. Berlin: Springer Verlag 1985, pp. 266–278.

von Zeersen D. Clinical self-rating scales of the Munich psychiatric information system (PSYCHIS München). In: Sartorius N, Ban TA (eds). Assessment of Depression. Berlin, Springer, 1986, pp. 270–303.

Watson M. Development of a questionnaire measure of adjustment to cancer: the MAC Scale. Psychol Med 1988; 18: 203–209.

Zigmond AS, Snaith RP. The Hospital Anxiety and Depression Scale. Acta Psychiat Scand 1983; 67: 361–370.

Zung WWK. A self-rating depression scale. Arch Gen Psychiat 1965; 12: 63–70.

Zung WWK. A rating instrument for anxiety disorders. Psychosom 1971; 12: 371–379.

Zung WWK. The Depression Status Inventory: an adjunct to the Self-rating Depression Scale. J Clin Psychol 1972; 28: 539–543.

5 Psychopathological Personality Rating Scales

From a psychopathological point of view axis 2 in DSM-III or DSM-III-R should be considered as a dimension closely related to the clinical syndromes, (described in Chaps. 2–4 in this compendium). A continuum between personality disorders and clinical syndromes was proposed by Kretschmer (1921), Bleuler (1922), Jung (1923) and Schneider (1923). Kretschmer suggested that the spectrum of schizophrenia ranges from slight schizothymia (just above the upper extreme of normal variation) to schizophrenic degrees of autism, the depressive spectrum from dysthymia (just above the upper extreme of normal variation) to psychotic degrees of melancholia, and the spectrum of mania from cyclothymia (just above the upper extreme of normal variation) to psychotic degrees of mania.

Bleuler (1922) regarded each person as having both schizothymic and dysthymic/cyclothymic dispositions, but in different loadings. Jung (1923) suggested that extraversion and introversion were present in each person as latent components of neuroticism. On clinical grounds Schneider (1923), often considered as the 'last classicist of psychiatry' (Pichot 1983), described the third group of personality diagnoses, the psychopathic personalities, which he considered as statistical extreems of the normal personality. However, as discussed by Pichot (1978), Schneider included a total of ten different subtypes of psychopathy, of which only the following three cover the basic components: (a) unstable dysphoria, (b) social maladjustment, and (c) failure to accept responsibility for one's own actions. These components are included in the concept of 'aggressive psychopath', as shown by Storr (1968).

As discussed by Eysenck (1952), the concept of personality 'type' (as used by Kretschmar and Jung) is often contrasted with the concept of personality 'trait', and it has been suggested that the 'type' approach implies a bimodal form of distribution and the 'trait' approach a unimodal. This argument has inter alia been used by Kendell (1975) among others in his biological approach to the classification of mental disorders. However, as already noted by Eysenck (1952), this view is fallacious, at least in regard to the classical psychometric theories. Kretschmer (1921) regarded the concept of type as follows:

Nature does not work with sharp contrasts and precise definitions, which derive from our own thought and our own need for comprehension. In nature, fluid transitions are the rule, but it would not be true to say that, in this infinite sea of fluid empirical forms, nothing clear and objective could be seen; quite on the contrary. In certain fields, groupings arise which we encounter again and again; when we study them objectively, we realize that we are dealing here with focal points of frequently occurring groups of characteristics, con-

Table 5.1. Personality syndromes and their corresponding components

Personality syndromes	ICD-10 components		DSM-III-R components		Rating scales
Psychoticism (Kretschmer 1921)	Paranoid Schizoid Borderline	F 60.0 F 60.1 F 60.31	Paranoid Schizoid Schizotypal Borderline Narcissism	301.00 301.20 301.22 301.83 301.81	Suspiciousness Expansiveness Emptiness Narcissism Nonempathia Amotivation
Psychopathia (Schneider 1923)	Dissocial Impulsive	F 60.2 F 60.32	Antisocial Passive aggressive	301.70 301.84	Low frustration tolerance Impulsivity Unstable dysphoria Social maladjustment Failure to accept responsibility for own actions Aggressive behaviour
Neuroticism (Jung 1921)	Anankastic Anxious Dependent Histrionic	F 60.5 F 60.6 F 60.7 F 60.4	Obsessive-compulsive Avoidant Dependent Histrionic	301.40 301.82 301.60 301.50	Introversion: depressed, tension, anxiety, neurasthenia, obsessive compulsive Extraversion: sociable, dissociative, hysteria General: moody, low self-esteem, guilt feelings

centrations of correlated traits.... What is essential in biology, as in clinical medicine, is not a single correlation, but groups of correlations; only those lead to the innermost connections.... What we call, mathematically, focal points of statistical correlations, we call, in more descriptive prose, constitutional types. The two are identical.

In other words, a personality type covers a group of components ('traits') which should be structurally interconnected.

The work of Eysenck and Eysenck (1976) in the Eysenck Personality Questionnaire (EPQ) provides an elegant example of using factor analysis to measure types (or personality syndromes/diagnoses) with the rating scale method. By this approach, three types or dimensions have been studied: neuroticism in general, introversion and extraversion, and psychoticism. Among self-rating scales the EPQ is the most relevant from a psychopathological point of view. This compendium also takes the dimensional approach regarding personality diagnoses. Likert scales (i.e. brief rating scales) have been preferred, as have Likert items (i.e. items defined 0–4). The components of such unidimensional Likert scales have been neuroticism, schizoid borderline, and psychopathia.

It is beyond the scope of this compendium to discuss rating scales measuring the many (too many) personality diagnoses included in DSM-III or DSM-III-R. The most appropriate instrument for obtaining axis 2 diagnoses in accordance with DSM-III or DSM-III-R is the Structured Interview for Personality Diagnoses (Spitzer and Williams 1983). Another scale for making DSM-III personality diagnoses is the Millon Clinical Multiaxial Inventory (MCMI; Millon 1983). The degree of concordance between the MCMI and the DSM-III is, however, a controversial issue (Widiger et al. 1985). In a recent review of the MCMI, Wetzler (1990) has demonstrated the problem of separating axis 1 and axis 2 syndromes with this self-rating scale.

The classical monograph on theories of personality and its measurement is Hall and Lindzey (1957); it is recommended that the reader consult this work.

Table 5.1 compares the personality syndromes of psychoticism, psychopathia and neuroticism using the ICD-10 and DSM-III-R codes as components or 'traits' rather than 'types'. There is some inconsistency in DSM-III-R, where dysthymia and cyclothymia are subsumed under axis 1 mood disorders and schizotypal disorder under axis 2 disorders. In ICD-10 only schizoid components are listed in personality diagnoses.

Table 5.2 shows the components of a personality 'borderline' scale measuring the schizoid dimensions. The original concept of borderline was considered a psychoneurotic form of schizophrenia (Hoch and Polatin 1949; Vanggaard 1979). With reference to these works the components have been collected from the DSM-III-R personality diagnoses listed under the psychoticism personality syndrome in Table 5.1. The components of ambivalence and anhedonia are those that differ especially from the Positive and Negative Syndrome Scale (PANSS; see Chap. 3). The items in the Schizoid Borderline Scale (SBS) have been selected from studies with health-related quality of life scales in psychosomatic research (see Chapter 9, especially Table 9.1). Such scales are based on the ability to experience pleasure (Watson et al. 1970), which Meehl has referred to as the 'hedonic capacity' (1962,

Table 5.2. Item distributions of rating scales: schizoid dimensions

Component	PANSS	SBS
Negative		
Autism	57%	28%
Ambivalence	0%	14%
Anhedonia	0%	14%
Cognitive impairment	43%	0%
Positive		
Psychotic symptoms	43%	0%
Cognitive beliefs	14%	14%
Motor symptoms	14%	0%
Aggression	14%	28%
Number of items	2x7	7

1975, 1987). In a recent study on the hedonic capacity in schizophrenics and their twins it was found that anhedonia is genetically influenced, however, less so than the full-blown schizophrenic syndrome (Berenbaum et al. 1990). In this study anhedonia was measured by a semi-structured interview including such questions as: How do you pass time? Who are your close friends? What kinds of nice things do you do yourself? What gives you the most pleasure?

However, if anhedonia is to be a major component in schizoid borderline personality it should be considered as a life-style attitude and not as a low score on well-being scales. Consequently the schizoid borderline syndrome differs, on the one hand, from dysthymia and depression in having no well-being symptoms and, on the other hand, from aggressive psychopathic components in the life-style attitude of emptiness and anhedonia. Psychopathic as well as neurotic persons are hedonics. Storr (1968) has formulated the hedonia-anhedonia problem most clearly: "The depressive person fears the withdrawal of love because it threatens his happiness. The schizoid person fears it because it seems to threaten his very existence." With reference to defence mechanisms (i.e. unconscious intrapsychic processes which provide relief from emotional conflicts and anxiety; Freud 1915) the hedonic dimension reflects neurotic defence mechanisms (e.g. denial, displacement, dissociation or sublimation) while the anhedonic dimension reflects narcissistic or paranoid defence mechanisms (e.g. protection).

The items comprising the SBS, together with their scoring instructions, are presented below. The scoring sheet is illustrated in "Appendix 5.1".

1 Excessive Social Anxiety
This item describes discomfort, tenseness and insecurity in social situations.
0. Not present.
1. Very mild or doubtful, questionable pathology.

2. Moderate discomfort in social situations, e.g. in a group of more than two or three people the patient don't know.
3. Social anxiety which is so marked that it interferes with the patient's daily life.
4. Extreme social anxiety.

2 Affective Instability
This item describes short but marked shifts from dysphoria to euphoria, i.e. from baseline mood to dysphoria and/or euphoria.
0. Not present.
1. Very mild or doubtful degree, questionable pathology.
2. The patient is "moody", i.e. often in changeable state from baseline mood to moderate dysphoria, and/or euphoria.
3. Markedly affective instability.
4. The patient shows extreme affective instability.

3 Inappropriate Anger or Lack of Control of Anger
This item describes unusually intense feelings of anger in response to disappointments or criticism.
0. Not present.
1. Present to a slight or doubtful degree, questionable pathology.
2. The patient experiences moderately inappropriate anger 'temper outbursts', but he is able to control it.
3. The patient describes severe anger which he/she can control only with difficulty.
4. The patient shows extreme anger which he cannot control.

4 Self-Mutilating Behaviour
This item describes non-life-threatening, self-inflicted damage, e.g. banging the head against the wall, scratching the skin, pricking with a needle, plucking out hair, swallowing things, burning oneself with a cigarette, etc.
0. Not present.
1. Doubtful whether present; questionable pathology.
2. Present to a mild to moderate degree.
3. Present to a moderate to marked degree.
4. Present to a severe to extreme degree.

5 Feelings of Emptiness or Boredom
This item describes deep and sustained feelings of emptiness, boredom and meaninglessness.
0. Not present.
1. Very mild or doubtful degree; questionable pathology.
2. The patient's ability to experience joy is moderately reduced.
3. The patient feels marked emptiness and boredom, e.g. feels empty inside.
4. The patient feels empty and bored to an extreme degree.

6 Lack of Empathy

This item describes the patient's inability to understand other people's experiences and feelings.

0. Not present.
1. Slightly or doubtfully decreased empathy, questionable pathology.
2. The patient shows moderate lack of interest in the feelings of others.
3. Marked lack of empathy.
4. Extreme lack of empathy.

7 Expansive Sense of Self-Importance

This item describes unrealistically elevated views of the patient on his/her own importance, e.g. the patient feels to be a person with special talents or abilities.

0. Not present.
1. Slightly or doubtfully elevated self-esteem; questionable pathology.
2. The patient feels to a moderate degree unrealistically superior to others, which does not, however, affect attitude or behaviour.
3. The patient has markedly increased self-esteem, which influences attitudes but not behaviour.
4. The patient has grandiose ideas of his own importance to a severe degree, influencing both attitudes and behaviour.

The Psychopathy Checklist (PCL; Hare 1980) is an observer-rating scale for measuring psychopathy as a dimension. Although no manual for item definitions has been published (each item is defined in Likert categories (0–4); as in the SBS, above), Hare (1980) has found an adequate inter-rater reliability. The content validity of psychopathy has been defined by Hare (1981):

'The behavior of the psychopath is directed almost entirely toward the satisfaction of personal needs, without any concern for the needs and welfare of others.... The psychopath is extremely impulsive, irresponsible, hedonistic, selfish, and intolerant of frustration. But perhaps his most important distinguishing features are an almost lack of empathy and affection for others, coupled with an absence of any genuine indications of guilt, anxiety, or remorse for his persistent pattern of unsocial and amoral behavior."

Factor analysis of the Psychopathy Checklist has shown (Harpur et al. 1988) that the scale contains two factors: the first taps the core items of the personality dimension of psychopathia (items 1, 3, 5, 6, 7, 8, 9, 20, 22) and the second chronic antisocial behaviour (items 4, 10, 11, 13, 14, 15, 16, 17, 18, 19, 21). Other factor analyses with the PCL (e.g. Rain 1985) have confirmed the two factor model of the scale. So far, latent structure analyses are lacking. The items of the PCL are presented below.

1. Glibness/superficial charm.
2. Previous diagnosis as psychopath.
3. Egocentricity.
4. Proneness/low frustration tolerance.
5. Pathological lying and deception.
6. Conning/lack of sincerity.
7. Lack of remorse or guilt.

8. Lack of affect and emotional depth.
9. Callous/lack of empathy.
10. Parasitic life-style.
11. Short-tempered/poor behavioural controls.
12. Promiscuous sexual relations.
13. Early behaviour problems.
14. Lack of realistic, long-term plans.
15. Impulsivity.
16. Irresponsible behaviour as parent.
17. Frequent extra marital relations.
18. Juvenile delinquency.
19. Poor probation or parole risk.
20. Failure to accept responsibility for own actions.
21. Many types of offense.
22. Drug/alcohol abuse not direct cause of antisocial behaviour.

The third personality dimension to be considered here is that of neuroticism. While the SBS is relevant for predicting schizophrenia disorders or psychotic defence mechanisms and the PCL for predicting aggressive behaviour or substance use disorders (including alcohol) the dimension of neuroticism is relevant for predicting neurotic defence mechanisms in psychosomatic disorders.

In psychosomatic research the interest in personality dimensions goes back to Hippocrates (460–377 BC), who found correlations between personality variables and the tendency to develop various diseases. Especially the dimension of *habitus apoplecticus* seemed of importance (the correlation between high vitality and arterial diseases). This personality variable was further described by Galen (129–210 AD) as the choleric temperament, and in our time type A behaviour refers to *habitus apoplecticus* (Jenkins et al. 1979). However, the first psychometric evidence was the study of Robinson et al. (1940), who demonstrated that the tendency to obesity may be the linking factor. In research on human stress factors the separation between chronic stress (personality dimension of anxiety) and acute stress (states of anxiety symptoms) has been made in Spielberger's State-Trait Anxiety Scale (Spielberger et al. 1970). The same has been done with aggression (Spielberger et al. 1986).

As discussed in Chapter 4, the Cornell Medical Index (CMI), has demonstrated high predictive validity for neurotic behaviour in patients with different degrees of somatic disorders. Neurotic personality scales have been derived from experience with the CMI, for example, the Eysenck Personality Questionnaire (EPQ; Eysenck and Eysenck 1976). The Neuroticism Scale from the EPQ has been found to have the highest convergent validity-compared to other self-rating scales for neurotic behaviour in a study in which the standard of validity was a clinical global assessment of neuroticism performed by an experienced psychiatrist (Bech et al. 1987). In a study on chronic benign pain disorder (Loldrup et al. 1991) it has been shown that in terms of Loevinger coefficients the total Neuroticism Scale was not homogeneous. However, Mokken coefficients pointed to the nine item subscale presented below. Scoring is 'yes' ('1') or 'no' ('0'). (CMI equivalents are inserted in parentheses.)

1. Do you worry about your health? (121)
2. Are you a worrier? (163)
3. Would you call yourself tense or 'high strung'? (188)
4. Are your feelings easily hurt? (174)
5. Have you often felt listless and tired for no reason? (108)
6. Would you call yourself a nervous person? (166)
7. Are you an irritable person? (180)
8. Do you suffer from nerves? (168)
9. Do you often feel lonely? (157)

Another neuroticism scale has been derived from the CMI. This scale was shown by Rawnsley (1966) to have high convergent validity using a clinical global assessment by experienced psychiatrists as index of neuroticism. Waters and O'Connor (1971) confirmed this result. The scale is presented below (scoring as above; CMI equivalents in parentheses).

1. Do you suffer from indigestion? (52)
2. Are you worried about your weight? (45)
3. Does every little thing get on your nerves and wear you out? (165)
4. Are you considered a nervous person? (166)
5. Are you extremely shy or sensitive? (172)
6. Are you considered a touchy person? (176)
7. Are you constantly keyed up and jittery? (188)
8. Do you suffer from severe nervous exhaustion? (113)
9. Do you wear yourself out worrying about your health? (121)

Whereas the Rawnsley subscale uses the original CMI questions, the Eysenck subscale has modified the questions on the basis of empirical research. Both scales are prone to a sense of 'yes-sayer' effect as the number of questions answered by 'yes' gives the rating on neuroticism. Table 5.3 compares the item distributions on

Table 5.3. Item distributions of rating scales: neuroticism

Components	Eysenck & Eysenck (1976)	Rawnsley (1966)
Digestive tract	0%	22%
Fatigability	11%	11%
Frequency of illness	11%	11%
Depression	11%	0%
Anxiety	33%	22%
Sensitivity	11%	22%
Anger	11%	0%
Tension	11%	11%

CMI components of these two scales. As mentioned in Chap. 4, experience with the CMI has shown that neurotic patients (in contrast to somatic patients) respond with 'yes' answers dispersed over the entire sample of sections. Eight of the 18 CMI sections are considered. The Rawnsley scale has items from the 'neurotic' organ of digestive trait. The Eysenck scale places the most weight on anxiety items.

The type A behaviour has been considered as a dimension very different from neuroticism. The Bortner Scale (Bortner 1969) is included in this compendium (Appendix 5.2) as a short rating scale for measuring type A behaviour (the Jenkins scale is a comprehensive scale). The Bortner Scale is based on items evaluated by visual analogue scales. As is evident, the opposite pole of the Bortner Scale type A is neuroticism. In other words, the type A dimension reflects the defence mechanism of reaction formation (blocking inacceptable wishes by 'contra-phobic behaviour'.

In the field of measuring personality with self-rating scales the Freiburg Personality Inventory (FPI; Fahrenberg et al. 1970) should also be considered, because intensive work with this scale has been made in the longitudinal Zürich studies (e.g. Angst and Clayton, 1986). The FPI comprises in its original version of 212 items based on personality scales like the MMPI (Minnesota Multiphasic Personality Inventory, Hathaway and McKinley 1951) and EPQ. In Appendix 5.3 is shown the three subscales of FPI identified by factor analysis consistently over the years in the Zürich studies (Angst and Clayton 1986). These scales are aggressivity, extraversion versus introversion, and psychosomatic or autonomic lability.

Although defence mechanisms are unconscious intrapsychic processes (and therefore most adequately should be tested by dynamic instruments such as the Thematic Apperception Test; Murray 1943), attempts have been made to develop self-rating scales measuring such constructs as denial, repression, regression, projection, etc. The most frequently used scale in this field is the Life Style Index developed by Plutchik et al. (1979). In a recent study Olff and Endresen (1991) made a factor analysis by which the scale was reduced to 45 items. This revised version is included. Below are indicated in parentheses the item numbers of the version published by Olff (1991).

Life Style Index (45 item version)

Instructions: Please indicate whether each of the following statements describes the way you usually feel or act. If the statement does not describe you, please mark a 'no'. If the statement does describe you, please mark a 'yes'.
 1. I am a very easy person to get along with (1)
 2. There has always been a person whom I wished I were like (3)
 3. When I want something I just can't wait to get it (5)
 4. One of my greatest assets is my self-control (7)
 5. I 'fly off the handle' easily (9)
 6. When someone shoves me in a crowd, I feel like killing him (10)
 7. People who boss other people around make me furious (12)
 8. I am an exceptionally fair person (14)

9. In my daydreams I am always the center of attention (16)
10. I get upset at the thought of members of my family walking around at home clothes on (17)
11. People who start rumours really annoy me (22)
12. I always see the brigt side of things (23)
13. I keep wanting or trying to change my appearance through exercise (24)
14. People have told me that I tend to be too impulsive (26)
15. I am annoyed by the fact that people show off too much (28)
16. I hate hostile people (29)
17. I am the type that never cries (31)
18. I have trouble giving up anything that belongs to me (33)
19. I have trouble remembering people's names (35)
20. I am always willing to listen to all sides of a problem even when I know I am right (37)
21. I never feel fed-up with people (38)
22. I can hardly remember anything that happened in my childhood (40)
23. People who try to get their way by yelling and screaming make me sick (44)
24. I am always optimistic (46)
25. When things don't go my way I sometimes sulk (49)
26. I feel outraged at dirty movies (52)
27. People tell me I am not very emotional (54)
28. When I drive a car, I sometimes get an urge to hit another car (57)
29. When I hear dirty jokes I feel very embarrassed (64)
30. I have dreams in which something repulsive appears (65)
31. Pornography is disgusting (68)
32. My bad temper has caused me trouble on my jobs (69)
33. One of the things I hate about people is that they are insincere (70)
34. When I read or hear about a tragedy it never seems to affect me (72)
35. Touching anything slimy make me feel nauseous (73)
36. I seem to have a lot of arguments with people (74)
37. I never feel emotional at funerals or funeral homes (75)
38. I hate people who always try to be center of attention (76)
39. Using public bathrooms is very upsetting for me (78)
40. It is very difficult for me to use dirty words (79)
41. I am irritated because people can't be trusted (80)
42. I have a strong need to have people tell me that I am sexually appealing (81)
43. I always try to wear clothes that make me as attractive as possible (83)
44. When someone bumps into me, I go into a rage (87)
45. When I see someone who is bloody, it almost never bothers me (90)

The item combinations are as follows: The factor of repression includes items 17, 19, 22, 27, 34, 37, 45. The factor of denial/intellectualization includes items 1, 4, 8, 12, 20, 21, 24. The factor of regression displacement includes items 3, 5, 6, 14, 25, 28, 32, 36, 44. The factor of reaction formation includes items 10, 26, 29, 30, 31, 35, 39, 40. The factor of compensation includes items 2, 9, 13, 18, 42, 43. The factor of projection includes items 7, 11, 15, 16, 23, 33, 38, 41.

The Task Force on DSM-IV (APA 1991) has suggested a new axis of defence or coping, because axis 2 in DSM-III seems excessively relying on descriptive psychopathology. The proposed DSM-IV Defensive Styles Rating Scale includes the following categories:

High Adaptive Level (= 7): Reflecting optimal adaption in the handling of stressors (e.g. anticipation, affiliation, altruism, humor, self-observation, sublimation, suppresion).

Mental Inhibition Level (= 6): Defensive functioning at this level keeps potentially threatening things out of awareness (e.g. obsessional defences as isolation of affect, intellectualization, undoing; hysterical defences such as reprssion or dissociation; other defences such as reaction formation, displacement or neurotic denial).

Minor Image-Distorting Level (= 5): Characterized by image distortions of self (e.g. devaluation, idealization, omnipotence).

Disavowal Level (= 4): Characterized by the disavowal of awareness of stressors (e.g. denial, rationalization, projection).

Major Image-Distorting Level (= 3): Characterized by wholesale fantastic distortion or gross misattributions of self and others (e.g. splitting of self and others' image, projective identification, autistic fantasy).

Action Level (= 2): Characterized by defensive functioning that deals with internal or external stressors by loss of inhibition leading to taking action without regard to the consequences (e.g. acting out, hypochondriasis, provocative passive aggression, apathetic withdrawal).

Level of Defensive Dysregulation (= 1): Characterized by failure of defensive regulation to contain the individual's reaction to stressors, leading to a pronounced break with objective reality (e.g. psychotic denial, psychotic distortion, delusional projection).

DSM-IV seems, thus, to include defence mechanisms as an axis 2 area. Most of the defensive styles rating scale items are ultimately defined in terms of symptom related to neurosis and psychosis. The measurement of coping with illness has in this compendium been treated in Chapter 8. In Chapter 5 is included scales measuring DSM-III axis 2 dimensions, and the DSM-IV scale of defence mechanism is considered also in this compendium as an axis 2 component or facet. It is, however, of interest that DSM-IV will include rating scales.

References

Angst J, Clayton P. Premorbid personality of depressive, bipolar, and schizophrenic patients with special reference to suicidal issues. Compreh Psychiat 1986; 27: 511–532.

Bech P, Jørgensen B, Jeppesen K, Loldrup D, Vanggaard T. Personality in depression. Concordance between clinical assessment and questionnaires. Acta Psychiat Scand 1986; 74: 263–268.

Berenbaum H, Oltmanns TF, Gottesman II. Hedonic capacity in schizophrenics and their twins. Psychol Med 1990; 20: 367–374.

Bleuler, E. Die Probleme der Schizoidie und der Syntonie. Zeitschr f d ges Neur u Psych 1922; 78: 122–129.

Bortner RW. A short scale as a potential measure of pattern A behaviour. J Chron Dis 1969; 22: 87–91.

Buss AH, Durkee A. An inventory for assessing different kinds of hostility. J Consult Psychiat 1957; 21: 343–349.

Coccaro EF, Siever LJ, Klar HM. Serotonergic studies in affective and personality disorder patients. Correlates with suicidal and impulsive behaviour. Arch Gen Psychiat 1989; 46: 587–599.

Cook WN, Medley DM. Proposed hostility and pharisaic-virtue scales for the MMPI. J Appl Psychol 1954; 38: 414–418.

Eysenck HJ. The scientific study of personality. London, Routledge & Kegan Paul, 1952.

Eysenck HJ, Eysenck SBG. Psychoticism as a Dimension of Personality. London, Hodder and Stoughton, 1976.

Fahrenberg J, Selg H, Hampel R. Das Freiburger Persönlichkeitsinventar (FPI). Göttingen, Hogrefe, 1970.

Freud S. Repression (First published in Zeitschrift 1915). Collected Papers. New York, Basic Books, 1959, Vol 4, pp. 84–97.

Gentry TA, Wakefield JA, Friedman AF. MMPI scales measuring Eysenck's personality factors. J Pers Ass 1985; 49: 146–149.

Griffin J. Well-being. Its Meaning, Measurement and Moral Importance. Oxford, Clarendon Press, 1988.

Hall CS, Lindzey G. Theories of Personality. New York, John Wiley & Sons, 1957.

Hare RD. A research scale for the assessment of psychopathy in criminal populations. Pers Indiv Diff 1980; 1: 111–119.

Hare RD. Psychopathy and violence. In: Hays JR, Roberts TK, Solway KS (eds). Violence and the Violent Individual. New York: Spectrum Publications 1981, pp. 53–74.

Harpur TJ, Hakstian AR, Hare RD. Factor structure of the psychopathy checklist. J Consult Clin Psychol 1988; 56: 741–747.

Hathaway SR, McKinley JC. Minnesota Multiphasic Personality Inventory. New York, The Psychological Corporation, 1951.

Hoch PH, Polatin P. Pseudoneurotic forms of schizophrenia. Psychiat Quart 1949; 23: 248–276.

Jenkins CD, Zymanski SJ, Rosenbaum RH. Jenkins Activity Survey. New York, The Psychological Corporation, 1979.

Jung CG. Psychological Types. London, Routledge & Kegan Paul, 1923.

Kendell RE. The Role of Diagnosis in Psychiatry. Oxford, Blackwell, 1975.

Kretschmer E. Körperbau und Charakter. Berlin, Springer 1921 and 1948.

Loldrup D, Langemark M, Hansen HJ, Kastrup M, Jeppesen K, Elsborg L, Bonnevie O, Olesen J, Bech P. The validity of the Melancholia Scale (MES) in predicting outcome of antidepressants in chronic idiopathic pain disorders. Eur Psychiat 1991; 6: 119–125.

Meehl PE. Schizotaxia, schizotypy, schizophrenia. Am Psychol 1962; 17: 827–838.

Meehl PE. Hedonic capacity: some conjectures. Bull Menninger Clinic 1975; 39: 295–307.

Meehl PE. Hedonic capacity ten years later: some clarifications. In: Clark DG, Fawcett J (eds). Anhedonia and Affective Deficit States. New York, Pergamon 1987, pp. 935–944.

Millon T. Millon Clinical Multiaxial Inventory Manual (Third edition). Minneapolis, Nat Computer System, 1983.

Murray HA. Manual of Thematic Apperception Test. Cambridge, Massachusetts, Harvard Univ Press, 1943.

Olff M, Endresen I. The Dutch and Norwegian translations of the Plutchik questionnaire for psychological defence. In: Olff M, Godaert G, Ursin H (eds). Qualification of Human Defence Mechanisms. Heidelberg, Springer 1991.

Pichot P. A Century of Psychiatry. Paris, Roger Dacosta, 1983.

Pichot P. Psychopathic behaviour: a historical overview. In: Hare RD, Schalling D (eds). Psychopathic Behaviour: Approaches to Research. Chichester, John Wiley & Sons, 1978, pp. 55–70.

Plutchik R, Kellerman H, Conte HR. A structural theory of ego defences and emotions. In: Izard CE (ed). Emotions and Psychopathology. New York, Plenum, 1979.

Raine A. A psychometric assessment of Hare's checklist for psychopathy on an English prison population. Br J Clin Psychol 1985; 24: 247–258.

Rawnsley K. Congruence of independent measures of psychiatric morbidity. J Psychosom Res 1966; 10: 84–93.

Robinson SC, Brucer M, Mass J. Hypertension and obesity. J Lab Clin Med 1940; 25: 807–822.

Schneider K. Psychopathic Personalities (First Version, 1923). English Version. London. Cassell, 1958.

Spielberger CD, Gorsuch RL, Lusheme RE. State-Trait Anxiety Inventory. Palo Alto, Consulting Psychologists Press, 1970.

Spielberger CD, Johnson EH, Jacobs GA, Krasner SS, Oesterle SE, Worden TJ. The State-Trait Anger Inventory. Palo Alto, Consulting Psychologists Press, 1986.

Spitzer RL, Williams JBW. Structured Clinical Interview for DSM-III (SCID). New York, Biometrics Research Department, New York State Psychiatric Inst, 1983.

Spitzer RL, Williams JBW, Gibbon M, First MB. Structured Clinical Interview for DSM-III-R. Washington, American Psychiatric Press, 1990.

Storr A. Human Aggression. London, Allen Lane Press, 1968.

Vanggaard T. Borderlands of Sanity. Copenhagen: Munksgaard 1979.

Waters WE, O'Connor PJ. Epidemiology of headache and migraine in women. J Neurol Neurosurg Psychiat 1971; 34: 148–153.

Watson CG, Klett WG, Lorei TW. Toward an operational definition of anhedonia. Psychol Bull 1970; 26: 371–376.

Wetzler S. The Millon Clinical Multiaxial Inventory (MCMI): a review. J Pers Ass 1990; 55: 445–464.

Widiger T, Williams J, Spitzer R, Frances A. The MCMI as a measure of DSM-III. J Pers Ass 1985; 49: 366–378.

Wistedt B, Rasmussen A, Pedersen L, Malm U, Träskman-Bendz L, Berggren M, Wakelin J, Bech P. The development of an observer scale measuring social dysfunction and aggression (SDAS). Pharmacopsychiat 1990; 23: 249–252.

Appendix 5.1   *Scoring sheet for the SBS*

DSM-III-R elements	No.	Item	Score
Schizotypal	1	Excessive social anxiety (extreme discomfort in social situations)	
Borderline	2	Affective instability (short but marked shifts from baseline mood to dysphoria and/or euphoria)	
Borderline	3	Inappropriate anger or lack of control of anger	
Borderline	4	Self-mutilating behaviour	
Borderline	5	Feelings of emptiness or boredom	
Narcissism	6	Lack of empathy	
Narcissism	7	Expansive sense of self-importance	
		Total score	

Appendix 5.2   Bortner Scale

Instructions: Each of us belongs somewhere between two extremes. For example most of us are neither the most solemn nor the most humorous person we know. What we would like you to do, is to look at this list and for each pair of items, make a vertical line where you think you belong between these extremes.

Example: Solemn ———————|——————— *Humorous*

1 *	Never late	1	Casual about appointments
2	Not competitive	2 *	Very competitive
3 *	Anticipates what others are going to say	3	Good listener, hears others out
4 *	Always rushed	4	Never feels rushed, even under pressure
5	Can wait patiently	5 *	Impatient when waiting
6 *	Goes all out	6	Casual
7	Take things one at a time	7 *	Tries to do many things at once, thinks about what he is going to do next
8 *	Emphatic in speech (may pound desk)	8	Slow, deliberate talker
9 *	Wants good job, recognition from others	9	Only cares about satisfying self no matter what others may think
10*	Fast (e.g. eating, walking)	10	Slow doing things
11	Easy going	11*	Hard driving
12	Sits on feelings	12*	Expresses feelings
13*	Many interests	13	Few interests outside work
14	Satisfied with job	14*	Ambitious

*Type-A behaviour

Appendix 5.3   *The Freiburg Personality Inventory (FBI)*

Scale 1: Aggressivity - Irritability

No.	Orig. item no.	Item
1	(11)	I easily lose my temper but I recover again quickly
2	(23)	If someone has been unjust to me, I wish him to be strictly punished
3	(82)	If someone does wrong to a friend of mine, I will join in the revenge
4	(93)	It amuses me to point out other people's mistakes
5	(105)	If I get really angry, I am capable of slapping someone in the face
6	(114)	I don't know why, but sometimes I feel like smashing something to bits
7	(115)	It sometimes calms me down to imagine at least that things go badly for nasty people
8	(122)	I often let inadvertent comments slip out which I had better kept to myself
9	(128)	After a party, I often feel like joining the others and annoying people somehow
10	(131)	Whoever seriously insults me can count on getting a slap in his face
11	(133)	When I am furious, I say impertinent things
12	(149)	Unfortunately, I am one of those people who frequently flies into a rage
13	(152)	I am rather moody
14	(171)	I like to make fun of other people
15	(190)	Now and again, I am a bit malicious
16	(191)	I often get upset at others too quickly

Degree of aggressivity: number of items scored yes

Appendix 5.3   *cont.*

Scale 2: Extraversion - Introversion

No.	Orig. item no.	Item
1	(7)	I have difficulty finding the right subjects to discuss when I want to get acquainted with someone.
2	(15)	I blush or turn pale easily
3	(19)	I feel a bit uneasy if people on the street or in shops are watching me
4	(34)	I can quickly bring a rather dull party to life
5	(35)	I get embarrassed rather easily
6	(40)	I have a bad knack for dealing with people
7	(57)	I like tasks that call for quick action
8	(65)	I can usually make quick and firm decisions
9	(102)	I am rather lively
10	(124)	If I behaved improperly at a party, I can easily forget about it afterwards
11	(125)	I have only a few close acquaintances
12	(142)	It's not in my nature to tell jokes and amusing stories
13	(151)	I have difficulty speaking in front of or addressing a large group of people
14	(172)	I almost always have a good answer ready to shoot back
15	(202)	I have trouble making important decisions, even after a long time considering the alternatives

Degree of extraversion: yes answers on items 4, 7, 8, 9, 10, 14
Degree of introversion: yes answers on items 1, 2, 3, 5, 6, 11, 12, 13, 15

Appendix 5.3   *cont.*

Scale 3: Autonomic Lability

No.	Orig. item no.	Item
1	(8)	I have frequent headaches
2	(21)	I sometimes feel a pulsation or my heart beating in my veins
3	(27)	I easily get dizzy and sometimes have black spots before my eyes if I sit up or get up suddenly from a lying position
4	(30)	I daydream more often than is good for me
5	(38)	I frequently have pins and needles or numbness in my hands, arms and legs, or they frequently fall asleep
6	(41)	I sometimes feel rather miserable for no reason
7	(48)	I sometimes get short of breath even without having done any hard work
8	(88)	I sometimes feel low without really knowing why
9	(116)	My hands and feet are often restless
10	(127)	At times, or even in general, I am so sensitive to light and noise that intensive light, 'load' colours or certain noises 'hurt' me physically
11	(153)	I get tired faster than most of the people around me
12	(154)	I feel it in my whole body when I get very angry or excited about
13	(157)	something
14	(189)	I am frequently bothered by useless thoughts which keep running through my head
15	(196)	I am frequently lost in thought
		I am often worn out, tired and exhausted

Degree of autonomic lability: number of items scored yes

6 Rating Scales for Somatic Disorders

While axes 1 and 2 syndromes of DSM-III should be referred to as psychopathological disability dimensions, axis 3 disorders should be seen as somatic disability syndromes, where the term disability covers the clinical symptoms resulting from an organic (somatic) disease. Feinstein (1987) has differentiated between an ailment-oriented index (disability which is the characteristic focus of attention in clinical care) and disorder-specific indices (where the clinical symptoms have diagnostic properties).

In chronic somatic disorders the ailment-orientated index has close associations with social functioning (including activity of daily life); this dimension is treated in Chapter 8 (axis 5 related problems). Chapter 6 is devoted to a rating scale approach to disorder-specific indices of somatic disability. DSM-III and DSM-III-R refer to the various chapters in ICD-9 by using the codes of somatic diagnoses. It is common to use a topographical approach by dividing the body into a series of sections or domains. Thus, the Cornell Medical Index (CMI; see Chapters 3 and 4) includes sections with reference to individual organs (e.g. eyes and ears), channels (e.g. gastro-intestinal tract) or systems (e.g. respiratory, cardiovascular, nervous systems). It is, however, beyond the scope of this compendium to cover all the somatic illnesses. What is of interest here is the principle of using the rating scale method in somatic disorders and using the language of clinical symptoms in psychomatic research.

6.1 Psychosomatic Language

In a medical sense symptoms such as sadness, fatigue and sleep disturbance are systemic symptoms, i.e. they may lack localization in the body as relevant for a specific somatic syndrome. Such symptoms can be produced either by somatic disorders or by primary psychopathological disorders. Hence, their diagnostic specificity is low. For example, sadness and fatigue can be important indicators of cancer severity if ascribable to cancer itself, but they have another overall impact if due to severe melancholic states with self-destructive or psychotic behaviour. Tension headache is, according to ICD-9, a subtype of chronic (psychogenic) pain disorder and therefore an axis 1 disorder. However, ICD-10, DSM-III and DSM-III-R list tension headache as an axis 3 disorder because pain associated with mus-

Table 6.1. Moods, emotions and sensations

Elements	Moods	Emotions	Sensations
Tied to characteristic body manifestations	Yes (e.g. motor retardation)	Yes (e.g. muscular tension)	Yes (e.g. food seeking behaviour)
Genuine duration	Weeks to months	Hours to days	Minutes to hours
Localized to parts of the body	No	No	Yes
Information about somatic illness	No	No	Yes
Colour thoughts (beliefs)	Yes (self-assessment, e.g. guilt feelings)	Yes (self-assessment, e.g. demoralization)	No
Directed to objects	No (free-floating)	Yes (e.g avoidance actions)	No

cle contraction headache has a pathophysiological mechanism that can account for the pain.

The feeling of pain is related to various dimensions, as emphasized by philosophers of mind (e.g. Ryle 1949, 1951; Wittgenstein 1953; Strawson 1959; Armstrong 1962; Budd 1989; Kenny 1989). Among the different meanings of pain are sensations, emotions and moods. As a sensation the presence or abscence of anginal pain is an important factor in ischaemic heart disease. More long lasting 'psychic' types of pain are often seen in mood disorders. Since the publication of Ryle's *Concept of mind* (1949) the body-mind dualism postulated by Descartes in the seventeenth century has been referred to as Descartes' myth. According to Ryle (1949) and Wittgenstein (1953), the connection between mental processes and their manifestations in behaviour is not a causal one. The somatic expression of a mental process is a criterion for that process, i.e. it is an indicator of the dimension being assessed. The most important chapters of Ryle's treatise in this respect are those on emotions and sensations. These chapters (recently reviewed by Kenny 1989) as well as Wittgenstein's philosophy of psychology (recently reviewed by Budd 1989) are important for clarifying the concepts of moods, emotions and sensations.

Table 6.1 shows the relationship between moods, emotions and sensations. The actual duration of bodily sensations is shorter than that of emotions, which again last a shorter period than moods. Wittgenstein emphasized that 'states of consciousness' have genuine durations as an essential component. Strawson (1959) has further discussed the problem of reidentification when sensations or emotions are interrupted by a break in consciousness (e.g. sleep) or withdrawal of attention from it. In this context it is of interest that epileptic fits or attacks of panic anxiety are protected in states of intense consciousness, for example during car driving (and is provoked during sleep). Psychic or mental pain has, like moods, longer duration than bodily pain. Sensations are, unlike emotions or moods, localized to parts of the body, thereby giving some information about the illness. From a medical point of view emotions or moods may even be misleading for the physician.

Emotions and moods colour thoughts (cognitive beliefs). Unlike moods, an object relation of emotion is often seen. Thus, fear as an emotion is fear of something, while fear as a mood is a free-floating uncertainty of psychic anxiety. The definition of pain according to the International Association for the Study of Pain (IASP 1979) is: "An unpleasant sensory and emotional experience associated with actual or potential tissue damage, or described in terms of such damage." As emphasized by Merskey (1991), the phenomenological description of pain (organic or psychological in origin) is a non-behavioural, subjective state, which is an unpleasant sensation, i.e. includes both sensation and emotions (unpleasantness). Thus, at the phenomenological level the monism of Ryle and Wittgenstein is valid, but at the ethiological level pain might be dualistic, or even multiplistic (as discussed by Merskey 1991). In the words of Ryle (1949): "Pains do not arrive already hallmarked rheumatic..."

Hence, pain is a purely subjective experience which to a varying degree takes both sensations and emotions (or moods) into account. From a rating scale point of view pain is most appropriately assessed globally by the patients themselves, for example by use of a visual analogue scale. A recent study, Allerup et al. 1992, found that a 10 cm visual analogue scale in patients with chronic (psychogenic) pain disorders fulfilled the Rasch criteria if the raw scores were transformed into categories of no pain (0–2 cm), minor pain (3–7 cm) and major pain (8–10 cm).

Research in the area of temporal quantifiers like 'always', 'mostly', 'often', 'seldom', 'sometimes', 'never' in clinimetrics is still only beginning. Thus, in somatic forms of pain the temporal expressions of pain are refered to discrete occasions, e.g. 'how often have you experienced pains in the last three days?' In psychic forms of pain (e.g. in depression) the continuous aspect is inherently conceived, resulting in questions such as: 'Is your pain experience worse in the morning?'

6.2 Disorder-Specific Scales

As an example of the rating scale approach applied to a somatic condition with aspects of chronic states versus attacks the Waters Headache Questionnaire (WHQ; Table 6.2) is presented below. The development of this scale has been described by Waters (1986). Both an interviewer version and a self-administered version have been constructed and no evidence of any significant differences between the two version was detected (Waters 1970). The scale differentiates between chronic tension headache and attacks of migraine. The scale illustrates the multidimensional method by covering the following dimensions: A, symptoms of general severity; B, diagnostic items (B_1, migraine; B_2, non-migraine items); and C, personality items. The personality items are derived from CMI, and these have been found (see Chapter 5) to have a high concordance with ratings of neurotic traits by experienced psychiatrists (Rawnsley 1966; Waters and O'Connor 1971). The modified version of the WHQ included below has been described by Bech et al. (1986). Factor analysis has shown that migraine and tension headache are not mutually exclusive conditions. The WHQ is as follows.

Introductory Question:
1. Have you had a headache within the past year?
   no = 0, yes = 1

A Severity Items (I–IV)
I Intensity of Pain
2. Are your headaches 1 = mild, 2 = severe, 3 = both?
3. My headaches are 1 = very mild, 2 = mild, 3 = not usually severe, 4 = quite severe, 5 = very severe, 6 = terribly severe, 7 = almost unbearable.
II Work Activity
4. 1 = I hardly notice my headache, 2 = my headaches rarely inconvenience me, 3 = my headaches sometimes distract me from what I am doing, 4 = sometimes I am unable to continue my normal activities because of my headaches,

Table 6.2. Psychometric description: WHQ

Type	Diagnostic scale for migraine versus tension headache.

Content validity	The scale consists of three parts or dimensions:
	    Severity of headache
	    Diagnostic items
	    Personality items

Administration	There exists both a questionnaire version (included in this compendium) and an interviewer version to be used by a non-professional interviewer.
Time frame	Inspective and retrospective items according to the dimension being assessed.
Item selection	Based on general knowledge and textbooks.
Number of items	The severity scale includes eight items, and the personality scale nine items.

Item distribution	The severity scale:
	    Pain (severity) 25%
	    Work activity 37%
	    Iatrogenic level 13%
	    Progressiveness 25%
	Migraine subscale:
	    Pain (type) 17%
	    Lateralization 17%
	    Warnings 17%
	    Vegetative symptoms 50%
	Non-migraine subscale:
	    Duration 33%
	    Frequency 33%
	    Location 33%
	Personality items:
	    Nine items, a yes answer scores neurotic (as on the Eysenck Neuroticism scale).

Construct validity	Factor analysis has indicated that the scale contains more than three factors. It is therefore recommended to use the subscale scores. The migraine score (dimension) and the non-migraine score (dimension) are not mutually exclusive dimensions. Rasch analysis to evaluate the suffiency of the subscale scores has so far not been investigated.
Reliability	The scale has been found reliable in terms of test-retest correlation.

5 = my headaches sometimes interfere a lot with what I am doing, 6 = I can hardly do anything when I have headache, 7 = I am fit for absolutely nothing when I have a headache.

6a. When you have a headache, do you usually have to: 1 = lie down, 2 = rest, 3 = take things easy?

6b. Have you missed work during the past year because of a headache? no = 0, yes = number of days

III Iatrogenic Level

15. Have you seen a doctor about the headaches? no = 0, yes = 1 IV Progressiveness
16. Over the years have your headaches become: 2 = more painful, 1 = less painful, 0 = not noticed any change?
17. Over the years have your headaches been: 2 = more frequent, 1 = less frequent, 0 = not noticed any change?

B Diagnostic Items (B1, B2)
B1 Migraine Items (I–IV)
I Type of Pain

8. Are your headaches throbbing or thumping? 0 = never, 1 = sometimes, 2 = usually, 3 = always

II Lateralization

10. Are your headaches one-sided only? 0 = never, 1 = sometimes, 2 = usually, 3 = always

III Warnings

11. Before you get a headache, do you know that one is coming? 0 = no, 1 = yes

IV Vegetative Symptoms

12. When you have a headache, do you notice any changes in your sight? 0 = no, 1 = yes
13. When you have a headache, do you: 1 = lose your appetite, 2 = feel dizzy, 3 = feel sleepy, 4 = hear singing in your ears, 5 = find that light hurts your eyes, 6 = notice tingling or any strange feeling in any part of your body?
14. When you have a headache, do you: 0 = never feel sick or vomit, 1 = ever feel sick, 2 = usually feel sick, 4 = usually vomit?

B2 Non-migraine Headache Items (I–III)
I Duration

5. How long does your headache last: 1 = less than half a day, 2 = one day, 3 = more than one day, 4 = more than two days?

II Frequency

7. Do you get a headache: 1 = about once a year, 2 = several times a year, 3 = about once a month, 4 = several times a month, 5 = about once a week, 6 = several times a week?

III Location

9. Where do you usually feel the headaches? 1 = temples, 2 = forehead/behind the eyes, 3 = back of head, 4 = top of head, 5 = all over head, 6 = elsewhere

C Neurotic Personality Items (1–9) (yes/no)

1. Do you suffer from indigestion?
2. Are you worried about your weight?
3. Does every little thing get on your nerves and wear you out?
4. Are you considered a nervous person?
5. Are you extremely shy and sensitive?

6. Are you considered a touchy person?
7. Are you constantly keyed-up end jittery?
8. Do you suffer from severe nervous exhaustion?
9. Do you wear yourself out worrying about your health?

Another somatic condition which has given rise to the use of rating scales is thyrotoxicosis. Two different scales have been considered here. The Diagnostic Scale for Clinical Thyrotoxicosis was developed by Crooks et al. (1959; see below) analogously to the Newcastle diagnostic scales for depression (see Chapter 3). Discriminant function analysis has produced positive and negative weights of the 22 items for toxic versus non-toxic thyrotoxicosis. The inter-observer reliability of the Diagnostic Scale for Clinical Thyrotoxicosis has been found to be higher than that between clinical diagnoses made by physicians without the aid of the scale (Crooks et al. 1959). The first 21 items are scored as 'yes' ('1') or 'no' ('0'); in the list of items below the respective calculated values are inserted in parentheses. A total calculated score of 10 or less indicates non-toxicity, and one of 20 or more indicates toxicity.

1. Dyspnoea on effort (+1, 0)
2. Palpitations (+2, 0)
3. Tiredness (+2, 0)
4. Preference for heat (0, −5)
5. Preference for cold (+5, 0)
6. Excessive sweating (+3, 0)
7. Nervousness (+2, 0)
8. Appetite increased (+3, 0)
9. Appetite decreased (−3, 0)
10. Weight increased (−3, 0)
11. Weight decreased (+3, 0)
12. Palpable thyroid (+3, −3)
13. Bruit over thyroid (+2, −2)
14. Exophthalmus (+2, 0)
15. Lid retraction (+2, 0)
16. Lid lag (+1, 0)
17. Hyperkinetic movements (+4, −2)
18. Fine finger tremor (+1, 0)
19. Hands hot (+2, −2)
20. Hands moist (+1, −2)
21. Auricular fibrillation (+4, 0)
22. Pulse rate (under 80, −3; 80–90, 0; over 90, +3)

A follow-up questionnaire for patients at risk of hypothyroidism during treatment for thyrotoxicosis has been constructed by Barker and Bishop (1969). This short scale (scored 'yes' or 'no') is included here to illustrate the use of rating scales in long-term treatment conditions. (The scale might be useful in patients on long-term lithium treatment.)

1. Do you feel as well as you did a year ago?
2. Do you now feel the cold more than ever before, so that you cannot get properly warm?
3. Is your appetite as good as it was a year ago?
4. Do you feel less energetic than usual?
5. Do you think you have put on weight in the last year?
6. Have you or any of your family or friends noticed that your voice has recently become huskier or weaker?
7. Are you getting any fuller in the face?
8. Has the skin of your arms or legs become more dry or rough during the past year?
9. Has your hair recently become unruly or more difficult to manage?

A review of questionnaires in medicine has been published by Bennett and Ritchie (1975).

6.3. Ailment-Oriented Scales

The term ailment-oriented has been used by Feinstein (1987) to refer to the dimension of symptoms that are the characteristic focus of attention in clinical care. Ailment-oriented scales are distinguished from general scales of health status that are used without reference to specific clinical manifestations. Chapter 8 deals with general health functional scales; these are often used for the measurement of several different ailments, including the general impact of the illness on the psychosocial functioning. An example of an ailment-oriented scale is the New York Heart Association scale for cardiac disability (Criteria Committee of the New York Heart Association 1964). Its four categories are the following:

1. Patients with cardiac disease but without resulting in limitations of physical activity. Ordinary physical activity does not cause fatigue, palpitation, dyspnoea, or anginal pain.
2. Patients with cardiac disease resulting in slight limitation of physical activity. They are comfortable at rest. Ordinary physical activity results in fatigue, palpitation, dyspnoea, or anginal pain.
3. Patients with cardiac disease resulting in marked limitation of physical activity. They are comfortable at rest. Less than ordinary physical activity causes fatigue, palpitation, dyspnoea, or anginal pain.
4. Patients with cardiac disease resulting in inability to carry on any physical activity without discomfort. Symptoms of cardiac insufficiency or of the anginal syndrome may be present even at rest. If any physical activity is undertaken discomfort is increased.

References

Allerup P, Bech P, Loldrup D. The dynamic Rasch model in the analysis of improvement curves based on single item visual analogue scales in patients with chronic pain disorders. Internat J Educ Research 1992 (in press).

Armstrong DM. Body Sensations. London: Routledge and Kegan Paul, 1962.

Barker DJP, Bishop JM. Computer-based screening system for patients at risk of hypothyreoidism. Lancet 1969; ii: 835–836.

Bech P, Kastrup M, Loldrup D. Use of headache rating scales: a multiaxial approach. Cephalalgia 1986; 6: 69–80.

Bennett AE, Ritchie K. Questionnaires in Medicine. London: Oxford Univ Press, 1975.

Brodman K, Erdmann AJ, Lorge I, Wolff HG. The Cornell Medical Index: An adjunct to medical intervension. JAMA 1949; 140: 530–536.

Budd M. Wittgenstein's Philosophy of Psychology. London: Routledge, 1989.

Criteria Committee of the New York Heart Association. Diseases of the Heart and Blood Vessels: Nomenclature and Criteria for Diagnosis. Boston: Little, Brown, and Co., 1964.

Crooks J, Murray IPC, Wayne EJ. Statistical methods applied to the clinical diagnosis of thyrotoxicosis. Quart J Med 1959; 28: 211–234.

Feinstein AR. Clinimetrics. New Haven: Yale Univ Press, 1987.

International Association for the Study of Pain. Pain terms: A list with definitions and notes on usage. Recommended by an IASP subcommittee on taxonomy. Pain 1979; 6: 249–252.

Kellner R, Sheffield BF. A self-rating scale of distress. Psychol Med 1973; 3: 88–97.

Kellner R. The symptom-rating test. In: Sartorius N, Ban TA (eds). Assessment of Depression. Berlin: Springer, 1986, pp. 213–220.

Kenny A. The Metaphysics of Mind. Oxford: Clarendon Press, 1989.

Merkey H. The defintion of pain. Eur Psychiat 1991; 6: 153–159.

Pichot P. Problems raised by the application of psychometric methods to transversal and longitudinal studies. Adv Cardiol 1982; 29: 10–17.

Rawnsley K. Congruence of independent measures of psychiatric morbidity. J Psychosom Res 1966; 10: 84–93.

Ryle G. The Concept of Mind. London: Hutchinson, 1949.

Ryle G. Feelings. Phil Quart 1951; 1: 102–116.

Strawson PF. Individuals: An Essay in Descriptive Metaphysics. London: Methuen, 1959.

Waters WE. Community studies of the prevalence of headache. Headache, 1970; 9: 178–186.

Waters WE. Migraine: Intelligence, social class, and family prevalence. Br Med J 1971; 2: 77–81.

Waters WE. Headache. London: Croom Helm, 1986.

Waters WE, O'Connor PJ. The epidemiology of headache and migraine in women. J Neurol Neurosurg Psychiat 1971; 34: 148–153.

Wittgenstein L. Philosophical Investigations. Oxford: Basil Blackwell, 1953.

World Health Organisation. Mental Disorders: Glossary and Guide to their Classification in Accordance with the Ninth Revision of the International Classification of Diseases. Geneva: World Health Organization, 1978.

7 Rating Scales for Psychosocial Stressors

The role of psychosocial factors in the development of mental disorders was first considered by Pinel in the late eighteenth century but was formulated most clearly by Esquirol in 1845 in his treatise on insanity. Esquirol emphasized that the causes of mental alienation are numerous: general or specific, physical or moral, primary or secondary, predisposing or exciting: "Not only do climate, season, age, sex, temperament, profession and mode of life have an influence upon the frequency, character, duration, crises and treatment of insanity; but this malady is still modified by laws, civilization, morals, and the political condition of people." (Esquirol, 1845). Winter depression, for example, was considered by Esquirol to be a seasonally pathogenic depression.

Although Wimmer (1916) had published a more comprehensive monography, it is generally agreed that Birnbaum (1911, 1923) was the first to integrate the various axes of psychopathology (psychiatric syndromes and personality), somatic illness and life events in making the conclusive psychiatric diagnosis. Birnbaum (1923) emphasized the principle which has been followed in this compendium: "First there is a purely descriptive phase, when research consists mainly in collecting, recording, and faithfully portraying phenomena as they are encountered. Then comes the stage of analytical enquiry, when inner relationships are examined, the laws that govern them are involved." He postulated a structured form of clinical disorders, among which he analysed psychogenic (psychosocial) factors. He differentiated between pathogenic factors (i.e. necessary and sufficient, 'this and no other') and pathoplastic factors (i.e. those that do shape the disorder in that they give content, colour, and contour to individual illnesses). To these factors Birnbaum (1923) added provoking factors which may be of great practical account, but which "are of minor clinical importance... in as much as they simply activate and mobilize clinical phenomena which have been pathogenically or pathoplastically determined."

Table 7.1 describes the relationship between life events and psychiatric (axis 1) syndromes regarding subclassification of the stressors in accordance with Birnbaum's principle. Psychosocial stressors can provoke dementia, but they have, of course, no pathogenetic or pathoplastic impact (personality traits may have a pathoplastic influence). Negative symptoms of schizophrenia resemble dementia in this respect. Positive symptoms, however, may be not only provoked but also coloured or even caused by life events (psychogenic paranoid psychosis); however, in this case the schizoid borderline personality is a constitutional factor as also

Table 7.1. Life events in relation to psychiatric syndromes

| | Organic mental disorders | Schizophrenia | | Mood disorders | Anxiety neurosis | Aggression |
		Negative	Positive			
Pathogenic factors	-	-	(+)	(+)	+	+
Pathoplastic factors	-	-	(+)	+	+	+
Provoking factors	+	+	+	+	+	+

emphasized by Birnbaum. Post-traumatic stress disorders are those in which the psychosocial stressor is the pathogenetic and pathoplastic factor. This clinical dimension includes both anxiety and depression (or mania). According to Birnbaum, the clinical states in which psychosocial stressors show pathogenic evidence are characterized by fluctuations in the state (instability), irritability and dissociation (hysterical features). Among pathoplastically determined cases Birnbaum included simulative states such as Ganser states (Ganser 1898). The relationship between the initial symptoms of post-traumatic stress neurosis (e.g. panic anxiety) and the chronic symptoms (e.g. generalized anxiety, dysthymia or less than major depression) was first described by Wimmer (1923).

The three aspects of a psychosocial stressor (provoking, pathoplastic and pathogenetic) are often unsystematically weighted in the different life event rating scales. Thus, Dohrenwend and Shrout (1985) have demonstrated that the Hassles Scale (Kanner et al. 1980) measures a combination of life events and subjective distress. A further analysis of this problem has been published elsewhere (Bech 1990).

The first life event scale was constructed by Holmes and Rahe (1967) as a self-rating scale. The selection of items was made by a judgement analysis using 'subjective stress' as the dimension of selection. In a review of methods for measuring life events it was found (Cohen and Wills 1985) that approximately 90% of the scales, including that of Holmes-Rahe, measure the external life event as such.

When Murray (1938) defined a psychosocial stressor as an external press having the power to affect the well-being of the subject, he found it important to distinguish between the significance of the external event as such (alpha press) and the perceived or interpreted stress (beta press). The list of items proposed by Murray (1938) is largely similar to that of psychosocial stressors described by Brown and Harris (1978, 1989). For the alpha press items Brown and Harris (1989) have developed the following 12-point scale of independence:

1. Completely independent events.
2. Events whose immediate origin is unconnected with the subject, but where it is impossible to rule out entirely that some aspect of the subject's behaviour might have influenced it.
3. Negligence by subject impossible to rule out, but not obvious.
4. All physical illnesses of the subjects.
5. Possibly independent.
6. Intentional actions, e.g. moved to a new house or planned pregnancy.
7. Events that have occurred as a result of subject's negligence.
8. Events where contact with a key person is disrupted after an argument.
9. Events where contact with a key person is disrupted without an argument.
10. Events stemming from the subject's romantic susceptibilities.
11. Events that derive from the romatic susceptibilities of the subject's partner.
12. Completely dependent events.

Table 7.2. Severity of psychosocial stressors scale in DSM-III and DSM-III-R

| DSM-III | | DSM-III-R | |
Term	Events (examples)	Term	Acute events	Enduring circumstances
1 None	No apparent stressor	1 None	No acute events that may be related to the disorder	No enduring circumstances that may be relevant to the disorder
2 Minimal	Minor violation of the law			
3 Mild	Change in work hours	2 Mild	Broke up with boyfriend or girlfriend; started or graduated from school; child left home	Family arguments; job dissatisfaction
4 Moderate	New career; death of close friend; pregnancy			
5 Severe	Serious illness in self or family; major financial loss; marital separation; birth of child	3 Moderate	Marriage; marital separation; loss of job; retirement; miscarriage	Marital discord; serious financial problems; trouble with the boss; being a single parent
6 Extreme	Death of close relative; divorce	4 Severe	Divorce; birth of first child	Unemployment, poverty
		5 Extreme	Death of spouse; serious physical illness diagnosed; victim of rape	Serious chronic illness in self or child
7 Catastrophic	Concentration camp experience; devastating natural disaster	6 Catastrophic	Death of child; suicide of spouse; devastating natural disaster	Captivity as hostage; concentration camp experience

The types of beta events can be classified into the following eight groups.
1. Changes in a role for the subject, e.g. changing a job.
2. Major changes in a role for close ties or household members.
3. Major changes in subject's health.
4. Major changes in health for close ties or household members.
5. Residence changes or any marked change in amount of contact with close ties or household members.
6. Forecasts of change, e.g. being told about being rehoused.
7. Fulfilments or disappointments of a valued goal.
8. Other dramatic events involving either the subject or a close tie.

Table 7.2 compares the measurement of severity of psychosocial stressors, axis 4, in DSM-III and in DSM-III-R. DSM-III-R appears superior to DSM-III in distinguishing between acute events and enduring circumstances. Axis 4 in DSM-III or DSM-III-R should be considered as rating scales. In other words, DSM-III and DSM-III-R have adopted the rating scale principle concerning axis 4 (and to some extent also concerning axis 5; see Chapter 8).

From a psychometric point of view life events, as interviewer scales, should be preferred to self-report scales (Brown and Harris 1978; Paykel 1983). An interviewer version of Holmes and Rahe's Social Readjustment Rating Scale has been developed by Bech et al. (1990). This version is included in this compendium to illustrate alpha items and their corresponding beta weights in terms of life-change units after Holmes and Rahe (1967). The questions of the Social Readjustment Rating Scale are as follow:
1. During the last 6 months have there been any change in relation to work? If yes, describe the alpha item (1.1–1.10). If the event is not appropriately described in the manual, please specify.
2. Has there been any change in relation to family or friends? Please specify.
3. Has there been any change in relation to leisure time or habits? Please specify.
4. Has there been any change in relation to economy/finances? Please specify.
Three responses are allowed for each question. These are assigned beta weights according to the schema presented in Table 7.3. The list of items in the Holmes-Rahe scale has been criticized by Kanner et al. (1981) for its preoccupation with dramatic events or severely taxing situations. It may well be that severity of stressors is closely related to pathogenetic factors. Kanner et al. (1981) constructed the Hassles Scale, which, however, seems to be a beta press scale.

The task force on DSM-IV (APA 1991) has under axis 4 suggested a psychosocial problem checklist as shown in Table 7.4. This proposal differs from DSM-III-R in which one overall severity rating is made. Table 7.3 can in this context be considered a compromise between the rating scale approach and the DSM-IV approach.

The DSM-IV task force (APA 1991) has also suggested a supplement to axis 4 including the two personal resources scales shown in Table 7.5. The reliability and validity of these scales have not yet been systmatically studied.

Table 7.3. Alpha items and beta weights in the Social Readjustment Rating Scale

Alpha items	Beta weights	Alpha items	Beta weights
1 Relations to work		*2 Relations to family*	
1.1 Fired at work	47	2.1 Death of spouse	100
1.2 Retirement	45	2.2 Divorce	73
1.3 Business readjustment	39	2.3 Marital seperation	65
1.4 Change to different kind of work	36	2.4 Death of close family member	63
1.5 Change in responsibility at work	29	2.5 Personal injury or illness	53
		2.6 Marriage	50
1.6 Outstanding personal achievement	28	2.7 Marital reconciliation	45
1.7 Beginning or ending education/training	26	2.8 Change in health of family members	44
1.8 Trouble with boss	23	2.9 Pregnancy	40
1.9 Change in work hours or conditions	20	2.10 Sex difficulties	39
		2.11 Gaining new family member	39
1.10 Other Specify _____			37
		2.12 Death of a close friend	
		2.13 Change in number of arguments with spouse	35
		2.14 Son/daughter leaving home	29
		2.15 Trouble with in-laws	29
		2.16 Wife begins/stops work	26
		2.17 Changes in residence	20
		2.18 Other Specify _____	

Alpha items	Beta weights	Alpha items	Beta weights
3 Relations to leisure time/habits		*4 Relations to finances*	
3.1 Change in living condition	25	4.1 Change in financial state	38
3.2 Revision of personal habits	24	4.2 Mortgage or loan (major)	31
3.3 Change in recreation	19	4.3 Foreclosure or mortgage/loan	30
3.4 Change in social activities	18	4.4 Mortgage or loan (minor)	17
3.5 Change in sleeping habits	16	4.5 Other Specify _____	
3.6 Change in eating habits	15		
3.7 Vacation			
3.8 Other Specify _____			

Table 7.4. Psychosocial Problem Checklist (DSM-IV)

Items (Problem areas)	Score Absent = 0 Present = 1	List the specific problems
Educational problems	☐	_____
Occupational problems		
- unemployment	☐	_____
- job dissatisfaction	☐	_____
- exposure to hazards	☐	_____
Environmental problems		
- inadequate housing	☐	_____
- inadequate food	☐	_____
- inadequate finances	☐	_____
- unsafe environment	☐	_____
Inadequate access to health	☐	_____
Inadequate social supports or interpersonal losses		
- family	☐	_____
- friends	☐	_____
- sociocultural/community group	☐	_____
Legal problems	☐	_____
Other areas (e.g. immigration)	☐	_____

Axis 4 in DSM-III-R is considered nondiagnostic in content and has not been widely used (APA 1991). In contrast, the structural analysis proposed by Birnbaum (1923) is an attempt not only to clarify the clinical syndromes but also to look beyond the usual features of clinical symptoms. It is an important approach to assess whether the clinical picture is changeable or varying in kind or quantity and argues for using rating scales to cover the current state (least 3–7 days). The registration of minor and major life events is pertinent in this perspective.

Table 7.5. Personal Resources Scale (DSM-IV)

Social Support Scale	Score	Environmental Resources Scale
Optimal (relationships provide extensive social support with little or no conflict).	= 5 =	*Optimal* (no significant financial problems, comfortable housing, easy access to health services).
Adequate (relationships provide an average amount of social support, with occasional social conflict).	= 4 =	*Adequate* (adequate finances to meet basic needs).
Somewhat inadequate (relationships provide adequate social support, with frequent social conflict).	= 3 =	*Somewhat inadequate* (finances adequate for necesities only, somewhat cramped or decrepit housing, limited access to health services).
Clearly deficient (social relationships provide little nurturance or support).	= 2 =	*Clearly deficient* (income regularly inadequate for meeting basic needs, housing extremely decrepit, health services not available without extreme effort).
Markedly deficient (social relationships are nonexistent or, if present, are generally unsupportive or abusive).	= 1 =	*Markedly deficient* (no sources of income, homeless).

References

American Psychiatric Association (APA): DSM-IV Options Book: Work in Progress. Washington DC: American Psychiatric Association 1991.

Bech P. Measurement of psychological distress and well-being. Psychother Psychosom 1990; 54: 77–89.

Bech P, Loldrup D, Garre K. Livskvalitet som effektstørrelse ved behandling af essentiel arterial hypertension. Ugeskr Laeger 1990; 152: 383–386.

Birnbaum K. Die Aufbau der Psychose. Berlin: Springer, 1923 pp. 1–46.

Brown GW, Harris TO (eds). Life Events and Illness.

Brown GW, Harris TO. Social Origins of Depression. London: Tavistock, 1978.

Cohen S, Wills TA. Stress, social support and the buffering hypothesis. Psycholog Bull 1985; 98: 310–357.

Dohrenwend BP, Shrout PE. Hassles in the conceptualization and measurement of life event stress variables. Ans Psychol 1985; 40: 780–785.

Esquirol JED. Mental Maladies. A Treatise of Insanity. Philadelphia: Lea and Blanchard, 1845.

Ganser SJM. A peculiar hysterical state. Acta Psychiat Nerv Krankh. 1898; 30: 633–639.

Holmes TH, Rahe RH. The social readjustment rating scale. J Psychosom Res 1967; 11: 213–218.

Kanner AD, Coyne JC, Schaefer C. Comparison of two models of stress measurement: Daily hassles and uplifts versus major life events. J Beh Med 1981; 4: 1–39.

Murray HA. Exploration in Personality. New York: Oxford Univ Press, 1938.

Paykel ES. Methodological aspects of life event research. J Psychosom Res 1983; 27: 341–352.

Wimmer A. Psykogene sundssygdomsformer. In: Sct. Hans Hospital 1816–1916, Jubilee Publication. Copenhagen: Gad 1916, pp. 85–216.

Wimmer A. Psykogene forstyrrelser efter ulykkestilfælde, "traumatisk neurose" (posttraumatic neurosis). Meddelelser fra Universitets Psykiatriske Laboratorium. Copenhagen: M. P. Madsen 1923, pp. 1–12.

8 Social Functioning and Coping Scales

The disease-specific ailment-oriented scales discussed in Chapter 6 cover the clinical symptoms that are characteristic focus of attention in medical care of chronic or subchronic disorders mainly of somatic type. The New York Heart Association scale for cardiac disability is included there to illustrate ailment-oriented scales. In Chapter 3 ward behavioural rating scales are discussed in relation to such components as self-care (personal hygiene) and cooperativeness (aggressiveness). In this context the Global Assessment of Functioning (GAF) from DSM-III-R is shown. It is emphasized there that GAF includes symptoms of both clinical axis 1 syndromes and adaptive social functioning, it is recommended to separate these dimensions.

In his influential paper on health as a social concept, Lewis (1953) concluded that social criteria play no part in defining disease (impairments) or illness (clinical symptoms which conform to the impairments and/or to a recognizable clinical syndrome). This holds for both somatic and mental disorders. The capacity to meet social demands, for example, the ability to work, may, according to Lewis, provoke such questions as: Is this man ill? or Is he relapsing? Lewis emphasizes that we cannot ignore social considerations because illness may lead to social maladaption.

Chapter 8 covers both health-performance scales and coping-with-illness scales, considering social adjustment as the major factor.

8.1 Health Performance Scales

General scales for measuring physical health include components of self-care (personal hygiene) and general physical activity (physical performance). The classical scale is the Karnofsky Performance Status Scale (Karnofsky and Burchenal 1949) which was originally designed for patients with cancer treated with chemotherapeutic agents. It consists of three general levels of condition, each with a number of subclasses. The scale is presented below (with performance status given in parentheses).

A   Able to carry on normal activity and to work. No special care needed.
   Normal. No complaints. No evidence of disease. (100%)
   Able to carry on normal activity. Minor signs or symptoms. (90%)
   Normal activity with effort. Some signs or symptoms. (80%)

B   Unable to work. Able to live at home, care for most personal needs. A varying
     degree of assistance is needed.
     Cares for self. Unable to carry on normal activity or to do active work. (70%)
     Requires occasional assistance but is able to care for most of his or her needs.
     (60%)
     Requires considerable assistance and frequent medical care. (50%)
C   Unable to care for self. Requires equivalent of institutional or hospital care.
     Disease may be progressing rapidly.
     Disabled. Requires special care and assistance. (40%)
     Severely disabled. Hospitalization is indicated. (30%)
     Hospitalization necessary. (20%)
     Moribund. (10%)
     Dead. (0%)

Basically this scale measures the nursing requirements in the ward, and the term
'symptoms' covers ailment-oriented symptoms.

It is an observer scale to be filled in by physicians. This scale is still the most
widely used for measuring health-related quality-of-life problems (Grieco and
Long 1984), but it is a health-performance scale, not a quality-of-life scale. However, even when used properly as a health performance index some psychometric
problems with the scale have been found (e.g. Hutchinson et al. 1979). The three
components – (A) ability to work, (B) ability to carry on normal activities without
assistance, and (C) ability to care for personal needs – are not an exhaustive set,
which is a requirement for the construct validity of a scale. For example, Hutchinson et al. (1979) have shown that the scale contains no score representing the state
of a paraplegic musician who can work succesfully but needs aid in other activities. This seems to be the reason for the low inter-observer reliability found by
Hutchinson et al (1979). However, Grieco and Long (1984) inter-observer reliability to be acceptable using trained observers with a modified version. A modification of the Karnofsky Performance Status Scale made by Grieco and Long (1984)
is provided below (scores in parentheses).
–   Normal, no complaints. (100%)
–   Does usual activities, but with some effort. Work not adversely affected.
     (90%)
–   Does usual activities, but with effort. Work or social activities mildly im-
     paired. (80%)
–   Self-help skills intact. May work part-time but does not work full or does not
     carry out usual activities. (70%)
–   Self-help skills intact but does not work, attend school, or carry out routine
     housework. Social, family, and marital or sexual relationship may be impaired.
     (60%)
–   Self-help skills mildly impaired. Requires considerable asistance and frequent
     medical care. Ordinary social relationship may be prohibited or significantly
     impaired. Does a few chores beyond self-care, such as light housework. (50%)
–   Disabled. Requires special care and assistance. One self-help skill is prohibited
     or significantly impaired. (40%)

- Severely disabled, hospitalization or institutionalization is indicated. More than one self-help skill prohibited or significantly impaired. (30%)
- Hospitalization or institutionalization is necessary, actual supportive treatment is necessary. Severely restricted behaviour. Poor awareness of environment. (20%)
- Unconscious or in stupor, near death. Little or no movement or awareness of surroundings. (10%)
- Dead. (0%)

The background for including axis 5 (adaptive social functioning) in DSM-III was its prognostic significance. According to DSM-III, this axis permits "the clinician to indicate his or her judgment of an individual's highest level of adaptative functioning (for at least a few months) during the past year." The prognostic validity of this information was thought obvious "because usually an individual returns to his or her previous level of adaptive functioning after an episode of illness." An empirical literature review of the predictive validity of axis 5 in DSM-III is still lacking.

The components of adaptive functioning in DSM-III were (a) social relations (covering both breath and quality of interpersonal relationship), (b) occupational functioning (covering amount, complexity and quality of the work accomplished), and (c) use of leisure time (covering both breath and depth of involvement and pleasure derived from recreational activities or hobbies). A most interesting statement in DSM-III was added: "The highest level of adaptive functioning should be used only when high productivity is not associated with a high level of subjective discomfort." In other words, subjective discomfort should be considered, although the axis 5 in principle is a social performance scale. Table 8.1 shows the DSM-III scale for highest level of adaptive functioning (axis 5).

In DSM-III-R axis 5 should be used for two time periods (a) current (the level of functioning at the time of evaluation) and (b) the past year (the highest level of functioning for at least a few months during the past year). According to DSM-III-R: "Ratings of current functioning will generally reflect the current need for treatment or care. Ratings of highest level of functioning during the past year frequently will have prognostic significance." However, axis 5 in DSM-III-R is very different from axis 5 in DSM-III. In DSM-III-R the components of adaptive functioning includes impairment in psychological functioning as well as impairments in social and occupational functioning. The measurement is made by use of a rating scale, the GAF. In Chapter 3 the impairment of psychological functioning is considered as a dimension in its own right. The social and occupational functioning part of GAF is shown in Table 8.2. A modification of DSM-III axis-5 assessment of social functioning is as follows (scores in parentheses):

- Good functioning, i.e. no impairment in social relations and/or occupational functioning. ('0')
- Fair functioning, i.e. moderate impairment in either social relations or occupational functioning, or mild to moderate impairment in both. ('1')
- Poor functioning, i.e. marked impairment in either social relations or occupational functioning, or moderate impairment in both. ('2')

Table 8.1. DSM-III: highest level of adaptive functioning (axis 5)

	Definitions of scale items	Examples
1 Superior	Unusually effective functioning in social relations, occupational functioning, and use of leisure time.	Single parent living in deteriorating neighbourhood, takes excellent care of children and home, has warm relations with friends, and finds time for pursuit of hobby.
2 Very good	Better than average functioning in social relations, occupational functioning, and use of leisure time.	A 65-year old retired widower, does some volunteer work, often sees old friends, and pursues hobbies.
3 Good	No more than slight impairment in either social or occupational functioning.	A woman with many friends, functions extremely well at a difficult job, but says "the strain is too much".
4 Fair	Moderate impairment in either social relations or occupational functioning or slight impairment in both.	A lawyer, has trouble carrying through assignments, has several acquaintances, but hardly any close friends.
5 Poor	Marked impairment in either social relations or occupational functioning, or moderate impairment in both.	A man with one or two friends, has trouble keeping a job for more than a few weeks.
6 Very poor	Marked impairment in both social relations and occupational functioning.	A woman unable to do any of her housework and has violent outbursts towards family and neighbours.
7 Grossly impaired	Gross impairment in virtually all areas of functioning.	An elderly man needs supervision to maintain minimal personal hygiene and is usually incoherent.

Table 8.2. GAF: social functioning dimension

Performance code	Comments
90-81	Good functioning both socially and occupationally
80-71	Slight impairment in occupational or social functioning
70-61	Slight to moderate difficulty in occupational or social functioning
60-51	Moderate difficulty in occupational or social functioning
50-41	Any serious impairment in occupational or social functioning
40-31	Major impairment in several social areas
30-21	Inability to function in almost all social areas
20-11	Occasionally fails to maintain even minimal personal hygiene
10-1	Persistent inability to maintain personal hygiene

- Very poor functioning, i.e. marked impairment in both social relations or occupational functioning. ('3')
- Grossly impaired functioning, i.e. gross impairment in virtually all areas of functioning. ('4')

The first major social status scale was developed by Barrabee et al. (1955). They defined social adjustment as the degree to which a person fulfils the normative social expectations of behaviour that constitute his or her roles. They focused on social adjustment as areas of behaviour to be evaluated, i.e. they excluded the process of subjective feeling (well-being). The areas of behaviour considered by Barrabee et al. (1955) for scaling social adjustments were: employment, economics, family life and community. From the scale developed by Barrabee et al. (1955) the Instrumental Activities of Daily Living Scale (IADL) was designed by Lawton and Brody (1969). However, it was Katz and coworkers (Staff of the Benjamin Rose Hospital 1959; Katz et al. 1963) who first developed a rating scale, termed Index of Independence in Activities of Daily Living. Studies on both scales (Lawton 1988; Spector and Katz 1987) have confirmed a hierarchical structure in the components of self-care. Table 8.3 presents results of a Guttman analysis by Lawton (1988) showing that having difficulties on scale items is closely related to the need for help.

Table 8.3. Percentage of population aged 65 or over with activity limitations. (Modified after Lawton 1988)

Self-care	Difficulty performing activity (%)	Received help with activity (%)
Eating	1.8	1.1
Using toilet	4.3	2.2
Dressing	6.2	4.3
Getting outside	9.6	5.3
Bathing	9.8	6.0

In a recent review on the components relevant for patients with persistent mental illness Schinnar et al. (1990) collected the items shown in Table 8.4; this table compares the Karnofsky scale and the DSM-III-R scale.

The social adjustment scale constructed by Barrabee et al. (1955) was meant to measure outcome of psychotherapy and not self-care in terms of independence in activities of daily living. Other scales can be considered as modifications of the Barrabee scale, for example that of Weissman (1975). Scales for more severely psychiatric patients include the Social Interview Scale (Claire et al. 1978) the Social Performance Schedule (Hurry and Sturt 1981) and the Social Behaviour Schedule (Platt et al. 1980). These scales are too comprehensive to be discussed in this compendium.

It is recommended to use the DSM-III-R modification consisting of the following items: occupational functioning, social relations, family relations, leisure time, and all things considered. A visual analogue scale reaching from 'no trouble at all' to 'a lot of trouble' should be used for scoring. A ward behaviour scale in psychogeriatric patients fulfilling the Rasch models might be considered (Verstraten 1988).

8.2 Coping with Illness Scales

Ischaemic heart disease has been used by Pichot (1982) to illustrate the interaction between the psychopathological and somatic performance axes that gives rise to the hypotheses as to their interactions: (a) patients suffering from ischaemic heart disease are predisposed because of certain personality traits (i.e. a special psychological vulnerability existing long before the somatic disease developed, e.g. type A behaviour); (b) there is a correlation between the onset of an acute ischae-

Table 8.4. Components of disability in rating scales. (From Schinnar et al. 1990)

Component	Karnofsky Performance Status Scale	DSM-III-R GAF (social dimension)	Modified DSM-III Global Social Functioning Scale	Visual analogue scales of reliance on treatment
Self-sufficiency	+			+
Limited self-control	+			+
Reliance on treatment (psychosocial, drugs, etc.)	+			+
Limited performance in non-work (leisure time)	+	+	+	
Limited performance in employment	+	+	+	
Limited social functions	+	+	+	
Limited activities of daily living and basic needs	+	+	+	
Lack of self-care (maximum dependence)	+	+	+	

mic attack and a psychosocial stressor; (c) the onset of an acute myocardial attack is attended by psychological change in the patient, e.g. secondary depression.

The personality scales included in Chapter 5 were selected as psychopathological scales with the most weight on the psycho-pathological process. Personality defined as a patho-psychological process has been outlined most convicting in Murray's classical work (1938) on the exploration in personality. This can be summarized as follows: (a) personality is an unobservable construct; (b) it refers to a series of events which in the ideal case span the entire life time of the person being examined ("the history of the personality *is* the personality"); (c) it is an integration of the disparate impulses and constrains to which the individual is exposed.

The study of experience and behaviour of persons diagnosed as ill was first scientifically approached two decades ago. Before that time psychosomatic research was devoted to pathogenic relationships. The concept of coping with illness was defined by Lipowski (1970) as all cognitive and motor activities which an ill person employs to preserve his bodily and psychic integrity, to recover reversibly impaired function and compensate as much as possible for any irreversible impairment. In this definition Lipowski integrates the psychological elements of Lazarus (1966) and the sociological elements of Mechanic (1968). Lipowski (1970) distinguished between (a) coping styles and (b) coping strategies.

Coping style refers to a person's enduring disposition to deal with challenges and stressors. Among subtypes of coping styles are denial, vigilant focusing (patients who must know what is happening to them, what the implications of their illness are, etc), fighting, capitulating, avoiding. Rating scales constructed for measuring the personality behaviour of coping styles include the Millon Behaviour Health Inventory (MBHI; Millon et al. 1982) and the Mental Adjustment to Cancer (MAC scale; Morris et al. 1977; Greer et al. 1979; Watson et al. 1988). The MBHI measures such dimensions as introversive, inhibited, cooperative, sociable, confident, forceful, respectful and sensitive. The MAC scales measures such dimensions as fighting spirit, denial, stoic acceptance and helplessness. Empirical studies have shown the MAC to be most valid in predicting outcome of illness (Pettingale et al. 1985). While the MBHI is a general scale for measuring coping styles, the MAC scale (shown below) is a specific scale (Watson et al. 1988). The scoring is: 1, definitely does not apply to me; 2, does not apply to me; 3, applies to me; 4, definitely applies to me.

1. I have been doing things that I believe will improve my health, e.g. changed my diet.
2. I feel I can't do anything to cheer myself up.
3. I feel that problems with my health prevent me from planning ahead.
4. I believe that my positive attitude will benefit my health.
5. I don't dwell on my illness.
6. I firmly believe that I will get better.
7. I feel that nothing I can do will make any difference.

8. I've left it all to my doctors.
9. I feel that life is hopeless.
10. I have been doing things that I believe will improve my health, e.g. exercised.
11. Since my cancer diagnosis I now realise how precious life is and I'm making the most of it.
12. I've put myself in the hands of God.
13. I have plans for the future, e.g. holiday, jobs, housing.
14. I worry about the cancer returning or getting worse.
15. I've had a good life, what's left is a bonus.
16. I think my state of mind can make a lot of difference to my health.
17. I feel that there is nothing I can do to help myself.
18. I try to carry on my life as I've always done.
19. I would like to make contact with others in the same boat.
20. I am determined to put it all behind me.
21. I have difficulty in believing that this happened to me.
22. I suffer great anxiety about it.
23. I am not very hopeful about the future.
24. At the moment I take on day at a time.
25. I feel like giving up.
26. I try to keep a sense of humour about it.
27. Other people worry about me more than I do.
28. I think of other people who are worse off.
29. I am trying to get as much information as I can about cancer.
30. I feel that I can't control what is happening.
31. I try to have a very positive attitude.
32. I keep quite busy, so I don't have time to think about IT.
33. I avoid finding out more about it.
34. I see my illness as a challenge.
35. I feel fatalistic about it.
36. I feel completely at a loss about what to do.
37. I feel very angry about what has happened to me.
38. I don't really believe I had cancer.
39. I count my blessings.
40. I try to fight the illness.

The MAC scale includes the following subscales: (a) Fighting spirit (items 4, 5, 6, 11, 13, 16, 18, 20, 26, 27, 31, 32, 34, 39, 40); (b) Helpless or hopeless (items 2, 9, 17, 23, 25, 30, 36,); (c) Anxious preoccupation (items 1, 3, 10, 14, 19, 21, 22, 29, 37); (d) Fatalism (items 7, 8, 12, 15, 24, 28, 33, 35); and (e) Avoidance (item 38).

Coping strategies refer to the techniques used by ill persons to deal with their illness and its consequences. The concept includes intrapsychic activities as well as communications and actions of the ill persons aimed at reduction of distress and suffering caused by the disease.

Table 8.5. Coping strategies, coping styles and clinical diagnosis

Coping strategies (Lipowski 1970)	Coping styles (Watson et al. 1988)	Clinical diagnosis
Illness as a challenge	Fighting spirit	No pathology
Illness as a relief	Stoic acceptance	
Illness as a weakness Illness as a punishment Illness as an irreparable loss	Helpless or hopeless	Depression Neuroticism
Illness as an enemy		Borderline (anhedonia)
Illness as a strategy	Denial	Hysteria (dissociative)

Table 8.5 compares the coping strategies postulated by Lipowski (1970) and the coping styles as measured by Morris et al. (1977); the table also indicates a correspondence to psychopathology. Morris et al. (1977) used the Hamilton Depression Scale and the Eysenck Neuroticism Scale to measure the degree of helplessness/hopelessness and neuroticism. They found that both scales predicted the coping style of helplessness/hopelessness, which again predicts a poor outcome of the treatment of breast cancer (Pettingale et al. 1985). The cut-off score on the Hamilton Scale was 10.

Life-event scales consider psychosocial stressors as relatively static events compared to coping with stress behaviour as defined by Lipowski (1970). From a dynamic point of view the interaction between personality styles (coping styles) and the impact of illness on coping strategies should be taken into account. Thus, whereas the type A behaviour measured by the Bortner Scale (see Chapter 5) is a dispositional personality scale, the MAC is a reaction-to-illness scale. Watson et al. have discussed whether mental coping responses are transient reactions rather than traitlike dispositions. If so, the scale is a disease specific coping scale as opposed to the Beck Depression Inventory (see Chapter 4) which by Cassileth et al. (1984) is considered a generic (non-specific) coping scale. Among personality dispositions it seems that the concept of hardiness (commitment, control and challenge) is most relevant (Kobasa et al. 1982).

Among scales focusing on the impact of the illness on the patient (in which the different stages of the illness should be considered as having different effect on coping strategies) is the Ways of Coping Scale (Folkman and Lazarus 1980). This measures 68 cognitive and behavioural strategies that a person may use when con-

Table 8.6. Applicability of the health status scales

Clinical disability	Scale

Original:
    Chronic heart disease
 	
Application:
    Severe chronic disease, e.g.
    Parkinson's disease
	Sickness Impact Profile, Bergner et al.
	(1976)
	
	Wilson and Goetz (1990)

Original:
    Chronic osteoarthritis
 	
Application:
    Severe chronic disease, e.g.
    Parkinson's disease
	Nottingham Health Profile, Hunt et al.
	(1981)
	
	Schindler et al. (1987)

Original:
    Cancer disease
 	
Application:
    Moderate to severe chronic disease
	Psychosocial Adjustment to Illness Scale,
	Morrow et al. (1978), Derogatis (1986)

Original:
    Chronic disease, e.g. diabetes
    mellitus
	McMaster Health Index Questionnaire
	section B, Chambers (1982)

fronted with a specific stimulus. However, so far little research on specific groups of patients has been carried out with this scale.

The Sickness Impact Profile (SIP; Bergner et al. 1976) began in 1972 as a collaborative effort between Berger, a sociologist, and Gilson, a physician. The first phase involved collection of statements describing the effect of illness upon behavioural function. An original pool of 788 items was differentiated into different components. Of these, 312 were retained and tested in a variety of different studies. Finally, the scale that was developed included 136 items (Bergner et al. 1981). Table 8.6 lists scales derived from the SIP; these include the Nottingham Health Profile (Martini and Hunt 1977; Hunt et al. 1981), the Psychosocial Adjustment to Illness Scale (PAIS; Morrow et al. 1978; Derogatis 1986) and the McMaster Health Index Questionnaire (Chambers 1982).

The Nottingham Health Profile was a non-patient derived scale which in the clinical field was originally used in patients with osteoarthritis, but the scale has since been used in a variety of chronic disorders such as Parkinson's disease. The SIP was originally applied to patients with chronic heart disease, but it has also been used in patients with Parkinson's disease (Wilson and Goetz 1990). Likewise, the PAIS (Derogatis 1986) was originally developed in chronic cancer disorders, but should also be considered for patients with diabetes mellitus or epilepsy. However, section B of the McMaster Health Index (Chambers 1982) was originally applied in patients with diabetes mellitus. The rank order indicated in Table 8.6 is meant to reflect the severity of the chronic somatic disorders. Thus, Parkinson's disease has been selected as one of the most clinically severe disorders, and the SIP is considered more of a disability-oriented scale than is the Nottingham Health Profile.

Assessing the generalizability of a scale originally constructed for a specific disease is a major problem. The applicability of a scale outside its original range has been tested by the Rasch model, where transferability indicates the extent to which the total score reflects a dimension across different populations. The PAIS has been standardized for lung cancer patients, but studies are ongoing to standardize the scale for separate disorders. Results have shown that chronic haemodialysis patients are among those with poorest adjustment scores (Guadagnoli and Mor 1990).

Table 8.7 presents the number of items per component and the relative item distribution of the SIP, PAIS and Nottingham Health Profile. The components are not easily translated in each other, which prevents a closer comparison for construct validity. Both the SIP and the Nottingham scale are more performance orientated, but the Nottingham scale includes a part 2 covering recreational and social environment. These scales, however, are not Likert scales. The Nottingham scale is a Thurstone scale (see Chapter 1) in which each item is subjectively weighted, but is often used by the unweighted raw scores (McDowell and Newell 1987).

The PAIS is a Likert scale and has been psychometrically most evaluated in terms of classical statistics (e.g. factor analysis). The results have been published by Derogatis (1986).

The prognostic validity of axis 5 in DSM-III seems to be derived from the concept of coping. Olff (1991) defines coping both as the positive response outcome expectances and the behavioural strategies involved. In their monography on stress, productivity and the reconstruction of working life, Karasek and Theorell (1990) defines 'creative anxiety' as a positive behavioural spiral: (1) active job setting, (2) increased feeling of mastery and confidence, (3) which helps coping with the inevitable strain-inducing situations of the job, (4) increased capacity to accept still more challenging situations. Likewise, they describe the negative behavioural spiral inducing clinical anxiety: (1) long-term accumulated strain, (2) diminishing feeling of mastery over situations, (3) restricted coping mechanisms, (4) clinical anxiety. Karasek (1985) has constructed a Job Contest Questionnaire, but it is outside the scope of this compendium to discuss this scale in detail. However, it measure coping as a stress-related concept to be distinguished from health-related quality of life which takes defence mechanisms into account.

Table 8.7. Number of items and relative item distribution of rating scales: SIP, PAIS and Nottingham Health Profile

SIP components	No.	%	PAIS components	No.	%	Nottingham Health Profile	No.	%
1 Sleep and rest	7	5				Sleep	5	13
2 Eating	9	7				Pain	8	21
3 Work	9	7	2 Vocation environment	6	14	(Work)	(1)	
4 Home management	10	7	3 Domestic environment	7	16	(Home)	(1)	
5 Recreation and pastimes	8	6	6 Social environment	6	14	(Hobbies, social life, homelife, vacation)	(4)	
6 Ambulation	12	9				Energy	3	8
7 Morbidity	10	7				Physical morbidity	8	21
8 Body care	23	17	1 Health care	8	18			
9 Social interaction	20	15	5 Extended family relations	4	9	Social isolation	5	13
10 Alertness behaviour	10	7						
11 Emotional behaviour	9	7	7 Psychological distress	7	16	Emotional reaction	9	24
12 Communication	9	7						
			4 Sexual relations	6	14	(Sex life)	(1)	
Total	136	100	Total	44	100	Total - part 1	38	100

Part 2 in parenthesis

References

Barrabee P, Barrabee EL, Finesinger JE. A normative social adjustment scale. Am J Psychiat 1955; 112: 252–259.

Bergner M, Bobbitt RA, Carter WB, Gilson BS. The Sickness Impact Profile: Development and final revision of a health status measure. Med Care 1981; 19: 787–806.

Cassileth BR, Lusk EJ, Stronse TB. Psychosocial status in chronic illness. New Wngl J Med 1984; 311: 506–511.

Chambers LW. The McMaster Health Index Questionnaire (MHIQ). Methodological Documentation and Report of Second Generation of Investigation. Dept. Clin. Epidemiology and Biostatistics, McMaster Univ, Hamilton, Ontario, 1982.

Claire WS, Cairns VE. Design, development and use of a standard interview to assess social maladjustment and dysfunction in community studies. Psychol Med 1978; 8: 589–604.

Derogatis LR. The psychological adjustment to illness scale (PAIS). J Psychosom Res 1986; 30: 77–91.

Folkman S, Lazarus RS. An analysis of coping in a middle-aged community sample. J Health Soc Beh 1980; 21: 219–239.

Goldberger L, Breznitz S (eds). Handbook of Stress. New York: Free Press, 1982.

Greer HS, Morris T, Pettingale KW. Psychological response to breast cancer: Effects of outcome. Lancet 1979; 2: 785–787.

Grieco A, Long CJ. Investigation of the Karnofsky Performance Status as a measure of quality of life. Health Psycholog 1984; 3: 129–143.

Guadagnoli E, Mor V. Social interaction tests and scales. In: Spilker B (ed). Quality of Life Assessment in Clinical Trials. New York: Raven Press 1990, pp. 85–94.

Hunt SM, McKenna SP, McEwen J. Reliability of a population survey tool: A study of patients with osteoarthrosis. J Epidemiol Community Health 1981; 35: 297–300.

Hurry J, Sturt E. Social performance in a population sample. Relation to psychiatric symptoms. In. Wing JK. What Is a Case. London, Grant McInture, 1981.

Hutchinson TA, Boyd NF, Feinstein AR. Scientific problems in clinical scales as demonstrated in the Karnofsky index of performance status. J Chron Dis 1979; 32: 661–666.

Karasek R. Job Content Questionnaire. Department of Industrial and Systems Engineering, Univ of South Carolina, Los Angeles, 1985.

Karasek R, Theorell T. Health Work. Stress, Productivity, and the Reconstructions of Working Life. New York, Basic Books, 1990.

Karnofsky DA, Burchenal JH. The clinical evaluation of chemotherapeutic agents in cancer. In: MacLeod CM (ed). Evaluation of Chemotherapeutic Agents. New York: Columbia Univ Press, 1949 pp. 191–205.

Katz S, Ford AB, Moskowitz RW, Jackson BA, Jaffe MW. Studies of illness in the aged. J AMA 1963; 185: 914–919.

Kobasa S, Maddi SR, Kahn S. Hardiness and health: A prospective study. J Pers Soc Psychol 1982; 42: 168–177.

Lawton MP. Scales to measure competence in everyday activities. Psychopharmacol Bull 1988; 24: 609–614.

Lawton MP, Brody EM. Assessment of older people: Self-maintaining and instrumental activities of daily living. Gerontologist 1969; 9: 179–186.

Lawton MP, Moss M, Fulcomer M, Kleban MH. A research and service-oriented Multilevel Assessment Instrument. J Gerontol 1982; 37: 91–99.

Lazarus RS. Psychological Stress and Coping Process. New York: McGraw-Hill, 1966.

Lewis A. Health as a social concept. Brit J Sociol 1953; 4: 109–124.

Lipowski ZJ. Physical illness, the individual and the coping processes. Int J Psychiat in Med 1970; 1: 91–102.

McDowell I, Newell C. Measuring health. New York: Oxford University Press 1987.

Mechanic D. Medical Sociology. New York: Free Press, 1968.

Millon T, Green C, Meagher R. Millon Behavioural Health Inventory Manual. Minneapolis: National Computer Systems, 1982.

Morris T, Greer HS, White P. Psychological and social adjustment to mastectomy. Cancer 1977; 40: 2381–2387.

Morrow GR, Chiarello RJ, Derogatis LR. A new scale for measuring patients' psychosocial adjustment to medical illness. Psychol Med 1978; 8: 605–610.

Murray HA. Exploration in personality. 1938. National Intitute of Mental Health. Community Support Systems for Persons With Long-Term Mental Illness: Questions and answers. Rockville: National Institute of Mental Health; 1987.

Olff M. Defence and Coping: Self-reported Health and Psychological Correlated. Utrecht, ISOR, 1991.

Pettingale KW, Morris T, Greer S, Haybittle JL. Mental attitudes to cancer: An additional prognostic factor. Lancet 1985; 1: 750.

Pichot P. Problems raised by the application of psychometric methods to transversal and longitudinal studies. Adv Cardiol 1982; 29: 10–17.

Platt S, Weymann A, Hirsh S, Hewett S. The Social Behaviour Assessment Schedule (SBAS). Rationale, contents, scoring and reliability of a new interview schedule. Soc Psychiat 1980; 15: 455–465.

Schinnar AP, Rothbard AB, Kanter R, Jung YS. An empirical literature review of definitions of severe and persistent mental illness. Am J Psychiatr 1990; 147: 1602–1608.

Shindler JS, Brown R, Welburn P, Parkes JD. Measuring the quality of life of patients with Parkinson's disease. In: Walker SR, Rosser RM (eds). Quality of Life: Assessment and Application. Lancaster: MTR Press, 1987, pp. 223–234.

Spector N, Katz S. The hierarchical relationship between activities of daily living and instrumental activities of daily living. J Chronic Dis 1987; 40: 481–490.

Staff of the Benjamin Rose Hospital. Multidisciplinary studies of illness in aged persons. A new classification of functional status in activities of daily living. J Chronic Dis 1959; 9: 55–62.

Verstraten PFJ. The GIP: An observational ward behaviour scale. Psychopharmacol Bull 1988; 24: 717–719.

Watson M, Greer S, Bliss JM. Mental Adjustment to Cancer (MAC) Scale. User's Manual Survey. The Institute of Cancer Research, 1989.

Watson M, Greer S, Young J, Inayat Q, Burges C, Robertson B. Development of a questionnaire measure of adjustment to cancer: The MAC scale. Psychol Med 1988; 18: 203–209.

Wilson RS, Goetz G. Neurological Illness. In: Spilker B (ed.). Quality of Life Assessments in Clinical Trials. New York, Raven Press 1990, pp. 347–356.

9 Health-Related Quality of Life Rating Scales

This compendium has followed DSM-III or DSM-III-R in using a multi-axial approach to mental as well as somatic disorders in their clinical description. Thus, Chapters 2–4 have referred to axis 1 (mental disorders), Chapter 5 to axis 2 (personality disorders), Chapter 6 to axis 3 (somatic disorders), Chapter 7 to axis 4 (psychosocial stressors), and Chapter 8 to axis 5 (social functioning and coping with illness). Chapter 9 deals with quality of life, which has no direct reference to an individual DSM-III axis. Quality of life is an integration of all five axis, is a hollistic concept, which has a close relationship to the concept of global improvement of illness during treatment as experienced by the patients themselves (Bech 1990a). In other words, health-related quality of life is a metaconcept which, inter alia, includes coping with illness.

In his influential paper on health Lewis (1953) emphasized that "The adequate performance of the body working as a whole is highly individual. (...) In clinical practice the physician must take the patient pretty much as supplying his own norm of total performance or behaviour. (...) Even in regard to physical illness we cannot disregard total behaviour, which is a psychological concept."

Moral philosophers (e.g. Plato, Aristotle, Epicurus, Hobbes, Spinoza, Kant, Schopenhauer, Bentham, James) took it for granted the fact that men have certain aims, purposes, and desires which they wish to achieve, fulfil, and satisfy. As discussed by Nowell-Smith (1967) the achievement of these aims is variously called 'The Good Life', 'The Good for Man', 'Happiness', and 'Felicity'. The task for the moral philosopher was to depict this state in broad outline and to tell others how they achieve it.

The ethical theories are, as stated by Nowell-Smith (1967), often divided into teleological theories (according to which the notions of duty, rightness, and obligation are supposed to be defined in terms of, or in some other way dependent on the notions of goodness or purpose) and deontological theories (according to which the notion of obligation is incapable of being analysed or made dependent on items of purpose).

Health-related quality of life has on the one hand a teleological approach (goals of improvement) and, on the other hand, a deontological approach (the type of life the patient want to lead will depend on the sort of man he or she is).

Health-related quality-of-life is what the patient himself feels is an improvement globally, the incremental validity of health. It is a subjective, psychological dimension. The dimension of subjective well-being was first recognized and measured by Bentham (1834). In fact, Bentham (1789) opened his treatise on *An Introduction of the Principles of Morals and Legislation* with the declaration that "Nature has placed mankind under the governance of two sovereign masters, pain and pleasure. It is for them alone to point out what we ought to do, as well as to determine what we shall do. On the one hand the standard of right and wrong, on the other the chain of causes and effects, are fastened to their throne." Using the terminology of this compendium 'pain' versus 'pleasure' should be referred to as 'clinical disability' versus 'quality of life'. Three decades ago, when the ecological movement in support of the 'green' quality of life style began as a reaction against the uncritical use of pesticides, Bentham's works were reconsidered (Bech 1991). The 'green' approach involved placing things in context, taking the whole situation into account. The principle that ecological laws dictate human morality inspired O'Riordan (1981) to distinguish between 'soft' and 'hard' technologists. The 'hard' technologist believes that scientific and technological expertise provides the basics for advice on matters related to public health and safety. In contrast, the 'soft' technologist believes that materialism for its own sake is wrong, and that economic growth can be adapted to integrate basic needs and subjective well-being through a process of personal as well as communal improvement.

Health-related quality of life is subjective well-being associated with disease, accidents or treatment and its side effects. It is generally considered (Bech 1987) that it was the late United States President, Lyndon B. Johnson, who stimulated research into quality of life when at a political meeting in 1964 he declared that "Goals cannot be measured in the size of our bank balance. They can only be measured in the quality of the lives that our people lead." However, Galbraith (1958) had earlier noted the need to measure the effect of the health care system in terms of quality of life.

Comparing the components of the first 50 rating scales measuring quality of life (published between 1966 and 1985), Joyce (1987) showed that 84% measured clinical disability (axis 1 or 3 components) or social adjustment (axis 5 components) rather than self-perceived health status in relation to subjective well-being. The components of the 50 rating instruments collected by Joyce (1987) covered physical, cognitive, affective, social and economic issues, which at a consensus meeting (Walker and Assher 1986) were considered the essential components of quality of life (PCASE). The disadvantages of illness as perceived by the patient in terms of the impact of health status on well-being includes both doing and feeling. It is the ongoing activity by which a patient attempts to satisfy his needs in terms of the pre-illness position, or in relation to his intended goals. The normative social adjustment scale constructed by Barrabee et al. (1955) explicitly excluded the dynamic processes of the disadvantage of illness as discussed in Chapter 8. The dynamic defence mechanisms as briefly mentioned in Chapter 5 are important aspects of quality of life.

9.1 Self-Report Scales Measuring Demoralization, Disadvantage or Discomfort (Handicap)

The first study to measure the dynamic processes of disadvantage during illness was published Parloff et al. (1954), who endeavoured to define the dimension of decreased subjective well-being (discomfort). For Parloff and coworkers this was taken as a dimension of improvement during psychotherapy, and in attempting to define it sought to use a language other than that of symptoms (which can confound problems of clinical disability components and quality-of-life problems). However, they found no alternative to the language of symptoms in communication with the patient. Later, Veroff et al. (1981) concluded that symptoms are interesting and important indicators of psychological experience: "They represent the presenting complaints people have, ones that they commonly use in conversations about everyday stressors and strains of modern living."

Frank (1974), who was a co-author of the classical paper by Parloff et al. (1954) preferred the term 'demoralization' to 'discomfort' emphasizing that:

Demoralization describes the state of candidates for psychotherapy, whatever their diagnostic label. They are conscious of having failed to meet their own expectations or those of others, or being unable to cope with some pressing problem. They feel powerless to change the situation or themselves. Their life space is constricted both in space and time ... The demoralized person is prey to anxiety and depression (the two most common complaints of persons seeking psychotherapy).

Patients with a wide range of somatic or mental disorders thus have a common dimension across these diagnoses, a pathopsychological non-specific dimension of discomfort or demoralization. Psychotherapy is, of course, the only proper therapeutic way out of this situation, and Parloff et al. (1954) emphasized that most patients seek psychotherapy to be relieved of distress rather than move from a satisfactory state of comfort to a better one.

Most of the published scales for measuring quality of life in relation to health measure degrees of discomfort or demoralization and find their applicability in hedonic personalities (including psychopathological personalities with neurotic and psychopathic traits). However, little (or no) research has been devoted to this problem (Bech 1990a), although one of the first inventories for measuring mental health (Seashore 1916) included the following important statements to be responded to by the patient: (1) I am a bodily being; (2) I am an intellectual being; (3) I am a social being; (4) I am a moral being; (5) I am an aesthetic being; and (6) I am a religious being.

Quality of life became a heading in the Index Medicus in 1977. However, most papers published before 1977 were health status measurements describing the impact of the disease on functions (disability). In 1986 the *New England Journal of Medicine* accepted the dimension of quality of life as an outcome criterion for a pharmaceutical product (Croog et al., 1986). Of the many scales included in this study the scale discriminating most validly between the treatments was the Psychological General Well-Being Schedule (Dupuy 1984). The papers in the medical literature from 1977 to 1986 have been more concerned with measuring the construct of quality of life as an intrapsychic dimension including components of life satisfactions in cognitive and emotional terms.

The World Health Organization (WHO) introduced the term 'handicap' to cover the disadvantages experienced by the patient as a result of illness (WHO 1980). It was emphasized that the dimension of handicap should reflect purely subjective statements on the part of the patient, but early results with this dimension have proven rather disappointing (Wood 1990). However, WHO has recently initiated new studies emphasizing the emotional aspects of handicap or disadvantage of illness (Sartorius 1987). Furthermore, Sartorius accepted the 'gap' or 'distance' approach in which life satisfaction is considered as a distance between 'as I was before illness', 'as I am now', and 'as I wish to be' (e.g. Michalos 1986; Bech 1990b). In discussing the meaning, measurement and moral importance of well-being, Griffin (1988) has emphasized that at least four components should be considered, namely 'deep personal relations' (interpersonal sensitivity), 'autonomy' (self-control), 'accomplishment in life' (doing things well) and 'understanding of life' (feeling to play a useful part in things).

In this compendium the concept of coping with illness (Chapter 8) is separated from defence mechanisms (Chapter 5). Health-related quality of life is an attempt to integrate the different axes of DSM-III into a global (psychological) concept. Defence mechanisms are therefore parts of the concept of quality of life. The defence mechanisms in situations with severe psychosocial stressors such as being ill are very different in hedonic personalities (the disposition or proneness to react with depression) compared to schizoid personalities. The hedonic personality fears that the illness threatens his happiness. The schizoid personality fears that illness threatens his or her very existence (Bech and Hjortsø 1990). These reactions are of a general nature as formulated by Storrr (1968): "The depressive person fears the withdrawal of love because it threatens his happiness. The schizoid person fears it because it seems to threaten his very existence." (See also Chapter 5.)

Table 9.1 shows the structure of discomfort in hedonic and schizoid persons. The pathoplastic reaction in the schizoid is an activation of the schizoid symptoms

Table 9.1. The structur of discomfort in hedonia and of distress in anhedonia in terms of the components of Griffin (1988)

Elements of quality of life or well-being	Structure of discomfort in hedonia	Structure of distress in anhedonia
Deep personal relations	Introversion	Suspiciousness
Autonomy	Decreased self-esteem	Increased self-esteem
Accomplishment in life	Retardation	Emptiness
Understanding of life	Guilt feelings	Narcissism

mainly by use of projection. The concept of anhedonia, defined as a narcissistic problem of existence without any basic reference to hedonia, was considered as early as Bleuler (1911) and Kraepelin (1913) to be a fundamental dimension in schizophrenia. Rado (1962) considered the 'flat and apathetic' feature of schizophrenia as an anhedonic picture. Since 1962 Meehl (1962, 1975, 1987) has used the term 'hedonic capacity' to describe a dimension in which anhedonia constitutes the lowest end of the score distribution. In a recent study on the lack of hedonic capacity in schizophrenics and their twins it was found that anhedonia is genetically influenced, but less so than schizophrenia (Berenbaum et al. 1990).

This compendium considers it essential to differentiate between anhedonia as a symptom of depression and anhedonia as a defence mechanism in health-related quality-of-life scales. In the former sense the concept has been measured by Watson et al. (1970); in the latter sense the scale of borderline schizoid personality (see Chapter 5) should be considered.

Table 9.2 shows the components of the various quality-of-life scales compared to clinical disability scales. Joyce (1987) was among the first to illustrate that the components of quality-of-life scales are similar to those of clinical disability scales (i.e. the scales treated in the other chapters of this compendium). These components are physical, cognitive, affective, social and economic (PCASE) issues. Following Joyce (1987) the disability scales measure health status aspects while quality-of-life scales measure handicap (demoralization, disadvantage or discomfort). Table 9.2 includes among the components 'ego-function' and a global assessment the PCASEE model (Bech 1992). The corresponding DSM-III axes are also shown in Table 9.2 emphasizing that DSM-III is a health status system. Analogous to the alpha and beta situations for psychosocial stressors (see Chapter 7) the health status components are alpha (objective) measurements and quality-of-life components and beta (subjective) measurements. As an example, the GHQ-12 consisting of both alpha and beta items is shown in Table 9.2. The alpha/beta dimension is a dimension of description of PCASEE components.

Table 9.3 compares the item distribution on components of demoralization, disadvantage or discomfort relevant for measuring health-related quality of life in hedonic personalities. These components are: (a) general (subjective) health items, (b) emotional items (depression and anxiety), (c) cognitive items (concentration and memory), (d) vegetative items (tiredness and sleep), (e) personal items (interpersonal sensitivity), (f) autonomy items (decision making, self-control), (g) accomplishment items (subjective performance, doing thing well) and (h) understanding (playing a meaningful part in things, time experience). The difference in the concept of clinical disability and subjective experience of illness has perhaps been most elegantly expressed by James (1890). According to James the law-like paradox in time experience shows that "Time filled with varied and interesting experience seems short in passing, but long as we look back. On the other hand, a tract of time empty of experience seems long in passing, but in retrospect short." James then explains that time experience should be excluded from clinical disability: "A night of pain will seem terribly long. What we feel is the long time of suffering, not the suffering of the long time." In other words, the suffering of the long

Table 9.2. The repertoire of PCASEE measured at four different levels (health status system, observer rating scales, self-rating scales and repertory grid). The PCASEE equals DSM-III axes and the levels the WHO classification of impairment, disability and handicap

	Levels of reference	P Physical	C Cognitive	A Affective	S Social	E Economic	E Ego functioning	Global (total) scores
1	DSM-III axes (diagnoses)	(axis 3) Somatic disorders	(axis 1 & 3) Organic mental disorders	(axis 1) Psychiatric disorders	(axis 5) Social functioning	(axis 4) Psychosocial stressors	(axis 2) Personality disorders	
2	Symptom rating scales (e.g. Hamilton with melancholia) Health status	Pains Tiredness Sleep	Concentration Memory Decision	Depression Anxiety	Lack of interests			HDS/MES
3	Quality of life							GHQ-12
	Symptoms (objective) Alpha situation	Energy 16)*	Concentration (7) Decision (36)		Lack of interests (23) Been busy (21)			
	Satisfaction (subjective) Beta situation	Good health (1)		Feels warmth (31) Reasonably happy (54)	Does things well (28) Satisfied with tasks (30) Enjoys normal activities (42)		Plays useful part in things (35)	
4	Repertory Grid (Beta situation)	Feels sound and fit	Uses experience and knowledge to solve problems	Has good contact with family/friends (love)	Has a meaningful job	Has economic basis for good condition of life	Feels OK in own eyes (self-confidence)	Percentage of improvement

* in parentheses the original GHQ item numbering

Table 9.3. Item distribution of rating scales: components of aggression

Components of demoralization, disadvantage, discomfort (handicap)	CHQ/QL-12 %	SCL/QL-17 %	General Well-being Schedule %	Nottingham Health Profile Part 1 - %	Demoralization Scale (modified Dohrenwend) %
General health	8	0	9	0	6
Emotional (depression, anxiety)	25	24	45	13	30
Cognitive (concentration, memory)	8	12	0	0	6
Vegetative (tiredness, sleep)	8	12	18	21	6
Personal (interpersonal sensitivity)	8	24	0	11	12
Autonomy (decisions, self-control)	8	18	9	5	6
Accomplishment (performance)	17	6	9	3	12
Understanding (self-acceptance)	17	6	9	3	24
Disability (clinical symptoms)	0	0	0	45	0

time in itself by inspection is a component of discomfort, not of clinical disability. Janet (1928) has noticed that our first encounter with duration occurred every time a delay was imposed between a desire and its realization, and he suggested that the most complex forms of adaptation to time involving conceptual and symbolic processes would derive from basic properties of waiting behaviour.

In chronic disorders where quality of life scales have their main applicability the waiting behaviour is an essential component with a delay been the hope of improvement and its realization. Illustrated by a novelist, this aspect of time experience in relation to illness has also been elegantly described by Mann (1924). In existential psychology (e.g. May 1986) it has been observed that the most profound psychological experiences are peculiarly those which shake the individual's relation to time. It is not time experienced in spatialized terms (time estimation) but time awareness (the subjective impression that time is passing rapidly or slowly, as shown by James (1890)) that is altered in depressive states (Bech 1975). In the definition of health-related quality of life as a teleological concept the patient's general orientation toward the flow of time (time perspective) is essential and is, therefore, closely connected with existential psychology (developed by such "time researchers" as von Gebsattel (1954), Minkowski (1955) or Straus (1960)). The concept of improvement (making something better) refers to such phrases as 'to improve the occassions' or 'to improve the hour'. The perception of the passing of time is an "immediate given experience" in terms of phenomenological ratings (Bech 1975) and is a private, individual experience within the field of quality of life.

The General Health Questionnaire (GHQ; Goldberg 1972) was constructed on the basis of the Cornell Medical Index and with reference to the subjective adjustment scale developed by Veroff et al. (1962). The GHQ contains a total of 60 items of which a subscale of 11 has been selected for the dimensional approach to quality of life (Bech 1990a). An additional item is included to cover the aspect of time experience. The GHQ/QL-12 (see below) should be considered as a scale with a reasonable item distribution across the quality-of-life components. This has been confirmed by a preliminary Rasch analysis and in a study showing a Loevinger coefficient of 0.52 (Loldrup et al. 1991). Of the 12 items fives are symptoms measuring physical (item 16), cognitive (items 7, 36) and social (items 21, 23) aspects that can be considered in some situations to be indicators of disability rather than quality of life. The remaining seven items describe more precisely the level of demoralization or health-related quality of life when covering the physical (item 1), affective (items 31, 54), social (items 28, 30, 42) and ego function (item 36) aspects of the PCASE features. In other words the GHQ/12-QL covers both disability (alpha) and pure quality-of-life items (beta; see Table 9.2). The application of GHQ in chronic disorders has raised problems in some studies because the item definition refers to 'as usual'. Is the 'as usual' the situation before illness, a year ago, a month ago? To solve this problem several suggestions have been made. Thus, when measuring quality of life in patients with long-term astma disorders Hyland et al. (1991) found it most appropriate to use items defined in degrees of probability (definitely applies, applies, does not apply, definitely does not apply). When accepting that quality of life measurements are temporal quantifiers, items should be defined by adverbs such as 'mostly', 'often', 'seldom', 'never'. The twelve GHQ items with high content validity have in the following been listed (numbering of items is that of the original GHQ) with the three alternatives of quantifiers ('original', 'probability', 'frequency').

Have you recently:

1. Been feeling perfectly well and in good health?
   Better than usual/definitely applies/mostly
   Same as usual/applies/often
   Worse than usual/does not apply/seldom
   Much worse than usual/definitely does not apply/never
7. Been able to concentrate on whatever you're doing?
   Better than usual/definitely applies/mostly
   Same as usual/applies/often
   Less than usual/does not apply/seldom
   Much less than usual/definitely does not apply/never
16. Been feeling full of energy?
    Better than usual/definitely applies/mostly
    Same as usual/applies/often
    Less energy than usual/does not apply/seldom
    Much less than usual/definitely does not apply/never
21. Been managing to keep yourself busy and occupied?
    More so than usual/definitely applies/mostly
    Same as usual/applies/often
    Rather less than usual/does not apply/seldom
    Much less than usual/definitely does not apply/never
23. Tended to lose interest in your ordinary activities
    Not at all/definitely does not apply/never
    No more than usual/does not apply/seldom
    Rather more than usual/applies/often
    Much more than usual/definitely applies/mostly
28. Felt on the whole you were doing things well?
    Better than usual/definitely applies/mostly
    About the same/applies/often
    Less well than usual/does not apply/seldom
    Much less well/definitely does not apply/never
30. Been satisfied with the way you've carried out your task?
    More satisfied than usual/definitely applies/mostly
    About the same as usual/applies/often
    Less satisfied than usual/does not apply/seldom
    Much less satisfied/definitely does not apply/never
31. Been able to feel warmth and affection for those near to you?
    Better than usual/definitely applies/mostly
    About same as usual/applies/often

Less well than usual/does not apply/seldom
Much less well/definitely does not apply/never
35. Felt that you are playing a useful part in things?
More so than usual/definitely applies/mostly
Same as usual/applies/often
Less useful than usual/does not apply/seldom
Much less useful/definitely does not apply/never
36. Felt capable of making decisions about things?
More so than usual/definitely applies/mostly
Same as usual/applies/often
Less so than usual/does not apply/seldom
Much less capable/definitely does not apply/never
42. Been able to enjoy your normal day-today activities?
More so than usual/definitely applies/mostly
Same as usual/applies/often
Less so than usual/does not apply/seldom
Much less than usual/definitely does not apply/never
54. Been feeling reasonably happy, all things considered?
More so than usual/definitely applies/mostly
About the same as usual/applies/often
Less so than usual/does not apply/seldom
Much less than usual/definitely does not apply/never

The Hopkins Symptom Checklist (SCL) was originally designed as a discomfort scale (Parloff et al. 1954; Guy 1976; Bech 1987). In a previous study 17 items were selected to measure quality of life (Bech et al. 1992). These items were not found to fulfil the Rasch model when tested across several different cultures. However, the subscale of items 1, 6, 8, 14, 15, 17 does fulfil the Rasch model (Bech et al. 1992). As seen in Table 9.3, the distribution of the SCL/QL-17 places the most weight on emotional and interpersonal sensitivity. Scoring is as follows: 0, not at all; 1, a little bit; 2, moderately; 3, quite a bit; 4, extremely. (Original SCL item numbers are inserted in parentheses.)

1. Blaming yourself for things (26)
2. Feeling critical of others (6)
3. Your feelings being easily hurt (34)
4. Feeling irritable (11)
5. Feeling hopeless about future (54)
6. Feeling blue (30)
7. Feeling lonely (29)
8. Temper outburst (24)
9. Thoughts ending your life (15)
10. Trouble remembering things (9)
11. Having to do things very slowly (38)
12. Difficulty making decisions (46)
13. Trouble concentrating (55)
14. Your mind going blank (51)

15. Sexual interest (5)
16. Trouble falling asleep (44)
17. Feeling low in energy (14)

It is recommended to use the SCL/QL-17 with temporal quantifiers (e.g. 0 = never; 1 = seldom; 2 = often; 3 = mostly; 4 = always), because this way of asking questions does not imply a persistent, psychopathological state, but rather a fluctuating emotion. The same approach has been adopted by the Health Status Questionnaire (SF-36) by Stewart et al. (1988); see Sect. 9.2.

The Psychological General Well-Being Schedule (Monk 1980; Dupuy 1984) is included here because this scale was used in the so far most influential publication of health-related quality of life (Croog et al. 1986). It has, however, a heterogenous item distribution across the various quality-of-life components (Table 9.3). On the other hand, among the various scales or tests included in the study by Croog et al. (1986) the Psychological General Well-Being Schedule is the most relevant quality of life scale and had a better differentiation between treatments than subscales of the Hopkins SCL. (Scores in parentheses.)

1. How have you been feeling in general (during the past month)?
   In excellent spirits (5)
   In very good spirits (4)
   In good spirits mostly (3)
   I have been up and down in spirits a lot (2)
   In low spirits mostly (1)
   In very low spirits (0)

2. How often were you bothered by any illness, bodily disorder, aches or pains (during the past month)?
   Every day (0)
   Almost every day (1)
   About half the time (2)
   Now and then, but less than half the time (3)
   Rarely (4)
   None of the time (5)

3. Did you feel depressed (during the past month)?
   Yes – to the point that I felt like taking my life (0)
   Yes – to the point that I did not care about anything (1)
   Yes – very depressed almost every day (2)
   Yes – quite depressed several times (3)
   Yes – a little depressed now and then (4)
   No – never felt depressed at all (5)

4. Have you been in firm control of your behaviour, thoughts, emotions, or feelings (during the past month)?
   Yes, definitely so (5)
   Yes, for the most part (4)
   Generally so (3)
   Not too well (2)

No, and I am somewhat disturbed (1)
No, and I am very disturbed (0)

5. Have you been bothered by nervousness or your 'nerves' (during the past month)?
   Extremely so – to the point where I could not work or take care of things (0)
   Very much so (1)
   Quite a bit (2)
   Some – enough to bother me (3)
   A little (4)
   Not at all (5)

6. How much energy, pep, or vitality did you have or feel (during the past month)?
   Very full of energy – lots of pep (5)
   Fairly energetic most of the time (4)
   My energy level varied quite a bit (3)
   Generally low in energy or pep (2)
   Very low in energy or pep most of the time (1)
   No energy or pep at all – I felt drained, sapped (0)

7. I felt downhearted and blue during the past month.
   None of the time (5)
   A little of the time (4)
   Some of the time (3)
   A good bit of the time (2)
   Most of the time (1)
   All of the time (0)

8. Were you generally tense or did you feel any tension (during the past month)?
   Yes – extremely tense, most or all of the time (0)
   Yes – very tense most of the time (1)
   Not generally tense, but did feel fairly tense several times (2)
   I felt a little tense a few times (3)
   My general tension level was quite low (4)
   I never felt tense or any tension at all (5)

9. How happy, satisfied, or pleased have you been with your personal life (during the past month)?
   Extremely happy – could not have been more satisfied or pleased (5)
   Very happy most of the time (4)
   Generally satisfied – pleased (3)
   Sometimes fairly happy, sometimes fairly unhappy (2)
   Generally dissatisfied, unhappy (1)
   Very dissatisfied or unhappy most or all of the time (0)

10. Did you feel healthy enough to carry out the things you like to do or had to do (during the past month)?
    Yes – definitely so (5)
    For the most part (4)
    Health problems limited me in some important ways (3)

I was only healthy enough to take care of myself (2)

I needed some help in taking care of myself (1)

I needed someone to help me with most or all of the things I had to do (0)

11. Have you felt so sad, discouraged, hopeless, or had so many problems that you wondered if anything was worthwhile (during the past month)?

Extremely so – to the point that I have just about given up (0)

Very much so (1)

Quite a bit (2)

Some – enough to bother me (3)

A little bit (4)

Not at all (5)

12. I woke feeling fresh and rested during the past month.

None of the time (0)

A little of the time (1)

Some of the time (2)

A good bit of the time (3)

Most of the time (4)

All of the time (5)

13. Have you been concerned, worried, or had any fears about your health (during the past month)?

Extremely so (0)

Very much so (1)

Quite a bit (2)

Some, but not a lot (3)

Practically never (4)

Not at all (5)

14. Have you had any reason to wonder if you were losing your mind, or losing control over the way you act, talk, think, feel or of your memory (during the past month)?

Not at all (5)

Only a little (4)

Some – but not enough to be concerned or worried about (3)

Some and I have been a little concerned (2)

Some and I am quite concerned (1)

Yes, very much so and I am very concerned (0)

15. My daily life was full of things that were interesting to me during the past month.

None of the time (0)

A little of the time (1)

Some of the time (2)

A good bit of the time (3)

Most of the time (4)

All of the time (5)

16. Did you feel active vigorous, or dull, sluggish (during the past month)?

Very active, vigorous every day (5)

Mostly active, vigorous – never really dull, sluggish (4)
Fairly active, vigorous – seldom dull, sluggish (3)
Fairly dull, sluggish – seldom active, vigorous (2)
Mostly dull, sluggish – never really active, vigorous (1)
Very dull, sluggish every day (0)

17. Have you been anxious, worried, or upset (during the past month)?
Extremely so – to the point of being sick or almost sick (0)
Very much so (1)
Quite a bit (2)
Some – enough to bother me (3)
A little bit (4)
Not at all (5)

18. I was emotionally stable and sure of myself during the past month.
None of the time (0)
A little of the time (1)
Some of the time (2)
A good bit of the time (3)
Most of the time (4)
All of the time (5)

19. Did you feel relaxed, at ease, or high strung, tight, or keyed-up (during the past month)?
Felt relaxed and at ease the whole month (5)
Felt relaxed and at ease most of the time (4)
Generally felt relaxed but at times felt fairly high strung (3)
Generally felt high strung but at times felt fairly relaxed (2)
Felt high strung, tight and keyed-up most of the time (1)
Felt high strung, tight, or keyed-up the whole month (0)

20. I felt cheerful, lighthearted during the past month.
None of the time (0)
A little of the time (1)
Some of the time (2)
A good bit of the time (3)
Most of the time (4)
All of the time (5)

21. I felt tired, worn out, used up, or exhausted during the past month.
None of the time (5)
A little of the time (4)
Some of the time (3)
A good bit of the time (2)
Most of the time (1)
All of the time (0)

22. Have you been under or felt you were under any strain, stress, or pressure (during the past month)?
Yes – almost more than I could bear or stand (0)
Yes – quite a bit of pressure (1)

Yes some – more than usual (2)
Yes some – but about usual (3)
Yes – a little (4)
Not at all (5)

The item definitions of the Psychological General Well-Being Schedule are, thus, individualized so that some items have quantifiers of intensity, others have temporal quantifiers.

To correlate the scale with the experience of time dimension an extra item has been added (Bech 1991): 23. Have you during the past month felt time passed on slowly? Not at all (5); Yes, but very rarely (4); Yes, but rarely (3); Yes, often (2); Yes, very often (1); Yes, constantly so (0).

The Psychological General Well-being Schedule has been validated both by comparing the total score with scales like the Beck Depression Inventory, the Zung Depression Scale and the Hopkins SCL-90. The correlation coefficients have been around 0.70 (Dupuy 1984). The homogeneity of the scale in terms of coeffecient alpha has been evaluated in many studies and the values have been around 0.90 (Dupuy 1984). However, the following subscales are recommended by Dupuy: Anxiety subscale (items 5, 8, 17, 19, 22); Depression subscale (items 3, 7, 11); Positive well-being (items 1, 9, 15, 20); Self-control (items 4, 14, 18); General health (items 2, 10, 13); and Vitality (items 6, 12, 16, 21). Using the alpha/beta distinction introduced in the compendium, where alpha items measure performance or symptoms, and beta items measure subjective satisfaction or colouring of thoughts, the Psychological General Well-Being Schedule have the following alpha items: 2, 3, 5, 6, 7, 8, 11, 17, 19, and 21. Consequently, the beta items are: 1, 4, 9, 10, 12, 13, 14, 15, 16, 18, 20, and 22.

The Nottingham Health Profile consists of a part 1 with 38 items and a part 2 with 7 items. Part 1 is the most relevant quality-of-life scale from a psychometric point of view, but, as shown in Table 9.3, approximately half of the items measure clinical disability. It should be emphasized that this scale is not a Likert scale.

The Psychiatric Epidemiology Research Interview (PERI) was developed with reference to Frank's concept of demoralization (Dohrenwend et al. 1981) in the same way as SCL-17 (Frank 1974; Parloff et al. 1954). From a total sample of 27 items a modified version is presented below that includes 17 items, the Demoralization Scale-17. As can be seen in Table 9.3 this scale has an item distribution (content validity) very similar to that of the GHQ-12. Because the Demoralization Scale was developed as an epidemiological research instrument, in reference to time frame it asks: "Since what date, how often have you...?" Only a self-report version of the Demoralization subscale is relevant in the area of quality of life assessments.

1. How often have you felt confident?
    0, very often
    1, fairly often
    2, sometimes
    3, almost never
    4, never

2. How often have your felt useless?
   4, very often
   3, fairly often
   2, sometimes
   1, almost never
   0, never
3. Think of a person who feels that he/she is a failure generally in life. Is this person
   4, very much like you
   3, much life you
   2, somewhat like you
   1, very little like you
   0, not at all like you?
4. Think of a person who feels he/she has much to be proud of. Is this person
   0, very much like you
   2, much like you
   3, somewhat like you
   4, very little like you
   5, not at all like you?
5. In general, if you had to compare yourself with the average (man/woman) your age, what grade would you give yourself?
   0, excellent
   1, good
   2, average
   3, below average
   4, a lot below average
6. In general, how satisfied are you with yourself?
   0, very satisfied
   1, somewhat satisfied
   2, neither satisfied or dissatisfied
   3, somewhat dissatisfied
   4, very dissatisfied
7. How often have you had times when you could'nt help wondering if any thing was worthwhile any more?
   4, very often
   3, fairly often
   2, sometimes
   1, almost never
   0, never
8. How often have you felt that nothing turns out for you the way you want it to, would you say
   4, very often
   3, fairly often
   2, sometimes

1, almost never

0, never?

9. How often have you felt completely helpless?

   4, very often

   3, fairly often

   2, sometimes

   1, almost never

   0, never

10. How often have you felt completely hopeless about everything, would you say

   4, very often

   3, fairly often

   2, sometimes

   1, almost never

   0, never?

11. How often have you feared going crazy; loosing your mind?

   4, very often

   3, fairly often

   2, sometimes

   1, almost never

   0, never

12. How often have you had attacks of sudden fear or panic?

   4, very often

   3, often

   2, sometimes

   1, almost never

   0, never

13. How often have you feared something terrible would happen to you?

   4, very often

   3, fairly often

   2, sometimes

   1, almost never

   0, never

14. How often have you had trouble concentrating or keeping your mind on what you were doing?

   4, very often

   3, fairly often

   2, sometimes

   1, almost never

   0, never

15. How often have you felt lonely?

   4, very often

   3, fairly often

   2, sometimes

   1, almost never

   0, never

16. How often have you feared being left alone or abandoned?
    4, very often
    3, fairly often
    2, sometimes
    1, almost never
    0, never
17. How often have you felt you were bothered by all different kinds of ailments
    in different parts of your body?
    4, very often
    3, fairly often
    2, sometimes
    1, almost never
    0, never

The total score of this scale is considered as a measure of demoralisation. Using the alpha/beta dichotomy, the first eleven items (1–11) are beta items, the remaining six (12–17) alpha items.

However, health authorities remain in the position of considering the dimension of health-related quality of life as a relevant indicator of improvement, but lacking as yet a scale with sufficient construct validity (e.g. Johnson 1990; Shoemaker et al. 1990). Only a scale with sufficient construct validity can confirm a genuine change during treatment, as emphasized by Shoemaker et al. (1990). Although the Index Medicus, the *New England Journal of Medicine*, and WHO have accepted the dimension of quality of life in medicine as an outcome criterion of treatment, the United States Food and Drug Administration (FDA; Shoemaker et al. 1990) has still found no evidence of its construct validity. Thus, Shoemaker et al. (1990) have called for scales fulfilling the following criteria if they are to be considered for measuring quality of life in trials with a pharmaceutical product:
−   The scale should be linear over the range of measurement (unidimensional, which in the terms of this compendium means a Likert rating scale).
−   The scale should be sensitive to change, and the change should have clinical meaning (Likert rating scale with discriminant validity).
−   The scale should measure the same thing in different patients within the indication of the product (Likert scale with transferability).
−   The scale should measure a dimension different from scales for severity of illness and different from side-effects of the pharmaceutical product (e.g. divergent validity when compared to disability scales).

These criteria are very relevant to the principle of rating scales in this compendium. They are modern psychometric criteria. Of the self-rating scales included in this compendium for measurement of health-related quality of life the GHQ/QL-12 and the SCL/QL-17 have so far been most validated. However, the Psychological General Well-Being Scale and the modified Dohrenwend Demoralization Scale should be considered as alternative measures of the relevant components of quality of life. Many studies are in progress to find alternative measures to the Likert rating scale approach (Bech, 1991). However, this topic is beyond the scope of this compendium.

The dimension closest to that of quality of life in relation to the clinical evaluation of pharmaceutical products consists of side effects components. This dimension is discussed in Chapter 10. In other words, convergent validity between quality-of-life scales and side-effect scales might be expected.

Among non-rating scale approaches to health-related quality of life, decision theory as advocated by Kaplan (1985) and Kaplan and Anderson (1990) is the most impressive. The components of this health-related decision model include the following steps:
– Function status (morbidity, physical activity, social activity)
– Adjustment to symptoms and problems
– Preference weights for the quality of well-being
– Healthy life expectancy
– Cost-effectiveness ratio

This approach constitues a general health policy model expressing the benefits of medical care, behavioural intervention or preventive programmes in terms of healthy years. This model integrates mortality and morbidity in health status terms of equivalents of healthy years of life. Others have chosen to describe outcome as Quality-Adjusted Life-Years (QALY; e.g. Weinstein and Stason 1976). It is, however, beyond the scope of this compendium to analyse the decision theory models, which apparently have no psychometric structure. It should only be recalled in this context that 'improvement' and 'time awareness' refer to an increase of quality of time as discussed earlier in this section.

The components of health-related quality-of-life scales are not only similar to health status components (however measured at different levels as indicated in Table 9.2) but are also analogous in being essential aspects of the concept of clinical improvement during treatment (see Chapter 2). This aspect of quality of life scales has been discussed in detail elsewhere (Bech 1990b). Hence, quality of life should be considered in a dialectic perspective. On the one hand, it is a dimension or construct and the scales measuring it should fulfil the FDA criteria as outlined above. On the other hand, quality of life is also a global approach to treatment emphasizing the fact that various features are intercorrelated. The use of quality-of-life scales has, inter alia, resulted in a better understanding of that which health status scales measure – again, an important consequence of a dialectic process. The principles of rating by Likert scales illustrate this process: items excluded from one dimension can give important information of other, related dimensions. Finally, the problem of item quantifiers (intensity versus frequency) has been discussed and has been illustrated for the GHQ-12. For a further discussion of the semantics of temporal quantifiers see Michon and Jackson (1985).

Among the rating scales included in this section the Psychological General Well-Being Schedule is recommended. A psychometric description of this scale is shown in Table 9.4.

Table 9.4. Psychometric description of Psychological General Well-Being Scale (PGWB)

Type	Quality of life scale.
Content validity	Covers the PCASEE components of quality of life. The alpha vs. beta situations (see Table 9.2) is balanced.
Administration	A self-rating scale.
Time frame	The original scale recommends one month, but shorter periods can be used.
Item selection	From studies in the normal population. It is therefore not a disease-specific scale, but a generic scale.
Item calibration	Likert definitions, 0-5. Notice that 5 equals well and 0 equals very poorly.
Number of items	Twenty-two.
Construct validity	Cronbach's alpha around 0.90 (Dupuy 1984).
Discriminant validity	Appropriate (Croog et al. 1986).
Concurrent validity	Acceptable (e.g. with SCL-90, Dupuy 1984).
Comments	The scale can be used both as an index of quality of life (total score of the 22 items) and as a profile (subscores). Further studies in this field are needed.

9.2 Health Status and Quality of Life Questionnaire

An application of methods tapping the aspects dealt with in Chapter 8 and 9 for monitoring the results of medical care in a rather simple way has been published by Stewart et al. (1988), by Tarlov et al. (1989) and by Wells et al. (1989). This method is referred to as the Health Status Questionnaire (SF-36), modified here to a Health Status and Quality-of-Life Questionnaire (HSQL). By doing this the various aspects of measuring medical care are considered. However, for the use of the original SF-36 the readers are recommended to consult Stewart and Ware (1992).

The Health Status Questionnaire is a health status instrument in the sense that it is a measure of an individual's functioning in terms of physical, social and mental disability (Chapter 8). The additional items in the HSQL underline two aspects of the concept of quality of life: (a) The level of well-being and satisfaction associated with an individual's life and how this is affected by disease, accidents and treatments evaluated by the questionnaire method; and (b) the hollistic approach inherent in quality of life taking health status, life events and side effects into account. The HSQL therefore contains an axis of life events and an axis of side effects. Furthermore, the items for daily activities have been modified to fulfil the hierarchical structure described in Chapter 8. Finally, the items concerning components of quality of life have been extended to cover the essential Hopkins items described in Section 9.1.

1. In general, would you say your health is?:
   Excellent
   Very good
   Good
   Fair
   Poor
2. Compared to one year ago, how would you rate your health in general now?
   Much better than 1 year ago
   Somewhat better than 1 year ago
   Somewhat worse now than 1 year ago
   Much worse now than 1 year ago
3. The following questions are about activities you might do during a typical day. Does your health now limit you in these activities? If so, how much? (Possible answers are: Yes, limited a lot; Yes, limited a little; No, not limited at all)
   a When eating
   b Using the toilet
   c When dressing
   d When bathing
   e Getting outside
   f Walking more than a mile
   g Moderate activities, such as moving a table, bowling, playing golf, etc.
   h Vigorous activities, such as running, lifting heavy objects, participating in sports?

4. During the past 4 weeks, have you had any of the following problems with your work or other regular daily activities as a *result of your physical health*? (Answer 'yes' or 'no')

a Cut down the amount of time you spent on work or other activities

b Accomplished less than you would like

c Were limited in the kind of work or other activities

d Had difficulty performing the work or other activities (e.g. it took extra effort)

5. During the past 4 weeks, have you had any of the following problems with your work or other regular daily activities as a *result of any emotional problems* (such as feeling depressed or anxious)? (Answer 'yes' or 'no')

a Cut down the amount of time you spent on work or other activities

b Accomplished less than you like

c Didn't do work or other activities as carefully as usual

6. During the past 4 weeks, to what extent has your physical health or emotional problems interfered with your normal social activities with family, friends, neighbours or groups?

Not at all

Slightly

Moderately

Quite a bit

Extremely

7. How much bodily pain have you had during the past 4 weeks?

None

Very mild

Mild

Moderate

Severe

Very severe

8. During the past 4 weeks how much did pain interfere with your normal work (including both work outside the home and housework)?

A little bit

Moderately

Quite

Extremely

9. These questions are about how you feel and how things have been with you during the past 4 weeks. For each question please give the one answer that comes closest to the way you have been feeling. How much of the time during the past 4 weeks (possible answers are: all of the time, most of the time, a good part of the time, some of the time, a little of the time and none of the time):

a Did you feel full of pep?

b Have you been a very nervous person?

c Have you felt so down in the dumps nothing could cheer you up?

d Have you felt calm and peaceful?

    e Did you have a lot of energy?

    f Have you felt downhearted and blue?

    g Did you feel worn out?

    h Have you been a happy person?

    i Did you feel tired?

    j Have you lost sexual interest?

    k Did you feel annoyed?

    l Did you blame yourself for things?

    m Have you been feeling lonely?

    n Have you been feeling easily hurt?

    o Did you have difficulty making decisions?

    p Have you been hopeless about future?

    q Did you have trouble falling or staying asleep?

10. During the past 4 weeks, how much of the time has your physical health or emotional problems interfered with your social activities (like visiting with friends, relatives, etc)?

    All of the time

    Most of the time

    Some of the time

    A little of the time

    None of the time

11. Please choose the answer that best describes how true or false each of the following statements is for you? (Possible answers are: definitely true, mostly true, not sure, mostly false, definitely false)

    a I seem to get sick a little easier than other people

    b I am as healthy as anybody I know

    c I expect my health to get worse

    d My health is excellent

12. During the past 4 weeks have you received any treatment? (Answer 'yes' or 'no')

    If yes, please specify:

13. During the past 4 weeks have you been troubled by side effects of the treatment as the following? (Answer 'yes' or 'no')

    a Headache

    b Sweating

    c Sleepy

    d Decreased appetite or weight loss

    e Increased appetite or weight gain

    f Other, please specify:

14. During the past 4 weeks, have you experienced stressful life events as the following? (Answer 'yes' or 'no')

    a Family arguments; job dissatisfaction

    b New career; death of close friend/relative

    c Marital separation; loss of job; retirement

    d Divorce; death of close friend/relative; unemployment

    e Death of spouse; victim of rape
    f Other, please specify:
15. Have you ever filled out this form before?
    Yes
    No
    Don't remember

The modification of the Health Status Questionnaire (SF-36) used in this compendium concerns item 3 (where the subscale in the modified version fulfills the
Guttman criteria for a perfect scale, i.e. the total score is a sufficient statistic) and
item 9 (where the first nine items (a–i) are the original items, and the remaining
items are new, derived from the SCL-90 subscale for quality of life). This modified SF-36 can, if the SCL-90 also has been used, give information of the consistency of the patient's report. Thus, the following items of SCL-90 and SF-36 are
duplicates: SF-36 item f = SCL-90 item 30; i = 14; j = 5; k = 11; l = 26; m = 29;
n = 34; o = 46; p = 54; q = 44.

The rating scale method takes a simultaneous account of the whole PCASEE
repertoire. The self-rating scales included in this compendium might, however, be
limited the fact that they have been standardized upon groups of patients who, obviously, are not those currently being studied. The individual, idiographic aspect
of quality of life might be overseen by the group-orientated self-rating standardi-
zations.

Among methods used in cognitive psychology is the Repertory Grid Technique
(Bech 1990b) which recently has been used by Thunedborg et al. (1991) to
measure individual quality of life in patients with anxiety disorders. The Repertory Grid was here adjusted to the PCASEE model.

Attempts have recently been made to develop a computer system to evaluate
the PCASEE model by the Repertory Grid Technique (van Dam et al. 1991). It is
outside the scope of this compendium to discuss this interesting approach further,
but in Table 9.5 is shown a self-rating scale version that illustrates the Stoker approach to some extent (Bech et al. 1993).

In Table 9.6 is shown the PCASEE model for the illustration of selected items
can be measured by quantifiers that covers the different levels of impairment
(diagnosis), disability (severity of symptoms), and quality of life (emotions and
demoralization).

In a recent review Schumacher et al. (1991) collected 127 articles on quality of
life from the following journals: Cancer, Journal of Clinical Oncology, American
Heart Journal, American Journal of Cardiology, Circulation, and British Heart
Journal. They found that within oncology and cardiology disability scales were
wrongly called quality of life scales in 47% and 36% respectively. A multidimensional PCASEE approach of quality of life was used in 36% and 27% respectively. A one-dimensional well-being index was used in 18% and 36% respectively.
Compared to the first comparative study by Joyce (1987) where, as previously
mentioned 84% of the scales measured disability, the development is promizing.

In an overview of meta-analyses of clinical trials that agree and disagree
Chalmers et al. (1987) found three on antidepressants versus placebo where the

Table 9.5. Patients's PCASEE evaluation (questionnaire version)

Below is a list of problems or complaints that people sometimes have. They are arranged so that there are five statements in each group. Please read each statement carefully. After you have done so, please fill in one of the boxes to the right that best describes how much that problem has bothered or distressed you during the past weeks including today.

group P		group C		group A	
physical problems		cognitive problems		affective problems	
I sleep	☐ badly ☐ ☐ ☐ ☐ well	I concen-trate	☐ badly ☐ ☐ ☐ ☐ well	I am anxious	☐ severely ☐ ☐ ☐ ☐ no
I feel physically	☐ unwell ☐ ☐ ☐ ☐ well	My memory is	☐ poor ☐ ☐ ☐ ☐ good	I want to get away from it all	☐ definitely ☐ ☐ ☐ ☐ no
My appetite is	☐ poor ☐ ☐ ☐ ☐ good	I am able to make decisions	☐ poorly ☐ ☐ ☐ ☐ well	I feel comfortable with myself	☐ no ☐ ☐ ☐ ☐ definitely
I experience physical pain	☐ severe ☐ ☐ ☐ ☐ no	I feel in control of life	☐ badly ☐ ☐ ☐ ☐ well	I am sad	☐ severely ☐ ☐ ☐ ☐ no
My energy is	☐ lacking ☐ ☐ ☐ ☐ full	My thinking is	☐ unclear ☐ ☐ ☐ ☐ clear	I am irritable	☐ severely ☐ ☐ ☐ ☐ no

Table 9.5 (cont.)

group S		group E		group E	
social	dysfunction	economical	problems	ego	problems
For my work I get	☐ no appre- ☐ ciation ☐ ☐ much ☐ appre- ☐ ciation	I am worried about my money	☐ definitely ☐ ☐ ☐ ☐ no	My self-confidence is	☐ poor ☐ ☐ ☐ ☐ good
I am doing household	☐ poorly ☐ ☐ ☐ ☐ well	I am able to make ends meet	☐ poorly ☐ ☐ ☐ ☐ well	I feel sexually	☐ unattrac- ☐ tive ☐ ☐ attrac- ☐ tive
I perform my work	☐ poorly ☐ ☐ ☐ ☐ well	I am able to buy what I want	☐ no ☐ ☐ ☐ ☐ definitely	My feelings are hurt	☐ too easily ☐ ☐ ☐ ☐ adequately
My interest in leisure activities is	☐ poor ☐ ☐ ☐ ☐ well	I am able to buy what I need	☐ definitely ☐ ☐ ☐ ☐ no	I can forgive myself	☐ poorly ☐ ☐ ☐ ☐ well
My social life is	☐ poor ☐ ☐ ☐ ☐ well	I need financial assistance	☐ definitely ☐ ☐ ☐ ☐ no	What I want from life is	☐ unclear ☐ ☐ ☐ ☐ clear

agreement concerned 'statistical evidence' while the disagreement concerned 'clinical evidence'. Thus, is a 19% superiority of tricyclic antidepressants over placebo in improvement after four weeks of treatment of clinical significance? The impact of health-related quality of life in clinical trials is to ask the patients whether the improvement is of significance for them. In his Talks to Teachers on what makes a life significant James (1899) concluded: "...The thing of deepest – or, at any rate, of comparatively deepest – significance in life does seem to be its character of progress...". Health-related quality of life refers to improvement during treatment.

Table 9.6. The PCASEE approach for measuring the different levels (diagnosis, disability, and quality of life)

Quantifiers of items	P (physical)	C (cognitive)	A (affective)	S (social)	E (economical)	E (ego strength)
Diagnosis (duration)	How long have you experienced insomnia?	How long have you had concentration problems?	How long have you been depressed?	How long have you had social dysfunction?	How long have you had economic problems?	How long have you had lowered self-confidence?
Clinical disability (intensity)	My insomnia is ☐ marked ☐ mild	My concentration problems are ☐ marked ☐ mild	My depression is ☐ marked ☐ mild	My social dysfunction is ☐ marked ☐ mild	My economic problems are ☐ marked ☐ mild	My self-confidence problem is ☐ marked ☐ mild
Quality of life (a) (frequency)	I have insomnia ☐ mostly ☐ seldom	I have concent-ration problems ☐ mostly ☐ seldom	I am depressed ☐ mostly ☐ seldom	I am socially disturbed ☐ mostly ☐ seldom	I have economic problems ☐ mostly ☐ seldom	I have self-confi-dence problems ☐ mostly ☐ seldom
Quality of life (b) (demoralization)	I sleep ☐ badly ☐ well	I concentrate ☐ poorly ☐ well	I feel comfortable with myself ☐ poorly ☐ well	I perform socially ☐ bad ☐ well	I am able to make ends meet ☐ poorly ☐ well	My self-confidence is ☐ poor ☐ good

References

Barrabee P, Barrabee EL, Finesinger JE. A normative social adjustment scale. Am J Psychiat 1955; 112: 252–259.

Bech P. Depression: Influence on time estimation and time experience. Acta Psychiatr Scand 1975; 51: 42–50.

Bech P. Quality of life in psychosomatic research, Psychopathol 1987; 20: 169–179.

Bech P. Methodological problems in assessing quality of life as outcome in psychopharmacology. A multi-axial approach. In: Benkert O, Maier W, Rickels K (eds). Methodology and Evaluation of Psychotropic Drugs. Heidelberg: Springer 1990a.

Bech P. Measurement of psychological distress and well-being. Psychother Psychosom 1990b, 54: 77–89.

Bech P. Changing definitions of quality of life. 1991 (in preparation).

Bech P. Measuring quality of life in the medical setting. Int J Psychiat Res Methods 1992 (in press).

Bech P, Hjortsø S. Problems in measuring quality of life in schizophrenia. Nord Psychiatr Tidsskr 1990.

Bech P, Allerup P, Maier W, Albus M, Lavori P, Ayuso JL. The Hamilton Scales and the Hopkins Symptom Checklist (SCL-90): A cross-national validity study in patients with panic disorders. Br J Psychiat 1992; 160: 206–211.

Bech P, Dunbar GC, Stoker MJ. Developing an instrument to measure the changes in Psychiatric patients' quality of life. In: Jonsson B, Rosenbaum J (eds). The Health Economics of Depression. Chichester; Wiley, 1993 (in press).

Bentham J. Introduction to the principles of morals and legislation. London: Univ of London, 1789.

Bentham J. Deontology or the science of morality. London: Univ of London, 1834.

Berenbaum H, Oltmanns TF, Gottesman II. Hedonic capacity in schizophrenics and their twins. Psychol Med 1990; 20: 367–374.

Bleuler E. Dementia praecox oder Gruppe der Schizophrene. In Aschaffenburg T (ed). Handbuch der Psychiatrie. Leipzig: Deuticke 1911.

Cassileth BR, Lusk EJ, Strouse TB. Psychosocial status in chronic illness. New Engl J Med 1984; 311: 506–511.

Chalmers TC, Berrier J, Sacks HS et al. Meta-analysis of clinical trials as a scientific discipline. Replicate variability and comparison of studies that agree and disagree. Statistics in Medicine 1987; 6: 733–744.

Croog SH, Levine S, Testa M. The effects of antihypertensive therapy on the quality of life. New Engl J Med 1986; 314: 1657–1664.

Dohrenwend BP, Lerav I, Strout PE. Screening scales from the psychiatric epidemiology research interview (PERI). In: Weissman MM, Myers JK, Ross CE (eds). Community Surveys of Psychiatric Disorders. New Brunswick: Rutgers Univ Press, 1981.

Dupuy HJ. Self-representation of general psychological well-being of American adults. Paper presented at American Public Health Association Meeting. Los Angeles, California, October 17, 1978.

Dupuy HJ. The Psychological General Well-being (PGWB) Index. In: Wenger NK, Mattson ME, Furberg CD, Elinson J (eds). Assessment of Quality of Life in Clinical Trials of Cardiovascular Therapies. New York: Le Jacq Publishing, 1984, pp. 184–188.

Frank JD. Persuasion and healing. New York: Schocken, 1974.

Freud S. Collected Papers. New York: Basic Books 1959.

Galbraith J. The Affluent Society. Boston: Houghton-Mifflin, 1958.

Goldberg D. The detection of psychiatric illness by questionnaire. Oxford: Oxford Univ Press, 1972.

Greer S. The psychological dimension in cancer treatment. Soc Sci Med 1984; 4: 345–349.

Griffin J. Well-being. Its Meaning, Measurement and Moral Importance. Oxford: Clarendon Press, 1988.

Guy W. Early Clinical Drug Evaluation (ECDEU) Assessment Manual for Psychopharmacology. Rockville: Nat Inst Mental Health, 1976.

Hunt SM, McKenna SP, McEven J, Williams J, Papp E. The Nottingham Health Profile: Subjective health status and medical consultations. Soc Sci Med 1981; 15A: 221–229.

Hyland ME, Finnis S, Irvine SH. A scale for assessing quality of life in adult asthma sufferers. J Psychosom Rec 1991; 35: 99–110.

James W. Principles of Psychology. New York: Holt 1890.

James W. Talks to Teachers. New York: Holt, 1899.

Janet P. L'évolution de la mémoire et de la notion de temps. Paris: Chahine, 1928.

Johnson JR. US/FDA perspective on quality of life measurement in clinical trials with cancer drugs. Paper presented at Management Forum, London, 17 September, 1990.

Joyce CRB. Quality of life: The state of the art in clinical assessment. In: Walker SR, Rosser RM (eds). Quality of Life: Assessment and Application. Lancaster: MTR Press, 1987 pp. 169–179.

Kaplan RM. Quality of life measurement. In: Karoly P (ed). Measurement strategies in health psychology. New York: John Wiley 1985, pp. 115–146.

Kaplan RM, Anderson JP. The general health policy model: An integrated approach. In: Spilker B (ed). Quality of Life Assessments in Clinical Trials. New York: Raven Press 1990, pp. 131–149.

Kraepelin E. Psychiatrie. Leipzig: Barth 1913.

Lewis A. Health as a social concept. Brit J Sociol 1953; 4: 109–124.

Likert RA. A technique for the measurement of attitudes.
Arch Psychol 1932; 140: 1–55.

Lipowski I. Physical illness, the individual and the coping process. Int J Psychiat Med 1970; 1: 91–102.

Loldrup D, Langemark M, Hansen HJ, Bonnevie O, Elsborg L, Olesen J, Bech P. The validity of the Melancholia Scale in predicting outcome of antidepressants in chronic idiopathic pain disorders. European Psychiatry 1991; 6: 119–125.

Mann T. Der Zauberberg. Frankfurt: S. Fischer, 1924 (English edition: The Magic Mountain, London: Penguin Books, 1960).

May R. The Discovery of Being. New York: Norton, 1986.

McDowell I, Newwell C. Measuring Health. New York: Oxford Univ Press, 1987.

McGlynn EA, Ware JE. Functional status and well-being of patients with chronic conditions. Results from the medical outcomes study. JAMA, 1989,; 262: 907–913.

Meehl PE. Schizotaxia, schizotypy, schizophrenia. Am Psychol 1962; 17: 827–838.

Meehl PE. Hedonic capacity: Some conjectures. Bull Menninger Clinic 1975; 39: 295–307.

Meehl PE. Hedonic capacity ten years later: Some clarifications. In Clark DC, Fawcett J (eds). Anhedonia and Affective Deficit States. New York: Pergamon 1987 pp. 935–944.

Michalos AC. Job satisfaction, marital satisfaction and the quality of life: A review and a preview. In: Andrews FM (ed). Research on the Quality of Life. Michigan: Univ of Michigan, 1986.

Michon JA, Jackson JL (eds). Time, mind, and behaviour. Berlin: Springer, 1985.

Minkowski E. Zum Problem der erlebten Zeit. Studium Gen 1955; 2: 601–615.

Monk M. Psychological status and hypertension. Am J Epidemiology 1980; 112: 200–208.

Nowell-Smith PH. Ethics. London: Penguin Books, 1967.

O'Riordan T. Environmentalism. London: Pion, 1981.

Parloff MB, Kelman HC, Frank JD. Comfort, effectiveness and self-awareness as criteria of improvement in psychotherapy. Am J. Psychiat 1954; 111: 343–351.

Rado S. Psychoanalysis of behavior: Collected Papers. Vol 2: 1956–1961. New York: Joune and Stratton, 1962.

Sartorius N. Cross-cultural comparisons of data about quality of life: A sample of issues. In: Aaronsen NK, Beckmann J (eds). The Quality of Life in Cancer Patients. New York: Raven Press 1987 pp. 19–24.

Schumacher M, Olschewski M, Schulgen G. Assessment of quality of life in clinical trials. Statistics in Medicine 1991; 10: 1915–1930.

Seashore CE. Psychology in daily life. New York: D. Appleton, 1916.

Shoemaker D, Burke G, Dorr A, Temple R, Friedman MA. A regulatory perspective. In: Spilker R (ed). Quality of Life in Clinical Trials. New York: Raven Press, 1990, pp. 193–201.

Spielberger CD, Gorsuch RL, Lushene RE. The State-Trait Anxiety Inventory. Palo Alto, Calif.: Consulting Psychologists Press, 1970.

Sprigge TLS. The Rational Foundations of Ethics. London: Routledge and Kegan Paul, 1988.

Stewart AL, Ware JE (eds). Measuring Functioning and Well-Being. Durham and London: Duke University Press, 1992.

Stewart AL, Greenfield S, Hays RD, Wells K, Rogers WH, Berry SD, Stewart AL, Hays RD, Ware JE. The MOS short form general health survey. Med Care 1988; 26: 724–735.

Storr A. Human Aggression. London: Allen Lane Press, 1968.

Straus E. Psychologie der Menschlichen Welt. Berlin: Springer Verlag 1960.

Tarlov AR, Ware JE, Greenfield S, Nelson C, Perrin E, Zubkoff M. The medical outcomes study. An application of methods for monitoring the results of medical care. JAMA 1989; 262: 925–930.

Thunedborg K, Allerup P, Bjerrum H, Joyce CRB, Bech P. Dissimination between treatments of generalized anxiety disorder by measurement of individual and group quality of life. 1992 (in preparation).

Thurstone L. Attitudes can be measured.

van Dam FSAM, Somers R, van Beek-cousijn AL. Quality of Life: Some Theoritical Issues. J Clin Pharmacol 1991; 21: 1665–1685.

Veroff J, Fels S, Gurin G. Dimensions of subjective adjustment. J Abnorm Soc Psychol 1962; 64: 192–198.

Veroff J, Douran E, Kulka RA. The inner American. New York: Basic Books, 1981.

von Gebsattel V. Prologomena einer Medizinischen Antropologie. Berlin: Springer Verlag 1954.

Walker SR, Asscher W (eds). Medicius and risk/benefit decisions. Lancaster: MTR Press, 1986.

Watson CG, Klett WG, Lorei TW. Toward an operational definition of anhedonia. Psychol Bull 1970; 26: 371–376.

Weinstein MC, Stason WB. Hypertension: A Policy Perspective.

Cambridge, Mass.: Harvard Univ Press, 1976.

Wells KB, Stewart A, Hays RD et al. The functioning and well-being of depressed patients. Results from the medical outcomes study. JAMA 1989; 262: 914–919.

Wood PHN. The international classification of impairments, disabilities, and handicaps of the World Health Organization. In: Leidl R, Potthoff P, Schwefel D (eds). European Approaches to Patient Classification Systems. Berlin: Springer 1990, pp. 83–101.

World Health Organization: The International Classification of Impairments, Disabilities, and Handicaps (ICIDH/WHO). Geneva: World Health Organization, 1980.

10 Rating Scales for Adverse Drug Reactions

For the various treatment modalities in psychiatry (e.g. psychotherapy or pharmacotherapy) the monitoring of adverse drug reactions has been a subject of intense interest, although scales for measuring side effects of psychopharmacological drugs have only recently been designed. On the other hand, the confession of 'non-existent' life events as a rational part of some types of psychoanalytical therapy has only very rarely been studied in terms of side effects of treatment, although Janet (1923) early observed problems in treating depressed patients with confessional psychoanalysis, a method Frank (1984) has compared to 'brain washing'.

10.1 Pharmacological Side Effects

In the cost-effectiveness ratio of a drug the cost factor includes negative attitudes to treatment in general as well as unpleasant side effects. Health-related quality-of-life scales include emotional or cognitive items of discomfort and functional limitations brought about by chronic disorders and long-term treatments (see Chapter 9). In contrast, adverse drug reactions should be considered as purely biological phenomena. In this context it is necessary to distinguish between ontology, causation and epistemology. Ontology refers to the mode of existence of the phenomena, and it is the biological aspects of the drug which are considered in this chapter – the dose-related, pharmacological causation and not the idiosyncrasy (i.e. an uncharacteristic response of a particular patient to a drug not normally occurring on administration of this drug) or the hypersensitivity (i.e. a reaction not explained by the pharmacological effects of the drug caused by an altered reactivity of this patient and generally considered to be an allergic phenomenon). Table 10.1 differentiates between pharmacological (type A) and idiosyncratic or allergic (type B) drug reactions. It is recommended to use spontaneous reports in assessing type B reactions, while rating scales are most appropriate for assessing type A reactions. The epistemological approach concerns questions such as 'How do we find out about the various phenomena?' In this compendium it is the clinical disability manifestations of adverse drug reactions and not the laboratory indicators that are of epistemological interest – and the rating scale measurements of pharmacological side effects.

The World Health Organization (WHO) defines adverse drug reaction as any response to a drug that is noxious and unintended and that occurs at doses used in humans for prophylaxis, diagnosis or therapy (Stephens 1988). The Conduct of Clinical Trials of Medical Products (CPMP) in the European Community has adopted this definition but states that "In the case of clinical trials injuries by overdosing, abuse or dependence and interactions with other medical products should be considered as adverse drug reactions"(CPMP 1990). In this chapter it is the WHO definition that is used. Thus, intoxications after overdosing are not considered.

10.2 Psychometric Considerations

The rating scale approach is more appropriate for measuring pharmacological side effects than for measuring idiosyncratic or allergic reactions (Table 10.1). Pharmacological side effects are usually discovered before the marketing of a drug because they are common reactions requiring fewer patients than evaluations of allergic drug reactions. The content validity of a side effect rating scale depends on the stage in the developing of a drug. In the early stages a more comprehensive scale is recommended, in the later stages a Likert scale. The self-rating approach is most appropriate in measuring emotional side effects, including sexual disturbances. In this area it might be difficult to distinguish between side-effects and treatment-related quality-of-life aspects. Thus, in measuring patient compliance in long-term lithium treatment items for both positive and negative attitudes are included (Cochran and Gitlin 1988). Among the negative items are the following: being reminded of having manic-melancholic illness, having medical control mood, suffering from unpleasant side effects, having long-term negative health consequences, being bothered by medication regimens, and being unable to carry

Table 10.1. Characteristics of adverse drug reactions: type A versus type B. (Modified after Stephens 1988)

Type A side effects (rating scale method)	Type B side effects (spontaneous rapport)
Common	Rare
Usually not serious	Usually serious
Relatively low mortality	Relatively high mortality
Discovered before marketing	Discovered after marketing
Dose related (pharmacological)	Not dose related (hypersensitivity or idiosyncrasy)

normal activities due to the interference of lithium treatment. Many of these are quality-of-life items (Bech 1988).

In Chapter 4 the psychometric problems of using self-rating scales are discussed, including those of response set (acquiescence, 'yes'-sayer effects) and social undesirability ('sick set' response). As is also noted there, Carroll et al. (1973) have argued that the patients' own feelings, beliefs or emotional states are not particularly relevant for purposes of defining a disease entity or for differential diagnosis. Pharmacological side effects could be evaluated using the patient's report as an important source of information, but the treating physician should be consulted for evaluation of the cause.

The United States Food and Drug Administration (FDA 1980) defines adverse drug reaction as any experience associated with the use of a drug whether or not considered drug-related, and includes any side effect, injury, toxicity or sensitivity reaction or significant failure of expected pharmacological action. As discussed by Stephens (1988), the FDA definition could be more suitable for adverse event. CPMP (1990) defines adverse event as follows:

Any undesirable experience occurring to a subject, during a clinical trial, whether or not considered related to the investigational product. Serious adverse event means an adverse experience that is fatal, life-threating, disabling or which results in inpatient hospitalization or prolongation of hospitalization. (...) An unexpected adverse event is an experience not previously reported (severity or incidence). (...) When an adverse event has been assessed and causal relation to the investigational product established, it must be considered as an adverse drug reaction.

Attempts have been made to compare the advantages and disadvantage of methods for assessing clinical adverse events and reactions (e.g. Cocchetto and Nardi 1986). Table 10.2 summarizes features of observer scales for assessing pure pharmacological side effects. Self-rating scales may be appropriate, on the other hand, in reference to the FDA requirements of adverse events. The potential bias with the rating scale method (e.g. response set) compared to spontaneous reports can be evaluated in placebo-controlled trials. In a study comparing the two methods Drowning et al. (1970) showed that the rating scale approach but not spontaneous reporting obtained active drug – placebo differences, although the frequency of side effects on placebo was highest in the rating scale method.

In a review of 67 publications on adverse placebo (drug) reactions Pogge (1965) showed that drowsiness, headache and insomnia were the most common placebo side effects, followed by nausea and constipation. The construct validity of placebo side effects as determined by one-dimensional Likert scales is fragile, as is that of adverse reactions to psychopharmacological drugs (Lingjærde et al. 1987). The individual items of a side effect rating scale should always be considered separately.

Table 10.2. Comparison of methods for assessing adverse drug reactions

Issues and requirements	Methods		
	Self-rating scales	Observer scales	Spontaneous reports, e.g. diary cards
Quantification of items	Minor degrees	Full range	Problematic
Observable behaviours	Minimal	Well	Minimal
Circumstances	Requires patient cooperation, ability to concentrate and read	Bed-side oriented	Requires patient cooperation, ability to concentrate and read
Response set	Present	Might be present	Might be present
Cross-national reliability	Less adequate	Adequate	Problematic
Content validity	Adverse events	Pharmacological side effects	Idiosyncratic or allergic side effects

10.3 Content Validity of Side-Effect Scales
for Psychopharmacological Drugs

When Cade (1949) introduced lithium salts for the treatment of mania, he noticed side effects such as anorexia, nausea and vomiting. Schou et al. (1954) performed the first placebo-controlled trial in psychopharmacology when they evaluated the effect of lithium salts in mania. They considered nausea, diarrhoea and tremor as specific clinical indicators of intoxication.

When Delay and Deniker (1952) demonstrated the antipsychotic effect of chlorpromazine (on agitation, aggressiveness and delusive symptoms in schizophrenia), they found no major side-effects. It was Steck (1954) who demonstrated that chlorpromazine induced a syndrome resembling parkinsonism (e.g. tremor) but also a non-parkinsonian symptoms such as akathisia (inability of the patient to remain seated). Tardive dyskinesia (abnormal involutary movements associated with prolonged chlorpromazine therapy) was first shown by Hall et al. (1956) and Schonecker (1957). It was later that the induction of pigmentation in light-exposed skin by chlorpromazine was observed, which has been estimated to occur in less than 0.1% of all patients treated with chlorpromazine for 2 years or more (Ayd 1970). However, this pigmentation is an idiosyncrasic or allergic type B reaction and is consequently beyond the scope of this compendium.

In the 50's it was observed that isoniazid and iproniazid used in the treatment of tuberculosis had euphoriant properties. This effect was originally considered as a side-effect because the patients seemed to feel too good and thereby overexerted themselves, ignoring the medical safeguards their condition required. This side-effect was considered as a wanted effect in patients with primary depressive illness, and studies carried out in the mid 50's confirmed that iproniazid (a monoamine oxydase inhibitor) had antidepressive properties, especially in depressed outpatients (Kline 1970). However, iproniazid induced so many somatic side-effects that it was soon replaced by safer monoamine oxydase inhibitors like phenelzine and isocarboxazide.

When Kuhn (1957, 1958) demonstrated the antidepressive action of imipramine, he observed no major side effects. However, in a later review (1970) he reported that imipramine after its marketing in 1958 "brought a disappointment in that the side effects were manifestly more troublesome than our original studies had suggested." Kuhn noticed that the side effects (mainly neurovegetative or autonomic) were much less serious in hospitalized patients than in those who had to cope with the stresses of daily life outside hospitals. Kuhn (1970) regarded the sedative side effects as the most negative features of tricyclic antidepressants: "an ideal antidepressive agent should possess no sedative activity."

Sedation can be considered as an intended (wanted) effect of a drug in the treatment of severe psychotic states and in agitated depression. However, in long-term treatment of psychiatric patients sedation is an unintended (unwanted) side effect. Table 10.3 shows the various side effects reported during treatment with lithium, chlorpromazine (example of typical neuroleptics), clozapine (atypical

Table 10.3. Content validity of psychopharmacological side effects

	Autonomic	Neurological			Sedative	Appetite stimulation	Polyuria
		Akathisia	Tremor	Dyskinesia			
Lithium	0	0	+	0	0	+	+
Chlorpromazine	+	+	+	+	+	+	0
Imipramine	+	0	+	0	(+)	+	0
MAO inhibitors (atypical)	0	0	0	0	0	+	0
Serotonin re-uptake, inhibitors (specific)	(+)	0	(+)	0	0	0	0
Clozapine (atypical)	+	0	0	0	+	+	0
Dopamine blockers (specific), e.g. savoxamine	0	(+)	(+)	(+)	0	0	0

neuroleptics) and savoxamine (selective dopamine blocker), imipramine (typical antidepressant), isocarboxazide (typical antidepressant), and fluvoxamine or citalopram (specific serotonin re-uptake inhibitors). The relationship between intended (wanted) and unintended (unwanted) effects is complex as seen in Table 10.3. Thus, the neurological side effects of chlorpromazine seems not to be a necessary condition for the antipsychotic action. Likewise, the autonomic side effects of imipramine seem not to be essential for its antidepressive action. In long-term studies the appetite stimulation that leads to significant weight gain in many patients is the most frequent reason for non-compliance (Bech et al. 1976).

The overall evaluation of side effects should be related to the therapeutic effect of the treatment under investigation. The first attempt in psychopharmacology to develop an index score of efficacy (efficacy index) was made by Guy and Bonato (1970). The therapeutic effect was regarded as benefit and the side effects as cost. The efficacy index expressed the net profit. Specific rating scales for therapeutic effects (e.g. the Hamilton–Melancholia Scales, HDS/MES) and specific side-effect scales could be used to express the efficacy index. Guy and Bonato, however, used global ratings. In the conception of the benefit–risk relationship in Figure 10.1 the ordinate is the global improvement scale (see Sect. 1.6) and the abscissa is a global side-effect scale. According to Guy and Bonato (1970), the global improvement scale should ideally express the improvement caused exclusively by the drug. On the other hand, Guy (1976) admits that in many studies the total improvement and the improvement due to drug are one and the same. The problem of assessing side effects globally was not discussed by Guy (1976).

In the scale developed by Lingjærde et al. (1987) two different aspects of assessing global side effects are used (Appendix 10.1). A combination of these two scales (A and B in Appendix 10.1) gives a score from 0 to 4. Figure 10.1 combines these scores and uses the result as abscissa for measuring global side effects (risks). Both dimensions in Figure 10.1 are scored 0–4; however, in calculating the benefit-risk ratio the scores have been squared. In cell A the drug brings an extreme illness improvement without side effects. Drug A is therefore a breakthrough. Drug B shows an excellent clinical improvement but also extreme side effects that cause discontinuation. Drug B is therefore speculative. Drug D is a disaster. Drug C is simply poor without any clinical effect although apparently also without side effects. Figure 10.1 indicates how difficult it is to evaluate cost–benefit relationships. However, it is recommended to include both a global improvement scale for therapeutic benefit and a global side effect scale for side effects (costs) such as here. (As indicated in Appendix 10.1 the performance scale can be administered both by the patient as self-rating scale and by the physician observer rating scale.)

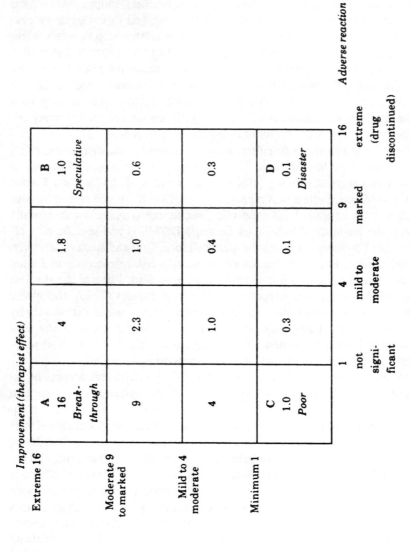

Fig. 10.1. The benefit-risk ratio in terms of clinical improvement versus pharmalogical adverse reactions

10.4 WHO Adverse Reaction Terminology

The World Health Organization (WHO) has developed an adverse reaction terminology for use in its programme for International Monotoring of Adverse Reactions to Drugs. This programme was initiated in 1968, and the latest version is that
from August 1990 (WHO 1990). The WHO terminology has been adopted by the
United States Food And Drug Administration (FDA, Gelberg et al. 1991). However, the WHO system is a terminology of classification, not a dictionary.

The organization of the WHO system includes three levels: (a) system organ
classes, (b) preferred terms and (c) included terms. System organ classes consists
of groups of preferred terms (items) pertaining to the same organ. A total of 18
organ classes are listed (Table 10.4). A preferred term can be allocated to a maximum of three different classes of system organs. Thus, the item of tremor is a preferred term (WHO code 0154). In terms of system organ classes, chlorpromazine-
induced tremor should be allocated to the central nervous system, lithium-induced
tremor to the peripheral nervous system, and imipramine-induced tremor to
unknown pathology. However, such a classification is as yet not possible according to WHO. Preferred terms are the principal terms for describing adverse reactions. Included terms are closely related to preferred terms and are used to assist in
finding the proper coding of the reverse reactions.

In principle, all side-effect scales should be translated into the WHO terminology. In this compendium the UKU side effect scale (see below) for antidepressants has been translated into the WHO system.

10.5 Comprehensive Versus Specific Scales
for Measuring Adverse Drug Reactions

In the evaluation of pharmacological side effects in the early stage of drug testing,
comprehensive scales are recommended. Among the observer scales of this type
the scale of the Udvalg for Kliniske Undersøgelser (UKU, Committee for Clinical
Investigations; Lingjærde et al. 1987) is recommended. This is presented below.
Another comprehensive side-effect scale is the somatic part of the scale of the Association for Methology and Documentation in Psychiatry (AMPD; Guy and Ban
1982; Bobon et al. 1983). The AMDP system includes comprehensive scales for
life events, psychopathology and somatic complaints. These AMDP dimensions
are recommended at the early stage of drug evaluations (Bishoff et al. 1990).

As a comprehensive self-rating scale for somatic complaints during psychopharmacological treatment in early stages of drug evaluation, the self-administered version of the Checklist for the Evaluation of Somatic Symptoms (see
Chapter 4) is recommended. The 42-item Beck Depression Inventory (see Chapter
4) should also be considered, although this scale was originally constructed for

Table 10.4. WHO system organ classes

No.	System Organ Classes
0100	Skin and appendage disorders
0200	Musculoskeletal system disorders
0300	Collagen disorders
0410	Central and peripheral nervous system disorders
0420	Autonomic nervous system disorders
0431	Vision disorders
0432	Hearing and vestibular disorders
0433	Special senses other, disorders
0500	Psychiatric disorders
0600	Gastro-intestinal system disorders
0700	Liver and biliary system disorders
0800	Metabolic and nutritional disorders
0900	Endocrine disorders
1010	Cardiovascular disorders, general
1020	Myo-, endo-, peri-cardial and valve disorder
1030	Heart rate and rhythm disorders
1040	Vascular (extracardiac) disorders
1100	Respiratory system disorders
1210	Red blood cell disorders
1220	White cell disorders
1230	Platelet, bleeding and clotting disorders
1300	Urinary system disorders
1410	Reproductive disorders, male
1420	Reproductive disorders, female
1500	Foetal disorders
1600	Neonatal and infancy disorders
1700	Neoplasm
1810	Body as a whole - general disorders
1820	Application site disorders
1830	Resistance mechanism disorders

measuring side effects of long-term treatment with lithium and cyclic antidepressants (Bech et al. 1976; Bech 1988).

In later stages of drug development specific rating scales should be used.

Udvalg for Kliniske Undersøgelser Scale (UKU scale)

Assessment of the individual symptoms is best accomplished by a goal directed interview with the patient during which the scale is completed point by point (but no necessarily in the order given in the form). The interview should be supplemented by clinical observation and information obtained from the ward staff, relatives or case records. As appears from the manual, most of the symptoms call for a 'here and now' assessment, but it is often appropriate to assess the patient's condition during the preceding 3 days. For some symptoms the basis of assessment is a longer period than 72 h, as specified in the manual (for instance changes in weight). Particularly in the case of items belonging to the group of psychic side effects there may be discrepancies between the patient's complaints and clinical signs or findings during the interview. As a general rule the clinical observations should be given precedence. It is important that the rating be independent of whether the symptom is regarded as being drug-induced.

Each item is defined by a four-point-scale (0–1–2–3). In general, degree '0' means 'not or doubtfully present' and refers to the 'normal' (the average of healthy people), not to the usual condition of the patient. Exceptions to this rule are made for some items where it is clinically more meaningful to refer to the usual condition, i.e. the condition before the patient became ill. This applies to sleep, dream activity, weight. In general 1, 2 and 3 indicate that a symptom is present to a mild, moderate or severe degree, respectively. The examples given for some items as illustrations of the scale points in question are to be regarded as guidelines and not as obligatory components of the operational definition of the items. In the global assessment of side effects an independent assessment by both the patient and the interviewer should, if possible, be carried out. The global assessment should be made on the basis of the degree to which the side effects interfere with the patient's daily performance.

The scoring sheet for the UKU scale is illustrated in Appendix 10.2. Instructions for scoring its 26 items are presented below.

1 Concentration Difficulties
Difficulties in ability to concentrate, to collect one's thoughts, or to sustain one's attention.
0. No or doubtful difficulties in concentrating.
1. The patient must try harder than usual to collect his thoughts, but not to the degree that it hampers him in his everyday life.
2. The difficulties in concentrating are pronounced enough to hamper the patient in his everyday life.
3. The patient's difficulties in concentrating are obvious to the interviewer during the interview.

2 Sedation

Diminished ability to stay awake during the day. The assessment is based on clinical signs during the interview.

0. No or doubtful sleepiness.
1. Slightly sleepy/drowsy as regards facial expression and speech.
2. More markedly sleepy/drowsy. The patient yawns and tends to fall asleep when there is a pause in the conversation.
3. Difficult to keep the patient awake and to wake the patient, respectively.

3 Failing Memory

Impaired memory. Assessment should be independent of any concentration difficulties.

0. No or doubtful disturbances of memory.
1. Slight, subjective feeling of reduced memory compared with the patient's usual condition; however, not interfering with functioning.
2. The failing memory hampers the patient or slight signs of this are observed during the interview.
3. The patient shows clear signs of failing memory during the interview.

4 Tension/Inner Unrest

Inability to relax, nervous restlessness. This item is to be assessed on the basis of the patient's experience and must be distinguished from motor akathisia.

0. No or doubtful tension/nervous restlessness.
1. The patient states that he is slightly tense and restless; however, this does not interfere with his functioning.
2. Considerable tension and inner unrest; however, without this being so intense or constant that the patient's daily life is influenced to any marked degree.
3. The patient feels tension or restlessness that is so marked that his daily life is clearly affected.

5 Increased Duration of Sleep

This should be assessed on the basis of the average of sleep over the three preceding nights. The assessment is to be made in relation to the patient's usual pre-illness state.

0. No or doubtful increase of the duration of sleep.
1. Sleeps up to 2 h longer than usual.
2. Sleeps 2–3 h longer than usual.
3. Sleeps more than 3 h longer than usual.

6 Reduced Duration of Sleep

This should be assessed on the basis of the average of sleep over the preceding 3 nights. The assessment is to be made in relation to the patient's usual pre-illness state.

0. No or doubtful reduction of the duration of sleep.
1. Sleeps up to 2 h less than usual.

2. Sleeps 2–3 h less than usual.
3. Sleeps more than 3 h less than usual.

7 Increased Dream Activity

This should be assessed independently of dream content and based on the average of sleep over the preceding 3 nights in relation to the usual pre-illness dream activity.

0. No or doubtful change in the dream activity.
1. Slightly increased dream activity but does not disturb the night's sleep.
2. More pronounced increase in dream activity.
3. Very pronounced increase in dream activity.

8 Emotional Indifference

A diminution of the patient's empathy, leading to apathy.

0. No or doubtful emotional indifference.
1. Slight subduing of the patient's empathy.
2. Obvious emotional indifference.
3. Pronounced indifference so that the patient behaves apathetically in relation to his surroundings.

9 Confusion

This deals with the degree of cloudedness of consciousness. This may be accompanied by loss of orientation, including time, place and personal data in different degrees and may be accompanied by psychotic symptoms.

0. The patient is fully orientated in time and place and personal data. The patient shows clearness of consciousness, answers relevantly and is fully orientated in time and place and personal data.
1. The patient may occasionally lack clearness of consciousness and full orientation, he may occasionally answer irrelevantly, but he is capable of correcting errors.
2. The patient frequently shows clouded consciousness, answers irrelevantly and shows signs of lack of orientation, he may for example correcly state month or year, but not the day of the week, or he may show problems naming the place, even if he without help can find his way around the ward.
3. The patient answers in a noticeably irrelevant manner. He is not orientated, neither in time, place, nor in personal data.

10 Tremor

This item comprises all forms of tremor.

0. No or doubtful tremor.
1. Very slight tremor that does not hamper the patient.
2. Clear tremor hampering the patient, the amplitude of finger tremor being less than 3 cm.
3. Clear tremor with an amplitude of more than 3 cm and which cannot be controlled by the patient.

11 Accommodation Disturbances

Difficulty in seeing clearly or distinctly at close quarters (with or without glasses), although the patient sees clearly at a long distance. If the patient uses bifocal glasses, the condition must be assessed on the basis of the use of the distance glasses.

0. No difficulty in reading an ordinary newspaper text.
1. Newspaper text can be read, but the patient's eyes tire rapidly or he must hold the paper further away.
2. The patient cannot read an ordinary newspaper text, but still manages to read texts printed in larger types.
3. The patient can read large type, such as a headline, only with aid, such as a magnifying glass.

12 Increased Salivation

Increased, non-stimulated salivation.

0. No or doubtful increase of salivation.
1. Salivation clearly increased, but not bothersome.
2. Disturbing increase of salivation; need for spitting or frequent swallowing of saliva; only exceptional dribbling.
3. Frequent or constant dribbling, perhaps concomitant speech disturbances.

13 Reduced Salivation (Dryness of Mouth)

Dryness of mouth because of diminished salivation. This may result in increased consumption of liquids, but it must be distinguished from thirst.

0. No or doubtful dryness of mouth.
1. Slight dryness of mouth, not disturbing the patient.
2. Moderate and slightly disturbing dryness of mouth.
3. Marked dryness of mouth which clearly disturbs the patient's daily life.

14 Nausea/Vomiting

To be recorded on the basis of the past 3 days.

0. No or doubtful nausea.
1. Slight nausea.
2. Disturbing nausea, but without vomiting.
3. Nausea with vomiting.

15 Diarrhoea

Increased frequency and/or thinner consistency of faeces.

0. No or doubtful diarrhoea.
1. Clearly present, but does not disturb work or other performance.
2. Disturbing, with need for several daily, inconvenient stools.
3. Marked, imperative need for defaecation, threatening or actual incontinence, results in frequent interruptions of work.

16 Constipation
Reduced frequency of defaecation and/or thicker consistency of faeces.
0. No or doubtful constipation.
1. Slight constipation, but bearable.
2. More marked constipation which hamper the patient.
3. Very pronounced constipation.

17 Micturition Disturbances
Feeling of difficulty in starting and of resistance to micturition, weaker stream or increased time of micturition. Should be assessed on the basis of the past 3 days.
0. No or doubtful micturition disturbances.
1. Clearly present, but bearable.
2. Poor stream, considerably increased time of micturition, feeling of incomplete emptying of bladder.
3. Retention of urine with high volume residual urine and/or threatened or actual acute retention.

18 Polyuria/Polydipsia
Increased urine production resulting in increased frequency of micturition and discharge of an abundant quantity of urine at each micturition; secondarily increased consumption of fluid.
0. No or doubtful.
1. Clearly present, but not hampering; nocturia at most once a night (in young people).
2. Moderately hampering because of frequent thirst, nocturia two or three times a night, or micturition more frequent than every 2 h.
3. Very hampering, almost constant thirst, nocturia at least four times a night, or micturition at least every hour.

19 Orthostatic Dizziness
Feeling of weakness, everything going black, buzzing in the ears, increasing tendency to faint when changing from supine or sitting position to upright position.
0. No or doubtful.
1. Clearly present, but requires no special countermeasures.
2. Hampering, but can be neutralized by slow and/or stagewise change to upright position.
3. Threatening fainting or real episodes of fainting despite careful change of position, with a tendency to this type of dizziness as long as the patient is in a upright position.

20 Palpitations/Tachycardia
Palpitation, feeling of rapid, strong and/or irregular heartbeats.
0. No or doubtful.
1. Clearly present, but not hampering, only short occassional attacks or more constant, but not marked palpitation.

2. Hampering frequent or constant palpitation that worries the patient or disturbs his night's sleep; however, without concomitant symptoms.
3. Suspicion of real tachycardia, for instance because of concomitant feeling of weakness and need to lie down, dyspnoea, tendency to fainting, or precordial pain.

21 Increased Tendency to Sweating
Localized to the whole body, not only palms and soles of the foot.
0. No or doubtful.
1. Clearly present, but mild, for example a profuse outburst of sweat only after considerable effort.
2. Hampering, requires frequent change of clothes, profuse sweating after moderate activity, for instance walking up stairs.
3. Profuse outbursts of sweat after slight activity or when resting, the patient is constantly wet, must change clothes several times a day and must also change night clothes or bedclothes.

22 Weight Gain
Rating is to be made on the basis of the preceding month.
0. No or doubtful weight gain during the preceding month.
1. Weight gain of 1–2 kg during the preceding month.
2. Weight gain of 3–4 kg during the preceding month.
3. Weight gain of more than 4 kg during the preceding month.

23 Weight Loss
0. No or doubtful weight loss.
1. Weight loss of 1–2 kg during the preceding month.
2. Weight loss of 3–4 kg during the preceding month.
3. Weight loss of more than 4 kg during the preceding month.

24 Diminished Sexual Desire
Reduced desire for sexual activity.
0. No or doubtful.
1. The desire for sexual activity is slightly diminished, but without hampering the patient.
2. A distinct reduction of the patient's desire for and interest in sexual activities so that is becomes a problem for the patient.
3. Desire and interest have diminished to such an extent that sexual intercourse occurs extremely seldom or has stopped.

25 Orgastic Dysfunction
Difficulty in obtaining and experiencing satisfactory orgasm.
0. No or doubtful.
1. It is more difficult for the patient than usual to obtain orgasm or the experience of orgasm is slightly influenced.

2. The patient states that there is a clear change in the ability to obtain orgasm or in the experience of orgasm. This change has reached such a degree that it troubles the patient.
3. When the patient rarely or never can obtain orgasm or the experience of orgasm is markedly reduced.

26 Headache

On the scoring sheet headache is classified as: (a) tension headache, (b) migraine, (c) other forms of headache.

0. No or doubtful headache.
1. Slight headache.
2. Moderate, hampering headache which does not interfere with the patient's daily life.
3. Pronounced headache interfering with the patient's daily life.

10.6 Specific Observer Side-Effect Scales

10.6.1 Scales for Neuroleptics

Among the most frequently used scales for neuroleptics is the Simpson-Angus scale, which was constructed essentially as a parkinsonism scale (Simpson and Angus 1970; see below). A modification of this scale, including an item of akathisia, was constructed by Bech and was first used in a study on the antipsychotic effect of haloperidol in relationship to the plasma concentration of this drug (Gjerris et al. 1983).

Another frequently used rating scale for measuring side-effects during neuroleptic treatment is the Abnormal Involuntary Movement Scale (AIMS; see below) published by Guy (1976). The inter-observer reliability of this scale has been found to be adequate (Gerlach et al. 1992), but its repeatability in clinical trials has been questionned by Bergen et al. (1988).

A third scale covering most appropriately the range of relevant side-effects of neuroleptic drugs is the Sanct Hans Rating Scale for Extrapyramidal Syndromes (SHRS; Gerlach and Korsgaard 1983). The scale contains four main categories: (a) hyperkinesia/dyskinesia (eight items); (b) parkinsonism (eight items); dystonia (one item); and akathisia (two items). The inter-rater reliability of the SHRS has been found adequate, and the parkonsonism subscale has an acceptable construct validity (in terms of Loevinger coefficients; Gerlach et al. 1992). Finally, the Chovinard Extrapyramidal Symptom Rating Scale has been included.

Simpson-Angus Scale (short version)

The scoring sheet for the Simpson-Angus scale is illustrated in Appendix 10.3. Instructions for scoring its six items are presented below.

1 Tremor
Patient is observed during the interview.
0. Absent.
1. Mild finger tremor, obvious to sight and touch.
2. Moderate tremor of hand or arm occurring spasmodically.
3. Marked tremor or one or more limbs.
4. Whole body tremor.

2 Salivation
Patient is observed while talking and then asked to open his mouth and elevate his tongue. The following ratings are given.
0. Absent.
1. Slight salivation to the extent that pooling takes place if the mouth is open and the tongue raised.
2. Moderate salivation is present and might occasionally result in difficulty in speaking.
3. Speaking with difficulty because of marked salivation.
4. Frank drooling.

3 Rigidity
This represents increased muscle tone of a uniform and general nature. It is observed on the basis of a uniform, steady resistance to passive movements of the limbs. Special importance is attached to the muscles around the elbow joints.
0. Absent.
1. Doubtful or very slight rigidity.
2. Moderate rigidity in neck, shoulder, and extremities. It must be possible to observe the rigidity on the basis of resistance to passive movements of elbow joints.
3. Marked rigidity assessed on the basis of resistance to passive movements of for instance elbow joints.
4. Very marked rigidity.

4 Gait
The patient is examined as he walks into the examining room, his gait, the swing of his arms, his general posture, all form the basis for an overall score for his item.
0. Absent.
1. Diminution in swing while the patient is walking.
2. Moderate diminution in swing with obvious rigidity in the arm.
3. Stiff gait with arms held rigidly before the abdomen.
4. Stooped shuffling gait with propulsion and retropulsion.

5 Dystonic Reaction
Dystonia in form of tonic muscular contractions localized to one or several muscle groups, particularly in the mouth, tongue, or neck. The assessment is to be made on the basis of the 72 h preceding the examination.

0. Absent.
1. Doubtful or very slight dystonia.
2. Moderate and short spasms, for instance, in the musculature of the jaws or the neck.
3. More markedly pronounced contractions of a longer duration or of a wider localization.
4. Very marked forms, for instance, oculogyric crises or opistotomia.

6 Akathisia

This represents the subjective feeling of muscle unrest, particularly in the lower extremities, so that it may be difficult for the patient to remain seated. The assessment of this item is based on clinical signs observed during the interview, as well as on the patient's report.

0. Absent.
1. Doubtful or very slight akathisia.
2. Moderate akathisia, however, the patient can keep still without effort.
3. Marked akathisia; the patient can, however, with an effort remain sitting during the interview.
4. The patient rises several times during the interview because of akathisia.

Abnormal Involuntary Movement Scale

Evaluation for the AIMS is to be made on the basis of the highest level of severity observed and refers to factual and oral movements (items 1–4), extremity movements (items 5, 6), trunk movement (item 7) and global judgement (items 8–10). Scoring instructions for items 1–9 are; 0, normal; 1, minimal; 2, mild; 3, moderate; 4, severe. Item 10 is scored: 0, no awareness; 1, aware bu no distress; 2, mild distress; 3, moderate distress; 4, severe distress. A discription of the recommended examination procedure is provided in Appendix 10.4. The items and their description are as follows.

1. Muscles of Facial Expression: Movements of forehead, eyebrows, periorbital area, cheeks; including frowning, blinking, smiling grimacing.
2. Lips and Perioral Area: Puckering, pouting, smacking.
3. Jaw: Biting, clenching, chewing, mouth opening, lateral movement.
4. Tongue: Rate only increase in movements both in and out of mouth, NOT inability to sustain movement.
5. Upper Extremities: arms, wrists, hands, fingers. Include choreic movements (i.e. rapid, objectively purposeless, irregular, spontaneous), athetoid movements (i.e. slow, irregular, complex, serpentine). Do NOT include tremor (i.e. repetitive regular, rhythmic).
6. Lower Extremities: Legs, knees, ankles, toes. Lateral knee movement, foot tapping, heel dropping, foot squirming, inversion and eversion of foot.
7. Neck, shoulders, hips: Rocking, twisting, squirming, pelvic gyrations.
8. Severity of Abnormal Movements
9. Incapacitation due to Abnormal Movements
10. Patient's Awareness of Abnormal Movements: Rate only patient's report

Sanct Hans Rating Scale

The original version of the SHRS prescribed scores of 0–6: 0, absent; 1, dubious; 2, mild; 3, mild–moderate; 4, moderate; 5, moderate–severe; 6, severe. A modified version with scores of 0–4 is: 0, absent; 1, dubious, very mild; 2, mild–moderate; 3, moderate–marked; 4, extreme. the items are as follows:
Hyperkinesia (Passive, Active)
Jaw
Tongue
Lips
Face
Head
Trunk
Upper Extremities
Lower Extremities
− Parkinsonism
Facial Expression
Bradykinesia
Tremor
Posture
Arm Swing
Gait
Rigidity
Salivation
− Dystonia
− Akathisia
Psyche
Motor

Extrapyramidal Symptom Rating Scale (Chovinard)

This scale was constructed by Chovinard and Ross-Chovinard (1979) and consists of the following parts.

I. Parkinsonism, Dystonia and Dyskinesia Scale
The items are scored 0 (absent), 1 (mild), 2 (moderate) and 3 (severe):
  1 Impression of slowness or weakness; difficulty in carrying out routine tasks.
  2 Difficulty walking or with balance
  3 Difficulty swallowing or talking.
  4 Stiffness, stiff posture.
  5 Cramps or pains in limbs, back or neck.
  6 Restless, nervous, unable to keep still.
  7 Tremors, shaking.
  8 Oculogyric crisis, abnormal sustained posture.
  9 Increased salivation.

10 Abnormal involuntary movements (dyskinesia) of extremities or trunk

11 Abnormal involuntary movements (dyskinesia) of tongue, jaw, lips or face.

12 Dizziness when standing up (especially in the morning).

II. Parkinsonism: Physician's Examination

1 Expressive automatic movements (0, normal; 1, very mild decrease in facial expressiveness; 2, mild decrease in facial expressiveness; 3, rare spontaneous smile, decrease blinking, voice slightly monotonous; 4, no spontaneous smile, staring gaze, low monotonous speech, mumbling; 5, marked facial mask, unable to frown, slurred speech; 6, extremely severe facial mask with unintellible speech).

2 Bradykinesia (0, normal; 1, global impression of slowness in movements; 2, definite slowness in movements; 3, very mild difficulty in initiating movements; 4, mild to moderate difficulty in initiating movements; 5, difficulty in starting or stopping any movement, or freezing on initiating voluntary act; 6, rare voluntary movement, almost completely immobile).

3 Rigidity, total, right arm, left arm, right leg, left leg (0, normal muscle tone; 1, very mild, barely perceptible; 2, mild (some resistance to passive movements); 3, moderate (definite resistance to passive movements); 4, moderately severe (moderate resistance but still easy to move the limb); 5, severe (marked resistance with definite difficulty to move the limb); 6, extremely severe (nearly frozen)).

4 Gait & posture (0, normal; 1, mild decrease of pendular arm movement; 2, moderate decrease of pendular arm movement, normal steps; 3, no pendular arm movement, head flexed, steps more or less normal; 4, stiff posture (neck, back), small step (shuffling gait); 5, more marked, festination or freezing on turning; 6, triple flexion, barely able to walk).

5 Tremor, total, right upper limb, left upper limb, right lower limb, left lower limb, head, jaw/chin, tongue, lips (0, none; 1, borderline; small aptitude (2, occasionnel; 3, frequent; 4, constant or almost so); moderate amplitude (3, occasionnel; 4, frequent, 5, constant or almost so); large amplitude (4, occasionnel; 5, frequent; 6, constant or almost so)).

6 Akathisia (0, none; 1, looks restless, nervous, impatient, uncomfortable; 2, needs to move at least one extremity; 3, often needs to move one extremity or to change position; 4, moves one extremity almost constantly if sitting, or stamp feet when standing; 5, unable to sit down for more than a short period of time; 6, moves or walks constantly).

7 Sialorrhea (0, absent; 1, very mild; 2, mild; 3, moderate, impairs speech; 4, moderately severe; 5, severe; 6, extremely severe, drooling).

8 Postural stability (0, normal; 1, hesitation when pushed but no retropulsion; 2, retropulsion but recovers unaided; 3, exaggerated retropulsion without falling; 4, absence of postural response, would fall if not caught by examiner; 5, unstable while standing, even without pushing; unable to stand without assistance).

III. Dystonia: Physician's Examination

1   Acute torsion dystonia, right upper limb, left upper limb, right lower limb, left lower limb, head, jaw, tongue, lips, eyes, trunk, total (=, absent; 1, very mild; 2, mild; 3, moderate; 4, moderately severe; 5, severe; 6, extremely severe).

2   Non acute or chronic or tardive dystonia, right upper limb, left upper limb, right lower limb, left lower limb, head, jaw, tongue, lips, eyes, trunk, total (=, absent; 1, very mild; 2, mild; 3, moderate; 4, moderately severe; 5, severe; 6, extremely severe).

IV. Dyskinetic Movements: Physician's Examination

1   Lingual movements (slow lateral or torsion movement of tongue) (0, none; 1, borderline; clearly present, within oral cavity (2, occasional – when activated or rarely spontaneous; 3, frequent – frequently spontaneous and present when activated; 4, constant or almost so); with occasional partial protrusion (3, occasional – when activated or rarely spontaneous; 4, frequent – frequently spontaneous and present when activated; 5, constant or almost so); with complete protrusion (4, occasional – when activated or rarely spontaneous; 5, frequent – frequently spontaneous and present when activated; 6, constant or almost so)).

2   Jaw movements (lateral movement, chewing, biting, clenching) (0, none; 1, borderline; clearly present, small amplitude (2, occasional – when activated or rarely spontaneous; 3, frequent – frequently spontaneous and present when activated; 4, constant or almost so); moderate amplitude, but without mouth opening (3, occasional – when activated or rarely spontaneous; 4, frequent – frequently spontaneous and present when activated; 5, constant or almost so); large amplitude, with mouth opening (4, occasional – when activated or rarely spontaneous; 5, frequent – frequently spontaneous and present when activated; 6, constant or almost so)).

3   Bucco-labial movements (puckering, pouting, smacking, etc) (0, none; 1, borderline; clearly present, small amplitude (2, occasional – when activated or rarely spontaneous; 3, frequent – frequently spontaneous and present when activated; 4, constant or almost so); moderate amplitude, forward movement of lips (3, occasional – when activated or rarely spontaneous; 4, frequent – frequently spontaneous and present when activated; 5, constant or almost so); large amplitude, marked, noisy smacking of lips (4, occasional – when activated or rarely spontaneous; 5, frequent – frequently spontaneous and present when activated; 6, constant or almost so)).

4   Truncal movements (rocking, twisting, pelvic gyrations) (0, none; 1, borderline; clearly present, small amplitude (2, occasional – when activated or rarely spontaneous; 3, frequent – frequently spontaneous and present when activated; 4, constant or almost so); moderate amplitude (3, occasional – when activated or rarely spontaneous; 4, frequent – frequently spontaneous and present when activated; 5, constant or almost so); greater amplitude (4, occasional – when activated or rarely spontaneous; 5, frequent – frequently spontaneous and present when activated; 6, constant or almost so)).

5 Upper extremities (choreoathetoid movements only: arms, wrists, hands, fingers) (0, none; 1, borderline; clearly present, small amplitude, movements of one limb (2, occasional – when activated or rarely spontaneous; 3, frequent – frequently spontaneous and present when activated; 4, constant or almost so); moderate amplitude, movement of one limb or movement of small amplitude involving two limbs (3, occasional – when activated or rarely spontaneous; 4, frequent – frequently spontaneous and present when activated; 5, constant or almost so); greater amplitude, movement involving two limbs (4, occasional – when activated or rarely spontaneous; 5, frequent – frequently spontaneous and present when activated; 6, constant or almost so).

6 Lower extremities (choreoathetoid movements only: legs, knees, ankles, toes) (0, none; 1, borderline; clearly present, small amplitude, movements of one limb (2, occasional – when activated or rarely spontaneous; 3, frequent – frequently spontaneous and present when activated; 4, constant or almost so); moderate amplitude, movement of one limb or movement of small amplitude involving two limbs (3, occasional – when activated or rarely spontaneous; 4, frequent – frequently spontaneous and present when activated; 5, constant or almost so); greater amplitude, movement involving two limbs (4, occasional – when activated or rarely spontaneous; 5, frequent – frequently spontaneous and present when activated; 6, constant or almost so).

7 Other involuntary movements (swallowing, irregular respiration, frowning, blinking, grimacing, sighing, etc) (0, none; 1, borderline; clearly present, small amplitude (2, occasional -when activated or rarely spontaneous; 3, frequent – frequently spontaneous and present when activated; 4, constant or almost so); moderate amplitude (3, occasional – when activated or rarely spontaneous; 4, frequent – frequently spontaneous and present when activated; 5, constant or almost so); greater amplitude (4, occasional – when activated or rarely spontaneous; 5, frequent – frequently spontaneous and present when activated; 6, constant or almost so).

V. Clinical Global Impression of Severity of Dyskinesia
Considering your clinical experience, how severe is the dyskinesia at this time? (0, absent; 1, borderline; 2, very mild; 3, mild; 4, moderate; 5, moderately severe, 6, marked; 7, severe; 8, extremely severe).

VI. Clinical Global Impression of Severity of Parkinsonism
Considering your clinical experience, how severe is the parkinsonism at this time? (0, absent; 1, borderline; 2, very mild; 3, mild; 4, moderate; 5, moderately severe, 6, marked; 7, severe; 8, extremely severe).

VII. Clinical Global Impression of Severity of Dystonia
Considering your clinical experience, how severe is the dystonia at this time? (0, absent; 1, borderline; 2, very mild; 3, mild; 4, moderate; 5, moderately severe, 6, marked; 7, severe; 8, extremely severe).

10.6.2 Scales for Antidepressants

No scale for antidepressants has been established. The subscale used by the Danish University Antidepressant Group (DUAG) is the most appropriate and is represented in Table 10.5. This scale has also been used as an example for translating items into the WHO definitions. Table 10.6 shows the complete translation from UKU terminology to WHO terms, including organ classes.

10.6.3 Scales for Lithium

The first scale developed specifically for measuring clinical side effects induced by lithium was constructed by Bech et al. (1979). The scale was based on a review of symptoms claimed to be associated with long term lithium therapy. The scale was evaluated in a study on mentally healthy subjects suffering from Meniere's disease. They participated in a double-blind, placebo-controlled study of 6 months' duration. Scale items are presented below. Scoring is as follows: 0, not present; 1, very slight or doubtful; 2, clearly present.

1. Hunger
2. Thirst
3. Polyuria
4. Goiter
5. Metal Taste
6. Diarrhoea
7. Gastralgia
8. Nausea
9. Blurred Vision
10. Hand Tremor
11. Muscle Pain
12. Difficulties in Memory
13. Difficulties in Concentration
14. Loss of Initiative and Inspiration
15. Insomnia: Initial
16. Insomnia: Middle
17. Change in Drinking Habits

10.7 Specific Self-Rating Scales for Side Effects

Many ad hoc self-rating scales exist for assessing side effects. Because it is often difficult for the patient to distinguish between symptoms of illness and side effects of treatment, it is usually accepted to combine these potential symptoms in the same scale (Bech et al. 1976). The enlarged Beck Depression Scale includes, for

Table 10.5. Item distribution of rating scales: components of aggression

	UKU items for antidepressants	WHO preferred terms	Code WHO	WHO included terms
1	Concentration difficulties	Concentration impaired	1127	Concentration impaired
2	Sedation	Somnolence	0197	Sedation excessive
3	Failing memory	Amnesia	0164	Memory impairment/disturbance/loss
4	Tension/inner unrest	Nervousness	0188	Nervous tension
5	Increased duration of sleep	Insomnia	0183	Sleep increased
6	Reduced duration of sleep	Insomnia	0183	Sleep decreased
7	Increased dream activity	Dreaming abnormal	1243	Dreaming abnormal
8	Emotional indifference	Apathy	0167	Apathy
9	Confusion	Confusion	0092	Confusional state
10	Tremor	Tremor	0154	Tremor
11	Accommodation disturbances	Accommodation abnormal	0202	Accommodation abnormal
12	Increased salivation	Saliva increased	0222	Saliva increased
13	Reduced salivation	Mouth dry	0218	Saliva decreased
14	Nausea	Nausea	0308	Nausea
15	Diarrhoea	Diarrhoea	0205	Diarrhoea
16	Constipation	Constipation	0204	Constipation
17	Micturia disturbances	Micturition disorder	0605	Micturition disorder
18	Polyuria	Polyuria	0613	Polyuria
19	Orthostatic dizziness	Dizziness	0101	Dizziness postural
20	Palpitations	Palpitation	0221	Palpitation
21	Increased sweating	Sweating increased	0043	Sweating increased
22	Weight gain	Weight increase	0408	Weight increase
23	Weight loss	Weight decrease	0407	Weight decrease
24	Diminished sexual desire	Libido decreased	0184	Libido decreased
25	Sexual dysfunction	Impotence/orgastic dysfunction	0182	Impotence/orgastic dysfunction
26	Headache	Headache	0109	Headache

Table 10.6. The complete translation from UKU terminology to WHO terms including system organ class

UKU terminology		WHO preferred term		System organ class	
Code	Psychic	Psychiatric disorders	Code	Code	Text
1.1	Concentration difficulties	Concentration impaired	P 1127.001	0050	Psychiatric disorders
1.2	Asthenia/ Lassitude/Increased fatigability	Asthenia Fatigue	P 0716.001 P 0724.001	1810 1810	Body as a whole - general disorders
1.3	Sleepiness/Sedation	Somnolence (Sedation excessive)	P 0197.001 I 0197.004	0500 0500)	Psychiatric disorders
1.4	Failing memory	Amnesia (Memory impairment)	P 0164.001 I 0164.003	0500 0500)	
1.5	Depression	Depression	P 0172.001	0500	
1.6	Tension/Inner unrest	Nervousness	P 0188.001	0500	
1.7	Increased duration of sleep		x		
1.8	Reduced duration of sleep	Insomnia	P 0183.001	0500	
1.9	Increased dream activity	Dreaming abnormal	P 1243.001	0500	
1.10	Emotional indifference	Apathy	P 0167.001	0500	

Table 10.6 (cont.)

UKU terminology		WHO preferred term		System organ class	
Code	Neurologic	Central and peripheral nervous system disorders	Code	Code	Text
2.1	Dystonia	Dystonia	P 0068.001	0410	Central and peripheral nervous system disorders
2.2	Rigidity	Hypertonia	P 0116.001	0410	
2.3	Hypokinesia/Akinesia	Hypokinesia	P 0118.001	0410	
2.4	Hyperkinesia	Hyperkinesia	P 0114.001	0410	
2.5	Tremor	Tremor	P 0154.001	0410	
2.6	Akathisia	Hyperkinesia (Akathisia)	P 0114.001 I 0114.004	0410 0410)	
2.7	Epileptic seizures	Convulsions	P 0093.001	0410	
2.8	Paraesthesias	Paraesthesias	P 0137.001	0410	

Table 10.6 (cont.)

UKU terminology		WHO preferred term		System organ class	
Code	Autonomic	Autonomic nervous system disorders	Code	Code	Text
3.1	Accommodation disturbances	Accommodation abnormal	P 0202.001	0431	Vision disorders
3.2	Increased salivation	Saliva increased	P 0222.001	0600	Gastro-intestinal system disorders
3.3	Reduced salivation	Mouth dry	P 0218.001	0600	
3.4	Nausea/Nausea Vomiting	Vomiting	P 0308.001 P 0228.001	0600 0600	
3.5	Diarrhoea	Diarrhoea	P 0205.001	0600	
3.6	Constipation	Constipation	P 0204.001	0600	
3.7	Micturition disturbances	Micturition disorder	P 0605.001	1300	Urinary system disorders
3.8	Polyuria/ Polydipsia	Polyuria Thirst	P 0613.001 P 0405.001	1300 0800	Metabolic and nutritional disorders
3.9	Orthostatic dizziness Dizziness postural	Dizziness (Dizziness postural	P 0101.001 I 0101.007	0410 0410)	Central and peripheral nervous system disorders
3.10	Palpitations/ Tachycardia	Palpitation Tachycardia	P 0221.001 P 0224.001	1030 1030	Heart rate and rhythm disorders
3.11	Increased tendency to sweating	Sweating increased	P 0043.001	0100	Skin and appendage disorders

Table 10.6 (cont.)

UKU terminology		WHO preferred term		System organ class	
Code	Other	Skin and appendage disorder	Code	Code	Text
4.1	Rash	Rash	P 0027.001	0100	Skin and appendage disorders
4.1a	Rash morbilliform	Rash maculopapular	P 0030.001	0100	
4.1b	Rash petechial	Purpura	P 0459.001	1230	Platelet, bleeding and clotting dis.
4.1c	Rash urticarial	Urticaria	P 0044.001	0100	Skin and appendage disorders
4.1d	Rash psoriatic	Rash psoriaform	P 0031.001	0100	
4.2	Pruritus	Pruritus	P 0024.001	0100	
4.3	Photosensitivity	Photosensitivity reaction	P 0022.001	0100	
4.4	Increased pigmentation	Pigmentation abnormal	P 0973.001	0100	
4.5	Weight gain	Weight increase	P 0408.001	0800	Metabolic and nutritional disorders
4.6	Weight loss	Weight decrease	P 0407.001	0800	
4.7	Menorrhagia	Menorrhagia	P 0656.001	1420	Reproductive disorders, female
4.8	Amenorrhoea	Amenorrhoea	P 0636.001	1420	
4.9	Galactorrhoea	Lactation nonpuerperal	P 0652.001	1420	

Table 10.6 (cont.)

UKU terminology		WHO preferred term		System organ class	
Code	Autonomic	Autonomic nervous system disorders	Code	Code	Text
4.10	Gynaecomastia	Gynaecomastia	P 0346.001	0900	Endocrine disorders
4.11	Increased sexual desire	Libido increased	P 0185.001	0500	Psychiatric disorders
4.12	Diminished sexual desire	Libido decreased	P 0184.001	0500	
4.13	Erectile dysfunction	Impotence	P 0182.001	0500	
4.14	Ejaculatory dysfunction	Ejaculation disorder	P 1217.001	1410	Reproductive disorders, male
4.15	Orgastic dysfunction		x		
4.16	Dry vagina		P 0670.001	1420	Reproductive disorders, female
4.17	Headache	Headache	P 0109.001	0410	Central and periph. nerv. syst. dis.
4.17a	Headache, tension headache	Headache	P 0109.001	0410	
4.17b	Headcahe, migraine	Migraine	P 0121.001	0410	
4.17c	Headache, other forms	Headache	P 0109.001	0410	
4.18	Physical dependence	Drug dependence	P 0174.001	0500	Psychiatric disorders
4.19	Psychic dependence	Drug dependence	P 0174.001	0500	

example, a subscale of vegetative symptoms considered to be side effects of anti-depressants (see Chapter 4) and the lithium side-effect scale by Bech et al. (1979).

10.8 General Remarks on the Statistical Analysis of Side-Effect Scales

The scales for side effects of psychopharmacological treatments are analogous to symptom-rating scales in that the scales focus on clinical disability induced by the treatment under examination. From a statistical point of view the items of a side-effect scale should be analysed in terms of at least three different questions: (a) Are the items indicators of illness? (b) Are the items true side effects? (c) Do some items reflect a mixture of (a) and (b)? A psychometric analysis of side-effect scales often shows that only very few items have an additive relationship if considered as true side effects. Total scores are therefore not generally recommended; single item analysis should be performed. However, the parkinsonism subscale of the SHRS is a Likert Scale. The analysis of side-effect scales also entails another problem: the interventional problem. As indicated in Appendix 10.1, an immediate consequence of a side-effect (the action to be taken) may be the reduction in dosage. Against this background the non-interventional versus the interventional approach to data analysis is discussed below.

In the non-interventional approach no dosage regulations are made. The problem in this approach is to include a corrected score, which means that 'side effects' before treatment are considered and balanced out in the statistical analysis. The longitudinal analysis of each item can then be performed (e.g. Lingjærde et al. 1987). The most useful method is that using the area under curve, as shown in Figure 10.2, where the patient has a score of '1' on the item before treatment. After 3 days of treatment this was increased to '2', and after a further 3 days of treatment to '3'. The corrected area under curve is the most appropriate expression statistically. From Figure 10.2 it appears that the time unit is 3 days, which is the retrospective period used by the UKU scale. Chapter 6 discusses psychosomatic language in relation to the actual duration of symptoms; it was shown that emotions last for hours and moods for days. For the non-interventional approach the pharmacological side effects are tolerated without changes in drug dosage, i.e. the fixed-dose approach. In this situation the actual duration of 3 days is appropriate. In other words, the beginning and end measurements are not important.

The interventional approach is illustrated in Figure 10.3 where an intervention (reduction in dosage) has been made after 6 days of treatment. The patient was not able to tolerate the side effect in its severe degree (score '3'). After the intervention the score decreased to '2' (moderate), which the patient accepted taking the positive effects of the drug into account (cost-effectiveness score). An intention-to-treat method is here to use the end-point score in the statistical analysis. An explanatory method is to show that an intolerable side effect emerged after 6 days of treatment. In this context a more precise statement of the beginning and end of the

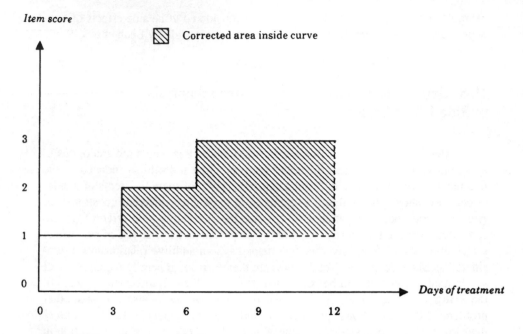

Fig. 10.2. The non-interventional approach to analysing side-effect items of a scale

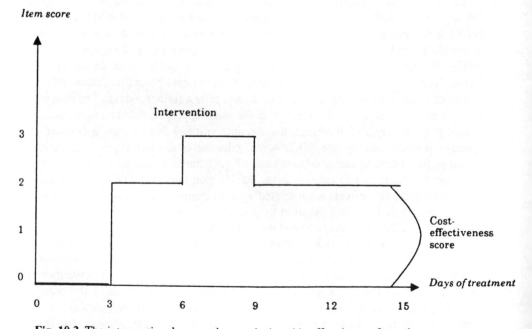

Fig. 10.3. The interventional approach to analysing side-effect items of a scale

intolerable reaction may be claimed. However, because such registrations are usually performed retrospectively, evaluations every 3 days, as in Figure 10.3, may be sufficient.

10.9 Compliance Scales

Side-effects are one of the major reasons for medical non-compliance in the out-patient treatment of affective disorders (Bech et al. 1976). Compliance has been investigated in this setting by Cochran (1984) who viewed compliance broadly as maintenance of a lithium regimen, obtaining scheduled blood tests, and attending medical appointments in order to assure adequate supervision of a drug that can have toxic side effects. A compliance index (Gordis 1976) was used modified to lithium treatment. This Compliance Index included a 3-point ordinal scale: 0, compliance (a consensus across measures that the patient was adhering to the re-gimen); 1, minor noncompliance (when there was failure to obtain blood levels, missed appointments without notifying the clinic, or forgotten dosages); 2, major noncompliance (if the patient significantly departed from the treatment regimen by terminating lithium against medical advice, dropping out of treatment, or being too chaotic in lithium consumption to maintain adequate blood levels).

Cochran (1984) showed that the Compliance Index had high inter-psychiatrist reliability, but the self-report score as well as the informant report score of this in-dex correlated only mildly to the psychiatrist's score. Side-effects were found as the major reason for noncompliance (Cochran 1984).

As discussed by Harvey (1988) the term 'compliance' has some negative con-notations, e.g. implying that the patient 'ought' to be doing what the doctor tells him to do, and that if not, then the patient is somehow in the wrong. From a qual-ity of life perspective the patient should not always be obedient. Harvey (1988) prefer 'adherence' to 'compliance', and he defines adherence as the extent to which a person's behaviour coincides with medical or health advice. The general reasons for lithium non-adherence have been summarized by Goodwin and Jamison (1990): From the patient's point of view the following reasons were given: a dis-like of medication controlling their moods; a dislike of the idea of having a chronic illness; feeling depressed; side-effects. From the doctor's point of view the following reasons were given: felt well, no need to continue medication; patient missed hypomanic episodes; patient felt bothered by the idea of having a chronic illness. As discussed by Bech et al. (1976) most patients seem to refer to side-ef-fects rather than insufficiency of lithium when they want to stop treatment.

Scales measuring attitudinal areas of medical non-adherence have been dis-cussed by Cochran and Gitlin (1988)

References

Ayd FJ. The impact of biological psychiatry. In: Ayd FJ, Blackwell B. (eds). Discoveries in Biological Psychiatry. Philadelphia: Lippincott, 1970, pp. 230–243.

Bech P. Rating scales for mood disorders: applicability, consistency and construct validity. Acta Psychiat Scand 1988; 78 (suppl. 345): 45–55.

Bech P, Vendsborg PB, Rafaelsen OJ. Lithium maintenance treatment of manic-melancholic patients: its role in the daily routine. Acta Psychiat Scand 1976; 53: 70–81.

Bech P, Thomsen J, Prytz S, Vendsborg PB, Zilstorff K, Rafaelsen OJ. The profile and severity of lithium-induced side effects in mentally healthy subjects. Neuropsychobiology 1979; 5: 160–166.

Bischoff R, Bobon D, Görtelmeyer R, Horn R, Müller AA, Stoll KD, Cade JFJ. Lithium salts in the treatment of psychotic excitement. Med J Aust 1949; 36: 349–351.

Bobon D, Baumann U, Angst J, Helmchen H, Hippius H. AMDP-system in pharmacopsychiatry. Basel: Karger, 1983.

Carroll BJ, Fielding JM, Blaski TG. Depression rating scales: a critical review. Arch Gen Psychiat 1973; 28: 361–366.

Chouinard G, Ross-Chouinard A, Annable L, Jones BD. Extrapyramidal Symptom Rating Scale. Can J Neurol Sci 1980; 7: 233–239.

Cocchetto DM, Nardi RV. Benefit-risk assessment of investigational drugs: Current methodology, limitations and alternative approaches. Science for clinicians. Pharmacology 1986; 6: 286–303.

Cochran SD. Preventing medical noncompliance in the outpatient treatment of bipolar affective disorders. J Cons Clin Psychol 1984; 5: 873–878.

Cochran SD, Gitlin MJ. Attitudinal correlates of lithium compliance in bipolar affective disorders. J Nerv Ment Dis 1988; 176: 457–464.

Conduct of Clinical Trials of Medical Products (CPMP). Good clinical practice for trials on medical products in the European Community. Brussels: Commission of the European Communities, 1990.

Delay J, Deniker P. 38 cas de psychose traitées par la cure prolongée et continué de 4560 RP. Le Congres de Psychiat Neurol de Langue Francaise. Luxembourg: Masson, 1952, pp. 503–513.

Drowning RW, Rickels K, Meyers F. Side reactions in neurotics: a comparison of two methods of assessment. J Clin Pharmacology 1970; 10: 289–297.

Faich GA. Adverse drug reaction monitoring. N Engl J Med 1986; 314: 1589–1592.

Food and Drug Administration (FDA). Procedural manual for handling drug experience reports. Glossary paper flow and algorithms. Rockville: Dept Health Human Serv, 1980.

Frank JD. The effects of psychotherapy. In.: Meyers JM (ed). Cures by Psychotherapy. New York, Praeger Publishers, 1984.

Gelberg A, Armstrong GD, Dreis MB, Anello C. Technology developments with the FDA adverse drug reaction file system. Drug Inform J 1991; 25: 19–28.

Gerlach J, Korsgaard S. Classification of abnormal involuntary movements in psychiatric patients. Neuropsychiat Clin 1983; 2: 201–208.

Gerlach J, Korsgaard S, Clemmesen P. The Sanct Hans Rating Scale for Extrapyramidal Syndromes: Reliability and Validity. Acta Psychiat Scand 1992 (in press).

Gjerris A, Bech P, Broen-Christensen C, Geisler A, Klysner R, Rafaelsen OJ. Haloperidol plasma levels in relation to antimanic effect. In: Usdin E, Dahl S, Gram LF (eds). Clinical Pharmacology in Psychiatry. London, MacMillan Press, 1980.

Goodwin FK, Jamison KR. Manic-Depressive Illness. New York, Oxford University Press 1990.

Gordis L. Conceptual and methodological problems in measuring compliance. In: Haynes RB, Taylor DW, Sackett DL (eds). Compliance in Health Care. Baltimore: Johns Hopkins University Press, 1979, pp. 23–45.

Guy W. Early Clinical Drug Evaluation (ECDEU) assessment manual for psychopharmacology. Rockville, Nat Inst Ment Health, 1976.

Guy W, Bonato RR. Manual for the Early Clinical Drug Evaluation (ECDEU) assessment battery. Maryland, Nat Inst Ment Health, 1970.

Guy W, Ban TA. The assessment and documentation of psychopathology. Berlin, Springer, 1982.

Hall RA, Jackson RB, Swain JM. Neurotoxic reactions resulting from chlorpromazine administration. J Am Med Ass 1956; 161: 214–218.

Harvey P. Health Psychology. London, Longman 1988.

Janet P. La medicine psychologique. Paris, Alcan, 1923.

Kline NS. Monoamine oxydase inhibitors: An unfinished picaresque tale. In: Ayd FJ, Blackwell B (eds.). Discoveries in Biological Psychiatry. Philadelphia, J. B. Lippincott 1970, pp. 459–464.

Kuhn R. The imipramine story. In: Ayd FJ, Blackwell B (eds). Discoveries in Biological Psychiatry. Philadelphia, Lippincott, 1970, pp. 205–217.

Kuhn R. Über die Wandlung depressiver Zustände mit einem Iminodibenzylderivat (G 22355). Schw Med Wschr 1957; 87: 1135–1140.

Kuhn R. The treatment of depressive states with G 22355 (imipramine hydrochloride). Am J Psychiatry 1958; 115: 459–464.

Levine J. Assessment of side-effects. In: Benkert O, Maier W, Rickels K (eds). Methodology of the evaluation of psychotropic drugs. Berlin, Springer 1990, pp. 130–135.

Lingjærde O, Ahlfors UG, Bech P, Dencker SJ, Elgen K. The UKU side effect rating scale. Acta Psychiat Scand 1987; 76 (suppl 334): 1–100.

Pogge RC. The toxic placebo. Medical Times 1963; 91: 773–781.

Schonecker M. Ein eigentümliches Syndrome im oralen Bereich bei Megaphenaplikation. Nervenartz 1957; 28: 35.

Schou M, Juel-Nielsen N, Strömgren E, Voldby H. The treatment of manic psychoses by the administration of lithium salts. J Neurol Neurosurg Psychiat 1954; 17: 250–260.

Simpson GM, Angus JWS. A rating scale for extrapyramidal side effects. Acta Psychiat Scand 1970; 46 (suppl 212): 11–19.

Steck, 1954 (cited by Deniker P.). Introduction of neuroleptic chemotherapy into psychiatry. In: Ayd FJ, Blackwell B (eds). Discoveries in biological psychiatry. Philadelphia, Lippincott, 1979, pp. 155–164.

Stephens MDB. The detection of new adverse drug reactions. London, The MacMillan Press, 1988.

Woggon B. Rating scales for psychiatry. European Edition. Hembach, Beltz Test, 1990.

World Health Organization. WHO Adverse Reaction Terminology. Geneva, World Health Organization, 1990.

Appendix 10.1   *Global Clinical Assessment of Severity of Side-effects*

A

	Clinical side effects-functioning	Patient	Physician
0	No side effects		
1	Mild side effects that do not interfere with patient's performance		
2	Side effects that interfere moderately with patient's performance		
3	Side effects that interfere markedly with patient's performance		

B

	Consequences for the drug therapy	Physician
0	No actions	
1	More frequent assessment of patients, but no reduction in dose	
2	Reduction in dose of drug	
3	Discontinuation of drug	

Appendix 10.2 *Scoring Sheet for the UKU Scale*

Item no.		Symptoms	Score	WHO codes
(1.1)	1	Concentration difficulties		1127
(1.2)	2	Sedation		0197
(1.4)	3	Failing memory		0164
(1.6)	4	Tension/inner unrest		0188
(1.7)	5	Increased duration of sleep		0183
(1.8)	6	Reduced duration of sleep		0183
(1.9)	7	Increased dream activity		1243
(1.10)	8	Emotional indifference		0167
(1.11)	9	Confusion		0092
(2.7)	10	Tremor		0154
(3.1)	11	Accommodation disturbances		0202
(3.2)	12	Increased salivation		0222
(3.3)	13	Reduced salivation		0218
(3.4)	14	Nausea/vomiting		0308
(3.5)	15	Diarrhoea		0205
(3.6)	16	Constipation		0204
(3.7)	17	Micturition disturbances		0206
(3.8)	18	Polyuria/polydipsia		0613
(3.9)	19	Orthostatic dizziness		0101
(3.10)	20	Palpitations/tachycardia		0221
(3.11)	21	Increased tendency to sweating		0043
(4.5)	22	Weight gain		0408
(4.6)	23	Weight loss		0407
(4.12)	24	Diminished sexual desire		0184
(4.13-15)	25	Orgastic dysfunction		0182
(4.17)	26	Headache		0109
Total score				

Appendix 10.3   *Scoring Sheet for the Simpson-Angus Scale*

No.	Item (WHO terms)	Score
1	Tremor (tremor; 0154)	
2	Salivation (saliva increased; 0222)	
3	Rigidity (hypertonia; 0116)	
4	Gait (hypokinesia; 0118)	
5	Dystonic reactions (dystonia; 0068)	
6	Akathisia (akathisia; 0114)	
Total score		

Appendix 10.4   *Examination procedure for AIMS*

Either before or after completing the examination procedure, observe the patient unobtrusively, at rest (e.g. in waiting room).
The chair to be used in this examination should be a hard, firm one without arms.

1. Ask patient to remove shoes and socks.

2. Ask patient whether there is anything in his/her mouth (i.e. gum, candy, etc.), and if there is, to remove it.

3. Ask patient about the current condition of his/her teeth. Ask patient if he/she wears dentures. Do teeth or dentures bother patient now?

4. Ask patient whether he/she notices movements in mouth, face, hands, or feet. If yes, ask to describe and to what extent they currently bother patient or interfere with his/her activities.

5. Have patient sit in chair with hands on knees, legs slightly apart, and feet flat on floor. (Look at entire body for movements while in this position).

6. Ask patient to sit with hands hanging unsupported. If male, between legs; if female and wearing a dress, hanging over knees. (Observe hands and other body areas.)

7. Ask patient to open mouth (observe tongue at rest in mouth). Do this twice.

8. Ask patient to protrude tongue. (Observe abnormalities of tongue movement). Do this twice.

9. Ask patient to tap thumb, with each finger, as rapidly as possible for 10-15 s; separately with right hand, then with left hand. (Observe facial and leg movements).

10. Flex and extend patient's left and right arms (one at a time). (Note any rigidity).

11. Ask patient to stand up. (Observe in profile. Observe all body areas again, hips included).

12. Ask patient to extend both arms outstretched in front with palms down. (Observe trunk, legs, and mouth).

13. Have patient walk a few paces, turn, and walk back to chair. (Observe hands and gait). Do this twice.

11 Epilogue

Cronbach (1957) has differentiated between two major disciplines of scientific psychology, namely between experimental psychology and correlation psychology. In experimental psychology the scientist changes conditions systematically in order to observe their consequences. The psychophysical studies in Wundt's laboratory in Leipzig a century ago started experimental psychology (Wundt 1888). In correlation psychology the scientist studies "correlations presented by Nature (...) and the correlator finds his interest in the already existing variation between individuals, social groups, and species. By 'correlation psychology' I do not refer to studies relying on one statistical procedure only..." (Cronbach 1957).

This compendium is correlation psychology where the target syndromes have been analysed by their shared phenomenology as presented by Nature. The basic principle of grouping symptoms into syndromes by shared phenomenology is also adopted by DSM-III-R and ICD-10. However, the procedural algorithms of DSM-III-R are resistant to quantification, which, for instance, is illustrated in Chapter 5 between personality 'type' versus personality 'trait' as emphasized already by Kretschmer (1921).

In this compendium the two most useful methods statistically for the demonstration of shared phenomenology have been referred to, namely factor analysis and latent structure analysis. Factor analysis is in Cronbach's meaning correlational but latent structure analysis (which mainly has been developed after 1957) is also 'correlational' in Cronbach's meaning of correlation psychology. Likert scale item definition with a rather narrow range of categories has been preferred to adhere most appropriately with these psychometric methods.

This compendium is a collection of rating scales measuring health components (physical, cognitive, affective, social, economic and ego-functional, PCASEE). Table 11.1 shows a listing of the scales within the PCASEE repertoire. The Likert type scales have been recommended in this compendium, i.e. short scales (10–20 items) with few anchoring steps for each item (0, not present to 4, present in an extreme degree). The total scores of such scales have been considered as a sufficient statistic of the syndrome being measured.

The descriptive level of the PCASEE model has been studied with reference to diagnostic aspects (diagnostic scales), outcome aspects (symptom scales), and predictive aspects (personality scales, coping strategies and defense mechanisms). It has been argued in this compendium that health-related quality of life scales either are attempts globally to integrate the various levels of the PCASEE model

Table 11.1. Health components and corresponding rating scales

P (physical)	C (cognitive)	A (affective)	S (social)	E (econ./stress)	E (ego function)
Withdrawal Syndrome Scale (WSA)	Brief Dementia Scale (BDS)	Mania Scale (MAS)	Global Assessment of Functioning (GAF)	Stressor Scale (Brown & Harris)	Coping strategies, e.g.
Waters Headache Questionnaire (WHQ)	Mini-Mental Scale (MMS)	Melancholia Scale (MES)	Activities of Daily Living Scale (ADL)	Social readjustment Scale (Holmes & Rahe)	Mental Adjustment to cancer (MAC)
St. Mary's Sleep Questionnaire (MSQ)	Alzheimer's Disease (ADAS)	Hamilton Depression Scale (HDS)	Job Content Questionnaire (Karasek)	Axis 4 (DSM-III-R)	* Defense mechanisms, e.g.
Diagnostic Scale for Clinical Thyrotoxicosis (CROOK)	Gottfries-Bråne-Steen (GBS)	Hamilton Anxiety Scale (HAS)			Life Style Index (LSI)
	Brief Psychiatric Rating Scale (BPRS)	Sheehan Panic Scale (SPS)			* Personality scales. e.g.
		Yale-Brown Obsessive-Compulsive Scale (Y-BOCS)			Neuroticism (EPQ)
		Social Dysfunction and Aggression Scale (SDAS)			Anhedonia (SBS)

or to look for a specific dimension of well-being taking the patient's own goals into consideration. In this connection side effects of treatment have been considered as essential dimensions.

Table 11.2 shows a scoring sheet which incorporates the various chapters of this compendium resulting in a multiaxial profile. Because health-related quality of life, *inter alia*, is an attempt to integrate the various axes the problem of profile versus index has been discussed. Thus, Rosser (1987) has developed a health index in which she has multiplied social disability with mental and physical disability. Using the Rosser index approach the rating scores of axis 1 (cognitive and affective disability), axis 2 (personality disability), axis 3 (physical disability), axis 4 (distress), axis 5 (current social disability), axis 6 (coping with illness), axis 7 (subjective quality of life), and axis 8 (side effects) should be added to a total health index. Likewise, a prognostic health index should be calculated, e.g. by adding axis 5 social function (past) and axis 2 (defence mechanisms).

Table 11.2. Multiaxial profile of patient: _____

Axis 1 **(Cognitive**	Clinical psychiatric syndrome	Codes: _____ DSM-III R/ICD-10
or Affective)	Appropriate rating scale	Score: ☐☐
Axis 2 **(Ego**	Personality disorder	Codes: _____ DSM-III R
functions)	Appropriate rating scale (personality)	Score: ☐☐
	Appropriate rating scale (defence mechanism)	Score: ☐☐
Axis 3 **(Physical)**	Physical disorder	Codes: _____ ICD 10
	Appropriate rating scale	Score: ☐☐
Axis 4 **(Economic,**	Psychological stressors	Codes: _____ DSM III R
Stressors)	Appropriate rating scale	Score: ☐☐
Axis 5 **(Social)**	Social functioning (currently)	Codes: _____ IDSM III R
	Appropriate rating scale (currently)	Score: ☐☐
Axis 6	Coping with illness	
	Appropriate rating scale	Score: ☐☐
Axis 7	Health-related quality of life	
	Appropriate rating scale	Score: ☐☐
Axis 8	Side-effects of treatment	Codes: _____ WHO
	Appropriate rating scale	Score: ☐☐

The psychopathological approach of this compendium has balanced between psychological pathology (i.e. dealing with mental phenomena appearing *de novo* in the evolution of mental illness) and pathological psychology (i.e. dealing with cognitive and behavioural phenomena that result from extreme variations of 'normal' mental functions or behaviour).

Because the 'correlator' in Cronbach's sense must await 'correlations presented by Nature' it is a time consuming method but also a method with higher validity that experimental psychology. The borderland between psychological pathology and pathological psychology is still a field that needs to be explored. Thus, autonomic thoughts and emotions which are essential elements of cognitive psychology can be considered either as primarily pathological events or as unwanted events by their frequency or intensity. Table 11.3 shows eight different autonomic thoughts or emotions (which in Chapter 3 were referred to as intrusive mental events) in relation to the PCASEE model. Studies analysing this approach are on-going.

The PCASEE model should, finally, be seen as a repertoire for the communication between the patient and the therapist. Thus, the model stimulates the doctor to translate signs and symptoms into clinical target syndromes (Table 11.1), and Table 11.2 stimulates the doctor to make a holistic description of the patient. Table 11.3 stimulates new ways of capturing unwanted mental events which may be indicators of the patient's existential problems in relation to his illness.

In his 'Existential Psychotherapy' Yalom (1980) says that psychotherapy is a bridge between wishing (the goal of treatment) and the patient's treatment behaviour. This bridge is passable if the therapist effectively provides the patient with an explanation helping him "to order previous unfamiliar phenomena and to experience them as being under his or her control. (...) The implication of this sequence is that it is primarily the process (that is, the provision of insight), rather than the precise content of the insight, that is important. The function of the interpretation is to provide the patient with a sense of mastery, accordingly, the value of an interpretation should be measured by this criterion" (Yalom 1980).

However, the content of the insight should not be discarded. As early as 1953, Lewis warned that psychoanalytical concepts of mental health and illness often concentrate on inner psychological data implying that some of the terms psychoanalysts use for their definition "would make it impossible to tell whether an individual is mentally healthy unless he has been psychoanalysed or his behaviour interpreted on psychoanalytic lines: the criteria, in short, are technical pschoanalytical ones. (...) Partly because such language leaves room for honest but absurdly wide differences of opinion between a psychoanalyst and other persons – say a psychiatrist, a general practitioner, or a relative of the patient – about whether a psychoanalysed patient, or indeed anybody at all, is mentally healthy. (...) Partly because it has not been settled we are still without exact information about the comparative effects of psychoanalysis or other methods of psychotherapy" (Lewis 1953).

The hope is that this compendium will help the therapist or other decision makers (including the patient) to obtain insight into psychometric theories of

Table 11.3. Automatic unwanted thoughts or emotions (intrusive events)

Automatic unwanted thoughts or emotions (intrusive events)	Health components (0, no; 1, yes)						Patient's rating Severity VAS (0-10)	Doctor's rating Category (0, no; 1, minor; 2, major)
	P physical	C cognitive	A affective	S social	E economic	E ego		
Preoccupation							frequency	"hypochondriasis"
Worry							intensity	panic attacks
Emotional lability							intensity	aggressive incidents
Tiredness							intensity	neurasthenia
Hopelessness							intensity	suicidal impulses
Pain							intensity	headache - other specify
Obsessions							frequency	discomfort
Compulsions							frequency	discomfort

psychopathology, of health state dimensions, and of quality of life problems. The rating scales included in this compendium are tools for measuring outcome of treatment, and not in themselves treatment modalities. However, the synchony or dyschony of rating scales scores during treatment should guide the therapist to adjust therapy, in order to give his patient the best form of treatment.

It is a century since James (1890) published his textbook on scientific psychology. Throughout this compendium the works of James have been referred to. This compendium will finish with a quotation from James's essay on pragmatism (James 1907):

"The ancient problem of 'the one and the many' (...) is (...) the most central of all philosophic problems (...) (because it) is the classification with the maximum number of consequences. (...) Philosophy has (...) been defined as the quest of the world's unity (...) But how about the variety in things? If we instead of using the term philosophy, we talk in general of our intellect and its needs, we quickly see that unity is only one of them. Acquaintance with the details of facts is always reckoned, along with their reduction to systems, as an indispensable mark of mental greatness (...) What our intellect really aims at is neither variety nor unity taken singly, but totality. In this, acquaintance with reality's diversities is as important as understanding their connexion. Curiosity goes pari passu with the systematizing passion."

The one versus multiple end-point measures illustrate our "intellect and its needs" in therapeutic studies of psychopathology, health status and quality of life.

Diagnosticians are often classified as lumpers or splitters. The treatment of rating scales illustrated in this compendium has, hopefully, resulted in a 'lumping' approach to the DSM-III-R or the WHO-systems. Therefore, 'compendium' has been preferred to 'handbook' or 'textbook'. The reduction of items representing the DSM-III-R or the WHO syndromes into Likert scales is not a reduction ad absurdum, but a reduction ad necessitatem by use of sufficient statistics. This compendium, then, represents Quine's doctrine: "To be is to be the value of a variable" (Quine 1953).

References

Cronbach LJ. The two disciplines of scientific psychology. American Psychologist 1957; 12: 671–684.

James W. The Principles of Philosophy. New York: Holt 1890.

James W. Pragmatism: A New Name for Some Old Ways of Thinking. New York: Holt 1907.

Kretschmer E. Körperbau und Charakter. Berlin: Springer 1921.

Lewis A. Health as a social concept. Brit J Sociol 1953; 4: 109–124.

Quine WV. From a Logical Point of View. Cambridge, Mass: Harvard University Press 1953.

Rosser RM. A health index and output measure. In: Walker SR, Rosser RM (eds). Quality of Life: Assessment and Application. Lancaster: MTP 1987, pp. 133–160.

Wundt W. Selbstbeobachtung und innere Wahrnehmung. Philos Stud 1888; 4: 292–309.

Yalom ID. Existential Psychotherapy. New York: Basic Books 1980, pp. 342–343.

Subject Index

Scales are listed under their complete name

List of Authors

List of Scales

Abnormal Involuntary Movement Scale – AIMS: Guy
ADAS Cognitive Subscale: Mohs, Cohen
Adjective Mood Scale (Befindlichkeitsskala): von Zerssen
Alzheimer's Disease Assessment Scale – ADAS: Rosen et al.
Anger-Hostility Scale from the Hopkins Symptom Checklist – SCL-6: Guy
Arbeitsgemeinschaft für Methodik und Dokumentation in der Psychiatrie (Association for Methodology and Documentation in Psychiatry) – AMDP: Ban, Guy, Pietzcker et al.
Barker and Bishop Follow-up Questionnaire: Barker, Bishop
Bech-Hey Asthenia Scale: Bech, Hey
Beck Anxiety Inventory – BAI: Beck et al.
Beck Depression Inventory – BDI-21: Beck
Behavioural Rating Scale for Mental Patients: Shatin, Freed
Binet Scale: Binet
Bonn Scale for the Assessment of Negative Symptoms of Schizophrenia – BSABS: Gross et al.
Borderline Anhedonia Scale – BAS: Bech
Bortner Scale: Bortner
Brief Cognitive Rating Scale – BCRS: Reisberg
Brief Dementia Scale – BDS: Lauritzen, Bech
Brief Psychiatric Rating Scale – BPRS: Overall, Gorham
Brown and Harris Life Event Scale of Independence: Brown, Harris
Buss-Durkee Self-rating Inventory – B-D SI: Buss, Durkee
Cambridge Dementia Scale – CAMDEX: Roth et al.
Carroll Scale: Carroll, Feinberg
Center for Epidemiologic Studies Scale for Depression – CES-D: Radloff
Checklist for the Evaluation of Somatic Symptoms – CHESS: Guelfi et al.
Clinical Anxiety Scale: Snaith et al.
Clinical Global Improvment Scale – CGIS: Guy
Clinical Global Impression Scale for Severity of Illness – CGI-SI: Guy
Clinical Syndrome Circle – CSC: Bech et al.
Clyde Mood Scale: Guy
Compliance Index: Gordis
Comprehensive Phychopathological Rating Scale – CPRS: Åsberg et al.
Cornell Medical Index – CMI: Brodman
Cornell Medical Index (CMI):
– Anger Scale
– Fatigability Index
– Neuroticism Scale
Defensive Styles Rating Scale: Task Force of DSM-IV
Depressive Retardation Rating Scale: Widlöcher
Diagnostic and Statistical Manual. Mental Disorders (First edition) – DSM-I: American Psychiatric Association

Diagnostic and Statistical Manual of Mental Disorders (Second edition) – DSM-II: American Psychiatric Association

Diagnostic and Statistical Manual of Mental Disorders. Third edition – DSM-III: American Psychiatric Association

Diagnostic and Statistical Manual of Mental Disorders. Third edition (revised) – DSM-III-R: American Psychiatric Association

Diagnostic and Statistical Manual of Mental Disorders. Fourth edition (draft) DSM-IV: American Psychiatric Association

Diagnostic Interview Schedule – DIS: Robins et al.

Diagnostic Melancholia Scale – DMS: Bech et al.

Diagnostic Scale for Clinical Thyrotoxicosis: Crooks

Discretized Analogue Scale – Discan: Singh, Bilsbury

Extrapyramidal Symptom Rating Scale – ESRS: Chovinard

Eysenck Personality Questionnaire – EPQ: Eysenck

Fear Scale: Marks, Mathew

Fatigability Index (CMI subscale): Brodman

Freiburg Personality Inventory – FPI: Fahrenberg et al.

Gelder-Marks Phobia Questionnaire: Gelder, Marks

General Health Questionnaire – GHQ: Goldberg

General Health Questionnaire – GHQ-30: Goldberg

General Health Questionnaire/Quality of Life – GHQ/QL-12: Bech

Generalized Anxiety Scale – GEAS: Bech

Global Assessment of Functioning (DSM-III-R) – GAF: – modified version (symptoms); – modified version (social): Bech

Global Clinical Assessment Scale for Severity of Illness – GCSI: Bech et al.

Global Clinical Assessment of Severity of Side-Effects: Lingjærde et al.

Glossary of Mental Disorders and Guide to their Classification for Use in Conjunction with the International Classification of Diseases. Eighth revision – ICD-8: WHO

Gottfries-Bråne-Steen Scale – GBS: Gottfries, Bråne, Steen

Hamilton Anxiety Scale – Panic Attacks – HAS-P: Hamilton

Hamilton Anxiety Scale – Generalized Anxiety – HAS-G: Hamilton

Hamilton Anxiety Scale – HAM-A: Hamilton

Hamilton Anxiety Scale – HAS: Hamilton

Hamilton Depression Scale – HDS: Hamilton

Hamilton Depression Scale – HAM-D: Hamilton

Hamilton/Melancholia Scale – HDS/MES – HDS/MES self rating scale; HDS/MES strucutred interview: Hamilton, Bech, Williams

Handicaps, Behaviour and Skills Schedule – HBS: Wing

Hassles Scale: Kanner et al.

Health Status and Quality of Life Questionnaire – HSQL: Bech

Health Status Questionnaire – SF-36: McGlynn, Ware

Holmes and Rahe's Social Readjustment Rating Scale (observer version): Bech et al.

Hopkins Symptom Checklist – SCL: Parloff et al.

Hopkins Symptom Checklist (SCL-90):
- Original scale SCL-41 (Parloff)
- Anger-hostility scale – SCL-6 (Guy)
- Phobic anxiety factor – SCL-9 (Guy)
- Obsessive-compulsive factor – SCL-10 (Guy)
- Anxiety factor – SCL-11 (Guy)
- Discomfort subscale – SCL-17 (Bech et al.)
- Generalized anxiety SCL-19 (Bech)
- Anxiety subscale (Bech et al.)
- Depression factor (Guy)
- Harvard anxiety subscale (Mollica et al.)

- Harvard depression subscale (Mollica et al.)
- Interpersonal sensitivity factor (Guy)
- Paranoid ideation factor (Guy)
- Phobia subscale (Bech et al.)
- Psychoticism factor (Guy)
- Somatization factor (Guy)

Hospital Anxiety and Depression Scale – HAD: Zigmond and Snaith
Index of Independence in Activity of Daily Living: Katz et al.
Instrumental Activities of Daily Living Scale – IADL: Lawton and Brody
International Classification of Diseases. Tenth Revision – ICD-10: WHO
International Classification of Impairments, Disabilities and Handicaps – ICIDH: WHO
Irritability Scale: Snaith, Taylor
Job Contest Questionnaire: Karasek
Karnofsky Performance Status Scale: Karnofsky, Burchenal
Karnofsky Performance Status Scale (modified version): Grieco, Long
Leeds Sleep Evaluation Questionnaire – SEQ: Hindmarch
Leyton Obsessional Inventory: Cooper
Life Style Index: Plutchik et al.
Lithium Side-Effect Scale: Bech et al.
Manchester Scale: Krawiecka et al.
Mania Rating Scale: Young et al.
Mania Scale – MAS: Bech
Mania State Rating Scale: Beigel et al.
Manual of the Internation Statistical Classification of Diseases, Injuries, and Causes of Death – ICD-6: WHO
Marks-Sheehan Phobia Scale: Marks, Sheehan
Martin et al. Withdrawal Scale: Martin et al.
Maudsley Obsessive-Compulsive Inventory (modified): Sanovio, Vidotto
McMaster Health Index Questionnaire: Chambers
Melancholia Scale (original see HDS/MES) – MES: Bech
Melancholia Scale for General Practice – MES-GP: Bech
Melancholia Scale with Arousal Symptoms – MES-A: Bech
Mental Adjustment to Cancer – MAC: Morris et al.
Mental Disorders: Glossary and Guide to their Classification in accordance with the Ninth Revision of the International Classification of Diseases – ICD-9: WHO
Mental Status Checklist – MSCL: Lifshitz
Millon Behaviour Health Inventory – MBHI: Millon et al.
Millon Clinical Multiaxial Inventory – MCMI: Millon
Mini Mental State Examination – MMSE: Folstein et al.
Minnesota Multiphasic Personality Inventory – MMPI: Hathaway, McKinley
Montgomery-Åsberg Depression Rating Scale – MADRS: Montgomery, Åsberg
Multi-dimensional scale for rating psychiatric patients: Lorr
Neuroticism Scale (CMI): Rawnsley
Neuroticism Scale (EPQ): Eysenck
New York Heart Association Scale for Cardiac Disability: Criteria Committee of the New York Heart Association
Newcastle Depression Diagnostic Scale (1965): Carney et al.
Newcastle Depression Diagnostic Scale (1971): Gurney
Normative Social Adjustment Scale: Barrabee, Finesinger
Nottingham Health Profile – NHP: Martini, Hunt
Nurses' Observation Scale for Inpatient Evaluation – NOSIE: Honigfeld, Klett
Obsessive-Compulsive Subscale of CPRS – OCS: Thoren et al.
Overt Aggression Scale – OAS: Yudofsky et al.

Overt Aggression Scale/Staff Oberservation Aggression Scale – modified – OAS/SOAS:
  Bech
Panic Attack Scale – PAS: Sheehan
Patient-Rated Anxiety Scale – PRAS: Sheehan
Patient-rated Scale for Generalized Anxiety: Bech
Personal Resources Scale (DSM-IV) American Psychiatric Association
Pichot-Brun Asthenia Scale: Pichot, Brun
Positive and Negative Syndrome Scale – PANSS: Kay et al.
Post-traumatic Anxiety Scale: Suchman
Present State Examination – PSE-10: Wing et al.
Profile of Mood States – POMS: McNair et al.
Psychiatric Epidemiology Research Interview – PERI: Dohrenwend et al.
Psychological General Well-Being Schedule: Dupuy
Psychopathy Checklist – PCL: Hare
Psychosocial Adjustment to Illness Scale – PAIS: Morrow, Derogatis
Psychosocial Problem Checklist (DSM-IV): American Psychiatric Association
Psychotic Disintregation Scale (BPRS) – PDS: Bech et al.
Sanct Hans Rating Scale for Extrapyramidal Syndromes – SHRS: Gerlach, Korsgaard
Sandoz Clinical Assessment – Geriatric – SCAG: Shader et al.
Scale for the Assessment of Negative Symptoms – SANS: Andreasen
Scale for the Assessment of Positive Symptoms – SAPS: Andreasen
Schedule for Affective Disorders and Schizophrenia – SADS: Spitzer et al.
Schizoid Borderline Scale – SBS: Bech
Self-rating Depression Scale – SDS: Zung
Sheehan Clincian-Rated Anxiety Scale: Sheehan
Sickness Impact Profile – SIP: Bergner et al.
Simpson-Angus Scale: Simpson, Angus
Social Beaviour Schedule: Platt et al.
Social Dysfunction and Aggression Scale – SDAS: European Rating Aggression Group
Social Interview Scale: Claire et al.
Social Performance Schedule: Hurry and Sturt
St. Mary's Hospital Sleep Questionnaire – SMH Sleep Questionnaire: Ellis et al.
Staff Observation Aggression Scale – SOAS: Palmstierna, Wistedt
State-Trait Anxiety Inventory – STAI: Spielberger
State-Train Scale (Assessment of anger): Spielberger
Structured Interview for Personality Diagnoses: Spitzer, Williams
Symptom Checklist/Quality of life – SCL/QL-17: Bech
Symptom Rating Scale for Depression and Anxiety: Bech
–   BDI-13 Beck Depression Scale (Beck, Beamesderfer)
–   BDI-21 Beck Depression Scale (Beck et al.)
–   Melancholia Inventory (Bech)
–   Asthenia Scale (Bech, Hey)
–   Anxiety Subscale (Bech)
–   Mania Subscale (Bech)
Symptom Rating Test: Kellner
Thematic Apperception Test: Murray
Thomas and Freedman Scale: Thomas, Freedman
Thurstone's attitude scales: Thurstone
UKU Side Effect Rating Scale: Lingjærde et al.
Visual Analogue Scale – VAS
Waters Headache Questionnaire – WHQ: Waters
Ways of Coping Scale: Folkman, Lazarus
Wechsler Adult Intelligence Subtest Scale – WAIS: Wechsler
Wessely Fatigue Questionnaire: Wessely

Withdrawal Syndrome Scale – WSA: Bech
WSA Nursing Staff Scale: Kristensen
Yale-Brown Obsessive Compulsive Scale – Y-BOCS: Goodman et al.
Zung Anxiety Scale: Zung
Zung Anxiety Self-Rating Scale – SAS: Zung
Zung Depression Scale: Zung
Zung Depression Self-Rating Scale: Zung
Zung Pain and Distress Scale: Zung

List of Items Occurring in Rating Scales

List of Abbreviations

ADAS	Alzheimer's Disease Assessment Scale
AIMS	Abnormal Involuntary Movement Scale
AMDP	Arbeitsgemeinschaft für Methodik und Dokumentation in der Psychiatrie (Association for Methodology and Documentation in Psychiatry)
B-D SI	Buss-Durkee Self-rating Inventory
BAI	Beck Anxiety Inventory
BAS	Borderline Anhedonia Scale
BCRS	Brief Cognitive Rating Scale
BDI-21	Beck Depression Inventory
BDS	Brief Dementia Scale
BPRS	Brief Psychiatric Rating Scale
BSABS	Bonn Scale for the Assessment of Negative Symptoms of Schizophrenia
CAMDEX	Cambridge Dementia Scale
CES-D	Center for Epidemiologic Studies Scale for Depression
CGI-SI	Clinical Global Impression Scale for Severity of Illness
CGIS	Clinical Global Improvement Scale
CHESS	Checklist for the Evaluation of Somatic Symptoms
CMI	Cornell Medical Index
CPRS	Comprehensive Psychopathological Rating Scale
CSC	Clinical Syndrome Circle
DIS	Diagnostic Interview Schedule
Discan	Discretized Analogue Scale
DMS	Diagnostic Melancholia Scale
DSM-I	Diagnostic and Statistical Manual. Mental Disorders (First edition)
DSM-II	Diagnostic and Statistical Manual of Mental Disorders (Second edition)
DSM-III	Diagnostic and Statistical Manual of Mental Disorders. Third edition
DSM-III-R	Diagnostic and Statistical Manual of Mental Disorders. Third edition (revised)
DSM-IV	Diagnostic and Statistical Manual of Mental Disorders. Fourth edition
EPQ	Eysenck Personality Questionnaire
ESRS	Extrapyramidal Symptom Rating Scale
FPI	Freiburg Personality Inventory
GAF	Global Assessment of Functioning (DSM-III-R)
GBS	Gottfries-Bråne-Steen Scale
GCSI	Global Clinical Assessment Scale for Severity of Illness
GEAS	Generalized Anxiety Scale
GHQ	General Health Questionnaire
GHQ/QL-12	General Health Questionnaire/Quality of Life
HAD	Hospital Anxiety and Depression Scale
HAM-A	Hamilton Anxiety Scale
HAM-D	Hamilton Depression Scale
HAS	Hamilton Anxiety Scale

HAS-G	Hamilton Anxiety Scale – Generalized Anxiety
HAS-P	Hamilton Anxiety Scale – Panic Attacks
HBS	Handicaps, Behaviour and Skills Schedule
HDS	Hamilton Depression Scale
HDS/MES	Hamilton/Melancholia Scale
HSQL	Health Status and Quality of Life Questionnaire
IADL	Instrumental Activities of Daily Living Scale
ICD-10	International Classification of Disease. Tenth Revision
ICD-6	Manual of the International Statistical Classification of Diseases, Injuries, and Causes of Death
ICD-8	Glossary of Mental Disorders and Guide to their Classification for Use in Conjunction with the International Classification of Diseases. Eighth revision
ICD-9	Mental Disorders: Glossary and Guide to their Classification in accordance with the Ninth Revision of the International Classification of Diseases
ICIDH	International Classification of Impairments, Disabilities and Handicaps
MAC	Mental Adjustment to Cancer
MADRS	Montgomery-Åsberg Depression Rating Scale
MAS	Mania Scale
MBHI	Millon Behaviour Health Inventory
MCMI	Millon Clinical Multiaxial Inventory
MES	Melancholia Scale (original see HDS/MES)
MES-A	Melancholia Scale with Arousal Symptoms
MES-GP	Melancholia Scale for General Practice
MMPI	Minnesota Multiphasic Personality Inventory
MMSE	Mini Mental State Examination
MSCL	Mental Status Checklist
NHP	Nottingham Health Profile
NOSIE	Nurses' Observation Scale for Inpatient Evaluation
OAS	Overt Aggression Scale
OAS/SOAS	Overt Aggression Scale/Staff Observation Aggression Scale – modified
OCS	Obsessive-Compulsive Subscale of CPRS
PAIS	Psychosocial Adjustment to Illness Scale
PANSS	Positive and Negative Syndrome Scale
PAS	Panic Attack Scale
PCL	Psychopathy Checklist
PDS	Psychotic Disintegration Scale (BPRS)
PERI	Psychiatric Epidemiology Research Interview
POMS	Profile of Mood States
PRAS	Patient-Rated Anxiety Scale
PSE-10	Present State Examination
SADS	Schedule for Affective Disorders and Schizophrenia
SANS	Scale for the Assessment of Negative Symptoms
SAPS	Scale for the Assessment of Positive Symptoms
SAS	Zung Anxiety Self-Rating Scale
SBS	Schizoid Borderline Scale
SCAG	Sandoz Clinical Assessment – Geriatric
SCL	Hopkins Symptom Checklist
SCL/QL-17	Symptom Checklist/Quality of life
SCL-6	Anger-hostility Scale from the Hopkins Symptom Checklist
SDAS	Social Dysfunction and Aggression Scale
SDS	Self-rating Depression Scale
SEQ	Leeds Sleep Evaluation Questionnaire

SF-36	Health Status Questionnaire
SHRS	Sanct Hans Rating Scale for Extrapyramidal Syndromes
SIP	Sickness Impact Profile
SMH Sleep Questionnaire	St.Mary's Hospital Sleep Questionnaire
SOAS	Staff Observation Aggression Scale
STAI	State-Trait Anxiety Inventory
VAS	Visual Analogue Scale
WAIS	Wechsler Adult Intelligence Subtest Scale
WHQ	Waters Headache Questionnaire
WSA	Withdrawal Syndrome Scale
Y-BOCS	Yale-Brown Obsessive Compulsive Scale

Springer-Verlag
and the Environment

$\mathbf{W}$e at Springer-Verlag firmly believe that an international science publisher has a special obligation to the environment, and our corporate policies consistently reflect this conviction.

$\mathbf{W}$e also expect our business partners – paper mills, printers, packaging manufacturers, etc. – to commit themselves to using environmentally friendly materials and production processes.

$\mathbf{T}$he paper in this book is made from low- or no-chlorine pulp and is acid free, in conformance with international standards for paper permanency.

Printing: Weihert-Druck GmbH, Darmstadt
Binding: Verlagsbuchbinderei Georg Kränkl, Heppenheim